Read, for the first time
while in captivity,
Moral and physical –
    at Fort Sills, and
        Camp Gruber //

Everyman, I will go with thee, and be thy guide,
In thy most need to go by thy side.

This is No. 542 of Everyman's Library. A
list of authors and their works in this series
will be found at the end of this volume. The
publishers will be pleased to send freely to all
applicants a separate, annotated list of the
Library.

J. M. DENT & SONS LIMITED
10–13 BEDFORD STREET LONDON W.C.2

E. P. DUTTON & CO. INC.
286–302 FOURTH AVENUE
NEW YORK

EVERYMAN'S LIBRARY
EDITED BY ERNEST RHYS

HISTORY

THE HISTORY OF ROME
BY THEODOR MOMMSEN · INTRO-
DUCTION BY E. A. FREEMAN, LL.D.
TRANSLATED BY W. P. DICKSON
IN 4 VOLS.   VOL. 1

THEODOR MOMMSEN, born in 1817 in Schleswig-Holstein. From 1848 was professor of Roman Law and Ancient History at Berlin and other universities. From 1873 to 1895 was secretary to the Berlin Academy of Sciences. From 1873 to 1888 was a member of the Prussian House of Representatives. Died in 1903.

THE HISTORY OF ROME

VOLUME ONE

THEODOR MOMMSEN

LONDON: J. M. DENT & SONS LTD.
NEW YORK: E. P. DUTTON & CO. INC.

INTRODUCTION

By Edward Augustus Freeman[1]

THE history of Rome is the greatest of all historical subjects, for this simple reason, that the history of Rome is in truth synonymous with the history of the world. If history be read not as a mere chronicle of events, recorded as a form and remembered as a lesson, but as the living science of causes and effects, it will be found, that rightly to understand the destiny of what is truly called the Eternal City, our researches must be carried up to the very beginnings of history and tradition, and must be continued uninterruptedly to the present hour. Palestine, Greece, and Italy are the three lands whose history contains the history of man. From Palestine we draw our religion; from Greece comes art and literature, and, in a manner, law and freedom. But the influence of Palestine and Greece is, to a large extent, a mere influence of example and analogy; and where it is a real influence of cause and effect, it is at best an indirect influence, propagated by the voices and the arms of strangers. The history of civilised man goes on in one unbroken tale from Theseus to our own day: but the drama shifts its scene and changes its actors; Greece can only reach us by way of Italy; the Athenian speaks to modern Europe almost wholly through a Roman interpreter. We profess a religion of Hebrew origin; but the oracles of that religion speak the language of Greece, and reached us only through the agency of Rome. Of the old states of the world, the history of Carthage and of Palestine merges itself for ever in that of Rome. Greece, like one of her own subterranean rivers, merges herself also for a while, shrouds herself under the guise and title of her conqueror, and at last reappears at such a distance that some refuse to recognise her identity.

To understand Roman history aright, we must know the history of the Semitic and Hellenic races which Rome absorbed, and of those races of the farther East which Rome herself

[1] *Römische Geschichte* von Theodor Mommsen. Erster Band: Bis zur Schlacht von Pydna. Leipzig, 1854. Zweiter Band: Von der Schlacht von Pydna bis auf Sullas Tod. Berlin, 1855. Dritter Band: Von Sullas Tod bis zur Schlacht von Thapsus. Berlin, 1856. [*Roman History*, by Theodor Mommsen. 3 vols. Leipzig and Berlin, 1854-6.]

never could subdue. We must go yet farther back; we must, by the aid of philological research, grope warily beyond the domain of history or legend. We must go back to unrecorded days, when Greek and Italian were one people; and to days more ancient still, when Greek, Italian, Celt, Teuton, Slave, Hindoo, and Persian were as yet members of one undivided brotherhood. And if the historian of Rome is bound to look back, still more is he bound to look onwards. He has but to cast his eye upon the world around him to see that Rome is a still living and abiding power. The tongue of Rome is the groundwork of the living speech of south-western Europe. The tongue of Rome is still the ecclesiastical language of half Christendom; the days are hardly past when it was the common language of science and learning. The law of Rome is still quoted in our courts and taught in our universities; in other lands it forms the source and groundwork of their whole jurisprudence. Little more than half a century has passed since an Emperor of the Romans, tracing his unbroken descent from Constantine and Augustus, still held his place among European sovereigns, and, as Emperor of the Romans, still claimed precedence over every meaner potentate.[1] And the title of a Roman office, the surname of a Roman family, still remains the highest object of human ambition, clutched at alike by worn-out dynasties and by successful usurpers. Go eastward, and the whole diplomatic skill of Europe is taxed to settle the affairs of a Roman colony, which, cut off alike by time and distance, still clings to its Roman language and glories in its Roman name. We made war but yesterday upon a potentate whose badge is the Roman eagle, on behalf of one whose capital has not yet lost the official title of New Rome. Look below the surface, and the Christian subjects of the Porte are found called and calling themselves Romans; go beyond the Tigris, and their master himself is known to the votary of Ali simply as the Roman Cæsar. Even facts like these, which hardly rise above the level of antiquarian curiosities, still bespeak an abiding influence such as no other city or kingdom ever knew. And, far above them all, in deep and vast significance, towers the yet living phenomenon of the Roman Church and the Roman pontiff. The city of the Cæsars has for ages been, still is, and, as far as man can judge, will still for ages be, the religious centre, the holy place,

[1] We must remember that Freeman was writing half a century ago, on the first appearance of Mommsen's work in England.—[ED.]

the sacred hearth and home, of the faith and worship of millions on each side of the Atlantic. The successor of the Fisherman still in very truth sits on the throne of Nero, and wields the sceptre of Diocletian. It is indeed a throne rocked by storms; Frank and German may do battle for its advocacy; they have done so in ages past, and may do so for ages to come; but the power which has lived through the friendship and the enmity of Justinian and Liutprand, of Charlemagne and Otto, of the Henrys and the Fredericks, of Charles of Austria and Napoleon of France, may well live to behold the extinction, however distant it may be, of both the rival lines of Corsica and Hapsburg. Look back to the first dim traditions of the European continent, and you look not too far back for the beginnings of Roman history. Ask for the last despatch and the last telegram, and it will tell you that the history of Rome has not yet reached its end. It is in Rome that all ancient history loses itself; it is out of Rome that all modern history takes its source. Her native laws and language, her foreign but naturalised creed, still form the most important element in the intellectual life of every European nation; and, in a large portion of the European continent, they not only form an important element, but are the very groundwork of all.

The history of Rome dies away so gradually into the general history of the middle ages, that it is hard to say at what point a special Roman history should terminate. Arnold proposed to continue his history to the coronation of Charlemagne. Something may doubtless be said for this point, and something also for other points, both earlier and later. The Roman history gradually changes from the history of a city to the history of an empire. The history of the Republic is the history of a municipality, bearing sway over an ever-increasing subject territory; it differed only in scale from the earlier dominion of Athens and Carthage, from the later dominion of Bern and Venice. Under the Empire this municipal character died away, the Roman citizen and the provincial became alike the subjects of Cæsar; in process of time the rights, such as they were, of the Roman citizen were extended to all the subjects of the Roman monarchy. During the middle ages, the strange spectacle was exhibited of a Greek and a German disputing the title of Roman Emperor, while Rome itself was foreign ground to both alike. But this was only the full development of a state of things which had begun to arise, which indeed could not fail to arise, long before the period commonly assigned for the termination of the genuine Roman Empire. The importance of the capital even under the Emperors far surpassed that of the capital of a modern state. But it was no longer what it had been under the Republic. When from the Atlantic to the Euphrates all were alike Romans, the common sovereign of all ceased to be bound to Rome itself by the same tie as the old Consuls and Dictators. Rome gradually ceased to be an imperial residence. Constantine can hardly be said to have transferred the seat of empire from Rome to Constantinople. He fixed at Constantinople a throne which had already left Rome, but which had as yet found no other permanent resting-place. His predecessors had reigned at Milan and Nikomedeia; his successors reigned at Ravenna and Constantinople. Constantius and Honorius did but occasionally visit Rome; more peacefully, indeed, but quite as transiently, as the Ottos and Henrys of a later age. And when the seat of government— always for a large part, sometimes for the whole—of the Roman Empire was permanently transferred to Constantinople, it is wonderful to see how truly that city became, as it was called, the New Rome. Greece, indeed, eventually asserted her rights over the old Megarian city; the Byzantine Empire gradually changed from a Roman to a Greek state; but at what moment the change was accomplished it is impossible to say. Up to the coronation of Charlemagne, the Byzantine monarch was at least nominal lord of the Old as well as the New Rome. With Charlemagne begin the various dynasties of German Cæsars, keeping up more local connection with Old Rome, but much less of the true Roman tradition, than their rivals at Byzantium. There is at least thus much to be said for the point chosen by Arnold, that down to the coronation of Charlemagne there was still one undisputed Roman Empire and Roman Emperor. Heraclius and Leo ruled Italy from Constantinople, as Diocletian had ruled it from Nikomedeia. After the year 800 East and West are formally divided; there are two Roman Empires, two Roman Emperors. Of these, the one is rapidly tending to become definitively German, the other to become definitively Greek.

Mommsen shows how one Italian city contrived to conquer the whole Mediterranean world, and how inadequate the municipal government of that city proved itself to be to the task of ruling it. This is indeed a subject, and a very great subject, by itself; it is one of the greatest of political lessons; it is, in fact, the whole history of the City of Rome as the conquering and governing municipality; what follows is the history of the Empire, deriving its name from the city, but becoming gradually divorced from it. The point which Mommsen has now reached might almost be the termination of a " Geschichte von Rom; " but his work calls itself a " Römische Geschichte," and may therefore be fairly continued to almost any point which the historian may choose to select.

Mommsen's *Roman History* is, beyond all doubt, to be ranked among those really great historical works which do so much honour to our own day. We can have little hesitation in pronouncing it to be the best complete Roman history in existence. For a complete history, as we have just shown, we may call it, even as it now stands; it is not a mere fragment, like those of Niebuhr and Arnold. And even the ages with which Niebuhr and Arnold have dealt may be studied again with great advantage under Mommsen's guidance. And the important period between the close of Arnold's third volume and the opening of Mr. Merivale's history, Mommsen has pretty well to himself among writers who have any claim to be looked upon as his peers. In short, we have now, for the first time, the complete history of the Roman Republic really written in a way worthy of the greatness of the subject. Mommsen is a real historian; his powers of research and judgment are of a very high order; he is skilful in the grasp of his whole subject, and vigorous and independent in his way of dealing with particular portions. And an English critic may be allowed to add, that his book is far easier and more pleasant to read than many of the productions of his learned fellow-countrymen.

At the same time, there are certain inherent disadvantages in the form and scale of the work. Mommsen's work is the first of a series, the aim of which seems to be to popularise— we do not use the word in a depreciatory sense—the study of classical antiquity among the general German public.

The writer speaks as a master to an audience whose business it is to accept and not to dispute his teaching. But this mode of writing has its disadvantages when applied by a bold and independent writer like Mommsen to a period of the peculiar character which belongs to the early history of Rome. That history, we need not say, is one which does not rest on contemporary authority. That Rome was taken by the

Gauls appears to be the solitary event in the annals of several centuries which we can be absolutely sure was recorded by a writer who lived at the time.[1] Yet of these ages Dionysius and Livy give us a history as detailed as Thucydides can give of the Peloponnesian War, or Eginhard of the campaigns of Charles the Great. Till the time of Niebuhr, none but a solitary sceptic here and there hesitated to give to the first decade of Livy a credence as unhesitating as they could have given to Thucydides or Eginhard. And such sceptics commonly carried their unbelief to so unreasonable an extent as rather to favour the cause of a still more unreasonable credulity. Till Arnold wrote, Hooke's was the standard English History of Rome; there are apparently some even in our own generation who regard it as still entitled to the place of honour. Now, though Hooke's four stately quartos stand in due order on our shelves, we cannot boast of so intimate an acquaintance with them as with the smaller volumes of Arnold and Mommsen; but we do know enough of their contents to perceive that Hooke had no more idea of doubting the existence of Romulus than he had of doubting the existence of Cæsar. Then came the wonderful work of Niebuhr, which overthrew one creed and set up another. The tale which our fathers had believed on the authority of Livy sank to the level of a myth, the invention of a poet, the exaggeration of a family panegyrist; but in its stead our own youth was called upon to accept another tale, told with almost equal minuteness, on the personal authority of a German doctor who had only just passed away from among men. Niebuhr's theory, in fact, acted like a spell; it was not to argument or evidence that it appealed; his followers avowedly claimed for him a kind of power of "divination." Since that time there has been, both in Germany and in England, a reaction against Niebuhr's authority. The insurrection has taken different forms: one party seem to have quietly relapsed into the unreasoning faith of our fathers. Others are content to adopt Niebuhr's general mode of inquiry, and merely to reverse his judgment on particular points. This is the case with the able but as yet fragmentary work of Dr. Ihne.[2] Finally, there comes the

---

[1] See the latter part of the 12th chapter of Sir G. C. Lewis's *Credibility of Early Roman History*. It seems clear that Greek contemporary writers did record the Gaulish invasion ; possibly the account of Polybius may fairly represent their version of the event.

[2] *Researches into the History of the Roman Constitution.* By W. Ihne, Ph.D. London, 1853.

party of absolute unbelief, whose champion is no less a person than the late Chancellor of the Exchequer. Beneath the Thor's hammer of Sir George Cornewall Lewis the edifice of Titus Livius and the edifice of Barthold Niebuhr fall to the ground side by side. Almost every child has wept over the tale of Virginia, if not in Livy, at least in Goldsmith. Niebuhr and Arnold connect the tragic story with profound historical and political lessons; but Sir Cornewall coldly asks, "Who saw her die?" and as nobody is ready to make the same answer as the fly in the nursery legend,—as Virginius and Icilius did not write the story down on a parchment roll, or carve it on a table of brass,—he will have nothing to say to any of them. "That the basis" of the decemviral story "is real, need not be doubted." [1] But that is all; how much is real basis, how much is imaginary superstructure, Sir Cornewall Lewis cannot undertake to determine.

To that large body of English scholars who have been brought up at the feet of Niebuhr, but who have since learned partially to reject his authority, there will be found something unsatisfactory, or perhaps more truly something disappointing, in Mommsen's way of dealing with the kings and the early republic. The spell of Niebuhr's fascination is one not easily broken: it is, in fact, much more than a spell; the faith with which we looked up to him in our youth was exaggerated, but it was not wholly misplaced. Sir G. C. Lewis has, beyond all doubt, done a permanent service to historical truth by convicting Niebuhr of an enormous amount of error in detail—of inaccuracies, inconsistencies, hasty inductions, instances of arrogant dogmatism; but we cannot think that he has shown Niebuhr's general system to be a wrong one. His method, at once destructive and constructive, is surely essentially sound. His doctrine that the current statement, probably far removed from literal truth, still contains a basis of truth, Sir Cornewall Lewis himself does not venture wholly to deny. That a process, not indeed of "divination," but of laborious examination and sober reflection, may in many cases distinguish the truth from the falsehood, does not seem in itself unreasonable. Our own belief is, that Niebuhr's arrogant and self-sufficient dogmatism did but damage a cause which was essentially sound. Sir G. C. Lewis, while successfully demolishing the outworks, has made, in our judgment, no impression upon Niebuhr's main fortress. In such a state of mind, we cannot help looking at every page of the early

[1] *Credibility of Early Roman History*, vol. ii. p. 292.

Roman history as essentially matter of controversy; every step must be taken warily, no assertion must either be lightly accepted or lightly rejected, and no decision come to without weighing the arguments on one side and the other. It is therefore somewhat disappointing, not to say provoking, when in Mommsen's history of this period we find difficulties passed over *sicco pede ;* when we find statements made which sometimes command our assent, sometimes excite our incredulity, but which, in either case, we never heard before, and Mommsen's grounds for adopting which we should, in either case, like to know. It is easy to see that Mommsen is quite capable of defending his own ground against either Niebuhr or Sir G. C. Lewis. We feel sure that he has gone carefully through every point of controversy in his own mind; we only wish that we ourselves might be admitted to witness the process as well as the result. We attribute no sort of blame to Mommsen for a defect which is inseparable from the scale and nature of his work. To have treated the whole subject controversially, to have examined every statement at length and cited every authority in full, would have swelled the book to an extent which would have been quite unpalatable either to the " upper classes of public schools " or to the " weitere Kreise " of the German advertisement. But it has the effect of rendering this part of Mommsen's work less valuable to the professed scholar than either that which precedes or that which follows it. He shines most in one portion in which he himself exercises a " divination " as ingenious and more sound than that of Niebuhr, and in another in which the whole business of the historian is to narrate and to comment upon facts whose general truth has never been called in question. The two subjects in dealing with which Mommsen has been most successful, and in truth equally successful, are the prehistoric age of the Italian nations, and the processes, military and diplomatic, by which a single city of one of them attained to universal empire. It is greatly to his credit that he should have achieved such striking success in two subjects requiring such different modes of treatment.

It was from the chapters on the first subject, first published in an English translation, that we first became acquainted with Mommsen's history, and formed our own impression of its merits. And though these chapters are, we think, the very best portion of the book, yet the impression thus formed has not on the whole been diminished by our present more extended acquaintance with its original form. These chapters form one of the very best applications that we have ever seen of the growing science of comparative philology. They show how much we may learn, from evidence which cannot deceive, of the history of nations for ages before a single event was committed to writing. We are thus enabled to go back to days earlier even than those which are, in a manner, chronicled by poetry and tradition. In the Homeric poems we have our first written record of the Greek people; a record undoubtedly setting before us a real state of things, and, far more probably than not, some real events and some real persons. But the whole is embellished with so much that is clearly fabulous, that we cannot undertake to assert how much of truth there is at the bottom. We can hardly doubt that Greeks, in a certain stage of social progress, warred on the coast of Asia; their leader may very probably have been a king of Mykenæ, and he is just as likely to have been called Agamemnon as anything else. The Homeric poems probably contain far more of real history than this; but much farther than this we cannot venture to go; the very abundance of our materials overwhelms us. But comparative philology goes far beyond the tale of Troy, far beyond the settlement of the Hellenes in the land of the many islands and of all Argos. And its evidence is the surest evidence of all, evidence thoroughly unconscious. Comparative philology and pre-historic archæology do for man what geology does for his dwelling-place.

We do not remember to have read anything for a long time past with a more intense interest than these portions of Mommsen's book. His general conclusions with regard to the earliest inhabitants of Italy are these. Ancient Italy contained three distinct races: 1st, the Iapygians in the south; 2nd, those whom Mommsen distinctively calls "Italians" in the middle; and 3rd, the Etruscans in the north and north-west. Their geographical position would seem to show that this was the order in which the three nations entered the peninsula. Of the Iapygians we know but little; history presents them to us only in a decaying state, and all we know of their language is derived from certain as yet uninterpreted inscriptions. This evidence, however, tends to show that their language was Arian, distinct from the Italian,[1] and

---

[1] We are here merely expressing Mommsen's views, without binding ourselves either to accept or to refute them. We think, however, that he

possessing certain affinities with the Greek. With this also
falls in the fact that in historic times they adopted Greek
civilisation with extraordinary ease. The Italians of Mommsen's nomenclature are the historical inhabitants of the
greater portion of the peninsula. This is the nation the history
of whose tongue and government becomes identical with that
of civilised man; for of their language the most finished type
is the Latin, and of their cities the greatest was Rome. The
Etruscans Mommsen holds to be totally alien from the Italian
nations; their language is probably Arian, but that is all
that can be said. He rejects the story of their Lydian origin,
and seems inclined to look upon Rhætia as the cradle of their
race. He makes two periods of the Etruscan language, of
which the former one is to be found in those inscriptions on
vases at Cære, or Agylla, which Mr. Francis Newman [1] quotes
as Pelasgian. Into the interminable Pelasgian controversy
Mommsen hardly enters at all. For that controversy turns
almost wholly on points of legend or tradition, hardly at all
on comparative philology. On the other hand, he passes by
in silence yet more complete some theories the evidence
adduced for which is wholly of a philological kind. We mean
the theory, supported by Mr. Newman and others,[2] which sees
a Celtic, and specially a Gaelic element in the old Italian
population, and that [3] which supposes a race of Basque or
Iberian aborigines to have occupied Italy before the entrance
of its historical inhabitants.

The Italians, in Mommsen's special sense, were then a people
closely allied to the Hellenes, and had made considerable
advances in cultivation before the two stocks separated.
The Italian stock again divides itself into two, the Latin and
the Umbro-Samnite, the difference between which he compares
to that between Ionic and Doric Greek. The Umbro-Samnite
again divides itself into the Oscan and the Umbrian, analogous,
according to our author, to the Doric of Sicily and the Doric
of Sparta. In Mommsen's own words:

" Each of these philological phenomena (Spracherscheinungen) is
the result of, and the testimony to, an historical event; it may be
inferred from them with complete certainty that a stock was
separated from the common parent-stem of peoples and languages

should at least have noticed the apparent identity of the names *Iapyges*,
Apuli, and *Opici*, which, so far as it goes, tells against him.
   [1] *Regal Rome*, p. 7. It is certainly hard to see how this sort of language
can, as Mommsen supposes, have developed into the later Etruscan.
   [2] *Ibid.*, pp. 17 et seqq.   [3] See Prichard, iii. 43.

which included within itself the ancestors at once of the Greeks and of the Italians; that from this stock next the Italians branched away, and that they again parted into the Western and Eastern stock, and then the Eastern again into the Umbrians and Oscans. Where and when these separations took place, language certainly cannot tell us; and scarce does our audacious thought dare try to grope its way along the course of these revolutions (diesen Revolutionen ahnend zu folgen), of which the earliest doubtless happened long before that immigration which led the forefathers of the Italians across the Apennines."

Rome is, according to Mommsen, a city purely Latin, and the head of Latium. The Tiber was at once the boundary of Latium against the Etruscan stranger, and the natural highway for the primitive commerce of the early Latins. The site of Rome thus marks it out as at once the commercial capital of Latium and the great bulwark of the land against the Etruscan. Such were the earliest duties of Rome. It may have been merely by a happy accident that one of the Latin cities was placed on a site which enabled it to assume them; it may have been founded expressly to discharge them, either by the common will of the Latin confederacy, or by the wisdom of some clear-sighted founder of unrecorded times. Rome may have been either the eldest or the youngest of Latin cities. But probability seems greatly in favour of her being rather the child than the parent of the League. All tradition represents Rome as an Alban, that is a Latin, colony. As soon as we get anything like a glimpse of real history, we find Rome essentially a Latin city, we find her unmistakably predominant among the cities of Latium. But Rome is not only far greater than any other Latin city; she appears as something in a manner outside the League, in the very position, in short, likely to be assumed by a younger state which had outstripped its elders. She is a Latin city, she is closely connected with the other Latin cities; but she is hardly an integral member of their confederacy; in the times of her greatest recorded weakness she treats with the League as an equal; the single city of Rome is placed on an equal footing with the aggregate of the other thirty. And from the advantage which a single powerful state always has over a confederacy of smaller ones, the equal alliance between Rome and Latium grew into a practical supremacy of Rome over Latium. Rome under her kings clearly possessed this power, and, if she lost it by her revolution, she recovered it by the league of Spurius Cassius. Rome and Latium were formerly equal allies; the Hernicans were united in the league on the same terms; but it is impossible to doubt that Rome was the soul of the confederacy during the whole time of its existence. The Æquian and Volscian invasions, again, fell far more heavily upon the Latin allies than upon Rome herself. Many Latin cities were wholly lost, others were greatly weakened. These processes would of course greatly increase the proportionate importance of Rome; they would bring the Latins to look more and more to Rome as the natural head of their nation, and to demand, not independence, but union on closer and juster terms. The demands of the Latin allies at the outbreak of the great Latin War are a sufficient commentary on the relations between Rome and Latium. The feeling towards Rome was clearly that of excluded citizens under an oligarchy, rather than that of an oppressed nation under a foreign government. They do not ask to shake off the Roman yoke, to forsake the Roman alliance; they ask instead to become wholly Roman themselves. They are ready to abolish the Latin name and the separate existence of the Latin League. Their demands are almost identical with those of the plebeians in Rome itself hardly a generation earlier. As the Licinian laws required one consul to be a plebeian, the Latins now require that one consul shall be a Latin. The senate was to be half Latin; the Latin cities would probably have assumed the position of Roman tribes. Terms like these Rome held it beneath her dignity to grant; but after the conquest of Latium, the mass of the Latin nation did gradually acquire Roman citizenship in one way or another. This is, in short, the constantly repeated history of Rome and her allies, from the earliest to the latest period. Men do not seek to get rid of Rome as their ruler; they wish to become Romans, and, in that character, to help to rule both themselves and others. The first recorded struggle, that between patrician and plebeian, is in its origin much more truly a struggle between distinct nations than between different orders in the same nation. But the demand of the plebeians is not to abolish the patrician government, but to obtain a share in it for themselves. It is only in some desperate moment, when every demand is refused, that they resort to the extreme measure of a " secession; " that is, in short, of leaving Rome, and founding a new city for themselves.

To the struggle between patrician and plebeian succeeds the struggle between Roman and Latin; the Latin is only driven into a war against Rome when he cannot obtain his desire of incorporation with Rome. The Samnite wars, including those with their Etruscan, Gaulish, and Epeirot allies, reduce the whole of Italy to the condition of dependent alliance with Rome. Italy is now gradually Latinised; but at the same time the yoke of Rome is found to be no light one. But no indications appear of any desire to throw it off, except in such strange exceptional cases as the solitary revolts of Falerii and Fregellæ. The Italians gradually assume the feelings of Romans; like the plebeians, like the Latins, they demand not independence, but complete incorporation. The claims of the Italian allies formed one of the most important political questions of the seventh century of the city. The rights of the Italians, admitted by the best men both of the senatorial and of the democratic party, were opposed to the vulgar prejudices of Senate and People alike. When each party had equally failed them, then the allies took arms, not for Samnite or Marsian independence, but for a new Rome of their own, a premature republican Constantinople, the city Italy.

This new Rome, like the old, had its senate, its consuls, its prætors, its citizenship shared by every member of an allied commonwealth. Like the Latins of the fifth century, the Italians of the seventh were at last admitted piecemeal to the rights for which they contended. Every Italian was now a Roman; save where Hellenic influence had taken permanent root, all Italy was now Latinised. But by this time vast regions out of Italy had begun to be Latinised also. Latin civilisation spread over Spain, Gaul, and Africa; the policy of the Emperors tended to break down the distinction between citizen and provincial, and at length the franchise of the Roman city was extended to all the subjects of the Roman empire. Western Europe became thoroughly Romanised; even the Greek and his eastern proselytes became Roman in political feeling, and gloried in that Roman name which some of them still retain. In Syria and Egypt alone did the old national feelings abide. Elsewhere, save some wild tribe here and there, the Mediterranean world was wholly Roman. Its unity was constantly rent by civil wars, by the claims of rival Emperors, by peaceful division between imperial colleagues. But from the Atlantic to Mount Taurus no Roman citizen thought of divesting himself of his Roman character. Emperors reigned in Gaul and Britain; but they were not Gallic or British sovereigns; they were still Roman Cæsars, holding a portion of the Roman Empire, and striving after the possession of the whole. During the whole history of Rome, both Old and New, from the first mythical King to the last phantom Emperor, it would be hard to find a case of a city or province, once thoroughly incorporated into the Roman system, which voluntarily separated itself from its Roman allegiance. Provinces might helplessly submit to foreign conquerors, but they never asserted their own national independence.[1] Till Monophysite Egypt welcomed a deliverer in the Mussulman Arab, it does not appear that barbarian invaders ever met with actual co-operation within the Roman territory. Italy, indeed, in the seventh century of our era, revolted against the Eastern Emperor, and gave herself of her own free will to a Frankish master; but he came as a Roman Patrician, a Roman Cæsar, to assert the rights of the Old Rome against the usurpations of the New. Through the whole of this long series of centuries, all who come in contact with the original Romulean city—the plebeian, the Latin, the Italian, at last the inhabitants of the whole Mediterranean world—all gradually obtained the Roman name; and none of them willingly forsook it.

The workings of a law which remained in full force for above two thousand years have carried us far away from Mommsen's immediate subject. And yet we have perhaps not mentioned the earliest instance of its working. Rome, as we have said, is in his view strictly a Latin city. He indignantly rejects the notion of the Romans being a mongrel race, " ein Mischvolk," a union of elements from the three great races of Italy. Of the three old patrician tribes, the Titienses are, indeed, probably of Sabine origin; but they were Sabines thoroughly Latinised, who at most, as other incorporated nations did in later times, introduced some Sabine rites into the Roman religion. The really Latin character of Rome was no more affected than when, under the early Republic, the Sabine Attus Clausus, with his clan and following, were converted into the Claudian tribe. Here, then, in days totally unrecorded, before the struggles of Latin or of plebeian, we find the first instance of that inherent power of assimilation or incorpora-

---

[1] Whether the so-called revolt of Britain and Armorica in the fifth century is to be counted as a solitary exception, depends on two very difficult questions: 1st, How far had Britain and Armorica really become Roman? 2nd, What is the meaning of the not very intelligible narrative in the last book of Zosimus?

tion on the part of the Roman commonwealth, which continued alike under kings, consuls, and Cæsars. The legend
of Romulus is, in Mommsen's view, a comparatively late one,
as is shown by the name of the eponymous hero being formed
from the later form of the name of the city and people. The
oldest form is not *Romani*, but *Ramnes*, that of the first
patrician tribe; and that form points to the name of the
Eternal City as being originally synonymous with our own
Woottons and Bushburys: " so dass der Name *Roma* oder
Rama vielleicht ursprünglich die Wald- oder Buschstadt
bezeichnet."

The other point, besides the primeval archæology, where
we thought Mommsen's treatment of his subject worthy of
special admiration, was what we may call the diplomatic
history of Rome. In Rome's gradual acquisition of universal
empire two great stages are marked, the complete subjugation
of Italy, and the conquest of Macedonia at the battle of Pydna.
Our author quite rejects the notion that any deliberate and
systematic scheme of universal dominion actuated the Roman
Senate and People through successive centuries. War and
conquest were undoubtedly as agreeable to them as they have
commonly been to most other nations; but their distant
acquisitions were in some cases almost forced upon them, and
they continually drifted into foreign wars as much through
the result of circumstances as from any deliberate intent.
Thus it would certainly seem to have been throughout the
period of Rome's greatest glory. Rome was at the true
summit of her greatness, within and without, in the fifth and
sixth centuries of her existence. The days of her early dissensions were over, those of her later dissensions had not yet
arrived. The old political struggle between patrician and
plebeian had become a thing of the past, the far more fearful
struggle between rich and poor was still a thing of the future.
The Romans of those ages not only knew how to win victories,
they had learned the far harder lesson how to endure defeat.
The victories of Pyrrhus and Hannibal would have broken
the spirit of almost every other nation of any age. But the
endurance of Rome was never shaken; she could endure to
proclaim publicly in her forum, " We have been overcome in
a great battle," and her senators could go forth to thank the
defeated demagogue [1] who had not despaired of the Republic.

[1] Mommsen seems to us unduly harsh on M. Terentius Varro, as well
as on C. Flaminius. Arnold does them far more justice.

Her political constitution may seem an anomaly; the sovereign senate side by side with the no less sovereign popular assembly, the consul all-powerful to act, the tribune all-powerful to forbid, may seem inconsistent, impracticable, unable to be worked. But the proof is in two centuries with nothing worthy to be called a civil commotion; the proof is in the conquest of Italy, in the repulse of Pyrrhus and of Hannibal, in tributary Carthage and tributary Macedonia. What the Roman system in these ages really was, is shown by the men whom it provided; men always great enough, and never too great; men ready to serve their country, but never dreaming of enslaving it. What was the true Roman national being is revealed to us in the hereditary virtues of the Decii and the Fabii, in the long-descended Scipio and in the lowly-born Curius and Regulus; we see it allied with Grecian culture in Titus Quinctius Flamininus, and standing forth in old Italian simplicity in Marcus Porcius Cato. Rome in these ages bore her full crop of statesmen and soldiers, magistrates and orators, ready to be the rulers of one year and the subjects of the next. But as yet she produced neither a traitor nor a tyrant, nor, in any but the older and nobler sense, a demagogue. We are not quite sure that Mommsen does full justice to this splendid period; he understands, but he does not always feel; his narrative constantly seems cold and tame after that of Arnold. We miss the brilliant picture of the great men of the fifth century,[1] we miss the awful vision of Hannibal,[2] we miss the pictures of Gracchus and his enfranchised slaves, and of Nero's march to the "fateful stream" of the Metaurus. Both tell us how the old Marcellus died by a snare which a youth might have avoided; but in how different a strain! Mommsen gives us, indeed, the facts with all truth and clearness:

" When out on an insignificant reconnaissance, both consuls were surprised by a party of African cavalry; Marcellus, already a sexagenarian, fought boldly the unequal battle till he sank dying from his horse; Crispinus escaped, but died of the wounds received in the skirmish." [3]

Turn we now to Arnold:

" Crispinus and the young Marcellus rode in covered with blood and followed by the scattered survivors of the party; but Marcellus, six times consul, the bravest and stoutest of soldiers, who had

---

[1] Arnold, ii. 272.   [2] *Ibid.*, iii. 70.   [3] Mommsen, ii. p. 161.

dedicated the spoils of the Gaulish king, slain by his own hand, to Jupiter Feretrius in the Capitol, was lying dead on a nameless hill; and his arms and body were Hannibal's." [1]

The policy of Rome during these two glorious ages had, according to Mommsen, for its primary object, first the acquisition, and then the retention, of a firm dominion in Italy. Its dealings with the provinces and with foreign states were simply means to secure this primary end. Italy was won; its various states were reduced to the condition of dependent allies. This condition deprived them of all practical sovereignty, and made them in all their external relations the passive subjects of Rome. But they retained their own communal governments; they served Rome with men, not with money; and Rome's constant wars gave their individual citizens many opportunities of acquiring both wealth and honour. Doubtless, as they had constantly more and more to do with distant nations, they began to feel a wider Italian patriotism, and to glory in the triumphs which they helped to win for the greatest of Italian cities. This feeling on the one hand, and on the other hand the occasional excesses of Roman officers in more degenerate times, combined to bring about that yearning after full Roman citizenship which we have so often mentioned already. The old Latin League no longer existed; it had partly vanished from the earth, partly had been incorporated with Rome. But its place was in a manner filled by those Latin colonies, those children of Rome, which, for some not very apparent reason, were invested with the Latin, and not the full Roman franchise. These were, in fact, Roman garrisons, scattered over the peninsula, serving to watch over the allied states, and to keep them in due dependence. Such was the state of things from the Rubicon to the Strait of Messina. But the full and safe possession of Italy involved something more. Italy had no natural frontier nearer than the Alps; Cisalpine Gaul had therefore to be conquered. And looking beyond the Adriatic and the Libyan Sea, Rome had to settle her relations with the Carthaginian republic and the Macedonian kingdom. The balance of power was in those days an idea altogether unknown. To a modern statesman, transported into the third century B.C., the great problem would have been to preserve such a balance between Rome, Carthage, and Macedonia. No rational English, French, or Russian diplomatist wishes to make any one of the

[1] Arnold, iii. 354.

other countries subject or tributary to his own; his object
is not positively to weaken the rival state, but merely to
repress any undue encroachment.   But from a Roman point
of view, for Rome to be strong, it was necessary that Carthage
and Macedonia should be absolutely weak.   It may possibly
be doubted whether the modern system does not bring about
just as many material evils as the other; but the theory is
quite different.   A war between Rome and Carthage could
terminate only in the destruction, or at least the deep humiliation, of one or other of the contending powers.   But let
France and Austria go to war to-morrow, and the result will
not be that either Paris or Vienna will cease to be the capital
of a powerful and independent state; those who pay the price
will be the unhappy scapegoats of Lombardy or Wallachia.
But in the view of a Roman statesman, Italy could only be
strong at the direct expense of Carthage and Macedonia.

A first war with Rome, like a modern war, involved at
most only pecuniary compensation, or the loss of a distant
dependency; but a second carried with it the loss of political
independence; a third involved total destruction.   Thus the
first Punic war cost Carthage Sicily and Sardinia, the second
made Carthage a dependent state, the third swept her away
from the face of the earth.   The first Macedonian war had
results little more than diplomatic; the second reduced
Macedonia to a dependent condition; the third annihilated
the kingdom, cutting it up into four separate commonwealths;
the fourth, if it deserve the name, made Macedonia a Roman
province.   The difference in the processes of the two conquests
is a good commentary on Mommsen's theory.   The problem
was for Rome to preserve a direct and unshaken dominion
over Italy; everything beyond was only means to this end.
But Sicily and Sardinia were natural appendages of Italy;
their possession by a state of equal rank might be directly
dangerous.   Rome therefore required their cession; that of
Sicily by the terms of peace with Carthage, that of Sardinia
as the price of its continuance a few years after.   Their
possession was almost as necessary as the possession of Cisalpine Gaul.   But Macedonia had no such threatening possessions.   The first treaty with Philip was concluded nearly on
equal terms; the Macedonian frontier was simply " rectified "
by the loss of some points and the addition of others.
Macedonia, again, had to pass through a more gradual descent
than Carthage.   Even the third war, the war of Pydna, did

not involve desolation, or even formal incorporation with the Roman dominion; clearly because Macedonia had sent no Hannibal to Cannæ, and her total humiliation was not so clearly an Italian necessity as that of Carthage.

The original Roman system, then, was to maintain direct rule in Italy; to tolerate no equal power, but to weaken all neighbouring states, to reduce them to what Mommsen calls the condition of clientage. But it is evident that this system could not fail to lead Rome more and more into the vortex of distant conquest. It is just like our own dominion in India, where we have our immediate provinces and our client princes exactly analogous to those of Rome. In either case, when intermeddling has once began, there is no way to stop it. Policy, or even sheer self-defence, leads to one conquest, that conquest leads to another; till at last annexation is loved for its own sake, the independent state becomes a dependency, and the dependency becomes a province. The Roman policy of surrounding Italy with a circle of weak states did not answer; it exposed her all the sooner to the necessity of a struggle with the powerful states which still remained behind. Make Macedonia first a dependency and then a province; that process only involves the next stage of doing the like by Syria: do the like by Syria; that only involves an attempt to do the like by Parthia, with which the like cannot be done. In this last particular case, Mommsen shows very clearly that the result of the Roman policy was most hurtful alike to the immediate interests of Rome and to the general interests of the world. The monarchy of the Seleucidæ, the truest heirs of Alexander's empire, whatever else it was, was at least, then and there, champion of European cultivation. It was the bulwark of the West against the East, the successor of Miltiades and Agesilaos, the precursor of Leo the Isaurian and Don John of Austria. Now the policy of Rome brought the Syrian monarchy to precisely that point in which the King of Antioch could not defend his own eastern borders, and in which it was not as yet either the palpable duty or the palpable interest of Rome to defend them for him. The effect of this is pointed out by Mommsen in a brilliant passage, which shows how well he understands the relation of his own immediate subject to the general history of the world.

" This transposition (Umwandlung) of international relations in central Asia is the turning-point in the history of antiquity. In place of the flowing tide of peoples which had hitherto poured from

West to East, and which had found its last and highest expression in the great Alexander, the ebb now begins. From the date of the foundation of the Parthian kingdom all the Hellenic elements, which might yet have held their ground in Bactria and on the Indus, are not only lost, but even western Iran shrinks back again into the track abandoned centuries ago, but not yet obliterated. *The Roman Senate sacrifices the first essential fruit of the policy of Alexander, and therewith initiates that reactionary movement whose last offshoots end in the Alhambra of Granada and in the great Mosque of Constantinople.* So long as the country from Ragæ and Persepolis to the Mediterranean still obeyed the King of Antiochia, so long Rome's power too extended to the border of the Great Desert; the Parthian kingdom, not because it was so very powerful, but because its centre of gravity was far away from the coast, in central Asia, could never become one of the dependencies of the Mediterranean empire. Since the time of Alexander, the world had belonged to the Western nations alone, and the East appeared to be, in relation to them, only what America and Australia became in later times in relation to the European nations. With Mithridates I. the East again entered the circle of political movement. The world had again two masters." [1]

But mixed up with much of the policy of Rome's eastern dealings there was, according to Mommsen, a large amount of what would nowadays be called philhellenic feeling. That the Roman senate, as Bishop Thirlwall says, surpassed all recorded governments in diplomatic skill, we can readily admit; and yet it need not be necessary to attribute all their doings to some unfathomably subtle line of policy. To hold that Rome acted, through a long series of years, on a deliberate plan of gradual conquest; that she systematically made use of her allies, and cast them off when they were done with; that she formed a league with a state with the settled purpose of reducing it to a dependency in the next generation, and to a province in the generation after that,—is really attributing to what is, after all, an abstraction rather too much of the attributes of a living and breathing man. The characteristics both of the Roman nation and of particular Roman families have so strong a tendency to pass on from father to son, that Rome does assume something more like a personal existence than almost any other state. Venice and Bern are the two nearest parallels in recent times. But the policy even of

[1] Vol. iii. p. 60. We are not quite sure, however, that Mommsen has not too closely identified the Parthian dominion with the native Persian race and religion. The rise of Parthia was, as he describes it, a great reaction of the East against the West. But the Parthians seem to have been not quite impervious either to Christianity or to Greek cultivation. The final blow was struck by the re-establishment of a really national Persian state in the third century A.D.

Rome or Venice still, after all, means the policy of the men who at successive times took the lead in the Roman and Venetian republics. Even in those grave senates everything was not so much matter of precedent and tradition that no fluctuating circumstances, no individual passions could ever affect their deliberations. States, like individuals—for the decisions of states are really the decisions of individuals—commonly act from mixed motives; and as most men would feel no small difficulty in analysing their own motives, we may feel still more difficulty in analysing those of the Roman senate. So much generosity as to exclude all care for self, so much selfishness as to exclude all thought for others, are both of them the exception in human affairs. Act generously, provided it does not seriously damage yourself, is, we fancy, the commonest rule both with rulers and with private men.

There is no occasion to suppose that when Flamininus proclaimed liberty to Greece it was mere hypocrisy on the part either of him or of his government. But we cannot suppose that either Flamininus or the Roman senate would have knowingly sacrificed a jot of Rome's real power or real interest to any dream of philhellenic generosity. It is easy, however, to see that a strong philhellenic feeling did really exist in the mind of Flamininus and of many other Romans of his day. Greece was then newly opened to Roman inquirers; Greek civilisation and literature were beginning to make a deep impression upon the Roman mind, both for good and for evil. The famous cities of Greece were already places of intellectual pilgrimage. The natural result was that, for at least a generation, both Greek allies and Greek enemies received better treatment than allies or enemies of any other race. Achaia and Athens were favoured and, as it were, humoured to the highest degree not clearly inconsistent with Roman interests. But the tide must have turned considerably before Mummius destroyed Cornith, even before L. Æmilius Paullus was required, against his will, to destroy the Epeirot cities. The phenomenon may well have been analogous to one of our own days with regard to the same land. A generation back men looked for results from the emancipation of Greece which were utterly extravagant and chimerical. The fashion is now to decry everything to do with independent Greece, and to deny the real progress she has made, because impossible expectations have not been realised. In short, a generation of Mummii has, among ourselves, succeeded to a generation of Flaminini. Mommsen, we should observe, by no means shares or approves of the philhellenism of the victor of Kynoskephalai. He has throughout a way of dealing more freely with established heroes, of casting about censure with a more unsparing hand, than is altogether consistent with the sort of vague and half superstitious reverence with which one cannot help regarding the men of old. Indeed, he sometimes passes from criticism and censure into the regions of actual sarcasm, almost of mockery; he deliberately quizzes " Plutarch's men " with as little compunction as *Punch* quizzes the men of our own time. Contemporary events have brought this home very strongly to our mind. While reading Mommsen's account of what we may call the Lord High Commissionership of T. Quinctius Flamininus, we could more than once have fancied we were reading an attack in the *Times* or the *Saturday Review* on him whom modern Hellas delights to honour as ὁ περίφημος καὶ φιλέλλην Γλάδστων.

Mommsen, following Polybius, makes the battle of Pydna one great stage in his history. Rome's work of conquest was now practically over; there remained little to do but to gather in the spoil. She had yet many battles to fight, many provinces to win, but there was no longer any Mediterranean power able to contend with her on equal terms for the lordship of the Mediterranean world. And now she began to show how little adapted her constitution was to administer a universal empire. Men generally look to this period of Roman history for arguments for or against monarchy, aristocracy, or democracy. Possibly all such may be found; but the most truly distinctive lesson which it teaches is one into which those questions do not immediately enter. That lesson is one which, to the nineteenth century, has become almost matter of curiosity; but it was a practical one as long as Venice ruled over Corfu and Kephallenia, as long as the Pays de Vaud obeyed the mandates of the oligarchy of Bern. That lesson is this, one well set forth by Mommsen in several passages, that a municipal government is unfitted to discharge imperial functions. Such a municipal government may be either aristocratic or democratic; but in either case it governs solely in the interest of the ruling city. It need not be tyrannical—Bern was eminently the reverse; but the subject states, the provinces or dependencies, have no share in their own government, and their interest is not the object of those who rule them. This warning will of course apply to all states possessing colonies or dependencies; but the cause is not the same. The Roman government, with its senate, its popular assembly, its annually elected magistrates, was a government essentially municipal; it was fitted only for the government of a single city. It had, indeed, as if its founders had foreseen the danger, something of a representative element from the beginning. The ruling principle of the ancient city governments, aristocratic and democratic alike, was, we need hardly say, that every member of the ruling class, be that class the widest democracy or the narrowest oligarchy, should have his personal share in the government, should give his direct vote in the sovereign assembly. But the territory of the Roman city extended, at a very early period, over a region far too wide to have allowed every Roman citizen to have habitually appeared in the *comitia*. Had the voting gone by heads, the residents in the city would have had it all their own way. This was obviated by the tribe system. Each of the thirty-five tribes had one vote. On the day of election or legislation, half a dozen citizens from a distant tribe had the same voice as the hundreds or thousands of a nearer one. In fact, as Niebuhr suggests, those half-dozen rural voters might really be the chosen delegates of the hundreds or thousands of their neighbours. Hence the importance of the legislation of Appius Claudius, and of the counter-legislation of Fabius and Decius. Appius divided the freedmen, the *turba forensis*, the Lambeth and Tower Hamlets of Rome, among all the then existing tribes; that is, he put the votes of all the tribes into their hands. Fabius and Decius removed them all into the four city tribes, so that they could command four votes only.

Even with this modification, the Roman popular assembly became, what it never became at Athens, a body utterly unmanageable, which could only cry "Yea, yea," to the proposals of the magistrates, and in which debate was out of the question. And, after all, senate and assembly alike represented purely Roman interests; the allies, still less the provinces, had no voice in either. It was as if the liverymen of London passed laws and appointed to offices for the whole United Kingdom. Under the municipal system of Rome there was no remedy. Had Italy and the world been received into the old tribes, or mapped out into new ones, it would only have made the assembly yet more unwieldy than it was already. A representative or a federal system would have solved the problem without any sacrifice of liberty. But

a representative system the ancient world never knew; though
the Achaian, the Lycian, though, as we have seen, the Roman
system itself, hovered on the verge of it. Federalism was,
indeed, at work in its most perfect form in Lycia and Achaia;
but it would have been in vain to ask Roman pride to have
allowed conquered nations to set up senates and assemblies
of equal rank with those of Rome herself. The monarchy of
the Cæsars cut the knot another way: the provincial could
not be raised to the level of the citizen, but the citizen could
be degraded to the level of the provincial. They both now
found a common master. The provincials no doubt benefited
by the change. It is, indeed, true that the municipal origin
of the Roman Empire, and the covert way in which monarchy
gradually crept in under republican forms, caused the capital
to retain an undue importance, and made first Rome and then
Constantinople to flourish at the cost of the provinces. But
the evil was far less under the Empire than under the Republic.
The best Emperors did what they could to govern in the
interest of the whole Empire, and the worst Emperors were
most terrible to those to whom they were nearest. The overthrow of the Roman Republic, the establishment of the
Cæsarean despotism, was the overthrow of the very life of
the Roman city; but to the Roman Empire it was a bitter
remedy for a yet more bitter disease. It proves nothing
whatever in favour of despotism against liberty; it establishes
no law that democracy must lead to military monarchy.
Athens and Schwitz had to bend to foreign invaders; but no
Prytanis or Landamman ever accomplished a *coup-d'état*.
What it does prove is, that a single city cannot govern an
empire; that for a subject province one master is less formidable than 700,000. Those 700,000 citizens were, among themselves, a frantic mob rather than a legitimate democracy:
as against the millions of Roman subjects from the Atlantic
to the Euphrates, they were an oligarchy as narrow and
exclusive as if they had all been written in the Golden Book
of Venice.

The experience of the last age of Roman history proves
nothing against any form of liberty, be it Athenian democracy, English monarchy, or Swiss or Achaian federalism. If
it gives us any immediate practical warning, it is a warning
against the claims of overgrown capitals. It has lately become
the fashion to call the seat of government the " metropolis,"
and the rest of the kingdom the " provinces; " names unknown

to English law, and alien to all English feeling. If we begin
to give eight members to the Tower Hamlets, the words may
possibly begin to have a meaning; and Manchester and
Arundel, Caithness and Tipperary, may alike have to look
out for a Fabius and a Decius to deliver them from the *turba
forensis* of a single overgrown city.

*[Although the references to the quotations from Mommsen in this
introduction are made to refer to the present edition, the wording will be
found to differ slightly, as they are Freeman's own translation.]*

The following is a list of the works of Theodor
Mommsen:—

Chief Works: Ad Legem de Scribis et viatoribus et de auctoritate, 1843;
De Collegiis et Sodaliciis Romanorum, 1843; Die römischen Tribus in
administrativer Beziehung, 1844; Oskische Studien, 1845; Supplement,
1846; Epigraphische Analekten, 1849, etc.; Die Unteritalischen Dialekte,
1850; Geschichte des römischen Munzwesens, 1850; 2nd edition, 1860;
Ueber den Chronographen vom Jahre 354, 1850; Römische Urkunden,
1850; Inscriptiones regni Neapolitani Latinae, 1851; Das Edit. Diokletian,
1851, 1893; Die Römische Feldmesser, 1852; Volusii Maeciani dis-
tributio partium, 1853; Inscriptiones Confaederationis Helveticae Latinae,
1854; Römische Geschichte, 1854-7, and many later editions; Die Stadt-
rechte der latinischen Gemeinden Salpensa ü Malaca, 1855; Die Rechts-
frage Zwischen Caesar und dem Senat, 1857; Die Römische Chronologie
bis auf Caesar, 1858; 2nd edition, 1860; Juris Antejustiniani fragmenta,
1861; Verzeichniss der römischen Provinzen Aufgesetzt um 297, 1862;
Römische Forschungen, 1863; Res Gestae divi Augusti, 1865; Justiniani
Digestorum seu Pandectarum libri, 1866, etc.; Römisches Staatsrecht,
1871, etc.; Observationes epigraphicae, 1872, etc.; Das Militär system
Caesars, 1877; Jordanis Romana et Getica (edited by), 1882; Con-
scriptionsordnung der Römischen Kaiserzeit, 1884; Das römische
militärwesen seit Diocletian, 1889; Chronica Minora Saeculi iv. v. vi.
vii., 1891 (edited by). Many of Mommsen's writings appeared first in
Mem. Soc. Royale de Saxe.

Mommsen was chief editor of Corpus inscriptionum latinarum, 1863,
etc.; and joint editor of Collectio Librorum juris Antejustiniani, 1884, etc.

Among the works edited by him were:—Polemii Silvii Laterculus, 1857;
C. Julii Solinii Collectanea, 1864, 1895; Plinii Epistulae et panegyricus,
1870; the History of Cassiodorus and Epistulae Theodericianae, and works
by Eusebius.

Works:—Collected Edition, with preface by H. O. Hirschfeld, 1905, etc.
English Translation of History:—W. P. Dickson, 4 vols. 1862-75; new
revised edition, 5 vols, 1894; The Provinces from Caesar to Diocletian,
2 vols. 1868-86; Dickson's translation, revised by F. Haverfeld, 2 vols.,
1909. The Earliest Inhabitants of Italy (from the History), translated
by G. Robertson, 1858.

Abridged edition by C. Bryans and F. J. R. Hendy, 1888.

TRANSLATOR'S NOTE TO THE EDITION
OF 1868

IN preparing this new edition, I have incorporated all the additions and alterations which are introduced in the *fourth* edition of the German; some of which, especially in the first volume, are of considerable importance, such as the fuller view given of the constitution and functions of the senate, the earlier paragraphs of the chapter on Religion, and the note on the history of the Greek alphabet at p. 213.   I have also embraced the opportunity of correcting various errors of my own or of the printer that had formerly escaped notice; and I have subjected the translation, particularly in the earlier portion, to careful revision, so as to make the rendering more accurate and consistent, and in not a few instances, I trust, more idiomatic.

GLASGOW COLLEGE, *October* 1868.

TO

MY FRIEND

MORIZ HAUPT

OF

BERLIN

EXTRACT FROM DR. MOMMSEN'S PREFACE

THE Varronian computation by years of the City is given as well as the corresponding year before the birth of Christ—the U.C. being above and the B.C. below the line.

In calculating the corresponding years, the year 1 of the City has been assumed as identical with the year 753 B.C., and with Olymp. 6, 4; although, if we take into account the circumstance that the Roman solar year began with the 1st day of March, and the Greek with the 1st day of July, the year 1 of the City would according to more exact calculation correspond to the last ten months of 753 and the first two months of 752 B.C., and to the last four months of Ol. 6, 3 and the first eight of Ol. 6, 4.

The Roman and Greek money has uniformly been commuted on the basis of assuming the libral *as* and *sestertius,* and the *denarius* and Attic *drachma,* respectively as equal, and taking for all sums above 100 *denarii* the present value in gold, and for all sums under 100 *denarii* the present value in silver, of the corresponding weight. The Roman pound (=327.45 *grammes*) of gold, equal to 4000 sesterces, has thus, according to the ratio of gold to silver 1: 15.5, been reckoned at 304½ Prussian *thalers* [about £43], and the *denarius,* according to the value of silver, at 7 Prussian *groschen* [about 8*d.*].[1]

[1] [I have deemed it, in general, sufficient to give the value of the Roman money approximately in round numbers, assuming for that purpose 100 sesterces as equivalent to £1.—TR.]

CONTENTS

BOOK FIRST

THE PERIOD ANTERIOR TO THE ABOLITION OF THE MONARCHY

BOOK SECOND

FROM THE ABOLITION OF THE MONARCHY IN ROME TO THE UNION OF ITALY

APPENDIX

BOOK FIRST

THE PERIOD ANTERIOR TO THE ABOLITION
OF THE MONARCHY

Τὰ παλαιότερα σαφῶς μὲν εὑρεῖν διὰ χρόνου πλῆθος ἀδύνατα ἦν· ἐκ δὲ τεκμηρίων ὧν ἐπὶ μακρότατον σκοποῦντί μοι πιστεῦσαι ξυμβαίνει οὐ μεγάλα νομίζω γενέσθαι, οὔτε κατὰ τοὺς πολέμους οὔτε ἐς τὰ ἄλλα.

THUCYDIDES.

THE HISTORY OF ROME

BOOK FIRST

CHAPTER I

INTRODUCTION

THE Mediterranean Sea with its various branches, penetrating
far into the great Continent, forms the largest gulf of the ocean,
and, alternately narrowed by islands or projections of the land
and expanding to considerable breadth, at once separates and
connects the three divisions of the Old World. The shores of
this inland sea were in ancient times peopled by various nations
belonging in an ethnographical and philological point of view
to different races, but constituting in their historical aspect one
whole. This historic whole has been usually, but not very
appropriately, entitled the history of the ancient world. It is
in reality the history of civilisation among the Mediterranean
nations; and, as it passes before us in its successive stages, it
presents four great phases of development—the history of the
Coptic or Egyptian stock dwelling on the southern shore, the
history of the Aramaean or Syrian nation which occupied the
east coast and extended into the interior of Asia as far as the
Euphrates and Tigris, and the histories of the twin-peoples, the
Hellenes and Italians, who received as their heritage the
countries on the European shore. Each of these histories was
in its earlier stages connected with other regions and with other
cycles of historical evolution; but each soon entered on its own
distinctive career. The surrounding nations of alien or even of
kindred extraction—the Berbers and Negroes of Africa, the
Arabs, Persians, and Indians of Asia, the Celts and Germans of
Europe—came into manifold contact with the peoples inhabiting the borders of the Mediterranean, but they neither imparted
unto them nor received from them any influences exercising
decisive effect on their respective destinies. So far, therefore,
as cycles of culture admit of demarcation at all, the cycle which
has its culminating points denoted by the names Thebes, Carthage, Athens, and Rome, may be regarded as an unity. The four

nations represented by these names, after each of them had
attained in a path of its own a peculiar and noble civilisation,
mingled with one another in the most varied relations of reciprocal intercourse, and skilfully elaborated and richly developed
all the elements of human nature. At length their cycle was
accomplished. New peoples who hitherto had only laved the
territories of the states of the Mediterranean, as waves lave the
beach, overflowed both its shores, severed the history of its
south coast from that of the north, and transferred the centre
of civilisation from the Mediterranean to the Atlantic Ocean.
The distinction between ancient and modern history, therefore,
is no mere accident, nor yet a mere matter of chronological convenience. What is called modern history is in reality the formation of a new cycle of culture, connected in several stages of its
development with the perishing or perished civilisation of the
Mediterranean states, as this was connected with the primitive
civilisation of the Indo-Germanic stock, but destined, like the
earlier cycle, to traverse an orbit of its own. It too is destined
to experience in full measure the vicissitudes of national weal and
woe, the periods of growth, of maturity, and of age, the blessed-
ness of creative effort in religion, polity, and art, the comfort of
enjoying the material and intellectual acquisitions which it has
won, perhaps also, some day, the decay of productive power in
the satiety of contentment with the goal attained. And yet
this goal will only be temporary: the grandest system of civilisation has its orbit, and may complete its course; but not so the
human race, to which, just when it seems to have reached its
goal, the old task is ever set anew with a wider range and with
a deeper meaning.

Our aim is to exhibit the last act of this great historical drama,
to relate the ancient history of the central peninsula projecting from the northern continent into the Mediterranean. It is
formed by the mountain-system of the Apennines branching off ·
in a southern direction from the western Alps. The Apennines
take in the first instance a south-eastern course between the
broader gulf of the Mediterranean on the west, and the narrow
one on the east; and in the close vicinity of the latter they
attain their greatest elevation, which, however, scarce reaches
the line of perpetual snow, in the Abruzzi. From the Abruzzi
the chain continues in a southern direction, at first undivided
and of considerable height; after a depression which forms a
hill-country, it splits into a somewhat flattened succession of
heights towards the south-east and a more rugged chain towards

the south, and in both directions terminates in the formation of narrow peninsulas.

The flat country on the north, extending between the Alps and the Apennines as far down as the Abruzzi, does not belong geographically, nor until a very late period even historically, to the southern land of mountain and hill, the Italy whose history is here to engage our attention. It was not till the seventh century of the city that the coast-district from Sinigaglia to Rimini, and not till the eighth that the basin of the Po, became incorporated with Italy. The ancient boundary of Italy on the north was not the Alps but the Apennines. This mountain-system nowhere rises abruptly into a precipitous chain, but, spreading broadly over the land and enclosing many valleys and table-lands connected by easy passes, presents conditions which well adapt it to become the settlement of man. Still more suitable in this respect are the adjacent slopes and the coast-districts on the east, south, and west. On the east coast the plain of Apulia, shut in towards the north by the mountain-block of the Abruzzi and only broken by the steep isolated ridge of Garganus, stretches in an uniform level with but a scanty development of coast and stream. On the south coast, between the two peninsulas in which the Apennines terminate, extensive lowlands, poorly provided with harbours but well watered and fertile, adjoin the hill-country of the interior. The west coast presents a far-stretching domain intersected by considerable streams, in particular by the Tiber, and shaped by the action of the waves and of the once numerous volcanoes into manifold variety of hill and valley, harbour and island. Here the regions of Etruria, Latium, and Campania, form the very flower of the land of Italy. South of Campania, the land in front of the mountains gradually diminishes, and the Tyrrhenian Sea almost washes their base. Moreover, as the Peloponnesus is attached to Greece, so the island of Sicily is attached to Italy—the largest and fairest isle of the Mediterranean, having a mountainous and partly desert interior, but girt, especially on the east and south, by a broad belt of the finest coast-land, mainly the result of volcanic action. Geographically the Sicilian mountains are a continuation of the Apennines, hardly interrupted by the narrow "rent" (Ρήγιον) of the straits; and in its historical rela-tions Sicily was in earlier times quite as decidedly a part of Italy as the Peloponnesus was of Greece,—a field for the struggles of the same races, and the seat of a similar superior civilisation.

The Italian peninsula resembles the Grecian in the temperate

climate and wholesome air that prevail on the hills of moderate
height, and on the whole, also, in the valleys and plains.   In
development of coast it is inferior; it wants, in particular, the
island-studded sea which made the Hellenes a seafaring nation.
Italy on the other hand excels its neighbour in the rich alluvial
plains and the fertile and grassy mountain-slopes, which are
requisite for agriculture and the rearing of cattle.   Like Greece
it is a noble land which calls forth and rewards the energies of
man, opening up alike for restless adventure the way to distant
lands and for quiet exertion modes of peaceful gain at home.

But, while the Grecian peninsula is turned towards the east,
the Italian is turned towards the west.   As the coasts of Epirus
and Acarnania had but a subordinate importance in the case of
Hellas, so had the Apulian and Messapian coasts in that of Italy;
and, while the regions on which the historical development of
Greece has been mainly dependent—Attica and Macedonia—
look to the east, Etruria, Latium, and Campania look to the west.
In this way the two peninsulas, so close neighbours and almost
sisters, stand as it were averted from each other.   Although the
naked eye can discern from Otranto the Acroceraunian mountains, the Italians and Hellenes came into earlier and closer
contact on every other pathway rather than on the nearest
across the Adriatic Sea.   In their instance, as has happened so
often, the historical vocation of the nations was prefigured in
the relations of the ground which they occupied; the two great
stocks, on which the civilisation of the ancient world grew,
threw their shadow as well as their seed, the one towards the east,
the other towards the west.

We intend here to relate the history of Italy, not simply the
history of the city of Rome.   Although, in the formal sense of
political law, it was the civic community of Rome which gained
the sovereignty first of Italy and then of the world, such a view
cannot be held to express the higher and real meaning of history.
What has been called the subjugation of Italy by the Romans
appears rather, when viewed in its true light, as the consolidation
into an united state of the whole Italian stock—a stock of which
the Romans were doubtless the most powerful branch, but still
were a branch only.

The history of Italy falls into two main sections: (1) its
internal history down to its union under the leadership of the
Latin stock, and (2) the history of its sovereignty over the
world.   Under the first section, which will occupy the first two
books, we shall have to set forth the settlement of the Italian

stock in the peninsula; the imperilling of its national and political existence, and its partial subjugation, by nations of other descent and older civilisation, Greeks and Etruscans; the rebellion of the Italians against the strangers, and the annihilation or subjection of the latter; finally, the struggles between the two chief Italian stocks, the Latins and the Samnites, for the hegemony of the peninsula, and the victory of the Latins at the end of the fourth century before the birth of Christ—or of the fifth century of the city. The second section opens with the Punic wars; it embraces the rapid extension of the dominion of Rome up to and beyond the natural boundaries of Italy, the long *status quo* of the imperial period, and the collapse of the mighty empire. These events will be narrated in the third and following books.

CHAPTER II

THE EARLIEST MIGRATIONS INTO ITALY

WE have no information, not even a tradition, concerning the first migration of the human race into Italy. It was the universal belief of antiquity that in Italy, as well as elsewhere, the first population had sprung from the soil. We leave it to the province of the naturalist to decide the question of the origin of different races, and of the influence of climate in producing their diversities. In an historical point of view it is neither possible, nor is it of any importance, to determine whether the oldest recorded population of a country were autochthones or immigrants. But it is incumbent on the historical inquirer to bring to light the successive strata of population in the country of which he treats, in order to trace, from as remote an epoch as possible, the gradual progress of civilisation to more perfect forms, and the suppression of races less capable of, or less advanced in, culture by nations of higher standing.

Italy is singularly poor in memorials of the primitive period, and presents in this respect a remarkable contrast to other fields of civilisation. The results of Germanic antiquarian research lead to the conclusion that in England, France, the North of Germany and Scandinavia, before the settlement of the Indo-Germans in those lands, there must have dwelt, or rather roamed, a people, perhaps of Mongolian race, gaining their subsistence by hunting and fishing, making their implements of stone, clay, or bones, adorning themselves with the teeth of animals and with amber, but unacquainted with agriculture and the use of the metals. In India, in like manner, the Indo-Germanic settlers were preceded by a dark-coloured population less susceptible of culture. But in Italy we neither meet with fragments of a supplanted nation, such as the Finns and Lapps in the Celto-Germanic domain and the black tribes in the Indian mountains; nor have any remains of an extinct primitive people been hitherto pointed out there, such as appear to be revealed in the peculiarly-formed skeletons, the places of assembling, and the burial mounds of what is called the stone-period of Germanic antiquity. Nothing has hitherto been brought to light to warrant the supposition that mankind existed in Italy at a period anterior to the knowledge of agriculture and of the smelting of the metals; and if the human race ever within the bounds of Italy really occupied the level of that primitive stage of culture which we are accustomed to call the savage state, every trace of such a fact has disappeared.

Individual tribes, or in other words, races or stocks, are the constituent elements of the earliest history. Among the stocks which in later times we meet with in Italy, the immigration of some, of the Hellenes for instance, and the denationalisation of others, such as the Bruttians and the inhabitants of the Sabine territory, are historically attested. Setting aside both these classes, there remain a number of stocks whose wanderings can no longer be traced by means of historical testimony, but only by *à priori* inference, and whose nationality cannot be shown to have undergone any radical change from external causes. To establish the national individuality of these is the first aim of our inquiry. In such an inquiry had we nothing to fall back upon but the chaotic mass of names of tribes and the confusion of what professes to be historical tradition, the task might well be abandoned as hopeless. The conventionally-received tradition, which assumes the name of history, is composed of a few serviceable notices by civilised travellers, and a mass of mostly worthless legends, which have usually been combined with little discrimination of the true character either of legend or of history. But there is another source of tradition to which we may resort, and which yields information fragmentary but authentic; we mean the indigenous languages of the stocks settled in Italy from time immemorial. These languages, which have grown with the growth of the peoples themselves, have had the stamp of their process of growth impressed upon them too deeply to be wholly effaced by subsequent civilisation. One only of the Italian languages is known to us completely; but the remains which have been preserved of several of the others are sufficient to afford a basis for historical inquiry regarding the existence, and the degrees, of family relationship among the several languages and peoples.

In this way philological research teaches us to distinguish three primitive Italian stocks, the Iapygian, the Etruscan, and that which we shall call the Italian. The last is divided into two main branches,—the Latin branch, and that to which the dialects of the Umbri, Marsi, Volsci, and Samnites belong.

As to the Iapygian stock, we have but little information. At the south-eastern extremity of Italy, in the Messapian or

Calabrian peninsula, inscriptions in a peculiar extinct language [1]
have been found in considerable numbers; undoubtedly remains of the dialect of the Iapygians, who are very distinctly
pronounced by tradition also to have been different from the
and Latin and Samnite stocks.   Statements deserving of credit
numerous indications lead to the conclusion that the same
language and the same stock were indigenous also in Apulia.
What we at present know of this people suffices to show clearly
that they were distinct from the other Italians, but does not
suffice to determine what position should be assigned to them
and to their language in the history of the human race.   The
inscriptions have not yet been, and it is scarcely to be expected
that they ever will be, deciphered.   The genitive forms, *aihi*
and *ihi*, corresponding to the Sanscrit *asya* and the Greek οιο,
appear to indicate that the dialect belongs to the Indo-Germanic
family.   Other indications, such as the use of the aspirated
consonants and the avoiding of the letters *m* and *t* as terminal
sounds, show that this Iapygian dialect was essentially different
from the Italian and corresponded in some respects to the Greek
dialects.   The supposition of an especially close affinity between
the Iapygian nation and the Hellenes finds further support in
the frequent occurrence of the names of Greek divinities in the
inscriptions, and in the surprising facility with which that
people became Hellenised, presenting a striking contrast to the
shyness in this respect of the other Italian nations.   Apulia,
which in the time of Timaeus ($\frac{400}{350}$) [2] was still described as a
barbarous land, had in the sixth century of the city become a
province thoroughly Greek, although no direct colonisation from
Greece had taken place; and even among the ruder stock of the
Messapii there are various indications of a similar tendency.
With the recognition of such a general family relationship or
peculiar affinity between the Iapygians and Hellenes (a recognition, however, which by no means goes so far as to warrant our
taking the Iapygian language to be a rude dialect of Greek),
investigation must rest content, at least in the meantime, until
some more definite and better assured result be attainable. [3]

[1] Some of the epitaphs may give us an idea of its sound; as θεοτορας *arta-
hiaihi bennarrihino* and *dazihonas platorrihi bollihi*.

[2] In all cases throughout this work the Varonian computation by years
of the City is given, as also the corresponding year before the birth of
Christ—the U.C. above and the B.C. below the line.

[3] The hypothesis has been put forward of an affinity between the Iapygian language and the modern Albanian; based, however, on points of
linguistic comparison that are but little satisfactory in any case, and least
of all where a fact of such importance is involved.   Should this relation-

The lack of information, however, is not much felt; for this race, already on the decline at the period when our history begins, comes before us only when it is giving way and disappearing. The character of the Iapygian people little capable of resistance, easily merging into other nationalities, agrees well with the hypothesis, to which their geographical position adds probability, that they were the oldest immigrants or the historical autochthones of Italy. There can be no doubt that all the primitive migrations of nations took place by land; especially such as were directed towards Italy, the coast of which was accessible by sea only to skilful sailors and on that account was still in Homer's time wholly unknown to the Hellenes. But if the earlier settlers came over the Apennines, then, as the geologist infers the origin of mountains from the stratification, the historical inquirer may hazard the conjecture that the stocks pushed furthest towards the south were the oldest inhabitants of Italy; and it is just at its extreme south-eastern verge that we meet with the Iapygian nation.

The middle of the peninsula was inhabited, as far back as reliable tradition reaches, by two peoples or rather two branches of the same people, whose position in the Indo-Germanic family admits of being determined with greater precision than that of the Iapygian nation. We may with propriety call this people the Italian, since upon it rests the historical significance of the peninsula. It is divided into the two branch-stocks of the Latins and the Umbrians; the latter including their southern offshoots, the Marsians and Samnites, and the colonies sent forth by the Samnites in historical times. The philological analysis of the idioms of these stocks has shown that they together constitute a link in the Indo-Germanic chain of languages, and that the epoch in which they still formed an unity is a comparatively late one. In their system of sounds there appears the peculiar spirant *f*, in the use of which they agree with the Etruscans, but decidedly differ from all Hellenic and Helleno-barbaric races as well as from the Sanscrit itself. The aspirates, again, which are retained by the Greeks throughout, and the harsher of them also by the Etruscans, were originally foreign

ship be confirmed, and should the Albanians on the other hand—a race also Indo-Germanic and on a par with the Hellenic and Italian races—be really a remnant of that Helleno-barbaric nationality traces of which occur throughout all Greece and especially in the northern provinces, the nation that preceded the Hellenes would be demonstrated as identical with that which preceded the Italians. Still the inference would not immediately follow that the Iapygian immigration to Italy had taken place across the Adriatic Sea.

to the Italians, and are represented among them by one of their elements—either by the media, or by the breathing alone *f* or *h*. The finer spirants, *s, w, j*, which the Greeks dispense with as much as possible, have been retained in the Italian languages almost unimpaired, and have been in some instances still further developed. The throwing back of the accent and the consequent destruction of terminations are common to the Italians with some Greek stocks and with the Etruscans; but among the Italians this was done to a greater extent than among the former, and to a lesser extent than among the latter. The excessive disorder of the terminations in the Umbrian certainly had no foundation in the original spirit of the language, but was a corruption of later date, which appeared in a similar although weaker tendency also at Rome. Accordingly in the Italian languages short vowels are regularly dropped in the final sound, long ones frequently: the concluding consonants, on the other hand, have been tenaciously retained in the Latin and still more so in the Samnite; while the Umbrian drops even these. In connection with this we find that the middle voice has left but slight traces in the Italian languages, and a peculiar passive formed by the addition of *r* takes its place; and further that the majority of the tenses are formed by composition with the roots *es* and *fu*, while the richer terminational system of the Greeks along with the augment enables them for the most part to dispense with auxiliary verbs. While the Italian languages, like the Aeolic dialect, gave up the dual, they retained universally the ablative which the Greeks lost, and for the most part also the locative. The rigorous logic of the Italians appears to have taken offence at the splitting of the idea of plurality into that of duality and of multitude; while they have continued with much precision to express the relations of words by inflections. A feature peculiarly Italian, and unknown even to the Sanscrit, is the mode of imparting a substantive character to the verb by gerunds and supines,—a process carried out more completely here than in any other language.

These examples selected from a great abundance of analogous phenomena suffice to establish the individuality of the Italian stock as distinguished from the other members of the Indo-Germanic family, and at the same time show it to be linguistically the nearest relative, as it is geographically the next neighbour, of the Greek. The Greek and the Italian are brothers; the Celt, the German, and the Slavonian are their cousins. The essential unity of all the Italian as of all the Greek dialects and stocks must have dawned early and clearly on the consciousness of the two great nations themselves; for we find in the Roman language a very ancient word of enigmatical origin, *Graius* or *Graicus,* which is applied to every Greek, and in like manner amongst the Greeks the analogous appellation Ὀπικός, which is applied to all the Latin and Samnite stocks known to the Greeks in earlier times, but never to the Iapygians or Etruscans.

Among the languages of the Italian stock, again, the Latin stands in marked contrast with the Umbro-Samnite dialects. It is true that of these only two, the Umbrian and the Samnite or Oscan, are in some degree known to us, and these even in a manner extremely defective and uncertain. Of the rest some, such as the Marsian and the Volscian, have reached us in fragments too scanty to enable us to form any conception of their individual peculiarities or to classify the varieties of dialect themselves with certainty and precision, while others, like the Sabine, have, with the exception of a few traces preserved as dialectic peculiarities in provincial Latin, completely disappeared. A conjoint view, however, of the facts of language and of history leaves no doubt that all these dialects belonged to the Umbro-Samnite branch of the great Italian stock, and that this branch, although much more closely related to Latin than to Greek, was very decidedly distinct from the Latin. In the pronoun and other cases frequently the Samnite and Umbrian used *p* where the Roman used *q*, as *pis* for *quis*; just as languages otherwise closely related are found to differ; for instance, *p* is peculiar to the Celtic in Brittany and Wales, *k* to the Gaelic and Erse. Among the vowel sounds the diphthongs in Latin and in the northern dialects generally appear very much destroyed, whereas in the southêrn Italian dialects they have suffered little; and connected with this is the fact, that in composition the Roman weakens the radical vowel otherwise so strictly preserved,—a modification which does not take place in the kindred group of languages. The genitive of words in *a* is in this group as among the Greeks *as*, among the Romans in the matured language *ae ;* that of words in *us* is in the Samnite *eis*, in the Umbrian *es*, among the Romans *ei ;* the locative disappeared more and more from the language of the latter, while it continued in full use in the other Italian dialects; the dative plural in *bus* is extant only in Latin. The Umbro-Samnite infinitive in *um* is foreign to the Romans; while the Osco-Umbrian future formed from the root *es* after the Greek fashion (*her-est* like λέγ-σω) has almost, perhaps altogether, disappeared in Latin, and its place is supplied by the optative of the simple verb or by analogous formations from *fuo* (*amabo*). In many of these instances, however—in the forms of the cases, for example —the differences only exist in the two languages when fully formed, while at the outset they coincide. It thus appears that, while the Italian language holds an independent position by the side of the Greek, the Latin dialect within it bears a relation to the Umbro-Samnite somewhat similiar to that of the Ionic to the Doric; and the differences of the Oscan and Umbrian and kindred dialects may be compared with the differences between the Dorism of Sicily and the Dorism of Sparta.

Each of these linguistic phenomena is the result and the attestation of an historical event. With perfect certainty they guide us to the conclusion, that from the common cradle of peoples and languages there issued a stock which embraced in common the ancestors of the Greeks and the Italians; that from this, at a subsequent period, the Italians branched off; and that these again divided into the western and eastern stocks, while at a still later date the eastern became subdivided into Umbrians and Oscans.

When and where these separations took place, language of course cannot tell; and scarce may adventurous thought attempt to grope its conjectural way along the course of those revolutions, the earliest of which undoubtedly took place long before that migration which brought the ancestors of the Italians across the Apennines. On the other hand the comparison of languages, when conducted with accuracy and caution, may give us an approximate idea of the degree of culture which the people had reached when these separations took place, and so furnish us with the beginnings of history, which is nothing but the development of civilisation. For language, especially in the period of its formation, is the true image and organ of the degree of civilisation attained; its archives preserve evidence of the great revolutions in arts and in manners, and from its records the future will not fail to draw information as to those times regarding which the voice of direct tradition is dumb.

During the period when the Indo-Germanic nations which are now separated still formed one stock speaking the same language, they attained a certain stage of culture, and they had a vocabulary corresponding to it. This vocabulary the several nations carried along with them, in its conventionally established use, as a common dowry and a foundation for further structures of their own. In it we find not merely the simplest terms denoting existence, actions, perceptions, such as *sum, do, pater*, the original echo of the impression which the external world made on the mind of man, but also a number of words indicative of culture (not only as respects their roots, but in a form stamped upon them by custom) which are the common property of the Indo-Germanic family, and which cannot be explained either on the principle of an uniform development in the several languages, or on the supposition of their having subsequently borrowed one from another. In this way we possess evidence of the development of pastoral life at that remote epoch in the unalterably fixed names of domestic animals; the Sanscrit *gâus* is the Latin *bos*, the Greek βοῦς; Sanscrit *avis* is the Latin *ovis*, Greek ὄϊς; Sanscrit *açvas*, Latin *equus*, Greek ἵππος; Sanscrit *hañsas*, Latin *anser*, Greek χήν; Sanscrit *âtis*, Latin *anas*, Greek νῆσσα; in like manner *pecus, sus, porcus, taurus, canis*, are Sanscrit words. Even at this remote period accordingly the stock, on which from the days of Homer down to our own time the intellectual development of mankind has been dependent, had already advanced beyond the lowest stage of civilisation, the hunting and fishing epoch, and had attained at least comparative fixity of abode. On the other hand, we have as yet no certain proofs of the existence of agriculture at this period. Language rather favours the negative view. Of the Latin-Greek names of grain none occurs in Sanscrit with the single exception of ζεά, which philologically represents the Sanscrit *yavas*, but denotes in the Indian barley, in Greek spelt. It must indeed be granted that this diversity in the names of cultivated plants, which so strongly contrasts with the essential agreement in the appellations of domestic animals, does not absolutely preclude the supposition of a common original agriculture. In the circumstances of primitive times transport and acclimatising are more difficult in the case of plants than of animals; and the cultivation of rice among the Indians, that of wheat and spelt among the Greeks and Romans, and that of rye and oats among the Germans and Celts, may all be traceable to a common system of primitive tillage. On the other hand the name of one cereal common to the Greeks and Indians only proves, at the most, that before the separation of the stocks they gathered and ate the grains of barley and spelt growing wild in Mesopotamia,[1] not that they already cultivated

---

[1] Barley, wheat, and spelt were found growing together in a wild state on the right bank of the Euphrates, north-west from Anah (Alph. de Can-

grain. While, however, we reach no decisive result in this way, a further light is thrown on the subject by our observing that a number of the most important words bearing on this province of culture occur certainly in Sanscrit, but all of them in a more general signification. *Agras* among the Indians denotes a level surface in general; *kûrnu*, anything pounded; *aritram*, oar and ship; *venas*, that which is pleasant in general, particularly a pleasant drink. The words are thus very ancient; but their more definite application to the field (*ager*), to the grain to be ground (*granum*), to the implement which furrows the soil as the ship furrows the surface of the sea (*aratrum*), to the juice of the grape (*vinum*), had not yet taken place when the earliest division of the stocks occurred, and it is not to be wondered at that their subsequent applications came to be in some instances very different, and that, for example, the corn intended to be ground, as well as the mill for grinding it (Gothic *quairnus*, Lithuanian *girnôs*[1]), received their names from the Sanscrit *kûrnu*. We may accordingly assume it as probable, that the primeval Indo-Germanic people were not yet acquainted with agriculture, and as certain, that, if they were so, it played but a very subordinate part in their economy; for had it at that time held the place which it afterwards held among the Greeks and Romans, it would have left a deeper impression upon the language.

On the other hand the building of houses and huts by the Indo-Germans is attested by the Sanscrit *dam(as)*, Latin *domus*, Greek δόμος; Sanscrit *veças*, Latin *vicus*, Greek οἶκος; Sanscrit *dvaras*, Latin *fores*, Greek θύρα; further, the building of oar-boats by the names of the boat, Sanscrit *nâus*, Latin *navis*, Greek ναῦς, and of the oar, Sanscrit *aritram*, Greek ἐρετμός, Latin *remus, tri-res-mis ;* and the use of waggons and the breaking in of animals for draught and transport by the Sanscrit *akshas* (axle and cart), Latin *axis*, Greek ἄξων, ἄμ-αξα; Sanscrit *iugam*, Latin, *iugum*, Greek ζυγόν. The words signifying clothing—Sanscrit *vastra*, Latin *vestis*, Greek ἐσθής ; and sewing —Sanscrit *siv*, Latin *suo*; Sanscrit *nah*, Latin *neo*, Greek νήθω, are alike in all Indo-Germanic languages. This cannot, however, be equally affirmed of the higher art of weaving.[2] The know-

dolle, *Géographie Botanique Raisonnée*, ii. p. 934). The growth of barley and wheat in a wild state in Mesopotamia had already been mentioned by the Babylonian historian Berosus (*ap.* Georg. Syncell, p. 50, *Bonn*).

[1] [Scotch *quern.* Mr. Robertson.]

[2] If the Latin *vieo, vimen*, belong to the same root as our *weave* (German. *weben*) and kindred words, the word must still, when the Greeks and Italians separated, have had the general meaning " to plait," and it cannot have been until a later period, and probably in different regions inde-

ledge of the use of fire in preparing food, and of salt for season-
ing it, is a primeval heritage of the Indo-Germanic nations; and
the same may be affirmed regarding the knowledge of the earliest
metals employed as implements or ornaments by man. At
least the names of copper (*aes*) and silver (*argentum*), perhaps
also of gold, are met with in Sanscrit, and these names can
scarcely have originated before man had learned to separate
and to utilise the ores; the Sanscrit *asis*, Latin *ensis*, points in
fact to the primeval use of metallic weapons.

No less do we find extending back into those times the fundamental ideas on which the development of all Indo-Germanic
states ultimately rests; the relative position of husband and
wife, the arrangement in clans, the priesthood of the father of
the household and the absence of a special sacerdotal class as
well as of all distinctions of caste in general, slavery as a legitimate institution, the days of publicly dispensing justice at the
new and full moon. On the other hand the positive organisation of the body politic, the decision of the questions between
regal sovereignty and the sovereignty of the community, between
the hereditary privilege of royal and noble houses and the unconditional legal equality of the citizens, belong altogether to a
later age.

Even the elements of science and religion show traces of a
community of origin. The numbers are the same up to one
hundred (Sanscrit *çatam*, *êkaçatam*, Latin *centum*, Greek, ἑ-κατόν,
Gothic *hund*); and the moon receives her name in all languages
from the fact that men measure time by her (*mensis*). The
idea of Deity itself (Sanscrit *dêvas*, Latin *deus*, Greek θεός),
and many of the oldest conceptions of religion and of natural
symbolism, belong to the common inheritance of the nations.
The conception, for example, of heaven as the father and of
earth as the mother of being, the festal expeditions of the gods
who proceed from place to place in their own chariots along
carefully levelled paths, the shadowy continuation of the soul's
existence after death, are fundamental ideas of the Indian as
well as of the Greek and Roman mythologies. Several of the
gods of the Ganges coincide even in name with those worshipped
on the Ilissus and the Tiber:—thus the Uranus of the Greeks

pendently of each other, that it assumed that of " weaving." The cultivation of flax, old as it is, does not reach back to this period, for the
Indians, though well acquainted with the flax-plant, up to the present day
use it only for the preparation of linseed-oil. Hemp probably became
known to the Italians at a still later period than flax; at least *cannabis*
looks quite like a borrowed word of later date.

is the Varunas, their Zeus, Jovis pater, Diespiter is the Djâus
pitâ of the Vedas. An unexpected light has been thrown on
many an enigmatical form in the Hellenic mythology by recent
researches regarding the earlier divinities of India. The hoary
mysterious forms of the Erinnyes are no Hellenic invention;
they were immigrants along with the oldest settlers from the
East. The divine greyhound *Saramâ*, who guards for the Lord
of heaven the golden herd of stars and sunbeams and collects for
him the nourishing rain-clouds as the cows of heaven to the
milking, and who moreover faithfully conducts the pious dead
into the world of the blessed, becomes in the hands of the
Greeks the son of *Saramâ*, *Saramêyas*, or Hermeias; and the
enigmatical Hellenic story of the stealing of the cattle of Helios,
which is beyond doubt connected with the Roman legend about
Cacus, is now seen to be a last echo (with the meaning no longer
understood) of that old fanciful and significant conception of
nature.

The task, however, of determining the degree of culture
which the Indo-Germans had attained before the separation of
the stocks properly belongs to the general history of the ancient
world. It is on the other hand the special task of Italian history
to ascertain, so far as it is possible, what was the state of the
Graeco-Italian nation when the Hellenes and the Italians parted.
Nor is this a superfluous labour; we reach by means of it the
stage at which Italian civilisation commenced, the starting-
point of the national history.

While it is probable that the Indo-Germans led a pastoral
life and were acquainted with the cereals, if at all, only in their
wild state, all indications point to the conclusion that the
Graeco-Italians were a grain-cultivating, perhaps even a vine-
cultivating, people. The evidence of this is not simply the
knowledge of agriculture itself common to both, for this does
not upon the whole warrant the inference of community of
origin in the peoples who may exhibit it. An historical connection between the Indo-Germanic agriculture and that of the
Chinese, Aramaean, and Egyptian stocks can hardly be disputed; and yet these stocks are either alien to the Indo-Germans,
or at any rate became separated from them at a time when agriculture was certainly still unknown. The truth is, that the
more advanced races in ancient times were, as at the present
day, constantly exchanging the implements and the plants employed in cultivation; and when the annals of China refer the
origin of Chinese agriculture to the introduction of five species

of grain that took place under a particular king in a particular year, the story undoubtedly depicts correctly, at least in a general way, the relations subsisting in the earliest epochs of civilisation. A common knowledge of agriculture, like a common knowledge of the alphabet, of war chariots, of purple, and other implements and ornaments, far more frequently warrants the inference of an ancient intercourse between nations than of their original unity. But as regards the Greeks and Italians, whose mutual relations are comparatively well known, the hypothesis that agriculture as well as writing and coinage first came to Italy by means of the Hellenes may be characterised as wholly inadmissible. On the other hand, the existence of a most intimate connection between the agriculture of the one country and that of the other is attested by their possessing in common all the oldest expressions relating to it; *ager*, ἀγρός ; *aro aratrum*, ἀρόω ἄροτρον ; *ligo* alongside of λαχάινω ; *hortus*, χόρτος ; *hordeum*, κριθή ; *milium*, μελίνη ; *rapa*, ῥαφανίς ; *malva*, μαλάχη ; *vinum*, οἶνος. It is likewise attested by the agreement of Greek and Italian agriculture in the form of the plough, which appears of the same shape on the old Attic and the old Roman monuments; in the choice of the most ancient kinds of grain, millet, barley, spelt; in the custom of cutting the ears with the sickle and having them trodden out by cattle on the smooth-beaten threshing-floor; lastly, in the mode of preparing the grain *puls* πόλτος, *pinso* πτίσσω, *mola* μύλη ; for baking was of more recent origin, and on that account dough or pap was always used in the Roman ritual instead of bread. That the culture of the vine too in Italy was anterior to the earliest Greek immigration, is shown by the appellation " wine-land " (Οἰνωτρία), which appears to reach back to the oldest visits of Greek voyagers. It would thus appear that the transition from pastoral life to agriculture, or, to speak more correctly, the combination of agriculture with the earlier pastoral economy, must have taken place after the Indians had departed from the common cradle of the nations, but before the Hellenes and Italians dissolved their ancient communion. Moreover, at the time when agriculture originated, the Hellenes and Italians appear to have been united as one national whole not merely with each other, but with other members of the great family; at least, it is a fact, that the most important of those terms of cultivation, while they are foreign to the Asiatic members of the Indo-Germanic family, are used by the Romans and Greeks in common with the Celtic as well as the Germanic, Slavonic, and Lithuanian stocks.[1]

The distinction between the common inheritance of the nations and their own subsequent acquisitions in manners and in language is still far from having been wrought out in all the variety of its details and gradations. The investigation of languages with this view has scarcely begun, and history still in the main derives its representation of primitive times, not from the rich mine of language, but from what must be called for the most part the rubbish-heap of tradition. For the present, therefore, it must suffice to indicate the differences between the culture of the Indo-Germanic family in its earliest entireness, and the culture of that epoch when the Graeco-Italians still lived together. The task of discriminating the results of culture which are common to the European members of this family, but foreign to its Asiatic members, from those which the several European groups, such as the Graeco-Italian and the Germano-Slavonic, have wrought out for themselves, can only be accomplished, if at all, after greater progress has been made in philological and historical inquiries. But there can be no doubt that, with the Graeco-Italians as with all other nations, agriculture became and in the mind of the people remained the germ and core of their national and of their private life. The house and the fixed hearth, which the husbandman constructs instead of the light hut and shifting fireplace of the shepherd, are represented in the spiritual domain and idealised in the goddess Vesta or Ἑστία, almost the only divinity not Indo-Germanic yet from the first common to both nations. One of the oldest legends of the Italian race ascribes to king Italus, or, as the Italians must have pronounced the word, Vitalus or Vitulus, the introduction of the change from a pastoral to an agricultural life, and shrewdly connects with it the original

---

[1] Thus *aro, aratrum* reappear in the old German *aran* (to plough, dialectically *eren*), *erida*, in Slavonian *orati, oradlo*, in Lithuanian *arti, arimnas*, in Celtic *ar, aradar*. Thus alongside of *ligo* stands our *rake* (German *rechen*), of *hortus* our *garden* (German *garten*), of *mola* our *mill* (German *mühle*, Slavonic *mlyn*, Lithuanian *malunas*, Celtic *malin*).

With all these facts before us, we cannot allow that there ever was a time when the Greeks in all Hellenic cantons subsisted by purely pastoral husbandry. If it was the possession of cattle, and not of land, which in Greece as in Italy formed the basis and the standard of all private property, the reason of this was not that agriculture was of later introduction, but that it was at first conducted on the system of joint possession. Of course a purely agricultural economy cannot have existed anywhere before the separation of the stocks; on the contrary, pastoral husbandry was (more or less according to locality) combined with it to an extent relatively greater than was the case in later times.

Italian legislation. We have simply another version of the same belief in the legend of the Samnite race which makes the ox the leader of their primitive colonies, and in the oldest Latin national names which designate the people as reapers (*Siculi*, perhaps also *Sicani*), or as field-labourers (*Opsci*). It is one of the characteristic incongruities which attach to the so-called legend of the origin of Rome, that it represents a pastoral and hunting people as founding a city. Legend and faith, laws and manners, among the Italians as among the Hellenes are throughout associated with agriculture.[1]

Cultivation of the soil cannot be conceived without some measurement of it, however rude. Accordingly, the measures of surface and the mode of setting off boundaries rest, like agriculture itself, on a like basis among both peoples. The Oscan and Umbrian *versus* of one hundred square feet corresponds exactly with the Greek *plethron*. The principle of marking off boundaries was also the same. The land-measurer adjusted his position with reference to one of the cardinal points, and proceeded to draw in the first place two lines, one from north to south, and another from east to west, his station being in their point of intersection (*templum*, τέμενος from τέμνω); then he drew at certain fixed distances lines parallel to these, and by this process produced a series of rectangular pieces of ground, the corners of which were marked by boundary posts (*termini*, in Sicilian inscriptions τέρμονες, usually ὅροι). This mode of defining boundaries, which is indeed also Etruscan but is hardly of Etruscan origin, we find among the Romans, Umbrians, Samnites, and also in very ancient records of the Tarentine Heracleots, who are as little likely to have borrowed it from the Italians as the Italians from the Tarentines: it is an ancient possession common to all. A peculiar characteristic of the Romans, on the other hand, was their rigid carrying out of the principle of the square; even where the sea or a river formed a natural boundary, they did not accept it, but wound up their allocation of the land with the last complete square.

It is not solely in agriculture, however, that the especially

---

[1] Nothing is more significant in this respect than the close connection of agriculture with marriage and the foundation of cities during the earliest epoch of culture. Thus the gods in Italy immediately concerned with marriage are Ceres and (or?) Tellus (Plutarch, *Romul.* 22; Servius on *Aen.* iv., 166; Rossbach, *Röm. Ehe*, 257, 301), in Greece Demeter (Plutarch, *Conjug. Praec. init.*); in old Greek formulas the procreation of children is called ἄροτος (p. 24, *note*); indeed, the oldest Roman form of marriage, *confarreatio*, derives its name and its ceremony from the cultivation of corn. The use of the plough in the founding of cities is well known.

close relationship of the Greeks and Italians appears; it is unmistakably manifest also in the other provinces of man's earliest activity. The Greek house, as described by Homer, differs little from the model which was always adhered to in Italy. The essential portion, which originally formed the whole interior accommodation of the Latin house, was the *atrium*, that is, the " blackened " chamber, with the household altar, the marriage bed, the table for meals, and the hearth; and precisely similar is the Homeric *megaron*, with its household altar and hearth and smoke-begrimed roof. We cannot say the same of ship-building. The boat with oars was an old common possession of the Indo-Germans; but the advance to the use of sailing vessels can scarcely be considered to have taken place during the Graeco-Italian period, for we find no nautical terms originally common to the Greeks and Italians except such as are also general among the Indo-Germanic family. On the other hand the primitive Italian custom of the husbandmen having common midday meals, the origin of which the myth connects with the introduction of agriculture, is compared by Aristotle with the Cretan Syssitia; and the ancient Romans further agreed with the Cretans and Laconians in taking their meals not, as was afterwards the custom among both peoples, in a reclining, but in a sitting posture. The method of kindling fire by the friction of two pieces of wood of different kinds is common to all peoples; but it is certainly no mere accident that the Greeks and Italians agree in the appellations which they give to the two portions of the touch-wood, " the rubber " (τρύπανον, *terebra*), and the " under-layer " (στόρευς, ἐσχάρα, *tabula*, probably from *tendere*, τέταμαι). In like manner the dress of the two peoples is essentially identical, for the *tunica* quite corresponds with the *chiton*, and the *toga* is nothing but a fuller *himation*. Even as regards weapons of war, liable as they are to frequent change, the two peoples have this much at least in common, that their two principal weapons of attack were the javelin and the bow, —a fact which is clearly expressed, as far as Rome is concerned, in the earliest names for warriors (*quirites, samnites, pilumni— arquites*),[1] and is in keeping with the oldest mode of fighting which was not properly adapted to a close struggle. Thus, in the language and manners of Greeks and Italians, all that relates

---

[1] Among the oldest names of weapons on both sides scarcely any can be shown to be certainly related; *lancea*, although doubtless connected with λόγχη, is, as a Roman word, recent, and perhaps borrowed from the Germans or Spaniards; and the Greek σαυνίον is in a similar position.

to the material foundations of human life may be traced back to the same primary elements; the oldest problems which the world proposes to man had been jointly solved by the two peoples at a time when they still formed one nation.

It was otherwise in the spiritual domain. The great problem of man—how to live in conscious harmony with himself, with his neighbour, and with the whole to which he belongs—admits of as many solutions as there are provinces in our Father's kingdom; and it is in this, and not in the material sphere, that individuals and nations display their divergences of character. The exciting causes which gave rise to this intrinsic contrast must have been in the Graeco-Italian period as yet wanting; it was not until the Hellenes and Italians had separated that that deep-seated diversity of mental character became manifest, the effects of which continue to the present day. The family and the state, religion and art, received in Italy and in Greece respectively a development so peculiar and so thoroughly national, that the common basis, on which in these respects also the two peoples rested, has been so overgrown as to be almost concealed from our view. That Hellenic character, which sacrificed the whole to its individual elements, the nation to the township, and the township to the citizen; which sought its ideal of life in the beautiful and the good, and, but too often, in the enjoyment of idleness; which attained its political development by intensifying the original individuality of the several cantons, and at length produced the internal dissolution of even local authority; which in its view of religion first invested the gods with human attributes, and then denied their existence; which allowed full play to the limbs in the sports of the naked youth, and gave free scope to thought in all its grandeur and in all its awfulness;—and that Roman character, which solemnly bound the son to reverence the father, the citizen to reverence the ruler, and all to reverence the gods; which required nothing and honoured nothing but the useful act, and compelled every citizen to fill up every moment of his brief life with unceasing work; which made it a duty even in the boy modestly to cover the body; which deemed every one a bad citizen who wished to be different from his fellows; which regarded the state as all in all, and a desire for the state's extension as the only aspiration not liable to censure,—who can in thought trace back these sharply-marked contrasts to that original unity which embraced them both, prepared the way for their development, and at length produced them? It would

be foolish presumption to desire to lift this veil; we shall only
endeavour to indicate in brief outline the beginnings of Italian
nationality and its connections with an earlier period; to direct
the guesses of the discerning reader rather than to express
them.

All that may be called the patriarchal element in the state
rested in Greece and Italy on the same foundations. Under
this head comes especially the moral and decorous arrangement
of the relations of the sexes,[1] which enjoined monogamy on
the husband and visited with heavy penalties the infidelity of
the wife, and which recognised the equality of woman and the
sanctity of marriage in the high position which it assigned to
the mother within the domestic circle. On the other hand the
rigorous development of the marital and still more of the
paternal authority, regardless of the natural rights of persons
as such, was a feature foreign to the Greeks and peculiarly
Italian; it was in Italy alone that moral subjection became
transformed into legal slavery. In the same way the principle
of the slave being completely destitute of legal rights—a principle involved in the very nature of slavery—was maintained
by the Romans with merciless rigour and carried out to all its
consequences; whereas among the Greeks alleviations of its
harshness were early introduced both in practice and in legislation, the marriage of slaves, for example, being recognised
as a legal relation.

On the household was based the clan, that is, the community
of the descendants of the same progenitor; and out of the clan
among the Greeks as well as the Italians arose the state. But
while under the weaker political development of Greece the
clan maintained itself as a corporate power, in contradistinction to that of the state, far even into historical times, the state
in Italy made its appearance at once in complete efficiency,
inasmuch as in presence of its authority the clans were neutralised and it exhibited an association not of clans, but of citizens.
Conversely, again, the individual attained relatively to the clan
an inward independence and freedom of personal development
far earlier and more completely in Greece than in Rome—a fact
reflected with great clearness in the Greek and Roman proper
names, which, originally similar, came to assume very different

---

[1] Even in details this agreement appears; *e.g.*, in the designation of lawful wedlock as " marriage concluded for the obtaining of lawful children "
(γάμος ἐπὶ) παιδων γνησίων ἀρότῳ —*matrimonium liberorum quaerendorum
causa*).

forms. In the more ancient Greek names the name of the clan was very frequently added in an adjective form to that of the individual; while, conversely, Roman scholars were aware that their ancestors bore originally only one name, the later *prae-nomen*. But while in Greece the adjective name of the clan early disappeared, it became, among the Italians generally and not merely among the Romans, the principal name; and the distinctive individual name, the *praenomen*, became subordinate. It seems as if the small and ever diminishing number and the meaningless character of the Italian, and particularly of the Roman, individual names, compared with the luxuriant and poetical fulness of those of the Greeks, were intended to illustrate the truth that it was characteristic of the one nation to reduce all features of distinctive personality to an uniform level, of the other freely to promote their development.

The association in communities of families under patriarchal chiefs, which we may conceive to have prevailed in the Graeco-Italian period, may appear different enough from the later forms of Italian and Hellenic polities; yet it must have already contained the germs out of which the future laws of both nations were moulded. The "laws of king Italus," which were still applied in the time of Aristotle, may denote the institutions essentially common to both. These laws must have provided for the maintenance of peace and the execution of justice within the community, for military organisation and martial law in reference to its external relations, for its government by a patriarchal chief, for a council of elders, for assemblies of the freemen capable of bearing arms, and for some sort of constitution. Judicial procedure (*crimen, κρίνειν*), expiation (*poena, ποίνη*), retaliation (*talio, ταλάω, τλῆναι*), are Graeco-Italian ideas. The stern law of debt, by which the debtor was directly responsible with his person for the repayment of what he had received, is common to the Italians, for example, with the Tarentine Heracleots. The fundamental ideas of the Roman constitution—a king, a senate, and an assembly entitled simply to ratify or to reject the proposals which the king and senate should submit to it—are scarcely anywhere expressed so distinctly as in Aristotle's account of the earlier constitution of Crete. The germs of larger state-confederacies in the political fraternising or even amalgamation of several previously independent stocks (symmachy, synoikismos) are in like manner common to both nations. The more stress is to be laid on this fact of the common foundations of Hellenic and Italian polity,

that it is not found to extend to the other Indo-Germanic
stocks; the organisation of the Germanic communities, for
example, by no means starts, like that of the Greeks and Romans,
from an elective monarchy.　But how different the polities were
that were constructed on this common basis in Italy and Greece,
and how completely the whole course of their political development belongs to each as its distinctive property,[1] it will be the
business of the sequel to show.

It is the same in religion.　In Italy, as in Hellas, there lies
at the foundation of the popular faith the same common treasure
of symbolic and allegorical views of nature: on this rests that
general analogy between the Roman and the Greek world of
gods and of spirits, which was to become of so much importance
in later stages of development.　In many of their particular
conceptions also,—in the already mentioned forms of Zeus-
Diovis and Hestia-Vesta, in the idea of the holy space (τέμενος,
templum), in many offerings and ceremonies—the two modes of
worship do not by mere accident coincide.　Yet in Hellas, as in
Italy, they assumed a shape so thoroughly national and peculiar,
that but little of the ancient common inheritance was preserved
in a recognisable form, and that little was for the most part
misunderstood or not understood at all.　It could not be otherwise; for, just as in the peoples themselves the great contrasts,
which during the Graeco-Italian period had lain side by side
undeveloped, were after their division distinctly evolved, so in
their religion also a separation took place between the idea and
the image, which had hitherto been one whole in the soul.
Those old tillers of the ground, when the clouds were driving
along the sky, probably expressed to themselves the phenomenon by saying that the hound of the gods was driving together
the startled cows of the herd.　The Greek forgot that the cows
were really the clouds, and converted the son of the hound of
the gods—a form devised merely for the particular purposes of
that conception—into the adroit messenger of the gods ready
for every service.　When the thunder rolled among the mountains, he saw Zeus brandishing his bolts on Olympus; when the
blue sky again smiled upon him, he gazed into the bright eye of
Athenaea, the daughter of Zeus; and so powerful over him was

---

[1] Only we must, of course, not forget that like pre-existing conditions
lead everywhere to like institutions.　For instance, nothing is more certain
than that the Roman plebeians were a growth originating within the
Roman commonwealth, and yet they everywhere find their counterpart
where a body of *metoeci* has arisen alongside of a body of burgesses.　As a
matter of course, chance also plays in such cases its provoking game.

the influence of the forms which he had thus created, that he soon saw nothing in them but human beings invested and illumined with the splendour of nature's power, and freely formed and transformed them according to the laws of beauty. It was in another fashion, but not less strongly, that the deeply implanted religious feeling of the Italian race manifested itself; it held firmly by the idea and did not suffer the form to obscure it. As the Greek, when he sacrificed, raised his eyes to heaven, so the Roman veiled his head; for the prayer of the former was contemplation, that of the latter reflection. Throughout the whole of nature he adored the spiritual and the universal. To everything existing, to the man and to the tree, to the state and to the store-room, was assigned a spirit which came into being with it and perished along with it, the counterpart of the natural phenomenon in the spiritual domain; to the man the male Genius, to the woman the female Juno, to the boundary Terminus, to the forest Silvanus, to the circling year Vertumnus, and so on to every object after its kind. In occupations the very steps of the process were spiritualised: thus, for example, in the prayer for the husbandman there was invoked the spirit of fallowing, of ploughing, of furrowing, sowing, covering-in, harrowing, and so forth down to the in-bringing, up-storing, and opening of the granaries. In like manner marriage, birth, and every other natural event were endowed with a sacred life. The larger the sphere embraced in the abstraction, the higher rose the god and the reverence paid by man. Thus Jupiter and Juno are the abstractions of manhood and womanhood; Dea Dia or Ceres, the creative power; Minerva, the power of memory; Dea Bona or among the Samnites Dea Cupra, the good deity. While to the Greek everything assumed a concrete and corporeal shape, the Roman could only make use of abstract, completely transparent formulae; and while the Greek for the most part threw aside the old legendary treasures of primitive times, because they embodied the idea in too transparent a form, the Roman could still less retain them, because the sacred conceptions seemed to him dimmed even by the lightest veil of allegory. Not a trace has been preserved among the Romans even of the oldest and most generally diffused myths, such as that current among the Indians, the Greeks, and even the Semites, regarding a great flood and its survivor, the common ancestor of the present human race. Their gods could not marry and beget children, like those of the Hellenes; they did not walk about unseen among mortals; and they needed no

nectar. But that they, nevertheless, in their spirituality—
which only appears tame to dull apprehension—gained a
powerful hold on men's minds, a hold more powerful perhaps
than that of the gods of Hellas created after the image of man,
would be attested, even if history were silent on the subject, by
the Roman designation of faith (the word and the idea alike
foreign to the Hellenes), *Religio*, that is to say, " that which
binds." As India and Iran developed from one and the same
inherited store, the former, the richly varied forms of its sacred
epics, the latter, the abstractions of the Zend-Avesta; so in the
Greek mythology the person is predominant, in the Roman the
idea, in the former freedom, in the latter necessity.

Lastly, what holds good of real life is true also of its counterfeit
in jest and play, which everywhere, and especially in the earliest
period of full and simple existence, do not exclude the serious,
but veil it. The simplest elements of art are in Latium and
Hellas quite the same; the decorous armed dance, the " leap "
(*triumpus θρίαμβος, δι-θύραμβος*); the masquerade of the
" full people " (*σάτυροι, satura*), who, enveloped in the skins of
sheep or goats, wound up the festival with their jokes; lastly,
the pipe, which with suitable strains accompanied and regulated
the solemn as well as the merry dance. Nowhere, perhaps, does
the especially close relationship of the Hellenes and Italians
come to light so clearly as here; and yet in no other direction
did the two nations manifest greater divergence as they became
developed. The training of youth remained in Latium strictly
confined to the narrow limits of domestic education; in Greece
the yearning after a varied yet harmonious training of mind
and body created the sciences of Gymnastics and Paideia,
which were cherished by the nation and by individuals as their
highest good. Latium in the poverty of its artistic development stands almost on a level with uncivilised peoples; Hellas
developed with incredible rapidity out of its religious conceptions the myth and the worshipped idol, and out of these that
marvellous world of poetry and sculpture, the like of which
history has not again to show. In Latium no other influences
were powerful in public and private life but prudence, riches,
and strength; it was reserved for the Hellenes to feel the blissful
ascendancy of beauty, to minister to the fair boy-friend with an
enthusiasm half sensuous, half ideal, and to reanimate their lost
courage with the war-songs of the divine singer.

Thus the two nations in which the civilisation of antiquity
culminated stand side by side, as different in development as

they were in origin identical.   The points in which the Hellenes
excel the Italians are more universally intelligible and reflect a
more brilliant lustre; but the deep feeling in each individual
that he was only a part of the community, a rare devotedness
and power of self-sacrifice for the common weal, an earnest
faith in its own gods, form the rich treasure of the Italian nation.
Both nations received a one-sided, and therefore each a complete, development; it is only a pitiful narrowmindedness that
will object to the Athenian that he did not know how to mould
his state like the Fabii and the Valerii, or to the Roman that he
did not learn to carve like Phidias and to write like Aristophanes.
It was in fact the most peculiar and the best feature in the
character of the Greek people, that rendered it impossible for
them to advance from national to political unity without at
the same time exchanging their polity for despotism.   The
ideal world of beauty was all in all to the Greeks, and compensated them to some extent for what they wanted in reality.
Wherever in Hellas a tendency towards national union appeared,
it was based not on elements directly political, but on games and
art: the contests at Olympia, the poems of Homer, the tragedies
of Euripides, were the only bonds that held Hellas together.
Resolutely, on the other hand, the Italian surrendered his own
personal will for the sake of freedom, and learned to obey his
father that he might know how to obey the state.   Amidst this
subjection individual development might be marred, and the
germs of fairest promise in man might be arrested in the bud;
the Italian gained in their stead a feeling of fatherland and of
patriotism such as the Greek never knew, and alone among all
the civilised nations of antiquity succeeded in working out
national unity in connection with a constitution based on self-
government—a national unity, which at last placed in his hands
the mastery not only over the divided Hellenic stock, but over
the whole known world.

CHAPTER III

THE SETTLEMENTS OF THE LATINS

THE home of the Indo-Germanic stock lay in the western portion of central Asia; from this it spread partly in a south-eastern direction over India, partly in a north-western over Europe. It is difficult to determine the primitive seat of the Indo-Germans more precisely: it must, however, at any rate have been inland and remote from the sea, as there is no name for the sea common to the Asiatic and European branches. Many indications point more particularly to the regions of the Euphrates; so that, singularly enough, the primitive seats of the two most important civilised stocks,—the Indo-Germanic and the Aramaean,—almost coincide as regards locality. This circumstance gives support to the hypothesis that these races also were originally connected, although, if there was such a connection, it certainly must have been anterior to all traceable development of culture and language. We cannot define more exactly their original locality, nor are we able to accompany the individual stocks in the course of their migrations. The European branch probably lingered in Persia and Armenia for some considerable time after the departure of the Indians; for, according to all appearance, that region has been the cradle of agriculture and of the culture of the vine. Barley, spelt, and wheat are indigenous in Mesopotamia, and the vine to the south of the Caucasus and of the Caspian Sea: there too the plum, the walnut, and others of the more easily transplanted fruit trees are native. It is worthy of notice that the name for the sea is common to most of the European stocks—Latins, Celts, Germans, and Slavonians; they must probably therefore before their separation have reached the coast of the Black Sea or of the Caspian. By what route from those regions the Italians reached the chain of the Alps, and where in particular they were settled while still united with the Hellenes alone, are questions that can only be answered when the problem is solved by what route—whether from Asia Minor or from the regions of the Danube—the Hellenes arrived in Greece. It may at all events be regarded as certain that the Italians, like the Indians, migrated into their peninsula from the north (p. 11).

The advance of the Umbro-Sabellian stock along the central mountain-ridge of Italy, in a direction from north to south, can still be clearly traced; indeed its last phases belong to purely historical times. Less is known regarding the route which the Latin migration followed. Probably it proceeded in a similar direction along the west coast, long, in all likelihood, before the first Sabellian stocks began to move. The stream only overflows the heights when the lower grounds are already occupied; and only through the supposition that there were Latin stocks already settled on the coast are we able to explain why the Sabellians should have contented themselves with the rougher mountain districts, from which they afterwards issued and intruded, wherever it was possible, between the Latin tribes.

It is well known that a Latin stock inhabited the country from the left bank of the Tiber to the Volscian mountains; but these mountains themselves, which appear to have been neglected on occasion of the first immigration when the plains of Latium and Campania still lay open to the settlers, were, as the Volscian inscriptions show, occupied by a stock more nearly related to the Sabellians than to the Latins. On the other hand, Latins probably dwelt in Campania before the Greek and Samnite immigrations; for the Italian names *Novla* or *Nola* (new-town), *Campani Capua*, *Volturnus* (from *volvere*, like *Iuturna* from *iuvare*), *Opsci* (labourers), are demonstrably older than the Samnite invasion, and show that, at the time when Cumae was founded by the Greeks, an Italian and probably Latin stock, the Ausones, were in possession of Campania. The primitive inhabitants of the districts which the Lucani and Bruttii subsequently occupied, the *Itali* proper (inhabitants of the land of oxen), are associated by the best observers not with the Iapygian, but with the Italian stock; and there is nothing to hinder our regarding them as belonging to its Latin branch, although the Hellenising of these districts which took place even before the commencement of the political development of Italy, and their subsequent inundation by Samnite hordes, have in this instance totally obliterated all traces of the older nationality. Very ancient legends bring the similarly extinct stock of the Siculi into connection with Rome. For instance, the earliest historian of Italy Antiochus of Syracuse tells us that a man named Sikelos came a fugitive from Rome to Morges king of Italia (*i.e.* the Bruttian peninsula). Such stories appear to be founded on the identity of race recognised by the narrators as subsisting between the Siculi (of whom there were some still

in Italy in the time of Thucydides) and the Latins. The striking
affinity of certain dialectic peculiarities of Sicilian Greek with
the Latin is probably to be explained rather by the old commercial connections subsisting between Rome and the Sicilian
Greeks, than by the ancient identity of the languages of the
Siculi and the Romans. According to all indications, however,
not only Latium, but probably also the Campanian and Lucanian
districts, Italia proper between the gulfs of Tarentum and
Laus, and the eastern half of Sicily were in primitive times
inhabited by different branches of the Latin nation.

Destinies very dissimilar awaited these different branches.
Those settled in Sicily, Magna Graecia, and Campania came into
contact with the Greeks at a period when they were unable to
offer resistance to a civilisation so superior, and were either
completely Hellenised, as in the case of Sicily, or at any rate so
weakened that they succumbed without marked resistance to
the fresh energy of the Sabine tribes. In this way the Siculi, the
Itali and Morgetes, and the Ausonians never came to play an
active part in the history of the peninsula. It was otherwise
with Latium, where no Greek colonies were founded, and the
inhabitants after hard struggles were successful in maintaining
their ground against the Sabines as well as against their northern
neighbours. Let us cast a glance at this district, which was
destined more than any other to influence the fortunes of the
ancient world.

The plain of Latium must have been in primeval times the
scene of the grandest conflicts of nature, while the slowly
formative agency of water deposited, and the eruptions of
mighty volcanoes upheaved, the successive strata of that soil
on which was to be decided the question to what people the
sovereignty of the world should belong. Latium is bounded
on the east by the mountains of the Sabines and Aequi which
form part of the Apennines; and on the south by the Volscian
range rising to the height of 4000 feet, which is separated
from the main chain of the Apennines by the ancient territory of the Hernici, the table-land of the Sacco (Trerus, a
tributary of the Liris), and stretching in a westerly direction
terminates in the promontory of Terracina. On the west its
boundary is the sea, which on this part of the coast forms but
few and indifferent harbours. On the north it imperceptibly
merges into the broad highlands of Etruria. The region thus
enclosed forms a magnificent plain traversed by the Tiber, the
" mountain-stream " which issues from the Umbrian, and by

the Anio, which rises in the Sabine mountains. Hills here and there emerge, like islands, from the plain; some of them steep limestone cliffs, such as that of Soracte in the north-east, and that of the Circeian promontory on the south-west, as well as the similar though lower height of the Janiculum near Rome; others volcanic elevations, whose extinct craters had become converted into lakes which in some cases still exist; the most important of these is the Alban range, which, free on every side, stands forth from the plain between the Volscian chain and the river Tiber.

Here settled the stock which is known to history under the name of the Latins, or, as they were subsequently called by way of distinction from the Latin communities beyond the bounds of Latium, the " Old Latins " (*prisci Latini*). But the territory occupied by them, the district of Latium, was only a small portion of the central plain of Italy. All the country north of the Tiber was to the Latins a foreign and even hostile domain, with whose inhabitants no lasting alliance, no public peace, was possible, and such armistices as were concluded appear always to have been for a limited period. The Tiber formed the northern boundary from early times; and neither in history nor in the more reliable traditions has any reminiscence been preserved as to the period or occasion of the establishment of a frontier line so important in its results. We find, at the time when our history begins, the flat and marshy tracts to the south of the Alban range in the hands of Umbro-Sabellian stocks, the Rutuli and Volsci; Ardea and Velitrae are no longer in the number of originally Latin towns. Only the central portion of that region between the Tiber, the spurs of the Apennines, the Alban Mount, and the sea—a district of about 700 square miles, not much larger than the present canton of Zurich—was Latium proper, the " plain," [1] as it appears to the eye of the observer from the heights of Monte Cavo. Though the country is a plain it is not monotonously flat. With the exception of the sea-beach, which is sandy and formed in part by the accumulations of the Tiber, the level is everywhere broken by hills of tufa moderate in height though often somewhat steep, and by deep fissures of the ground. These alternating elevations and depressions of the surface lead to the formation of lakes in winter;

---

[1] Like *lătus* (side) and πλᾰτύς (flat); it denotes therefore the flat country in contrast to the Sanbie mountain-land, just as Campania, the " plain," forms the contrast to Samnium. *Lātus*, formerly *stlātus*, has no connection with *Latium*.

and the exhalations proceeding in the heat of summer from
the putrescent organic substances which they contain engender
that noxious fever-laden atmosphere, which in ancient times
tainted the district as it taints it at the present day. It is a
mistake to suppose that these miasmata were first occasioned
by the neglect of cultivation, which was the result of misgovernment in the last century of the Republic and is so still.
Their course lies rather in the want of natural outlets for the
water; and it operates now as it operated thousands of years
ago. It is true, however, that the malaria may to a certain
extent be banished by thoroughness of tillage—a fact which
has not yet received its full explanation, but may be partly
accounted for by the circumstance that the working of the surface accelerates the drying up of the stagnant waters. It must
always remain a remarkable phenomenon, that a dense agricultural population should have arisen in regions where no healthy
population can at present subsist, and where the traveller is
unwilling to tarry even for a single night, such as the plain of
Latium and the lowlands of Sybaris and Metapontum. We
must bear in mind that man in a lower stage of civilisation has
generally a quicker perception of what nature demands, and a
greater readiness in conforming to her requirements; perhaps,
also, a more elastic physical constitution, which accommodates
itself more readily to the conditions of the soil where he
dwells.

In Sardinia agriculture is prosecuted under physical conditions precisely similar even at the present day; the pestilential
atmosphere exists, but the peasant avoids its injurious effects
by caution in reference to clothing, food, and the choice of his
hours of labour. In fact, nothing is so certain a protection
against the " aria cattiva " as wearing the fleece of animals and
keeping a blazing fire; which explains why the Roman countryman went constantly clothed in heavy woollen stuffs, and never
allowed the fire on his hearth to be extinguished. In other
respects the district must have appeared attractive to an
immigrant agricultural people: the soil is easily laboured with
mattock and hoe and is productive even without being manured,
although, tried by an Italian standard, it does not yield any
extraordinary return: wheat yields on an average about fivefold.[1] Good water is not abundant; the higher and more

---

[1] A French statist, Dureau de la Malle (*Econ. Pol. des Romains*, ii. 226),
compares with the Roman Campagna the district of Limagne in Auvergne,
which is likewise a wide, much intersected, and uneven plain, with a super-

sacred on that account was the esteem in which every fresh spring was held by the inhabitants.

No accounts have been preserved of the mode in which the settlements of the Latins took place in the district which has since borne their name; and we are left to gather what we can almost exclusively from *à posteriori* inference regarding them. Some knowledge may, however, in this way be gained, or at any rate some conjectures that wear an aspect of probability.

The Roman territory was divided in the earliest times into a number of clan-districts, which were subsequently employed in the formation of the earliest " rural wards " (*tribus rusticae*). Tradition informs us as to the *tribus Claudia*, that it originated from the settlement of the Claudian clansmen on the Anio; and that the other districts of the earliest division originated in a similar manner is indicated quite as certainly by their names.

These names are not, like those of the districts added at a later period, derived from the localities, but are formed without exception from the names of clans; and the clans who thus gave their names to the wards of the original Roman territory are, so far as they have not become entirely extinct (as is the case with the *Camilii, Galerii, Lemonii, Pollii, Pupinii, Voltinii*), the very oldest patrician families of Rome, the *Aemilii, Cornelii, Fabii, Horatii, Menenii, Papirii, Romilii, Sergii, Veturii*. It is worthy of remark, that not one of these clans can be shown to have taken up its settlement in Rome only at a later epoch. Every Italian, and doubtless also every Hellenic, canton must, like that of Rome, have been divided into a number of groups associated at once by locality and by clanship; such a clan-settlement is the " house " (οἰκία) of the Greeks, from which very

ficial soil of decomposed lava and ashes—the remains of extinct volcanoes. The population, at least 2500 to the square league, is one of the densest to be found in purely agricultural districts: property is subdivided to an extraordinary extent. Tillage is carried on almost entirely by manual labour, with spade, hoe, or mattock; only in exceptional cases a light plough is substituted drawn by two cows, the wife of the peasant not unfrequently taking the place of one of them in the yoke. The team serves at once to furnish milk and to till the land. They have two harvests in the year, corn and vegetables; there is no fallow. The average yearly rent for an arpent of arable land is 100 francs. If instead of such an arrangement this same land were to be divided among six or seven large landholders, and a system of management by stewards and day labourers were to supersede the husbandry of the small proprietors, in a hundred years the Limagne would doubtless be as waste, forsaken, and miserable as the Campagna di Roma is at the present day.

frequently the κῶμαι and δῆμοι originated among them, like the *tribus* in Rome. The corresponding Italian terms "house" (*vicus*) or "building" (*pagus*, from *pangere*) indicate, in like manner, the joint settlement of the members of a clan, and thence come by an easily understood transition to signify in common use hamlet or village. As each household had its own portion of land, so the clan-household or village had clan-lands belonging to it, which, as will afterwards be shown, were managed up to a comparatively late period after the analogy of household-lands, that is, on the system of joint-possession. Whether it was in Latium itself that the clan-households became developed into clan-villages, or whether the Latins were already associated in clans when they immigrated into Latium, are questions which we are just as little able to answer as we are to determine how far, in addition to the original ground of common ancestry, the clan may have been based on the incorporation or co-ordination from without of individuals not related to it by blood.

These clanships, however, were from the beginning regarded not as independent societies, but as the integral parts of a political community (*civitas, populus*). This first presents itself as an aggregate of a number of clan-villages of the same stock, language, and manners, bound to mutual observance of law and mutual legal redress and to united action in aggression and defence. A fixed local centre was quite as necessary in the case of such a canton as in that of a clanship; but as the members of the clan, or in other words the constituent elements of the canton, dwelt in villages, the centre of the canton cannot have been a town or place of joint settlement in the strict sense. It must, on the contrary, have been simply a place of common assembly, containing the seat of justice and the common sanctuary of the canton, where the members of the canton met every eighth day for purposes of intercourse and amusement, and where, in case of war, they obtained a safer shelter for themselves and their cattle than in the villages: in ordinary circumstances this place of meeting was not at all or but scantily inhabited. Ancient places of refuge, of a kind quite similar, may still be recognised at the present day on the tops of several of the hills in the highlands of east Switzerland. Such a place was called in Italy "height" (*capitolium*, like ἄκρα, the mountain-top), or "stronghold" (*arx*, from *arcere*); it was not a town at first, but it became the nucleus of one, as houses naturally gathered round the stronghold and were afterwards surrounded with the " ring " (*urbs*, connected with *urvus*, *curvus*, perhaps also with *orbis*).   The stronghold and town were visibly distinguished from each other by the number of gates, of which the stronghold had as few as possible, and the town many, the former ordinarily but one, the latter at least three.   Such fortresses were the bases of that cantonal constitution which prevailed in Italy anterior to the existence of towns: a constitution[1] the nature of which may still be recognised with some degree of clearness in those provinces of Italy which did not until a late period reach, and in some cases have not yet fully reached, the stage of aggregation in towns, such as the land of the Marsi and the small cantons of the Abruzzi.   The country of the Aequiculi, who even in the imperial period dwelt not in towns, but in numerous open hamlets, presents a number of ancient ringwalls, which, regarded as " deserted towns " with their solitary temples, excited the astonishment of the Roman as well of modern archaeologists, who have fancied that they could find accommodation there, the former for their " primitive inhabitants " (*aborigines*), the latter for their Pelasgians.   We shall certainly be nearer the truth in recognising these structures not as walled towns, but as places of refuge for the inhabitants of the district, such as were doubtless found in more ancient times over all Italy, although constructed in less artistic style.   It was natural that at the period when the stocks that had made the transition to urban life were surrounding their towns with stone walls, those districts whose inhabitants continued to dwell in open hamlets should replace the earthen ramparts and palisades of their strongholds with buildings of stone.   When in later ages peace was securely established throughout the land and such fortresses were no longer needed, these places of refuge were abandoned and soon became a riddle to after generations.

These cantons accordingly, having their rendezvous in some stronghold, and including a certain number of clanships, form the primitive political unities with which Italian history begins. At what period, and to what extent, such cantons were formed in Latium, cannot be determined with precision; nor is it a matter of special historical interest.   The isolated Alban range, that natural stronghold of Latium, which offered to settlers the most wholesome air, the freshest springs, and the most secure position, would doubtless be first occupied by the new comers. Here accordingly, along the narrow plateau above Palazzuola, between the Alban lake (*Lago di Castello*) and the Alban mount (*Monte Cavo*), extended the town of Alba, which was universally

regarded as the primitive seat of the Latin stock, and the mother
city of Rome as well as of all the other Old Latin communities;
here, too, on the slopes lay the very ancient Latin canton-centres
of Lanuvium, Aricia, and Tusculum.   Here are found some of
those primitive works of masonry, which usually mark the
beginnings of civilisation and seem to stand as a witness to
posterity that in reality Pallas Athene, when she does appear,
comes into the world full grown.   Such is the escarpment of the
wall of rock below Alba in the direction of Palazzuola, whereby
the place, which is rendered naturally inaccessible by the steep
declivities of Monte Cavo on the south, is rendered equally un-
approachable on the north, and only the two narrow approaches
on the east and west, which are capable of being easily defended,
are left open for traffic.   Such, above all, is the large subterranean tunnel cut—so that a man can stand upright within it—
through the hard wall of lava, 6000 feet thick, by which the
waters of the lake formed in the old crater of the Alban Mount
were reduced to their present level and a considerable space was
gained for tillage on the mountain itself.

The summits of the last offshoots of the Sabine range form
natural fastnesses of the Latin plain; and the canton-strong-
holds there gave rise at a later period to the considerable towns
of Tibur and Praeneste.   Labici too, Gabii, and Nomentum in
the plain between the Alban and Sabine hills and the Tiber,
Rome on the Tiber, Laurentum and Lavinium on the coast,
were all more or less ancient centres of Latin colonisation, not
to speak of many others less famous and in some cases almost
forgotten.

All these cantons were in primitive times politically sovereign,
and each of them was governed by its prince with the co-
operation of the council of elders and the assembly of warriors.
Nevertheless the feeling of fellowship based on community of
descent and of language not only pervaded the whole of them,
but manifested itself in an important religious and political
institution—the perpetual league of the collective Latin cantons.
The presidency belonged originally, according to the universal
Italian as well as Hellenic usage, to that canton within whose
bounds lay the meeting-place of the league; in this case it was
the canton of Alba, which, as we have said, was generally
regarded as the oldest and most eminent of the Latin cantons.
The communities entitled to participate in the league were in
the beginning thirty—a number which we find occurring with
singular frequency as the sum of the constituent parts of a

commonwealth in Greece and Italy. What cantons originally made up the number of the thirty old Latin communities or, as with reference to the metropolitan rights of Alba they are also called, the thirty Alban colonies, tradition has not recorded, and we can no longer ascertain. The rendezvous of this union was, like the Pamboeotia and the Panionia among the similar confederacies of the Greeks, the " Latin festival " (*feriae Latinae*), at which, on the " Mount of Alba " (*Mons Albanus, Monte Cavo*), upon a day annually appointed by the chief magistrate for the purpose, an ox was offered in sacrifice by the assembled Latin stock to the " Latin god " (*Jupiter Latiaris*). Each community taking part in the ceremony had to contribute to the sacrificial feast its fixed proportion of cattle, milk, and cheese, and to receive in return a portion of the roasted victim. These usages continued down to a late period, and are well known: respecting the more important legal bearings of this association we can do little else than institute conjectures.

From the most ancient times there were held, in connection with the religious festival on the Mount of Alba, assemblies of the representatives of the several communities at the neighbouring Latin seat of justice at the source of the Ferentina (near Marino). Indeed such a confederacy cannot be conceived to exist without having a certain power of superintendence over the associated body, and without possessing a system of law binding on all. Tradition records, and we may well believe, that the league exercised jurisdiction in reference to violations of federal law, and that it could in such cases pronounce even sentence of death. The equality in respect of legal rights and of intermarriage that subsisted among the Latin communities at a later date may perhaps be regarded as an integral part of the primitive law of the league, so that any Latin man could beget lawful children with any Latin woman and acquire landed property and carry on trade in any part of Latium. The league may have also provided a federal tribunal of arbitration for the mutual disputes of the cantons; on the other hand, there is no proof that the league imposed any limitation on the sovereign right of each community to make peace or war. In like manner there can be no doubt that the constitution of the league implied the possibility of its waging defensive or even aggressive war in its own name; in which case, of course, it would be necessary to have a federal commander-in-chief. But we have no reason to suppose that in such an event each community was compelled by law to furnish a contingent for the army, or that, conversely, any one was interdicted from undertaking a war on its own account even against a member of the league. There are, however, indications that during the Latin festival, just as was the case during the festivals of the Hellenic leagues, "a truce of God" was observed throughout all Latium;[1] and probably on that occasion even tribes at feud granted safe-conducts to each other.

It is still less in our power to define the privileges of the presiding canton; only we may safely affirm that there is no reason for recognising in the Alban presidency a real political hegemony over Latium, and that possibly, nay probably, it had no more significance in Latium than the honorary presidency of Elis had in Greece.[2] On the whole it is probable that the extent of this Latin league, and the amount of its jurisdiction, were somewhat unsettled and fluctuating; yet it remained throughout not an accidental aggregate of various communities, more or less alien to each other, but the just and necessary expression of the relationship of the Latin stock. The Latin league may not have at all times included all Latin communities, but it never at any rate granted the privilege of membership to any that were not Latin. Its counterpart in Greece was not the Delphic Amphictyony, but the Boeotian or Aetolian confederacy.

These very general outlines must suffice: any attempt to draw the lines more sharply would only falsify the picture. The manifold play of mutual attraction and repulsion among those earliest political atoms, the cantons, passed away in Latium without witnesses competent to tell the tale. We must now be content to realise the one great abiding fact that they possessed a common centre, to which they did not sacrifice their

---

[1] The Latin festival is expressly called "armistice" (*indutiae*, Macrob. *Sat.* i. 16; ἐκεχειρίαι, Dionys. iv. 49); and a war was not allowed to be begun during its continuance (Macrob. *l. c.*).

[2] The assertion often made in ancient and modern times, that Alba once ruled over Latium under the forms of a symmachy, nowhere finds on closer investigation sufficient support. All history begins not with the union, but with the disunion of a nation; and it is very improbable that the problem of the union of Latium, which Rome finally solved after some centuries of conflict, should have been already solved at an earlier period by Alba. It deserves to be remarked too that Rome never asserted in the capacity of heiress of Alba any claims of sovereignty proper over the Latin communities, but contented herself with an honorary presidency; which no doubt, when it became combined with material power, afforded a handle for her pretensions of hegemony. Testimonies, strictly so called, can scarcely be adduced on such a question; and least of all do such passages as Festus *v. praetor*, p. 241, and Dionys. iii. 10, suffice to stamp Alba as a Latin Athens.

individual independence, but by means of which they cherished and increased the feeling of their belonging collectively to the same nation. By such a common possession the way was prepared for their advance from that cantonal individuality, with which the history of every people necessarily begins, to the national union with which the history of every people ends or at any rate ought to end.

CHAPTER IV

THE BEGINNINGS OF ROME

ABOUT fourteen miles up from the mouth of the river Tiber, hills of moderate elevation rise on both banks of the stream, higher on the right, lower on the left bank. With the latter group there has been closely associated for at least two thousand five hundred years the name of the Romans. We are unable, of course, to tell how or when that name arose; this much only is certain, that in the oldest form of it known to us the inhabitants of the canton are called not Romans, but (by a shifting of sound that frequently occurs in the earlier period of a language, but fell very early into abeyance in Latin[1]) Ramnians (Ramnes), a fact which constitutes an expressive testimony to the immemorial antiquity of the name. Its derivation cannot be given with certainty; possibly "Ramnes" may mean "foresters" or "bushmen."

But they were not the only dwellers on the hills by the bank of the Tiber. In the earliest division of the burgesses of Rome a trace has been preserved of the fact that that body arose out of the amalgamation of three cantons once probably independent, the Ramnians, Tities, and Luceres, into a single commonwealth —in other words, out of such a *synoikismos* as that from which Athens arose in Attica.[2] The great antiquity of this threefold division of the community [3] is perhaps best evinced by the fact

[1] A similar change of sound is exhibited in the case of the following formations, all of them of a very ancient kind: *pars portio*, *Mars mors*, *farreum* ancient form for *horreum*, *Fabii Fovii*, *Valerius Volesus*, *vacuus vocivus*.

[2] The *synoikismos* did not necessarily involve an actual settlement together at one spot; but while each resided as formerly on his own land, there was thenceforth only one council-hall and court-house for the whole. Thucyd. ii. 15; Herodot. i. 170.

[3] We might even, looking to the Attic τριττύς and the Umbrian *trifo*, raise the question whether a triple division of the community was not a fundamental principle of the Graeco-Italians: in that case the triple division of the Roman community would not be referable to the amalgamation of several once independent tribes. But, in order to the establishment of an hypothesis so much at variance with tradition, such a threefold division would require to present itself more generally throughout the Graeco-Italian field than seems to be the case, and to appear uniformly everywhere as the ground-scheme. The Umbrians may possibly have adopted the word *tribus* only when they came under the influence of Roman rule; it cannot with certainty be traced in Oscan.

that the Romans, in matters especially of constitutional law, regularly used the forms *tribuere* (" to divide into three ") and *tribus* (" a third ") in the general sense of " to divide " and " a part," and the latter expression (*tribus*), like our " quarter," early lost its original signification of number. After the union each of these three communities—once separate, but now forming subdivisions of a single community—still possessed its third of the common domain, and had its proportional representation in the burgess-force and in the council of the elders. In ritual also, the number divisible by three of the members of almost all the oldest colleges—of the Vestal Virgins, the Salii, the Arval Brethren, the Luperci, the Augurs—probably had reference to that three-fold partition. These three elements into which the primitive body of burgesses in Rome was divided have had theories of the most extravagant absurdity engrafted upon them. The irrational opinion that the Roman nation was a mongrel people finds its support in that division, and its advocates have striven by various means to represent the three great Italian races as elements entering into the composition of the primitive Rome, and to transform a people which has exhibited in language, polity, and religion, a pure and national development such as few have equalled into a confused aggregate of Etruscan and Sabine, Hellenic and, forsooth! even Pelasgian fragments.

Setting aside self-contradictory and unfounded hypotheses, we may sum up in a few words all that can be said respecting the nationality of the component elements of the primitive Roman commonwealth. That the Ramnians were a Latin stock cannot be doubted, for they gave their name to the new Roman commonwealth and therefore must have substantially determined the nationality of the united community. Respecting the origin of the Luceres nothing can be affirmed, except that there is no difficulty in the way of our assigning them, like the Ramnians, to the Latin stock. The second of these communities, on the other hand, is with one consent derived from Sabina; and this view can at least be traced to a tradition preserved in the Titian brotherhood, which represented that priestly college as having been instituted, on occasion of the Tities being admitted into the collective community, for the preservation of their distinctive Sabine ritual. It would appear, therefore, that at a period very remote, when the Latin and Sabellian stocks were beyond question far less sharply contrasted in language, manners, and customs than were the Roman and the Samnite of a later age, a Sabellian community entered into a

Latin canton-union; and, as in the older and more credible
traditions without exception the Tities take precedence of the
Ramnians, it is probable that the intruding Tities compelled
the older Ramnians to accept the *synoikismos*. A mixture of
different nationalities certainly therefore took place; but it
hardly exercised an influence greater than the migration, for
example, which occurred some centuries afterwards of the
Sabine Attus Clauzus or Appius Claudius and his clansmen and
clients to Rome. The earlier admission of the Tities among
the Ramnians does not entitle us to class the community among
mongrel peoples any more than does that subsequent reception
of the Claudii among the Romans. With the exception, perhaps,
of isolated national institutions handed down in connection with
ritual, the existence of Sabellian elements can nowhere be
pointed out in Rome; and the Latin language in particular
furnishes absolutely no support to such an hypothesis.[1] It
would in fact be more than surprising, if the Latin nation should
have had its nationality in any sensible degree affected by the
insertion of a single community from a stock so very closely
related to it; and, besides, it must not be forgotten that at the
time when the Tities settled beside the Ramnians, Latin nationality rested on Latium as its basis, and not on Rome. The
new tripartite Roman commonwealth was, notwithstanding
some incidental elements which were originally Sabellian, just
what the community of the Ramnians had previously been—
a portion of the Latin nation.

Long, in all probability, before an urban settlement arose on
the Tiber, these Ramnians, Tities, and Luceres, at first separate,
afterwards united, had their stronghold on the Roman hills,
and tilled their fields from the surrounding villages. The
"wolf-festival" (*Lupercalia*), which the *gens* of the Quinctii
celebrated on the Palatine hill, was probably a tradition from
these primitive ages—a festival of husbandmen and shepherds,
which more than any other preserved the homely pastimes of
patriarchal simplicity, and, singularly enough, maintained itself
longer than all the other heathen festivals in Christian Rome.

[1] Although the older opinion, that Latin is to be viewed as a mixed
language made up of Greek and non-Greek elements, has been now abandoned on all sides, judicious inquirers even (*e.g.* Schwegler, *R. G.* i. 184, 193)
still seek to discover in Latin a mixture of two nearly related Italian
dialects. But we ask in vain for the linguistic or historical facts which
render such an hypothesis necessary. When a language presents the
appearance of being an intermediate link between two others, every philo-
logist knows that the phenomenon may quite as probably depend, and
more frequently does depend, on organic development than on external
intermixture.

From these settlements the later Rome arose.   The founding
of a city in the strict sense, such as the legend assumes, is of
course to be reckoned altogether out of the question: Rome was
not built in a day.   But the serious consideration of the historian
may well be directed to the inquiry, in what way Rome could so
early attain the prominent political position which it held in
Latium—so different from what the physical character of the
locality would have led us to anticipate.   The site of Rome is
less healthy and less fertile than that of most of the old Latin
towns.   Neither the vine nor the fig succeed well in the immediate environs, and there is a want of springs yielding a
good supply of water; for neither the otherwise excellent
fountain of the Camenae before the Porta Capena, nor the
Capitoline well, afterwards enclosed within the Tullianum,
furnish it in any abundance.   Another disadvantage arises
from the frequency with which the river overflows its banks.
Its very slight fall renders it unable to carry off the water,
which during the rainy season descends in large quantities from
the mountains, with sufficient rapidity to the sea, and in consequence it floods the low-lying lands and the valleys that open
between the hills, and converts them into swamps.   For a
settler the locality was anything but attractive.   In antiquity
itself an opinion was expressed that the first body of immigrant
cultivators could scarce have spontaneously resorted in search
of a suitable settlement to that unhealthy and unfruitful spot
in a region otherwise so highly favoured, and that it must have
been necessity, or rather some special motive, which led to the
establishment of a city there.   Even the legend betrays its
sense of the strangeness of the fact: the story of the foundation
of Rome by refugees from Alba under the leadership of the sons
of an Alban prince, Romulus and Remus, is nothing but a
naïve attempt of primitive quasi-history to explain the singular
circumstance of the place having arisen on a site so unfavour-
able, and to connect at the same time the origin of Rome with
the general metropolis of Latium.   Such tales, which profess
to be historical but are merely improvised explanations of no
very ingenious character, it is the first duty of history to dis-
miss; but it may perhaps be allowed to go a step further, and
after weighing the special relations of the locality to propose a
positive conjecture not regarding the way in which the place
originated, but regarding the circumstances which occasioned
its rapid and surprising prosperity and led to its occupying its
peculiar position in Latium.

Let us notice first of all the earliest boundaries of the Roman territory. Towards the east the towns of Antemnae, Fidenae, Caenina, Collatia, and Gabii lie in the immediate neighbourhood, some of them not five miles distant from the gates of the Servian Rome; and the boundary of the canton must have been in the close vicinity of the city gates. On the south we find at a distance of fourteen miles the powerful communities of Tusculum and Alba; and the Roman territory appears not to have extended in this direction beyond the *Fossa Cluilia*, five miles from Rome. In like manner, towards the south-west, the boundary betwixt Rome and Lavinium was at the sixth milestone. While in a landward direction the Roman canton was thus everywhere confined within the narrowest possible limits, from the earliest times, on the other hand, it extended without hindrance on both banks of the Tiber towards the sea. Between Rome and the coast there occurs no locality that is mentioned as an ancient canton-centre, and no trace of any ancient canton-boundary. The legend indeed, which has its definite explanation of the origin of everything, professes to tell us that the Roman possessions on the right bank of the Tiber, the " seven hamlets " (*septem pagi*), and the important salt-works at its mouth, were taken by king Romulus from the Veientes, and that king Ancus fortified on the right bank the *tête du pont*, the " mount of Janus " (*Ianiculum*), and founded on the left the Roman Peiraeus, the seaport at the river's " mouth " (*Ostia*). But in fact we have evidence more trustworthy than that of legend, that the possessions on the Etruscan bank of the Tiber must have belonged to the original territory of Rome; for in this very quarter, at the fourth milestone on the later road to the port, lay the grove of the creative goddess (*Dea Dia*), the primitive chief seat of the Arval festival and Arval brotherhood of Rome. Indeed from time immemorial the clan of the Romilii, the chief probably of all the Roman clans, was settled in this very quarter; the Janiculum formed a part of the city itself, and Ostia was a burgess colony or, in other words, a suburb.

This cannot have been the result of mere accident. The Tiber was the natural highway for the traffic of Latium; and its mouth, on a coast scantily provided with harbours, became necessarily the anchorage of seafarers. Moreover, the Tiber formed from very ancient times the frontier defence of the Latin stock against their northern neighbours. There was no place better fitted for an emporium of the Latin river and sea traffic, and for a maritime frontier fortress of Latium, than Rome. It combined the advantages of a strong position and of immediate vicinity to the river; it commanded both banks of the stream down to its mouth; it was so situated as to be equally convenient for the river navigator descending the Tiber or the Anio, and for the seafarer with vessels of so moderate a size as those which were then used; and it afforded greater protection from pirates than places situated immediately on the coast. That Rome was indebted accordingly, if not for its origin, at any rate for its importance, to these commercial and strategical advantages of its position, there are numerous indications to show—indications which are of very different weight from the statements of quasi - historical romances. Thence arose its very ancient relations with Caere, which was to Etruria what Rome was to Latium, and accordingly became Rome's most intimate neighbour and commercial ally. Thence arose the unusual importance of the bridges over the Tiber, and of bridge-building generally in the Roman commonwealth. Thence came the galley in the city arms; thence, too, the very ancient Roman port-duties on the exports and imports of Ostia, which were from the first levied only on what was to be exposed for sale (*promercale*), not on what was for the shipper's own use (*usuarium*), and which were therefore in reality a tax upon commerce. Thence, to anticipate, the comparatively early occurrence in Rome of coined money, and of commercial treaties with transmarine states. In this sense, then, it is certainly not improbable that Rome may have been, as the legend assumes, a creation rather than a growth, and the youngest rather than the oldest among the Latin cities. Beyond doubt the country was already in some degree cultivated, and the Alban range as well as various other heights of the Campagna were occupied by strongholds, when the Latin frontier emporium arose on the Tiber. Whether it was a resolution of the Latin confederacy, or the clear-sighted genius of some unknown founder, or the natural development of traffic, that called the city of Rome into being, it is vain even to surmise.

But in connection with this view of the position of Rome as the emporium of Latium another observation suggests itself. At the time when history begins to dawn on us, Rome appears, in contradistinction to the league of the Latin communities, as a compact urban unity. The Latin habit of dwelling in open villages, and of using the common stronghold only for festivals and assemblies or in case of special need, was subjected to

restriction at a far earlier period, probably, in the canton of
Rome than anywhere else in Latium. The Roman did not
cease to manage his farm in person, or to regard it as his proper
home; but the unwholesome atmosphere of the Campagna
could not but induce him to take up his abode as much as
possible on the more airy and salubrious city hills; and by the
side of the cultivators of the soil there must have been a numerous non-agricultural population, partly foreigners, partly native,
settled there from very early times. This to some extent
accounts for the dense population of the old Roman territory,
which may be estimated at the utmost at 115 square miles,
partly of marshy or sandy soil, and which, even under the
earliest constitution of the city, furnished a force of 3300 freemen; so that it must have numbered at least 10,000 free inhabitants. But further, every one acquainted with the Romans and
their history is aware that it is their urban and mercantile
character which forms the basis of whatever is peculiar in their
public and private life, and that the distinction between them
and the other Latins and Italians in general is pre-eminently
the distinction between citizen and rustic. Rome, indeed, was
not a mercantile city like Corinth or Carthage; for Latium was
an essentially agricultural region, and Rome was in the first
instance, and continued to be, pre-eminently a Latin city. But
the distinction between Rome and the mass of the other Latin
towns must certainly be traced back to its commercial position,
and to the type of character produced by that position in its
citizens. If Rome was the emporium of the Latin districts, we
can readily understand how, along with and in addition to Latin
husbandry, an urban life should have attained vigorous and
rapid development there and thus have laid the foundation for
its distinctive career.

It is far more important and more practicable to follow out
the course of this mercantile and strategical growth of the city
of Rome, than to attempt the useless task of analysing the
insignificant and but little diversified communities of primitive
times. The course of this development may still be so far
recognised in the traditions regarding the successive circumvallations and fortifications of Rome, the formation of which necessarily kept pace with the growth of the Roman commonwealth
in importance as a city.

The town, which in the course of centuries grew up as Rome,
in its original form embraced according to trustworthy testimony
only the Palatine, or " square Rome " (*Roma quadrata*), as it

was called in later times from the irregularly quadrangular form of the Palatine hill. The gates and walls that enclosed this original city remained visible down to the period of the empire: the sites of two of the former, the Porta Romana near S. Giorgio in Velabro, and the Porta Mugionis at the Arch of Titus, are still known to us, and the Palatine ring-wall is described by Tacitus from his own observation at least on the sides looking towards the Aventine and Caelian. Many traces indicate that this was the centre and original seat of the urban settlement. On the Palatine was to be found the sacred symbol of that settlement, the " outfit vault " (*mundus*) as it was called, in which the first settlers deposited a sufficiency of everything necessary for a household and added a clod of their dear native earth. There, too, was situated the building in which all the curies assembled for religious and other purposes, each at its own hearth (*curiae veteres*). There stood the meeting-house of the " Leapers " (*curia Saliorum*) in which also the sacred shields of Mars were preserved, the sanctuary of the " Wolves " (*Lupercal*), and the residence of the priest of Jupiter. On and near this hill the legend of the founding of the city placed the scenes of its leading incidents, and the straw-covered house of Romulus, the shepherd's hut of his foster-father Faustulus, the sacred fig-tree towards which the cradle with the twins had floated, the cornelian cherry-tree that sprang from the shaft of the spear which the founder of the city had hurled from the Aventine over the valley of the Circus into this enclosure, and other such sacred relics were pointed out to the believer. Temples in the proper sense of the term were still at this time unknown, and accordingly the Palatine has nothing of the sort to show belonging to the primitive age. The public assemblies of the community were early transferred to another locality, so that their original site is unknown; only it may be conjectured that the free space round the *mundus*, afterwards called the *Area Apollinis*, was the primitive place of assembly for the burgesses and the senate, and the stage erected over the *mundus* itself the primitive seat of justice of the Roman community.

The " festival of the Seven Mounts " (*septimontium*), again, preserved the memory of the more extended settlement which gradually formed round the Palatine. Suburbs grew up one after another, each protected by its own separate though weaker circumvallation and joined to the original ring-wall of the Palatine, as in fen districts the outer dikes are joined on to the main dike. The " Seven Rings " were, the Palatine

itself; the Cermalus, the slope of the Palatine in the direction
of the morass that in the earliest times extended between it and
the Capitoline (*velabrum*); the Velia, the ridge which connected
the Palatine with the Esquiline, but in subsequent times was
almost wholly obliterated by the buildings of the empire; the
Fagutal, the Oppius, and the Cispius, the three summits of the
Esquiline; lastly, the Sucusa, or Subūra, a fortress constructed
outside of the earthen rampart which protected the new town
on the Carinae, in the low ground between the Esquiline and
the Quirinal beneath S. Pietro in Vincoli. These additions,
manifestly the results of a gradual growth, clearly reveal to a
certain extent the earliest history of the Palatine Rome, especially
when we compare with them the Servian arrangement of
districts which was afterwards formed on the basis of this
earliest division.

The Palatine was the original seat of the Roman community,
the oldest and originally the only ring-wall. The urban settlement, however, began at Rome as well as elsewhere not within,
but under the protection of, the stronghold; and the oldest
settlements with which we are acquainted, and which afterwards
formed the first and second regions in the Servian division of the
city, lay in a circle round the Palatine. These included the
settlement on the declivity of the Cermalus with the " street
of the Tuscans "—a name which was probably a memorial
of the commercial intercourse that subsisted between the
Caerites and Romans and was already perhaps carried on with
vigour in the Palatine city—and the settlement on the Velia;
both of which subsequently along with the stronghold-hill itself
constituted a region of the Servian city. Further, there were
the component elements of the subsequent second region—
the suburb on the Caelian, which probably embraced only its
extreme point above the Colosseum; that on the Carinae, the
spur which projects from the Esquiline towards the Palatine;
and, lastly, the valley and outwork of the Subura, from which
the whole region receivèd its name. These two regions jointly
constituted the incipient city; and the Suburan region, which
extended at the base of the stronghold, nearly from the Arch
of Constantine to S. Pietro in Vincoli, and over the valley beneath,
appears to have been more considerable and perhaps older than
the settlements incorporated by the Servian arrangement in the
Palatine region, because in the order of the regions the former
takes precedence of the latter. A remarkable memorial of the
distinction between these two portions of the city was preserved

in one of the oldest sacred customs of the later Rome, the sacrifice of the October horse yearly offered in the *Campus Martius*: down to a late period a struggle took place at this festival for the horse's head between the men of the Subura and those of the Via Sacra, and according as victory lay with the former or with the latter, the head was nailed either to the Mamilian Tower (site unknown) in the Subura, or to the king's palace under the Palatine. It was the two halves of the old city that thus competed with each other on equal terms. At that time, accordingly, the Esquiliae (which name strictly used is exclusive of the Carinae) were in reality what they were called, the "outer buildings" (*ex-quiliae*, like *inquilinus*, from *colere*) or suburb: this became the third region in the later city division, and it was always held in inferior consideration as compared with the Suburan and Palatine regions. Other neighbouring heights also, such as the Capitol and the Aventine, may probably have been occupied by the community of the Seven Mounts; the "bridge of piles" in particular (*pons sublicius*), thrown over the natural pier of the island in the Tiber, must have existed even then—the pontifical college alone is sufficient evidence of this—and the *tête du pont* on the Etruscan bank, the height of the Janiculum, would not be left unoccupied; but the community had not as yet brought either within the circuit of its fortifications. The regulation which was adhered to as a ritual rule down to the latest times, that the bridge should be composed simply of wood without iron, manifestly shows that in its original practical use it was to be merely a flying bridge, which must be capable of being easily at any time broken off or burnt. We recognise in this circumstance how insecure for a long time and liable to interruption was the command of the passage of the river on the part of the Roman community.

No relation is discoverable between the urban settlements thus gradually formed and the three communities into which from an immemorially early period the Roman commonwealth was in political law divided. As the Ramnes, Tities, and Luceres appear to have been communities originally independent, they must have had their settlements originally apart; but they certainly did not dwell in separate circumvallations on the Seven Hills, and all fictions to this effect in ancient or modern times must be consigned by the intelligent inquirer to the same fate with the battle of the Palatine and the charming tale of Tarpeia. On the contrary each of the three tribes of Ramnes, Tities, and Luceres must have been distributed throughout the two regions of the oldest city, the Subura and Palatine, and the suburban region as well: with this may be connected the fact, that afterwards not only in the Suburan and Palatine, but in each of the regions subsequently added to the city, there were three pairs of Argean chapels. The Palatine city of the Seven Mounts may have had a history of its own; no other tradition of it has survived than simply that of its having once existed. But as the leaves of the forest make room for the new growth of spring, although they fall unseen by human eyes, so has this unknown city of the Seven Mounts made room for the Rome of history.

But the Palatine city was not the only one that in ancient times existed within the circle afterwards enclosed by the Servian walls; opposite to it, in its immediate vicinity, there lay a second city on the Quirinal. The "old strong-hold" (*Capitolium vetus*) with a sanctuary of Jupiter, Juno, and Minerva, and a temple of the goddess of Fidelity in which state treaties were publicly deposited, forms the evident counterpart of the later Capitol with its temple to Jupiter, Juno, and Minerva, and with its shrine of Fides Romana likewise destined as it were for a repository of international law, and furnishes clear proof that the Quirinal also was once the centre of an independent commonwealth. The same fact may be inferred from the double worship of Mars on the Palatine and the Quirinal; for Mars was the type of the warrior and the oldest chief divinity of the burgess communities of Italy. With this is connected the further circumstance that his ministers, the two primitive colleges of the "Leapers" (*Salii*) and of the "Wolves" (*Luperci*), existed in the later Rome in duplicate: by the side of the Salii of the Palatine there were also Salii of the Quirinal; by the side of the Quinctian Luperci of the Palatine there was a Fabian guild of Luperci, which in all probability had their sanctuary on the Quirinal.[1]

---

[1] That the Quinctian Luperci had precedence in rank over the Fabian is evident from the circumstance that the fabulists attribute the Quinctii to Romulus, the Fabii to Remus (Ovid. *Fast.* ii. 373, *seq.*; Vict. *De Orig.* 22). That the Fabii belonged to the Hill-Romans is shown by the sacrifice of their *gens* on the Quirinal (Liv. v. 46, 52), whether that sacrifice may or may not have been connected with the Lupercalia.

Moreover, the Lupercus of the former college is called in inscriptions (Orelli, 2253) *Lupercus Quinctialis vetus ;* and the *praenomen* Kaeso, which was most probably connected with the Lupercal worship (see *Röm. Forschungen,* i. 17), is found exclusively among the Quinctii and Fabii: the form commonly occurring in authors, *Lupercus Quinctilius* and *Quinctilianus*, is therefore a misnomer, and the college belonged not to the comparatively recent Quinctilii, but to the far older Quinctii. When, again,

All these indications, which even in themselves are of great weight, become more significant when we recollect that the accurately known circuit of the Palatine city of the Seven Mounts excluded the Quirinal, and that afterwards in the Servian Rome, while the first three regions corresponded to the former Palatine city, a fourth region was formed out of the Quirinal along with the neighbouring Viminal. Thus, too, we discover an explanation of the reason why the strong outwork of the Subura was constructed beyond the city wall in the valley between the Esquiline and Quirinal; it was at that point, in fact, that the two territories came into contact, and the Palatine Romans, after having taken possession of the low ground, were under the necessity of constructing a stronghold for protection against those of the Quirinal.

Lastly, even the name has not been lost by which the men of the Quirinal distinguished themselves from their Palatine neighbours. As the Palatine city took the name of "the Seven Mounts," its citizens called themselves the "mount-men" (*montani*), and the term "mount," while applied to the other heights belonging to the city, was above all associated with the Palatine; so the Quirinal height—although not lower, but on the contrary somewhat higher, than the former—as well as the adjacent Viminal never in the strict use of the language received any other name than "hill" (*collis*). In the ritual records, indeed, the Quirinal was not unfrequently designated as the "hill" without further addition. In like manner the gate leading out from this height was usually called the "hill-gate" (*porta collina*); the priests of Mars settled there were called those "of the hill" (*Salii collini*) in contrast to those of the Palatine (*Salii Palatini*), and the fourth Servian region formed out of this district was termed the hill-region (*tribus collina*).[1] The name of Romans primarily associated

the Quinctii (Liv. i. 30), or Quinctilii (Dion. iii. 29), are named among the Alban clans, the latter reading is to be preferred, and the Quinctii are to be regarded rather as an old Roman *gens*.

[1] Although the name "Hill of Quirinus" was afterwards ordinarily used to designate the height where the Hill-Romans had their abode, we need not on that account regard the name "Quirites" as having been originally reserved for the burgesses on the Quirinal. For the earliest indications point, as regards them, to the name *Collini*; while it is indisputably certain that the name *Quirites* denoted from the first, as well as subsequently, simply the full burgess, and had no connection with the distinction between *montani* and *collini* (comp. chap. v. *infra*). In fact, Mars *quirinus*, the spear-bearing god of Death, was originally worshipped as well on the Palatine as on the Quirinal; the oldest inscriptions found at what was afterwards called the Temple of Quirinus designate this divinity

with the locality was probably appropriated by these " Hill-
men " as well as by those of the " Mounts; " and the former
perhaps designated themselves as "Romans of the Hill "
(*Romani collini*). That a diversity of race may have lain at
the foundation of this distinction between the two neighbouring
cities is possible; but evidence sufficient to warrant our pronouncing a community established on Latin soil to be of alien
lineage is, in the case of the Quirinal community, totally wanting.[1]

Thus the site of the Roman commonwealth was still at this
period occupied by the Mount-Romans of the Palatine and the
Hill-Romans of the Quirinal as two separate communities confronting each other and doubtless in many respects at feud, in
some degree resembling the Montigiani and the Trasteverini in
modern Rome. That the community of the Seven Mounts
early attained a great preponderance over that of the Quirinal
may with certainty be inferred both from the greater extent of
its newer portions and suburbs, and from the position of inferiority in which the former Hill-Romans were obliged to
acquiesce under the later Servian arrangement. But even
within the Palatine city there was hardly a true and complete
amalgamation of the different constituent elements of the

simply as Mars, but at a later period for the sake of distinction the god of
the Mount-Romans more especially was called Mars, the god of the Hill-
Romans more especially Quirinus.
  When the Quirinal is called *collis agonalis*, " hill of sacrifice," it is so
designated merely as the centre of the religious rites of the Hill-Romans.
  [1] The evidence alleged for this (comp. *e.g.* Schwegler, *R. G.* i. 480) mainly
rests on an etymologico-historical hypothesis started by Varro and as
usual unanimously echoed by later writers, that the Latin *quiris* and
quirinus are akin to the name of the Sabine town *Cures*, and that the
Quirinal hill accordingly had been peopled from *Cures*. The linguistic
affinity of these words is probable; but how little warrant there is for
deducing from it such an historical inference must be obvious at once. That
the old sanctuaries on this eminence (where, besides, there was also a
" *Collis Latiaris* ") were Sabine, has been asserted, but has not been proved.
Mars quirinus, Sol, Salus, Flora, Semo Sancus or Deus fidius were indeed
Sabine, but they were also Latin, divinities, formed evidently during the
epoch when Latins and Sabines still lived undivided. If a name like that
of Semo Sancus (which moreover occurs in connection with the Tiber-
island) is especially associated with the sacred places of the Quirinal which
afterwards diminished in its importance (comp. the *Porta Sanqualis* deriving its name therefrom), every unbiassed inquirer will recognise in such a
circumstance only a proof of the high antiquity of that worship, not a
proof of its derivation from a neighbouring land. In so speaking we do
not mean to deny that it is possible that old distinctions of race may have
co-operated in producing this state of things; but if such was the case,
they have, so far as we are concerned, totally disappeared, and the views
current among our contemporaries as to the Sabine element in the constitution of Rome are only fitted seriously to warn us against such baseless
speculations leading to no result.

settlement. We have already mentioned how the Subura and the Palatine annually contended for the horse's head; the several Mounts also, and even the several curies (there was as yet no common hearth for the city, but the various hearths of the curies subsisted side by side, although in the same locality) probably felt themselves to be as yet more separated than united; and Rome as a whole was probably rather an aggregate of urban settlements than a single city. It appears from many indications that the houses of the old and powerful families were constructed somewhat after the manner of fortresses and were rendered capable of defence—a precaution, it may be presumed, not unnecessary. It was the magnificent structure ascribed to king Servius Tullius that first surrounded not merely those two cities of the Palatine and Quirinal, but also the heights of the Aventine and the Capitoline which were not comprehended within their enclosure, with a single great ring-wall, and thereby created the new Rome—the Rome of history. But ere this mighty work was undertaken, the relations of Rome to the surrounding country had beyond doubt undergone a complete revolution. As the period, during which the husbandman guided his plough on the seven hills of Rome just as on the other hills of Latium, and the usually unoccupied places of refuge on particular summits alone presented the germs of a more permanent settlement, corresponds to the earliest epoch of the Latin stock, an epoch barren of traffic and barren of action; as thereafter the flourishing settlement on the Palatine and in the "Seven Rings" was coincident with the occupation of the mouths of the Tiber by the Roman community, and with the progress of the Latins to a more stirring and freer inter-course, to an urban civilisation in Rome more especially, and perhaps also to a more consolidated political union in the individual states as well as in the confederacy; so the Servian wall, which was the foundation of a single great city, was connected with the epoch at which the city of Rome was able to contend for, and at length to achieve, the sovereignty of the Latin league.

CHAPTER V

THE ORIGINAL CONSTITUTION OF ROME

FATHER and mother, sons and daughters, home and homestead, servants and chattels—such are the natural elements constituting the household in all cases, where polygamy has not obliterated the distinctive position of the mother. But the nations that have been most susceptible of culture have diverged widely from each other in their conception and treatment of the natural distinctions which the household thus presents. By some they have been apprehended and wrought out more profoundly, by others more superficially; by some more under their moral, by others more under their legal aspects. None has equalled the Roman in the simple but inexorable embodiment in law of the principles pointed out by nature herself.

The family formed an unity. It consisted of the free man who upon his father's death had become his own master, and the spouse whom the priests by the ceremony of the sacred salted cake (*confarreatio*) had solemnly wedded to share with him water and fire, with their sons and sons' sons and the lawful wives of these, and their unmarried daughters and sons' daughters, along with all goods and substance pertaining to any of its members. The children of daughters on the other hand were excluded, because, if born in wedlock, they belonged to the family of the husband; and if begotten out of wedlock, they had no place in a family at all. To the Roman citizen a house of his own and the blessing of children appeared the end and essence of life. The death of the individual was not an evil, for it was a matter of necessity; but the extinction of a household or of a clan was injurious to the community itself, which in the earliest times therefore opened up to the childless the means of avoiding such a fatality by their adopting, in presence of the people, the children of others as their own.

The Roman family from the first contained within it the conditions of a higher culture in the moral adjustment of the mutual relations of its members. Men alone could be head of a family. Woman did not indeed occupy a position inferior to man in the acquiring of property and money; on the contrary the daughter inherited an equal share with her brother, and the mother an equal share with her children. But woman always and necessarily belonged to the household, not to the community; and in the household itself she necessarily held a position of domestic subjection—the daughter to her father, the wife to her husband,[1] the fatherless unmarried woman to her nearest male relatives; it was by these, and not by the king, that in case of need woman was called to account. Within the house, however, woman was not servant but mistress. Exempted from the tasks of corn-grinding and cooking which according to Roman ideas belonged to the menials, the Roman housewife devoted herself in the main to the superintendence of her maid-servants, and to the accompanying labours of the distaff, which was to woman what the plough was to man.[2] In like manner, the moral obligations of parents towards their children were fully and deeply felt by the Roman nation; and it was reckoned a heinous offence if a father neglected or corrupted his child,

[1] This was not merely the case with the old religious marriage (*matrimonium confarreatione*) ; the civil marriage also (*matrimonium consensu*), although not in itself giving to the husband proprietary power over his wife, opened up the way for his acquiring this proprietary power, inasmuch as the legal ideas of " formal delivery " (*coemptio*), and " prescription " (*usus*), were applied without ceremony to such a marriage. Until its acquisition, and in particular therefore during the period which elapsed before the completion of the prescription, the wife was (just as in the later marriage by *causae probatio*, until that took place), not *uxor*, but *pro uxore*. Down to the period when Roman jurisprudence became a completed system the principle maintained its ground, that the wife who was not in her husband's power was not a married wife, but only passed as such (*uxor tantummodo habetur*. Cicero, *Top*. 3, 14).

[2] The following epitaph, although belonging to a much later period, is not unworthy to have a place here. It is the stone that speaks:—

> *Hospes, quod deico, paullum est. Asta ac pellige.*
> *Heic est sepulcrum haud pulcrum pulcrai feminae,*
> *Nomen parentes nominarunt Claudiam,*
> *Suom mareitum corde dilexit sovo,*
> *Gnatos duos creavit, horunc alterum*
> *In terra linquit, alium sub terra locat ;*
> *Sermone lepido, tum autem incessu commodo,*
> *Domum servavit, lanam fecit. Dixi. Abei.*
>
> (*Corp. Inscr. Lat.* 1007.)

Still more characteristic, perhaps, is the introduction of wool-spinning among purely moral qualities; which is no very unusual occurrence in Roman epitaphs. Orelli, 4639: *optima et pulcherrima, lanifica pia pudica frugi casta domiseda.* Orelli, 4861: *modestia probitate pudicitia obsequio lanificio diligentia fide par similisque cetereis probeis femina fuit.* Epitaph of Turia: *domestica bona pudicitiae, opsequi, comitatis, facilitatis, lanificiis [tuis adsiduitatis, religionis] sine superstitione, ornatus non conspiciendi, cultus modici.*

or if he even squandered his property to his child's disadvantage.

In a legal point of view, however, the family was absolutely
guided and governed by the single all-powerful will of the
" father of the household " (*pater familias*).   In relation to him
all in the household were destitute of legal rights—the wife and
the child no less than the bullock or the slave.   As the virgin
became by the free choice of her husband his wedded wife, so
it rested with his own free will to rear or not to rear the child
which she bore to him.   This maxim was not suggested by
indifference to the possession of a family; on the contrary,
the conviction that the founding of a house and the begetting
of children were a moral necessity and a public duty had a
deep and earnest hold of the Roman mind.   Perhaps the only
instance of support accorded on the part of the community in
Rome is the enactment that aid should be given to the father
who had three children presented to him at a birth; while their
views regarding exposure are indicated by its religious prohibition
so far as concerned all the sons—deformed births excepted—
and at least the first daughter.   Censurable, however, and
injurious to the public weal as exposure might be, a father
could not be divested of his right to resort to it; for he was,
above all, thoroughly and absolutely master in his household,
and it was intended that he should remain so.   The father
of the household not only maintained the strictest discipline
over its members, but he had the right and duty of exercising
judicial authority over them and of punishing them as he
deemed fit in life and limb.   The grown-up son might establish
a separate household or, as the Romans expressed it, maintain
his " own cattle " (*peculium*) assigned to him by his father;
but in law all that the son acquired, whether by his own labour
or by gift from a stranger, whether in his father's household
or in his own, remained the father's property.   So long as the
father lived, the persons legally subject to him could never hold
property of their own, and therefore could not alienate unless
by him so empowered, or bequeath.   In this respect wife and
child stood quite on the same level with the slave, who was
not unfrequently allowed to manage a household of his own,
and who was likewise entitled to alienate when commissioned
by his master.   Indeed a father might convey his son as well
as his slave in property to a third person: if the purchaser was
a foreigner, the son became his slave; if he was a Roman, the
son, while as a Roman he could not become a Roman's slave,

stood at least to his purchaser in a slave's stead (*in mancipii causâ*).

In reality the paternal and marital power was subject to no legal restrictions at all. Religion, indeed, pronounced its anathema on some of the worst cases of abuse. For example, besides the already mentioned restriction of the right of exposure, whoever sold his wife or married son was declared accursed; and in a similar spirit it was enacted that in the exercise of domestic jurisdiction the father, and still more the husband, should not pronounce sentence on child or wife without having previously consulted the nearest blood-relations, his wife's as well as his own. But such provisions as these involved no legal diminution of his powers, for the execution of the anathemas was the province of the gods, not of earthly justice, and the blood-relations called in to the domestic judgment were present not to judge, but simply to advise the father of the household in his judicial office.

But not only was the power of the master of the house unlimited and responsible to no one on earth; it was also, as long as he lived, unchangeable and indestructible. According to the Greek as well as Germanic laws the grown-up son, who was practically independent of his father, was also independent legally; but the power of the Roman father could not be dissolved during his life either by age or by insanity, or even by his own free will, except where a daughter passed by a lawful marriage out of the hand of her father into the hand of her husband and, leaving her own *gens* and the protection of her own gods to enter into the *gens* of her husband and the protection of his gods, became thenceforth subject to him as she had hitherto been to her father. It was easier, according to Roman law, for the slave to obtain release from his master than for the son to obtain release from his father; the manumission of the former was permitted at an early period, and by simple forms; the release of the latter was only rendered possible at a much later date, and by very circuitous means. Indeed, if a master sold his slave and a father his son and the purchaser released both, the slave obtained his freedom, but the son by the release simply reverted into his father's power as before. The inexorable consistency with which the Romans carried out their conception of the paternal and marital power converted it into a real right of property.

Closely, however, as the power of the master of the household over wife and child approximated to his proprietary power over slaves and cattle, the members of the family were nevertheless separated by a broad line of distinction, not merely in fact but in law, from the family property. The power of the house-master—even apart from the fact that it appeared in operation only within the house—was of a transient, and in some degree of a representative, character. Wife and child did not exist merely for the house-father's sake in the sense in which property exists only for the proprietor, or in which the subjects of an absolute state exist only for the king; they were the objects indeed of a legal right on his part, but they had at the same time capacities of right of their own; they were not things, but persons. Their rights were dormant in respect of exercise, simply because the unity of the household demanded that it should be governed by a single representative; but when the master of the household died, his sons at once came forward as its masters and now obtained on their own account over the women and children and property the rights hitherto exercised over these by the father. On the other hand the death of the master occasioned no change in the legal position of the slave.

So strongly was the unity of the family realised, that even the death of the master of the house did not entirely dissolve it. The descendants, who were rendered by that occurrence independent, regarded themselves as still in many respects an unity; a principle which was made use of in arranging the succession of heirs and in many other relations, but especially in regulating the position of the widow and unmarried daughters. As according to the older Roman view a woman was not capable of having power either over others or over herself, the power over her, or, as it was in this case more mildly expressed, the "guardianship" (*tutela*) remained with the house to which she belonged, and was now exercised in the room of the deceased house-master by the whole of the nearest male members of the family; ordinarily, therefore, by sons over their mother, and by brothers over their sisters. In this sense the family, once founded, endured unchanged till the male stock of its founder died out; only the bond of connection must of course have become practically more lax from generation to generation, until at length it became impossible to prove the original unity. On this, and on this alone, rested the distinction between family and clan, or, according to the Roman expression, between *agnati* and *gentiles*. Both denoted the male stock; but the family embraced only those individuals who, mounting up from generation to generation, were able to exhibit the successive steps of their descent from a common progenitor; the clan (*gens*) on the other hand comprehended all those who, while claiming to be descended from a common ancestor, were no longer able fully to point out the intermediate links and thereby to establish the degree of their relationship. This is very clearly expressed in the Roman names: when they speak of " Quintus, son of Quintus, grandson of Quintus and so on, the Quintian," the family reaches as far as the ascendants are designated individually, and where the family terminates the clan is introduced supplementarily, indicating derivation from the common ancestor who has bequeathed to all his descendants the name of the " children of Quintus."

To these strictly closed unities—the family or household united under the control of a living master, and the clan which originated out of the breaking-up of such households—there further belonged the dependents or " listeners " (*clientes*, from *cluere*). This term denoted not the guests, that is, the members of similar circles who were temporarily sojourning in another household than their own, and still less the slaves who were looked upon in law as the property of the household and not as members of it, but those individuals who, while they were not free burgesses of any commonwealth, yet lived within one in a condition of protected freedom. The class included refugees who had found a reception with a foreign protector, and those slaves in respect to whom their master had for the time being waived the exercise of his rights, and so conferred on them practical freedom. This relation had not properly the character of a relation *de jure*, like the relation of a man to his guest or to his slave: the client remained non-free, although good faith and use and wont alleviated in his case the condition of non-freedom. Hence the " listeners " of the household (*clientes*) together with the slaves strictly so called formed the " body of servants " (*familia*) dependent on the will of the " burgess " (*patronus*, like *patricius*). Hence according to original right the burgess was entitled partially or wholly to resume the property of the client, to reduce him on emergency once more to the state of slavery, to inflict even capital punishment on him; and it was simply in virtue of a distinction *de facto*, that these patrimonial rights were not asserted with the same rigour against the client as against the actual slave, and that on the other hand the moral obligation of the master to provide for his own people and to protect them acquired a greater importance in the case of the client, who was practically in a more free position, than in the case of the slave. Especially must the *de facto* freedom of the client have approximated to freedom *de jure* in those cases where the relation had subsisted for several generations: when the releaser and the released had themselves died, the *dominium* over the descendants of the released person could not be without flagrant impiety claimed by the heirs at law of the releaser; and thus there was gradually formed within the household itself a class of persons in dependent freedom, who were different alike from the slaves and from the members of the *gens* entitled in the eye of the law to full and equal rights.

On this Roman household was based the Roman state, as respected both its constituent elements and its form. The community of the Roman people arose out of the junction (in whatever way brought about) of such ancient clanships as the Romilii, Voltinii, Fabii, etc.; the Roman domain comprehended the united lands of those clans (p. 35). Whoever belonged to one of these clans was a burgess of Rome. Every marriage concluded in the usual forms within this circle was valid as a true Roman marriage, and conferred burgess-rights on the children begotten of it. Whoever was begotten in an illegal marriage, or out of marriage, was excluded from the membership of the community. On this account the Roman burgesses assumed the name of the "fathers' children" (*patricii*), inasmuch as they alone in the eye of the law had a father. The clans with all the families that they contained were incorporated with the state just as they stood. The spheres of the household and the clan continued to subsist within the state; but the position which a man held in these did not affect his relations towards the state. The son was subject to the father within the household, but in political duties and rights he stood on a footing of equality. The position of the protected dependents was naturally so far changed that the freedmen and clients of every patron received on his account toleration in the community at large; they continued indeed to be immediately dependent on the protection of the family to which they belonged, but the very nature of the case implied that the clients of members of the community could not be wholly excluded from its worship and its festivals, although, of course, they were not capable of the proper rights or liable to the proper duties of burgesses. This remark applies still more to the case of the protected dependents of the community at large. The state thus consisted, like the household, of persons properly belonging to it and of dependents—of " burgesses " and of " inmates " or *metoeci*.

As the clans resting upon a family basis were the constituent elements of the state, so the form of the body-politic was modelled after the family both generally and in detail. The household was provided by nature herself with a head in the person of the father with whom it originated, and with whom it perished. But in the community of the people, which was designed to be imperishable, there was no natural master; not at least in that of Rome, which was composed of free and equal husbandmen and could not boast of a nobility by the grace of God. Accordingly one from its own ranks became its " leader " (*rex*) and " commander " (*dictator*), " master of the people " (*magister populi*) and lord in the household of the Roman community. That this was indeed the true nature of his position is evident, for at a later period there were to be found in or near to his residence the always blazing hearth and the well-barred store-chamber of the community, the Roman Vesta and the Roman Penates—indications of the visible unity of that supreme household which included all Rome. The regal magistracy began at once and by right, when the successor had been designated and the office had become vacant; but the community did not owe fidelity and obedience to the king until he had convoked the assembly of freemen capable of bearing arms and had formally challenged its allegiance. Then he possessed in its entirety that power over the community which belonged to the house-father in his household; and, like him, he ruled for life. He held intercourse with the gods of the community, whom he consulted and appeased (*auspicia publica*), and he nominated all the priests and priestesses. The agreements which he concluded in name of the community with foreigners were binding upon the whole people; although in other instances no member of the community was bound by an agreement with a non-member. His " command " (*imperium*) was all-powerful in peace and in war, on which account " messengers " (*lictores*, from *licere*, to summon) preceded him with axes and rods on all occasions when he appeared officially. He alone had the right of publicly addressing the burgesses, and it was he who kept the keys of the public treasury. He had the same right as a father had to exercise discipline and jurisdiction. He inflicted penalties for breaches of order, and, in particular, flogging for military offences. He sat in judgment in all private and in all criminal processes, and decided absolutely regarding life and death as well as regarding freedom; he might hand over one burgess to fill the place of a slave to another; he might even order a burgess to be sold into actual slavery or, in other words, into banishment. When he had pronounced sentence of death, he was entitled, but not obliged, to allow an appeal to the people for pardon. He called out the people for service in war and commanded the army; but with these high functions he was no less bound, when an alarm of fire was raised, to appear in person at the scene of the burning.

As the house-master was not simply the greatest but the only power in the house, so the king was not merely the first but the only holder of power in the state. He might indeed form colleges of men of skill composed of those specially conversant with the rules of sacred or of public law, and call upon them for their advice; he might, to facilitate his exercise of power, entrust to others particular functions, such as the making communications to the burgesses, the command in war, the decision of processes of minor importance, the inquisition of crimes; he might in particular, if he was compelled to quit the bounds of the city, leave behind him a " city-warden " (*praefectus urbi*) with the full powers of an *alter ego ;* but all magisterial power existing by the side of the king's was derived from the latter, and every magistrate held his office by the king's appointment and during the king's pleasure. All the officials of the earliest period, the extraordinary city-warden as well as those who were probably nominated regularly—the " trackers of foul murder " (*quaestores paricidii*), and the " leaders of division " (*tribuni*, from *tribus*, part) of the infantry (*milites*) and of the cavalry (*celeres*)—were mere royal commissioners, and not magistrates in the subsequent sense of the term. The regal power had not and could not have any external checks imposed upon it by law: the master of the community had no judge of his acts within the community, any more than the house-father had a judge within his household. Death alone terminated his power; and in view of that event it was, to all appearance, not only his lawful prerogative but probably part of his duty to nominate a successor to himself of his own free choice. A formal co-operation in the election of king was not requisite on the part of the council of elders, and the burgesses only concurred after the nomination;[1] *de jure* the new king was always appointed by his

[1] Evidence of a direct nature regarding the constitutional preliminaries of the election of king in Rome is not to be looked for. But the nomination of the dictator took place exactly in the mode here described; the

predecessor, and thus " the august blessing of the gods, with which renowned Rome was founded," was transmitted from its first regal recipient in regular succession to his followers in office, and the unity of the state was preserved unchanged notwithstanding the personal change of the holders of power.

This unity of the Roman people, represented in the field of religion by the Roman Diovis, was in the field of law represented by the prince, and therefore his costume was the same as that of the supreme god; the chariot even in the city, where every one else went on foot, the ivory sceptre with the eagle, the vermilion-painted face, the chaplet of oaken leaves in gold, belonged alike to the Roman god and to the Roman king. It would be a great error, however, to regard the Roman constitution on that account as a theocracy: among the Italians the ideas of god and king never faded away into each other, as they did in Egypt and the East. The king was not the god of the people; it were much more correct to designate him as the proprietor of the state. Accordingly the Romans knew nothing of special divine grace granted to a particular family, or of any other sort of mystical charm by which a king should be made of different stuff from other men: noble descent and relationship with earlier rulers were recommendations, but were not necessary conditions; the office might be lawfully filled by any Roman come to years of discretion and sound in body and mind.[1] The king was simply an ordinary burgess, whom merit or fortune, and the primary necessity of having one as master in every house, had placed as master over his equals—a husbandman set over husbandmen, a warrior set over warriors. As the son absolutely obeyed his father and yet

nomination of the consul varied from it only in so far as the succession in this case had reference of course not to the death of the predecessor but to his retirement, and there was conceded to the community a binding right of proposal and to the senate its correlative right of confirmation—an arrangement which beyond dispute bears the stamp of a later origin—while the nomination itself in the case of the consulate was without exception made by the predecessor in office or the interrex; and, as the consulate and the dictatorship were in substance simply continuations of the regal office, the hypothesis which we have embodied above must be regarded as quite certain. Even according to the traditional accounts the previous election by the curies was admissible merely, but by no means legally necessary, as the story of Servius Tullius proves. It was probably the custom to make the nomination in public (*contione advocata*), and the acclamation with which it was received might easily be viewed by later writers in the light of an election.

[1] Dionysius affirms (v. 25) that lameness excluded from the supreme magistracy. That Roman citizenship must have formed an indispensable condition for the regal office as well as for the consulate, is so self-evident as to make it scarcely worth while to refute formally the fictions respecting the burgess of Cures.

did not esteem himself inferior, so the burgess submitted to his
ruler without precisely accounting him his better. This constituted the moral and practical limitation of the regal power.
The king might, it is true, do much that was inconsistent with
equity without exactly breaking the law of the land: he might
diminish his fellow-combatants' share of the spoil; he might
impose exorbitant task-works, or otherwise by his imposts
unreasonably encroach upon the property of the burgess; but
if he did so, he forgot that his plenary power came not from
God, but under God's consent from the people, whose representative he was; and who was there to protect him if the
people should in return forget the oath of allegiance which they
had sworn? The legal limitation, again, of the king's power
lay in the principle that he was entitled only to execute the law,
not to alter it. Every deviation from the law had to receive
the previous approval of the assembly of the people and the
council of elders; if it was not so approved, it was a null and
tyrannical act carrying no legal effect. It thus appears that the
power of the king in Rome was, both morally and legally,
altogether different from the sovereignty of the present day.
There is no counterpart in modern life either to the Roman
household or to the Roman state.

The division of the body of burgesses was based on the
primitive normal principle, that ten houses formed a clan
(*gens*), ten clans or a hundred households formed a wardship
(*curia*, probably related to *curare* = *coerare*, κοίρανος), ten wardships or a hundred clans or a thousand households formed the
community; and further, that every household furnished a
foot-soldier (hence *mil-es*, like *equ-es*, thousand-walker), and
every clan a horseman and a senator. When communities
combined, each of course appeared at a part (*tribus*) of the whole
community (*tota* in Umbrian and Oscan), and the original unit
became multiplied by the number of such parts. This division
had reference primarily to the personal composition of the
burgess-body, but it was applied also to the domain so far as
the latter was apportioned at all. That the curies had their
lands as well as the tribes, admits of the less doubt, since among
the few names of the Roman curies that have been handed down
to us we find along with some apparently derived from *gentes*,
e.g. Faucia, others certainly of local origin, *e.g. Veliensis*.
Besides we meet with a very old measure of land corresponding
to the *curia* of a hundred households, the " hundred " (*centuria*),
comprising a hundred homesteads of two *jugera* each. The

clan's lands, of which we have already spoken (p. 35), must in this primitive period of joint possession have been the smallest unit in the division of land.

We find this constitution under its simplest form in the scheme of the Latin or burgess communities that subsequently sprang up under the influence of Rome; these had uniformly the number of a hundred acting councillors (*centumviri*) and each of these councillors was called "head of ten households" (*decurio*).[1] But the same normal numbers make their appearance throughout in the earliest tradition regarding the tripartite Rome, which assigns to it thirty curies, three hundred clans, three hundred horsemen, three hundred senators, three thousand households, and as many foot-soldiers.

Nothing is more certain than that this earliest constitutional scheme did not originate in Rome: it was a primitive institution common to all the Latins, and perhaps reached back to a period long anterior to the separation of the stocks. The Roman constitutional tradition quite deserving of credit in such matters, while it accounts historically for the other divisions of the burgesses, makes the division into curies alone originate with the origin of the city; and in entire harmony with that view not only does the curial constitution present itself in Rome, but in the recently discovered scheme of the organisation of the Latin communities it appears as an essential part of the Latin municipal system.

It is difficult, on the other hand, to arrive at a satisfactory view of the object and practical value of the scheme now before us. The distribution into curies manifestly constituted its essence. The tribes ("parts") cannot have been an element of essential importance for the simple reason that their occurrence at all was, not less than their number, the result of accident; where there were tribes, they certainly had no other significance than that of preserving the remembrance of an epoch when such tribes had themselves been wholes.[2] There is no tradition that the individual tribes had special presiding magistrates or special

[1] Even in Rome, where the simple constitution of ten curies otherwise early disappeared, we still discover one practical application of it, and that singularly enough in the very same formality which we have other reasons for regarding as the oldest of all those that are mentioned in our legal traditions, the *confarreatio*. It seems scarcely doubtful that the ten witnesses in that ceremony had the same relation to the constitution of ten curies as the thirty lictors had to the constitution of thirty curies.

[2] This is implied in their very name. The "part" (*tribus*) is, as jurists know, simply that which has once been or may hereafter come to be a whole, and so has no real standing of its own in the present.

assemblies of their own; and it is extremely probable that in the interest of the unity of the commonwealth the tribes which had joined together to form it were never in reality allowed to have such institutions. In the army, it is true, the infantry had as many pairs of leaders as there were tribes; but each of these pairs of military tribunes did not command the contingent of a tribe; on the contrary each individually, as well as all in conjunction, exercised command over the whole infantry. The clans and families also must in like manner with the tribes, although for reasons very different, have had a theoretical more than a practical significance under this type of constitution. The limits of the stock and of the household were furnished by nature. The legislative power might interfere with these groups in the way of modification; it might subdivide a large clan and count it as two, or it might join several weak ones together; and it might enlarge or diminish even the household in a similar way. Nevertheless affinity in blood always appeared to the Romans to lie at the root of the connection between the members of a clan and still more between those of a family; and the Roman community can only have interfered with those groups to a limited extent consistent with the retention of their fundamental character of affinity. While, accordingly, the number of households and clans in the Latin communities was perhaps originally conceived as fixed, it must very soon have come to vary amidst the accidents of human affairs; and the normal scheme of exactly a thousand households and exactly a hundred clans cannot have had more than a theoretical significance except, at the most, in its earliest infancy—the infancy of an institution which meets us matured on the threshold of history.[1] The practical unimportance of these numbers is palpably evinced by the entire absence of instances where they were really applied. It is not affirmed by tradition, nor is it credible, that one foot-

---

[1] In Slavonia, where the patriarchal economy is retained up to the present day, the whole family, often to the number of fifty or even a hundred, remains together in the same house under the control of the house-father chosen by the whole family for life (Goszpodár). The property of the household, consisting chiefly of cattle, is managed by the house-father; the surplus is distributed according to the family branches. Private acquisitions by industry and trade remain separate property. Instances of quitting the household occur, even in the case of men, *e.g.* by marrying into a stranger household (Csaplovics, *Slavonien*, i. 106, 179).

Under such circumstances, which probably are not very widely different from the earliest condition of Rome, the household approximates in character to the community, and a fixed number of households can certainly be conceived. We may even connect with such a state of things the primitive *adrogatio*.

soldier precisely was taken from each house, and one horseman precisely from each clan; although three thousand of the former and three hundred of the latter were selected in all, the selection in detail was doubtless determined from the remotest times wholly by practical considerations, and if the Romans did not allow these normal numbers to fall entirely into abeyance, the reason of their retention lay simply in the tendency so deeply implanted in the Latin character towards a logical or rather systematic adjustment of proportions. If these views be correct, the only member that remains, and that really fulfilled important functions in this primitive constitutional organisation, is the *curia*. Of these there were ten, or, where there were several tribes, ten to each tribe. Such a " wardship " was a real corporate unity, the members of which assembled at least for holding common festivals. Each wardship was under the charge of a special warden (*curio*), and had a priest of its own (*flamen curialis*); beyond doubt also the levies and valuations took place according to curial divisions, and in judicial matters the burgesses met by curies and voted by curies. This organisation, however, cannot have been introduced primarily with a view to voting, for in that case they would certainly have made the number of subdivisions uneven.

Sternly defined as was the contrast between burgess and non-burgess, the equality of rights within the burgess-body was complete. No people has ever perhaps equalled that of Rome in the inexorable rigour with which it has carried out these principles, the one as fully as the other. The strictness of the Roman distinction between burgesses and non-burgesses is nowhere perhaps brought out with such clearness as in the treatment of the primitive institution of honorary citizenship, which was originally designed to mediate between the two. When a stranger was, by resolution of the community, adopted into the circle of the burgesses,[1] he might surrender his previous citizenship, in which case he passed over wholly into the new community; but he might also combine his former citizenship with that which had just been granted to him. Such was the primitive custom, and such it always remained in Hellas, where in later ages the same person not unfrequently held the freedom of several communities at the same time. But the greater

---

[1] The original expression for this was *patronum cooptari*, which, as *patronus* just like *patricius* in itself denoted simply the full burgess (p. 61), did not differ from the *in patricios cooptari* (Liv. iv. 4; Sueton. *Tib.* 1) or the later *in patricios adlegi*.

vividness with which the conception of the community as such was realised in Latium could not tolerate the idea that a man might simultaneously belong in the character of a burgess to two communities; and accordingly, when the newly-chosen burgess did not intend to surrender his previous franchise, it attached to the nominal honorary citizenship no further meaning than that of an obligation to befriend and protect the guest (*ius hospitii*), such as had always been recognised as incumbent in reference to foreigners.

But this rigorous retention of barriers against those that were without was accompanied by an absolute banishment of all differences of rights among the members included in the burgess community of Rome. We have already mentioned that the distinctions existing in the household, which of course could not be set aside, were at least ignored in the community; the son who as such was subject in property to his father might, in the character of a burgess, come to have command over his father as master. There were no class-privileges: the fact that the Tities took precedence of the Ramnes, and both ranked before the Luceres, did not affect their equality in all legal rights. The burgess cavalry, which at this period was used for single combat in front of the line on horseback or even on foot, and was rather a select or reserved corps than a special arm of the service, and which accordingly contained by far the wealthiest, best-armed, and best-trained men, was naturally held in higher estimation than the burgess infantry; but this was a distinction purely *de facto*, and admittance to the cavalry was doubtless conceded to any patrician. It was solely the constitutional subdivision of the burgess-body that gave rise to distinctions recognised by the law. The legal equality of all the members of the community was carried out even in their external appearance. Dress indeed served to distinguish the president of the community from its members, the senator from the burgess who did not belong to the senate, the grown-up man under obligation of military service from the boy not yet capable of enrolment; but otherwise the rich and the noble as well as the poor and low-born were only allowed to appear in public in the like simple wrapper (*toga*) of white woollen stuff. This complete equality of rights among the burgesses had beyond doubt its original basis in the Indo-Germanic type of constitution; but in the precision with which it was thus apprehended and embodied it formed one of the most characteristic and influential peculiarities of the Latin nation. And in connection with this we may recall the fact that in Italy we do not meet with any race of earlier settlers less capable of culture, that had become subject to the Latin immigrants (p. 9). They had no conquered race to deal with, and therefore no such condition of things as that which gave rise to the Indian system of caste, to the nobility of Thessaly and Sparta and perhaps of Hellas generally, and probably also to the Germanic distinction of ranks.

The maintenance of the state economy devolved, of course, upon the burgesses. The most important function of the burgess was his service in the army; for the burgesses alone had the right and duty of bearing arms. [The burgesses were at the same time the " body of warriors " (*populus*, related to *populari*, to lay waste, and *popa*, the butcher);] in the old litanies it is upon the " spear-armed body of warriors " (*pilumnus poplus*) that the blessing of Mars is invoked; and the king, when he addressed them, called them " lance-men " (*quirites*).[1] We have already stated how the army of aggression, the " gathering " (*legio*), was formed. In the tripartite Roman community

[1] *Quiris*, *quiritis*, or *quirinus*, literally means " lance-bearer," from *quiris* or *curis*=lance and *ire*, and in that respect agrees with *samnis*, *samnitis* and *sabinus*, which even among the ancients was derived from σαύνιον, spear. Kindred forms are *arquites*, *milites*, *pedites*, *equites*, *velites*, those respectively who *go* with the *bow*, in bodies of a *thousand*, on *foot*, on *horseback*, without armour in their mere *over-garment*; only in the latter forms, as in *dederitis*, *hominis*, and numerous other words, the *i*, originally long, has been shortened. In this way Juno quiritis, (Mars) quirinus, Janus quirinus are primarily characterised by that epithet as divinities that hurl the spear; and employed in reference to men *quiris* denotes the warrior, that is, the full burgess. With this view the *usus loquendi* coincides. Where the locality was to be referred to, " *Quirites* " was never used, but always " Rome " and " Romans " (*urbs Roma*, *populus*, *civis*, *ager Romanus*), because the term *quiris* had as little of a local meaning as *civis* or *miles*. For the same reason these designations could not be combined; they did not say *civis quiris*, because both denoted, though from different points of view, the same legal conception. On the other hand the solemn announcement of the funeral of a burgess ran in the words " this warrior has departed in death " (*ollus quiris leto datus*); and in like manner he who was injured employed this word in calling the burgesses to aid him (*quiritare*); the king addressed the assembled community by this name, and, when he sat in judgment, gave sentence according to the law of the warrior-freemen (*ex iure quiritium*, quite similar to the later *ex iure civili*). The phrase *populus Romanus*, *quirites*, thus means " the community and the individual burgesses," and therefore in an old formula (Liv. i. 32) to the *populus Romanus* are opposed the *prisci Latini*, to the *quirites* the *homines prisci Latini* (Bekker, *Handb.* ii. 20 seq.); *populus Romanus quiritium* corresponds to the well-known phrases *colonia colonorum*, *municipium municipum*.

In the face of these facts nothing but ignorance of language and of history can still adhere to the idea that the Roman community was once confronted by a Quirite community of a similar kind, and that after their incorporation the name of the recently received community supplanted in ritual and legal phraseology that of the receiver.—Comp. p. 53 note.

it consisted of three "hundreds" (*centuriae*) of horsemen (*celeres,* "the swift," or *flexuntes,* "the wheelers") under the three leaders-of-division of the horsemen (*tribuni celerum*),[1] and three "thousands" of footmen (*milites*) under the three leaders-of-division of the infantry (*tribuni militum*); the latter were probably from the first the flower of the general levy. To these there may perhaps have been added a number of light-armed men, archers especially, fighting outside of the ranks.[2] The general was regularly the king himself. Besides service in war, other personal burdens might devolve upon the burgesses; such as the obligation of undertaking the king's commissions in peace and in war (p. 64), and the task-work of tilling the king's lands or of constructing public buildings. How heavily in particular the burden of building the walls of the city pressed upon the community, is evidenced by the fact that the ring-walls retained the name of "tasks" (*moenia*). There was no regular direct taxation, nor was there any direct regular expenditure on the part of the state. Taxation was not needed for defraying the burdens of the community, since the state gave no recompense for serving in the army, for task-work, or for public service

[1] Among the eight ritual institutions of Numa Dionysius (ii. 64) after naming the Curiones and Flamines specifies as the third the leaders of the horsemen (οἱ ἡγεμόνες τῶν Κελερίων). According to the Praenestine calendar a festival was celebrated at the Comitium on the 19th March [*adstantibus pon*]*tificibus et trib*(*unis*) *celer*(*um*). Valerius Antias (in. Dionys. ii. 13, comp. iii. 41) assigns to the earliest Roman cavalry a leader, Celer, and three centurions; whereas in the treatise *De Viris Ill.* 1, Celer himself is termed *centurio*. Moreover Brutus is affirmed to have been *tribunus celerum* at the expulsion of the kings (Liv. i. 59), and according to Dionysius (iv. 71) to have even by virtue of this office made the proposal to banish the Tarquins. And, lastly, Pomponius (Dig. i. 2, 2, 15, 19) and Lydus in a similar way, partly perhaps borrowing from him (*De Mag.* i. 14, 37), identify the *tribunus celerum* with the Celer of Antias, the *magister equitum* of the dictator under the republic, and the *Praefectus praetorio* of the empire.

Of these—the only statements which are extant regarding the *tribuni celerum*—the last mentioned not only proceeds from late and quite untrustworthy authorities, but is inconsistent with the meaning of the term, which can only signify "divisional leaders of horsemen." The master of the horse of the republican period, who was nominated only on extraordinary occasions and was in later times no longer nominated at all, cannot possibly have been identical with the magistracy that was required for the annual festival of the 19th March and was consequently a standing office. Laying aside, as we necessarily must, the account of Pomponius, which has evidently arisen solely out of the anecdote of Brutus dressed up with ever increasing ignorance as history, we reach the simple result that the *tribuni celerum* entirely correspond in number and character to the *tribuni militum*, and that they were the leaders-of-division of the horsemen, consequently quite distinct from the *magister equitum.*

[2] This is indicated by the evidently very old forms *velites* and *arquites* and by the subsequent organisation of the legion.

generally; so far as there was any such recompense at all, it was
given to the person who performed the service by the district
primarily concerned in it, or by the person who could not or
would not serve himself. The victims needed for the public
service of the gods were procured by a tax on actions at law;
the defeated party in an ordinary process paid down to the state
⌐a cattle-fine (*sacramentum*) proportioned to the value of the
object in dispute.⌐ There is no mention of any regular presents
to the king on the part of the burgesses; but the non-burgesses
settled in Rome (*aerarii*) appear to have paid to him a tax for
protection. Besides this there flowed into the royal coffers the
port-duties (p. 47), as well as the income from the domains—in
particular, the pasture tribute (*scriptura*) from the cattle driven
out upon the common pasture, and the quotas of produce
(*vectigalia*), which the lessees of the lands of the state had to pay
instead of rent. To this was added the produce of cattle fines
and confiscations and the gains of war. In cases of need a contribution (*tributum*) was imposed, which was looked upon,
however, as a forced loan and was repaid when the times improved; whether it fell upon the inhabitants without distinction,
or upon the burgesses alone, cannot be determined; the latter
supposition is, however, the more probable.

The king managed the finances. The property of the state,
however, was not identified with the private property of the
king; which, judging from the statements regarding the extensive landed possessions of the last Roman royal house, the
Tarquins, must have been considerable. The ground won by
arms, in particular, appears to have been constantly regarded
as property of the state. Whether and how far the king was
restricted by use and wont in the administration of the public
property, can no longer be ascertained; but we may infer from
the subsequent course of procedure that the burgesses can never
have been consulted regarding it, whereas it was probably the
custom to consult the senate in the imposition of the *tributum*
and in the distribution of the lands won in war.

The burgesses, however, do not merely come into view as
furnishing contributions and rendering service; they also bore
a part in the public government. For this purpose all the
members of the community (with the exception of the women,
and the children still incapable of bearing arms)—in other
words, the " spearmen," as in addressing them they were
designated—assembled at the seat of justice, when the king
convoked them for the purpose of making a communication

(*conventio, contio*), or formally bade them meet (*comitia*) for the third week (*in trinum noundinum*), to consult them by curies. He appointed such formal assemblies of the community to be held regularly twice a year, on the 24th of March and the 24th of May, and as often besides as seemed to him necessary. The burgesses, however, were always summoned not to speak, but to hear; not to ask questions but to answer them. No one spoke in the assembly but the king, or he to whom the king saw fit to grant liberty of speech; and the speaking of the burgesses consisted of a simple answer to the question of the king, without discussion, without reasons, without conditions, without breaking up the question into parts. Nevertheless the Roman burgess-community, like the Germanic and not improbably the primitive Indo-Germanic communities in general, was the real and ultimate basis of the political idea of sovereignty. But in the ordinary course of things this sovereignty was dormant, or only had its expression in the fact that the burgess-body voluntarily bound itself to render allegiance to its president. For that purpose the king, after he had entered on his office, addressed to the assembled curies the question whether they would be true and loyal to him and would according to use and wont acknowledge himself as well as his servants, the trackers (*quaestores*) and messengers (*lictores*); a question which undoubtedly might no more be answered in the negative than the parallel homage in the case of a hereditary monarchy might be refused.

It was in thorough consistency with constitutional principles that the burgesses, as being the sovereign power, should not on ordinary occasions take part in the course of public business. So long as public action was confined to the carrying into execution of the existing constitutional regulations, the power which was, properly speaking, sovereign in the state could not and might not interfere: the laws governed, not the lawgiver. But it was different where a change of the existing legal arrangements or even a mere deviation from them in a particular case was necessary. In every such instance the Roman constitution exhibits the burgesses as exercising their power; so that each act of the sovereign authority is accomplished by the co-operation of the burgesses and the king or *interrex*. As the legal relation between ruler and ruled was itself ratified in the manner of a contract by oral question and answer, so every sovereign act of the community was accomplished by means of a question (*rogatio*), which the king—but only he, never his deputy (p. 64)—addressed to the burgesses, and to which the majority of the curies gave an affirmative answer. In this case their consent might undoubtedly be refused. Among the Romans, therefore, law was not primarily, as we conceive it, a command addressed by the sovereign to the whole members of the community, but primarily a contract concluded between the constitutive powers of the state by address and counter-address.[1] Such a legislative contract was *de jure* requisite in all cases which involved a deviation from the ordinary consistency of the legal system. In the ordinary course of law any one might without restriction give away his property to whom he would, but only upon condition of its immediate transfer: that the property should continue for the time being with the owner, and at his death pass over to another, was a legal impossibility—unless the community should allow it; a permission which in this case the burgesses could grant not only when assembled in their curies, but also when drawn up for battle. [This was the origin of testaments.] In the ordinary course of law the freeman could not lose or surrender the inalienable blessing of freedom, and therefore one who was subject to no house-master could not subject himself to another in the place of a son—unless the community should grant him leave to do so. This was the *adrogatio*. In the ordinary course of law burgess-rights could only be acquired by birth and could never be lost—unless the community should confer the patriciate or allow its surrender; neither of which acts, doubtless, could be validly done originally without a decree of the curies. In the ordinary course of law the criminal whose crime deserved death, when once the king or his deputy had pronounced sentence according to judgment and justice, was inexorably executed; for the king could only judge, not pardon—unless the condemned burgess appealed to the mercy of the community and the judge allowed him the opportunity of pleading for pardon. This was the beginning of the *provocatio*, which for that reason was especially permitted not to the transgressor who had refused to plead guilty and had been convicted, but to him who confessed his crime and urged reasons in palliation

---

[1] *Lĕx* (obscure in its origin, but related to *lēgare*, " to depute, to appoint ") denotes, as is well known, a contract in general, along, however, with the connotation of a contract whose terms the proposer dictates and the other party simply accepts or declines; as was usually the case, *e.g.* with public *licitationes*. In the *lex publica populi Romani* the proposer was the king, the acceptor the people; the limited co-operation of the latter was thus significantly indicated in the very language.

of it. In the ordinary course of law the perpetual treaty concluded with a neighbouring state might not be broken— unless the burgesses deemed themselves released from it on account of injuries inflicted on them. Hence it was necessary that they should be consulted when an aggressive war was contemplated, but not on occasion of a defensive war, where the other state had broken the treaty, nor on the conclusion of peace; it appears, however, that the question was in such a case addressed not to the usual assembly of the burgesses, but to the army. Thus, in general, it was necessary to consult the burgesses whenever the king meditated any innovation, any change of the existing public law; and in so far the right of legislation was from antiquity a right of the community, not of the king. In these and all similar cases the king could not act with legal effect without the co-operation of the community; the man whom the king alone declared a patrician remained a non-burgess as before, and the invalid act could only carry consequences *de facto*, not *de jure*. Thus far the assembly of the community, restricted and hampered as it at first appears, was yet from antiquity a constituent element of the Roman commonwealth, and was in law superior to, rather than co-ordinate with, the king.

But by the side of the king and of the burgess-assembly there appears in the earliest constitution of the community a third original power, not destined for action like the former, nor for legislation like the latter, and yet co-ordinate with both and within its own rightful sphere placed over both. This was the council of elders or *senatus*. Beyond doubt it had its origin in the clan-constitution: the old tradition that in the original Rome the senate was composed of all the heads of households is correct in state-law to this extent, that each of the clans of the later Rome which had not merely migrated thither at a more recent date referred its origin to one of those household-fathers of the primitive city as its ancestor and patriarch. If, as is probable, there was once in Rome or at any rate in Latium a time when, like the state itself, each of its ultimate constituents, that is to say, each clan had virtually a monarchical organisation and was under the rule of an elder—whether raised to that position by the choice of the clansmen or of his predecessor, or in virtue of hereditary succession—the senate of that time must have been simply the collective body of these clan-elders; and if so, it was an institution altogether independent of the king and of the burgess-assembly and, in contradistinction

to the latter which was directly composed of the whole body
of the burgesses, it had in some measure the character of an
indirect representation of the people. Certainly that stage of
independence when each clan was virtually a state was surmounted in the Latin stock at an immemorially early period,
and the first and perhaps most difficult step towards developing
the community out of the clan-organisation—the setting aside
of the clan-elders—had possibly been taken in Latium long
before the foundation of Rome; the Roman clan, as we know
it, is without any visible head, and no one of the living clansmen is especially called to represent the common patriarch
from whom all the clansmen descended or profess to descend,
so that even inheritance and guardianship, when they fall
by death to the clan, devolve on the clan-members as a whole.
Nevertheless the original character of the council of elders
bequeathed many and important legal consequences to the
Roman senate. To express the matter briefly, the position
of the senate as something other and more than a mere state-
council—than an assemblage of a number of trusty men whose
advice the king found it fitting to obtain—hinged entirely on
the fact that it was once an assembly like that, described by
Homer, of the princes and rulers of the people sitting for deliberation in a circle round the king. The number of members in the
original council of elders was necessarily a fixed one, corresponding to the number of the clans that formed the state; and
membership was necessarily for life. In both respects the
Roman senate was similar. The number of the senatorial
stalls in Rome not only remained at all times a fixed one,
but was also at the outset necessarily equal to the number
of clanships belonging to the state, so that the amalgamation of the three primitive communities, each of which was
assumed to consist of a hundred clanships, was in state-law
necessarily accompanied by an increase of the senatorial seats
to the normal number of three hundred, which thenceforth
became fixed. Moreover the senators were at all times called
to sit for life; and if at a later period the life-long tenure
subsisted more *de facto* than *de jure*, and the revisions of the
senatorial list that took place from time to time afforded an
opportunity to remove the unworthy or the unacceptable
senator, it can be shown that this arrangement only arose in
the course of time. The selection of the senators was certainly
at all times vested in the king, nor could it be otherwise after
the clan-elders had ceased to exist; but in this selection during

the earlier epoch, so long as the people retained a vivid sense of the individuality of the clans, it was probably the established rule that, when a senator died, the king should call another experienced and aged man of the same clanship to fill his place, and that there should be no Roman clan unrepresented and none with a double representation in the senate of the Roman community. It was only in all probability when the community became more thoroughly amalgamated and inwardly united, that this usage was departed from and the selection of the senators was left entirely to the free judgment of the king, so that he was only regarded as failing in his duty when he omitted to fill up vacancies.

The prerogatives of this council of elders were based on the view that the rule over a community composed of clans rightfully belonged to the collective clan-elders, although in accordance with the monarchical principle of the Romans, which found so stern an expression in the household, that rule could only be exercised for the time being by one of these elders, namely the king. Every member of the senate accordingly was as such, not in practice but in prerogative, likewise king of the community; and therefore his insignia, though inferior to those of the king, were quite of a similar character: he wore the purple on his dress and the red shoe like the king; but the whole robe of the king was purple, whereas that of the senator had merely a purple border (*latus clavus*), and the red shoes of the king were higher and more handsome than those of the senators. On this ground, moreover, the royal power in the Roman community could never be left vacant. If the king died without having himself nominated a successor, the elders at once took his place and exercised the prerogatives of regal power. According to the immutable principle however that only one can be master at a time, even now it was only one of them that ruled, and such a "temporary king" (*interrex*) was distinguished from the king nominated for life simply in respect to the duration, not in respect to the plenitude, of his authority. The duration of the office of *interrex* was fixed for the individual holder at not more than five days; it circulated accordingly among the senators on the footing that, until the royal office was again permanently filled up, the temporary holder at the expiry of his term nominated a successor to himself for a similar term of five days agreeably to the order of succession fixed by lot. There was, it may readily be conceived, no declaration of allegiance to the *interrex* on the part of the community. Nevertheless the *interrex* was

entitled and bound not merely to perform all the official acts
otherwise pertaining to the king, but even to nominate a king
for life—with the single exception that this right was not vested
in the first who held the office, probably because the first was
regarded as defectively appointed inasmuch as he was not
nominated by his predecessor. Thus this assembly of elders
was the ultimate holder of the ruling power (*imperium*) and the
divine protection (*auspicia*) of the Roman commonwealth, and
furnished the guarantee for the uninterrupted continuance
of that commonwealth and of its monarchical—though not
hereditarily monarchical—organisation. If therefore the senate
subsequently seemed to the Greeks to be an assembly of kings,
this was only what was to be expected; it had in fact been such
originally.

But it was not merely in so far as the idea of a perpetual
kingdom found its living expression in this assembly, that it
was an essential member of the Roman constitution. The
council of elders, indeed, had no title to interfere with the official
functions of the king. The latter doubtless, in the event of his
being unable personally to lead the army or to decide a legal
dispute, took his deputies at all times from the senate; for which
reason subsequently the chief posts of command were regularly
bestowed on senators alone, and senators were likewise employed
by preference as jurymen. But the senate, in its collective
capacity, was never consulted in the leading of the army or in
the administration of justice; and therefore there was no right
of military command and no jurisdiction vested in the senate
of the later Rome. On the other hand the council of elders
was reckoned the appointed guardian of the existing constitution
with reference to the encroachments of the king and the
burgesses. On the senate devolved the duty of examining
every resolution adopted by the burgesses at the suggestion
of the king, and of refusing to confirm it if it seemed to violate
existing rights; or, which was the same thing, in all cases where a
resolution of the community was constitutionally requisite—
as on every alteration of the constitution, on the reception of
new burgesses, on the declaration of an aggressive war—the
council of elders had a right of veto. This must not indeed be
regarded in the light of legislation pertaining jointly to the
burgesses and the senate, somewhat in the same way as to the
two chambers in the constitutional state of the present day;
the senate was not so much law-maker as law-guardian, and
could only cancel a decree when the community seemed to have

exceeded its competence—to have violated by its decree existing obligations towards the gods or towards foreign states or organic institutions of the community. But still it was a matter of the greatest importance that—to take an example—when the Roman king had proposed a declaration of war and the burgesses had converted it into a decree, and when the satisfaction which the foreign community seemed bound to furnish had been demanded in vain, the Roman envoy invoked the gods as witnesses of the wrong and concluded with the words, " But on these matters we shall consult the elders at home how we may obtain our rights; " it was only when the council of elders had declared its consent, that the war now decreed by the burgesses and approved by the senate was formally declared. Certainly it was neither the design nor the effect of this rule to occasion a constant interference of the senate with the resolutions of the burgesses, and by such guardianship to divest them of their sovereign power; but, as in the event of a vacancy in the supreme office the senate secured the continuance of the constitution, we find it here also as the shield of legal order in opposition even to the supreme power in the community.

With this arrangement was probably connected the apparently very ancient usage, in virtue of which the king previously submitted to the senate the proposals that were to be brought before the burgesses, and caused all its members one after another to give their opinion on the subject. As the senate had the right of cancelling the resolution adopted, it was natural for the king to assure himself beforehand that no opposition was to be apprehended from that quarter. Moreover, it was not in accordance with Roman habits to decide matters of importance without having taken counsel with other men; and the senate was called, in virtue of its very composition, to act as a state council to the ruler of the community. It was from this usage of giving counsel, far more than from the prerogatives which we have previously described, that the subsequent extensive powers of the senate were developed; but it was in its origin insignificant and really amounted only to the prerogative of the senators to answer, when they were asked a question. It may have been usual to ask the previous opinion of the senate in affairs of importance which were neither judicial nor military, as, for instance—apart from the proposals to be submitted to the assembly of the people—in the imposition of task works and extraordinary services generally, and in the disposal of the conquered territory; but such a previous consultation, though

usual, was not legally necessary.   The king convoked the senate
when he pleased, and laid before it his questions; no senator
might declare his opinion unasked, still less might the senate
meet without being summoned, except in the single case of its
meeting on occasion of a vacancy to settle by lot the order of
succession in the office of *interrex*.   That the king was moreover
at liberty to call in and consult other men whom he trusted
alongside of, and at the same time with, the senators, cannot
be proved by positive facts, but yet can hardly be doubted.
The advice was not a command; the king might omit to comply
with it, while the senate had no other means for giving practical
effect to its views except the already-mentioned right of cassation,
which was far from being universally applicable.   "I have
chosen you, not that ye may be my guides, but that ye may
do my bidding:" these words, which a later author puts into
the mouth of king Romulus, certainly express with substantial
correctness the position of the senate in this respect.

Let us now sum up the results.   Sovereignty, as conceived
by the Romans, was inherent in the community of burgesses;
but the burgess-body was never entitled to act alone, and was
only entitled to co-operate in action, when there was to be a
departure from existing rules.   By its side stood the assembly
of the elders of the community appointed for life, virtually a
college of magistrates with regal power, called in the event of
a vacancy in the royal office to administer it by means of their
own members until it should be once more definitely filled, and
entitled to overturn the illegal decrees of the community.   The
royal power itself was, as Sallust says, at once absolute and
limited by the laws (*imperium legitimum*); absolute, in so far
as the king's command, whether righteous or not, must in the
first instance be unconditionally obeyed; limited, in so far as
a command contravening established usage and not sanctioned
by the true sovereign—the people—carried no permanent legal
consequences.   The oldest constitution of Rome was thus in
some measure constitutional monarchy inverted.   In that form
of government the king is regarded as the possessor and vehicle
of the plenary power of the state, and accordingly acts of grace,
for example, proceed solely from him, while the administration
of the state belongs to the representatives of the people and to
the executive responsible to them.   In the Roman constitution
the community of the people exercised very much the same
functions as belong to the king in England: the right of pardon,
which in England is the prerogative of the crown, was in Rome

the prerogative of the community; while all government was vested in the president of the state.

If, in conclusion, we inquire as to the relation of the state itself to its individual members, we find the Roman polity equally remote from the laxity of a mere defensive combination and from the modern idea of an absolute omnipotence of the state. The community doubtless exercised power over the person of the burgess in the imposition of public burdens, and in the punishment of offences and crimes; but any special law inflicting, or threatening to inflict, punishment on an individual on account of acts not universally recognised as penal always appeared to the Romans, even when there was no flaw in point of form, an arbitrary and unjust proceeding. Far more restricted still was the power of the community in respect of the rights of property and the rights of family which were coincident, rather than merely connected, with these; in Rome the household was not absolutely annihilated and the community aggrandised at its expense, as was the case in the police organisation of Lycurgus. It was one of the most undeniable as well as one of the most remarkable principles of the primitive constitution of Rome, that the state might imprison or hang the burgess, but might not take away from him his son or his field or even lay taxation on him. In these and similar things the community itself was restricted from encroaching on the burgess, nor was this restriction merely ideal; it found its expression and its practical application in the constitutional veto of the senate, which was certainly entitled and bound to annul any resolution of the community contravening such an original right. No community was so all-powerful within its own sphere as the Roman; but in no community did the burgess who conducted himself unblameably live in an equally absolute security from the risk of encroachment on the part either of his fellow-burgesses or of the state itself.

These were the principles on which the community of Rome governed itself—a free people, understanding the duty of obedience, disowning all mystical ideas of divine right, absolutely equal in the eye of the law and one with another, bearing the sharply defined impress of a nationality of their own, while at the same time (as will be afterwards shown) they wisely as well as magnanimously opened their gates wide for intercourse with other lands. This constitution was neither manufactured nor borrowed; it grew up amidst and along with the Roman people. It was based, of course, upon the earlier constitutions—the

Italian, the Graeco-Italian, and the Indo-Germanic; but a long succession of phases of political development must have intervened between such constitutions as the poems of Homer and the Germania of Tacitus delineate and the oldest organisation of the Roman community. In the acclamation of the Hellenic and in the shield-striking of the Germanic assemblies there was involved an expression of the sovereign power of the community; but a wide interval separated forms such as these from the organised jurisdiction and the regulated declaration of opinion of the Latin assembly of curies. It is possible, moreover, that as the Roman kings certainly borrowed the purple mantle and the ivory sceptre from the Greeks (not from the Etruscans), the twelve lictors also and various other external arrangements were introduced from abroad. But that the development of the Roman constitutional law belonged decidedly to Rome or, at any rate, to Latium, and that the borrowed elements in it are but small and unimportant, is clearly demonstrated by the fact that all its ideas are uniformly expressed by words of Latin coinage.

This constitution practically established the fundamental conceptions on which the Roman commonwealth was thenceforth to be based; for, as long as there existed a Roman community, in spite of changes of form it was always held that the magistrate had absolute command, that the council of elders was the highest authority in the state, and what every exceptional resolution required the sanction of the sovereign or, in other words, of the community of the people.

THE history of every nation, and of Italy more especially, is a *Synoikismos* on a great scale. Rome, in the earliest form in which we have any knowledge of it, was already triune, and similar incorporations only ceased when the spirit of Roman vigour had wholly died away. Apart from that primitive process of amalgamation of the Ramnes, Tities, and Luceres, of which hardly anything beyond the bare fact is known, the earliest act of incorporation of this sort was that by which the Hill-burgesses became merged in the Palatine Rome. The organisation of the two communities, when they were about to be amalgamated, may be conceived to have been substantially similar; and in solving the problem of union they would have to choose between the alternatives of retaining duplicate institutions or of abolishing one set of these and extending the other to the whole united community. They adopted the former course with respect to all sanctuaries and priesthoods. Thenceforth the Roman community had its two guilds of Salii and two of Luperci, and as it had two forms of Mars, it had also two priests for that divinity—the Palatine priest, who afterwards usually took the designation of priest of Mars, and the Colline, who was termed priest of Quirinus. It is likely, although it can no longer be proved, that all the old Latin priesthoods of Rome— the Augurs, Pontifices, Vestals, and Fetials—originated in the same way from a combination of the priestly colleges of the Palatine and Quirinal communities. In the division into local regions the town on the Quirinal hill was added as a fourth region to the three belonging to the Palatine city, viz. the Suburan, Palatine, and suburban (*Esquiliae*). In the case of the original *Synoikismos* the annexed community was recognised after the union as at least a tribe (part) of the new burgess-body, and thus had in some sense a continued political existence; but this course was not followed in the case of the Hill-Romans or in any of the later processes of annexation. After the union the Roman community continued to be divided as formerly into three tribes, each containing ten wardships (*curiae*); and the Hill-Romans—whether they were or were not previously distributed into tribes of their own—must have been inserted into the existing tribes and wardships. This insertion was probably so arranged that, while each tribe and wardship received its assigned proportion of the new burgesses, the new burgesses in these divisions were not amalgamated completely with the old; the tribes henceforth presented two ranks: the Tities, Ramnes, and Luceres being respectively subdivided into first and second (*priores, posteriores*). With this division was connected in all probability that arrangement of the organic institutions of the community in pairs, which meets us everywhere. The three pairs of Sacred Virgins are expressly described as representatives of the three tribes with their first and second ranks; and it may be conjectured that the six Argean chapels that belonged to each of the four urban regions (p. 52), and the pair of Lares worshipped in each street, had a similar origin. This arrangement is especially apparent in the army: after the union each half-tribe of the tripartite community furnished a hundred horsemen, and the Roman burgess cavalry was thus raised to six " hundreds," and the number of its captains probably from three to six. There is no tradition of any corresponding increase to the infantry; but to this origin we may refer the subsequent custom of calling out the legions regularly two by two, and this doubling of the levy probably led to the rule of having not three, as was perhaps originally the case, but six leaders-of-division to command the legion. It is certain that no corresponding increase of seats in the senate took place: on the contrary, the primitive number of three hundred senators remained the normal number down to the seventh century. It may, however, be reasonably presumed that a number of the more prominent men of the newly annexed community would be received into the senate of the Palatine city. The same course was followed with the magistracies: a single king presided over the united community, and there was no change as to his principal deputies, particularly the warden of the city. It thus appears that the ritual institutions of the Hill-city were continued, and that the doubled burgess-body was required to furnish a military force of double the numerical strength; but in other respects the incorporation of the Quirinal city into the Palatine was really a subordination of the former to the latter. There is reason to conjecture that originally this distinction between the Palatine old and the Quirinal new burgesses was identical with the distinction between the first and second

Tities, Ramnes, and Luceres, and consequently that it was the
gentes of the Quirinal city that formed the "second." The
distinction was certainly more an honorary than a legal
precedence; somewhat after the manner in which subsequently
at the voting in the senate the senators taken from the old
clans were always asked before those of the "lesser."[1] In like
manner the Colline region ranked as inferior even to the suburban
(Esquiline) region of the Palatine city; the priest of the Quirinal
Mars as inferior to the priest of the Palatine Mars; the Quirinal
Salii and Luperci as inferior to those of the Palatine. It thus
appears that the *Synoikismos*, by which the Palatine community
incorporated that of the Quirinal, marked an intermediate stage
between the earliest *Synoikismos* by which the Tities, Ramnes,
and Luceres became blended, and all those that took place
afterwards. The annexed community was no longer allowed
to form a separate tribe in the new whole, but it was permitted
to furnish at least a distinct portion of each tribe; and its
ritual institutions were not only allowed to subsist—as was
afterwards done in other cases, after the capture of Alba for
example—but were elevated into institutions of the united
community, a course which was not pursued in any subsequent
instance.

This amalgamation of two substantially similar commonwealths produced rather an increase in the size than a change
in the intrinsic character of the existing community. A second
process of incorporation, which was carried out far more gradually and had far deeper effects, may be traced back, so far as the
first steps in it are concerned, to this epoch; we refer to the
amalgamation of the burgesses and the *metoeci*. At all times
there existed side by side with the burgesses in the Roman
community persons who were protected, the "listeners"
(*clientes*), as they were called from their being dependents on
the several burgess-households, or the "multitude" (*plebes*,

---

[1] The appellation of "lesser clans" appears to have pertained not to
these "second," but to the clans that came in subsequently, especially
those of Alba. As to the *minores gentes*, apart from conjectures of little
historical value as to the time of their admission into the burgess-body
(Cic. *de Rep.* ii. 20, 25; Liv. i. 35; Tacit. *Ann.* xi. 25; Victor, *Viri Ill.* 6),
nothing is recorded by tradition, except that they had a secondary position
in voting in the senate (Cic. *l. c.*)—for which reason the *princeps senatus*
could only be taken from the *maiores gentes*—and that the Papirii belonged
to them (Cic. *ad Fam.* ix. 21). The latter circumstance is remarkable, for
a canton derived its name from this *gens* (p. 35). As the Fabii seem to
have belonged to the Hill-city (p. 53), and yet furnished several *principes
senatus*, some distinction must be drawn between the Colline clans and the
minores.

from *pleo, plenus*), as they were termed negatively with reference to their want of political rights.[1] The elements of this intermediate stage between the freeman and the slave were, as has been shown (p. 61), already in existence in the Roman household: but in the community this class necessarily acquired greater importance *de facto* and *de jure*, and that from two reasons. In the first place the community might itself possess half-free clients as well as slaves; especially after the conquest of a town and the breaking up of its commonwealth it might often appear to the conquering community advisable not to sell the mass of the burgesses formally as slaves, but to allow them the continued possession of freedom *de facto*, so that in the capacity as it were of freedmen of the community they entered into relations of clientship to the state, or in other words to the king. In the second place the very nature of the community as such, and its authority over the individual burgesses, implied a power of protecting their clients against an abusive exercise of the *dominium* still vested in them *de jure*. At an immemorially early period there was introduced into Roman law the principle on which rested the whole legal position of the *metoeci*, that, when a master on occasion of a public legal act—such as in the making of a testament, in an action at law, or in the census—expressly or tacitly surrendered his *dominium*, neither he himself nor his lawful successors should ever have power arbitrarily to recall that resignation or reassert a claim to the person of the freedman himself or of his descendants. The clients and their posterity did not by virtue of their position possess either the rights of burgesses or those of guests: for to constitute a burgess a formal bestowal of the privilege was requisite on the part of the community, while the relation of guest presumed the holding of burgess-rights in a community which had a treaty with Rome. What they did obtain was a legally protected possession of freedom, while they continued to be *de jure* non-free. Accordingly for a lengthened period their relations in all matters of property seem to have been, like those of slaves, regarded in law as relations of the patron, so that it was necessary that the latter should represent them in processes at law; in connection with which the patron might levy contributions from them in case of need, and call them to account before him criminally. By degrees, however, the body of *metoeci* outgrew these fetters; they began to acquire and to alienate in their own name, and to claim and obtain legal

---

[1] *Habuit plebem in clientelas principum descriptam.*   Cicero, *de Rep.* ii. 9.

redress from the Roman tribunals without the formal intervention of their patron.

In matters of marriage and inheritance, equality of rights with the burgesses was far sooner conceded to foreigners (p. 39) than to those who were strictly non-free and belonged to no community; but the latter could not well be prohibited from contracting marriages in their own circle and from forming the legal relations arising out of marriage—those of marital and paternal power, of *agnatio* and *gentilitas*, of heritage and of tutelage—after the model of the corresponding relations among the burgesses.

Similar consequences to some extent were produced by the exercise of the *jus hospitii*, in so far as by virtue of it foreigners settled permanently in Rome and established a household, and perhaps even acquired immovable estate there. In this respect the most liberal principles must have prevailed in Rome from primitive times. The Roman law knew no distinctions of quality in inheritance and no locking up of estates. It allowed on the one hand to every man capable of making a disposition the entirely unlimited disposal of his property during his lifetime; and on the other hand, so far as we know, to every one who was at all entitled to have dealings with Roman burgesses, even to the foreigner and the client, the unlimited right of acquiring movable, and (from the time when movables could be held as private property at all) also immovable, estate in Rome. Rome was in fact a commercial city, which was indebted for the commencement of its importance to international commerce, and which with a noble liberality granted the privilege of settlement to every child of an unequal marriage, to every manumitted slave, to every stranger who surrendering his rights in his native land emigrated to Rome, and in fact—to a great extent—even to the foreigner who retained his rights as a burgess in any friendly community.

At first, therefore, the burgesses were in reality the protectors, the non-burgesses were the protected; but in Rome, as in all communities which freely admit settlement but do not throw open the rights of citizenship, it soon became a matter of increasing difficulty to harmonise this relation *de jure* with the actual state of things. The flourishing of commerce, the right of settling in the capital secured to all Latins by the Latin league, the greater frequency of manumissions as prosperity increased, necessarily occasioned even in peace a disproportionate increase of the number of *metoeci*. That number was further augmented by the greater part of the population of the neighbouring towns subdued by force of arms and incorporated with Rome; which, whether it removed to the city or remained in its old home now reduced to the rank of a village, ordinarily exchanged its native burgess rights for those of a Roman *metoikos*. Moreover the burdens of war fell exclusively on the old burgesses and were constantly thinning the ranks of their patrician descendants, while the *metoeci* shared in the results of victory without having to pay for it with their blood.

Under such circumstances the only wonder is that the Roman patriciate did not disappear much more rapidly than it actually did. The fact of its still continuing for a prolonged period a numerous community can scarcely be accounted for by the bestowal of Roman burgess-rights on several distinguished foreign clans, which after emigrating from their homes or after the conquest of their cities received the Roman franchise—for such grants appear to have occurred but sparingly from the first, and to have become always the more rare as the privilege increased in value. A cause of greater influence, in all likelihood, was the introduction of the civil marriage, by which a child begotten of patrician parents living together as married persons, although without *confarreatio*, acquired full burgess-rights equally with the child of a *confarreatio* marriage. At least it is probable that the civil marriage, which already existed in Rome before the Twelve Tables but was certainly not an original institution, was introduced for the purpose of preventing the disappearance of the patriciate.[1] Connected with this were the measures which were already in the earliest times adopted with a view to maintain a numerous posterity in the several households (p. 58); and it is even not incredible that for a similar reason all children of patrician mothers, begotten in unequal marriage or out of marriage, were admitted in later times as members of the burgess-body.

Nevertheless the number of the *metoeci* was constantly on the

[1] The enactments of the Twelve Tables respecting *usus* show clearly that they found the civil marriage already in existence. In like manner the high antiquity of the civil marriage is clearly evident from the fact that it, equally with the religious marriage, necessarily involved the marital power (p. 57), and only differed from the religious marriage as respected the manner in which that power was acquired. The latter of itself necessarily gave full marital power to the husband; whereas, in the case of civil marriage, one of the general forms of acquiring property used on other occasions—delivery on the part of a person entitled to give away, or prescription—was requisite in order to lay the foundation of a valid marital power and thereby to constitute a valid marriage. The marital power was simply the husband's right of property in his wife.

increase and liable to no diminution, while that of the burgesses
was at the utmost perhaps not decreasing; and in consequence
the *metoeci* necessarily acquired by imperceptible degrees
another and a freer position. The non-burgesses were no
longer merely emancipated slaves or strangers needing protection; their ranks included the former burgesses of the Latin
communities vanquished in war, and more especially the Latin
settlers who lived in Rome not by the favour of the king or of
any other burgess, but by federal right. Legally unrestricted
in the acquiring of property, they gained money and estate in
their new home, and bequeathed, like the burgesses, their homesteads to their children and children's children. The vexatious
relation of dependence on particular burgess-households became
gradually relaxed. If the liberated slave or the immigrant
stranger still held an entirely isolated position in the state, such
was no longer the case with his children, still less with his grand-
children, and this very circumstance of itself rendered their
relations to the patron of less moment. While in earlier times
the client was exclusively left dependent for legal protection on
the intervention of the patron, the more the state became consolidated and the importance of the clanships and households
in consequence diminished, the more frequently must the
individual client have obtained justice and redress of injury,
even without the intervention of his patron, from the king. A
great number of the non-burgesses, particularly the members
of the dissolved Latin communities, were probably from the
first clients not of any private person at all, but of the king for
the time being, and thus served only the single master to whom
the burgesses also, although in different fashion, rendered
obedience. The king, whose sovereignty over the burgesses
was in truth ultimately dependent on the good-will of his
subjects, must have welcomed the means of forming out of
his own dependents a body bound to him by closer ties, whose
gifts and lapsed successions replenished his treasury—even the
protection-money which the *metoeci* paid to the king (p. 73)
may have been of this nature—whose taskwork he could lay
claim to in his own right, and whom he found always ready to
swell the train of their protector.

Thus there grew up by the side of the burgesses a second
community in Rome: out of the clients arose the Plebs. This
change of name is significant. In law there was no difference
between the client and the plebeian, the " dependent " and the
" man of the multitude; " but in fact there was a very important

one, for the former term brought into prominence the relation of dependence on a member of the politically privileged class; the latter suggested merely the want of political rights. As the feeling of special dependence diminished, that of political inferiority forced itself on the thoughts of the free *metoeci ;* and it was only the sovereignty of the king ruling equally over all that prevented the outbreak of political conflict between the privileged and the non-privileged classes.

The first step, however, towards the amalgamation of the two portions of the people scarcely took place in the revolutionary way which their antagonism appeared to foreshadow. The reform of the constitution, which bears the name of king Servius Tullius, is indeed, as to its historical origin, involved in the same darkness with all the events of a period respecting which we learn whatever we know not by means of historical tradition, but solely by means of inference from the institutions of later times. But its character testifies that it cannot have been a change demanded by the plebeians, for the new constitution assigned to them duties alone, and not rights. More probably it must have owed its origin either to the wisdom of one of the Roman kings, or to the urgent desire of the burgesses that they should no longer be exclusively liable to military service, and that the non-burgesses also should contribute to the levy. By the Servian constitution the duty of service and the obligation connected with it of making advances to the state in case of need (the *tributum*), instead of being imposed on the burgesses as such, were laid upon the possessors of land, the " domiciled " or " freeholders " (*adsidui*), or the " wealthy " (*locupletes*), whether they were burgesses or merely *metoeci ;* service in the army was changed from a personal burden into a burden on property. The details of the arrangement were as follow.

Every freeholder from the seventeenth to the sixtieth year of his age, including children in the household of fathers who were freeholders, without distinction of birth, was under obligation of service; so that even the manumitted slave had to serve, if in an exceptional case he had come into possession of landed property. We do not know how the strangers who held landed property in Rome were dealt with; probably there existed a regulation, according to which no foreigner was allowed to acquire land in Rome unless he actually transferred his residence thither and took his place among the *metoeci*, or in other words, among those bound to serve in war. The body of men liable to serve was distributed according to the size of their portions of

land into five " summonings " (*classes*, from *calare*). Of these,
however, only such as were liable to the first summoning, the
possessors of an entire hide [1] of land, were obliged to appear in
complete armour, and in that point of view were pre-eminently

[1] [*Hufe*, hide, as much as can be properly tilled with one plough, called
in Scotland a plough-gate.]

As to the question, whether the assessments of the Servian census were
originally reckoned in money or landed property, we may observe:

(1) Our information regarding it is derived from the scheme of the
census preserved in the archives of the censors, the *censoriae tabulae* (Cic.
Orat. c. 46, 156) or the *descriptio classium quam fecit Servius Tullius* (Fest.
s. v. procum, p. 249 Müll.). This scheme of course presented the Servian
constitution as it stood in the last period of its practical application, and
therefore with all the modifications which the course of time had introduced. As to the original arrangements we have no evidence; for the
statement of the later writers who in accordance with their usual custom
attribute that scheme to Servius Tullius has no claim to authority.

(2) It is unnecessary to dwell on the intrinsic improbability that in an
agricultural state like the Roman, and in a country where the growth of
money was so slow and difficult, the civil organisation would be based
upon a purely monetary rating. But it is of importance to note that, as
Boeckh in particular has most fully shown in his *Metrologische Untersuchungen*, the sums specified are for so early a period much too high.
100,000 heavy *asses* or pounds of copper—equal according to my investigations to 400 Roman pounds of silver, or about £1050—is an incredible
rating for a full burgess at a time when an ox was valued at 100 *asses*=£1, 1s.
Boeckh's hypothesis that the assessments are to be understood as referring
to the lighter *as* (an hypothesis, by-the-way, which rests on the same basis
as mine, viz. that the scheme before us is that of the later, and not that of
the original, census) has of necessity been abandoned, for there are positive
proofs that the sums of the census as given by tradition were reckoned by
the heavy *as* equal to the sestertius. Nothing remains but to assume that
the assessments were originally reckoned in land, and were converted into
money at a time when landed property had attained a high money-value.

(3) Landed property, as is well known, formed the qualification for the
tribus rusticae all along and for the *tribus urbanae* down to the censorship of
Appius Claudius in $\frac{442}{312}$. In my work on the Roman Tribes I have proved
that the centuries and classes proceeded from the tribes, and therefore
(setting aside the additional centuries of *liticines*, etc.) the qualification of
a *tribulis* supplied the basis for the proportional arrangement of the
classes.

(4) A direct and in the highest sense trustworthy testimony is furnished
by the Twelve Tables in the enactment: *adsiduo* [*civi*] *vindex adsiduus
esto ; proletario civi qui volet vindex esto*. The *proletarius* was the *capite
census* (Fest. *v. proletarium ;* Cic. *de Rep.* ii. 22), that is, the burgess not
included within the five classes; *adsiduus*, on the other hand, denoted any
burgess belonging to the five classes (Charisius, p. 58; Putsch, p. 75, Keil;
comp. Gell. xix. 8, 15; *classicus adsiduusque, non proletarius*) as indeed
necessarily follows from their being contrasted. Now *adsiduus*, as a comparison between it and *residuus, dividuus*, etc., incontestably shows, is
precisely identical in signification with the German *ansässig* (" settled on
the soil," " permanently domiciled "); and the same holds true of *locuples*,
which is put by the ancients as synonymous with *adsiduus* (Gell. xvi. 10,
15). Compare, moreover, the passage in Livy, xlv. 15; *eos, qui praedium
praediave rustica pluris sestertium triginta millium haberent, censendi ius
factum est ;* a formula in which, in my opinion, a full indication has been
preserved of the nature of the so-called Servian assessments.

regarded as " those summoned to war-service " (*classici*).   The four following ranks of smaller land-holders—the possessors respectively of three-fourths, of a half, of a quarter, or of an eighth of a normal farm—were required to render service, but not to equip themselves in complete armour.   As the land happened to be at that time apportioned, almost the half of the farms were entire hides, while each of the classes possessing respectively three-fourths, the half, and the quarter of a hide, amounted to scarcely an eighth of the freeholders, and those again holding an eighth of a hide amounted to fully an eighth of the whole number.   It was accordingly laid down as a rule that, in the case of the infantry, the levy should be in the proportion of eighty holders of an entire hide, twenty from each of the three next classes, and twenty-eight from the last.

The cavalry was similarly dealt with; the number of divisions in it was tripled, and the only difference in this case was that the six divisions already existing retained the old names (*Tities, Ramnes, Luceres primi* and *secundi*), although the non-burgesses were not excluded from serving in these, or the burgesses from serving in the twelve new divisions.   The reason for this difference is probably to be sought in the fact that at that period the divisions of infantry were embodied anew for each campaign and discharged on their return home, whereas in the cavalry horses as well as men were on military grounds kept together also in time of peace, and held their regular drills, which were perpetuated as festivals of the Roman equites down to the latest times.[1]   Accordingly the squadrons once constituted were allowed, even under this reform, to keep their ancient names. They chose for the cavalry the most opulent and considerable landholders among the burgesses and non-burgesses; and at an early period, perhaps from the very first, a certain measure of land seems to have been regarded as involving an obligation to serve in the cavalry.   Along with these, however, there existed a number of free places in the ranks, for the unmarried women, the boys under age, and the old men without children, who held land, were bound instead of personal service to provide horses for particular troopers (each trooper had two), and to furnish them with fodder.   As regards the whole, there was one horseman to nine foot-soldiers; but in actual service the horsemen were used more sparingly.   The non-freeholders (" children-

---

[1] For the same reason, when the levy was enlarged after the admission of the Hill-Romans, the equites were doubled, while in the infantry force instead of the single " gathering " (*legio*) two legions were called out (p. 85).

producers," *proletarii*) had to supply workmen and musicians for the army as well as a number of substitutes (*adcensi*, supernumeraries), who marched with the army unarmed (*velati*), and, when vacancies occurred in the field, took their places in the ranks equipped with the armour of the sick or of the fallen.

To facilitate the levying of the infantry, the city and its precincts were distributed into four " parts " (*tribus*); by which the old triple division was superseded, at least so far as concerned its local significance. These were the Palatine, which comprehended the height of that name along with the Velia; the Suburan, to which the street so named, the Carinae, and the Caelian belonged; the Esquiline; and the Colline, formed by the Quirinal and Viminal, the " hills " as contrasted with the " mounts " of the Capitol and Palatine. We have already spoken of the formation of these regions (p. 50), and shown how they originated out of the ancient double city of the Palatine and the Quirinal. Beyond the walls each region must have included the land-district adjacent to it, for Ostia was reckoned in the Palatine region. That the four regions were nearly on an equality in point of numbers is evident from their contributing equally to the levy. This division, which had primary reference to the soil alone and applied only inferentially to those who possessed it, was merely for administrative purposes, and never had any religious significance attached to it; for the fact that in each of the city-districts there were six chapels of the enigmatical Argei no more confers upon them the character of ritual districts than the erection of an altar to the Lares in each street implies such a character in the streets.

Each of these four levy-districts had to furnish the fourth part not only of the force as a whole, but of each of its military subdivisions, so that each legion and each century numbered an equal proportion of conscripts from each region; evidently for the purpose of merging all distinctions of a gentile and local nature in the one common levy of the community, and especially of blending, through the powerful levelling influence of the military spirit, the *metoeci* and the burgesses into one people.

In a military point of view, the male population capable of bearing arms was divided into a first and second levy, the former of which, the " juniors " from the commencement of the seventeenth to the completion of the forty-sixth year, were especially employed for service in the field, while the " seniors " guarded the walls at home. The military unit in the infantry continued as formerly to be the legion (p. 71), a phalanx arranged and armed exactly in the old Doric style, of three thousand men, who, six file deep, formed a front of five hundred heavy-armed soldiers; to which were attached twelve hundred " unarmed " (*velites*, see p. 72, *note*). The four first ranks of each phalanx were formed by the full-armed hoplites of the first class, the holders of an entire hide; in the fifth and sixth were placed the less completely equipped farmers of the second and third class; the two last classes were annexed as rear ranks to the phalanx or fought by its side as light-armed troops. Provision was made for readily supplying the accidental gaps which were so injurious to the phalanx. Thus there served in each legion forty-two centuries or 4200 men, of whom 3000 were hoplites, 2000 from the first class, 500 from each of the two following, and 1200 light-armed, of whom 500 belonged to the fourth and 700 to the fifth class; each levy-district furnished for every legion 1050, and for every century 25 men. In ordinary cases two legions took the field, while two others did garrison duty at home. The normal amount accordingly of the infantry reached four legions or 16,800 men, eighty centuries from the first class, twenty from each of the three following, and twenty-eight from the last class; not taking into account the two centuries of substitutes or those of the workmen and the musicians. To all these fell to be added the cavalry, consisting of 1800 horse; on taking the field, however, only three centuries were usually assigned to each legion. The normal amount of the Roman army of the first and second levy rose accordingly to close upon 20,000 men: which number must beyond doubt have corresponded on the whole to the effective strength of the serviceable population of Rome, as it stood at the time when the new organisation was introduced. As the population increased, the number of centuries was not augmented, but the several divisions were strengthened by supernumeraries, without altogether losing sight however of the fundamental number. Indeed the Roman corporations in general, strictly closed as to numbers, very frequently evaded the limits imposed upon them by admitting supernumerary members.

This new organisation of the army was accompanied by a more careful supervision of landed property on the part of the state. It was now either enacted for the first time or, if not, at any rate ordained more precisely, that a land-register should be established, in which the several proprietors of land should have their fields with all their appurtenances, servitudes, slaves, beasts of draught and of burden, duly recorded. Every act of

alienation, which did not take place publicly and before witnesses, was declared null; and a revision of the register of
landed property, which was at the same time the levy-roll, was
directed to be made every fourth year. The *mancipatio* and
the census thus arose out of the Servian military organisation.

It is evident at a glance that this whole institution was from
the outset of a military nature. In the whole detailed scheme
we do not encounter a single feature suggestive of any destination of the centuries to other than purely military purposes;
and this alone must, with every one accustomed to consider such
matters, form a sufficient reason for pronouncing its application
to political objects a later innovation. The regulation by which
every one who had passed his sixtieth year was excluded from
the centuries, becomes absolutely absurd, if they were intended
from the first to form a representation of the burgess-community
similar to and parallel with the curies. Although, however, the
organisation of the centuries was introduced merely to enlarge
the military resources of the burgesses by the inclusion of the
metoeci—so that there is no greater error than to represent that
organisation as the introduction of a timocracy in Rome—the
new obligation imposed upon the inhabitants to bear arms
exercised in its consequences a material influence on their
political position. He who is obliged to become a soldier must
also, wherever the state is not rotten, have it in his power to
become an officer; beyond question plebeians also could now be
nominated in Rome as centurions and as military tribunes.
Although, moreover, the institution of the centuries was not
intended to curtail the political privileges exclusively possessed
by the burgesses as hitherto represented in the curies, yet it was
inevitable that those rights, which the burgesses hitherto had
exercised not as the assembly of curies, but as the burgess-levy,
should pass to the new centuries of burgesses and *metoeci*.
Henceforward, accordingly, it was the centuries who authorised
the testaments of soldiers made before battle (p. 75), and whose
consent the king had to ask before beginning an aggressive war
(p. 76). It is important, on account of the subsequent course of
development, to note these first indications of the centuries
taking part in public affairs; but the centuries came to acquire
such rights at first more in the way of natural sequence than of
direct design, and subsequently to the Servian reform, as before,
the assembly of the curies was regarded as the proper burgess-
community, whose homage bound the whole people in allegiance
to the king. By the side of these full-burgesses stood the clients

having freeholds or, as they were afterwards called, the " burgesses without right of voting " (*cives sine suffragio*), as participating in the public burdens, the service of the army, tribute, and taskwork (hence *municipes*); but they ceased to pay protection-money, which was thenceforth paid only by the *metoeci* who were beyond the pale of the tribes, that is, who were non-freeholders (*aerarii*).

In this way, while hitherto there had been distinguished only two classes of members of the community, burgesses and clients, there were now established three political classes of active, passive, and protected members respectively—categories, which exercised a dominant influence over the constitutional law of Rome for many centuries.

When and how this new military organisation of the Roman community came into existence can only be conjectured. It presupposes the existence of the four regions; in other words, the Servian wall must have been erected before the reform took place. But the territory of the city must also have considerably exceeded its original limits, when it could furnish 8000 holders of entire hides and as many who held lesser portions, or sons of such holders, and in addition a number of larger landholders and their sons. We are not acquainted with the superficial extent of the normal Roman farm; but it is not possible to estimate it as under twenty *jugera*.[1] If we reckon as a minimum 10,000 full hides, this would imply a superficies of 190 square miles of arable land; and on this calculation, if we make a very moderate allowance for pasture, the space occupied by houses, and downs, the territory, at the period when this reform was carried out, must have had at least an extent of 420 square miles, probably an extent still more considerable. If we follow tradition, we must assume a number of 84,000 burgesses who were freeholders and capable of bearing arms; for such, we are told, were the

---

[1] Even about $\frac{480}{273}$, allotments of land seven *jugera* appeared to those that received them small (Val. Max. iii. 3, 5; Colum. i. *praef.* 14; i. 3, 11; Plin. *H. N.* xviii. 3, 18: fourteen *jugera*, Victor, 33; Plutarch, *Apophth. Reg. et Imp.* p. 235 Dübner, in accordance with which Plutarch, *Crass.* 2, is to be corrected).

A comparison of the Germanic proportions gives the same result. The *jugerum* and the *morgen* [nearly ⅝ of an English acre], both originally measures rather of labour than of surface, may be looked upon as originally identical. As the German hide consisted ordinarily of 30, but not unfrequently of 20 or 40 *morgen*, and the homestead frequently, at least among the Anglo-Saxons, amounted to a tenth of the hide, it will appear, taking into account the diversity of climate and the size of the Roman *heredium* of 2 *jugera*, that the hypothesis of a Roman hide of 20 *jugera* is not unsuitable to the circumstances of the case. It is to be regretted that on this very point tradition leaves us without information.

numbers ascertained by Servius at the first census. A glance
at the map, however, shows that this number must be fabulous;
it is not even a genuine tradition, but a conjectural calculation,
by which the 16,800 capable of bearing arms who constituted the
normal strength of the infantry appeared to yield, on an average
of five persons to each family, the number of 84,000 free burgesses active and passive,.and this number was confounded with
that of those capable of bearing arms. But even according to
the more moderate estimates laid down above, with a territory
of some 16,000 hides containing a population of nearly 20,000
capable of bearing arms and at least three times that number of
women, children, and old men, persons who had no land, and
slaves, it is necessary to assume not merely that the region
between the Tiber and Anio had been acquired, but that the
Alban territory had also been conquered, before the Servian
constitution was established; a result with which tradition
agrees. What were the numerical proportions of patricians and
plebeians originally in the army, cannot be ascertained.

Upon the whole it is plain that this Servian institution did
not originate in a conflict between the orders. On the contrary, it bears the stamp of a reforming legislator like the
constitutions of Lycurgus, Solon, and Zaleucus; and it has
evidently been produced under Greek influence. Particular
analogies may be deceptive, such as the coincidence noticed by
the ancients that in Corinth also widows and orphans were charged
with the provision of horses for the cavalry; but the adoption
of the armour and arrangements of the Greek hoplite system
was certainly no accidental coincidence. Now if we consider
the fact that it was in the second century of the city that the
Greek states in Lower Italy advanced from the pure clan-
constitution to a modified one, which placed the preponderance
in the hands of the landholders, we shall recognise in that movement the impulse which called forth in Rome the Servian
reform—a change of constitution resting in the main on the
same fundamental idea, and only directed into a somewhat
different course by the strictly monarchical form of the Roman
state.[1]

[1] The analogy also between the so-called Servian constitution and the
treatment of the Attic *metoeci* deserves to be particularly noticed. Athens,
like Rome, opened her gates at a comparatively early period to the *metoeci*,
and afterwards summoned them also to share the burdens of the state.
We cannot suppose that any direct connection existed in this instance
between Athens and Rome; but the coincidence serves all the more distinctly to show how the same causes—urban centralisation and urban
development—everywhere and of necessity produce similar effects.

CHAPTER VII

THE HEGEMONY OF ROME IN LATIUM

THE brave and impassioned Italian race doubtless never lacked
feuds among themselves and with their neighbours: as the
country flourished and civilisation advanced, feuds must have
become gradually changed into war and raids for pillage into
conquest, and political powers must have begun to assume
shape. No Italian Homer, however, has preserved for us a
picture of these earliest frays and plundering excursions, in
which the character of nations is moulded and expressed like the
mind of the man in the sports and enterprises of the boy; nor
does historical tradition enable us to form a judgment, with
even approximate accuracy, as to the outward development of
power and the comparative resources of the several Latin cantons.
It is only in the case of Rome, at the utmost, that we can trace
in some degree the extension of its power and of its territory.
The earliest demonstrable boundaries of the united Roman
community have been already stated (p. 46); in the landward
direction they were on an average just about five miles distant
from the capital of the canton, and it was only toward the coast
that they extended as far as the mouth of the Tiber (*Ostia*),
at a distance of somewhat more than fourteen miles from Rome.
" The new city," says Strabo, in his description of the primitive
Rome, " was surrounded by larger and smaller tribes, some of
whom dwelt in independent villages and were not subordinate to
any national union." It seems to have been at the expense of
these neighbours of kindred lineage in the first instance that the
earliest extensions of the Roman territory took place.

The Latin communities situated on the upper Tiber and
between the Tiber and the Anio—Antemnae, Crustumerium,
Ficulnea, Medullia, Caenina, Corniculum, Cameria, Collatia,
—were those which pressed most closely and sorely on Rome,
and they appear to have forfeited their independence in very
early times to the arms of the Romans. The only community
that retained independence in this district in after times was
Nomentum; which perhaps saved its freedom by alliance
with Rome. The possession of Fidenae, the *tête du pont* of

the Etruscans on the left bank of the Tiber, was contested
between the Latins and the Etruscans—in other words, between
the Romans and Veientes—with varying results. The struggle
with Gabii, which held the plain between the Anio and the
Alban hills, was for a long period equally balanced: down to
late times the Gabine dress was deemed synonymous with that
of war, and Gabine ground the prototype of hostile soil.[1] By
these conquests the Roman territory was probably extended
to about 190 square miles. Another very early achievement
of the Roman arms was preserved, although in a legendary
dress, in the memory of posterity with greater vividness than
those obsolete struggles: Alba, the ancient sacred metropolis
of Latium, was conquered and destroyed by Roman troops.
How the collision arose, and how it was decided, tradition does
not tell: the battle of the three Roman with the three Alban
brothers born at one birth is nothing but a personification of
the struggle between two powerful and closely related cantons,
of which the Roman at least was triune. We know nothing
at all beyond the naked fact of the subjugation and destruction
of Alba by Rome.[2]

It is not improbable, although wholly a matter of conjecture,
that, at the same period when Rome was establishing herself
on the Anio and on the Alban hills, Praeneste, which appears
at a later date as mistress of eight neighbouring townships,

---

[1] The formulae of accursing for Gabii and Fidenae are quite as characteristic (Macrob. *Sat.* iii. 9). It cannot, however, be proved and is extremely improbable that, as respects these towns, there was an actual
historical accursing of the ground on which they were built, such as really
took place at Veii, Carthage, and Fregallae. It may be conjectured that
old accursing formularies were applied to those two hated towns, and were
considered by later antiquaries as historical documents.

[2] There seems to be no good ground for the doubt recently expressed in
a quarter deserving of respect as to the destruction of Alba having really
been the act of Rome. It is true, indeed, that the account of the destruction of Alba is in its details a series of improbabilities and impossibilities;
but that is true of every historical fact inwoven into legend. To the
question as to the attitude of the rest of Latium towards the struggle
between Rome and Alba, we are unable to give an answer; but the question itself rests on a false assumption, for it is not proved that the constitution of the Latin league absolutely prohibited a separate war between
two Latin communities (p. 39). Still less is the fact that a number of
Alban families were received into the burgess-union of Rome inconsistent
with the destruction of Alba by the Romans. Why may there not have
been a Roman party in Alba just as there was in Capua? The circumstance, however, of Rome claiming to be in a religious and political point
of view the heir-at-law of Alba may be regarded as decisive of the matter;
for such a claim could not be based on the migration of individual clans
to Rome, but could only be based, as it actually was, on the conquest of
the town.

Tibur, and others of the Latin communities were similarly occupied in enlarging the circle of their territory and laying the foundations of their subsequent far from inconsiderable power.

We feel the want of accurate information as to the legal character and legal effects of these early Latin conquests, still more than we miss the records of the wars in which they were won. Upon the whole it is not to be doubted that they were treated in accordance with the system of incorporation, out of which the tripartite community of Rome had arisen; excepting that the cantons who were compelled by arms to enter the combination did not, like the primitive three, preserve some sort of relative independence as separate regions in the new united community, but became so entirely merged in the general whole as to be no longer traced (p. 84). However far the power of a Latin canton might extend, in the earliest times it tolerated no political centre except the proper capital; and still less founded independent settlements, such as the Phœnicians and the Greeks established, thereby creating in their colonies clients for the time being and future rivals to the mother city. In this respect, the treatment which Ostia experienced from Rome deserves special notice: the Romans could not and did not wish to prevent the rise *de facto* of a town at that spot, but they allowed the place no political independence, and accordingly they did not bestow on those who settled there any local burgess-rights, but merely allowed them to retain, if they already possessed, the general burgess-rights of Rome.[1] This principle also determined the fate of the weaker cantons, which by force of arms or by voluntary submission became subject to the stronger. The stronghold of the canton was razed, its domain was added to the domain of the conquerors, and a new home was instituted for the inhabitants as well as for their gods in the capital of the victorious canton. This must not be understood absolutely to imply a formal transportation of the conquered inhabitants to the new capital, such as was the rule at the founding of cities in the East. The towns of Latium at this time can have been little more than the strongholds and weekly markets of the husbandmen: it was sufficient in general that the market and the seat of justice should be transferred to the new capital.

---

[1] Hence was developed the conception, in political law, of the maritime colony or colony of burgesses (*colonia civium Romanorum*), that is, of a community separate in fact, but not independent or possessing a will of its own in law; a community which merged in the capital as the *peculium* of the son merged in the property of the father, and which as a standing garrison was exempt from serving in the legion.

That even the temples often remained at the old spot is shown
in the instances of Alba and of Caenina, towns which must
still after their destruction have retained some semblance of
existence in connection with religion. Even when the strength
of the place that was razed rendered it really necessary to remove
the inhabitants, they would be frequently settled, with a view
to the cultivation of the soil, in the open hamlets of their old
domain. That the conquered, however, were not unfrequently
compelled either as a whole or in part to settle in their new
capital, is proved, more satisfactorily than all the several stories
from the legendary period of Latium could prove it, by the
maxim of Roman state-law, that only he who had extended
the boundaries of the territory was entitled to advance the wall
of the city (the *pomerium*). Of course the conquered, whether
transferred or not, were ordinarily compelled to occupy the
legal position of clients;[1] but particular individuals or clans
occasionally had burgess-rights or, in other words, the patriciate
conferred upon them. In the time of the empire the Alban
clans were still recognised which were introduced among the
burgesses of Rome after the fall of their native seat; amongst
these were the Julii, Servilii, Quinctilii, Cloelii, Geganii, Curiatii,
Metilii: the memory of their descent was preserved by their
Alban family shrines, among which the sanctuary of the *gens*
of the Julii at Bovillae again rose under the empire into great
repute.

This centralising process, by which several small communities
became absorbed in a larger one, of course was not an idea
specially Roman. Not only did the development of Latium and
of the Sabellian stocks hinge upon the distinction between
national centralisation and cantonal independence; the case
was the same with the development of the Hellenes. Rome in
Latium and Athens in Attica arose out of a like amalgamation
of many cantons into one state; and the wise Thales suggested
a similar fusion to the hard-pressed league of the Ionic cities as
the only means of saving their nationality. But Rome adhered
to this principle of unity with more consistency, earnestness,
and success than any other Italian canton; and just as the

---

[1] To this the enactment of the Twelve Tables undoubtedly has reference:
Nex[i mancipiique] forti sanatique idem ius esto, that is, in dealings *privati
juris* the " sound " and the " recovered " shall be on a footing of equality.
The Latin allies cannot be here referred to, because their legal position was
defined by federal treaties, and the law of the Twelve Tables treated only
of the law of Rome. The *sanates* were the *Latini prisci cives Romani*, or
in other words, the communities of Latium compelled by the Romans to
enter the plebeiate.

prominent position of Athens in Hellas was the effect of her early centralisation, so Rome was indebted for her greatness solely to the same system far more energetically applied.

While the conquests of Rome in Latium may be mainly regarded as direct extensions of her territory and people presenting the same general features, a further and special significance attached to the conquest of Alba. It was not merely the problematical size and presumed riches of Alba that led tradition to assign a prominence so peculiar to its capture. Alba was regarded as the metropolis of the Latin confederacy, and had the right of presiding among the thirty communities that belonged to it. The destruction of Alba, of course, no more dissolved the league itself than the destruction of Thebes dissolved the Boeotian confederacy;[1] but, in entire consistency with the strict application of the *jus privatum* which was characteristic of the Latin laws of war, Rome now claimed the presidency of the league as the heir-at-law of Alba. What sort of crisis preceded or followed the acknowledgment of this claim, or whether there was any crisis at all, we cannot tell. Upon the whole the hegemony of Rome over Latium appears to have been speedily and generally recognised, although particular communities, such as Labici and above all Gabii, may for a time have declined to own it. Even at that time Rome was probably a maritime power in contrast to the Latin "land," a city in contrast to the Latin villages, and a single state in contrast to the Latin confederacy; even at that time it was only in conjunction with and by means of Rome that the Latins could defend their coasts against Carthaginians, Hellenes, and Etruscans, and maintain and extend their landward frontier in opposition to their restless neighbours of the Sabellian stock. Whether the accession to her material resources which Rome obtained by the subjugation of Alba was greater than the increase of her power by the capture of Antemnae or Collatia, cannot be ascertained: it is quite possible that it was not by the conquest of Alba that Rome was first constituted the most powerful community in Latium; she may have been so long before; but she did gain in consequence of that event the presidency at the Latin festival, which became the basis of the future

---

[1] The community of Bovillae appears even to have been formed out of part of the Alban domain, and to have been admitted in room of Alba among the autonomous Latin towns. Its Alban origin is attested by its having been the seat of worship for the Julian *gens* and by the name *Albani Longani Bovillenses* (Orelli-Henzen, 119, 2252, 6019); its autonomy by Dionysius, v. 61, and Cicero, *pro Planco*, 9, 23.

hegemony of the Roman community over the whole Latin confederacy. It is important to indicate as definitely as possible the nature of a relation so influential.

The form of the Roman hegemony over Latium was, in general, that of an alliance on equal terms between the Roman community on the one hand and the Latin confederacy on the other, establishing a perpetual peace throughout the whole domain and a perpetual league for offence and defence. " There shall be peace between the Romans and all communities of the Latins, as long as heaven and earth endure; they shall not wage war with each other, nor call enemies into the land, nor grant passage to enemies: help shall be rendered by all in concert to any community assailed, and whatever is won in joint warfare shall be equally distributed." The secured equality of rights in trade and exchange, in commercial credit and in inheritance tended, by the manifold relations of commercial intercourse to which it led, still further to interweave the interests of communities already connected by the ties of similar language and manners, and in this way produced an effect somewhat similar to that of the abolition of customs-restrictions in our own day. Each community certainly retained in form its own law: down to the time of the Social war Latin law was not necessarily identical with Roman: we find, for example, that the enforcing of betrothal by action at law, which was abolished at an early period in Rome, continued to subsist in the Latin communities. But the simple and purely national development of Latin law, and the endeavour to maintain as far as possible uniformity of rights, led at length to the result, that the law of private relations was in matter and form substantially the same throughout all Latium. This uniformity of rights comes very distinctly into view in the rules laid down regarding the loss and recovery of freedom on the part of the individual burgess. According to an ancient and venerable maxim of law among the Latin stock no burgess could become a slave in the state wherein he had been free, or suffer the loss of his burgess-rights while he remained within it: if he was to be punished with the loss of freedom and of burgess-rights (which was the same thing), it was necessary that he should be expelled from the state and should enter on the condition of slavery among strangers. This maxim of law was now extended to the whole territory of the league; no member of any of the federal states might live as a slave within the bounds of the league. Applications of this principle are seen in the enactment embodied in the Twelve

Tables, that the insolvent debtor, in the event of his creditor wishing to sell him, must be sold beyond the boundary of the Tiber, in other words, beyond the territory of the league; and in the clause of the second treaty between Rome and Carthage, that an ally of Rome who might be taken prisoner by the Carthaginians should be free so soon as he entered a Roman seaport. It has already (p. 39) been indicated as probable that the federal equality of rights also included intercommunion of marriage, and that every full burgess of a Latin community could conclude a legitimate marriage with any Latin woman of equal standing. Each Latin could of course only exercise political rights where he was enrolled as a burgess; but on the other hand it was implied in an equality of private rights, that any Latin could take up his abode in any place within the Latin bounds; or, to use the phraseology of the present day, there existed, side by side with the special burgess-rights of the individual communities, a general right of settlement co-extensive with the confederacy. It is easy to understand how this should have turned materially to the advantage of the capital, which alone in Latium offered the means of urban intercourse, urban acquisition, and urban enjoyment; and how the number of *metoeci* in Rome should have increased with remarkable rapidity, after the Latin land came to live in perpetual peace with Rome.

In constitution and administration the several communities not only remained independent and sovereign, so far as their federal obligations were not concerned, but, what was of more importance, the league of the thirty communities as such retained its autonomy in contradistinction to Rome. When we are assured that the position of Alba towards the federal communities was a position superior to that of Rome, and that on the fall of Alba these communities attained autonomy, this may well have been the case, in so far as Alba was essentially a member of the league, while Rome from the first had rather the position of a separate state confronting the league than of a member included in it; but, just as the states of the confederation of the Rhine were formally sovereign, while those of the German empire had a master, it is probable that the presidency of Alba was really an honorary right (p. 40) like that of the German emperors, and that the protectorate of Rome was from the first a supremacy like that of Napoleon. In fact Alba appears to have exercised the right of presiding in the federal council, while Rome allowed the Latin deputies to hold their consultations by themselves under the presidency, as it appears, of an officer selected from their own number, and contented herself with the honorary presidency at the federal festival where sacrifice was offered for Rome and Latium, and with the erection of a second federal sanctuary in Rome—the temple of Diana on the Aventine—so that thenceforth sacrifice was offered both on Roman soil for Rome and Latium, and on Latin soil for Latium and Rome. With equal deference to the interests of the league the Romans in the treaty with Latium bound themselves not to enter into a separate alliance with any Latin community — a stipulation which very clearly reveals the apprehensions not without reason felt by the confederacy with reference to the powerful community at their head. The position of Rome not so much within as alongside of Latium, and the footing of formal equality subsisting between the city on the one side and the confederacy on the other, are most clearly discernible in their military system. The federal army was composed, as the later mode of making the levy incontrovertibly shows, of a Roman and a Latin force of equal strength. The supreme command was to alternate between Rome and Latium; and on those years only when Rome appointed the commander the Latin contingent was to appear before the gates of Rome, and to salute at the gate by acclamation the elected commander as its general, after the Romans commissioned by the Latin federal council to take the auspices had assured themselves of the satisfaction of the gods with the choice that had been made. In like manner the land and other property acquired in the wars of the league were equally divided between Rome and Latium. While thus in all internal relations the most complete equality of rights and duties was insisted on with jealous strictness, the Romano-Latin federation can hardly have been at this period represented in its external relations merely by Rome. The treaty of alliance did not prohibit either Rome or Latium from undertaking an aggressive war on their own behoof; and if a war was waged by the league, whether pursuant to a resolution of its own or in consequence of a hostile attack, the Latin federal council must have had a right to take part in the conduct as well as in the termination of the war. Practically indeed Rome in all probability possessed the hegemony even then, for, wherever a single state and a federation enter into permanent connections with each other, the preponderance usually falls to the former.

The steps by which after the fall of Alba Rome—now mistress of a territory comparatively considerable, and probably the leading power in the Latin confederacy—extended still further her direct and indirect dominion, can no longer be traced. There was no lack of feuds with the Etruscans and more especially the Veientes, chiefly respecting the possession of Fidenae; but it does not appear that the Romans were successful in acquiring permanent mastery over that Etruscan outpost, which was situated on the Latin bank of the river not much more than five miles from Rome, or in expelling the Veientes from that formidable basis of offensive operations. On the other hand they maintained apparently undisputed possession of the Janiculum and of both banks of the mouth of the Tiber. As regards the Sabines and Aequi Rome appears in a more advantageous position; the connection which afterwards became so intimate with the more distant Hernici must have had at least its beginning under the monarchy, and the united Latins and Hernici enclosed on two sides and held in check their eastern neighbours. But on the south frontier the territory of the Rutuli and still more that of the Volsci were scenes of perpetual war. The earliest extension of the Latin land took place in this direction, and it is here that we first encounter those communities founded by Rome and Latium on the enemy's soil and constituted as autonomous members of the Latin confederacy—the Latin colonies, as they were called— the oldest of which appear to reach back to the regal period. How far the territory reduced under the power of the Romans extended at the close of the monarchy, can by no means be determined. Of feuds with the neighbouring Latin and Volscian communities the Roman annals of the regal period recount more than enough; but only a few detached notices, such as that perhaps of the capture of Suessa in the Pomptine plain, can be held to contain a nucleus of historical fact. That the regal period laid not only the political foundations of Rome, but the foundations also of her external power, cannot be doubted; the position of the city of Rome as contradistinguished from, rather than forming part of, the league of Latin states is already decidedly marked at the beginning of the republic, and enables us to perceive that an energetic development of external power must have taken place in Rome during the time of the kings. Successes certainly of no ordinary character have thus passed into oblivion; but the splendour of them lingers over the regal period of Rome, especially over the royal house of the Tarquins, like a distant evening twilight in which outlines disappear.

While the Latin stock was thus tending towards union under

the leadership of Rome and was at the same time extending its territory on the east and south, Rome itself, by the favour of fortune and the energy of its citizens, had been converted from a stirring commercial and rural town into the powerful capital of a flourishing country. The remodelling of the Roman military system and the political reform of which it contained the germ, known to us by the name of the Servian constitution, stand in intimate connection with this internal change in the character of the Roman community. But externally also the character of the city cannot but have changed with the influx of ampler resources, with the rising requirements of its position, and with the extension of its political horizon. The amalgamation of the adjoining community on the Quirinal with that on the Palatine must have been already accomplished when the Servian reform, as it is called, took place; and after this reform had united and consolidated the military strength of the community, the burgesses could no longer rest content with entrenching the several hills, as one after another they were filled with buildings, and with also perhaps keeping the island in the Tiber and the height on the opposite bank occupied so that they might command the river. The capital of Latium required another and more complete system of defence; they proceeded to construct the Servian wall. The new continuous city-wall began at the river below the Aventine, and included that hill, on which there have been brought to light recently (1855) at two different places, the one on the western slope towards the river, the other on the opposite eastern slope, colossal remains of those primitive fortifications—portions of wall as high as the walls of Alatri and Ferentino, built of large square hewn blocks of tufo in courses of unequal height—emerging as it were from the tomb to testify to the might of an epoch, whose structures are perpetuated in these walls of rock, and whose other achievements will continue to exercise an influence more lasting even than these. The ring-wall further embraced the Caelian and the whole space of the Esquiline, Viminal, and Quirinal, where a fortification likewise but recently brought to light on a great scale (1862)—on the outside composed of blocks of peperino and protected by a moat in front, on the inside forming a huge earthen rampart sloped towards the city and imposing even at the present day—supplied the want of natural means of defence. From thence it ran to the Capitoline, the steep declivity of which towards the Campus Martius served as part of the city wall, and it again abutted on the river above the island in the Tiber.

The Tiber island with the bridge of piles and the Janiculum did not belong strictly to the city, but the latter height was probably a fortified outwork. Hitherto the Palatine had been the stronghold, but now this hill was left open to be built upon by the growing city; and on the other hand upon the Tarpeian Hill, free on every side, and from its moderate extent easily defensible, there was constructed the new " stronghold " (*arx, capitolium*[1]), containing the stronghold-spring—the carefully enclosed " well-house " (*tullianum*)—the treasury (*aerarium*), the prison, and the most ancient place of assembling for the burgesses (*area Capitolina*), where still in after times the regular announcements of the changes of the moon continued to be made. Private dwellings of a permanent character were not permitted in earlier times on the stronghold-hill;[2] and the space between the two summits of the hill, the sanctuary of the evil god (*Vediovis*), or as it was termed in the later Hellenising epoch, the Asylum, was covered with wood and probably intended for the reception of the husbandmen and their herds, when inundations or war drove them from the plain. The Capitol was in reality as well as in name the Acropolis of Rome, an independent castle capable of being defended even after the city had fallen: its gate was probably placed towards what was afterwards the Forum.[3] The Aventine seems to have been fortified in a similar style, although less strongly, and to have been preserved free from permanent occupation. With this is connected the fact, that for purposes strictly urban, such as the distribution of the introduced water, the inhabitants of Rome were divided into the inhabitants of the city proper (*montani*), and those of the districts situated within the general

[1] Both names, although afterwards employed as proper names of locality (*capitolium* being applied to the summit of the stronghold-hill that lay next to the river, *arx* to that next to the Quirinal), were originally appellatives, corresponding exactly to the Greek ἄκρα and κορυφή: every Latin town had its *capitolium* as well as Rome. The proper local name of the Roman stronghold-hill was *mons Tarpeius*.

[2] The enactment *ne quis patricius in arce aut capitolio habitaret* probably prohibited only buildings of stone which apparently were often constructed in the style of fortresses, not the ordinary and easily removable dwelling-houses. Comp. Becker, *Top.* p. 386.

[3] For the chief thoroughfare, the *Via Sacra*, led from that quarter to the stronghold; and the bending in towards the gate may still be clearly recognised in the turn which this makes to the left at the arch of Severus. The gate itself must have disappeared under the huge structures which were raised in after ages on the Clivus. The so-called gate at the steepest part of the Capitoline Mount, which is known by the name of Janualis or Saturnia, or the " open," and which had to stand always open in the time of war, evidently had merely a religious significance, and never was a real gate

ring-wall, but yet not reckoned as strictly belonging to the city
(*pagani Aventinenses, Ianiculenses, collegia Capitolinorum et
Mercurialium*).[1] The space enclosed by the new city wall
thus embraced, in addition to the former Palatine and Quirinal
cities, the two city-strongholds of the Capitol and the Aventine,
and also the Janiculum;[2] the Palatine, as the oldest city proper,
was enclosed by the other heights along which the wall was
carried, as if encircled with a wreath, and the two castles occupied
the middle.

The work, however, was not complete so long as the ground,
protected by so laborious exertions from outward foes, was not
also reclaimed from the dominion of the water, which per-

---

[1] Four such guilds are mentioned: (1) the *Capitolini* (Cicero, *ad Q. fr.* ii.
5, 2), with *magistri* of their own (Henzen, 6010, 6011), and annual games
(Liv. v. 50; comp. *Corp. Inscr. Lat.* i. n. 805); (2) the *Mercuriales* (Liv. ii.
27; Cicero, *l. c.*; Preller, *Myth.* p. 597) with their *magistri* (Henzen, 6010),
the guild of the valley of the Circus, where the temple of Mercury stood;
(3) the *pagani Aventinenses* also with *magistri* (Henzen, 6010); and (4) the
pagani pagi Ianiculensis likewise with *magistri* (*C. I. L.* i. n. 801, 802). It
is certainly not accidental that these four guilds, the only ones of the sort
that occur in Rome, belong to the very two hills excluded from the four
local tribes but enclosed by the Servian wall, the Capitol and the Aventine, and the Janiculum belonging to the same fortification; and connected
with this is the further fact that the expression *montani paganive* is employed as a designation of the whole inhabitants in connection with the
city (comp. besides the well-known passage, Cic. *de Domo*, 28, 74, especially
the law as to the city aqueducts in Festus, *v. sifus*, p. 340; [*mon*]*tani
paganive si*[*fis aquam dividunto*]). The *montani*, properly the inhabitants
of the three regions of the Palatine town (p. 53), appear to be put here *a
potiori* for the whole population of the four regions of the city proper.
The *pagani* are, undoubtedly, the residents of the Aventine and Janiculum
not included in the tribes, and the analogous *collegia* of the Capitol and the
Circus valley.

[2] The Servian Rome, however, never looked upon itself as the "city of
the seven hills;" on the contrary, that name in the best ages of Rome
denoted exclusively the narrower Old Rome of the Palatine (p. 48). It
was not until the times of her decline, when the festival of the Septimontium, which was steadily retained and celebrated with great zest even
under the empire, began to be erroneously regarded as a festival for the
city generally, that ignorant writers sought for and accordingly found the
Seven Mounts in the Rome of their own age. The germ of such a misunderstanding may be already discerned in the Greek riddles of Cicero, *ad Att.*
vi. 5, 2, and in Plutarch, *Q. Rom.* 69 (comp. Tibullus, ii, 5, 55; Martial,
iv. 64, 11; Tertullian, *Apolog.* 35); but the earliest authority that actually
enumerates Seven Mounts (*montes*) of Rome is the description of the city
of the age of Constantine the Great. It names as such the Palatine, Aventine, Caelian, Esquiline, Tarpeian, Vatican, and Janiculum—where the
Quirinal and Viminal are, evidently as *colles*, omitted, and in their stead
two "*montes*" are introduced from the right bank of the Tiber. Other
still later and quite confused lists are given by Servius (*ad Aen.* vi. 783),
the Berne Scholia to Virgil's Georgics (ii. 535), and Lydus (*de Mens.* p. 118,
Bekker). The enumeration of the Seven Mounts as commonly made
in modern times, viz. Palatine, Aventine, Caelian, Esquiline, Viminal,
Quirinal, Capitoline, is unknown to any ancient author.

manently occupied the valley between the Palatine and the Capitol, so that there was a regular ferry there, and which converted the valleys between the Capitol and the Velia and between the Palatine and the Aventine into marshes. The subterranean drains still existing at the present day, composed of magnificent square blocks, which excited the astonishment of posterity as a marvellous work of regal Rome, must rather be reckoned to belong to the following epoch, for travertine is the material employed and we have many accounts of new structures of the kind in the times of the republic; but the scheme itself belongs beyond all doubt to the regal period, although to a later epoch probably than the designing of the Servian wall and the Capitoline stronghold. The spots thus drained or dried supplied large open spaces such as were required to meet the public wants of the newly enlarged city. The assembling-place of the community, which had hitherto been the Area Capitolina at the stronghold itself, was now transferred to the flat space, where the ground fell from the stronghold towards the city (*comitium*), and which stretched thence between the Palatine and the Carinae, in the direction of the Velia. At that side of the *comitium* which adjoined the stronghold, and upon the wall which arose above the *comitium* in the fashion of a balcony, the members of the senate and the guests of the city had a place of honour assigned to them on occasion of festivals and assemblies of the people; and not far from this there soon came to be built a special senate-house, which derived from its builder the name of the Curia Hostilia. The platform for the judgment-seat (*tribunal*), and the stage whence the burgesses were addressed (the later *rostra*), were erected on the *comitium* itself. Its prolongation in the direction of the Velia became the new market (*forum Romanorum*). On the west side of the Forum, beneath the Palatine, rose the community-house, which included the official dwelling of the king (*regia*) and the common hearth of the city, the rotunda forming the temple of Vesta; at no great distance, on the south side of the Forum, there was erected a second round building connected with the former, the store-room of the community or temple of the Penates, which still stands at the present day as the porch of the church Santi Cosma e Damiani. It is a feature significant of the new city now united in a way very different from the settlement of the " seven mounts," that, over and above the thirty hearths of the curies which the Palatine Rome had been content with associating in one building, the Servian Rome presented such a

single hearth for the city at large.[1] Along the two longer sides
of the Forum butchers' shops and other traders' stalls were
arranged. In the valley between the Palatine and Aventine a
space was staked off for races; this became the Circus. The
cattle-market was laid out immediately adjoining the river, and
this soon became one of the most densely peopled quarters of
Rome. Temples and sanctuaries arose on all the summits,
above all the federal sanctuary of Diana on the Aventine (p. 106),
and on the summit of the stronghold the far-seen temple of
Father Diovis, who had given to his people all this glory, and
who now, when the Romans were triumphing over the surrounding nations, triumphed along with them over the subject gods
of the vanquished.

The names of the men, at whose bidding these great buildings
of the city arose, are almost as completely lost in oblivion as
those of the leaders in the earliest battles and victories of Rome.
Tradition indeed assigns the different works to different kings—
the senate-house to Tullus Hostilius, the Janiculum and the
wooden bridge to Ancus Marcius, the great Cloaca, the Circus,
and the temple of Jupiter to the elder Tarquinius, the temple of
Diana and the ring-wall to Servius Tullius. Some of these
statements may perhaps be correct; and it is apparently not
the result of accident that the building of the new ring-wall is
associated both as to date and author with the new organisation
of the army, which in fact bore special reference to the regular
defence of the city walls. But upon the whole we must be content to learn from this tradition—what is indeed evident of
itself—that this second creation of Rome stood in intimate
connection with the commencement of her hegemony over
Latium and with the remodelling of her burgess-army, and that,
while it originated in one and the same great conception, its
execution was not the work either of a single man or of a single
generation. It is impossible to doubt that Hellenic influences
exercised a powerful effect on this remodelling of the Roman
community, but it is equally impossible to demonstrate the mode
or the degree of their operation. It has already been observed
that the Servian military constitution is essentially of an

---

[1] Both the situation of the two temples, and the express testimony of
Dionysius, ii. 65, that the temple of Vesta lay outside of the Roma quadrata, prove that these structures were connected with the foundation not
of the Palatine, but of the second (Servian) city. Posterity reckoned this
regia with the temple of Vesta as a scheme of Numa; but the cause which
gave rise to that hypothesis is too manifest to allow of our attaching any
weight to it.

Hellenic type (p. 98); and it will be afterwards shown that the games of the circus were organised on an Hellenic model.   The new *regia* with the city hearth was quite a Greek *prytaneion*, and the round temple of Vesta, looking towards the east and not so much as consecrated by the augurs, was constructed in no respect according to Italian, but wholly in accordance with Hellenic ritual.   With these facts before us, the statement of tradition appears not at all incredible that the Ionian confederacy in Asia Minor to some extent served as a model for the Romano-Latin league, and that the new federal sanctuary on the Aventine was for that reason constructed in imitation of the Artemision at Ephesus.

CHAPTER VIII

THE UMBRO-SABELLIAN STOCKS—BEGINNINGS OF THE SAMNITES

THE migration of the Umbrian stocks appears to have begun at a period later than that of the Latins. Like the Latin, it moved in a southerly direction, but it kept more in the centre of the peninsula and towards the east coast. It is painful to speak of it; for our information regarding it comes to us like the sound of bells from a town that has been sunk in the sea. The Umbrian people extended according to Herodotus as far as the Alps, and it is not improbable that in very ancient times they occupied the whole of Northern Italy, to the point where the settlements of the Illyrian stocks began on the east, and those of the Ligurians on the west. As to the latter, there are traditions of their contests with the Umbrians, and we may perhaps draw an inference regarding their extension in very early times towards the south from isolated names, such as that of the island of Ilva (Elba) compared with the Ligurian Ilvates. To this period of Umbrian greatness the evidently Italian names of the most ancient settlements in the valley of the Po, Hatria (black-town), and Spina (thorn-town), probably owe their origin, as well as the numerous traces of Umbrians in Southern Etruria (such as the river Umbro, Camars the old name of Clusium, Castrum Amerinum). Such indications of an Italian population having preceded the Etruscan especially occur in the most southern portion of Etruria, the district between the Ciminian forest (below Viterbo) and the Tiber. In Falerii, the town of Etruria nearest to the frontier of Umbria and the Sabine country, according to the testimony of Strabo, a language was spoken different from the Etruscan, and inscriptions bearing out that statement have recently been brought to light there, the alphabet and language of which, while presenting points of contact with the Etruscan, exhibit a general resemblance to the Latin.[1] The local worship also presents traces of a Sabellian

---

[1] In the alphabet the *r* especially deserves notice, being of the Latin (R) and not of the Etruscan form (Đ), and also the *z* (⊟); it can only be derived from the primitive Latin, and must very faithfully represent it.

character; and a similar inference is suggested by the primitive relations subsisting in sacred as well as other matters between Caere and Rome. It is probable that the Etruscans seized those southern districts from the Umbrians at a period considerably subsequent to their occupation of the country on the north of the Ciminian forest, and that an Umbrian population maintained itself there even after the Tuscan conquest. In this fact we may probably discover the ultimate explanation of the surprising rapidity with which the southern portion of Etruria became Latinised, as compared with the tenacious retention of the Etruscan language and manners in Northern Etruria, after the Roman conquest. That the Umbrians were after obstinate struggles driven back from the north and west into the narrow mountainous country between the two arms of the Apennines which they subsequently held, is clearly indicated by the very fact of their geographical position, just as the position of the inhabitants of the Grisons and that of the Basques at the present day indicates the similar fate that has befallen them. Tradition also has to report that the Tuscans deprived the Umbrians of three hundred towns; and, what is of more importance as evidence, in the national prayers of the Umbrian Iguvini, which we still possess, along with other stocks the Tuscans specially are cursed as public foes.

It was probably in consequence of this pressure exerted upon them from the north, that the Umbrians advanced towards the south, keeping in general upon the heights, because they found the plains already occupied by Latin stocks, but beyond doubt frequently making inroads and encroachments on the territory of the kindred race, and intermingling with them the more readily, that the distinction in language and habits could not have been at all so marked then as we find it afterwards. To the class of such inroads belongs the tradition of the entrance of the Reatini and Sabines into Latium and their contests with the Romans; similar phenomena were probably repeated all along the west coast. Upon the whole the Sabines maintained their footing in the mountains, as in the district bordering on Latium which has since been called by their name, and in the

The language likewise has close affinity with the oldest Latin; *Marci Acarcelini he cupa*, that is, *Marcius Acarcelinius heic cubat: Menerva A. Cotena La. f. . . . zenatuo sentem . . . dedet cuando . . . cuncaptum*, that is, *Minervae A(ulus ?) Cotena La(rtis) f(ilius) de senatus sententia dedit quando* (perhaps=*olim*) *conceptum.* At the same time with these and similar inscriptions there were found some other records in a different character and language, undoubtedly Etruscan.

Volscian land; probably because the Latin population did not extend thither or was there less dense, while on the other hand the well-peopled plains were better able to offer resistance to the invaders, although they were not in all cases able or desirous to prevent isolated bands from gaining a footing, such as the Tities and afterwards the Claudii in Rome (p. 44). In this way the stocks here became variously mingled, a state of things which serves to explain the numerous relations that subsisted between the Volscians and Latins, and how it happened that their district, as well as Sabina, afterwards became so speedily Latinised.

The chief branch, however, of the Umbrian stock migrated eastward from Sabina into the mountains of the Abruzzi, and the adjacent hill-country to the south of them. Here, as on the west coast, they occupied the mountainous districts, whose thinly scattered population gave way before the immigrants or submitted to their yoke; while in the plain along the Apulian coast the ancient native population, the Iapygians, upon the whole maintained their ground, although involved in constant feuds, in particular on the northern frontier about Luceria and Arpi. When these migrations took place cannot of course be determined; but it was probably about the period of the regal government in Rome. Tradition reports that the Sabines, pressed by the Umbrians, vowed a *ver sacrum,* that is, swore that they would give up and send beyond their bounds the sons and daughters born in the year of war, so soon as these should reach maturity, that the gods might at their pleasure destroy them or bestow upon them new abodes in other lands. One band was led by the ox of Mars; these were the Safini or Samnites, who in the first instance established themselves on the mountains adjoining the river Sagrus, and at a later period proceeded to occupy the beautiful plain on the east of the Matese chain, near the sources of the Tifernus. Both in their old and in their new territory they named their place of public assembly—which in the one case was situated near Agnone, in the other near Bojano—from the ox which led them Bovianum. A second band was led by the woodpecker of Mars; these were the Picentes, " the woodpecker-people," who took possession of what is now the March of Ancona. A third band was led by the wolf (*hirpus*) into the region of Beneventum; these were the Hirpini. In a similar manner the other small tribes branched off from the common stock—the Praetuttii near Teramo; the Vestini about the Gran Sasso; the Marrucini near Chieti; the

Frentani on the frontier of Apulia; the Paeligni about the Majella mountains; and lastly the Marsi about lake Fucinus, coming in contact with the Volscians and Latins. All of these tribes retained, as these legends clearly show, a vivid sense of their relationship and of their having come forth from the Sabine land. While the Umbrians succumbed in the unequal struggle and the western offshoots of the same stock became amalgamated with the Latin or Hellenic population, the Sabellian tribes prospered in the seclusion of their distant mountain land, equally remote from collision with the Etruscans, the Latins, and the Greeks. There was little or no development of an urban life amongst them; their geographical position almost wholly precluded them from engaging in commercial intercourse, and the mountain-tops and strongholds sufficed for the necessities of defence, while the husbandmen continued to dwell in open hamlets or wherever each found the spring and the forest or pasture that he desired. In such circumstances their constitution remained stationary; like the similarly situated Arcadians in Greece, their communities never became incorporated into a single state; at the utmost they only formed confederacies more or less loosely connected. In the Abruzzi especially, the strict seclusion of the mountain valleys seems to have debarred the several cantons from intercourse either with each other or with the outer world. They maintained but little connection with each other and continued to live in complete isolation from the rest of Italy; and in consequence, notwithstanding the bravery of their inhabitants, they exercised less influence than any other portion of the Italian nation on the development of the history of the peninsula.

On the other hand the Samnite people decidedly exhibited the highest political development among the eastern Italian stock, as the Latin nation did among the western. From an early period, perhaps from its first immigration, a comparatively strong political bond held together the Samnite nation, and gave to it the strength which subsequently enabled it to contend with Rome on equal terms for the supremacy of Italy. We are as ignorant of the time and manner of the formation of the league, as we are of its constitution; but it is clear that in Samnium no single community exercised a preponderating influence, and still less was there any town to serve as a central rallying point and bond of union for the Samnite stock, such as Rome was for the Latins. The strength of the land lay in its *communes* of husbandmen, and authority was vested in the assembly formed of their representatives; it was this assembly which in case of need nominated a federal commander-in-chief. In consequence of its constitution the policy of this confederacy was not aggressive like the Roman, but was limited to the defence of its own bounds; only in an united state is power so concentrated and passion so strong, that the extension of territory can be systematically pursued. Accordingly the whole history of the two nations is prefigured in their diametrically opposite systems of colonisation. Whatever the Romans gained was a gain to the state: the conquests of the Samnites were achieved by bands of volunteers who went forth in search of plunder and, whether they prospered or were unfortunate, were left to their own resources by their native home. The conquests, however, which the Samnites made on the coasts of the Tyrrhenian and Ionic seas, belong to a later age; during the regal period in Rome they seem to have been only gaining possession of the settlements in which we afterwards find them. As a single incident in the series of movements among the neighbouring peoples caused by the Samnite settlement may be mentioned the surprise of Cumae by Tyrrhenians from the Upper Sea, Umbrians, and Daunians in the year of the city $\frac{230}{524}$. If we may give credit to the accounts of the matter which present certainly a considerable colouring of romance, it would appear that in this instance, as was often the case in such expeditions, the intruders and those whom they supplanted combined to form one army, the Etruscans joining with their Umbrian enemies, and these again joined by the Iapygians whom the Umbrian settlers had driven towards the south. Nevertheless the undertaking proved a failure: on this occasion at least the superiority of the Greeks in the art of war, and the bravery of the tyrant Aristodemus, succeeded in repelling the barbarian assault on the beautiful seaport.

CHAPTER IX

THE ETRUSCANS

THE Etruscan people, or Ras,[1] as they called themselves, present a striking contrast to the Latin and Sabellian Italians as well as to the Greeks. They were distinguished from these nations by their very bodily structure: instead of the slender and symmetrical proportions of the Greeks and Italians, the sculptures of the Etruscans exhibit only short sturdy figures with large heads and thick arms. Their manners and customs also, so far as we are acquainted with them, point to the conclusion that this nation was originally quite distinct from the Graeco-Italian stocks. The religion of the Tuscans in particular, presenting a gloomy fantastic character and delighting in the mystical handling of numbers and in wild and horrible speculations and practices, is equally remote from the clear rationalism of the Romans and the genial image-worship of the Hellenes. The conclusion which these facts suggest is confirmed by the most important and authoritative evidence of nationality, the evidence of language. The remains of the Etruscan tongue which have reached us, numerous as they are and presenting so many data to aid in deciphering it, occupy a position of isolation so complete, that not only has no one hitherto succeeded in its interpretation, but no one has been able even to determine precisely its proper place in the classification of languages. Two periods in the development of the language may be clearly distinguished. In the older period the vocalisation of the language was completely carried out, and the collision of two consonants was almost without exception avoided.[2] By throwing off the vocal and consonantal terminations, and by the weakening or rejection of the vowels, this soft and melodious language was gradually changed in character, and became intolerably harsh and rugged.[3] They changed for example

[1] *Ras-ennae*, with the gentile termination mentioned at p. 120.
[2] To this period belong *e.g.* inscriptions on the clay vases of Caere, such as, *miniceθumamimaθumaramlisiaiθipurenaieθeeraisieepanamineθunastavhelefu*, or *mi ramuθaſ kaiuſinaia.*
[3] We may form some idea of the sound which the language now had from the commencement of the great inscription of Perusia; *eulat tanna larezul amevaχr lautn velθinase stlaafunas sleleθcaru.*

ramuθaf into *ramθa*, Tarquinius into *Tarchnaf*, Minerva into *Menrva*, Menelaos, Polydeukes, Alexandros, into *Menle*, *Pultuke*, *Elchsentre*. The indistinct and rugged nature of their pronunciation is shown most clearly by the fact that at a very early period the Etruscans ceased to distinguish *o* from *u*, *b* from *p*, *c* from *g*, *d* from *t*. At the same time the accent was, as in Latin and in the more rugged Greek dialects, uniformly thrown back upon the initial syllable. The aspirate consonants were treated in a similar fashion; while the Italians rejected them with the exception of the aspirated *b* or the *f*, and the Greeks, reversing the case, rejected this sound and retained the others *θ*, *φ*, *χ*, the Etruscans allowed the softest and most pleasing of them, the *φ*, to drop entirely except in words borrowed from other languages, but made use of the other three to an extraordinary extent, even where they had no proper place; Thetis for example became *Thethis*, Telephus *Thelaphe*, Odysseus *Utuze* or *Uthuze*. Of the few terminations and words, whose meaning has been ascertained, the greater part have not the most distant analogy to the Graeco-Italian languages; such as the termination *al* employed as a designation of descent, frequently of descent from the mother, *e.g. Canial*, which on a bilingual inscription of Chiusi is translated by *Cainia natus ;* and the termination *sa* in the names of women, used to indicate the clan into which they have married, *e.g. Lecnesa* denoting the spouse of a *Licinius. Cela* or *clan* with the inflection *clensi* means son; *seχ* daughter; *ril* year; the god Hermes becomes *Turms*, Aphrodite *Turan*, Hephaestos *Sethlans*, Bakchos *Fufluns*. Alongside of these strange forms and sounds there certainly occur isolated analogies between the Etruscan and the Italian languages. Proper names are formed, substantially, after the general Italian system. The frequent gentile termination *enas* or *ena* [1] recurs in the termination *enus* which is likewise of frequent occurrence in Italian, especially in Sabellian clan-names; thus the Etruscan names *Vivenna* and *Spurinna* correspond closely to the Roman *Vibius* or *Vibienus* and *Spurius*. A number of names of divinities, which occur as Etruscan on Etruscan monuments or in authors, have in their roots, and to some extent even in their terminations, a form so thoroughly Latin, that, if these names were really originally Etruscan, the

---

[1] Such as Maecenas, Porsena, Vivenna, Caecina, Spurinna. The vowel in the penult is originally long, but in consequence of the throwing back of the accent upon the initial syllable is frequently shortened and even rejected. Thus we find Porsèna as well as Porsèna, and Ceicne as well as Caecina.

two languages must have been closely related; such as *Usil* (sun and dawn, connected with *ausum, aurum, aurora, sol*), *Minerva* (*menervare*), *Lasa* (*lascivus*), *Neptunus, Voltumna*. As these analogies, however, may have had their origin in the subsequent political and religious relations between the Etruscans and Latins, and in the accommodations and borrowings to which these relations give rise, they do not invalidate the conclusion to which we are led by the other observed phenomena, that the Tuscan language differed as widely from all the Graeco-Italian dialects as did the languages of the Celts or of the Slavonians. So at least it sounded to the Roman ear; " Tuscan and Gallic " were the languages of barbarians, " Oscan and Volscian " were but rustic dialects.

But, while the Etruscans differed thus widely from the Graeco-Italian family of languages, no one has yet succeeded in connecting them with any other known race. All sorts of dialects have been examined with a view to discover affinity with the Etruscan, sometimes by simple interrogation, sometimes by torture, but all without exception in vain. The geographical position of the Basque nation would naturally suggest it as not unlikely to be cognate; but even in the Basque language no analogies of a decisive character have been brought forward. As little do the scanty remains of the Ligurian language which have reached our time, consisting of local and personal names, indicate any connection with the Tuscans. Even the extinct nation which has constructed those enigmatical sepulchral towers called *Nuraghe* by thousands in the islands of the Tuscan Sea, especially in Sardinia, cannot well be connected with the Etruscans, for not a single structure of the same character is to be met with in Etruria. The utmost we can say is that several traces, apparently reliable, point to the conclusion that the Etruscans may be on the whole included among the Indo-Germans. Thus *mi* in the beginning of many of the older inscriptions is certainly ἐμί, εἰμί, and the genitive form of consonantal stems *veneruf, rafuvuf* is exactly reproduced in old Latin, corresponding to the old Sanscrit termination *as*. In like manner the name of the Etruscan Zeus, *Tina* or *Tinia*, is probably connected with the Sanscrit *dina*, meaning day, as Ζάν is connected with the synonymous *diwan*. But, even granting those points of connection, the Etruscan people appears withal scarcely less isolated. " The Etruscans," Dionysius said long ago, " are like no other nation in language and manners; " and we have nothing to add to his statement.

It is equally difficult to determine from what quarter the Etruscans migrated into Italy; nor is much lost through our inability to answer the question, for this migration belonged at any rate to the infancy of the people, and their historical development began and ended in Italy. No question, however, has been handled with greater zeal than this, in accordance with the principle which induces antiquaries especially to inquire into what is neither capable of being known nor worth the knowing—to inquire " who was Hecuba's mother," as the emperor Tiberius is said to have done. As the oldest and most important Etruscan towns lay far inland—in fact we find not a single Etruscan town of any note immediately on the coast except Populonia, which we know for certain was not one of the old twelve cities—and the movement of the Etruscans in historical times was from north to south, it seems probable that they migrated into the peninsula by land. Indeed the low stage of civilisation in which we find them at first would ill accord with the hypothesis of their having migrated by sea. Nations even in the earliest times crossed a strait as they would a stream; but to land on the west coast of Italy was a very different matter. We must therefore seek for the earlier home of the Etruscans to the west or north of Italy. It is not wholly improbable that the Etruscans may have come into Italy over the Raetian Alps; for the oldest traceable settlers in the Grisons and Tyrol, the Raeti, spoke Etruscan down to historical times, and their name sounds similar to that of the Ras. These may no doubt have been a remnant of the Etruscan settlements on the Po; but it is at least quite as likely that they may have been a portion of the nation which remained behind in its earlier abode.

In glaring contradiction to this simple and natural view stands the story that the Etruscans were Lydians who had emigrated from Asia. It is very ancient: it occurs even in Herodotus; and it reappears in later writers with innumerable changes and additions, although several intelligent inquirers, such as Dionysius, emphatically declared their disbelief in it, and pointed to the fact that there was not the slightest apparent similarity between the Lydians and Etruscans in religion, laws, manners, or language. It is possible that an isolated band of pirates from Asia Minor may have reached Etruria, and that their adventure may have given rise to such tales; but more probably the whole story rests on a mere verbal mistake. The Italian Etruscans or the *Turs-ennae* (for this appears to be the original form and the basis of the Greek Τυρσ-ηνοί, Τυρρηνοί, of the Umbrian *Turs-ci*, and of the two Roman forms *Tusci*, *Etrusci*), nearly coincide in name with the Lydian people, the Τορρηβοί or perhaps also Τυρρ-ηνοί, so named from the town Τύρρα. This manifestly accidental resemblance in name seems to be in reality the only foundation for that hypothesis—not rendered more reliable by its great antiquity—and for all the pile of crude historical speculation that has been reared upon it. By connecting the ancient maritime commerce of the Etruscans with the piracy of the Lydians, and then by confounding Thucydides is the first who has demonstrably done so) the Torrhebian pirates, whether rightly or wrongly, with the buccaneering Pelasgians who roamed and plundered on every sea, there has been produced one of the most unhappy complications of historical tradition. The term Tyrrhenians denotes sometimes the Lydian Torrhebi—as is the case in the earliest sources, such as the Homeric hymns; sometimes under the form Tyrrheno-Pelasgians or simply that of Tyrrhenians, the Pelasgian nation; sometimes, in fine, the Italian Etruscans, although the latter never came into lasting contact with the Pelasgians or Torrhebians, nor were at all connected with them by common descent.

It is, on the other hand, a matter of historical interest to determine what were the oldest traceable abodes of the Etruscans, and what were their further movements when they left these. Various circumstances attest that before the great Celtic invasion they dwelt in the district to the north of the Po, being conterminous on the east along the Adige with the Veneti of Illyrian (Albanian?) descent, on the west with the Ligurians. This is proved in particular by the already mentioned rugged Etruscan dialect which was still spoken in the time of Livy by the inhabitants of the Raetian Alps, and by the fact that Mantua remained Tuscan down to a late period. To the south of the Po and at the mouths of that river Etruscans and Umbrians were mingled, the former as the dominant, the latter as the older race, which had founded the old commercial towns of Hatria and Spina, while the Tuscans appear to have been the founders of Felsina (Bologna) and Ravenna. A long time elapsed ere the Celts crossed the Po; hence the Etruscans and Umbrians left deeper traces of their existence on the right bank of the river than they had done on the left, which they had to abandon at an early period. All the districts, however, to the north of the Apennines passed too rapidly out of the hands of one nation into those of another to permit the formation of any continuous national development there.

Far more important in an historical point of view was the great settlement of the Tuscans in the land which still bears their name. Although Ligurians or Umbrians were probably at one time (p. 114) settled there, the traces of their occupation have been almost wholly effaced by the civilisation of their Etruscan successors. In this region, which extends along the coast from Pisae to Tarquinii and is shut in on the east by the Apennines, the Etruscan nationality found its permanent abode and maintained itself with great tenacity down to the time of the empire. The northern boundary of the proper Tuscan territory was formed by the Arnus; the region north from the Arnus as far as the mouth of the Macra and the Apennines was a debateable border land in the possession sometimes of Ligurians, sometimes of Etruscans, and for this reason larger settlements were not successful there. The southern boundary was probably formed at first by the Ciminian Forest, a chain of hills south of Viterbo, and at a later period by the Tiber. We have already (p. 115) noticed the fact that the territory between the Ciminian range and the Tiber with the towns of Sutrium, Nepete, Falerii, Veii, and Caere appears to have been taken possession of by the Etruscans at a period considerably later than the more northern district, possibly not earlier than in the second century of Rome, and that the original Italian population must have maintained its ground in this region, especially in Falerii, although in a relation of dependence.

From the time at which the river Tiber became the line of demarcation between Etruria on the one side and Umbria and Latium on the other, peaceful relations probably prevailed upon the whole in that quarter, and no essential change seems to have taken place in the boundary line, at least so far as concerned the Latin frontier. Vividly as the Romans were impressed by the feeling that the Etruscan was a foreigner, while the Latin was their countryman, they yet seem to have stood in much less fear of attack or of danger from the right bank of the river than, for example, from their kinsmen in Gabii and Alba; and this was natural, for they were protected in that direction not merely by the broad stream which formed a natural boundary, but also by the circumstance, so momentous in its bearing on the mercantile and political development of Rome, that none of the more powerful Etruscan towns lay immediately

n the river, as did Rome on the Latin bank. The Veientes
ere the nearest to the Tiber, and it was with them that Rome
nd Latium came most frequently into serious conflict, especially
or the possession of Fidenae, which served the Veientes as a
ort of *tête du pont* on the left bank just as the Janiculum served
he Romans on the right, and which was sometimes in the hands
f the Latins, sometimes in those of the Etruscans. The relations
f Rome with the somewhat more distant Caere were on the
hole far more peaceful and friendly than those which we usually
nd subsisting between neighbours in early times. There are
oubtless vague legends, reaching back to times of distant anti-
uity, about contests between Latium and Caere; Mezentius
he king of Caere, for instance, is asserted to have obtained
reat victories over the Latins, and to have imposed upon them
 wine-tax; but evidence much more definite than that which
ttests a former state of feud is supplied by tradition as to an
specially close connection between the two ancient centres
f commercial and maritime intercourse in Latium and Etruria.
Reliable traces of any advance of the Etruscans beyond the
Tiber, by land, are altogether wanting. It is true that Etruscans
re named in the first ranks of the great barbarian host, which
Aristodemus annihilated in $\frac{230}{524}$ under the walls of Cumae
p. 118); but, even if we regard this account as deserving credit
n all its details, it only shows that the Etruscans had taken
art in a great plundering expedition. It is far more important
o observe that south of the Tiber no Etruscan settlement can
e pointed out as having owed its origin to founders who came
y land; and that no indication whatever is discernible of any
erious pressure by the Etruscans upon the Latin nation. The
ossession of the Janiculum and of both banks of the mouth of
he Tiber remained, so far as we can see, undisputed in the
ands of the Romans. As to the migrations of bodies of
Etruscans to Rome, we find an isolated statement drawn from
Tuscan annals, that a Tuscan band, led by Caelius Vivenna of
Volsinii and after his death by his faithful companion Mastarna,
was conducted by the latter to Rome and settled there on the
Caelian Mount. We may hold the account to be trustworthy,
although the addition that this Mastarna became king in Rome
under the name of Servius Tullius is certainly nothing but an
mprobable conjecture of the archaeologists who busied them-
elves with legendary parallels. The name of the " Tuscan
quarter " at the foot of the Palatine (p. 50) points to a similar
settlement.

It can hardly, moreover, be doubted that the last regal family which ruled over Rome, that of the Tarquins, was of Etruscan origin, whether it belonged to Tarquinii, as the legend asserts, or to Caere, where the family tomb of the Tarchnas has recently been discovered. The female name Tanaquil or Tanchvil interwoven with the legend, while it is not Latin, is common in Etruria. But the traditional story—according to which Tarquin was the son of a Greek who had migrated from Corinth to Tarquinii, and came to settle in Rome as a *metoikos*—is neither history nor legend, and the historical chain of events is manifestly in this instance not entangled merely, but completely torn asunder. If anything at all can be deduced from this tradition beyond the bare and really unimportant fact that at last a family of Tuscan descent swayed the regal sceptre in Rome, it can only be held as implying that this dominion of a man of Tuscan origin ought not to be viewed either as a dominion of the Tuscans or of any one Tuscan community over Rome, or conversely as the dominion of Rome over southern Etruria. There is, in fact, no sufficient ground either for the one hypothesis or for the other. The history of the Tarquins has its theatre in Latium, not in Etruria; and Etruria, so far as we can see, during the whole regal period exercised no influence of any essential moment on either the language or customs of Rome, and did not at all interrupt the regular development of the Roman state or of the Latin league.

The cause of this comparatively passive attitude of Etruria towards the neighbouring land of Latium is probably to be sought partly in the struggles of the Etruscans with the Celts on the Po, which it is probable that the Celts did not cross until after the expulsion of the kings from Rome, and partly in the tendency of the Etruscan people towards seafaring and the acquisition of a supremacy on the sea and seaboard—a tendency decidedly exhibited in their settlements in Campania, and of which we shall speak more fully in the next chapter.

The Tuscan constitution, like the Greek and Latin, was based on the gradual transition of the community to an urban life. The early direction of the national energies towards navigation, trade, and manufactures appears to have called into existence urban commonwealths, in the strict sense of the term, earlier in Etruria than elsewhere in Italy. Caere is the first of all the Italian towns that is mentioned in Greek records. On the other hand we find that the Etruscans had on the whole less of the ability and the disposition for war than the Romans and Sabellians: the un-Italian custom of employing mercenaries to fight for them occurs among the Etruscans at a very early period. The oldest constitution of the communities must in its general outlines have resembled that of Rome. Kings or Lucumones ruled, possessing similar insignia and probably therefore a similar plenitude of power with the Roman kings. A strict line of demarcation separated the nobles from the common people. The resemblance in the clan-organisation is attested by the analogy of the systems of names; only, among the Etruscans, descent on the mother's side received much more consideration than in Roman law. The constitution of their league appears to have been very lax. It did not embrace the whole nation; the northern and the Campanian Etruscans were associated in confederacies of their own, just in the same way as the communities of Etruria proper. Each of these leagues consisted of twelve communities, which recognised a metropolis, especially for purposes of worship, and a federal head or rather a high priest, but appear to have been substantially equal in respect of rights; while some of them at least were so powerful that neither could a hegemony establish itself, nor could the central authority attain consolidation. In Etruria proper Volsinii was the metropolis; of the rest of its twelve towns we know by trustworthy tradition only Perusia, Vetulonium, Volci, and Tarquinii. It was, however, quite as unusual for the Etruscans really to act in concert, as it was for the Latin confederacy to do otherwise. Wars were ordinarily carried on by a single community, which endeavoured to interest in its cause such of its neighbours as it could; and when an exceptional case occurred in which war was resolved on by the league, individual towns very frequently kept aloof from it. The Etruscan confederations appear to have been from the first —still more than the other Italian leagues formed on a similar basis of national affinity—deficient in a firm and paramount central authority.

CHAPTER X

THE HELLENES IN ITALY—MARITIME SUPREMACY OF THE TUSCANS AND CARTHAGINIANS

IN the history of the nations of antiquity a gradual dawn ushered in the day; and in their case too the dawn was in the east. While the Italian peninsula still lay enveloped in the dim twilight of morning, the regions of the eastern basin of the Mediterranean had already emerged into the full light of a varied and richly developed civilisation. It falls to the lot of most nations in the early stages of their development to be taught and trained by some rival sister-nation; and such was destined to be in an eminent degree the lot of the peoples of Italy. The circumstances of its geographical position, however, prevented this influence from being brought to bear upon the peninsula by land. No trace is to be found of any resort in early times to the difficult route by land between Italy and Greece. There were in all probability from time immemorial tracks for purposes of traffic, leading from Italy to the lands beyond the Alps; the oldest route of the amber trade from the Baltic joined the Mediterranean at the mouth of the Po—on which account the delta of the Po appears in Greek legend as the native country of amber—and this route was joined by another leading across the peninsula over the Apennines to Pisae; but from these regions no elements of civilisation could come to the Italians. It was the seafaring nations of the east that brought to Italy whatever foreign culture reached it in early times.

The oldest civilised nation on the shores of the Mediterranean, the Egyptians, were not a seafaring people, and therefore they exercised no influence on Italy. But the same may be with almost equal truth affirmed of the Phoenicians. It is true that, issuing from their narrow home on the extreme eastern verge of the Mediterranean, they were the first of all known races to venture forth in floating houses on the bosom of the deep, at first for the purpose of fishing and dredging, but soon also for the prosecution of trade. They were the first to open up maritime commerce; and at an incredibly early period they traversed

he Mediterranean even to its furthest extremity in the west.
Maritime stations of the Phoenicians appear on almost all its
coasts earlier than those of the Hellenes: in Hellas itself, in
Crete and Cyprus, in Egypt, Libya, and Spain, and likewise on
the western Italian main.   Thucydides tells us that all around
Sicily, before the Greeks came thither or at least before they
had established themselves there in any considerable numbers,
the Phoenicians had set up their factories on the headlands and
islets, not with a view to territorial aggrandisement, but for the
sake of trading with the natives.   But it was otherwise in the
case of continental Italy.   No reliable indication has hitherto
been given of the existence of any Phoenician settlement there
excepting one, a Punic factory at Caere, the memory of which
has been preserved partly by the appellation *Punicum* given to
a little village on the Caerite coast, partly by the other name of
the town of Caere itself, *Agylla*, which is not, as idle fiction
asserts, of Pelasgic origin, but is a Phoenician word signifying
the " round town "—precisely the appearance which Caere
presents when seen from the sea.   That this station and any
similar establishments which may have elsewhere existed on the
coasts of Italy were neither of much importance nor of long
standing, is evident from their having disappeared almost
without leaving a trace.   We have not the smallest reason to
think them older than the Hellenic settlements of a similar kind
on the same coasts.   An evidence of no slight weight that
Latium at least first became acquainted with the men of Canaan
through the medium of the Hellenes is furnished by the Latin
name " Poeni," which is borrowed from the Greek.   All the
oldest relations, indeed, of the Italians to the civilisation of the
east point decidedly towards Greece; and the rise of the Phoenician factory at Caere may be very well explained, without
resorting to the pre-Hellenic period, by the subsequent well-
known relations between the commercial state of Caere and
Carthage.   In fact, when we recall the circumstance that the
earliest navigation was and continued to be essentially of a
coasting character, it is plain that scarcely any country on the
Mediterranean lay so remote from the Phoenicians as the
Italian mainland.   They could only reach it from the west
coast of Greece or from Sicily; and it is very probable that the
seamanship of the Hellenes became developed early enough to
anticipate the Phoenicians in braving the dangers of the Adriatic
and of the Tyrrhene seas.   There is no ground therefore for the
assumption that any direct influence was originally exercised

by the Phoenicians over the Italians. To the subsequent relations between the Phoenicians holding the supremacy of the western Mediterranean and the Italians inhabiting the shores of the Tyrrhene sea our narrative will return in the sequel.

To all appearance the Hellenic mariners were the first among the inhabitants of the eastern basin of the Mediterranean to navigate the coasts of Italy. Of the important questions however as to the region from which, and as to the period at which, the Greek seafarers came thither, only the former admits of being answered with some degree of precision and fulness. The Aeolian and Ionian coast of Asia Minor was the region where Hellenic maritime traffic first became developed on a large scale, and whence issued the Greeks who explored the interior of the Black Sea on the one hand and the coasts of Italy on the other. The name of the Ionian Sea, which was retained by the waters intervening between Epirus and Sicily, and that of the Ionian gulf, the term by which the Greeks in earlier times designated the Adriatic Sea, are memorials of the fact that the southern and eastern coasts of Italy were once discovered by seafarers from Ionia. The oldest Greek settlement in Italy, Kyme, was, as its name and legend tell, founded by the town of the same name on the Anatolian coast. According to trustworthy Hellenic tradition, the Phocaeans of Asia Minor were the first of the Hellenes to traverse the more remote western sea. Other Greeks soon followed in the paths which those of Asia Minor had opened up; Ionians from Naxos and from Chalcis in Euboea, Achaeans, Locrians, Rhodians, Corinthians, Megarians, Messenians, Spartans. After the discovery of America the civilised nations of Europe vied with one another in sending out expeditions and forming settlements there; and the new settlers when located amidst barbarians recognised their common character and common interests as civilised Europeans more strongly than they had done in their former home. So it was with the new discovery of the Greeks. The privilege of navigating the western waters and settling on the western land was not the exclusive property of a single Greek province or of a single Greek stock, but a common good for the whole Hellenic nation; and, just as in the formation of the new North American world, English and French, Dutch and German settlements became mingled and blended, Greek Sicily and " Great Greece " became peopled by a mixture of all sorts of Hellenic races often so amalgamated as to be no longer distinguishable. Leaving out of account some settlements occupying a more isolated position

—such as that of the Locrians with its offsets Hipponium and
Medama, and the settlement of the Phocaeans which was not
founded till towards the close of this period, Hyele (Velia, Elea)
—we may distinguish in a general view three leading groups.
The original Ionian group, comprehended under the name of
the Chalcidian towns, included in Italy Cumae with the other
Greek settlements at Vesuvius and Rhegium, and in Sicily
Zankle (afterwards Messana), Naxos, Catana, Leontini, and
Himera. The Achaean group embraced Sybaris and the greater
part of the cities of Magna Graecia. The Dorian group comprehended Syracuse, Gela, Agrigentum, and the majority of the
Sicilian colonies, while in Italy nothing belonged to it but Taras
(Tarentum) and its offset Heraclea. On the whole the preponderance lay with the immigrants who belonged to the more
ancient Hellenic influx, that of the Ionians and the stocks settled
in the Peloponnesus before the Doric immigration. Among
the Dorians only communities with a mixed population, such
as Corinth and Megara, took any leading part; the purely Doric
provinces had but a subordinate share in the movement. This
result was naturally to be expected, for the Ionians were from
ancient times a trading and seafaring people, while it was only
at a comparatively late period that the Dorian stocks descended
from their inland mountains to the seaboard, and they always
kept aloof from maritime commerce. The different groups of
immigrants are very clearly distinguishable, especially by their
monetary standards. The Phocaean settlers coined according
to the Babylonian standard which prevailed in Asia. The
Chalcidian towns followed in the earliest times the Aeginetan,
in other words, that which originally prevailed throughout all
European Greece, and more especially the modification of it
which is found occurring in Euboea. The Achaean communities
coined by the Corinthian standard; and lastly the Doric colonies
followed that which Solon introduced in Attica in the year
$\frac{160}{594}$, with the exception of Tarentum and Heraclea which
in their principal pieces adopted rather the standard of their
Achaean neighbours than that of the Dorians in Sicily.

The dates of the earlier voyages and settlements will probably
always remain enveloped in darkness. We may still, however,
distinctly recognise a certain order of sequence. In the oldest
Greek document, which belongs, like the earliest intercourse with
the west, to the Ionians of Asia Minor—the Homeric poems—
the horizon scarcely extends beyond the eastern basin of the
Mediterranean. Sailors driven by storms into the western sea

might have brought to Asia Minor accounts of the existence of a western land and possibly also of its whirlpools and island-mountains vomiting fire: but in the age of the Homeric poetry there was an utter want of reliable information respecting Sicily and Italy, even in that Greek land which was the earliest to enter into intercourse with the west; and the story-tellers and poets of the east could without fear of contradiction fill the vacant realms of the west, as those of the west in their turn filled the fabulous east, with their castles in the air. In the poems of Hesiod the outlines of Italy and Sicily appear better defined; there is some acquaintance with the native names of tribes, mountains, and cities in both countries; but Italy is still regarded as a group of islands. On the other hand in all the literature subsequent to Hesiod Sicily and even the whole coast of Italy appear as known, at least in a general sense, to the Hellenes. The order of succession of the Greek settlements may in like manner be ascertained with some degree of precision. Thucydides evidently regarded Cumae as the earliest settlement of note in the west; and certainly he was not mistaken. It is true that many a landing-place lay nearer at hand for the Greek mariner, but none were so well protected from storms and from barbarians as the island of Ischia, upon which the town was originally situated; and that such were the prevailing considerations that led to this settlement, is evident from the very position which was subsequently selected for it on the main land—the steep but well-protected cliff which still bears to the present day the venerable name of the Anatolian mother-city. Nowhere in Italy, accordingly, were the scenes of the legends of Asia Minor so vividly and tenaciously localised as in the district of Cumae, where the earliest voyagers to the west, full of those legends of western wonders, first stepped upon the fabled land and left the traces of that world of story which they believed that they were treading in the rocks of the Sirens and the lake of Avernus leading to the lower world. On the supposition, moreover, that it was in Cumae that the Greeks first became the neighbours of the Italians, it is easy to explain why the name of that Italian stock which was settled immediately around Cumae, the name of Opicans, came to be employed by them for centuries afterwards to designate the Italians collectively. There is a further credible tradition, that a considerable interval elapsed between the settlement at Cumae and the main Hellenic immigration into Lower Italy and Sicily, and that in this immigration Ionians from Chalcis and from Naxos took the lead. Naxos in Sicily is said

to have been the oldest of all the Greek towns founded by strict
colonisation in Italy or Sicily; the Achaean and Dorian colonisations followed, but not until a later period.

It appears, however, to be quite impossible to fix the dates
of this series of events with even approximate accuracy. The
founding of the Achaean city of Sybaris in $^{33}_{21}7$, and that of
the Dorian city Tarentum in $^{46}_{08}7$, may be taken as a basis in
such an enquiry—the most ancient dates in Italian history, the
correctness or at least approximation to correctness of which may
be looked upon as established.   But how far beyond that epoch
the earlier Ionian colonies reached back, is quite as uncertain
as is the age which gave birth to the poems of Hesiod or even
of Homer.   If Herodotus is correct in the period which he
assigns to Homer, the Greeks were still unacquainted with Italy
a century before the foundation of Rome. The date thus
assigned, however, like all other statements respecting the
Homeric age, is matter not of testimony, but of inference; and
any one who carefully weighs the history of the Italian alphabets
as well as the remarkable fact that the Italians had become
acquainted with the Greek nation before the newer name
"Hellenes" had supplanted the older national designation
"Graeci," [1] will be inclined to refer the earliest intercourse of
the Italians with the Greeks to an age considerably more remote.

The history of the Italian and Sicilian Greeks forms no part of
the history of Italy; the Hellenic colonists of the west always
retained the closest connection with their original home and
participated in the national festivals and privileges of Hellenes.
But it is of importance even as bearing on Italy, that we should
indicate the diversities of character that prevailed in the Greek

---

[1] The name Graeci is, like that of Hellenes, associated with the primitive
seat of Greek civilisation, the interior of Epirus and the region of Dodona.
In the Eoai of Hesiod it still appears a collective name for the nation,
although it is manifest that it is intentionally thrown into the shade and
rendered subordinate to that of Hellenes. The latter does not occur in
Homer, but in addition to Hesiod it is found in Archilochus about the
year 50 U.C., and it may very well have come into use considerably earlier
(Duncker, *Gesch. d. Alt.* iii. 18, 556). Before this period, therefore, the
Italians had already attained so extensive an acquaintance with the
Greeks, that they knew not only how to name the individual tribe, but
how to designate the nation by a collective term.   It is difficult to see how
we can reconcile with this fact the statement that a century before the
foundation of Rome Italy was still quite unknown to the Greeks of Asia
Minor.   We shall speak of the alphabet below; its history yields entirely
similar results.   It may perhaps be characterised as a rash step to reject
the statement of Herodotus respecting the age of Homer on the strength of
such considerations; but is there no rashness in following implicitly the
guidance of tradition in questions of this kind?

settlements there, and at least exhibit some of the leading features
which enabled the Greek colonisation to exercise so varied an
influence on Italy.

Of all the Greek settlements, that which retained most
thoroughly its distinctive character and was least affected by
influences from without was the settlement which gave birth
to the league of the Achaean cities, composed of the towns of
Siris, Pandosia, Metabus or Metapontum, Sybaris with its offsets
Posidonia and Laus, Croton, Caulonia, Temesa, Terina, and
Pyxus. These colonists, taken as a whole, belonged to a Greek
stock which steadfastly adhered to its own peculiar dialect (distinguished from the Doric, with which in other respects it had
most affinity, *e.g.* by the want of the *h*) and retained no less
steadfastly the old national Hellenic mode of writing, instead
of adopting the more recent alphabet which had elsewhere come
into general use; and which preserved its own nationality as distinguished from the barbarians and from other Greeks by the
firm bond of a federal constitution. The language of Polybius
regarding the Achaean symmachy in the Peloponnesus may be
applied also to these Italian Achaeans; " not only did they live
in federal and friendly communion, but they made use of the
same laws, and the same weights, measures, and coins, as well as
of the same magistrates, councillors, and judges."

This league of the Achaean cities was strictly a colonisation.
The cities had no harbours—Croton alone had a paltry roadstead—and they had no commerce of their own; the Sybarite
prided himself on growing grey between the bridges of his
lagoon-city, and Milesians and Etruscans bought and sold for
him. These Achaean Greeks, however, were not in possession
merely of a narrow belt along the coast, but ruled from sea to
sea in the " land of wine " and " of oxen " (Οἰνωτρία, 'Ιταλία)
or the " great Hellas; " the native agricultural population was
compelled to farm their lands and to pay to them tribute in the
character of clients or even of serfs. Sybaris—in its time the
largest city in Italy—exercised dominion over four barbarian
tribes and five-and-twenty townships, and was able to found
Laus and Posidonia on the other sea. The surprisingly fertile
low grounds of the Crathis and Bradanus yielded a super-
abundant produce to the Sybarites and Metapontines—it was
there perhaps that grain was first cultivated for exportation.
The height of prosperity which these states in a very short time
attained is strikingly attested by the only surviving works of art
of these Italian Achaeans, their coins of chaste antiquely beauti-

ful workmanship—the earliest monuments of art and writing in Italy which we possess, as it can be shown that they had already begun to be coined in $\frac{174}{580}$. These coins show that the Achaeans of the west did not simply participate in the noble development of plastic art that was at this very time taking place in the motherland, but were even superior in technical skill. For, while the silver pieces which were in use about that time in Greece proper and among the Dorians in Italy were thick, often stamped only on one side, and in general without inscription, the Italian Achaeans with great and independent skill struck from two similar dies partly cut in relief, partly sunk, large thin silver coins always furnished with inscriptions and displaying the advanced organisation of a civilised state in the mode of impression, by which they were carefully protected from the process of counterfeiting usual in that age—the plating of inferior metal with thin silver-foil.

Nevertheless this rapid bloom bore no fruit. Even Greeks speedily lost all elasticity of body and of mind in a life of indolence, in which their energies were never tried either by vigorous resistance on the part of the natives or by hard labour of their own. None of the brilliant names in Greek art or literature shed glory on the Italian Achaeans, while Sicily could claim ever so many of them, and even in Italy the Chalcidian Rhegium could produce its Ibycus and the Doric Tarentum its Archytas. With this people, among whom the spit was for ever turning on the hearth, nothing flourished from the outset but boxing. The rigid aristocracy which early gained the helm in the several communities, and which found in case of need a sure reserve of support in the federal power, prevented the rise of tyrants. The only danger to be apprehended was that the government of the best might be converted into a government of the few, especially if the privileged families in the different communities should combine to assist each other in carrying out their designs. Such was the predominant aim in the combination of mutually pledged " friends " which bore the name of Pythagoras. It enjoined the principle that the ruling class should be " honoured like gods," and that the subject class should be " held in subservience like beasts," and by such theory and practice provoked a formidable reaction, which terminated in the annihilation of the Pythagorean " friends " and the renewal of the ancient federal constitution. But frantic party feuds, insurrections *en masse* of the slaves, social abuses of all sorts, attempts to carry out in practice an impracticable state-philosophy, in short, all the evils of demoralised civilisation raged incessantly in the Achaean communities, till under the accumulated pressure their political power utterly broke down.

It is no matter of wonder therefore that the Achaeans settled in Italy exercised less influence on its civilisation than the other Greek settlements. An agricultural people, they had less occasion than those engaged in commerce to extend their influence beyond their political bounds. Within their own dominions they enslaved the native population and crushed the germs of their national development as Italians, while they refused to open up to them by means of complete Hellenisation a new career. In this way the Greek characteristics, which were able elsewhere to retain a vigorous vitality notwithstanding all political misfortunes, disappeared more rapidly, more completely, and more ingloriously in Sybaris and Metapontum, in Croton and Posidonia, than in any other region; and the bilingual mongrel people, which arose in subsequent times out of the remains of the native Italians and Achaeans and the more recent immigrants of Sabellian descent, never attained any real prosperity. This catastrophe, however, belongs in point of time to the succeeding period.

The settlements of the other Greeks were of a different character, and exercised a very different effect upon Italy. They by no means despised agriculture and the acquisition of territory; it was not the wont of the Hellenes, at least when they had reached their full vigour, to rest content after the manner of the Phoenicians with a fortified factory in the midst of a barbarian land. But all their cities were founded primarily and especially for the sake of trade, and accordingly, altogether differing from those of the Achaeans, they were uniformly established beside the best harbours and lading-places. These cities were very various in their origin and in the occasion and period of their respective foundations; but there subsisted among them certain points of common agreement or at least of contradistinction from the league of the Achaean cities—such as the common use by all of them of certain modern forms of the alphabet,[1] and the very Dorism of their language, which pervaded at an early

---

[1] Thus the three old Oriental forms of the *i* (⟨S⟩), *l* (⟨Λ⟩) and *r* (⟨P⟩) for which as apt to be confounded with the forms of the *s*, *g*, and *p* the signs Ι Ⅼ R were early proposed to be substituted, remained either in exclusive or preponderant use among the Achaean colonies, while the other Greeks of Italy and Sicily without distinction of race used either exclusively or chiefly the more recent forms.

date even those towns that, like Cumae for example,[1] originally spoke the soft Ionic dialect. These settlements were of very various degrees of importance in their bearing on the development of Italy: it is sufficient at present to notice those which exercised a decided influence over the destinies of the Italian races, the Doric Tarentum and the Ionic Cumae.

Of all the Hellenic settlements in Italy, Tarentum was destined to play the most brilliant part. The excellent harbour, the only good one on the whole southern coast, rendered the city the natural emporium for the traffic of the south of Italy, and for some portion even of the commerce of the Adriatic. The rich fisheries of its gulf, the production and manufacture of its excellent wool, and the dyeing of it with the purple juice of the Tarentine *murex*, which rivalled that of Tyre—both branches of industry introduced there from Miletus in Asia Minor— employed thousands of hands, and added to the carrying trade a traffic of export. The coins struck at Tarentum in greater numbers than anywhere else in Grecian Italy, many of them even composed of gold, furnish to us a significant attestation of the lively and widely extended commerce of the Tarentines. At this epoch, when Tarentum was still contending with Sybaris for the first place among the Greek cities of Lower Italy, its extensive commercial connections must have been already forming; but the Tarentines seem never to have steadily and successfully directed their efforts to the extension of their territory after the manner of the Achaean cities.

While the most easterly of the Greek settlements in Italy thus rapidly rose into splendour, those which lay furthest to the north, in the neighbourhood of Vesuvius, attained a more moderate prosperity. There the Cumaeans had crossed from the fertile island of Aenaria (Ischia) to the mainland, and had built a scond home on a hill close by the sea, from whence they founded the seaport of Dicaearchia (afterwards Puteoli) and the cities of Parthenope and Neapolis. They lived, like the Chalcidian cities generally in Italy and Sicily, in conformity with the laws which Charondas of Catana (about $\frac{100}{650}$) had established, under a constitution democratic but modified by a high qualification, which placed the power in the hands of a council of members selected from the wealthiest men—a constitution which proved lasting and kept these cities free, upon the whole, from the tyranny alike of usurpers and of the mob.

---

[1] *E.g.*, the inscription on an earthen vase of Cumae runs thus:—

Ταταίες ἐμὶ λέφυθος· Ϝὸς δ᾽ ἄν με κλέφσει θυφλὸς ἔσται.

We know little as to the external relations of these Campanian
Greeks. They remained, whether from necessity or from choice,
confined to a district of even narrower limits than the Tarentines;
and issuing from it not for purposes of conquest and oppression,
but for holding of peaceful commercial intercourse with the
natives, they created the means of a prosperous existence for
themselves, and at the same time occupied the foremost place
among the missionaries of Greek civilisation in Italy.

While on the one side of the straits of Rhegium the whole
southern coast of the mainland and its western coast as far as
Vesuvius, and on the other the larger eastern half of the island
of Sicily, were Greek territory, the west coast of Italy northward of Vesuvius and the whole of the east coast were in a
position essentially different. No Greek settlements arose on
the Italian seaboard of the Adriatic; a fact which has an evident
connection with the comparatively trifling number and subordinate importance of the Greek colonies planted on the
opposite Illyrian shore and on the numerous adjacent islands.
Two considerable mercantile towns, Epidamnus or Dyrrachium
(now Durazzo, $\frac{127}{627}$) and Apollonia (near Avlona, about $\frac{167}{587}$),
were founded upon the portion of this coast nearest to Greece
during the regal period of Rome; but no old Greek colony can
be pointed out further to the north, with the exception perhaps
of the insignificant settlement at Black Corcyra (Curzola, about
$\frac{174}{580}$?). No adequate explanation has yet been given why the
Greek colonisation developed itself in this direction to so meagre
an extent. Nature herself appeared to direct the Hellenes
thither, and in fact from the earliest times there existed a
regular traffic to that region from Corinth and still more from
the settlement at Corcyra (Corfu) founded not long after Rome
(about $\frac{44}{710}$); a traffic, which had as its emporia on the Italian
coast the towns of Spina and Hatria, situated at the mouth of the
Po. The storms of the Adriatic, the inhospitable character at
least of the Illyrian coasts, and the barbarism of the natives are
manifestly not in themselves sufficient to explain this fact. But
it was a circumstance fraught with the most momentous consequences for Italy, that the elements of civilisation which came
from the east did not exert their influence on its eastern provinces directly, but reached them only through the medium of
those that lay to the west. The Adriatic commerce carried on by
Corinth and Corcyra was shared by the most easterly mercantile
city of Magna Graecia, the Doric Tarentum, which by the possession of Hydrus (Otranto) had the command, on the Italian side,

of the entrance of the Adriatic. Since, with the exception of
the ports at the mouth of the Po, there were in those times no
emporia worthy of mention along the whole east coast—the rise
of Ancona belongs to a far later period, and later still the rise of
Brundisium—it is very probable that the mariners of Epidamnus
and Apollonia frequently discharged their cargoes at Tarentum.
The Tarentines had also much intercourse with Apulia by land;
all the Greek civilisation to be met with in the south-east of
Italy owed its existence to them. That civilisation, however,
was during the present period only in its infancy; it was not
until a later epoch that the Hellenism of Apulia became
developed.

It cannot be doubted, on the other hand, that the west coast
of Italy northward of Vesuvius was frequented in very early
times by the Hellenes, and that there were Hellenic factories on
its promontories and islands. Probably the earliest evidence
of such voyages is the localising of the legend of Odysseus on the
coasts of the Tyrrhene Sea.[1] When men discovered the isle of
Aeolus in the Lipari islands, when they pointed out at the
Lacinian cape the isle of Calypso, at the cape of Misenum that
of the Sirens, at the cape of Circeii that of Circe, when they
recognised in the steep promontory of Terracina the towering
mound of Elpenor, when the Laestrygones were provided with
haunts near Caieta and Formiae, when the two sons of Ulysses
and Circe, Agrius, that is the "wild," and Latinus, were made
to rule over the Tyrrhenes in the "inmost recess of the holy
islands," or according to a more recent conception Latinus was
called the son of Ulysses and Circe, and Auson the son of Ulysses
and Calypso—we recognise in these legends ancient sailors' tales
of the seafarers of Ionia, who thought of their native home as
they traversed the Tyrrhene Sea. The same noble vividness of
feeling which pervades the Ionic poem of the voyages of Odysseus
is discernible in this fresh localisation of its legend at Cumae
itself and throughout the regions frequented by the Cumaean
mariners.

Other traces of these very ancient voyages are to be found
in the Greek name of the island Aethalia (Ilva, Elba), which

---

[1] Among Greek writers this Tyrrhene legend of Ódysseus makes its
earliest appearance in the Theogony of Hesiod, in one of its more recent
sections, and then in authors of the period shortly before Alexander,
Ephorus (from whom the so-called Scymnus drew his materials), and the
writer known as Scylax. The first of these sources belongs to an age
when Italy was still regarded by the Greeks as a group of islands, and is
certainly therefore very ancient; so that the origin of these legends may,
on the whole, be confidently placed in the regal period of Rome.

appears to have been (after Aenaria) one of the places earliest occupied by Greeks, perhaps also in that of the seaport Telamon in Etruria; and further in the two towns on the Caerite coast, Pyrgi (near S. Severa) and Alsium (near Palo), the Greek origin of which is indicated beyond possibility of mistake not only by their names, but also by the peculiar architecture of the walls of Pyrgi, which differs essentially in character from that of the walls of Caere and the Etruscan cities generally. Aethalia, the "fire-island," with its rich mines of copper and especially of iron, probably sustained the chief part in this northern commerce, and there in all likelihood the foreigners had their central settlement and seat of traffic with the natives; the more especially as they could not have found the means of smelting the ores on a small and not well-wooded island without intercourse with the mainland. The silver mines of Populonia also on the headland opposite to Elba were perhaps known to the Greeks and wrought by them.

If, as was undoubtedly the case, the foreigners, ever in those times intent on piracy and plunder as well as trade, did not fail, when opportunity offered, to levy contributions on the natives and to carry them off as slaves, the natives on their part exercised the right of retaliation; and that the Latins and Tyrrhenes retaliated with greater energy and better fortune than their neighbours in the south of Italy, is attested not merely by the legends to that effect, but by the practical result. In these regions the Italians succeeded in resisting the foreigners and in retaining, or at any rate soon resuming, the mastery not merely of their own mercantile cities and seaports, but also of their own seas. The same Hellenic invasion which crushed and denationalised the races of the south of Italy, directed the energies of the peoples of Central Italy—very much indeed against the will of their instructors—towards navigation and the founding of towns. It must have been in this quarter that the Italians first exchanged the raft and the boat for the oared galley of the Phoenicians and Greeks. Here too we first encounter great mercantile cities, particularly Caere in southern Etruria and Rome on the Tiber, which, if we may judge from their Italian names as well as from their being situated at some distance from the sea, were—like the exactly similar commercial towns at the mouth of the Po, Spina and Hatria, and Ariminum further to the south—certainly not Greek, but Italian foundations. It is not in our power, as may easily be supposed, to exhibit the historical course of this earliest reaction of Italian nationality against foreign assault; but we can still recognise the fact, which was of the greatest importance as bearing upon the further development of Italy, that this reaction took a different course in Latium and in southern Etruria from that which it exhibited in the properly Tuscan and adjoining provinces.

Legend itself contrasts in a significant manner the Latin with the " wild Tyrrhenian," and the peaceful beach at the mouth of the Tiber with the inhospitable shores of the Volsci. This cannot mean that Greek colonisation was tolerated in some of the provinces of Central Italy, but not permitted in others. Northward of Vesuvius there existed no independent Greek community at all in historical times; if Pyrgi once was such, it must have already reverted, before the period at which our tradition begins, into the hands of the Italians or in other words of the Caerites. But in southern Etruria, in Latium, and likewise on the east coast, peaceful intercourse with the foreign merchants was protected and encouraged; and such was not the case elsewhere. The position of Caere was especially remarkable. " The Caerites," says Strabo, " were held in much repute among the Hellenes for their bravery and integrity, and because, powerful though they were, they abstained from robbery." It is not piracy that is thus referred to, for in this the merchant of Caere must have indulged like the rest. But Caere was a sort of free port for Phoenicians as well as Greeks. We have already mentioned the Phoenician station—subsequently called Punicum—and the two Hellenic stations of Pyrgi and Alsium (p. 129, 140). It was these ports that the Caerites refrained from robbing, and it was beyond doubt through this tolerant attitude that Caere, which possessed but a wretched roadstead and had no mines in its neighbourhood, early attained so great prosperity and acquired, in reference to the earliest Greek commerce, an importance even greater than the cities of the Italians destined by nature as emporia at the mouths of the Tiber and Po. The cities we have just named are those which appear as holding primitive religious intercourse with Greece. The first of all barbarians to present gifts to the Olympian Zeus was the Tuscan king Arimnus, perhaps a ruler of Ariminum. Spina and Caere had their special treasuries in the temple of the Delphic Apollo, like other communities that had regular dealings with the shrine; and the sanctuary at Delphi, as well as the Cumaean oracle, is interwoven with the earliest traditions of Caere and of Rome. These cities, where the Italians held peaceful sway and carried on friendly traffic with the foreign merchant, became pre-eminently wealthy and powerful, and were in reality marts not only for Hellenic merchandise, but also for the germs of Hellenic civilisation.

Matters stood on a different footing with the " wild Tyrrhenians." The same causes, which in the province of Latium, and in the districts on the right bank of the Tiber and along the lower course of the Po that were perhaps rather subject to Etruscan supremacy than strictly Etruscan, had led to the emancipation of the natives from the maritime power of the foreigner, led in Etruria proper to the development of piracy and maritime ascendancy, in consequence possibly of the difference of national character disposing the people to violence and pillage, or it may be for other reasons with which we are not acquainted. The Etruscans were not content with dislodging the Greeks from Aethalia and Populonia; even the individual trader was apparently not tolerated by them, and soon Etruscan privateers roamed over the sea far and wide, and rendered the name of the Tyrrhenians a terror to the Greeks. It was not without reason that the Greeks reckoned the grapnel as an Etruscan invention, and called the western sea of Italy the sea of the Tuscans. The rapidity with which these wild corsairs multiplied and the violence of their proceedings, in the Tyrrhene Sea in particular, are very clearly shown in their establishment on the Latin and Campanian coasts. The Latins indeed maintained their ground in Latium proper, and the Greeks at Vesuvius; but between them and by their side the Etruscans held sway in Antium and in Surrentum. The Volscians became clients of the Etruscans; their forests contributed keels for the Etruscan galleys; and seeing that the piracy of the Antiates was only terminated by the Roman occupation, it is easy to understand why the coast of the southern Volscians bore among Greek mariners the name of the Laestrygones. The high promontory of Sorrento with the cliff of Capri which is still more precipitous but destitute of any harbour—a station thoroughly adapted for corsairs on the watch, commanding a prospect of the Tyrrhene Sea between the bays of Naples and Salerno—was early occupied by the Etruscans. They are affirmed even to have founded a " league of twelve towns " of their own in Campania, and communities speaking Etruscan still existed in its inland districts in times quite historical. These settlements were probably indirect results of the maritime dominion of the Etruscans in the Campanian seas, and of their rivalry with the Cumaeans at Vesuvius.

The Etruscans however by no means confined themselves to robbery and pillage. The peaceful intercourse which they held with Greek towns is attested by the gold and silver coins which, at least from the year $\frac{200}{544}$, were struck by the Etruscan cities, and in particular by Populonia, after a Greek model and a Greek standard. The circumstance, moreover, that these coins are modelled not upon those of Magna Graecia, but rather upon those of Attica and even Asia Minor, is perhaps an indication of the hostile attitude in which the Etruscans stood towards the Italian Greeks. For commerce they in fact enjoyed a most favourable position, far more advantageous than that of the inhabitants of Latium. Inhabiting the country from sea to sea they commanded the great Italian free ports on the western waters, the mouths of the Po and the Venice of that time on the eastern sea, and the land route which from ancient times led from Pisae on the Tyrrhene Sea to Spina on the Adriatic, while in the south of Italy they commanded the rich plains of Capua and Nola. They were the holders of the most important articles of Italian export, the iron of Aethalia, the copper of Volaterrae and Campania, the silver of Populonia, and the amber which was brought to them from the Baltic (p. 128). Under the protection of their piracy, which constituted as it were a rude navigation act, their own commerce could not fail to flourish. It need not surprise us to find Etruscan and Milesian merchants competing in the market of Sybaris, nor need we be astonished to learn that the combination of privateering and commerce on a great scale generated an unbounded and senseless luxury, in which the vigour of Etruria early wasted away.

While in Italy the Etruscans and, in a lesser degree, the Latins thus stood opposed to the Hellenes, warding them off and partly treating them as enemies, this antagonism to some extent necessarily affected the rivalry which then pervaded the commerce and navigation of the Mediterranean—the rivalry between the Phoenicians and Hellenes. This is not the place to set forth in detail how, during the regal period of Rome, these two great nations contended for supremacy on all the shores of the Mediterranean, in Greece even and Asia Minor, in Crete and Cyprus, on the African, Spanish, and Celtic coasts. This struggle did not take place directly on Italian soil, but its effects were deeply and permanently felt in Italy. The fresh energies and more universal endowments of the younger competitor had at first the advantage everywhere. Not only did the Hellenes rid themselves of the Phoenician factories in their own European and Asiatic home, but they dislodged the Phoenicians also from Crete and Cyprus, obtained a footing in Egypt and Cyrene, and possessed themselves of Lower Italy and the larger eastern half of the island of Sicily. On all hands the small trading stations of the Phoenicians gave way before the more energetic colonisation of the Greeks. Selinus ($\frac{126}{628}$) and Agrigentum ($\frac{174}{580}$) were founded in Western Sicily; the more remote western sea was traversed, Massilia was built on the Celtic coast (about $\frac{150}{600}$), and the shores of Spain were explored, by the bold Phocaeans from Asia Minor. But about the middle of the second century the progress of Hellenic colonisation was suddenly arrested and there is no doubt that the cause of this arrest was the contemporary rapid development of Carthage, the most powerful of the Phoenician cities in Libya—a development manifestly due to the danger with which Hellenic aggression threatened the whole Phoenician race. If the nation which had opened up maritime commerce on the Mediterranean had been already dislodged by its younger rival from the sole command of the western half, from the possession of both lines of communication between the eastern and western basins of the Mediterranean, and from the monopoly of the carrying trade between east and west, the sovereignty at least of the seas to the west of Sardinia and Sicily might still be saved for the Orientals; and to its maintenance Carthage applied all the tenacious and circumspect energy peculiar to the Aramaean race. Phoenician colonisation and Phoenician resistance assumed an entirely different character. The earlier Phoenician settlements, such as those in Sicily described by Thucydides, were mercantile factories: Carthage subdued extensive territories with numerous subjects and powerful fortresses. Hitherto each Phoenician settlement had stood isolated in its opposition to the Greeks; now the powerful Libyan city centralised the whole warlike resources of the race within its reach with a vigour to which the history of the Greeks can produce nothing parallel. Perhaps the element in this reaction which exercised the most momentous influence in the sequel was the close relation into which the weaker Phoenicians entered with the natives of Sicily and Italy in order to resist the Hellenes. When the Cnidians and Rhodians made an attempt about $\frac{175}{579}$ to establish themselves at Lilybaeum, the centre of the Phoenician settlements in Sicily, they were expelled by the natives, the Elymi of Segeste, in concert with the Phoenicians. When the Phocaeans settled about $\frac{217}{537}$ at Alalia (Aleria) in Corsica opposite to Caere, there

appeared for the purpose of expelling them a combined fleet of
Etruscans and Carthaginians, numbering a hundred and twenty
sail; and although in the naval battle that ensued—one of the
earliest known in history—the fleet of the Phocaeans, which was
only half as numerous, claimed the victory, the Carthaginians
and Etruscans gained the object which they had in view in the
attack; the Phocaeans abandoned Corsica, and preferred to
settle at Hyele (Velia) on the less exposed coast of Lucania.   A
treaty between Etruria and Carthage not only established
regulations regarding the importation of goods and the redress
of rights, but included also an alliance-in-arms (συμμαχία), the
serious import of which is shown by that very battle of Alalia.
It is a significant indication of the position of the Caerites, that
they stoned the Phocaean captives in the market at Caere and
then sent an embassy to the Delphic Apollo to atone for the
crime.

Latium did not join in these hostilities against the Hellenes;
on the contrary we find friendly relations subsisting in very
ancient times between the Romans and the Phocaeans in Velia
as well as in Massilia, and the Ardeates are even said to have
founded in concert with the Zacynthians a colony in Spain, the
later Saguntum.   Much less, however, did the Latins range
themselves on the side of the Hellenes: the neutrality of their
position in this respect is attested by the close relations maintained between Caere and Rome, as well as by the traces of
ancient intercourse between the Latins and Carthaginians.   It
was through the medium of the Hellenes that the Canaanite race
became known to the Romans, for, as we have already seen
(p. 129), they always designated it by its Greek name; but the
fact that they did not borrow from the Greeks either the name
for the city of Carthage [1] or the national name of *Afri*,[2] and the
circumstance that among the earlier Romans Tyrian wares were
designated by the adjective *Sarranus* [3] which in like manner
precludes the idea of Greek intervention, demonstrate—what

---

[1] The Phoenician name was Karthada; the Greek, Karchedon; the
Roman, Cartago.

[2] The name *Afri*, already current in the days of Ennius and Cato (comp.
Scipio Africanus), is certainly not Greek, and is most probably related to
that of the Hebrews.

[3] The adjective *Sarranus* was from early times applied by the Romans
to the Tyrian purple and the Tyrian flute; and it was in use also as a surname, at least from the time of the war with Hannibal.   *Sarra*, which
occurs in Ennius and Plautus as the name of the city, was perhaps formed
from *Sarranus*, not directly from the native name *Sor*.   The Greek form,
Tyrus, Tyrius, seems not to occur in any Roman author anterior to
Afranius (ap. Fest. p. 355 M.).   Compare Movers, *Phön*. ii. 1, 174.

the treaties of a later period concur in proving—the direct com
mercial intercourse anciently subsisting between Latium and
Carthage.

The combined power of the Italians and Phoenicians actually
succeeded in substantially retaining the western half of the
Mediterranean in their hands. The north-western portion of
Sicily, with the important ports of Soluntum and Panormus on
the north-west, and Motya at the point which looks towards
Africa, remained in the direct or indirect possession of the
Carthaginians. About the age of Cyrus and Croesus, when the
wise Bias was endeavouring to induce the Ionians to emigrate
in a body from Asia Minor and settle in Sardinia (about $\frac{200}{550}$),
the Carthaginian general Malchus anticipated them, and subdued
a considerable portion of that important island by force of arms;
half a century later, the whole coast of Sardinia appears in the
undisputed possession of the Carthaginian community. Corsica
on the other hand, with the towns of Alalia and Nicaea, fell to
the Etruscans, and the natives paid them tribute of the products
of their poor island, pitch, wax, and honey. In the Adriatic
sea, moreover, the allied Etruscans and Carthaginians predominated, as in the waters to the west of Sicily and Sardinia.
The Greeks, indeed, did not give up the struggle. Those
Rhodians and Cnidians, who had been driven out of Lilybaeum,
established themselves on the islands between Sicily and Italy
and founded there the town of Lipara ($\frac{175}{579}$). Massilia flourished
in spite of its isolation, and soon monopolised the trade from
Nice to the Pyrenees. At the Pyrenees themselves Rhoda
(now Rosas) was established as an offset from Lipara, and it is
affirmed that Zacynthians settled in Saguntum, and even that
Greek dynasts ruled at Tingis (Tangier) in Mauretania. But
the Hellenes no longer gained ground; after the foundation of
Agrigentum they did not succeed in acquiring any important
additions of territory on the Adriatic or on the western sea, and
they remained excluded from the Spanish waters as well as from
the Atlantic Ocean. Every year the Liparaeans had their
conflicts with the Tuscan " sea-robbers," and the Carthaginians
with the Massiliots and the Cyrenaeans and above all with the
Sicilian Greeks; but no results of permanent moment were on
either side achieved, and the issue of struggles which lasted for
centuries was, on the whole, the simple maintenance of the
status quo.

Thus Italy was, indirectly at any rate, indebted to the
Phoenicians for the exemption of at least her central and

northern provinces from colonisation, and for the counter-development of a national maritime power there, especially in Etruria. But there are not wanting indications that the Phoenicians already found it expedient to manifest that jealousy which is usually associated with naval domination, if not in reference to their Latin allies, at any rate in reference to their Etruscan confederates, whose naval power was greater. The statement as to the Carthaginians having prohibited the sending forth of an Etruscan colony to the Canary islands, whether true or false, reveals the existence of a rivalry of interests in the matter.

CHAPTER XI

LAW AND JUSTICE

HISTORY, as such, cannot reproduce the life of a people in the infinite variety of its details; it must be content with exhibiting the development of that life as a whole. The doings and dealings, the thoughts and imaginings of the individual, however strongly they may reflect the characteristics of the national mind, form no part of history. Nevertheless it seems necessary to make some attempt to indicate—only in the most general outlines—the features of individual life in the case of those earlier ages which are, so far as history is concerned, all but lost in oblivion; for it is in this field of research alone that we acquire some idea of the breadth of the gulf which separates our modes of thinking and feeling from those of the civilised nations of antiquity. Tradition, with its confused mass of national names and its dim legends, resembles withered leaves which with difficulty we recognise to have once been green. Instead of threading that dreary maze and attempting to classify those shreds of humanity, the Chones and Oenotrians, the Siculi and the Pelasgi, it will be more to the purpose to inquire how the life of the people in ancient Italy expressed itself, practically, in their jurisprudence and, ideally, in their religion; how they farmed and how they traded; and whence the several nations derived the art of writing and other elements of culture. Scanty as our knowledge in this respect is in reference to the Roman people and still more so in reference to the Sabellians and Etruscans, even the slight and very defective information which is attainable will enable the mind to associate with these names some more or less clear conception of the once living reality. The chief result of such a view (as we may here mention by way of anticipation) may be summed up in saying that fewer traces comparatively of the primitive state of things have been preserved in the case of the Italians, and of the Romans in particular, than in the case of any other Indo-Germanic race. The bow and arrow, the war-chariot, the incapacity of women to hold property, the acquiring of wives by purchase, the primitive form of burial, blood-revenge, the clan-constitution conflicting

with the authority of the community, a fresh natural symbolism
—all these, and numerous phenomena of a kindred character,
must be presumed to have lain at the foundation of civilisation
in Italy as well as elsewhere; but at the epoch when that
civilisation comes clearly into view they have wholly disappeared, and only the comparison of kindred races informs us
that such things once existed. In this respect Italian history
begins at a far later stage of civilisation than *e.g.* the Greek or
the Germanic, and from the first it exhibits a comparatively
modern character.

The laws of most of the Italian stocks are lost in oblivion.
Some information regarding the law of the Latin land alone has
survived in Roman tradition.

All jurisdiction was vested in the community or, in other
words, in the king, who administered justice or " command "
(*ius*) on the " days of utterance " (*dies fasti*) at the " judgment-
platform " (*tribunal*) in the place of public assembly, sitting
on a " chariot-seat " (*sella curulis*);[1] by his side stood his
" messengers " (*lictores*), and before him the person accused or
the " parties " (*rei*). In the case of slaves the right of decision
lay immediately with the master, and in the case of women with
the father, husband, or nearest male relative (p. 57); but slaves
and women were not reckoned as being properly members of
the community. Over sons and grandsons who were *in potestate*
the power of the *pater familias* subsisted concurrently with the
royal jurisdiction; that power, however, was not a jurisdiction
in the proper sense of the term, but simply a consequence of the
father's inherent right of property in his children. We find no
traces of any jurisdiction appertaining to the clans as such, or of
any judicature at all that did not derive its authority from the
king. As regards the right of self-redress and in particular the
avenging of blood, we still find in legends an echo perhaps of the
original principle that a murderer, or any one who should
illegally protect a murderer, might justifiably be slain by the
kinsmen of the person murdered; but these very legends
characterise this principle as objectionable,[2] and from their

---

[1] This " chariot-seat "—no other explanation can well be given con-
sistently with philological rules (comp. *Serv. ad. Aen.* i. 16)—is most simply
explained by supposing that the king alone was entitled to ride in a
chariot within the city (p. 65)—whence originated the privilege subsequently accorded to the chief magistrate on solemn occasions—and that
originally, so long as there was no elevated tribunal, he rode to the comitium in his chariot and gave judgment from the chariot-seat.

[2] The story of the death of king Tatius, as given by Plutarch (*Rom.* 23,
24), viz. that kinsmen of Tatius had killed envoys from Laurentum; that

statements blood-revenge would appear to have been very early suppressed in Rome by the energetic assertion of the authority of the state. In like manner we perceive in the earliest Roman law no trace of that influence which under the oldest Germanic institutions the comrades of the accused and the people present were entitled to exercise over the pronouncing of judgment; nor do we find in the former any evidence of the usage so frequent in the latter, by which the mere will and power to maintain a claim with arms in hand were treated as judicially necessary or at any rate admissible.

Judicial procedure took the form of a public or a private process, according as the king interposed of his own motion or only when appealed to by the injured party. The former course was taken only in cases which involved a breach of the public peace. First of all, therefore, it was applicable in the case of public treason or communion with the public enemy (*proditio*), and in that of violent rebellion against the magistracy (*perduellio*). But the public peace was also broken by the foul murderer (*parricida*), the sodomite, the violator of a maiden's or matron's chastity, the incendiary, the false witness, by those, moreover, who with evil spells conjured away the harvest, or who without due title cut the corn by night in the field entrusted to the protection of the gods and of the people; all of these were therefore dealt with as though they had been guilty of high treason. The king opened and conducted the process, and pronounced sentence after conferring with the senators whom he had called in to advise with him. He was at liberty, however, after he had initiated the process, to commit the further handling and the adjudication of the matter to deputies who were, as a rule, taken from the senate. The commissioners for adjudicating on rebellion (*duoviri perduellionis*) were extraordinary deputies of this sort. The " trackers of murder " (*quaestores parricidii*) appear to have been standing deputies, whose primary duty was to search for and arrest murderers, and who

---

Tatius had refused the complaint of the kinsmen of the slain for redress; that they then put Tatius to death; that Romulus acquitted the murderers of Tatius, on the ground that murder had been expiated by murder; but that in consequence of the penal judgments of the gods that simultaneously fell upon Rome and Laurentum the perpetrators of both murders were in the sequel subjected to righteous punishment—this story looks very like an historical version of the abolition of blood-revenge, just as the introduction of the *provocatio* lies at the foundation of the myth of the Horatii. The versions of the same story that occur elsewhere certainly present considerable variations, but they seem to be confused or dressed up.

therefore acted as a sort of police. Imprisonment while the case was undergoing investigation was the rule; the accused might, however, be released on bail. Torture to compel confession was only applied to slaves. Every one convicted of having broken the public peace expiated his offence with his life. The modes of inflicting capital punishment were various: the false witness, for example, was hurled from the stronghold-rock; the harvest-thief was hanged; the incendiary was burnt. The king could not grant pardon, for that privilege was vested in the community alone; but the king might grant or refuse to the condemned permission to appeal for mercy (*provocatio*). In addition to this the law recognised an intervention of the gods in favour of the condemned criminal. He who had made a genuflection before the priest of Jupiter might not be scourged on the same day; any one under fetters who set foot in his house had to be released from his bonds; and the life of a criminal was spared if on his way to execution he accidentally met one of the sacred virgins of Vesta.

The king inflicted at his discretion fines payable to the state for trespasses against order and for police offences; they consisted in a definite number (hence the name *multa*) of cattle or sheep. It was in his power also to pronounce sentence of scourging.

In all other cases, where the individual alone was injured and not the public peace, the state only interposed upon the appeal of the party injured, who caused his opponent, or in case of need by laying violent hands on him compelled him, to appear personally along with himself before the king. When both parties had appeared and the plaintiff had orally stated his demand, while the defendant had in similar fashion refused to comply with it, the king might either investigate the cause himself or have it disposed of by a deputy acting in his name. The regular form of satisfaction for such an injury was a compromise arranged between the injurer and the injured; the state only interfered supplementarily, when the thief did not satisfy the person from whom he had stolen or the aggressor the party aggrieved by an adequate expiation (*poena*), when any one had his property detained or his just demand unfulfilled.

Whether or under what circumstances during this epoch theft was regarded as expiable, and what in such an event the person injured was entitled to demand from the thief, cannot be ascertained. But the injured party with reason demanded heavier compensation from a thief caught in the very act than from one detected afterwards, since the feeling of exasperation which had to be appeased was more vehement in the case of the former than in that of the latter. If the theft appeared incapable of expiation, or if the thief was not in a position to pay the value demanded by the injured party and approved by the judge, he was assigned by the judge to the person from whom he had stolen as a bondsman.

In cases of damage (*iniuria*) to person or to property, where the injury was not of a very serious description, the aggrieved party was obliged unconditionally to accept compensation; if, on the other hand, any member was lost in consequence of it, the maimed person could demand eye for eye and tooth for tooth.

Since the arable land among the Romans was long cultivated upon the system of joint possession, and was not distributed until a comparatively late age, the idea of property was primarily associated not with immovable estate, but with "estate in slaves and cattle" (*familia pecuniaque*). It was not the right of the stronger that was regarded as the foundation of a title to it; on the contrary, all property was considered as conferred by the community upon the individual burgess for his exclusive possession and use; and therefore it was only the burgesses and such as the community treated in this respect as equal to burgesses that were capable of holding property. All property passed freely from hand to hand. The Roman law made no substantial distinction between movable and immovable estate (from the time that the latter was regarded as private property at all), and recognised no absolute vested interest of children or other relatives in the paternal or family property. Nevertheless it was not in the power of the father arbitrarily to deprive his children of their right of inheritance, because he could neither dissolve the paternal power nor execute a testament except with consent of the whole community, which might be, and certainly under such circumstances often was, refused. In his lifetime no doubt the father might make dispositions disadvantageous to his children; for the law was sparing of personal restrictions on the proprietor and allowed, upon the whole, every grown-up man freely to dispose of his property. The regulation, however, under which he who alienated his hereditary property and deprived his children of it was placed by order of the magistrate under guardianship like a lunatic, was probably as ancient as the period when the arable land was first divided and in consequence private property generally acquired greater importance for the commonwealth. In this way the two antagonistic principles—the unlimited right of the owner to dispose of his own, and the preservation of the family property unbroken—were as far as possible harmonised in the Roman law. Permanent restrictions on property were in no case allowed, with the exception of servitudes such as those indispensable in husbandry. Heritable leases and ground-rents charged upon property could not legally exist. The law as little recognised mortgaging; but the same purpose was served by the immediate delivery of the property in pledge to the creditor as if he were its purchaser, who thereupon gave his word of honour (*fiducia*) that he would not alienate the object pledged until the payment fell due, and would restore it to his debtor when the sum advanced had been repaid.

Contracts concluded between the state and a burgess, particularly the obligation given by those who became sureties for a payment to the state (*praevides, praedes*), were valid without further formality. On the other hand, contracts between private persons under ordinary circumstances founded no claim for legal redress at the hands of the state. The only protection of the creditor was the debtor's word of honour which was held in high esteem after the wont of merchants, and possibly also, in those frequent cases where an oath had been added, the fear of the gods who avenged perjury. The only contracts legally actionable were those of betrothal (the effect of which was that the father, in the event of his failing to give the promised bride, had to furnish satisfaction and compensation), of purchase (*mancipatio*), and of loan (*nexum*). A purchase was held to be legally concluded when the seller delivered the article purchased into the hand of the buyer (*mancipare*), and the buyer at the same time paid to the seller the stipulated price in presence of witnesses. This was done, after copper superseded sheep and cattle as the regular standard of value, by weighing out the stipulated quantity of copper in a balance adjusted by a neutral person.[1] These conditions having been complied with, the

[1] The *mancipatio* in its fully developed form must have been more recent than the Servian reform, as the number of the witnesses proportioned to that of the classes, and the selection of mancipable objects which had for its aim the fixing of agricultural property, serve to show; even tradition must have assumed that such was the case, for it makes Servius the inventor of the balance. But in its origin the *mancipatio* must be far more ancient; for it primarily applies only to objects which are acquired by grasping with the hand, and must therefore in its earliest form have belonged to the epoch when property mainly consisted in slaves and cattle (*familia pecuniaque*). The number of the witnesses, and the enumeration

seller had to answer for his being the owner, and in addition seller and purchaser had to fulfil every stipulation specially agreed on; the party failing to do so made reparation to the other, just as if he had robbed him of the article in question. But a purchase only found an action in the event of its being a transaction for ready money: a purchase on credit neither gave nor took away the right of property, and constituted no ground of action. A loan was negotiated in a similar way; the creditor weighed over to the debtor in presence of witnesses the stipulated quantity of copper under the obligation (*nexum*) of repayment. In addition to the capital the debtor had to pay interest, which under ordinary circumstances probably amounted to ten per cent. per annum.[1] The repayment of the loan took place, when the time came, with similar forms.

If a debtor to the state did not fulfil his obligations, he was without further ceremony sold with all that he had; the simple demand on the part of the state was sufficient to establish the debt. If on the other hand a private person informed the king of any violation of his property (*vindiciae*), or if repayment of the loan received did not duly take place, the procedure depended on whether the facts relating to the cause had to be established by proof or were already clear. The latter cannot well be conceived in the case of actions as to property, but in actions as to loans the ground of action could be easily established according to the current rules of law by means of witnesses. The establishment of the facts assumed the form of a wager, in which each party made a deposit (*sacramentum*) against the contingency of his being worsted; in important causes when the value involved was greater than ten oxen, a deposit of five oxen, in causes of less amount, a deposit of five sheep. The judge then decided who had gained the wager, whereupon the deposit of the losing party fell to the priests for behoof of the public sacrifices. The party who lost the wager and allowed thirty days to elapse without giving due satisfaction to his

of those objects which had to be acquired by *mancipatio*, fall in this view to be ranked as Servian innovations; the *mancipatio* itself, and consequently the use also of the balance and of copper, are more ancient. Beyond doubt *mancipatio* was originally the universal form of purchase, and was the practice followed with all articles even after the Servian reform; it was only a misunderstanding of later ages which put upon the rule, that certain articles must be transferred by *mancipatio*, the construction that these articles alone could be so transferred.

[1] Viz. for the year of ten months one twelfth part of the capital (*uncia*), which amounts to 8½ per cent. for the year of ten, and 10 per cent. for the year of twelve, months.

opponent, and the party whose obligation to pay was established from the first—consequently, as a rule, the debtor who had got a loan and had no witnesses to attest repayment—became liable to proceedings in execution "by laying on of hands" (*manus iniectio*); the plaintiff seized him wherever he found him, and brought him to the bar of the judge simply to demand the acknowledged debt. The party seized was not allowed to defend himself; a third party might indeed intercede for him and represent this act of violence as unwarranted (*vindex*), in which case the proceedings were stayed; but such an intercession rendered the intercessor personally responsible, for which reason, in the case of freeholders, other freeholders alone could act as intercessors. If neither satisfaction nor intercession took place, the king assigned the party seized in execution to his creditor, so that he could lead him away and keep him like a slave. After the expiry of sixty days during which the debtor had been three times exposed in the market-place and proclamation had been made whether any one would have compassion on him, if these steps were without effect, his creditors had a right to put him to death and to divide his carcase, or to sell him with his children and his effects into foreign slavery, or to keep him at home in a slave's stead; he could not by the Roman law, so long as he remained within the bounds of the Roman community, become absolutely a slave (p. 104). Thus the Roman community protected every man's estate with unrelenting rigour as well from the thief and the injurer, as from the unauthorised possessor and the insolvent debtor.

Protection was in like manner provided for the estate of persons not capable of bearing arms and therefore not capable of protecting their own property, such as minors and lunatics, and above all for that of women; in these cases the nearest heirs were called to undertake the guardianship.

After a man's death his property fell to the nearest heirs: in the division all who were equal in proximity of relationship—women included—shared alike, and the widow along with her children was admitted to her proportional share. A dispensation from the legal order of succession could only be granted by the assembly of the people; previous to which the consent of the priests had to be obtained on account of the religious obligations attaching to property. Such dispensations appear nevertheless to have become at an early period very frequent. In the event of a dispensation not being procured, the want of it might be in some measure remedied by means of the completely free control which every one had over his property during his lifetime. His whole property was transferred to a friend, who distributed it after death according to the wishes of the deceased.

Manumission was unknown to the law of very early times. The owner might indeed refrain from exercising his proprietary rights; but this did not cancel the existing impossibility of master and slave contracting mutual obligations; still less did it enable the slave to acquire, in relation to the community, the rights of a guest or of a burgess. Accordingly manumission must have been at first simply *de facto*, not *de jure;* and the master cannot have been debarred from the possibility of again at pleasure treating the freedman as a slave. But there was a departure from this principle in cases where the master came under obligation not merely towards the slave, but towards the community, to leave him in possession of freedom. There was no special legal form, however, for thus binding the master— the best proof that there was at first no such thing as a manumission; but those methods which the law otherwise presented —testament, action, or census—were employed for this object. If the master had either declared his slave free when executing his last will in the assembly of the people, or had allowed his slave to claim freedom in his own presence before a judge or to get his name inscribed in the valuation-roll, the freedman was regarded not indeed as a burgess, but as free in relation to his former master and his heirs, and was accordingly looked upon at first as a client, and in later times as a plebeian (p. 86).

The emancipation of a son encountered greater difficulties than that of a slave; for while the relation of master to slave was accidental and therefore capable of being dissolved at will, the father could never cease to be father. Accordingly in later times the son was obliged, in order to get free from the father, first to enter into slavery and then to be set free out of this latter state; but in the period now before us no emancipation of sons can have as yet existed.

Such were the laws under which burgesses and clients lived in Rome. Between these two classes, so far as we can see, there subsisted from the beginning the fullest equality of private rights. The foreigner on the other hand, if he had not submitted to a Roman patron and thus lived as a client, was beyond the pale of the law both in person and in property. Whatever the Roman burgess took from him was as rightfully acquired as was the shell-fish, belonging to nobody, which was picked up by the sea-shore; but in the case of ground lying beyond the

Roman bounds, while the Roman burgess might take practical possession, he could not be regarded as in a legal sense its proprietor; for the individual burgess was not entitled to advance the bounds of the community. The case was different in war: whatever the soldier who was fighting in the ranks of the levy gained, whether movable or immovable property, fell not to him, but to the state, and accordingly here too it depended upon the state whether it would advance or contract its bounds.

Exceptions from these general rules were created by special state-treaties, which secured certain rights to the members of foreign communities within the Roman state. In particular, the perpetual league between Rome and Latium declared all contracts between Romans and Latins to be valid in law, and at the same time instituted in their case a speedy civil process before sworn " recoverers " (*reciperatores*). As, contrary to Roman usage, which in other instances committed the decision to a single judge, these always sat several in number and that number uneven, they are probably to be regarded as a court for the cognisance of commercial dealings, composed of arbiters from both nations and an umpire. They sat in judgment at the place where the contract was entered into, and were obliged to have the process terminated at latest in ten days. The forms, under which the dealings between Romans and Latins were conducted, were of course the general forms which regulated the mutual dealings of patricians and plebeians; for the *mancipatio* and the *nexum* were originally no mere formal acts, but the significant embodiment of legal ideas which held a sway at least as extensive as the range of the Latin language.

Dealings with countries strictly foreign were carried on in a different fashion and by means of other forms. In very early times treaties as to commerce and legal redress must have been entered into with the Caerites and other friendly peoples, and must have formed the basis of the international private law (*ius gentium*), which gradually became developed in Rome alongside of the law of the land. An indication of the formation of such a system is found in the remarkable *mutuum*, " exchange " (from *mutare* like *dividuus*)—a form of loan, which was not based like the *nexum* upon a binding declaration of the debtor expressly emitted before witnesses, but upon the mere transit of the money from one hand to another, and which as evidently originated in dealings with foreigners as the *nexum* in business dealings at home. It is accordingly a significant fact that the word reappears in Sicilian Greek as μοῖτον; and with this is to

be connected the reappearance of the Latin *carcer* in the Sicilian
κάρκαρον. Since it is philologically certain that both words
were originally Latin, their occurrence in the local dialect of
Sicily becomes an important testimony to the frequency of the
dealings of Latin traders in the island, which led to their borrowing money there and becoming liable to that imprisonment for
debt, which was everywhere in the earlier systems of law the
consequence of the non-repayment of a loan. Conversely the
name of the Syracusan prison, " stone-quarries " or λατομίαι,
was transferred at an early period to the enlarged Roman state
prison, the *lautumiae*.

We have derived our outline of these institutions mainly
from the earliest record of the Roman common law prepared
about half a century after the abolition of the monarchy; and
their existence in the regal period, while doubtful perhaps as
to particular points of detail, cannot be doubted in the main.
Surveying them as a whole, we recognise the law of a far-
advanced agricultural and mercantile city, marked alike by its
liberality and its consistency. In its case the conventional
language of symbols, such as *e.g.* the Germanic laws exhibit, has
already quite disappeared. There is no doubt that such a
symbolic language must have existed at one time among the
Italians. Remarkable instances of it are to be found in the
form of searching a house, wherein the searcher must, according
to the Roman as well as the Germanic custom, appear without
upper garment, merely in his shirt; and especially in the primitive Latin formula for declaring war, in which we meet with
at least two symbols occurring also among the Celts and the
Germans—the " pure herb " (*herba pura*, Franconian *chrene-
chruda*) as a symbol of the native soil, and the singed bloody staff
as a sign of commencing war. But with a few exceptions in
which reasons of religion protected the ancient usages—to which
class the *confarreatio* as well as the declaration of war by the
college of Fetiales belonged—the Roman law, as we know it,
uniformly and on principle rejects the symbol, and requires in all
cases neither more nor less than the full and pure expression of
will. The delivery of an article, the summons to bear witness,
the conclusion of marriage, were complete as soon as the parties
had in an intelligible manner declared their purpose; it was
usual, indeed, to deliver the article into the hand of the new
owner, to pull the person summoned as a witness by the ear, to
veil the bride's head and to lead her in solemn procession to her
husband's house; but all these primitive practices were already,

nder the oldest national law of the Romans, customs legally
vorthless. In a way entirely analogous to the setting aside of
llegory and along with it of personification in religion, every
ort of symbolism was on principle expelled from their law. In
ke manner that earliest state of things presented to us by the
Iellenic as well as the Germanic institutions, wherein the power
f the community still contends with the authority of the smaller
.ssociations of clans or cantons that are merged in it, is in Roman
aw wholly superseded; there is no alliance for the vindication
f rights within the state, to supplement the state's imperfect
.id by mutual offence and defence; nor is there any serious
race of vengeance for bloodshed, or of the family property
estricting the individual power of disposal. Such institutions
nust probably at one time have existed among the Italians;
races of them may perhaps be found in particular institutions
f ritual, *e.g.* in the expiatory goat, which the involuntary
iomicide was obliged to give to the nearest of kin to the slain;
iut even at the earliest period of Rome which we can conceive
his stage had long been passed. The clan and the family were
iot annihilated in the Roman community; but the theoretical
is well as the practical omnipotence of the state in its own
.phere was no more limited by them than by the freedom which
he state granted and guaranteed to the burgess. The ultimate
oundation of law was in all cases the state; freedom was simply
inother expression for the right of citizenship in its widest sense;
ill property was based on express or tacit transference by the
:ommunity to the individual; a contract was valid only so far
is the community by its representatives attested it, a testament
inly so far as the community confirmed it. The provinces of
iublic and private law were definitely and clearly discriminated:
he former having reference to crimes against the state, which
mmediately called for the judgment of the state and always
nvolved capital punishment; the latter having reference to
iffences against a fellow-burgess or a guest, which were mainly
lisposed of in the way of compromise by expiation or satisfaction
nade to the party injured, and were never punished with the
orfeit of life, but, at most, with the loss of freedom. The
greatest liberality in the permission of commerce and the most
rigorous procedure in execution went hand in hand; just as in
:ommercial states at the present day the universal right to draw
iills of exchange appears in conjunction with a strict procedure
n regard to them. The burgess and the client stood in their
lealings on a footing of entire equality; state-treaties conceded

a comprehensive equality of rights also to the guest; women were placed completely on a level in point of legal capacity with men, although restricted in administering their property; the boy had scarcely grown up when he received at once the most comprehensive powers in the disposal of his estate, and every one who could dispose at all was as sovereign in his own sphere as was the state in public affairs. A feature eminently characteristic was the system of credit. There did not exist any credit on landed security, but instead of a debt on mortgage the step which constitutes at present the final stage in mortgage-procedure—the delivery of the property from the debtor to the creditor—took place at once. On the other hand personal credit was guaranteed in the most summary, not to say extravagant, fashion; for the law entitled the creditor to treat his insolvent debtor like a thief, and granted to him in sober legislative earnest what Shylock, half in jest, stipulated for from his mortal enemy, guarding indeed by special clauses the point as to the cutting off too much more carefully than did the Jew. The law could not have more clearly expressed its design, which was to establish at once an independent agriculture free of debt and a mercantile credit, and to suppress with stringent energy all merely nominal ownership and all breaches of fidelity. If we further take into consideration the right of settlement recognised at an early date as belonging to all the Latins (p. 105), and the validity which was likewise early pronounced to belong to civil marriage (p. 89), we shall perceive that this state, which made the highest demands on its burgesses and carried the idea of subordinating the individual to the interest of the whole further than any state before or since has done, only did and only could do so by itself removing the barriers to intercourse and unshackling liberty quite as much as it subjected it to restriction. In permission or in prohibition the law was always absolute. As the foreigner who had none to intercede for him was like the hunted deer, so the guest was on a footing of equality with the burgess. A contract did not ordinarily furnish a ground of action, but where the right of the creditor was acknowledged, it was so all-powerful that there was no deliverance for the poor debtor, and no humane or equitable consideration was shown towards him. It seemed as if the law found a pleasure in presenting on all sides its sharpest spikes, in drawing the most extreme consequences, in forcibly obtruding on the bluntest understanding the tyrannic nature of the idea of right. The poetical form and the genial symbolism, which so pleasingly

prevail in the Germanic legal ordinances, were foreign to the
Roman; in his law all was clear and precise; no symbol was
employed, no institution was superfluous. It was not cruel;
everything necessary was performed without tedious ceremony,
even the punishment of death; that a free man could not be
tortured was a primitive maxim of Roman law, to obtain which
other peoples have had to struggle for thousands of years. Yet
this law was frightful in its inexorable severity, which we cannot
suppose to have been very greatly mitigated by humanity in
practice, for it was really the law of the people; more terrible
than Venetian *piombi* and chambers of torture was that series
of living entombments which the poor man saw yawning before
him in the debtors' towers of the rich. But the greatness of
Rome was involved in, and was based upon, the fact that the
Roman people ordained for itself and endured a system of law,
in which the eternal principles of freedom and of subordination,
of property and of legal redress, reigned and still at the present
day reign unadulterated and unmodified.

CHAPTER XII

RELIGION

THE Roman world of gods, as we have already indicated (p. 27) was a higher counterpart, an ideal reflection, of the earthly Rome, in which the little and the great were alike reproduced with painstaking exactness. The state and the clan, the individual phenomena of nature as well as the individual operations of mind, every man, every place and object, every act even falling within the sphere of Roman law, reappeared in the Roman world of gods; and, as earthly things come and go in perpetual flux, the circle of the gods underwent a corresponding fluctuation. The tutelary spirit, which presided over the individual act, lasted no longer than that act itself: the tutelary spirit of the individual man lived and died with the man; and eternal duration belonged to divinities of this sort only in so far as similar acts and similarly constituted men and therefore spirits of a similar kind were ever coming into existence afresh. As the Roman gods ruled over the Roman community, so every foreign community was presided over by its own gods; but strict as was the distinction between the burgess and non-burgess, between the Roman and the foreign god, both foreign men and foreign divinities might be admitted by resolution of the community to the freedom of Rome, and when the citizens of a conquered city were transported to Rome, the gods of that city were also invited to take up their new abode there.

We obtain information regarding the original cycle of the gods as it stood in Rome previous to any contact with the Greeks from the list of the public and duly named festival-days (*feriae publicae*) of the Roman community, which is preserved in its calendar and is beyond all question the oldest document which has reached us from Roman antiquity. The first place in it is occupied by the gods Jupiter and Mars along with the duplicate of the latter, Quirinus. All the days of full moon (*idus*) are sacred to Jupiter, besides all the wine-festivals and various other days to be mentioned afterwards; the 21st May (*agonalia*) is dedicated to his counterpart, the "bad Jovis" (*Vediovis*).

To Mars belongs the new-year of the 1st March, and generally the great warrior-festival in this month which derived its very name from the god; this festival, introduced by the horse-racing (*equirria*) on the 27th February, had during March its principal solemnities on the days of the shield-forger (*equirria* or *Mamuralia*, March 14), of the armed dance at the Comitium (*quinquatrus*, March 19), and of the consecration of trumpets (*tubilustrium*, March 23). As, when a war was to be waged, it began with this festival, so after the close of the campaign in autumn there followed a further festival of Mars, that of the consecration of arms (*armilustrium*, October 19). Lastly, to the second Mars, Quirinus, the 17th February was appropriated (*Quirinalia*). Among the other festivals those which related to the culture of corn and wine hold the first place, while the pastoral feasts play but a subordinate part. To this class belongs especially the great series of spring-festivals in April, in the course of which sacrifices were offered on the 15th to Tellus, the nourishing earth (*fordicidia*, sacrifice of the pregnant cow), on the 19th to Ceres, the goddess of germination and growth (*Cerialia*), on the 21st to Pales, the fecundating goddess of the flocks (*Palilia*), on the 23rd to Jupiter, as the protector of the vines and of the vats of the previous year's vintage which were first opened on this day (*Vinalia*), and on the 25th to the bad enemy of the crops, rust (*Robigus : Robigalia*). So after the completion of the work of the fields and the fortunate ingathering of their produce twin festivals were celebrated in honour of the god and goddess of inbringing and harvest, Consus (from *condere*) and Ops; the first immediately after the completion of cutting (August 21, *Consualia*; August 25, *Opiconsiva*); and the second in the middle of winter, when the blessings of the granary are especially manifest (December 15, *Consualia ;* December 19, *Opalia*); between these two latter days the thoughtful consideration of the old arrangers of the festivals inserted that of seed-sowing (*Saturnalia* from *Saëturnus* or *Saturnus*, December 17). In like manner the festival of must or of healing (*meditrinalia*, October 11), so called because a healing virtue was attributed to the fresh must, was dedicated to Jovis as the wine-god after the completion of the vintage; the original reference of the third wine-feast (*Vinalia*, August 19) is not clear. To these festivals were added at the close of the year the wolf-festival (*Lupercalia*, February 17) of the shepherds in honour of the good god, Faunus, and the boundary-stone festival (*Terminalia*, February 23) of the husbandmen, as also the summer grove-festival of two days (*Lucaria*, July 19, 21) which may have referred to the forest-gods (*Silvani*), the fountain festival (*Fontinalia*, October 13), and the festival of the shortest day, which brings in the new sun (*An-geronalia, Divalia*, December 21).

Of not less importance—as was to be expected in the case of the port of Latium—were the mariner-festivals of the divinities of the sea (*Neptunalia*, July 23), of the harbour (*Portunalia*, August 17), and of the Tiber stream (*Volturnalia*, August 27).

Handicraft and art, on the other hand, are represented in this cycle of the gods only by the god of fire and of smith's work, Volcanus, to whom besides the day named after him (*Volcanalia*, August 23) the second festival of the consecration of trumpets was dedicated (*tubilustrium*, May 23), and perhaps also by the festival of Carmentis (*Carmentalia*, January 11, 15), who probably was adored originally as the goddess of spells and of song and only inferentially as protectress of births.

Domestic and family life in general were represented by the festival of the goddess of the house and of the spirits of the storechamber, Vesta and the Penates (*Vestalia*, June 9); the festival of the goddess of birth [1] (*Matralia*, June 11); the festival of the bearing of children, dedicated to Liber and Libera (*Liberalia*, March 17); the festival of departed spirits (*Feralia*, February 21), and the three days' ghost-celebration (*Lemuria*, May 9, 11, 13); while those having reference to civil relations were the two—otherwise to us somewhat obscure— festivals of the king's flight (*Regifugium*, February 24) and of the people's flight (*Poplifugia*, July 5), of which at least the last day was devoted to Jupiter, and the festival of the Seven Mounts (*Agonia* or *Septimontium*, December 11). A special day (*agonia*, January 9) was also consecrated to Janus, the god of beginning. The real nature of some other days—that of Furrina (July 25), and that of the Larentalia devoted to Jupiter and Acca Larentia, perhaps a feast of the Lares (December 23) —is no longer known.

This table is complete for the immovable public festivals; and—although by the side of these standing festal days there

---

[1] This was, to all appearance, the original nature of the "morning-mother" or *Mater matuta* ; in connection with which we may recall the circumstance that, as the names *Lucius* and especially *Manius* show, the morning hour was reckoned as lucky for birth. *Mater matuta* probably became a goddess of sea and harbour only at a later epoch under the influence of the myth of Leucothea; the fact that the goddess was chiefly worshipped by women tells against the view that she was originally a harbour-goddess.

certainly occurred from the earliest times changeable and occasional festivals—this document, in what it says as well as in what it omits, opens up to us an insight into a primitive age otherwise almost wholly unknown. The union of the Old Roman community and the Hill-Romans had indeed already taken place when this table of festivals was formed, for we find in it Quirinus alongside of Mars; but when this list was drawn up the Capitoline temple was not yet in existence, for Juno and Minerva are absent; nor was the temple of Diana erected on the Aventine; nor was any notion of worship borrowed from the Greeks.

The central object not only of Roman but of Italian worship generally in that epoch when the Italian stock still dwelt by itself in the peninsula was, according to all indications, the god Maurs or Mars, the killing god,[1] pre-eminently regarded as the divine champion of the burgesses, hurling the spear, protecting the flock, and overthrowing the foe. Each community of course had its own Mars, and deemed him to be the strongest and holiest of all; and accordingly every " ver sacrum " setting out to found a new community marched under the protection of its own Mars. To Mars was dedicated the first month not only in the Roman calendar of the months, which in no other instance takes notice of the gods, but also probably in all the other Latin and Sabellian calendars: among the Roman proper names, which in like manner contain no allusion to any other god, Marcus, Mamercus, and Mamurius appear in prevailing use from very early times; with Mars and his sacred woodpecker was connected the oldest Italian prophecy; the wolf, the animal sacred to Mars, was the badge of the Roman burgesses, and such sacred national legends as the Roman imagination was able to produce referred exclusively to the god Mars and to his duplicate Quirinus. In the list of festivals certainly father Diovis—a purer and more civil than military reflection of the character of the Roman community—occupies a larger space than Mars, just as the priest of Jupiter has precedence over the two priests of the god of war; but the latter still plays a very prominent part in the list, and it is even quite likely that, when this arrangement of festivals was established, Jovis stood by the side of Mars like Ahuramazda by the side of Mithra, and that

---

[1] From *Maurs*, which is the oldest form handed down by tradition, there have been developed by different treatment of the u Mars, Mavors, Mors ; the transition to ŏ (like *Paula, Pola*, and the like) appears also in the double form *Mar-Mor* (comp. *Ma-mŭrius*) alongside of *Mar-Mar* and *Ma-Mers.*

the worship of the warlike Roman community still really centred at this time in the martial god of death and his March festival, while it was not the " care-destroyer " afterwards introduced by the Greeks, but father Jovis himself, who was regarded as the god of the heart-gladdening wine.

It is no part of our present task to consider the Roman deities in detail; but it is important, even in an historical point of view, to call attention to the peculiar narrowness of conception and at the same time the deeply-rooted earnestness that marked the Roman faith. Abstraction and personification lay at the root of the Roman as well as of the Hellenic mythology: the Hellenic as well as the Roman god was originally suggested by some natural phenomenon or some mental conception, and to the Roman just as to the Greek every divinity appeared a person. This is evident from their apprehending the individual gods as male or female; from their style of appeal to an unknown deity,—" Be thou god or goddess, man or woman; " and from the deeply cherished belief that the name of the proper tutelary spirit of the community ought to remain for ever unpronounced, lest an enemy should come to learn it and calling the god by his name should entice him beyond the bounds. A remnant of this strongly sensuous view clung to Mars in particular, the oldest and most national form of divinity in Italy. But while abstraction, which lies at the foundation of every religion, elsewhere endeavoured to rise to wider and more enlarged conceptions and to penetrate ever more deeply into the essence of things, the forms of the Roman faith remained at, or sank to, a singularly low level of conception and of insight. While in the case of the Greek every important notion speedily expanded into a group of forms and gathered around it a circle of legends and ideas, in the case of the Roman the fundamental thought remained stationary in its original naked rigidity. The religion of Rome had nothing of its own presenting even a remote resemblance to the religion of Apollo investing earthly morality with a halo of glory, to the divine intoxication of Dionysus, or to the Chthonian and mystical worships with their profound and hidden meanings. It had indeed its " bad god " (*Ve-diovis*), its apparitions and ghosts (*lemures*), and its deities of foul air, of fever, of diseases, perhaps even of theft (*laverna*); but it was unable to excite that mysterious awe after which the human heart has always a longing, or thoroughly to incorporate the incomprehensible and even the malignant elements in nature and in man, which must not be wanting in religion if it would reflect man as a whole. In the religion of Rome there was hardly anything secret except the names of the gods of the city, the Penates; the real character, moreover, even of these gods was manifest to every one.

The national Roman theology sought on all hands to form distinct conceptions of important phenomena and qualities, to express them in its terminology, and to classify them systematically—in the first instance according to that division of persons and things which also formed the basis of private law—that it might thus be able in due fashion to invoke the gods individually or by classes, and to point out (*indigitare*) to the multitude the modes of appropriate invocation. Of such notions, the products of outward abstraction—of the homeliest simplicity, sometimes venerable, sometimes ridiculous—Roman theology was in substance made up. Conceptions such as sowing (*saeturnus*) and field-labour (*ops*), ground (*tellus*) and boundary-stone (*terminus*), were among the oldest and most sacred of Roman divinities. Perhaps the most peculiar of all the forms of deity in Rome, and probably the only one for whose worship there was devised an effigy peculiarly Italian, was the double-headed Ianus; and yet it was simply suggestive of the idea so characteristic of the scrupulous spirit of Roman religion, that at the commencement of every act the "spirit of opening" should first be invoked, while it above all betokened the deep conviction that it was as indispensable to combine the Roman gods in sets as it was necessary that the more personal gods of the Hellenes should stand singly and apart.[1] Of all the worships of Rome that which perhaps had the deepest hold was the worship of the tutelary spirits that presided in and over the household and the storechamber: these were in public worship Vesta and the Penates, in family worship the gods of forest and field, the Silvani, and especially the gods of the household in its strict sense, the Lases or Lares, to whom their share of the family meal was regularly assigned, and before whom it was,

[1] The facts, that gates and doors and the morning (*ianus matutinus*) were sacred to Ianus, and that he was always invoked before any other god and was even represented in the series of coins before Jupiter and the other gods, indicate unmistakably that he was the abstraction of opening and beginning. The double-head looking both ways was connected with the gate that opened both ways. To make him god of the sun and of the year is the less justifiable, because the month that bears his name was originally the eleventh, not the first; that month seems rather to have derived its name from the circumstance, that at this season after the rest of the middle of winter the cycle of the labours of the field began afresh. It was, however, a matter of course that the opening of the year should also be included in the sphere of Ianus, especially after Ianuarius came to be placed at its head.

even in the time of Cato the Elder, the first duty of the father of the household on returning home to perform his devotions. In the ranking of the gods, however, these spirits of the house and of the field occupied the lowest rather than the highest place; it was—and it could not be otherwise with a religion which renounced all attempts to idealise—not the broadest and most general, but the simplest and most individual abstraction, in which the pious heart found most nourishment.

This indifference to ideal elements in the Roman religion was accompanied by a practical and utilitarian tendency, as is clearly enough apparent in the table of festivals which has been already explained. Increase of substance and of prosperity by husbandry and the rearing of flocks and herds, by seafaring and commerce—this was what the Roman desired from his gods; and it very well accords with this view, that the god of good faith (*deus fidius*), the goddess of chance and good luck (*fors fortuna*), and the god of traffic (*mercurius*), originating out of their daily dealings, although not occurring in that ancient table of festivals, appear very early as adored far and near by the Romans. Strict frugality and mercantile speculation were rooted in the Roman character too deeply not to find their thorough reflection in its divine counterpart.

Respecting the world of spirits little can be said. The departed souls of mortal men, the " good " (*manes*), continued to exist as shades haunting the spot where the body reposed (*dii inferi*), and received meat and drink from the survivors. But they dwelt in the depths beneath, and there was no bridge that led from the lower world either to men ruling on earth or upward to the gods above. The hero-worship of the Greeks was wholly foreign to the Romans, and the late origin and poor invention of the legend as to the foundation of Rome are shown by the thoroughly unRoman transformation of king Romulus into the God Quirinus. Numa, the oldest and most venerable name in Roman tradition, never received the honours of a god in Rome as Theseus did in Athens.

The most ancient priesthoods in the community bore reference to Mars; especially the priest of the god of the community, nominated for life, " the kindler of Mars " (*flamen Martialis*) as he was designated from presenting burnt-offerings, and the twelve " leapers " (*salii*), a band of young men who in March performed the war-dance in honour of Mars and accompanied it by song. We have already explained (p. 84) how the amalgamation of the Hill-community with that of the Palatine gave rise to the duplication of the Roman Mars, and thereby to the introduction of a second priest of Mars—the *flamen Quirinalis*—and a second guild of dancers—the *salii collini*.

To these were added other public worships (some of which probably had an origin far earlier than that of Rome), for which either single priests were appointed—as those of Carmentis, of Volcanus, of the god of the harbour and the river—or the celebration of which was committed to particular colleges or clans in name of the people. Such a college was probably that of the twelve " field-brethren " (*fratres arvales*) who invoked the creative goddess (*dea dia*) in May to bless the growth of the seed; although it is very doubtful whether they enjoyed at this period the peculiar consideration which we find subsequently accorded to them in the time of the empire. These were accompanied by the Titian brotherhood, which had to preserve and to attend to the distinctive *cultus* of the Roman Tities (p. 43), and by the thirty " curial kindlers " (*flamines curiales*), instituted for the hearths of the thirty curies. The " wolf festival " (*lupercalia*) already mentioned was celebrated for the protection of the flocks and herds in honour of the " favourable god " (*faunus*), by the Quinctian clan and the Fabii who were associated with them after the admission of the Hill-Romans, in the month of February—a genuine shepherds' carnival, in which the " wolves " (*luperci*) jumped about naked with a girdle of goatskin, and whipped the people with thongs. In like manner the community may be conceived as represented and participating in the case of other gentile worships.

To this earliest worship of the Roman community new rites were gradually added. The most important of these worships had reference to the city as newly united and virtually founded afresh by the construction of the great wall and stronghold. In it the highest and best Iovis of the Capitol—the genius of the Roman people—was placed at the head of all the Roman divinities, and his " kindler " thenceforth appointed, the *flamen Dialis*, formed in conjunction with the two priests of Mars the sacred triad of high-priests. Contemporaneously began the *cultus* of the new single city-hearth—Vesta—and the kindred *cultus* of the Penates of the community (p. 111). Six chaste virgins, daughters as it were of the household of the Roman people, attended to that pious service, and had to maintain the wholesome fire of the common hearth always blazing as an example (p. 34) and an omen to the burgesses. This worship, half-domestic, half-public, was the most sacred of all in Rome, and it accordingly was the latest of all the heathen worships there to give way before the ban of Christianity. The Aventine, moreover, was assigned to Diana as the representative of the Latin confederacy (p. 106), but for that very reason no special Roman priesthood was appointed for her; and the community gradually became accustomed to render definite homage to numerous other deified abstractions by means of general festivals or by representative priesthoods specially destined for their service; in particular instances—such as those of the goddess of flowers (*Flora*) and of fruits (*Pomona*)—it appointed also special *flamines*, so that the number of these was at length fifteen. But among them they carefully distinguished those three great kindlers (*flamines maiores*), who down to the latest times could only be taken from the ranks of the old burgesses, just as the old incorporations of the Palatine and Quirinal *Salii* always asserted precedence over all the other colleges of priests. Thus the necessary and stated observances due to the gods of the community were entrusted once for all by the state to fixed corporations or regular ministers; and the expense of sacrifices, which was probably not inconsiderable, was covered partly by the assignation of certain lands to particular temples, partly by the fines (pp. 73, 154).

It cannot be doubted that the public worship of the other Latin, and probably also of the Sabellian, communities was essentially similar in character. At any rate it can be shown that the Flamines, Salii, Luperci, and Vestales were institutions not special to Rome, but general among the Latins, and at least the first three colleges appear to have been formed in the kindred communities independently of the Roman model.

Lastly, as the state made arrangements in reference to its own gods, so each burgess might make similar arrangements in his individual sphere, and might not only present sacrifices, but might also consecrate set places and ministers, to his own divinities.

There was thus enough of priesthood and of priests in Rome. Those, however, who had business with a god resorted to the god, and not to the priest. Every suppliant and inquirer addressed himself directly to the divinity—the community of course by the king as its mouthpiece, just as the *curia* by the *curio* and the *equites* by their colonels; no intervention of a priest was allowed to conceal or to obscure this original and simple relation. But it was no easy matter to hold converse with a god. The god had his own way of speaking, which was intelligible only to those acquainted with it; but one who did rightly understand it knew not only how to ascertain, but also how to manage, the will of the god, and even in case of need to overreach or to constrain him. It was natural, therefore, that the worshipper of the god should regularly consult such men of skill and listen to their advice; and thence arose the corporations or colleges of men specially skilled in religious lore, a thoroughly national Italian institution, which had a far more important influence on political development than the individual priest or priesthoods. These colleges have been often, but erroneously, confounded with the priesthoods. The priesthoods were charged with the worship of a specific divinity; the skilled colleges, on the other hand, were charged with the preservation of traditional rules regarding those more general religious observances, the proper fulfilment of which implied a certain amount of information and rendered it necessary that the state in its own interest should provide for the faithful transmission of that information. These close corporations supplying their own vacancies, of course from the ranks of the burgesses, became in this way the depositaries of skilled arts and sciences.

Under the Roman constitution and that of the Latin communities in general there were originally but two such colleges; that of the augurs and that of the pontifices.[1] The six augurs were skilled in interpreting the language of the gods from the flight of birds; an art which was prosecuted with great earnestness and reduced to a quasi-scientific system. The five "bridge-builders" (*pontifices*) derived their name from their function, as

---

[1] The clearest evidence of this is the fact, that in the communities organised on the Latin scheme augurs and pontifices occur everywhere (*e.g.* Cic. *de Lege Agr.* ii. 35, 96, and numerous inscriptions), but the other colleges do not. The former, therefore, stand on the same footing with the constitution of ten curies and the Flamines, Salii, and Luperci, as very ancient heirlooms of the Latin stock; whereas the Duoviri *sacris faciundis*, the Fetiales, and other colleges, like the thirty curies and the Servian tribes and centuries, originated in, and remained therefore confined to, Rome. But in the case of the second college—the pontifices—the influence of Rome probably led to the introduction of that name into the general Latin scheme instead of some earlier, perhaps more variable, designation; or—an hypothesis which philologically has much in its favour—*pons* originally signified not "bridge," but "way" generally, and *pontifex* therefore meant "constructor of ways."

The statements regarding the original number of the augurs in particular vary. The view that it was necessary for the number to be an odd one is refuted by Cic. (*de Lege Agr.* ii. 35, 96); and Livy (x. 6) does not say so, but only states that the number of Roman augurs had to be divisible by three, and so must have had an odd number as its basis. According to Livy (*l.c.*) the number was six down to the Ogulnian law, and the same is virtually affirmed by Cicero (*de Rep.* ii. 9, 14) when he represents Romulus as instituting four, and Numa two, augural stalls.

sacred as it was politically important, of conducting the building and demolition of the bridge over the Tiber. They were the Roman engineers, who understood the mystery of measures and numbers; whence there devolved upon them also the duties of managing the calendar of the state, of proclaiming to the people the time of new and full moon and the days of festivals, and of seeing that every religious and every judicial act took place on the right day. As they had thus an especial supervision of all religious observances, it was to them in case of need —on occasion of marriage, testament, or *adrogatio*—that the preliminary question was addressed, whether the matter proposed did not in any respect offend against divine law; and it was they who fixed and promulgated the general exoteric precepts of ritual, which were known under the name of the " royal laws." Thus they acquired (although not probably to the full extent till after the abolition of the monarchy) the general oversight of Roman worship and of whatever was connected with it —and what was there that was not so connected? They themselves described the sum of their knowledge as " the science of things divine and human." In fact the rudiments of spiritual and temporal jurisprudence as well as of historical composition proceeded from this college. For the writing of history was associated with the calendar and the book of annals; and, as from the organisation of the Roman courts of law no tradition could originate in these courts themselves, it was necessary that the knowledge of legal principles and procedure should be traditionally preserved in the college of the pontifices, which alone was competent to give an opinion respecting court-days and questions of religious law.

By the side of these two oldest and most eminent corporations of men versed in spiritual lore may be to some extent ranked the college of the twenty state-heralds (*fetiales,* of uncertain derivation), destined as a living repository to preserve traditionally the remembrance of the treaties concluded with neighbouring communities, to pronounce an authoritative opinion on alleged infractions of treaty-rights, and in case of need to demand satisfaction and declare war. They had precisely the same position with reference to international, as the pontifices had with reference to religious, law; and were therefore, like the latter, entitled to point out the law, although not to administer it.

But in however high repute these colleges were, and important and comprehensive as were the functions assigned to them, it was never forgotten—least of all in the case of those which held the highest position—that their duty was not to command, but to tender skilled advice, not directly to obtain the answer of the gods, but to explain the answer when obtained to the inquirer. The highest of the priests was not merely inferior in rank to the king, but might not even give advice to him unasked. It was the province of the king to determine whether and when he would take an observation of birds; the " bird-seer " simply stood beside him and interpreted to him, when necessary, the language of the messengers of heaven. In like . manner the Fetialis and the Pontifex could not interfere in matters of international or common law except when those concerned therewith desired it. The Romans, notwithstanding all their zeal for religion, adhered with unbending strictness to the principle that the priest ought to remain completely powerless in the state and—excluded from all command—ought like any other burgess to render obedience to the humblest magistrate.

The Latin worship was grounded mainly on man's enjoyment of earthly pleasures, and only in a subordinate degree on his fear of the wild forces of nature; it consisted pre-eminently therefore in expressions of joy, in lays and songs, in games and dances, and above all in banquets. In Italy, as everywhere among agricultural tribes whose ordinary food consists of vegetables, the slaughter of cattle was at once a household feast and an act of worship: a pig was the most acceptable offering to the gods, just because it was the usual roast for a feast. But all extravagance of expense as well as all excess of rejoicing was inconsistent with the solid character of the Romans. Frugality in relation to the gods was one of the most prominent traits of the primitive Latin worship; and the free play of imagination was repressed with iron severity by the moral self-discipline which the nation maintained; so that the Latins remained strangers to the abominations which grow out of its unrestrained indulgence. At the very core of the Latin religion there lay that profound moral impulse which leads men to bring earthly guilt and earthly punishment into relation with the world of the gods, and to view the former as a crime against the gods, and the latter as its expiation. The execution of the criminal condemned to death was as much an expiatory sacrifice offered to the divinity as was the killing of an enemy in just war; the thief who by night stole the fruits of the field paid the penalty to Ceres on the gallows just as the enemy paid it to mother earth and the good spirits on the field of battle. The profound and fearful idea of substitution also meets us here: when the gods of the community were angry and nobody could be laid hold of as definitely guilty, they might be appeased by one who voluntarily gave himself up (*devovere se*); noxious chasms in the ground were closed, and battles half lost were converted into victories, when a brave burgess threw himself as an expiatory offering into the abyss or upon the foe. The "sacred spring" was based on a similar view; all the offspring whether of cattle or of men within a specified period were presented to the gods. If acts of this nature are to be called human sacrifices, then such sacrifices belonged to the essence of the Latin faith; but we are bound to add that, far back as our view reaches into the past, this immolation, so far as life was concerned, was limited to the guilty who had been convicted before a civil tribunal, or to the innocent who voluntarily chose to die. Human sacrifices of a different description, which are inconsistent with the fundamental idea of a sacrificial act, and which, wherever they have occurred among the Indo-Germanic stocks at least, have been the offspring of later degeneracy and barbarism, never gained admission among the Romans; hardly in a single instance were superstition and despair induced, even in times of extreme distress, to seek an extraordinary deliverance through means so revolting. Comparatively slight traces are to be found among the Romans of belief in ghosts, fear of enchantments, or dealing in mysteries. Oracles and prophecy never acquired the importance in Italy which they obtained in Greece, and never were able to exercise a serious control over public or private life.

But on the other hand the Latin religion sank into a singular insipidity and dulness, and early became shrivelled into an anxious and dreary round of ceremonies. The god of the Italian was, as we have already said, above all things an instrument for helping him to the attainment of very substantial earthly objects; this turn was given to the religious views of the Italian by his tendency towards the palpable and the real, and is no less distinctly apparent in the saint-worship of the modern inhabitants of Italy. The gods confronted man just as a creditor confronted his debtor; each of them had a duly acquired right to certain performances and payments; and as the number of the gods was as great as the number of the incidents in earthly life, and the neglect or wrong performance of the worship of each god revenged itself in the corresponding incident, it was a laborious and difficult task even to gain a knowledge of one's religious obligations, and the priests who were skilled in the law of divine things and pointed out its requirements—the *pontifices* —could not fail to attain an extraordinary influence. The upright man fulfilled the requirements of sacred ritual with the same mercantile punctuality with which he met his earthly obligations, and at times did more than was due, if the god had done so on his part. Man even dealt in speculation with his god; a vow was in reality as in name a formal contract between the god and the man, by which the latter promised to the former for a certain service to be rendered a certain equivalent return; and the Roman legal principle that no contract could be concluded by deputy was not the least important of the reasons on account of which all priestly mediation was excluded from the religious concerns of man in Latium. Nay, as the Roman merchant was entitled, without injury to his conventional rectitude, to fulfil his contract merely in the letter, so in dealing with the gods, according to the teaching of Roman theology, the copy of an object was given and received instead of the object itself. They presented to the lord of the sky heads of onions and poppies, that he might launch his lightnings at these rather than at the heads of men. In payment of the offering annually demanded by father Tiber, thirty puppets plaited of rushes were annually thrown into the stream.[1] The ideas of divine mercy and placability were in these instances inseparably mixed up with a pious cunning, which tried to delude and to pacify so formidable a master by means of a sham satisfaction. The Roman fear of the gods accordingly exercised powerful influence over the minds of the multitude; but it was by no means that sense of awe in the presence of an all-controlling nature or of an almighty God, that lies at the foundation of the views of pantheism and monotheism respectively; on the contrary, it was of a very earthly character, and scarcely different in any material respect from the trembling with which the Roman debtor approached his just, but very strict and very powerful creditor. It is plain that such a religion was fitted rather to stifle than to foster artistic and speculative views. When the Greek had clothed the simple thoughts of primitive times with human flesh and blood, the ideas of the gods so formed not only became the elements of plastic and poetic art, but acquired also that universality and elasticity which are the profoundest characteristics of human nature and for this very

[1] It is only an unreflecting misconception that can discover in this usage a reminiscence of ancient human sacrifices.

reason are essential to all religions that aspire to rule the world. Through such ideas the simple view of nature became expanded into the conception of a cosmogony, the homely moral notion became enlarged into a principle of universal humanity; and for a long period the Greek religion was enabled to embrace within it the physical and metaphysical views—the whole ideal development of the nation—and to expand in depth and breadth with the increase of its contents, until imagination and speculation rent asunder the vessel which had nursed them. But in Latium the embodiment of the conceptions of deity continued so wholly transparent that it afforded no opportunity for the training either of artist or poet, and the Latin religion always held a distant and even hostile attitude towards art. As the god was not and could not be aught else than the spiritualisation of an earthly phenomenon, this same earthly counterpart naturally formed his place of abode (*templum*) and his image; walls and effigies made by the hands of men seemed only to obscure and to embarrass the spiritual conception. Accordingly the original Roman worship had no images of the gods or houses set apart for them; and although the god was at an early period worshipped in Latium, probably in imitation of the Greeks, by means of an image, and had a little chapel (*aedicula*) built for him, such a figurative representation was reckoned contrary to the laws of Numa and was generally regarded as an impure and foreign innovation. The Roman religion could exhibit no image of a god peculiar to it, with the exception, perhaps, of the double-headed Ianus; and Varro even in his time derided the desire of the multitude for puppets and effigies. The utter want of productive power in the Roman religion was likewise the ultimate cause of the thorough poverty which always marked Roman poetry and still more Roman speculation.

The same distinctive character was manifest, moreover, in the domain of its practical use. The practical gain which accrued to the Roman community from their religion was a code of moral law gradually developed by the priests, and the *pontifices* in particular, side by side with the legal ordinances. This moral law on the one hand supplied the place of police regulations at a period when the state was still far from providing any direct police-guardianship for its citizens; and on the other hand it brought to the bar of the gods and visited with divine penalties the breach of those moral obligations which could not be reached at all, or could be but imperfectly enforced, by the law of the state. The regulations of the former class religiously inculcated the due observance of holidays and the cultivation of the fields and vineyards according to the rules of good husbandry, which we shall have occasion to notice more fully in the sequel. To this class belonged also the worship of the hearth or of the Lares which was connected with considerations of sanitary police (p. 167), and above all the practice of burning the bodies of the dead, adopted among the Romans at a singularly early period, far earlier than among the Greeks—a practice implying a rational conception of life and of death, which was foreign to primitive times and is even foreign to ourselves at the present day. It must be reckoned no small achievement that the national religion of the Latins was able to carry out these and similar improvements. But the moral effect of this law was still more important. Under this head we might include the fact itself that every sentence, at least every capital sentence, was primarily conceived as the curse of the divinity offended by the crime. But not only did that curse accompany the judgment pronounced by the community; it also supplemented its deficiencies. If a husband sold his wife, or a father sold his married son; if a child struck his father, or a daughter-in-law her father-in-law; if a patron violated his obligation to keep faith with his guest or dependent, the civil law had no penalty for such outrages, but the burden of the curse of the gods lay thenceforth on the head of the offender. Not that the person thus accursed (*sacer*) was outlawed; such an outlawry, inconsistent in its nature with all civil order, was only an exceptional occurrence in Rome—an aggravation of the religious curse at the time of the quarrels between the orders. It was not the province of the civil authorities, still less of the individual burgess or of the wholly powerless priest, to carry into effect the divine curse; the life of the person accursed was forfeited not to men but to the gods. But the pious popular faith, on which that curse was based, must in earlier times have had power even over natures frivolous and wicked; and the moral agency of religion must have exercised an influence deeper and purer precisely because it was not contaminated by any appeal to the secular arm.

But it performed no higher service in Latium than the furtherance of civil order and morality by such means as . these. In this field Hellas had an unspeakable advantage over Latium; it owed to its religion not merely its whole intellectual development, but also its national union, so far as such an union was attained at all; the oracles and festivals of the gods, Delphi and

Olympia, and the Muses, daughters of faith, were the centres round which revolved all that was great in Hellenic life and all in it that was the common heritage of the nation. And yet even here Latium had, as compared with Hellas, its own advantages. The Latin religion, reduced as it was to the level of ordinary perception, was completely intelligible to every one and accessible in common to all; and therefore the Roman community preserved the equality of its citizens, while Hellas, where religion rose to the level of the highest thought, had from the earliest times to endure all the blessing and curse of an aristocracy of intellect. The Latin religion like every other had its origin in the effort to fathom the abyss of thought; it is only to a superficial view, which is deceived as to the depth of the stream because it is clear, that its transparent spirit-world can appear to be shallow. This deeply-rooted faith disappeared with the progress of time as necessarily as the dew of morning disappears before the rising sun, and in consequence the Latin religion came at length to wither; but the Latins preserved their simplicity of faith longer than most peoples and longer especially than the Greeks. As colours are effects of light and at the same time dim it, so art and science are not merely the creations but also the destroyers of faith; and, much as this process at once of development and of destruction is swayed by necessity, by the same law of nature certain results have been reserved to the epoch of early simplicity—results which subsequent epochs make vain endeavours to attain. The mighty intellectual development of the Hellenes, which created their religious and literary unity (ever imperfect as that unity was), was the very thing that made it impossible for them to attain to a genuine political union; they sacrificed thereby the simplicity, the flexibility, the self-devotion, the power of amalgamation, which constitute the conditions of any such union. It is time therefore to desist from that childish view of history which believes that it can commend the Greeks only at the expense of the Romans, or the Romans only at the expense of the Greeks; and, as we allow the oak to hold its own beside the rose, so should we abstain from praising or censuring the two noblest organisations which antiquity has produced, and comprehend the truth that their distinctive excellences have a necessary connection with their respective defects. The deepest and ultimate reason of the diversity between the two nations lay beyond doubt in the fact that Latium did not, and that Hellas did, during the season of growth come into contact with the East. No people on earth was great enough by its own efforts to create either the marvel of Hellenic or at a later period the marvel of Christian culture; history has produced these most brilliant results only where the ideas of Aramaic religion have sunk into an Indo-Germanic soil. But if for this reason Hellas is the prototype of purely human, Latium is not less for all time the prototype of national, development; and it is the duty of us their successors to honour both and to learn from both.

Such was the nature and such the influence of the Roman religion in its pure, unhampered, and thoroughly national development. Its national character was not infringed by the fact that, from the earliest times, modes and systems of worship were introduced from abroad; no more than the bestowal of the rights of citizenship on individual foreigners denationalised the Roman state. An exchange of gods as well as of goods with the Latins must have taken place as a matter of course; the transplantation to Rome of gods and worships belonging to less cognate races is more remarkable. Of the distinctive Sabine worship maintained by the Tities we have already spoken (p. 169). Whether any of their conceptions of the gods were borrowed from Etruria is more doubtful: for the Lases, the older designation of the genii (from *lascivus*), and Minerva the goddess of memory (*mens, menervare*), which have been usually described as originally Etruscan, were on the contrary, judging from philological grounds, indigenous to Latium. It is at any rate certain, and in keeping with all that we otherwise know of Roman intercourse, that the Greek worship received earlier and more extensive attention in Rome than any other of foreign origin. The Greek oracles furnished the earliest occasion of its introduction. The language of the Roman gods was wholly confined to Yea and Nay or at the most to the making their will known by the method of casting lots, which appears in its origin Italian;[1] while from very ancient times—although not apparently until the impulse was received from the East— the more talkative gods of the Greeks imparted actual utterances of prophecy. The Romans made efforts, even at an early period, to treasure up such counsels, and copies of the leaves of the soothsaying priestess of Apollo, the Cumaean Sibyl, were accordingly a high valued gift on the part of their Greek

---

[1] *Sors* from *serere*, to place in a row. The *sortes* were probably small wooden tablets arranged upon a string, which when thrown formed figures of various kinds; an arrangement which puts one in mind of the Runic characters.

guest-friends from Campania. For the reading and interpretation of the fortune-telling book a special college, inferior in rank only to the augurs and pontifices, was instituted in early times consisting of two men of lore (*duoviri sacris faciundis*), who were furnished at the expense of the state with two slaves acquainted with the Greek language. To these custodiers of oracles the people resorted in cases of doubt, when an act of worship was needed in order to avoid some impending evil and they did not know to which of the gods or with what rites it was to be performed. But Romans in search of advice early betook themselves also to the Delphic Apollo himself. Besides the legends relating to such an intercourse already mentioned (p. 141), it is attested partly by the reception of the word *thesaurus* so closely connected with the Delphic oracle into all the Italian languages with which we are acquainted, and partly by the oldest Roman form of the name of Apollo, *Aperta*, the "opener," an etymological perversion of the Doric Apellon, the antiquity of which is betrayed by its very barbarism. The Greek Herakles was naturalised in Italy as Herclus, Hercoles, Hercules, at an early period and under a peculiar conception of his character, apparently in the first instance as the god of gains of adventure and of any extraordinary increase of wealth; for which reason the general was wont to present the tenth of the spoil which he had procured, and the merchant the tenth of the substance which he had obtained, to Hercules at the chief altar (*ara maxima*) in the cattle market. Accordingly he became the god of mercantile covenants generally, which in early times were frequently concluded at this altar and confirmed by oath, and in so far was identified with the old Latin god of good faith (*deus fidius*). The worship of Hercules was from an early date among the most widely diffused; he was, to use the words of an ancient author, adored in every hamlet of Italy, and altars were everywhere erected to him in the streets of the cities and along the country roads. The gods also of the mariner, Castor and Polydeukes, or among the Romans Pollux, the god of traffic Hermes—the Roman Mercurius, and the god of healing, Asklapios or Aesculapius, were early known to the Romans, although their public worship only began at a later period. The name of the festival of the "good goddess" (*bona dea*) *damium*, corresponding to the Greek δάμιον or δήμιον, may likewise reach back as far as this epoch. It must be the result also of ancient borrowing, that the old *Liber pater* of the Romans was afterwards conceived as "father deliverer"

and identified with the wine-god of the Greeks, the " releaser "
(*Lyaeos*), and that the Roman god of the lower regions was
called the " dispenser of riches " (*Pluto—Dis pater*), while his
spouse Persephone became converted at once by change of the
initial sound and by transference of the idea into the Roman
Proserpina, that is, " germinatrix." Even the goddess of the
Romano-Latin league, Diana of the Aventine, seems to have
been copied from the federal goddess of the Ionians of Asia
Minor, the Ephesian Artemis; at least her carved image in the
Roman temple was formed after the Ephesian type (p. 125).
It was in this way alone, through the myths of Apollo, Dionysus,
Pluto, Herakles, and Artemis which were early pervaded by
Oriental ideas, that the Aramaic religion exercised at this period
a remote and indirect influence on Italy. We clearly perceive
from these facts that the introduction of the Greek religion
was especially due to commercial intercourse—that it was
traders and mariners who primarily brought the Greek gods
to Italy.

These individual cases however of derivation from abroad
were but of secondary moment, while the remains of the
natural symbolism of primeval times, of which the legend of the
oxen of Cacus may perhaps be a specimen (p. 19) were verging
on extinction. In all its leading features the Roman religion
was an organic creation of the people among whom we find it.

The Sabellian and Umbrian worship, judging from the little
we know of it, rested upon quite the same fundamental views
as the Latin with local variations of colour and form. That
it was different from the Latin is very distinctly apparent
from the establishment of a special college at Rome for the
preservation of the Sabine rites (p. 48); but that very fact
affords an instructive illustration of the nature of the difference.
Observation of the flight of birds was with both stocks the
regular mode of consulting the gods; but the Tities observed
different birds from the Ramnian augurs. Similar relations
present themselves, wherever we have opportunity of comparing
them. Both stocks in common regarded the gods as abstractions
of the earthly and as of an impersonal nature; they differed
in expression and ritual. It was natural that these diversities
should appear of importance to the worshippers of those days;
we are no longer able to apprehend what was the characteristic
distinction, if any really existed.

The remains of the sacred rites of the Etruscans that have
reached us are marked by a different spirit. Their prevailing

characteristics are a gloomy and withal tiresome mysticism, ringing the changes on numbers, soothsaying, and that solemn enthroning of pure absurdity which at all times finds its own circle of devotees. We are far from knowing the Etruscan worship in such completeness and purity as we know the Latin; and it is not improbable—indeed it cannot well be doubted—that several of its features were only introduced by the minute subtlety of a later period, and that the gloomy and fantastic principles which were most alien to the Latin worship are those that have been especially handed down to us by tradition. But enough still remains to show that the mysticism and barbarism of this worship had their foundation in the essential character of the Etruscan people.

With our very unsatisfactory knowledge we cannot delineate the intrinsic contrast subsisting between the Etruscan conceptions of deity and the Italian; but it is clear that the most prominent among the Etruscan gods were the malignant and the mischievous. Their worship was cruel, including in particular the sacrifice of their captives; thus at Caere they slaughtered the Phocaean, and at Tarquinii the Roman, prisoners. Instead of a tranquil world of departed " good spirits " ruling peacefully in the realms beneath, such as the Latins had conceived, the Etruscan religion presented a veritable hell, in which the poor souls were doomed to be tortured by mallets and serpents, and to which they were conveyed by the conductor of the dead, a savage semi-brutal figure of an old man with wings and a large hammer—a figure which afterwards served in the gladiatorial games at Rome as a model for the costume of the man who removed the corpses of the slain from the arena. So fixed was the association of torture with this condition of the shades, that there was even provided a redemption from it, which after certain mysterious offerings transferred the poor soul to the society of the gods above. It is remarkable that, in order to people their lower world, the Etruscans early borrowed from the Greeks their gloomiest notions, such as the doctrine of Acheron and Charon, which play an important part in the Etruscan discipline.

But the Etruscan occupied himself above all in the interpretation of signs and portents. The Romans heard the voice of the gods in nature; but their bird-seer understood only the signs in their simplicity, and knew only in general whether the occurrence boded good or ill. Disturbances of the ordinary course of nature were regarded by him as boding evil, and put a stop to the business in hand, as when for example a storm of thunder and lightning dispersed the comitia; and he probably sought to get rid of them, as, for example, in the case of monstrous births, which were put to death as speedily as possible. But beyond the Tiber matters were carried much further. The penetrating Etruscan read off to the believer his future fortunes in detail from the lightning and from the entrails of animals offered in sacrifice; and the more singular the language of the gods, the more startling the portent or prodigy, the more confidently did he declare what they foretold and the means by which it was possible to avert the mischief. Thus arose the lore of lightning, the art of inspecting entrails, the interpretation of prodigies—all of them, and the science of lightning especially, devised with the hair-splitting subtlety which characterises the mind in pursuit of absurdities. A dwarf called Tages with the figure of a child but with grey hairs, who had been ploughed up by a peasant in a field near Tarquinii— we might almost fancy that practices at once so childish and so drivelling had sought to present in this figure a caricature of themselves—betrayed the secret of this lore to the Etruscans, and then straightway died. His disciples and successors taught what gods were in the habit of hurling the lightning; how the lightning of each god might be recognised by its colour and the quarter of the heavens whence it came; whether the lightning boded a permanent state of things or a single event; and in the latter case whether the event was one unalterably fixed, or whether it could be up to a certain limit artificially postponed: how they might convey the lightning away when it struck, or compel the threatening lightning to strike, and various marvellous arts of the like kind, with which there was incidentally conjoined no small desire of pocketing fees. How deeply repugnant this jugglery was to the Roman character is shown by the fact that, even when people came at a later period to employ the Etruscan lore in Rome, no attempt was made to naturalise it; during our present period the Romans were probably still content with their own, and with the Grecian, oracles.

The Etruscan religion occupied a higher level than the Roman, in so far as it developed at least the rudiments of what was wholly wanting among the Romans—speculation veiled under the forms of religion. Over the world and its gods there ruled the veiled gods (*Dii involuti*), consulted by the Etruscan Jupiter himself; that world moreover was finite, and, as it had come into being, so was it again to pass away after the expiry of a definite period of time, whose sections were the *saecula*. Respecting the intellectual value which may once have belonged to this Etruscan cosmogony and philosophy, it is difficult to form a judgment; they appear however to have been from the very first characterised by a dull fatalism and an insipid play upon numbers.

CHAPTER XIII

AGRICULTURE, TRADE, AND COMMERCE

AGRICULTURE and commerce are so intimately bound up with the constitution and the external history of states, that the former must frequently be noticed in the course of describing the latter. We shall here endeavour to supplement the detached notices which we have already given, by exhibiting a summary view of Italian and particularly of Roman economics.

It has been already observed (p. 19) that the transition from a pastoral to an agricultural economy preceded the immigration of the Italians into the peninsula. Agriculture continued to be the main support of all the communities in Italy, of the Sabellians and Etruscans no less than of the Latins. There were no purely pastoral tribes in Italy during historical times, although of course the various races everywhere combined pastoral husbandry, to a greater or less extent according to the nature of the locality, with the cultivation of the soil. The beautiful custom of commencing the formation of new cities by tracing a furrow with the plough along the line of the future ring-wall shows how deeply rooted was the feeling that every commonwealth is dependent on agriculture. In the case of Rome in particular—and it is only in its case that we can speak of agrarian relations with any sort of certainty—the Servian reform shows very clearly not only that the agricultural class originally preponderated in the state, but also that an effort was made permanently to maintain the body of freeholders as the pith and marrow of the community. When in the course of time a large portion of the landed property in Rome had passed into the hands of non-burgesses and thus the rights and duties of burgesses were no longer bound up with freehold property, the reformed constitution obviated this incongruous state of things, and the perils which it threatened, not merely temporarily but permanently, by dividing once for all the members of the community without reference to their political position into " freeholders " (*assidui*) and " producers of children " (*proletarii*), and imposing on the former the public burdens—a step

185

which in the natural course of things could not but be speedily followed by the concession of public rights. The whole policy of Roman war and conquest rested, like the constitution itself, on the basis of the freehold system; as the freeholder alone was of value in the state, the aim of war was to increase the number of its freehold members. The vanquished community was either compelled to merge entirely into the yeomanry of Rome, or, if not reduced to this extremity, it was required, not to pay a war-contribution or a fixed tribute, but to cede a portion (usually a third part) of its domain, which was thereupon regularly occupied by Roman farms. Many nations have gained victories and made conquests as the Romans did; but none has equalled the Roman in thus making the ground he had won his own by the sweat of his brow, and in securing by the ploughshare what had been gained by the lance. That which is gained by war may be wrested from the grasp by war again, but it is not so with the conquests made by the plough; while the Romans lost many battles, they scarcely ever on making peace ceded Roman soil, and for this result they were indebted to the tenacity with which the farmers clung to their fields and homesteads. The strength of man and of the state lies in their dominion over the soil; the greatness of Rome was built on the most extensive and immediate mastery of her citizens over her soil, and on the compact unity of the body which thus acquired so firm a hold.

We have already indicated (pp. 36, 67) that in the earliest times the arable land was cultivated in common, probably by the several clans; each clan tilled its own land, and thereafter distributed the produce among the several households belonging to it. There exists indeed an intimate connection between the system of joint tillage and the clan form of society, and even subsequently in Rome joint residence and joint management were of very frequent occurrence in the case of co-proprietors.[1] Even the traditions of Roman law furnish the information that wealth consisted at first in cattle and the usufruct of the soil,

[1] The system which we meet with in the case of the Germanic joint tillage, combining a partition of the land in property among the clansmen with its joint cultivation by the clan, can hardly ever have existed in Italy. Had each clansman been regarded in Italy, as among the Germans, in the light of proprietor of a particular spot in each portion of the collective domain that was marked off for tillage, the separate husbandry of later times would probably have set out from a minute subdivision of hides. But the very opposite was the case; the individual names of the Roman hides (*fundus Cornelianus*) show clearly that the Roman proprietor owned from the beginning a possession not broken up but united.

and that it was not till later that land came to be distributed among the burgesses as their own special property.[1] Better evidence that such was the case is afforded by the earliest designation of wealth as " cattle-stock " or " slave-and-cattle-stock " (*pecunia, familia pecuniaque*), and of the separate possessions of the children of the household and of slaves as " small cattle " (*peculium*); also by the earliest form of acquiring property, the laying hold of it with the hand (*mancipatio*), which was only appropriate to the case of movable articles (p. 153); and above all by the earliest measure of " land of one's own " (*heredium*, from *herus* lord), consisting of two *jugera* (about an acre and a quarter), which can only have applied to garden-ground, and not to the hide.[2] When and how the dis-

---

[1] Cicero (*de Rep.* ii. 9, 14, comp. Plutarch, *Q. Rom.* 15) states: *Tum* (in the time of Romulus) *erat res in pecore et locorum possessionibus, ex quo pecuniosi et locupletes vocabantur*—(*Numa*) *primum agros, quos bello Romulus ceperat, divisit viritim civibus.* In like manner Dionysius represents Romulus as dividing the land into thirty curial districts, and Numa as establishing boundary-stones and introducing the festival of the Terminalia (i. 7, ii. 74; and thence Plutarch, *Numa*, 16).

[2] Since this assertion still continues to be disputed, we shall let the numbers speak for themselves. The Roman writers on agriculture of the later republic and the imperial period reckon on an average five *modii* of wheat as sufficient to sow a *jugerum*, and the produce as fivefold. The produce of a *heredium* accordingly (even when, without taking into view the space occupied by the dwelling-house and farm-yard, we regard it as entirely arable land, and make no account of years of fallow) amounts to fifty, or deducting the seed forty, *modii*. For an adult hard-working slave Cato (c. 56) reckons fifty-one *modii* of wheat as the annual consumption. These data enable any one to answer for himself the question whether a Roman family could or could not subsist on the produce of a *heredium*. This result is not shaken by reckoning up the subsidiary produce yielded by the arable land itself and by the common pasture, such as figs, vegetables, milk, flesh (especially as derived from the ancient and zealously pursued rearing of swine), etc., for the Roman pastoral husbandry, though not in the older time unimportant, was yet of subordinate importance, and grain notoriously formed the chief substance of the people; nor is it much affected by the boasted thoroughness of the older cultivation. By assuming indeed that the return was on an average not fivefold but tenfold, and taking into account the after-crop of the arable land and the fig-harvest, a very considerable increase of the gross produce will no doubt be obtained—and it has never been denied that the farmers of this period drew a larger produce from their lands than the great landholders of the later republic and the empire obtained (p. 34); but moderation must be exercised in forming such estimates, because we have to deal with a question of averages and with a mode of husbandry conducted neither methodically nor with much capital, and in no case can the enormous deficit, which is left according to those estimates between the produce of the *heredium* and the requirements of the household, be covered by mere superiority of cultivation. The attempted counter-proof goes astray when it relies on the arguments that the slave of later times subsisted more exclusively on corn than the free farmer of the earlier epoch, and that the assumption of a fivefold return is too low for this epoch; both assumptions really lie at the foundation of the view here given. The counter-proof can

tribution of the arable land took place, can no longer be ascertained. This much only is certain, that the oldest form of the constitution was based not on freehold-tenure, but on clanship as a substitute for it, whereas the Servian constitution presupposes the distribution of the land. It is evident from the same constitution that the great bulk of the landed property consisted of middle-sized farms, which provided work and subsistence for a family and admitted of the keeping of cattle for tillage as well as of the application of the plough. The ordinary extent of such a Roman full hide has not been ascertained with precision, but can scarcely, as has already been shown (p. 97), be estimated at less than twenty jugera (12½ acres nearly).

Their husbandry was mainly occupied with the culture of the cereals. The usual grain was spelt (*far*);[1] but different kinds of pulse, roots, and vegetables were also diligently cultivated.

only be regarded as successful when it shall have produced a methodical calculation based on rural economics, according to which among a population chiefly subsisting on vegetables the produce of a piece of land of an acre and a quarter shall be proved sufficient on an average for the subsistence of a family.

It is indeed asserted that instances occur of colonies with allotments of two *jugera* founded even in historical times; but the only instance of the kind (Liv. iv. 47) is that of the colony of Labici in the year 336—an instance, which will certainly not be reckoned (by such scholars as are worth the arguing with) to belong to the class of traditions that are trustworthy in their historical details, and which is beset by other very serious difficulties (see book ii. ch. 5, note). It is no doubt true that in the noncolonial assignation of land to the burgesses collectively (*adsignatio viritana*) sometimes only a few *jugera* were granted (as *e.g.* Liv. viii. 11, 21). In these cases however it was not the intention to create new farms with the allotments, but, on the contrary, as a rule, the intention was to add to the existing farms new parcels from the conquered lands (comp. *C.I.L.* i. p. 88). At any rate, any supposition is better than an hypothesis which requires us to believe as it were in a miraculous multiplication of the food of the Roman household. The Roman farmers were far less modest in their requirements than their historiographers. They conceived, as has been already stated (p. 97), that they could not subsist even on allotments of seven *jugera* yielding a produce of one hundred and forty *modii*.

[1] Perhaps the latest, although probably not the last, attempt to prove that a Latin farmer's family might have subsisted on two *jugera* of land, finds its chief support in the argument that Varro (*de R.R.* i. 44, 1), reckons the seed requisite for the *jugerum* at five *modii* of wheat but ten *modii* of spelt, and estimates the produce as corresponding to this, whence it is inferred that the cultivation of spelt yielded a produce, if not double, at least considerably higher than that of wheat. But the converse is more correct, and the nominally higher quantity sown and reaped is simply to be explained by the fact that the Romans sowed and garnered the wheat already shelled, but the spelt still in the husk (Pliny, *H. N.*, xviii. 7, 61), which in this case was not separated from the fruit by threshing. For the same reason spelt is at the present day sown twice as thickly as wheat, and gives a produce twice as great by measure, but less than that of wheat after deduction of the husks. According to Würtemburg estimates

That the culture of the vine was not introduced for the first time into Italy by Greek settlers (p. 19), is shown by the list of the festivals of the Roman community which reaches back to a time preceding the Greeks, and which presents three wine-festivals to be celebrated in honour of " father Iovis," not in honour of the wine-god of more recent times who was borrowed from the Greeks, the " father deliverer " (*Liber*). The very ancient legend which represents Mezentius king of Caere as levying a wine-tax from the Latins or the Rutuli, and the various versions of the widely-spread Italian story which affirms that the Celts were induced to cross the Alps in consequence of their coming to the knowledge of the noble fruits of Italy, especially of the grape and of wine, are indications of the pride of the Latins in their glorious vine, the envy of all their neighbours. A careful system of vine-husbandry was early and generally inculcated by the Latin priests. In Rome the vintage did not begin until the supreme priest of the community, the *flamen* of Jupiter, had granted permission for it and had himself made a beginning; in like manner a Tusculan ordinance forbade the sale of new wine, until the priest had proclaimed the festival of opening the casks. The early prevalence of the culture of the vine is likewise attested not only by the general adoption of wine-libations in the sacrificial ritual, but also by the precept of the Roman priests promulgated as a law of king Numa, that men should present in libation to the gods no wine obtained from uncut grapes; just as, to introduce the beneficial practice of drying the grain, they prohibited the offering of grain undried.

furnished to me by G. Hannsen, the average produce of the Würtemburg *morgen* is reckoned in the case of wheat (with a sowing of ¼ to ½ *scheffel*) at 3 *scheffel* of the medium weight of 275 lbs. (=825 lbs.); in the case of spelt (with a sowing of ½ to 1½ *scheffel*) at least 7 *scheffel* of the medium weight of 150 lbs. (= 1050 lbs.), which are reduced by shelling to about 4 *scheffel*. Thus spelt compared with wheat yields in the gross more than double, with equally good soil perhaps triple the crop, but—by specific weight—before the shelling not much above, after shelling (as " kernel ") less than, the half. It was not by mistake, as has been asserted, but because it was fitting in computations of this sort to start from estimates of a like nature handed down to us, that the calculation instituted above was based on wheat; it may stand, because, when transferred to spelt, it does not essentially differ and the produce rather falls than rises. Spelt is less nice as to soil and climate, and exposed to fewer risks than wheat; but the latter yields on the whole, especially when we take into account the not inconsiderable expenses of shelling, a higher net produce (on an average of fifteen years in the district of Frankenthal in Rhenish Bavaria the *malter* of wheat stands at 11 *gulden* 3 *krz.*, the *malter* of spelt at 4 *gulden* 30 *krz.*), and, as in South Germany, where the soil admits, the growing of wheat is preferred and generally with the progress of cultivation comes to supersede that of spelt, so the analogous transition of Italian agriculture from the culture of spelt to that of wheat was undeniably a progress.

The culture of the olive was of later introduction, and certainly was first brought to Italy by the Greeks.[1] The olive is said to have been first planted in the countries of the western Mediterranean towards the close of the second century of the city; and this view accords with the fact that the olive-branch and the olive occupy in the Roman ritual a place very subordinate to the juice of the vine. The esteem in which both noble trees were held by the Romans is shown by the rearing of a vine and of an olive-tree in the middle of the Forum, not far from the Curtian lake.

The principal fruit-tree planted was the nutritious fig, which was probably a native of Italy. The legend of the origin of Rome wove its threads closely around the old fig-trees, several of which stood on the Palatine and in the Roman Forum.[2]

The farmer and his sons guided the plough, and performed generally the necessary labours of husbandry: it is not probable that slaves or free day-labourers were regularly employed in the work of the ordinary farm. The plough was drawn by the ox or by the cow; horses, asses, and mules served as beasts of burden. The rearing of cattle for the sake of meat or of milk did not exist at all as a distinct branch of husbandry, or was prosecuted only to a very limited extent, at least on land which remained the property of the clan; but, in addition to the smaller cattle which were driven out together to the common pasture, swine and poultry, particularly geese, were kept upon the farm. As a general rule, there was no end of ploughing and re-ploughing: a field was reckoned imperfectly tilled, in which the furrows were not drawn so close that harrowing could be dispensed with; but the method of culture was more earnest than intelligent, and no improvement took place in the defective plough or in the imperfect processes of reaping and of thrashing. This result is probably attributable rather to the scanty development of rational mechanics than to the obstinate clinging of the farmers to use and wont; for mere kindly attachment to the system of tillage transmitted with the patrimonial soil was far from influencing the practical Italian, and obvious improvements in agriculture, such as the cultivation of fodder-plants and the irrigation of meadows, were probably adopted from

---

[1] *Oleum* and *oliva* are derived from ἔλαιον, ἔλαια, and *amurca* (oil-lees) from ἀμόργη.

[2] But there is no proper authority for the statement that the fig-tree which stood in front of the temple of Saturn was cut down in the year 260 (Plin. *H. N.*, xv. 18, 77); the date CCLX. is wanting in all good manuscripts, and has been interpolated, probably with reference to Liv. ii. 21.

neighbouring peoples or independently developed by themselves at an early period—Roman literature itself in fact began
with the discussion of the theory of agriculture. Welcome rest
followed diligent and judicious labour; and here too religion
asserted her right to soothe the toils of life even to the humblest
by pauses of refreshment and of greater freedom of movement.
Four times a month, and therefore on an average every eighth
day (*nonae*), the farmer went to town to buy and sell and
transact his other business. But rest from labour, in the strict
sense, took place only on the several festival days, and especially
in the holiday-month after the completion of the winter sowing
(*feriae sementivae*): during these set times the plough rested by
command of the gods, and not the farmer only, but also his
slave and his ox, reposed in holiday idleness.

Such, probably, was the way in which the ordinary Roman
farm was cultivated in the earliest times. The next heirs had
no protection against bad management except the right of
having the spendthrift who squandered his inherited estate
placed under wardship like a lunatic (p. 152). Women moreover were in substance divested of their personal right of disposal, and, if they married, a member of the same clan was
ordinarily assigned as husband, in order to retain the estate
within the clan. The law sought to check the overburdening
of landed property with debt partly by ordaining, in the case of
a debt secured over the land, the immediate transference of the
ownership of the object pledged from the debtor to the creditor,
partly, in the case of a simple loan, by the rigour of the proceedings in execution which speedily led to actual bankruptcy; the
latter means however, as the sequel will show, attained its object
but very imperfectly. No restriction was imposed by law on
the free divisibility of property. Desirable as it might be that
co-heirs should remain in the undivided possession of their
heritage, even the oldest law was careful to keep the power of
dissolving such a partnership open at any time to any partner;
it was good that brethren should dwell together in peace, but to
compel them to do so was foreign to the liberal spirit of Roman
law. The Servian constitution moreover shows that even in
the regal period of Rome there were not wanting small cottagers
and garden-proprietors, with whom the mattock took the place
of the plough. It was left to custom and the sound sense of the
population to prevent excessive subdivision of the soil; and
that their confidence in this respect was not misplaced and the
landed estates ordinarily remained entire, is proved by the

universal Roman custom of designating them by permanen[t] individual names. The community exercised only an indirec[t] influence in the matter by the sending forth of colonies, whic[h] regularly led to the establishment of a number of new full hides and frequently perhaps also to the suppression of a number o[f] minor holdings, the small landholders being sent forth a[s] colonists.

It is far more difficult to perceive how matters stood wit[h] landed property on a larger scale. The fact that such large properties existed to no inconsiderable extent, cannot be doubte[d] from the position of the *equites* in the Servian constitution, an[d] may be easily explained partly by the distribution of the clan lands, which of itself must have produced a class of large landholders in consequence of the necessary inequality in th[e] numbers of the persons included in the several clans and parti[-] cipating in the distribution, and partly by the abundant influ[x] of mercantile capital to Rome. But farming on a large scal[e] in the proper sense, implying a considerable establishment o[f] slaves, such as we afterwards meet with at Rome, cannot b[e] supposed to have existed during this period. On the contrar[y] to this period we must refer the ancient definition, which repre[-] sents the senators as called fathers from the fields which the[y] parcelled out among the common people as a father among hi[s] children; and originally the landowner must have distribute[d] that portion of his land which he was unable to farm in person[,] or even his whole estate, into little parcels among his dependent[s] to be cultivated by them, as is the general practice in Italy a[t] the present day. The recipient might be the house-child o[r] slave of the granter; if he was a free man, his position was tha[t] which subsequently went by the name of " occupancy on sufferance " (*precarium*). The recipient retained his occupancy during pleasure, and had no legal means of protecting himsel[f] in possession; on the contrary the granter could eject him a[t] any time when he pleased. The relation did not necessarily involve any payment on the part of the person who had the usufruct of the soil to its proprietor; but such a payment beyond doubt frequently took place and, it is probable, consisted ordinarily in the delivery of a portion of the produce. The relation in this case approximated to the lease of subsequent times, but remained always distinguished from it partly by the absence of a term for its expiry, partly by its non-actionable character on either side and the legal protection of the claim for rent depending entirely on the lessor's right of ejection. It

s plain that it was essentially a relation based on mutual
fidelity, which could not subsist without the help of the powerful
sanction of custom consecrated by religion; and this was not
wanting. The institution of clientship, altogether of a moral-
religious nature, beyond doubt rested fundamentally on this
assignation of the profits of the soil. Nor was the introduction
of such an assignation dependent on the abolition of the system
of common tillage; for, just as after this abolition the individual,
so previous to it the clan might grant to dependents a joint use
of its lands; and beyond doubt with this very state of things
was connected the fact that the Roman clientship was not
personal, but that from the outset the client along with his clan
entrusted himself for protection and fealty to the patron and
his clan. This earliest form of Roman landholding serves to
explain how there sprang from the great landlords in Rome a
landed, and not an urban, nobility. As the pernicious institution of middlemen remained foreign to the Romans, the Roman
landlord found himself not much less chained to his land than
was the tenant and the farmer; he inspected and took part in
everything himself, and the wealthy Roman esteemed it his
highest praise to be reckoned a good landlord. His house was
on his land; in the city he had only a lodging for the purpose of
attending to his business there, and perhaps of breathing the
purer air that prevailed there during the hot season. Above
all however these arrangements furnished a moral basis for the
relation between the upper class and the common people, and
so materially lessened its dangers. The free tenants-on-sufferance, sprung from families of decayed farmers, dependents, and
freedmen, formed the great bulk of the proletariate (p. 88), and
were not much more dependent on the landlord than the petty
temporary tenant inevitably is with reference to the great proprietor. The slaves tilling the fields for a master were beyond
doubt far less numerous than the free tenants. In all cases
where an immigrant nation has not at once reduced to slavery
a population *en masse*, slaves seem to have existed at first only
to a very limited amount, and consequently free labourers seem
to have played a very different part in the state from that in
which they subsequently appear. In Greece " day-labourers "
($\theta\hat{\eta}\tau\epsilon s$) in various instances during the earlier period occupy the
place of the slaves of a later age, and in some communities,
among the Locrians for instance, there was no slavery down to
historical times. Even the slave, moreover, was ordinarily of
Italian descent; the Volscian, Sabine, or Etruscan war-captive

must have stood in a different relation towards his master from the Syrian and the Celt of later times. Besides as a tenant he had in fact, though not in law, land and cattle, wife and child, as the landlord had, and after manumission was introduced (p. 156) there was a possibility, not remote, of working out his freedom. If such then was the footing on which landholding on a large scale stood in the earliest times, it was far from being a manifest evil in the commonwealth; on the contrary it was of most material service to it. Not only did it provide subsistence, although scantier upon the whole, for as many families in proportion as the intermediate and smaller properties; but the landlords moreover, occupying a comparatively elevated and free position, supplied the community with its natural leaders and rulers, while the agricultural and unpropertied tenants-on-sufferance furnished the genuine material for the Roman policy of colonisation, without which it never would have succeeded; for while the state may furnish land to him who has none, it cannot impart to one who knows nothing of agriculture the spirit and the energy to wield the plough.

Ground under pasture was not affected by the distribution of the land. The state, and not the clanship, was regarded as the owner of the common pastures. It made use of them in part for its own flocks and herds, which were intended for sacrifice and other purposes and were always kept up by means of the cattle-fines; and it gave to the possessors of cattle the privilege of driving them out upon the common pasture for a moderate payment (*scriptura*). The right of pasturage on the public domains may have originally borne some relation *de facto* to the possession of land, but no connection *de jure* can ever have subsisted in Rome between the particular hides of land and a definite proportional use of the common pasture; because property could be acquired even by the *metoikos*, but the right to use the common pasture always remained a privilege of the burgess and was only granted exceptionally to the *metoikos* by the royal favour. At this period, however, the public land seems to have held but a subordinate place in the national economy generally, for the original common pasturage was not perhaps very extensive, and the conquered territory was probably for the most part distributed immediately as arable land among the clans or at a later period among individuals.

While agriculture was the chief and most extensively prosecuted occupation in Rome, other branches of industry did not fail to accompany it, as might be expected from the early development of urban life in that emporium of the Latins. In fact eight guilds of craftsmen were numbered among the institutions of king Numa, that is, among the institutions that had existed in Rome from time immemorial. These were the flute-blowers, the goldsmiths, the coppersmiths, the carpenters, the fullers, the dyers, the potters, and the shoemakers—a list which would substantially exhaust the class of tradesmen working to order on others' account in the very early times, when the baking of bread and the professional art of healing were not yet known and wool was spun into clothing by the women of the household themselves. It is remarkable that there appears no special guild of workers in iron. This affords a fresh confirmation of the fact that the manufacture of iron was of comparatively late introduction in Latium; and on this account in matters of ritual down to the latest times copper alone might be used, *e.g.* for the sacred plough and the shear-knife of the priests. These bodies of craftsmen must have been of great importance in early times for the urban life of Rome and for its position towards the Latin land—an importance not to be measured by the depressed condition of Roman handicraft in later times, when it was injuriously affected by the multitude of artisan-slaves working for their master or on his account, and by the increased importation of articles of luxury. The oldest lays of Rome celebrated not only the mighty war-god Mamers, but also the skilled armourer Mamurius, who understood the art of forging for his fellow-burgesses shields similar to the divine model shield that had fallen from heaven; Volcanus the god of fire and of the forge appears in the early list of Roman festivals (p. 164). Thus in the earliest Rome, as everywhere, the arts of forging and of wielding the plough-share and the sword went hand in hand, and there was nothing of that arrogant contempt for handicrafts which we afterwards meet with there. After the Servian organisation, however, imposed the duty of serving in the army exclusively on the freeholders, the industrial classes were excluded not by any law, but practically by virtue of their general want of a freehold qualification, from the privilege of bearing arms, except in the case of special subdivisions chosen from the carpenters, coppersmiths, and musicians and attached with a military organisation to the army; and this may perhaps have been the origin of the subsequent habit of depreciating the manual arts and of the position of political inferiority assigned to them. The institution of guilds doubtless had the same object as the colleges of priests that resembled them in name; the men of skill associated themselves in order more permanently and securely to preserve the tradition of their art. That there was some mode of excluding unskilled persons is probable; but no traces are to be met with either of monopolising tendencies or of protective steps against inferior manufactures. There is no aspect, however, of the life of the Roman people respecting which our information is so scanty as that of the Roman trades.

Italian commerce must, it is obvious, have been limited in the earliest epoch to the mutual dealings of the Italians themselves. Fairs (*mercatus*), which must be distinguished from the usual weekly markets (*nundinae*) were of great antiquity in Latium. Probably they were at first associated with international gatherings and festivals, and so perhaps were connected in Rome with the festival at the federal temple on the Aventine; the Latins, who came for this purpose to Rome every year on the 13th August, may have embraced at the same time the opportunity of transacting their business in Rome and of purchasing what they needed there. A similar and perhaps still greater importance belonged in the case of Etruria to the annual general assembly at the temple of Voltumna (perhaps near Montefiascone) in the territory of Volsinii; it served at the same time as a fair and was regularly frequented by Roman traders. But the most important of all the Italian fairs was that which was held at Soracte in the grove of Feronia, a situation than which none could be found more favourable for the exchange of commodities among the three great nations. That high isolated mountain, which appears to have been set down by nature herself in the midst of the plain of the Tiber as a goal for the traveller, lay on the boundary which separated the Etruscan and Sabine lands (to the latter of which it appears mostly to have belonged), and it was likewise easily accessible from Latium and Umbria. Roman merchants regularly made their appearance there, and the wrongs of which they complained gave rise to many a quarrel with the Sabines.

Beyond doubt dealings of barter and traffic were carried on at these fairs long before the first Greek or Phoenician vessel entered the western sea. When bad harvests had occurred, different districts supplied each other at these fairs with grain; there, too, they exchanged cattle, slaves, metals, and whatever other articles were deemed needful or desirable in those primitive times. Oxen and sheep formed the oldest medium of exchange, ten sheep being reckoned equivalent to one ox. The recognition of these objects as universal legal representatives of value or in other words as money, as well as the scale of proportion between the large and smaller cattle, may be traced back—as the occurrence of both among the Germans especially shows— not merely to the Graeco-Italian period, but beyond this even to the epoch of a purely pastoral economy.[1] In Italy, where metal in considerable quantity was everywhere required especially for agricultural purposes and for armour, but few of its provinces themselves produced the requisite metals, copper (*aes*) very early made its appearance alongside of cattle as a second medium of exchange; and so the Latins, who were poor in copper, designated valuation itself as " coppering " (*aestimatio*). This establishment of copper as a general equivalent recognised throughout the whole peninsula, as well as the simplest numeral signs of Italian invention to be mentioned more particularly below (p. 206), and the Italian duodecimal system, may be regarded as traces of this earliest international intercourse of the Italian peoples while they still had the peninsula to themselves.

We have already indicated generally the nature of the influence exercised by transmarine commerce on the Italians who continued independent. The Sabellian stocks remained almost wholly unaffected by it. They were in possession of but a small and inhospitable belt of coast, and received whatever reached them from foreign nations—the alphabet for instance— only through the medium of the Tuscans or Latins; a circumstance which accounts for their want of urban development. The intercourse of Tarentum with the Apulians and Messapians appears to have been at this epoch still unimportant. It was otherwise along the west coast. In Campania the Greeks and Italians dwelt peacefully side by side, and in Latium, and still more in Etruria, an extensive and regular exchange of commodities took place. What were the earliest articles of import, may be inferred partly from the objects found in the primitive tombs, particularly those at Caere, partly from indications preserved in the language and institutions of the

---

[1] The comparative legal value of sheep and oxen, as is well known, is proved by the fact that, when the cattle-fines were converted into money-fines, the sheep was rated at ten, and the ox at a hundred *asses* (Festus v. *peculatus*, p. 237, comp. p. 24, 144; Gell. xi. 1; Plutarch, *Poplicola*, 11). By a similar adjustment the Icelandic law makes twelve rams equivalent to a cow; only in this as in other instances the Germanic law has substituted the duodecimal for the older decimal system.

It is well known that the term denoting cattle was transferred to denote money both among the Latins (*pecunia*) and among the Germans (English *fee*).

Romans, partly and chiefly from the stimulus given to Italian industry; for of course they bought foreign manufactures for a considerable time before they began to imitate them. We cannot determine how far the development of handicrafts had advanced before the separation of the stocks, or what progress it thereafter made while Italy remained left to its own resources; it is uncertain how far the Italian fullers, dyers, tanners, and potters received their impulse from Greece or Phoenicia or had their own independent development. But it is certain that the trade of the goldsmiths, which existed in Rome from time immemorial, can only have arisen after transmarine commerce had begun and ornaments of gold had to some extent found sale among the inhabitants of the peninsula. We find, accordingly, in the oldest sepulchres of Caere and Vulci in Etruria and of Praeneste in Latium, plates of gold with winged lions stamped upon them, and similar ornaments of Babylonian manufacture. It may be a question in reference to the particular object found, whether it has been introduced from abroad or is a native imitation; but on the whole it admits of no doubt that all the west coast of Italy in early times imported metallic wares from the East. It will be shown still more clearly in the sequel, when we come to speak of the exercise of art, that architecture and modelling in clay and metal received a powerful stimulus in very early times from Greece, whence the oldest tools and the oldest models were derived. In the sepulchral chambers just mentioned, besides the gold ornaments, there were deposited vessels of bluish enamel or greenish clay, which, judging from the materials and style as well as from the hieroglyphics impressed upon them, were of Egyptian origin; perfume-vases of Oriental alabaster, several of them in the form of Isis; ostrich-eggs with painted or carved sphinxes and griffins; beads of glass and amber. These last may have come by the land-route from the north; but the other objects prove the importation of perfumes and articles of ornament of all sorts from the East. Thence came linen and purple, ivory and frankincense, as is proved by the early use of linen fillets, of the purple dress and ivory sceptre for the king, and of frankincense in sacrifice, as well as by the very ancient borrowed names for them (λίνον, *linum ;* πορφύρα, *purpura ;* σκῆπτρον, σκίπων, *scipio ;* perhaps also ἐλέφας, *ebur ;* θύος, *thus*). Of similar significance is the derivation of a number of words relating to articles used in eating and drinking, particularly the names of oil (comp. p. 190), of jugs (ἀμφορεύς, *amp(h)ora, ampulla ;*

κρατήρ, cratera), of feasting (κωμάζω, comissari), of a dainty (ὀψώνιον, obsonium), of dough (μᾶζα, massa), and various names of cakes (γλυκοῦς, lucuns ; πλακοῦς, placenta ; τυροῦς, turunda); while conversely the Latin names for dishes (patina, πατάνη) and for lard (arvina, ἀρβίνη) have found admission into Sicilian Greek. The later custom of placing in the tomb beside the dead Attic, Corcyrean, and Campanian vases proves, what these testimonies from language likewise show, the early market for Greek pottery in Italy. That Greek leather-work made its way into Latium at least in the shape of armour is apparent from the application of the Greek word for leather (σκῦτος), to signify among the Latins a shield (scutum; like lorica, from lorum). Finally, we deduce a similar inference from the numerous nautical terms borrowed from the Greek (although it is remarkable that the chief technical expressions in navigation —the terms for the sail, mast, and yard—are pure Latin forms);[1] and from the recurrence in Latin of the Greek designations for a letter (ἐπιστολή, epistula), a token (tessera, from τέσσαρα), a balance (στατήρ, statera), and earnest-money (ἀρραβών, arrabo, arra); and conversely from the adoption of Italian law-terms in Sicilian Greek (p. 157), as well as from the exchange of the proportions and names of coins, weights, and measures, which we shall notice in the sequel. The character of barbarism which all these borrowed terms obviously present, and especially the characteristic formation of the nominative from the accusative (placenta=πλακοῦντα; ampora=ἀμφορέα; statera= στατῆρα), constitute the clearest evidence of their great antiquity. The worship of the god of traffic (Mercurius) also appears to have been from the first influenced by Greek ideas; and his annual festival seems to have been fixed on the

---

[1] Velum is certainly of Latin origin; so is malus, especially as that term denotes not merely the mast, but the tree in general: antenna likewise may come from ἀνά (anhelare, antestari), and tendere=supertensa. Of Greek origin, on the other hand, are gubernare, to steer (κυβερνᾶν); ancora, anchor (ἄγκυρα); prora, ship's bows (πρῶρα); aplustre, ship's stern (ἄφλαστον); anquina, the rope fastening the yards (ἄγκοινα); nausea, sea-sickness (ναυσία).

The four principal winds—aquilo, the " eagle-wind," the north-easterly Tramontana; volturnus (of uncertain derivation, perhaps the " vulture-wind "), the south-easterly; auster the " scorching " south-west wind, the Sirocco; favonius, the " favourable " north-west wind blowing from the Tyrrhene Sea—have indigenous names bearing no reference to navigation; but all the other Latin names for winds are Greek (such as eurus, notus), or translations from the Greek (e.g. solanus = ἀπηλιώτης, Africus = λίψ).

ides of May, because the Hellenic poets celebrated him as the
son of the beautiful Maia.

It thus appears that Italy in very ancient times derived its
articles of luxury, just as imperial Rome did, from the East,
before it attempted to manufacture for itself after the models
which it imported. In exchange it had nothing to offer except
its raw produce, consisting especially of its copper, silver, and
iron, but including also slaves and timber for ship-building,
amber from the Baltic, and, in the event of bad harvests occurring
abroad, its grain.

From this state of things as to the commodities in demand
and the equivalents to be offered in return, we have already
explained why Italian traffic assumed in Latium a form differing
from that which it presents in Etruria. The Latins, who were
deficient in all the chief articles of export, could carry on only
a passive traffic, and were obliged even in the earliest times to
procure the copper of which they had need from the Etruscans
in exchange for cattle or slaves—we have already mentioned
the very ancient practice of selling the latter on the right bank
of the Tiber (p. 105). On the other hand the Tuscan balance
of trade must have been necessarily favourable at Caere and
Populonia, at Capua and Spina. Hence the rapid development
of prosperity in these regions and their powerful commercial
position; whereas Latium remained pre-eminently an agricultural country. The same contrast recurs in all their individual
relations. The oldest tombs constructed and furnished in the
Greek fashion, but with an extravagance to which the Greeks were
strangers, are to be found at Caere, while—with the exception
of Praeneste, which appears to have occupied a peculiar position
and to have been very intimately connected with Falerii and
southern Etruria—the Latin land exhibits not a single tomb
of this nature belonging to the earlier times; and there was among
the Sabellians a simple turf seemed sufficient as a covering for
any one's remains. The most ancient coins, of not much later
origin than those of Magna Graecia, belong to Etruria, and
to Populonia in particular: during the whole regal period
Latium had to be content with copper by weight, and had not
even introduced foreign coins, for the instances are very rare in
which such coins (*e.g.* one of Posidonia) have been found there.
In architecture, plastic art, and embossing, the same stimulants
acted on Etruria and on Latium, but it was only in the case of
the former that capital was brought to bear on them and led
to their being prosecuted extensively and with growing technical

skill. The commodities were upon the whole the same, which were bought, sold, and manufactured in Latium and in Etruria; but the southern land was far inferor to its northern neighbours in the energy with which its commerce was plied. The contrast between them in this respect is shown in the fact that the articles of luxury manufactured after Greek models in Etruria found a market in Latium, particularly at Praeneste, and even in Greece itself, while Latium hardly ever exported anything of the kind.

A distinction not less remarkable between the commerce of the Latins and that of the Etruscans appears in their respective routes or lines of traffic. As to the earliest commerce of the Etruscans in the Adriatic we can hardly do more than express the conjecture that it was directed from Spina and Hatria chiefly to Corcyra. We have already mentioned (p. 143) that the western Etruscans ventured boldly into the eastern seas, and trafficked not merely with Sicily, but also with Greece proper. An ancient intercourse with Attica is indicated by the Attic clay vases, which are so numerous in the more recent Etruscan tombs, and had been perhaps even at this time introduced for other purposes than the already-mentioned decoration of tombs, while conversely Tyrrhenian bronze candlesticks and gold cups were articles early in request in Attica. Still more definitely is such an intercourse indicated by the coins. The silver pieces of Populonia were struck after the pattern of a very old silver piece stamped on one side with the Gorgoneion, on the other merely presenting an incuse square, which has been found at Athens and on the old amber-route in the district of Posen, and which was in all probability the very coin struck by order of Solon in Athens. We have mentioned already that the Etruscans had also dealings, and perhaps after the development of the Etrusco-Carthaginian maritime alliance their principal dealings, with the Carthaginians. It is a remarkable circumstance that in the oldest tombs of Caere, besides native vessels of bronze and silver, there have been found chiefly oriental articles, which may certainly have come from Greek merchants, but more probably were introduced by Phoenician traders. We must not, however, attribute too great importance to this Phoenician trade, and in particular we must not overlook the fact that the alphabet, as well as the other influences that stimulated and matured native culture, were brought to Etruria by the Greeks, and not by the Phoenicians.

Latin commerce assumed a different direction. Rarely as

we have opportunity of instituting comparisons between the
Romans and the Etruscans as regards the reception of Hellenic
elements, the cases in which such comparisons can be instituted
exhibit the two nations as completely independent of each other.
This is most clearly apparent in the case of the alphabet. The
Greek alphabet brought to the Etruscans from the Chalcidico-
Doric colonies in Sicily or Campania varies not immaterially
from that which the Latins derived from the same quarter, so
that, although both peoples have drawn from the same source,
they have done so at different times and different places. The
same phenomenon appears in particular words: the Roman
Pollux and the Tuscan Pultuke are independent corruptions of
the Greek Polydeukes; the Tuscan Utuze or Uthuze is formed
from Odysseus, the Roman Ulixes is an exact reproduction of
the form of the name usual in Sicily; in like manner the Tuscan
Aivas corresponds to the old Greek form of this name, the
Roman Aiax to a secondary form that was probably also
Sicilian; the Roman Aperta or Apollo and the Samnite Appellun
have sprung from the Doric Apellon, the Tuscan Apulu from
Apollon. Thus the language and writing of Latium indicate
that the direction of Latin commerce was exclusively towards
the Cumaeans and Sicilians. Every other trace which has
survived from so remote an age leads to the same conclusion:
such as, the coin of Posidonia found in Latium; the purchase
of grain, when a failure of the harvest occurred in Rome, from
the Volscians, Cumaeans, and Siceliots (and, as was natural,
from the Etruscans as well); above all, the relation subsisting
between the Latin and Sicilian monetary systems. As the
local Dorico-Chalcidian designation of silver coin νόμος, and the
Sicilian measure ἡμίνα, were transferred with the same meaning
to Latium as *nummus* and *hemina,* so conversely the Italian
designations of weight, *libra, triens, quadrans, sextans, uncia,*
which arose in Latium for the measurement of the copper
which was used by weight instead of money, had found their way
into the common speech of Sicily in the third century of the
city under the corrupt and hybrid forms, λίτρα, τριᾶς, τετρᾶς,
ἑξᾶς, οὐγκία. Indeed, among all the Greek systems of weights
and moneys, the Sicilian alone was brought into a determinate
relation to the Italian copper-system; not only was the value
of silver set down conventionally and perhaps legally as two
hundred and fifty times that of copper, but the equivalent on
this computation of a Sicilian pound of copper ($\frac{1}{120}$th of the
Attic talent, $\frac{2}{3}$ of the Roman pound) was in very early times

struck, especially at Syracuse, as a silver coin ($\lambda i \tau \rho a$, $\dot{a} \rho \gamma \nu \rho i o \nu'$ *i.e.* " pound of copper in silver "). Accordingly it cannot be doubted that Italian bars of copper circulated also in Sicily instead of money; and this exactly harmonises with the hypothesis that the commerce of the Latins with Sicily was a passive commerce, in consequence of which Latin money was drained away thither. Other proofs of ancient intercourse between Sicily and Italy, especially the adoption in the Sicilian dialect of the Italian expressions for a commercial loan, a prison, and a dish, and the converse reception of Sicilian terms in Italy, have been already mentioned (p. 157, 199). We meet also with several, though less definite, traces of an ancient intercourse of the Latins with the Chalcidian cities in Lower Italy, Cumae and Neapolis, and with the Phocaeans in Velia and Massilia. That it was however far less active than that with the Siceliots is shown by the well-known fact that all the Greek words which made their way in earlier times to Latium exhibit Doric forms— we need only recall *Aesculapius, Latona, Aperta, marchina*. Had their dealings with the originally Ionian cities, such as Cumae (p. 137) and the Phocaean settlements, been on a similar scale with those which they had with the Sicilian Dorians, Ionic forms would at least have made their appearance along with the others; although certainly Dorism early penetrated into these Ionic colonies themselves, and their dialect varied greatly. While all the facts thus combine to attest the stirring traffic of the Latins with the Greeks of the western main generally, and especially with the Sicilians, there is scarcely found a single proof of intercourse with other peoples; in particular it is very remarkable that—if we leave out of account some local names— there is an utter absence of any evidence from language as to ancient intercourse between the Latins and the nations speaking the Aramaic tongue.[1]

If we further inquire how this traffic was carried on, whether by Italian merchants abroad or by foreign merchants in Italy,

---

[1] If we leave out of view *Sarranus, Afer*, and other local designations (p. 145), the Latin language appears not to possess a single word immediately derived in early times from the Phoenician. The very few words from Phoenician roots which occur in it, such as *arrabo* or *arra* and perhaps also *murra, nardus*, and the like, are plainly borrowed proximately from the Greek, which has a considerable number of such words of Oriental extraction as indications of its primitive intercourse with the Aramaeans. The same holds true of the enigmatical word *thesaurus ;* whether it may have been originally Greek or borrowed by the Greeks from the Phoenician or Persian, it is at any rate, as a Latin word, derived from the Greek, as the very retaining of its aspiration proves (p. 180).

the former supposition has all the probabilities in its favour, at least so far as Latium is concerned. It is scarcely conceivable that those Latin terms denoting the substitute for money and the commercial loan could have found their way into general use in the language of the inhabitants of Sicily through the mere resort of Sicilian merchants to Ostia and their receipt of copper in exchange for ornaments.

Lastly, in regard to the persons and classes by whom this traffic was carried on in Italy, no special superior class of merchants distinct from and independent of the class of landed proprietors developed itself in Rome. The reason of this surprising phenomenon was, that the wholesale commerce of Latium was from the beginning in the hands of the large landed proprietors—an hypothesis which is not so singular as it seems. It was natural that in a country intersected by several navigable rivers the great landholder, who was paid by his tenants their quotas of produce in kind, should come at an early period to possess barks; and there is evidence that such was the case. The transmarine traffic conducted on the trader's own account must therefore have fallen into the hands of the great landholder, seeing that he alone possessed the vessels for it and—in his produce—the articles for export.[1] In fact the distinction between a landed and a moneyed aristocracy was unknown to the Romans of earlier times; the great landholders were at the same time the speculators and the capitalists. In the case of a very active commerce such a combination certainly could not have been maintained; but, as the previous representation shows, while there was a comparatively vigorous traffic in Rome in consequence of the trade of the Latin land being there concentrated, Rome was by no means mainly a commercial city like Caere or Tarentum, but was and continued to be the centre of an agricultural community.

[1] Quintus Claudius, in a law issued shortly before 534, prohibited the senators from having sea-going vessels holding more than 300 *amphorae* (1 *amph.*=nearly 6 gallons): *id satis habitum ad fructus ex agris vectandos ; quaestus omnis patribus indecorous visus* (Liv. xxi. 63). It was thus an ancient usage, and was still permitted, that the senators should possess sea-going vessels for the transport of the produce of their estates: on the other hand, transmarine mercantile speculation (*quaestus*, traffic, fitting-out of vessels, etc.) on their part was prohibited. It is a curious fact that the ancient Greeks as well as the Romans expressed the tonnage of their sea-going ships constantly in *amphorae ;* the reason evidently being, that Greece as well as Italy exported wine at a comparatively early period, and on a larger scale than any other bulky article.

CHAPTER XIV

MEASURING AND WRITING

THE art of measuring brings the world into subjection to man; the art of writing prevents his knowledge from perishing along with himself; together they make man—what nature has not made him—all-powerful and eternal. It is the privilege and duty of history to trace the course of national progress along these paths also.

Measurement necessarily presupposes the development of the several ideas of units of time, of space, and of weight, and of a whole consisting of equal parts, or in other words of number and of a numeral system. The most obvious bases presented by nature for this purpose are, in reference to time, the periodic returns of the sun and moon, or the day and the month; in reference to space, the length of the human foot, which is more easily applied in measuring than the arm; in reference to gravity, the burden which a man is able to poise (*librare*) on his hand while he holds his arm stretched out, or the " weight " (*libra*). As a basis for the notion of a whole made up of equal parts, nothing so readily suggests itself as the hand with its five, or the hands with their ten, fingers; upon this rests the decimal system. We have already observed that these elements of all numeration and measuring reach back not merely beyond the separation of the Greek and Latin stocks, but even to the most remote primeval times. The antiquity in particular of the measurement of time by the moon is demonstrated by language (p. 17); even the mode of reckoning the days that elapse between the several phases of the moon, not forward from the phase on which it had entered last, but backward from that which was next expected, is at least older than the separation of the Greeks and Latins.

The most definite evidence of the antiquity and original exclusive use of the decimal system among the Indo-Germans is furnished by the well-known agreement of all Indo-Germanic languages in respect to the numerals as far as a hundred inclusive (p. 18). In the case of Italy the decimal system pervaded all the earliest arrangements: it may be sufficient to recall the number ten so usual in the case of witnesses, securities, envoys, and magistrates, the legal equivalence of one ox and ten sheep, the partition of the canton into ten curies and the pervading application generally of the decurial system, the *limitatio*, the tenth in offerings and in agriculture, decimation, and the praenomen *Decimus*. Among the applications of this most ancient decimal system in the sphere of measuring and of writing, the remarkable Italian ciphers claim a primary place. When the Greeks and Italians separated, there were still evidently no conventional signs of number. On the other hand we find the three oldest and most indispensable numerals, one, five, and ten, represented by three signs—I, V or Λ, X, manifestly imitations of the outstretched finger, and the open hand single and double— which were not derived either from the Hellenes or the Phoenicians, but were common to the Romans, Sabellians, and Etruscans. They were the first steps towards the formation of a national Italian writing, and at the same time evidences of the liveliness of that earlier inland intercourse among the Italians which preceded their transmarine commerce (p. 196). Which of the Italian stocks invented, and which of them borrowed, these signs, can of course no longer be ascertained. Other traces of the pure decimal system occur but sparingly in this field; among them are the *vorsus*, the Sabellian measure of surface of 100 square feet (p. 21), and the Roman year of 10 months.

Generally in the case of those Italian measures, which were not connected with Greek standards and were probably developed by the Italians before they came into contact with the Greeks, there prevailed the partition of the " whole " (*as*) into twelve " units " (*unciae*). The very earliest Latin priesthoods, the colleges of the Salii and Arvales (p. 168), as well as the leagues of the Etruscan cities, were organised on the basis of the number twelve. The same number predominated in the Roman system of weights and in the measures of length, where the pound (*libra*) and the foot (*pes*) were usually subdivided into twelve parts; the unit of the Roman measures of surface was the " driving " (*actus*) of 120 feet square, a combination of the decimal and duodecimal systems.[1] Similar arrangements as to the measures of capacity may have passed into oblivion.

[1] Originally both the *actus*, " driving," and its still more frequently occurring duplicate, the *iugerum*, " yoking," were, like the German " morgen," not measures of surface, but measures of labour; the latter denoting the day's work, the former the half-day's work, with reference to the peculiarly marked division of the day in Italy by the ploughman's rest at noon.

If we inquire into the basis of the duodecimal system and consider how it can have happened that, in addition to *ten*, *twelve* should have been so early and universally singled out from the equal series of numbers, we shall be able to find no other source to which it can be referred than a comparison of the solar and lunar periods. The double hand of ten fingers and the solar cycle of nearly twelve lunar periods first suggested to man the profound conception of an unit composed of equal units, and thereby originated the idea of a system of numbers, the first step towards mathematical thought. The consistent duodecimal development of this idea appears to have belonged to the Italian nation, and to have preceded the first contact with the Greeks.

But when at length the Hellenic trader had opened up the route to the west coast of Italy, the measures of surface remained unaffected, but the measures of length, of weight, and above all of capacity—in other words those definite standards without which barter and traffic are impossible—experienced the effects of the new international intercourse. The Roman foot, which in later times was a little smaller than the Greek,[1] but at that time was either equal in reality or was at any rate still reckoned equal to it, was, in addition to its Roman subdivision into twelve twelfths, divided after the Greek fashion into four hand-breadths (*palmus*) and sixteen finger-breadths (*digitus*). Further, the Roman weights were brought into a fixed proportional relation to the Attic system, which prevailed throughout Sicily but not in Cumae—another significant proof that the Latin traffic was chiefly directed to the island; four Roman pounds were assumed as equal to three Attic *minae*, or rather the Roman pound was assumed as equal to one and a half of the Sicilian *litrae*, or half-*minae* (p. 202). But the most singular and chequered aspect is presented by the Roman measures of capacity, as regards both their names and their proportions. Their names have come from the Greek terms either by corruption (*amphora, modius* after μέδιμνος, *congius* from χοεύς, *hemina, cyathus*) or by translation (*acetabulum* from ὀξύβαφον); while conversely ξέστης is a corruption of *sextarius*. All the measures are not identical, but those in most common use are so; among liquid measures the *congius* or *chus*, the *sextarius*, and the *cyathus*, the two last also for dry goods; the Roman *amphora* was equivalent in liquid measure to the Attic talent, and at the same time stood to the Greek *metretes* in the fixed ratio of 3 : 2, and to the Greek *medimnos* of 2 : 1. To one who can decipher

---

[1] $\frac{24}{25}$ of the Greek foot = one Roman foot.

the significance of such records, these names and numerical proportions fully reveal the activity and importance of the intercourse between the Sicilians and the Latins.

The Greek numeral signs were not adopted; but the Roman probably availed himself of the Greek alphabet, when it reached him, to form ciphers for 50 and 1000, perhaps also for 100, out of the signs for the three aspirated letters which he had no use for. In Etruria the sign for 100 at least appears to have been obtained in a similar way. Afterwards, as usually happens, the systems of notation among the two neighbouring nations became assimilated by the adoption in substance of the Roman system in Etruria.

In like manner the Roman calendar—and probably that of the Italians generally—began with an independent development of its own, but subsequently came under the influence of the Greeks. In the division of time the returns of sunrise and sunset, and of the new and full moon, most directly arrest the attention of man; and accordingly the day and the month, determined not by cyclic calculation but by direct observation, were long the exclusive measures of time. Down to a late age sunrise and sunset were proclaimed in the Roman market-place by the public crier, and in like manner it may be presumed that in early times, at each of the four phases of the moon, the number of days that would elapse from that phase until the next was proclaimed by the priests. The mode of reckoning therefore in Latium—and the like mode, it may be presumed, was in use not merely among the Sabellians, but also among the Etruscans —was by days, which, as already mentioned, were counted not forward from the phase that had last occurred, but backward from that which was next expected; by lunar weeks, which varied in length between 7 and 8 days, the average length being $7\frac{3}{8}$; and by lunar months, which in like manner were sometimes of 29, sometimes of 30 days, the average duration of the synodical month being 29 days 12 hours 44 minutes. For some time the day continued to be among the Italians the smallest, and the month the largest, division of time. It was not until afterwards that they began to distribute day and night respectively into four portions, and it was much later still when they began to employ the division into hours; which explains why even stocks otherwise closely related differed in their mode of fixing the commencement of day, the Romans placing it at midnight, the Sabellians and the Etruscans at noon. No calendar, of the year at any rate, had as yet been organised when the Greeks separated from the Italians, for the names for the year and its divisions in the two languages have been formed quite independently of each other. Nevertheless the Italians appear to have already in the pre-Hellenic period advanced, if not to the arrangement of a fixed calendar, at any rate to the institution of two larger units of time. The simplifying of the reckoning according to lunar months by the application of the decimal system, which was usual among the Romans, and the designation of a term of ten months as a "ring" (*annus*) or complete year, bear in them all the traces of a high antiquity. Later, but likewise at a period very early and undoubtedly previous to the operation of Greek influences, the duodecimal system (as we have already stated) was developed in Italy, and, as it derived its very origin from the observation of the fact that the solar period was equal to twelve lunar periods, it was certainly applied in the first instance to the reckoning of time. This view accords with the fact that the individual names of the months—which can only have originated after the month was viewed as part of a solar year—particularly those of March and of May, were similar among the different branches of the Italian stock, while there was no similarity between the Italian names and the Greek. It is not improbable therefore that the problem of laying down a practical calendar which should correspond at once to the moon and the sun—a problem which may be compared in some sense to the quadrature of the circle, and the solution of which was only recognised as impossible and abandoned after the lapse of many centuries—had already employed the minds of men in Italy before the epoch at which their contact with the Greeks began; these purely national attempts to solve it, however, have passed into oblivion.

What we know of the oldest calendar of Rome and of some other Latin cities—as to the Sabellian and Etruscan measurement of time we have no traditional information—is decidedly based on the oldest Greek arrangement, which was intended to answer both to the phases of the moon and to the seasons of the solar year, constructed on the assumption of a lunar period of $29\frac{1}{2}$ days and a solar period of $12\frac{1}{2}$ lunar months or $368\frac{3}{4}$ days, and on the regular alternation of a full month or month of 30 days with a hollow month or month of 29 days and of a year of 12 with a year of 13 months, but at the same time maintained in some sort of harmony with the actual celestial phenomena by arbitrary curtailments and intercalations. It is possible that this Greek arrangement of the year in the first instance

came into use among the Latins without undergoing any alteration; but the oldest form of the Roman year which can be
historically recognised varied materially from its model, not in
the cyclical result nor yet in the alternation of years of 12 with
years of 13 months, but in the designation and in the measuring
off of the individual months. The Roman year began with the
beginning of spring; the first month in it, and the only one which
bears the name of a god, was named from Mars (*Martius*), the
three following from sprouting (*aprilis*), growing (*maius*), and
thriving (*iunius*), the fifth and onward to the tenth from their
places in the order of arrangement (*quinctilis, sextilis, september,
october, november, december*), the eleventh from commencing
(*ianuarius*) (p. 167), with reference probably to the renewal of
agricultural operations that followed mid-winter and the season
of rest, the twelfth, and in an ordinary year the last, from
cleansing (*februarius*). To this series recurring in regular succession there was added in the intercalary year a nameless
" labour-month " (*mercedonius*) at the close of the year, viz.
after February. And, as the Roman calendar was independent
as respected the names of the months which were probably
taken from the old national ones, it was also independent as
regarded their duration. Instead of the four years of the Greek
cycle, each composed of six months of 30 and six of 29
days and an intercalary month inserted every second year alternately of 29 and 30 days (354 + 384 + 354 + 383 = 1475 days), the
Roman calendar substituted four years, each containing four
months—the first, third, fifth, and eighth—of 31 days and seven
of 29 days, with a February of 28 days during three years and
of 29 in the fourth, and an intercalary month of 27 days inserted
every second year (355 + 383 + 355 + 382 = 1475 days). In like
manner this calendar deviated from the original distribution of
the month into four weeks, sometimes of 7, sometimes of 8 days;
instead of this it permanently fixed the first quarter in the
months of 31 days on the seventh, in those of 29 on the fifth day,
and the full moon in the former on the fifteenth, in the latter on
the thirteenth day; so that the second and fourth weeks in the
month consisted of 8 days, the third ordinarily of 9 (only in the
case of the February of 28 days it consisted of 8, and in the
intercalary month of 27 days, of 7), the first of 6 where the
month consisted of 31, and in other cases of 4 days. As the
course of the last three weeks of the month was thus essentially
similar, it was henceforth necessary only to proclaim the length
of the first week in each month. Thence the first day of the

first week received the name of " proclamation-day " (*kalendae*). The first days of the second and fourth weeks, which were uniformly of 8 days, were—in conformity with the Roman custom of reckoning, which included the *terminus ad quem*—designated as " nine-days " (*nonae, noundinae*), while the first day of the third week retained the old name of *idus* (perhaps " dividing-day "). The chief motive lying at the bottom of this strange remodelling of the calendar seems to have been a belief in the salutary virtue of odd numbers; [1] and while in general it is based on the oldest form of the Greek year, its variations from that form distinctly exhibit the influence of the doctrines of Pythagoras, which were then paramount in Lower Italy, and which especially turned upon a mystic view of numbers. But the consequence was that this Roman calendar, clearly as it bears traces of the desire that it should harmonise with the course both of sun and moon, in reality by no means so corresponded with the lunar periods as did at least on the whole its Greek model, while, like the oldest Greek cycle, it could only follow the solar seasons by means of frequent arbitrary excisions, and did in all probability follow them but very imperfectly, for it is scarcely likely that the calendar would be handled with greater skill than was manifested in its original arrangement. The retention moreover of the reckoning by months or—which is the same thing—by years of ten months implies a tacit, but not to be misunderstood, confession of the irregularity and untrustworthiness of the oldest Roman solar year. This Roman calendar may be regarded, at least in its essential features, as that generally current among the Latins. As the time of beginning the year and the names of the months were universally liable to change, variations in the minor ordinal numbers and designations are quite compatible with the hypothesis of a common basis; and with such a calendar-system, which practically was quite irrespective of the lunar course, the Latins might easily come to have their months of arbitrary length, whose limits were possibly marked by annual festivals —as in the case of the Alban months, which varied between 16 and 36 days. It would appear probable therefore that the Greek *trieteris* had early been introduced from Lower Italy at least into Latium

---

[1] Censorin. 20. 4, 5; Macrob. *Sat.* i. 13, 5; Solin. 1. With reference to this belief in general, see Festus, *Ep. v. imparem*, p. 109, Müll.; Virgil, *Ecl.* viii. 75, and Servius thereon; Plin. xxviii. 2, 23 (*impares numeros ad omnia vehementiores credimus idque in febribus dierum observatione intellegimur*); Macrob. *Comm.* i. 2, 1; ii. 2, 17 (*impar numerus mas et par femina vocatur*); Plutarch, *Q.R.* 102.

and perhaps also among the other Italian stocks, and had there
after been subjected in the calendars of the several cities to
various subordinate alterations.

For the measuring of periods of more than one year the
regnal years of the kings may have been employed: but it is
doubtful whether that method of dating, which was in use in the
East, existed in Greece or Italy during earlier times. On the
other hand the intercalary period recurring every four years
and the census and lustration of the community connected with
it, appear to have suggested a reckoning by *lustra* similiar in
plan to the Greek reckoning by Olympiads—a mode of reckoning, however, which early lost its chronological importance in
consequence of the irregularities that were soon introduced by
the postponements of the census.

The art of expressing sounds by written signs was of later
origin than the art of measurement. The Italians did not any
more than the Hellenes develop such an art of themselves,
although we may discover attempts at such a development in
the Italian numeral signs (p. 206), and possibly also in the
primitive Italian custom—formed independently of Hellenic
influence—of drawing lots by means of wooden tablets. The
difficulty which must have attended the first individualising of
sounds—occurring as they do in so great a variety of combinations—is best demonstrated by the fact that a single alphabet
propagated from people to people and from generation to
generation has sufficed, and still suffices, for the whole of
Aramaic, Indian, Graeco-Roman, and modern civilisation; and
this most important product of the human intellect was the
joint creation of the Aramaeans and the Indo-Germans. The
Semitic family of languages, in which vowels have a subordinate
character and never can begin a word, presented special facilities
for the individualising of the consonants; and it was among
the Semites accordingly that the first alphabet—in which the
vowels, however, were wanting—was invented. It was the
Indians and Greeks who first independently of each other and
by very divergent methods created, out of the Aramaean consonantal writing introduced among them by commerce, a
complete alphabet by the addition of the vowels—which was
effected by the application of four letters, which the Greeks did
not use as consonantal signs, for the four vowels *a e i o*, and by
the formation of a new sign for *u*—in other words by the introduction of the syllable into writing instead of the mere con
sonant, or, as Palamedes says in Euripides,

Τὰ τῆς γε λήθης φάρμακ᾽ ὀρθώσας μόνος
Ἄφωνα καὶ φωνοῦντα, συλλαβάς τε θείς,
Ἐξεῦρον ἀνθρώποισι γράμματ᾽ εἰδέναι.

This Aramaeo-Hellenic alphabet was accordingly brought to the Italians through the medium of the Sicilian or Italian Hellenes; not, however, through the agricultural colonies of Magna Graecia, but through the merchants of Cumae or Naxos, by whom it must have been brought in the first instance to the very ancient emporia of international traffic in Latium and Etruria—to Rome and Caere. The alphabet received by the Italians was by no means the oldest Hellenic one; it had already experienced several modifications, particularly the addition of the three letters ξ φ χ and the alteration of the signs for ι γ λ.[1] We have already observed (p. 202) that the Etruscan

[1] The history of the alphabet among the Hellenes turns essentially on the fact that—assuming the primitive alphabet of 23 letters, that is to say, the Phoenician alphabet vocalised and enlarged by the addition of the *u*—proposals of very various kinds were made to supplement and improve it, and each of these has a history of its own. The most important of these, which it is interesting to keep in view as bearing on the history of Italian writing, are the following:—I. The introduction of special signs for the sounds ξ φ χ. This proposal is so old that all the Greek alphabets with the single exception of that of the islands Thera and Melos, and all derived from the Greek without exception, exhibit its influence. At first probably the aim was to append the signs Χ=ξι̂, Φ=φι̂, and Ψ=χι̂ to the close of the alphabet, and in this shape it was adopted on the continent of Hellas—with the exception of Athens and Corinth—and also among the Sicilian and Italian Greeks. The Greeks of Asia Minor on the other hand, of Crete and the islands of the Archipelago, and also the Corinthians on the mainland appear, when this proposal reached them, to have already had in use for the sound ξι̂ the fifteenth sign of the Phoenician alphabet Ξ (Samech); accordingly of the three new signs they adopted the Φ for φι̂, but employed the X not for ξι̂, but for χι̂. The third sign originally invented for χι̂ was probably allowed in most instances to drop; the Ionians of Asia Minor retained it, but gave to it the value of ψι̂. The mode of writing adopted in Asia Minor was followed also by Athens; only in its case not merely the ψι̂, but the ξι̂ also, was not received and in their room the two consonants continued to be written as before.—II. Equally early, if not still earlier, an effort was made to obviate the confusion that might so easily occur between the forms for *i* ⟨ and for *s* ⟨; for all the Greek alphabets known to us bear traces of the endeavour to distinguish them otherwise and more precisely. Already in very early times two such proposals of change must have been made, each of which found a field of its own. In the one case they employed for the sibilant—for which the Phoenician alphabet furnished two signs, the fourteenth for *sh* (Μ) and the eighteenth for *s* (Ϡ)—not the latter, which was in sound the more suitable, but the former; and such was in earlier times the mode of writing in the eastern islands, in Corinth and Corcyra, and among the Italian Achaeans. In the other case they substituted for the sign of *i* the simple stroke Ι, which was by far the more usual, and at no very late date became at least so far general that the broken *i* ⟨ everywhere disappeared, although individual communities retained the *s* in the form Μ alongside of the Ι.—III. Of later date is the substitution of ⋁

and Latin alphabets were not derived the one from the other, but both directly from the Greek; in fact the Greek alphabet came to Etruria in a form materially different from that which reached Latium. The Etruscan alphabet has a double sign *s* for $\wedge$ (λ) which might readily be confounded with Γ γ. This was done in Athens and Boeotia, while Corinth and the communities dependent on Corinth attained the same object by giving to the γ the semicircular form C instead of the hook-shape.—IV. The forms for ρ Γ and ρ P, likewise very liable to be confounded, were distinguished by transforming the latter into R; which more recent form was not used by the Greeks of Asia Minor, the Cretans, the Italian Achaeans, and a few other districts, but on the other hand greatly preponderated both in Greece proper and in Magna Graecia and Sicily. Still the older form of the ρ P did not so early and so completely disappear there as the older form of the *l*; this alteration therefore beyond doubt is to be placed later.—V. The distinction between the long and short *e* and the long and short *o* remained in the earlier times wholly confined to the Greeks of Asia Minor and of the islands of the Aegean Sea.

All these technical improvements are of a like nature and from an historical point of view of like value, in so far as each of them arose at a definite time and at a definite place and thereafter took its own mode of diffusion and found its special development. The excellent investigation of Kirchhoff (*Studien zur Geschichte des griechischen Alphabets*, 1863), which has thrown a clear light on the—previously so obscure—history of the Hellenic alphabet, and has furnished essential data for the earliest relations between the Hellenes and Italians, settling in particular incontrovertibly the previously uncertain home of the Etruscan alphabet, is affected by a certain one-sidedness in so far as it lays disproportionally great stress on a single one of these proposals. If systems are here to be distinguished at all, we may not divide the alphabets into two classes according to the value of the X as ξ or as χ, but we shall have to distinguish the alphabet of 23 from that of 25 or 26 letters, and perhaps further in this latter case to distinguish the Ionic of Asia Minor, from which the later common alphabet proceeded, from the common Greek of earlier times. In dealing, however, with the different proposals for the modification of the alphabet the several districts followed an essentially eclectic course, so that one was received here and another there; and it is just in this respect that the history of the Greek alphabet is so instructive, because it shows how particular groups of the Greek lands exchanged improvements in handicraft and art, while others exhibited no such reciprocity. As to Italy in particular we have already called attention to the remarkable contrast between the Achaean agricultural towns and the Chalcidic and Doric colonies of a more mercantile character (p. 136); in the former the primitive forms were throughout retained, in the latter the improved forms were adopted, even those which coming from different quarters were somewhat inconsistent, such as the C γ alongside of the $\vee$ *l*. The Italian alphabets proceed, as Kirchhoff has shown, wholly from the alphabet of the Italian Greeks and in fact from the Chalcidico-Doric; but that the Etruscans and Latins received their alphabet not the one from the other but both directly from the Greeks, is placed beyond doubt by the different form of the *r*. For, while of the four modifications of the alphabet above described which concern the Italian Greeks (the fifth was confined to Asia Minor) the first three were already carried out before the alphabet went to the Etruscans and Latins, the fuller distinction between ρ and *r* had not yet been introduced when it came to Etruria, but was complete when the Latins received it; for which reason the Etruscans are as little acquainted with the form R for *r* as the Latins or the Faliscans with the form P.

(sigma *s* and san *sh*) and only a single *k*,[1] and of the *r* only the older form P; the Latin has, so far as we know, only a single *s*, but a double sign for *k* (kappa *k* and koppa *q*), and of the *r* merely the more recent form R. The oldest Etruscan writing shows no knowledge of lines, and winds like the coiling of a snake; the more recent employs parallel broken off lines from right to left; the Latin writing, as far as our monuments reach back, exhibits only the latter form of parallel lines, which originally perhaps may have run at pleasure from left to right or from right to left, but subsequently ran among the Romans in the former, and among the Faliscans in the latter direction. The model alphabet brought to Etruria must notwithstanding its comparatively remodelled character reach back to an epoch very ancient, though not positively to be determined; for, as the two sibilants sigma and san were always used by the Etruscans as different sounds side by side, the Greek alphabet which came to Etruria must still have possessed both of them in this way as living signs of sound; but among all the monuments of the Greek language known to us not one presents sigma and san in simultaneous use.

The Latin alphabet certainly, as we know it, bears on the whole a more recent character; and it is not improbable that the Latins did not simply receive the alphabet once for all, as was the case in Etruria, but in consequence of their lively intercourse with Sicily kept pace for a considerable period with the alphabet in use there, and followed its variations. We find, for instance, that the earlier forms Σ and /W were not unknown to the Romans, but were superseded in common use by the later forms ⊆ and W—a circumstance which can only be explained

---

[1] That the Etruscans always were without the koppa, seems not doubtful; for not only is no sure trace of it to be met with elsewhere, but it is wanting in the model alphabet of the Galassi vase. The attempt to show its presence in the syllabarium of the latter is at any rate mistaken, for the syllabarium can and does only take notice of the Etruscan letters that were afterwards in common use, and to these the koppa notoriously did not belong; moreover the sign placed at the close cannot well from its position have any other value than that of the *f*, which was in fact the last letter in the Etruscan alphabet, and which could not be omitted in a syllabarium exhibiting the variations of that alphabet from its model. It is certainly surprising that the koppa should be absent from the Greek alphabet that came to Etruria, when it otherwise so long maintained its place in the Chalcidico-Doric; but this may well have been a local peculiarity of the town whose alphabet first reached Etruria. Caprice and accident have at all times had a share in determining whether a sign becoming superfluous shall be retained or dropped from the alphabet; thus the Attic alphabet lost the eighteenth Phoenician sign, but retained the others which had disappeared from the usual language.

by supposing that the Latins employed for a considerable period the Greek alphabet as such in writing either their mother-tongue or Greek. It is dangerous therefore to draw from the more recent character of the Greek alphabet which we meet with in Rome, as compared with that brought to Etruria, the inference that writing was practised earlier in Etruria than in Rome.

The powerful impression produced by the acquisition of the treasure of letters on those who received them, and the vividness with which they realised the power that slumbered in those humble signs, are illustrated by a remarkable vase from one of the oldest tombs of Caere (built before the invention of the arch), exhibiting the old Greek model alphabet as it came to Etruria, and also an Etruscan syllabarium formed from it, which may be compared to that of Palamedes—evidently a sacred relic of the introduction and acclimatisation of alphabetic writing in Etruria.

Not less important for history than the derivation of the alphabet is the further course of its development on Italian soil: perhaps it is even of more importance; for by means of it a gleam of light is thrown upon the inland commerce of Italy, which is involved in far greater darkness than the commerce with foreigners on its coast. In the earliest epoch of the Etruscan alphabet, when it was used without material altera-tion as it had been introduced, its use appears to have been restricted to the Etruscans on the Po and in what is now Tuscany. In course of time this alphabet, manifestly diffus-ing itself from Hatria and Spina, reached southward along the east coast as far as the Abruzzi, northward to the Veneti and subsequently even to the Celts at the foot of, amidst, and indeed beyond the Alps, so that its last offshoots reached as far as the Tyrol and Styria. The more recent epoch started with a reform of the alphabet, the chief features of which were the introduction of writing in interrupted lines, the suppression of the *o*, which was no longer distinguished in pronunciation from the *u*, and the introduction of a new letter *f*, for which the alphabet as received by them had no corresponding sign. This reform evidently arose among the western Etruscans, and while it did not find reception beyond the Apennines, became naturalised among all the Sabellian tribes, and especially among the Umbrians. In its further course the alphabet experienced various fortunes in connection with the several stocks of the Etruscans on the Arno and around Capua, the Umbrians and the Samnites; frequently the *mediae* were entirely or partially lost, while elsewhere again new vowels and consonants were developed. But that West-Etruscan reform of the alphabet was not merely as old as the oldest tombs found in Etruria; it was considerably older, for the syllabarium just mentioned as found probably in one of these tombs already presents the reformed alphabet in an essentially modified and modernised shape; and, as the reformed alphabet itself is relatively recent as compared with the primitive one, the mind almost fails in the effort to reach back to the time when that alphabet came to Italy.

While the Etruscans thus appear as the instruments in diffusing the alphabet in the north, east, and south of the peninsula, the Latin alphabet again was confined to Latium, and maintained its ground, upon the whole, there with but few alterations; only the letters γ κ and ζ σ gradually became coincident in sound, the consequence of which was, that in each case one of the homophonous signs (κ ζ) disappeared from writing. In Rome it can be shown that these were already laid aside when the Twelve Tables were committed to writing. Now when we consider that in the oldest abbreviations the distinction between γ *c* and κ *k* is still regularly maintained;[1] that the period, accordingly, when the sounds became in pronunciation coincident, and before that again the period during which the abbreviations became fixed, were far earlier than the origin of the Twelve Tables; and lastly, that a considerable interval must necessarily have elapsed between the introduction of writing and the establishment of a conventional system of abbreviation; we must, both as regards Etruria and Latium, carry back the commencement of the art of writing to an epoch which more closely approximates to the first incidence of the Egyptian Sirius-period within historical times, the year 1322 B.C., than to the year 776, with which the chronology of the Olympiads began in Greece.[2] The high antiquity of the art of writing in

[1] Thus C represents *Gaius*; CN *Gnaeus*; while K stands for *Kaeso*. With the more recent abbreviations of course this is not the case; in these γ is represented not by C, but by G (GAL *Galeria*), κ, as a rule, by C (C *centum*; COS *consul*; COL *Collina*), or before *a* by K (KAR *karmentalia*; MERK *merkatus*). For they expressed for a time the sound *c* before *a* by K, before the other vowels by C, just as our *q* is only written before *u*.

[2] If this view is correct, the origin of the Homeric poems (though of course not exactly in the form in which we now have them) must have been far anterior to the age which Herodotus assigns for the flourishing of Homer (100 before Rome); for the introduction of the Hellenic alphabet into Italy, as well as the beginning of intercourse at all between Hellas and Italy, belongs only to the post-Homeric period.

Rome is evinced otherwise by numerous and plain indications.
The existence of documents of the regal period is sufficiently
attested; such was the special treaty between Rome and Gabii,
which was concluded by a king Tarquinius and probably not by
the last of that name, and which, written on the skin of the
bullock sacrificed on the occasion, was preserved in the temple
of Sancus on the Quirinal, which was rich in antiquities and
probably escaped the conflagration of the Gauls; and such was
the alliance which king Servius Tullius concluded with Latium,
and which Dionysius saw on a copper tablet in the temple of
Diana on the Aventine. What he saw, however, was probably
a copy restored after the fire with the help of a Latin exemplar,
for it is not likely that engraving on metal was practised in the
time of the kings. But even then they scratched (*exarare*,
scribere, akin to *scrobes* [1]) or painted (*linere*, thence *littera*) on
leaves (*folium*), inner bark (*liber*), or wooden tablets (*tabula*,
album), afterwards also on leather and linen. The sacred
records of the Samnites as well as of the priesthood of Anagnia
were inscribed on linen rolls, and so were the oldest lists of the
Roman magistrates preserved in the temple of the goddess of
recollection (*Iuno moneta*) on the Capitol. It is scarcely necessary to recall further proofs in the primitive marking of the
pastured cattle (*scriptura*), in the mode of addressing the senate,
"fathers and enrolled" (*patres conscripti*), and in the great
antiquity of the books of oracles, the clan-registers, and the
Alban and Roman calendars. When Roman tradition speaks
of halls in the Forum, where the boys and girls of quality were
taught to read and write, as early as the time of the expulsion
of the kings, the statement may be, but is not necessarily to be
deemed, an invention. We have been deprived of information
as to the early Roman history, not in consequence of the want of
a knowledge of writing or even perhaps of the lack of documents,
but in consequence of the incapacity of the historians of the
succeeding age (which was called to investigate the history) to
work out the materials furnished by the archives, and of the
perversity which led them to ransack tradition for the delineation of motives and of characters, for accounts of battles and
narratives of revolutions, and in pursuit of these to miss such
information as it would not have refused to yield to the serious
and self-denying inquirer.

The history of Italian writing thus furnishes in the first place
a confirmation of the weak and indirect influence exercised by

[1] Just as the Old Saxon *wrītan* signifies properly to tear, thence to write.

he Hellenic character over the Sabellians as compared with
he more western peoples. The fact that the former received
heir alphabet from the Etruscans and not from the Romans is
probably to be explained by supposing that they had obtained
t before they entered upon their migration along the ridge of
he Apennines, and that the Sabines and Samnites took it with
hem when they were sent forth from the mother-land. On
he other hand this history of writing contains a salutary warn-
ng against the adoption of the hypothesis, originated by the
ater Roman culture in its devotedness to Etruscan mysticism
and antiquarian trifling, and patiently repeated by modern and
even very recent inquirers, that Roman civilisation derived its
germs and its main substance from Etruria. If this were the
ruth, some trace of it ought to be more especially apparent in
his field; but on the contrary the nucleus of the Latin art of
writing was Greek, and its development was so national, that
t did not even adopt the very desirable Etruscan sign for *f*.
Indeed, where there is an appearance of borrowing, as in the
numeral signs, it is on the part of the Etruscans, who derived
rom the Romans at least the sign for 50.

Lastly it is a significant fact, that among all the Italian stocks
he development of the Greek alphabet primarily consisted in
a process of corruption. Thus the *mediae* disappeared in the
whole of the Etruscan dialects, while the Umbrians lost γ and
d, the Samnites *d*, and the Romans γ; and among the latter *d*
also threatened to amalgamate with *r*. In like manner among
he Etruscans *o* and *u* early coalesced, and even among the
Latins we meet with a tendency to the same corruption. Nearly
he converse occurred in the case of the sibilants; for while the
Etruscan retained the three signs *z*, *s*, *sh*, and the Umbrian
ejected the last but developed two new sibilants in its room,
he Samnite and the Faliscan confined themselves like the
Greek to *s* and *z*, and the Roman of later times to *s* alone. It is
plain that the more delicate distinctions of sound were duly
elt by the introducers of the alphabet, men of culture and
masters of two languages; but after the national writing became
wholly detached from the Hellenic mother-alphabet, the *mediae*
and their *tenues* gradually came to coincide, and the sibilants
and vowels were thrown into disorder—transpositions or rather
destructions of sound, of which the first in particular is entirely
oreign to the Greek. The destruction of the forms of flexion
and derivation went hand in hand with this corruption of sounds.
The cause of this barbarisation was, upon the whole, simply the

necessary process of corruption which is continuously eating
away every language, where its progress is not checked by
literature and reason; only in this case indications of what has
elsewhere passed away without leaving a trace have been pre
served in the writing of sounds. The circumstance that this
barbarising process affected the Etruscans more strongly than
any other of the Italian stocks adds to the numerous proofs of
their inferior capacity for culture. The fact on the other hand
that, among the Italians, the Umbrians apparently were the
most affected by a similar corruption of language, the Romans
less so, the southern Sabellians least of all, probably finds its
explanation, at least in part, in the more lively intercourse
maintained by the former with the Etruscans, and by the latter
with the Greeks.

CHAPTER XV

ART

POETRY is impassioned language, and its modulation is melody. While in this sense no people is without poetry and music, some nations have received a pre-eminent endowment of poetic gifts. The Italian nation, however, was not and is not one of these. The Italian is deficient in the passion of the heart, and in the longing to idealise what is human and to give life to the things of the inanimate world, which form the very essence of poetic art. His acuteness of perception and his charming versatility enabled him to excel in irony and in the vein of tale-telling which we find in Horace and Boccaccio, in the graceful pleasantries of love and song which are presented in Catullus and in the best popular songs of Naples, above all in low comedy and in farce. Italian soil gave birth in ancient times to burlesque tragedy, and in modern times to burlesques of the poetry of chivalry. In rhetoric and histrionic art especially no other nation equalled or equals the Italians. But in the more perfect kinds of art they have hardly advanced beyond dexterity of execution, and no epoch of their literature has produced a true epos or a genuine drama. The very highest literary works that have been successfully produced in Italy, divine poems like Dante's Commedia, and historical treatises such as those of Sallust and Machiavelli, of Tacitus and Colletta, are pervaded by a passion more rhetorical than spontaneous. Even in music, both in ancient and modern times, real creative talent has been far less conspicuous than the cleverness which speedily assumes the character of virtuosoship, and enthrones in the room of genuine and genial art a hollow and heart-withering idol. The field of the inward in art—so far as we may in the case of art distinguish an inward and an outward at all—is not that which has fallen to the Italian as his special province; the power of beauty, to have its full effect upon him, must be placed not ideally before his mind, but sensuously before his eyes. Accordingly he is thoroughly at home in architecture, painting, and sculpture; in these he was during the epoch of ancient culture the best disciple of the Hellenes, and in modern times he has become the instructor of all nations.

From the defectiveness of our traditional information it is not possible to trace the development of artistic ideas among the several groups of nations in Italy; and in particular we are no longer in a position to speak of the poetry of Italy; we can only speak of that of Latium. Latin poetry, like that of every other nation, began in the lyrical form, or, to speak more correctly, sprang out of those primitive festal rejoicings, in which dance, music, and song were still inseparably blended. It is remarkable, however, that in the most ancient religious usages dancing, and next to dancing instrumental music, were far more prominent than song. In the great procession, with which the Roman festival of victory was opened, the chief place, next to the images of the gods and the champions, was assigned to the dancers grave and merry. The grave dancers were arranged in three groups of men, youths, and boys, all clad in red tunics with copper belts, with swords and short lances, the men being moreover furnished with helmets, and generally in full armed attire. The merry dancers were divided into two companies—" the sheep " in sheep-skins with a parti-coloured over-garment, and " the goats " naked down to the waist, with a buck's skin thrown over them. In like manner the " leapers " (*salii*) were perhaps the most ancient and sacred of all the priesthoods (p. 168), and dancers (*ludii, ludiones*) were indispensable in all public processions, and particularly at funeral solemnities; so that dancing became even in ancient times a common trade. But, wherever the dancers made their appearance, there appeared also the musicians or—which was in the earliest times the same thing—the pipers. They too were never wanting at a sacrifice, at a marriage, or at a funeral; and by the side of the primitive priesthood of the " leapers " there was ranged, of equal antiquity although of far inferior rank, the guild of the " pipers " (*collegium tibicinum*, p. 195), whose true character as strolling musicians is evinced by their ancient privilege—maintained even in spite of the strictness of Roman police—of wandering through the streets at their annual festival, wearing masks and full of sweet wine. While dancing thus presents itself as an honourable function and music as one subordinate but still necessary, so that public corporations were instituted for both of them, poetry appears more as an incidental and, so to speak, uncalled-for phenomenon, whether it may have come into existence on its own account or to serve as an accompaniment to the movements of the dancers.

The earliest chant, in the view of the Romans, was that which the leaves sang to themselves in the green solitude of the forest. The whispers and pipings of the " favourable spirit " (*faunus*, from *favere*) in the grove were reproduced to men, by those who had the gift of listening to him, in rhythmically measured language (*casmen*, afterwards *carmen*, from *canere*). Of a kindred nature to these soothsaying songs of inspired men and women (*vates*) were the incantations properly so called, the formulae for conjuring away diseases and other troubles, and the evil spells by which they prevented rain and called down lightning or even enticed the seed from one field to another; only in these instances, probably from the outset, formulae of mere sounds appear side by side with formulae of words.[1] More firmly rooted in tradition and equally ancient were the religious litanies which were sung and danced by the Salii and other priesthoods; the only one of which that has come down to us, a dance chant of the Arval Brethren in honour of Mars probably composed to be sung in alternate parts, deserves a place here.

> *Enos, Lases, iuvate !*
> *Neve lue rue, Marmar, sins incurrere in pleores !*
> *Satur fu, fere Mars ! limen sali ! sta ! berber !*
> *Semunis alternis advocapit conctos !*
> *Enos, Marmar, iuvato !*
> *Triumpe !*

Which may be thus interpreted:

To the gods.	*Nos, Lares, iuvate !* *Ne luem ruem* (=*ruinam*), *Mamers, sinas incurrere in plures !* *Satur esto, fere Mars !*
To the individual brethren.	*In limen insili ! sta ! verbera* (*limen ?*) *!*
To all the brethren.	*Semones alterni advocate cunctos !*
To the god.	*Nos, Mamers, iuvato !*
To the individual brethren.	*Tripudia !* [2]

The Latin of this chant and of kindred fragments of the

---

[1] Thus Cato the Elder (*de R. R.* 160), gives as potent against sprains the formula: *hauat hauat hauat ista pista sista damia bodannaustra*, which was probably quite as obscure to its inventor as it is to us. Of course, along with these there were also formulae of words; *e.g.* it was a remedy for gout, to think, while fasting, on some other person, and thrice nine times to utter the words, touching the earth at the same time and spitting:—
" I think of thee, mend my feet. Let the earth receive the ill, let health with me dwell " (*terra pestem teneto, salus hic maneto.* Varro *de R.R.* i. 2, 27).

[2] Each of the first five lines was repeated thrice, and the call at the close five times. Various points in the interpretation are uncertain, particularly as respects the third and fourth lines.

Salian songs, which were regarded even by the scholars of the Augustan age as the oldest documents of their mother-tongue, is related to the Latin of the Twelve Tables somewhat as the language of the Nibelungen is related to the language of Luther; and we may perhaps compare these venerable litanies, as respects both language and contents, with the Indian Vedas.

Lyrical panegyrics and lampoons belonged to a later epoch. We might infer from the national character of the Italians that satirical songs must have abounded in Latium in ancient times, even if their prevalence had not been attested by the very ancient measures of police directed against them. But the panegyrical chants became of more importance. When a burgess was borne to burial, the bier was followed by a female relative or friend, who, accompanied by a piper, sang his dirge (*nenia*). In like manner at banquets boys, who according to the fashion of those days attended their fathers even at feasts out of their own houses, sang by turns songs in praise of their ancestors, sometimes to the pipe, sometimes simply reciting them without accompaniment (*assa voce canere*). The custom of men singing in succession at banquets was probably borrowed from the Greeks, and that not till a later age. We know no further particulars of these ancestral lays; but it is self-evident that they must have attempted description and narration and thus have developed, along with and out of the lyrical element, the features of epic poetry.

Other elements of poetry were called into action in the primitive popular carnival, the comic dance or *satura* (p. 28), which beyond doubt reached back to a period anterior to the separation of the stocks. On such occasions song would never be wanting; and the circumstances under which such pastimes were exhibited, chiefly at public festivals and marriages, as well as the eminently practical shape which they certainly assumed, naturally suggested that several dancers, or sets of dancers, should take up reciprocal parts; so that the singing thus came to be associated with a species of acting, which of course was chiefly of a comical and often of a licentious character. In this way there arose not merely alternative chants, such as afterwards went by the name of Fescennine songs, but also the elements of a popular comedy—which were in this instance planted in a soil admirably adapted for their growth, as an acute sense of the outward and the comic, and a delight in gesticulation and masquerade have ever been leading traits of Italian character.

No remains have been preserved of these germs of the Roman epos and drama. That the ancestral lays were traditional is self-evident, and is abundantly demonstrated by the fact that they were regularly recited by children; but even in the time of Cato the Elder they had completely passed into oblivion. The comedies again, if it be allowable to apply to them such a name, were at this period and long afterwards altogether improvised. Consequently nothing of this popular poetry and popular melody could be handed down but the measure, the accompaniment of music and choral dancing, and perhaps the masks.

Whether what we call metre existed in the earlier times is doubtful; the litany of the Arval Brethren scarcely accommodates itself to an outwardly fixed metrical system, and presents to us rather the appearance of an animated recitation. On the other hand we find in subsequent times a very ancient rhythm, the so-called Saturnian [1] or Faunian metre, which is foreign to the Greeks, and may be conjectured to have arisen contemporaneously with the oldest Latin popular poetry. The following poem, belonging, it is true, to a far later age, may give an idea of it:—

> *Quod ré suá difeídens—ásperé afleícta*
> *Paréns timéns heic vóvit—vóto hóc solúto*
> *Decumá factá poloúcta—leíbereís lubéntes*
> *Donú danúnt—Hércoleí—máxsumé—méreto*
> *Semól te oránt se vóti—crébro cón—démnes.*

$$\smile\,\underline{\ }\,{}'\,\smile\,\underline{\ }\,{}'\,\smile\,\underline{\ }\,\overline{\ \ }\,\|\,\underline{\ }\,{}'\,\smile\,\underline{\ }\,{}'\,\smile\,\overline{\ \ }$$

That which, misfortune dreading—sharply to′ afflict him,
An anxious parent vowed here,—when his wish was granted,
A sacred tenth for banquet—gladly give his children
To Hercules a tribute—most of all deserving;
And now they thee beseech, that—often thou wouldst hear them.

Panegyrics as well as comic songs appear to have been uniformly sung in Saturnian metre, of course to the pipe, and probably in such a way that the *caesura* in particular in each line was strongly marked; and in alternate singing the second singer probably took up the verse at this point. The Saturnian

---

[1] The name probably denotes nothing but " the chant-measure," inasmuch as the *sátura* was originally the chant sung at the carnival. The god of sowing, *Saeturnus* or *Saiturnus*, afterwards *Sáturnus*, received his name from the same root; his feast, the Saturnalia, was certainly a sort of carnival, and it is possible that the farces were originally exhibited chiefly there. But there are no proofs of a relation between the Satura and the Saturnalia, and probably the immediate association of the *versus sáturnius* with the god Saturn, and the lengthening of the first syllable in connection with that view, belong only to later times.

measure is, like every other occurring in Roman and Greek antiquity, based on quantity; but of all the antique metres perhaps it is the least thoroughly elaborated, for besides many other liberties it allows itself the greatest licence in omitting the short syllables, and it is at the same time the most imperfect in construction, for these iambic and trochaic half-lines opposed to each other were but little fitted to develop a rhythmical structure adequate for the purposes of the higher poetry.

The fundamental elements of the national music and choral dancing of Latium, which must likewise have been established during this period, are buried in oblivion; except that the Latin pipe is reported to have been a short and slender instrument, provided with only four holes, and originally, as the name shows, made out of the light thigh-bone of some animal.

Lastly, the masks used in after times for the standing characters of the Latin popular comedy or the Atellana, as it was called: Maccus the harlequin, Bucco the glutton, Pappus the good papa, and the wise Dossennus—masks which have been cleverly and strikingly compared to the two servants, the *pantalon* and the *dottore*, in the Italian comedy of Punch—already belonged to the earliest Latin popular art. That they did so cannot of course be strictly proved; but as the use of masks for the face in Latium in the case of the national drama was of immemorial antiquity, while the Greek drama in Rome did not adopt them for a century after its first establishment, as moreover those Atellane masks were of decidedly Italian origin, and as, in fine, the origination as well as the execution of improvised pieces cannot well be conceived apart from fixed masks assigning once for all to the player his proper position throughout the piece, we must associate fixed masks with the rudiments of the Roman drama, or rather regard them as constituting those rudiments themselves.

If our information respecting the earliest indigenous civilisation and art of Latium is so scanty, it may easily be conceived that our knowledge will be still scantier regarding the earliest impulses imparted in this respect to the Romans from without. In a certain sense we may include under this head their becoming acquainted with foreign languages, particularly the Greek. To this latter language, of course, the Latins generally were strangers, as was shown by their enactment in respect to the Sibylline oracles (p. 180); but an acquaintance with it must have been not at all uncommon in the case of merchants. The same may be affirmed of the knowledge of reading and writing, closely connected as it was with the knowledge of Greek (p. 213). The culture of the ancient world, however, was not based either on the knowledge of foreign languages or on elementary technical accomplishments. An influence more important than any thus imparted was exercised over the development of Latium by the elements of the fine arts, which were already in very early times received from the Hellenes. For it was the Hellenes alone, and not the Phoenicians or the Etruscans, that in this respect exercised influence on the Italians. We nowhere find among the latter any stimulus of the fine arts which can be traced to Carthage or Caere, and the Phoenicians and Etruscans may be in general regarded as presenting barren and unproductive types of civilisation.[1] But the influence of Greece did not fail to bear fruit. The Greek seven-stringed lyre, the " strings " (*fides*, from σφιδη, gut; also *barbitus*, βάρβιτος), was not like the pipe indigenous in Latium, and was always regarded there as an instrument of foreign origin; but the early period at which it gained a footing is demonstrated partly by the barbarous mutilation of its Greek name, partly by its being employed even in ritual.[2] That some of the legendary stores of the Greeks during this period found their way into Latium, is shown by the ready reception of Greek works of sculpture with their representations based so thoroughly upon the poetical treasures

---

[1] The statement that " formerly the Roman boys were trained in Etruscan culture, as they were in later times in Greek " (Liv. ix. 36), is quite irreconcilable with the original character of Roman training, and it is not easy to discover what the Roman boys could have learnt in Etruria. Even the most zealous modern partisans of Tages-worship will not maintain that the study of the Etruscan language played such a part in Rome then as the learning of French does now with us; that one who was not an Etruscan should have any understanding of the art of the Etruscan *haruspices* was considered, even by those who availed themselves of that art, to be a disgrace or rather an impossibility (Müller, *Etr.* ii. 4). Probably the whole statement was concocted by the Etruscising antiquaries of the last age of the republic out of rationalistic stories of the older annals, such as that which makes Mucius Scaevola learn Etruscan when a child, for the sake of his conversation with Porsena (Dionysius, v. 28; Plutarch, *Poplicola*, 17; comp. Dionysius, iii. 70).

[2] The employment of the lyre in ritual is attested by Cicero *de Orat.* iii. 51, 197; *Tusc.* iv. 2, 4; Dionysius, vii. 72; Appian, *Pun.* 66; and the inscription in Orelli, 2448, comp. 1803. It was likewise used at the *neniae* (Varro *ap.* Nonium, *v. nenia* and *praeficae*). But playing on the lyre remained none the less unbecoming (Scipio *ap.* Macrob. *Sat.* ii. 10, *et al.*). The prohibition of music in 639 U.C. exempted only the " Latin player on the pipe along with the singer," not the player on the lyre, and the guests at meals sang only to the pipe (Cato in Cic. *Tusc.* i. 2, 3; iv. 2, 3; Varro *ap.* Nonium, *v. assa voce;* Horace, *Carm.* iv. 15, 30). Quintilian, who asserts the reverse (*Inst.* i. 10, 20), has inaccurately transferred to private banquets what Cicero (*de Orat.* iii. 51) states in reference to the feasts of the gods.

of the nation; and the old Latin barbarous conversions of Persephone into Prosepna, Bellerophontes into Melerpanta, Kyklops into Cocles, Laomedon into Alumentus, Ganymedes into Catamitus, Neilos into Melus, Semele into Stimula, enable us to perceive at how remote a period such stories had been heard and repeated by the Latins. Lastly and especially, the Roman chief festival or festival of the city (*ludi maximi, Romani*) must in all probability have derived, if not its origin, at any rate its later arrangements from a Greek source. It was an extraordinary thanksgiving festival celebrated in honour of the Capitoline Jupiter and the gods dwelling along with him, ordinarily in pursuance of a vow made by the general before battle, and therefore usually observed on the return home of the burgess-force in autumn. A festival procession proceeded towards the Circus staked off between the Palatine and Aventine, and furnished with an arena and places for spectators; in front the whole boys of Rome, arranged according to the divisions of the burgess-force, on horseback and on foot; then the champions and the groups of dancers whom we have described above, each with their own music; thereafter the servants of the gods with vessels of frankincense and other sacred utensils; lastly the biers with the images of the gods themselves. The spectacle itself was the counterpart of war as it was waged in primitive times, a contest with chariots, on horseback, and on foot. First there ran the war-chariots, each of which carried in Homeric fashion a charioteer and a combatant; then the combatants who had leaped off; then the horsemen, each of whom appeared after the Roman style of fighting with a horse which he rode and another lead by the hand (*desultor*); lastly, the champions on foot, naked to the girdle round their loins, measured their powers in racing, wrestling, and boxing. In each species of contest there was but one competition, and that between not more than two competitors. A chaplet rewarded the victor, and the honour in which the simple branch which formed the wreath was held is shown by the law permitting it to be laid on the bier of the victor when he died. The festival thus lasted only one day, and the competitions probably still left sufficient time on that day for the real carnival, at which the groups of dancers displayed their art and above all exhibited their farces; and perhaps other representations also, such as competitions in juvenile horsemanship, found a place.[1] The honours won

[1] The city festival can have only lasted at first for a single day, for in the sixth century it still consisted of four days of scenic and one day of

n real war also played their part in this festival; the brave
warrior exhibited on this day the equipments of the antagonist
whom he had slain, and was decorated with a chaplet by the
grateful community just as was the victor in the competition.

Such was the nature of the Roman festival of victory or
city-festival; and the other public festivities of Rome may be
conceived to have been of a similar character, although less
ample in point of resources. At the celebration of a public
funeral dancers regularly bore a part, and along with them,
if there was to be any further exhibition, horse-racers; in that
case the burgesses were specially invited beforehand to the
funeral by a public crier.

But this city-festival, so intimately bound up with the manners
and exercises of the Romans, coincides in all essentials with the
Hellenic national festivals: more especially in the fundamental
idea of combining a religious solemnity and a competition
in warlike sports; in the selection of the several exercises,
which at the Olympic festival, according to Pindar's testimony,
consisted from the first in running, wrestling, boxing, chariot-
racing, and throwing the spear and stone; in the nature of the
prize of victory, which in Rome as well as in the Greek national
festivals was a chaplet, and in the one case as well as in the other
was assigned not to the charioteer, but to the owner of the team;
and lastly in introducing the feasts and rewards of general
patriotism in connection with the general national festival.
This agreement cannot have been accidental, but must have
been either a remnant of the primitive connection between
the peoples, or a result of the earliest international intercourse;
and the probabilities preponderate in favour of the latter
hypothesis. The city-festival, in the form in which we are
acquainted with it, was not one of the oldest institutions of
Rome, for the Circus itself was only laid out in the later regal

Circensian sports (Ritschl, *Parerga*, i. 313) and it is well known that the
scenic amusements were only a subsequent addition. That in each kind of
contest there was originally only one competition, follows from Livy, xliv.
9; the running of five-and-twenty pairs of chariots in succession on one
day was a subsequent innovation (Varro *ap.* Serv. *Georg.* iii. 18). That
only two chariots—and likewise beyond doubt only two horsemen and
two wrestlers—strove for the prize, may be inferred from the circumstance
that at all periods in the Roman chariot-races only as many chariots competed as there were so-called factions; and of these there were originally
only two, the white and the red. The horsemanship-competition of
patrician youths which belonged to the Circensian games, the so-called
Troia, was, as is well known, revived by Caesar; beyond doubt it was
connected with the cavalcade of the boy-militia, which Dionysius mentions
(vii. 72).

period (p. 112); and just as the reform of the constitution then took place under Greek influence (p. 98), the city-festival may have been at the same time so far transformed as to combine Greek races with, and eventually to a certain extent to substitute them for, an older mode of amusement — the "leap" (*triumpus*, p. 28), and possibly swinging, which was a primitive Italian custom and long continued in use at the festival on the Alban mount. Moreover, while there is some trace of the use of the war-chariot in actual warfare in Hellas, no such trace exists in Latium. Lastly, the Greek term σταδιον (Doric σπαδιον) was at a very early period transferred to the Latin language, retaining its signification, as *spatium;* and there exists even an express statement that the Romans derived their horse and chariot races from the people of Thurii, although, it is true, another derives them from Etruria. It thus appears that, in addition to the impulses imparted by the Hellenes in music and poetry, the Romans were indebted to them for the fruitful idea of gymnastic competitions.

Thus there not only existed in Latium the same fundamental elements in which Hellenic culture and art originated, but Hellenic culture and art themselves exercised a powerful influence over Latium in very early times. Not only did the Latins possess the elements of gymnastic training, in so far as the Roman boy learned like every farmer's son to manage horses and waggon and to handle the hunting-spear, and as in Rome every burgess was at the same time a soldier; but the art of dancing was from the first an object of public care, and a powerful impulse was further given to such culture at an early period by the introduction of the Hellenic games. The lyrical poetry and tragedy of Hellas grew out of songs similar to the festival lays of Rome; the ancestral lay contained the germs of epos, the masked farce the germs of comedy; and in this field also Grecian influences were not wanting.

In such circumstances it is the more remarkable that these germs either did not spring up at all, or were soon arrested in their growth. The bodily training of the Latin youth continued to be solid and substantial, but it remained altogether alien form the idea of an artistic bodily culture, such as was the aim of Hellenic gymnastics. The public games of the Hellenes, when introduced into Italy, changed not so much their normal form as their essential character. While they were intended to be competitions of burgesses and beyond doubt were so at first in Rome, they became contests of trained riders and

trained boxers, and, while the proof of free and Hellenic descent
formed the first condition for participating in the Greek festal
games, those of Rome soon passed into the hands of freedmen
and foreigners and even of persons not free at all. Consequently
the circle of fellow-competitors became converted into a public
of spectators, and the chaplet of the victorious champion, which
has been with justice called the badge of Hellas, was afterwards
hardly ever mentioned in Latium.

A similar fate befell poetry and her sisters. The Greeks and
Germans alone possess a fountain of song that wells up
spontaneously; from the golden vase of the Muses only a few
drops have fallen on the green soil of Italy. There was no
formation of legend in the strict sense there. The Italian gods
were abstractions and remained such; they never became
elevated into or, as some may prefer to say, never were obscured
under, a true personal shape. In like manner men, even the
greatest and noblest, remained in the view of the Italians without
exception mortals, and were not, as in the longing recollection
and affectionately cherished tradition of Greece, elevated
in the conception of the multitude into godlike heroes. But
above all no development of national poetry took place in
Latium. It is the deepest and noblest effect of the fine arts
and above all of poetry, that they do away with the barriers
of civil communities and create out of tribes a nation and out
of the nations a world. As in the present day by means of our
cosmopolitan literature the distinctions of civilised nations are
done away, so Greek poetic art transformed the narrow and
egotistic sense of family relationship into the consciousness
of an Hellenic nation, and this again into the consciousness
of a broad humanity. But in Latium nothing similar occurred.
There might be poets in Alba and in Rome, but there arose no
Latin epos, nor even—what were still more conceivable—a
catechism for the Latin farmer of a kind similar to the Works
and Days of Hesiod. The Latin federal festival might well
have become a national festival of the Muses, like the Olympian
and Isthmian games of the Greeks. A cycle of legends might
well have gathered around the fall of Alba, such as was woven
around the conquest of Ilion, and every community and every
noble clan of Latium might have discovered or inserted the story
of its own origin there. But neither of these results took place,
and Italy remained without national poetry or art.

The inference which of necessity follows from these facts,
that the development of the fine arts in Latium was rather a

shrivelling up than an expanding into bloom, is confirmed in a
manner not to be mistaken by tradition. The beginnings of
poetry everywhere, perhaps, belong rather to women than to
men; the spell of incantation and the chant for the dead pertain
pre-eminently to the former, and not without reason the spirits
of song, the Casmenae or Camenae and the Carmentis of Latium,
like the Muses of Hellas, were conceived as feminine. But the
time came in Hellas, when the poet relieved the songstress and
Apollo took his place at the head of the Muses. In Latium
there was no national god of song, and the older Latin language
had no designation for the poet.[1] The power of song emerging
there was out of all proportion weaker, and was rapidly arrested
in its growth. The exercise of the fine arts was there early
restricted, partly to women and children, partly to incorporated
or unincorporated tradesmen. We have already mentioned
that funeral chants were sung by women and banquet-lays by
boys; the religious litanies also were chiefly executed by
children. The musicians formed an incorporated, the dancers
and the wailing women (*praeficae*) unincorporated, trades.
While dancing, music, and singing remained constantly in
Greece—as they were originally also in Latium—reputable
employments redounding to the honour of the burgess and of
the community to which he belonged, in Latium the better
portion of the burgesses stood more and more aloof from these
vain arts, and that the more decidedly in proportion as art
came to be more publicly exhibited and more thoroughly penetrated by the quickening impulses derived from other lands.
The use of the native pipe was sanctioned, but the lyre remained
despised; and while the national amusement of masks was
allowed, the foreign amusements of the *palaestra* were not only
regarded with indifference, but esteemed disgraceful. While
the fine arts in Greece became more and more the common
property of the Hellenes individually and collectively and
thereby became the means of diffusing a universal culture, they
gradually disappeared in Latium from the thoughts and feelings
of the people; and, as they degenerated into utterly insignificant
handicrafts, the idea of a general national culture to be communicated to youth never suggested itself at all. The educa-

---

[1] *Vates* probably denoted in the first instance the " leader of the singing "
(for so the *Vates* of the Salii must be understood) and thereafter in its older
usage approximated to the Greek προφήτης; it was a word belonging to
religious ritual, and even when subsequently used of the poet, always
retained the accessory idea of a divinely-inspired singer—the priest of the
Muses.

tion of youth remained entirely confined within the limits of the narrowest domesticity. The boy never left his father's side, and accompanied him not only to the field with the plough and the sickle, but also to the house of a friend or to the council-hall, when his father was invited as a guest or summoned to the senate. This domestic education was well adapted to train man wholly for the household and wholly for the state. The permanent intercommunion of life between father and son, and the mutual reverence felt by adolescence for ripened manhood and by the mature man for the innocence of youth, lay at the root of the steadfastness of the domestic and political traditions, of the closeness of the family bond, and in general of the grave earnestness (*gravitas*) and character of moral worth in Roman life. This mode of educating youth was in truth one of those institutions of homely and scarce conscious wisdom, which are as simple as they are profound. But amidst the admiration which it awakens we may not overlook the fact that it could only be carried out, and was only carried out, by the sacrifice of true individual culture and by a complete renunciation of the equally charming and perilous gifts of the Muses.

Regarding the development of the fine arts among the Etrus-cans and Sabellians our knowledge is little better than none.[1] We can only notice the fact that in Etruria the dancers (*histri, histriones*) and the pipe-players (*subulones*) early made a trade of their art, probably earlier even than in Rome, and exhibited themselves in public not only at home, but also in Rome for small remuneration and less honour. It is a circumstance more remarkable that at the Etruscan national festival, in the exhibi-tion of which the whole twelve cities were represented by a federal priest, games were given like those of the Roman city-festival; we are, however, no longer in a position to answer the question which it suggests, how far the Etruscans were more successful than the Latins in attaining a national art not con-fined to the narrow bounds of the individual communities. On the other hand a foundation probably was laid in Etruria, even in early times, for that insipid accumulation of learned lumber, particularly of a theological and astrological nature, by virtue of which afterwards, when amidst the general decay anti-quarian dilettantism began to flourish, the Tuscans divided with the Jews, Chaldeans, and Egyptians the honour of being accounted the primitive sources of divine wisdom. We know

---

[1] We shall show in due time that the Atellanae and Fescenninae belonged not to Campanian and Etruscan, but to Latin art.

still less, if possible, of Sabellian art; but that of course by no
means warrants the inference that the Sabellians were inferior
to the neighbouring stocks. On the contrary, it may be conjectured from what we otherwise know of the character of the
three chief races of Italy, that in artistic gifts the Samnites
approached nearest to the Hellenes and the Etruscans were
farthest removed from them; and a sort of confirmation of this
hypothesis is furnished by the fact, that the most gifted and
most original of the Roman poets, such as Naevius, Ennius,
Lucilius, and Horace, belonged to the Samnite lands, whereas
Etruria has almost no representatives in Roman literature
except the Arretine Maecenas, the most insufferable of · all
heartless and affected [1] court-poets, and the Volaterran Persius,
the true ideal of a conceited and languid, poetry-smitten, youth.

The elements of architecture were, as has been already
indicated, a primitive common possession of the stocks. The
dwelling-house constituted the first attempt of structural art;
and it was the same among Greeks and Italians. Built of
wood, and covered with a pointed roof of straw or shingles, it
formed a square dwelling-chamber, which let out the smoke
and let in the light by an opening in the roof corresponding
with a hole for carrying off the rain in the ground (*cavum
aedium*). Under this " black roof " (*atrium*) the meals were
prepared and consumed; there the household gods were worshipped, and the marriage bed and the bier were set out; there
the husband received his guests, and the wife sat spinning amid
the circle of her maidens. The house had no porch, unless we
take as such the uncovered space between the house door and
the street, which obtained its name *vestibulum, i.e.* dressing-
place, from the circumstance that the Romans were in the habit
of going about within doors in their tunics, and only wrapped the
toga around them when they went abroad. There was, moreover, no division of apartments except that sleeping and store
closets might be provided around the dwelling-room; and still
less were there stairs, or stories placed one above another.

Whether, or to what extent, a national Italian architecture
arose out of these beginnings can scarcely be determined, for in
this field Greek influence, even in the earliest times, had a very
powerful effect and almost wholly overgrew such national
attempts as possibly had preceded it. The very oldest Italian
architecture with which we are acquainted is not much less under
the influence of that of Greece than the architecture of the

---

[1] [Literally " word-crisping," in allusion to the *calamistri Maecenatis*.]

Augustan age. The primitive tombs of Caere and Alsium, and probably the oldest one also of those recently discovered at Praeneste, have been, exactly like the *thesauroi* of Orchomenos and Mycenae, roofed over with courses of stone placed one above another, gradually over-lapping, and closed by a large stone cover. A very ancient building at the city wall of Tusculum was roofed in the same way, and so was originally the well-house (*tullianum*) at the foot of the Capitol, till the top was pulled down to make room for another building. The gates constructed on the same system are entirely similar in Arpinum and in Mycenae. The tunnel which drains the Alban lake (p. 38), presents the greatest resemblance to that of lake Copais. What are called Cyclopean ring-walls frequently occur in Italy, especially in Etruria, Umbria, Latium, and Sabina, and decidedly belong in point of design to the most ancient buildings of Italy, although the greater portion of those now extant were probably not executed till a much later age, several of them certainly not till the seventh century of the city. They are, just like those of Greece, sometimes quite roughly formed of large unwrought blocks of rock with smaller stones inserted between them, sometimes disposed in square horizontal courses,[1] sometimes

[1] Of this character were the Servian walls, the remains of which recently discovered at the Aventine, both on the side towards S. Paolo in the Vigna Maccarana, and on the side towards the Tiber below S. Sabina, have been figured or described in the *Annali dell' Inst. Rom.* 1855, plates XXI.—XXV., p. 87, *seq.* The blocks of tufo are hewn in longish rectangles, and at some places, for the sake of greater solidity, are laid alternately with the long and with the narrow side outermost. At one place, in the upper part of the wall, a large regular arch has been inserted, which is similar in style, but appears to have been added at a later date. The portions of the wall preserved consist of about fourteen courses; the upper portion is wanting, and the lower is for the most part concealed by later buildings, and often covered over with *opus reticulatum*. The wall evidently stretched quite along the edge of the hill. The continuation of these excavations inwards showed that mines and sewers traversed the Aventine hill, just as they traversed the Capitoline, in all directions. The latter belong to the system of *cloacae*, the extent and importance of which in ancient Rome has been instructively discussed by Braun (*Annali dell' Inst.* 1852, p. 331).

The portion of the Servian wall near the Viminal gate, discovered in 1862 at the Villa Negroni, consists of regular courses of huge blocks of peperino, measuring as much as 3 metres in length, 1 metre on an average in breadth, and 0.75 of a metre in thickness, which are laid side by side in three rows, so that the whole thickness of the wall amounts to more than 3 metres, or fully 10 Roman feet. To this falls to be added the earthen rampart piled up behind it, which seems to have had on its upper surface a breadth of about 13 metres or fully 40 Roman feet. At intervals of about 5 metres there are seen the foundations of towers projecting outwards. Of another piece of the Servian wall found at an early date, not far from the Porta Capena, a representation is given in Gell (*Topography of Rome*, p. 494).

Essentially similar to the Servian walls are those discovered in the

composed of polygonal dressed blocks fitting into each other. The selection of one or other of these systems was doubtless ordinarily determined by the material, and accordingly the polygonal masonry does not occur in Rome, where in the most ancient times tufo alone was employed for building. The resemblance in the case of the two former and simpler styles may perhaps be traceable to the similarity of the materials employed and of the object in view in building; but it can hardly be deemed accidental that the artistic polygonal wall-masonry, and the gate with the path leading up to it universally bending to the left and so exposing the unshielded right side of the assailant to the defenders, belong to the Italian fortresses as well as to the Greek. It is a significant circumstance, that this wall-masonry was only usual in that portion of Italy which was neither reduced to subjection by the Hellenes nor cut off from intercourse with them, and that the true polygonal masonry is found in Etruria only at Pyrgi and at the towns, not very far distant from it, of Cosa and Saturnia; and as the design of the walls of Pyrgi, especially when we take into account the significant name ("towers"), may just as certainly be ascribed to the Greeks as that of the walls of Tiryns, in them most probably there still stands before our eyes one of the models from which the Italians learned how to build their walls. The temple in fine, which in the period of the empire was called the Tuscanic and was regarded as a kind of style co-ordinate with the various Greek temple-structures, not only generally resembled the Greek temple in being an enclosed space (*cella*) usually quadrangular, over which walls and columns raised aloft a sloping roof, but was also in details, especially in the column itself and its architectural features, thoroughly dependent on the Greek system. It is in accordance with all these facts probable, as it is credible of itself, that Italian architecture previous to its contact with the Hellenes was confined to wooden huts, abattis, and mounds of earth and stones, and that construction in stone was only adopted in consequence of the example and the better tools of the Greeks. It is scarcely to be doubted that the Italians first learned from them the use of iron, and derived from them the preparation of mortar (*cal[e]x calecare*, from χάλιξ), the machine (*machina*, μηχανή), the measuring-rod (*groma*, a corruption from γνώμων, γνῶμα), and the artificial

Vigna Nussiner, on the slope of the Palatine, towards the Capitoline (Braun, *l. c.*), which have been, probably with justice, pronounced to be remains of the primitive circumvallation of the *Roma quadrata* (p. 48).

lattice-work (*clathri*, κλῇθρον). Accordingly we can scarcely speak of an architecture peculiarly Italian, except that in the woodwork of the Italian dwelling-houses—alongside of altera- tions produced by Greek influence—many peculiarities were retained or were for the first time developed, and these again exercised a reflex influence on the building of the Italian temples. The architectural development of the house proceeded in Italy from the Etruscans. The Latin and even the Sabellian still adhered to the hereditary wooden hut and to the good old custom of assigning to the god or spirit not a consecrated dwelling, but only a consecrated space, while the Etruscan had already begun artistically to transform his dwelling-house, and to erect after the model of the dwelling-house of man a temple also for the god and a sepulchral chamber for the spirit. That the advance to such luxurious structures in Latium took place under Etruscan influence, is proved by the designation of the oldest style of temple architecture and of the oldest style of house architecture respectively as Tuscanic.[1] As concerns the character of this transference, the Grecian temple probably imitated the general outlines of the tent or dwelling-house; but it was essentially built of hewn stone and covered with tiles, and the nature of the stone and the baked clay suggested to the Greek the laws of necessity and beauty. The Etruscan on the other hand re- mained a stranger to the strict Greek distinction between the dwelling of man necessarily erected of wood and the dwelling of the gods necessarily formed of stone. The peculiar charac- teristics of the Tuscan temple—the outline approaching nearer to a square, the higher gable, the greater breadth of the intervals between the columns, above all, the increased inclination of the roof and the singular projection of the roof-corbels beyond the supporting columns—all arose out of the greater approxima- tion of the temple to the dwelling-house, and out of the peculiarities of wooden architecture.

The plastic and delineative arts are more recent than archi- tecture; the house must be built before any attempt is made to decorate gable and walls. It is not probable that these arts really gained a place in Italy during the regal period of Rome; it was only in Etruria, where commerce and piracy early gave rise to a great concentration of riches, that art or handicraft— if the term be preferred—obtained a footing in the earliest times. Greek art, when it acted on Etruria, was still, as its copy shows, at a very primitive stage, and the Etruscans pro-

[1] *Ratio Tuscanica : cavum aedium Tuscanicum.*

bably learned from the Greeks the art of working in clay and metal at a period not much later than that at which they borrowed from them the alphabet. The silver coins of Populonia, almost the only works that can be with any precision assigned to this period, give no very high idea of Etruscan artistic skill as it then stood. It is not unlikely, however, that the best of the Etruscan works in bronze, to which the later critics of art assigned so high a place, may have belonged to this primitive age; and the Etruscan terra-cottas also cannot have been altogether despicable, for the oldest works in baked clay placed in the Roman temples—the statue of the Capitoline Jupiter, and the four-horse chariot on the roof of his temple— were executed in Veii, and the large ornaments of a similar kind placed on the roofs of temples passed generally among the later Romans under the name of " Tuscanic works."

On the other hand, among the Italians—not among the Sabellian stocks merely, but even among the Latins—native sculpture and design were at this period only coming into existence. The most considerable works of art appear to have been executed abroad. We have just mentioned the statues of clay alleged to have been executed in Veii; and very recent excavations have shown that works in bronze made in Etruria, and furnished with Etruscan inscriptions, circulated in Praeneste at least, if not generally throughout Latium. The statue of Diana in the Romano-Latin federal temple on the Aventine, which was considered the oldest statue of a divinity in Rome,[1] exactly resembled the Massiliot statue of the Ephesian Artemis, and was perhaps manufactured in Velia or Massilia. The guilds, which from ancient times existed in Rome, of potters, coppersmiths, and goldsmiths (p. 195), are almost the only proofs of the existence of native sculpture and design there; respecting the position of their art it is no longer possible to gain any clear idea.

If we endeavour to obtain historical results from these archives of the tradition and practice of primitive art, it is in the first place manifest that Italian art, like the Italian measures and Italian writing, developed itself not under Phoeni-

[1] When Varro (*ap.* Augustin. *De Civ. Dei*, iv. 31; comp. Plutarch, *Num.* 8) affirms that the Romans for more than one hundred and seventy years worshipped the gods without images, he is evidently thinking of this primitive piece of carving, which, according to the conventional chronology, was dedicated between $\frac{176}{578}$ and $\frac{219}{535}$, and, beyond doubt, was the first statue of the gods, the consecration of which was mentioned in the authorities which Varro had before him.

cian, but exclusively under Hellenic influence. There is not a single one of the aspects of Italian art which has not found its definite model in the art of ancient Greece; and, so far, the legend is fully warranted which traces the most ancient form of painted clay figures, beyond doubt the most ancient form of art in Italy, to the three Greek artists, the "moulder," "fitter," and "draughtsman," Eucheir, Diopos, and Eugrammos, although it is more than doubtful whether this art came directly from Corinth or was brought directly to Tarquinii. There is as little trace of any immediate imitation of oriental models as there is of an independently-developed form of art. The Etruscan lapidaries adhered to the form of the beetle or *scarabaeus*, which was originally Egyptian; but *scarabaei* were also used as models in carving in Greece in very early times (*e.g.* such a beetle-stone, with a very ancient Greek inscription, has been found in Aegina), and therefore they may very well have come to the Etruscans through the Greeks. The Italians may have bought from the Phoenician; they learned only from the Greek.

To the further question, from what Greek stock the Etruscans in the first instance received their art-models, a categorical answer cannot be given; yet relations of a remarkable kind subsist between the Etruscan and the oldest Attic art. The three forms of art, which were practised in Etruria at least in after times very extensively, but in Greece only to an extent very limited, tomb-painting, mirror-designing, and graving on stone, have been hitherto met with on Grecian soil only in Athens and Aegina. The Tuscan temple does not correspond exactly either to the Doric or to the Ionic; but in the more important points of distinction, in the course of columns carried round the *cella*, as well as in the placing of a separate pedestal under each particular column, the Etruscan style follows the more recent Ionic; and it is this same Iono-Attic style of building still pervaded by a Doric element, which in its general design stands nearest of all the Greek styles to the Tuscan. In the case of Latium there is an almost total absence of any reliable traces of intercourse bearing on the history of art. If it was—as is indeed almost self-evident—the general relations of traffic and intercourse that determined also the introduction of models in art, it may be assumed with certainty that the Campanian and Sicilian Hellenes were the instructors of Latium in art, as in the alphabet; and the analogy between the Aventine Diana and the Ephesian Artemis is at least not inconsistent with such an hypothesis. Of course the older Etruscan art also served as a model for Latium. As to the Sabellian tribes, if Greek architectural and plastic art reached them at all, it must, like the Greek alphabet, have come to them only through the medium of the more western Italian stocks.

If, in conclusion, we are to form a judgment respecting the artistic endowments of the different Italian nations, we already at this stage perceive—what becomes indeed far more obvious in the later stages of the history of art—that while the Etruscans attained to the practice of art at an earlier period and produced more massive and rich workmanship, their works are inferior to those of the Latins and Sabellians in appropriateness and utility no less than in spirit and beauty. This certainly is apparent, in the case of our present epoch, only in architecture. The polygonal wall-masonry, as appropriate to its object as it was beautiful, was frequent in Latium and in the inland country behind it; while in Etruria it was rare, and not even the walls of Caere are constructed of polygonal blocks. Even in the religious prominence—remarkable also as respects the history of art— assigned to the arch (p. 167) and to the bridge (p. 171) in Latium, we may be allowed to perceive, as it were, an anticipation of the future aqueducts and consular highways of Rome. On the other hand, the Etruscans repeated, and at the same time corrupted, the ornamental architecture of the Greeks: for while they transferred the laws established for building in stone to architecture in wood, they displayed no thorough skill of adaptation, and by the lowness of their roof and the wide intervals between their columns gave to their temples, to use the language of an ancient architect, a "heavy, mean, straggling, and clumsy appearance." The Latins found in the rich stores of Greek art but very little that was congenial to their thoroughly realistic tastes; but what they did adopt they appropriated truly and heartily as their own, and in the development of the polygonal wall architecture perhaps excelled their instructors. Etruscan art is a remarkable evidence of dexterity mechanically acquired and mechanically retained, but it is, as little as the Chinese, an evidence even of genial receptivity. As scholars have long since desisted from the attempt to derive Greek art from that of the Etruscans, so they must, with whatever reluctance, make up their minds to transfer the Etruscans from the first to the lowest place in the history of Italian art.

BOOK SECOND

FROM THE ABOLITION OF THE MONARCHY
IN ROME TO THE UNION OF ITALY

—— δεῖ οὐκ ἐκπλήττειν τὸν συγγραφέα τερατευόμενον
διὰ τῆς ἱστορίας τοὺς ἐντυγχάνοντας.

POLYBIUS.

BOOK SECOND.

FROM THE ABOLITION OF THE MONARCHY
IN ROME TO THE UNION OF ITALY

BOOK SECOND

CHAPTER I

CHANGE OF THE CONSTITUTION—LIMITATION OF THE POWER OF THE MAGISTRATE

THE strict conception of the unity and omnipotence of the state in all matters pertaining to it, which was the central principle of the Italian constitutions, placed in the hands of the single president nominated for life a formidable power, which was felt doubtless by the enemies of the land, but was not less heavily felt by its citizens. Abuse and oppression could not fail to ensue, and, as a necessary consequence, efforts were made to lessen that power. It was, however, the grand distinction of the endeavours after reform and the revolutions in Rome, that there was no attempt to impose limitations on the community as such or even to deprive it of corresponding organs of expression—that there never was any endeavour to assert the so-called natural rights of the individual in contradistinction to the community—that, on the contrary, the attack was wholly directed against the form in which the community was represented. From the times of the Tarquins down to those of the Gracchi the cry of the party of progress in Rome was not for limitation of the power of the state, but for limitation of the power of the magistrates: nor amidst that cry was the truth ever forgotten, that the people ought not to govern, but to be governed.

This struggle was carried on within the burgess-body. Side by side with it another movement developed itself—the cry of the non-burgesses for equality of political privileges. Under this head are included the agitations of the plebeians, the Latins, the Italians, and the freedmen, all of whom—whether they may have borne the name of burgesses, as did the plebeians and the freedmen, or not, as was the case with the Latins and Italians —were destitute of, and laid claim to, political equality.

A third distinction was one of a still more general nature;

the distinction between the wealthy and the poor, especially such as had been dispossessed or were endangered in possession. The civil and political relations of Rome led to the rise of a numerous class of farmers—partly small proprietors who were dependent on the mercy of the capitalist, partly small temporary lessees who were dependent on the mercy of the landlord—and in many instances deprived individuals as well as whole communities of the lands which they held, without affecting their personal freedom. By these means the agricultural proletariate became at an early period so powerful as to have a material influence on the destinies of the community. The urban proletariate did not acquire political importance till a much later epoch.

On these distinctions hinged the internal history of Rome, and, as we may conjecture, not less the history—totally lost to us—of the other Italian communities. The political movement within the fully-privileged burgess-body, the warfare between the excluded and excluding classes, and the social conflicts between the possessors and the non-possessors of land —variously as they crossed and interlaced, and singular as were the alliances they often produced—were nevertheless essentially and fundamentally distinct.

As the Servian reform, which placed the *metoikos* on a footing of equality in a military point of view with the burgess, appears to have originated from considerations of an administrative nature rather than from any political party-tendency, we may assume that the first of the movements which led to internal crises and changes of the constitution was that which sought to limit the magistracy. The earliest achievement of this, the most ancient opposition in Rome, consisted in the abolition of the life-tenure of the presidency of the community; in other words, in the abolition of the monarchy. How necessarily this was the result of the natural development of things is strikingly demonstrated by the fact, that the same change of constitution took place in an analogous manner through the whole circuit of the Italo-Grecian world. Not only in Rome, but likewise among the other Latins as well as among the Sabellians, Etruscans, and Apulians—in fact, in all the Italian communities, just as in those of Greece—we find the rulers for life of an earlier epoch superseded in after times by annual magistrates. In the case of the Lucanian canton there is evidence that it had a democratic government in time of peace, and it was only in the event of war that the magistrates appointed a king, that is, a magistrate similar to the Roman dictator. The Sabellian civic communities, such as those of Capua and Pompeii, in like manner were in later times governed by a "community-manager" (*medix tuticus*) changed from year to year, and we may assume that similar institutions existed among the other national and civic communities of Italy. In this light the reasons which led to the substitution of consuls for kings in Rome need no explanation. The organism of the ancient Greek and Italian polity through its own action and by a sort of natural necessity produced the limitation of the life-presidency to a shortened, and for the most part an annual, term. Simple, however, as was the cause of the change, it might be brought about in various ways; a resolution might be adopted on the death of one life-ruler not to elect another—a course which the Roman senate is said to have attempted after the death of Romulus; or the ruler might voluntarily abdicate, as is affirmed to have been the intention of king Servius Tullius; or the people might rise in rebellion against a tyrannical ruler, and expel him.

It was in this last way that the monarchy was terminated in Rome. For however much the history of the expulsion of the last Tarquinius, "the proud," may have been interwoven with anecdotes and spun out into a romance, it is not in its leading outlines to be called in question. Tradition credibly enough indicates as the causes of the revolt, that the king neglected to consult the senate and to complete its numbers; that he pronounced sentences of capital punishment and confiscation without advising with his counsellors; that he accumulated immense stores of grain in his granaries, and exacted from the burgesses military labours and task-work beyond what was due. The exasperation of the people is attested by the formal vow which they made man by man for themselves and for their posterity that thenceforth they would never tolerate a king; by the blind hatred with which the name of king was ever afterwards regarded in Rome; and above all by the enactment that the "king for offering sacrifice" (*rex sacrorum* or *sacrificulus*)—whom they considered it their duty to create that the gods might not miss their accustomed mediator—should be disqualified from holding any further office, so that this official was at once the first in rank and the least in power of all the Roman magistrates. Along with the last king all the members of his clan were banished— a proof how close at that time gentile ties still were. The Tarquinii transferred themselves to Caere, perhaps their ancient home (p. 126), where their family tomb has recently been discovered. In the room of one president holding office for life two annual rulers were now placed at the head of the Roman community.

This is all that can be looked upon as historically certain in reference to this important event.[1] It may easily be conceived that in a great community with extensive dominion like the Roman the royal power, particularly if it had been in the same family for several generations, would be more capable of resistance, and the struggle would thus be keener, than in smaller states; but there is no certain indication of foreign states interfering in the struggle. The great war with Etruria—which possibly, moreover, has been placed so close upon the expulsion of the Tarquins only in consequence of chronological confusion in the Roman annals—cannot be regarded as an intervention of Etruria in favour of a countryman who had been injured in Rome, for the very sufficient reason that the Etruscans notwithstanding their complete victory neither restored the Roman monarchy, nor even brought back the Tarquinian family.

If we are left in ignorance of the historical connections of this important event, we are fortunately in possession of clearer light as to the nature of the change which was made in the constitution. The royal power was by no means abolished as is shown by the fact that, when a vacancy occurred, a " temporary king " (*interrex*) was nominated as before. The one life-king was simply replaced by two year-kings, who called themselves generals (*praetores*), or judges (*iudices*), or merely colleagues (*consules*).[2] The collegiate principle, from which this last—and subsequently most current—name of the annual kings was derived, assumed in their case an altogether peculiar form.

---

[1] The well-known fable for the most part refutes itself. To a considerable extent it has been concocted for the explanation of surnames (*Brutus, Poplicola, Scaevola*). But even its apparently historical ingredients are found on closer examination to have been invented. Of this character is the statement that Brutus was captain of horse (*tribunus celerum*) and in that capacity proposed the decree of the people as to the banishment of the Tarquins; for, according to the earliest constitution of Rome, it is quite impossible that a mere tribune should have had the right to convoke the curies, when that right was not accorded to the *alter ego* of the king, the city warden (p. 74). The whole of this statement has evidently been invented with the view of furnishing a basis of legitimacy for the Roman republic; and the invention is a very miserable one, for the *tribunus celerum* is confounded with the entirely different *magister equitum* (p. 72), and then the right of convoking the centuries which pertained to the latter by virtue of his praetorian rank is made to apply to this assembly of the curies.

[2] *Consules* are those who " leap or dance together," as *praesul* is one who " leaps before," *exul*, one who " leaps out " (ὁ ἐκπεσών), *insula*, a " leap into," primarily applied to a mass of rock fallen into the sea.

The supreme power was not entrusted to the two magistrates conjointly, but each consul possessed and exercised it for himself as fully and wholly as it had been possessed and exercised by the king; and, although a partition of functions doubtless took place from the first—the one consul for instance undertaking the command of the army, and the other the administration of justice—that partition was by no means binding, and each of the colleagues was legally at liberty to interfere at any time in the province of the other. When, therefore, supreme power confronted supreme power and the one colleague forbade what the other enjoined, the consular commands neutralised each other. This peculiarly Latin, if not peculiarly Roman, institution of co-ordinate supreme authorities—which in the Roman commonwealth on the whole approved itself as practicable, but to which it will be difficult to find a parallel in any other considerable state—manifestly sprang out of the endeavour to retain the regal power in legally undiminished fulness. They were thus led not to break up the royal office into parts or to transfer it from an individual to a college, but simply to double it and thereby, if necessary, to neutralise it through its own action.

A similar course was followed in reference to the termination of their tenure of office, for which moreover the earlier *interregnum* of five days furnished a legal precedent. The ordinary presidents of the community were bound not to remain in office longer than a year reckoned from the day of their entering on their functions;[1] but they ceased to be magistrates not upon expiry of the set term, but only upon their publicly and solemnly demitting their office: so that, in the event of their daring to disregard the term and to continue their magistracy beyond the year, their official acts were nevertheless valid, and in the earlier times they scarcely even incurred any other than a moral responsibility. The inconsistency between full rule over the community and a set term assigned to that rule by law was so vividly felt, that its tenure for life was only avoided by means of the magistrate declaring his own—in a certain sense free—

---

[1] The day of entering on office did not coincide with the beginning of the year (1st March), and was not at all fixed. The day of retiring was regulated by it, except when a consul was elected expressly in room of one who had died or abdicated (*consul suffectus*); in which case the substitute succeeded to the rights and consequently to the term of him whom he replaced. But these supplementary consuls in the earlier period only occurred when one of the consuls had died or abdicated: pairs of supplementary consuls are not found until the later ages of the republic. Ordinarily, therefore, the official year of a consul consisted of unequal portions of two civil years.

will in the matter; and the magistrate was not restricted directly by the law, but only induced by it to restrict himself. Nevertheless this tenure of the supreme magistracy for a set term, which its holders but once or twice ventured to overstep, was of the deepest importance. As an immediate consequence of it, the practical irresponsibility of the king was lost in the case of the consul. It is true that the king was always in the Roman commonwealth subject, and not superior, to the law; but, as according to the Roman view the supreme judge could not be prosecuted at his own bar, while the king might perpetrate a crime, there was for him no tribunal and no punishment. The consul, again, if he had committed murder or treason, was protected by his office only so long as it lasted; on his retirement he was liable to the ordinary penal jurisdiction like any other burgess.

To these changes of a prominent nature, affecting the principles of the constitution, other restrictions were added of a subordinate and administrative character, some of which nevertheless produced a deep effect. The privilege of the king to have his fields tilled by taskwork of the burgesses, and the special relation of clientship in which the *metoeci* as a body must have stood to the king, ceased of themselves with the life-tenure of the office.

Hitherto in criminal processes as well as in fines and corporal punishments it had been the province of the king not only to investigate and decide the cause, but also to decide whether the person found guilty should or should not be allowed to appeal for pardon. The Valerian law now (in $\frac{245}{509}$) enacted that the consul must allow the appeal of the condemned, where sentence of capital or corporal punishment had been pronounced otherwise than by martial law—a regulation which by a later law (of uncertain date, but passed before $\frac{303}{451}$) was extended to heavy fines. In token of this right of appeal, when the consul appeared in the capacity of judge and not of general, the consular lictors laid aside the axes which they had previously carried by virtue of the penal jurisdiction belonging to their master. The law however threatened the magistrate, who did not allow due course to the *provocatio*, with no other penalty than infamy—which, as matters then stood, was essentially nothing but a moral stain, and at the utmost only had the effect of disqualifying the infamous person from giving testimony. Here too the course followed was based on the same view, that it was in law impossible to diminish the old regal powers, and that the checks imposed upon the holder of the supreme authority in consequence of the revolution had, strictly viewed, only a practical and moral value. When therefore the consul acted within the old regal jurisdiction, he might in so acting perpetrate an injustice, but he committed no crime and consequently was not amenable for what he did to the penal judge.

A limitation similar in its tendency took place in the civil jurisdiction; for to this epoch probably belongs the change by which the right of the magistrates, after adjustment of a cause, to commit to a private person the investigation of its merits was converted into an obligation to do so. It is probable that this was accomplished by a general arrangement respecting the transference of magisterial power to deputies or successors. While the king had been absolutely at liberty to nominate deputies but had never been compelled to do so, in the case of the consul the right of delegating his powers seems to have been limited and legally restricted in a twofold manner. In the first place such comprehensive delegated powers—themselves partaking of the splendour that environed the king—as those of the warden of the city in relation to the administration of justice, and probably also the delegated command of the army (p. 64), virtually ceased upon the introduction of annual kings; for the appointment of a warden of the city, which still was made for the few hours during which the two consuls had to absent themselves from the city in order to take part in the Latin festival, was a mere form and was treated in that light. It was in fact one of the objects attained by putting the supreme magistracy into the collegiate form, that a magistrate-depute for the administration of justice was only required in rare exceptional cases; and although in war the commander-in-chief could not be prohibited from entrusting the command even of the whole army to another, such a deputy now took his place as simply the adjutant (*legatus*) of the general. The new republic tolerated neither king nor lieutenant with full regal powers; but the consul was at liberty, especially if a serious war seemed to require that the original unity of the magistracy should be restored, to suspend the collegiate equality of prerogatives, and to nominate a third colleague, with the title of dictator, whom both the nominating consul and his original colleague were bound to obey as a superior magistrate, and in whose person, as an extraordinary and temporary measure, the old regal powers again came into force in all their compass.

The second restriction imposed on the consuls as to the

delegation of their powers was perhaps still more important in
its effects. While the consul as commander-in-chief retained
undiminished the right of freely delegating all or any of his
functions, in the province of his urban duties delegation was
prescribed as to certain cases, and was prohibited with reference
to all others. The former class of cases, in which the president
of the community was theoretically competent but was at the
same time obliged to act only through the medium of deputies
—appointed, it is true, by himself—included not only civil
processes, but those criminal causes which the king had been
accustomed to dispose of through the two " trackers of murder "
(*quaestores*, pp. 64, 150), and also the important charge of the
state-treasure and of the state-archives, which these two
quaestors undertook in addition to their previous functions
Thus the quaestors now became in law—what they had for long
perhaps been in fact—standing magistrates; and as they were
now nominated by the consul just as formerly by the king, it
followed that they abdicated office along with him after the
expiry of a year. In other cases again, where his course was
not expressly prescribed, the chief magistrate in the capital had
either to act personally or not at all; for instance, no delegation
was admissible at the introductory steps of a process. This
diversity in the treatment of civil and military delegation explains why in the government of the Roman community proper
no delegated magisterial authority (*pro magistratu*) was possible,
nor were purely urban magistrates ever represented by non-
magistrates; and why, on the other hand, military deputies
(*pro consule, pro praetore, pro quaestore*) were excluded from all
action within the community proper.

Again the right of nominating his successor, which the king
had exercised absolutely, was by no means withdrawn from
the new head of the community; but he was bound to nominate
the person whom the community should designate to him.
Through this binding right of proposal the nomination of the
ordinary supreme magistrates in a certain sense passed substantially into the hands of the community; practically, however, there still existed a very considerable distinction between
that right of proposal and the right of formal nomination. The
consul conducting the election was by no means a mere returning officer. By virtue of his prerogative essentially similar to
the king's, he might reject particular candidates and disregard
votes tendered for them; at first he might even limit the choice
to a list of candidates proposed by himself; and—what was of

still more consequence—the community by no means obtained through its right of proposal the right of deposing a magistrate again, which it must necessarily have obtained had it really appointed him. On the contrary, as the successor was even now nominated solely by his predecessor and thus no actual magistrate ever derived his right from a magistrate still holding office, the old and important principle of Roman state-law, that the supreme magistrate could never be deposed, remained inviolably in force in the consular period also.

Lastly the nomination of the priests, which had been a prerogative of the kings (p. 63), was not transferred to the consuls; but the colleges of priests filled up the vacancies in their own ranks, while the Vestals and single priests were nominated by the pontifical college, on which devolved also the exercise of the paternal jurisdiction, so to speak, of the community over the priestesses of Vesta. With a view to the performance of these acts, which could only be properly performed by a single individual, the college probably about this period first nominated a president, the *Pontifex maximus*. This separation of the supreme authority in things sacred from the civil power—while the already-mentioned " king for sacrifice " had neither the civil nor the sacred powers of the king, but simply the title, conferred upon him—and the semi-magisterial position of the new high priest so decidedly contrasting with the character which otherwise marked the priesthood in Rome, form one of the most significant and important peculiarities of a state-revolution, the aim of which was to impose limits on the powers of the magistrates mainly in the interest of the aristocracy.

We have already mentioned that the outward state of the consul was far inferior to that of the regal office hedged round as it was with reverence and terror, that the regal name and the priestly consecration were withheld from him, and that the axe was taken away from his attendants. We have to add that, instead of the purple robe which the king had worn, the consul was distinguished from the ordinary burgess simply by the purple border of his *toga*, and that, while the king in all probability regularly appeared in public in his chariot, the consul was bound to accommodate himself to the general rule, and like every other burgess to go within the city on foot.

These limitations, however, of the plenary power and of the insignia of the magistracy applied in the main only to the ordinary presidency of the community. In extraordinary cases, as we have already said, the two presidents chosen by

the community were superseded by a single one, the master of
the army (*magister populi*) or commander (*dictator*). In the
election of dictator the community bore no part at all; his
nomination proceeded solely from one of the consuls for the time
being. There was no appeal from his sentence any more than
from that of the king, unless he chose to allow it. As soon as
he was nominated, all the other magistrates were by right subject to his authority. On the other hand the duration of the
dictator's office was limited in two ways: first, as the official
colleague of those consuls, one of whom had nominated him, he
might not remain in office beyond their legal term; and secondly,
a period of six months was fixed as the absolute maximum for
the duration of his office. It was a further arrangement peculiar
to the dictatorship, that the " master of the army " was bound to
nominate for himself immediately a " master of horse " (*magister
equitum*), who acted along with him as a dependent assistant
somewhat as did the quaestor along with the consul, and with
him retired from office—an arrangement undoubtedly connected
with the fact that the dictator, probably as being the leader of
the infantry, was constitutionally prohibited from mounting on
horseback. In the light of these regulations the dictatorship
is doubtless to be conceived as an institution which arose along
with the consulship, and which was designed especially, in the
event of war, to obviate for a time the disadvantages of divided
power and to revive temporarily the regal authority; for in
war more particularly the equality of rights in the consuls could
not but appear fraught with danger; and not only positive
testimonies, but the oldest names given to the magistrate himself and his assistant, as well as the limitation of the office to the
duration of a summer campaign, and the exclusion of the *provocatio*, attest the pre-eminently military design of the original
dictatorship.

On the whole, therefore, the consuls continued to be, as the
kings had been, the supreme administrators, judges, and
generals; and even in a religious point of view it was not the
rex sacrorum (who was only nominated that the name might
be preserved), but the consul, who offered prayers and sacrifices
for the community, and in its name ascertained the will of the
gods with the aid of those skilled in sacred lore. Against cases
of emergency a power was retained of reviving at any moment,
without previous consultation of the community, the full and
unlimited regal authority, so as to set aside the limitations
imposed by the collegiate arrangement and by the special curtail-

ments of jurisdiction. In this way the problem of legally retaining and practically restricting the regal authority was solved in genuine Roman fashion with equal acuteness and simplicity by the nameless statesmen who worked out this evolution.

The community thus acquired by the change of constitution rights of the greatest importance: the right of annually designating its presidents, and that of deciding in the last instance regarding the life or death of the burgess. But the body which acquired these rights could not possibly be the community as it had been hitherto constituted—the patriciate which had practically become an order of nobility. The strength of the nation lay in the "multitude" (*plebs*), which already comprehended in large numbers people of note and of wealth. The exclusion of this multitude from the public assembly, although it bore part of the public burdens, might be tolerated as long as that public assembly itself had no very material share in the working of the state machine, and as long as the royal power by the very fact of its high and free position remained almost equally formidable to the burgesses and to the *metoeci* and thereby maintained equality of legal redress in the nation. But when the community itself was called regularly to elect and to decide, and the president was practically reduced from its master to its commissioner for a set term, this relation could no longer be maintained as it stood; least of all when the state had to be re-modelled on the morrow of a revolution, which could only have been carried out by the co-operation of the patricians and the *metoeci*. An extension of that community was inevitable; and it was accomplished in the most comprehensive manner, inasmuch as the collective plebeiate, that is, all the non-burgesses who were neither slaves nor citizens of extraneous communities living at Rome under the *jus hospitii*, were admitted into the curies, and thereupon the old burgesses, who had hitherto formed the curies, lost altogether the right of meeting and of resolving in concert. But at the same time the curiate assembly, which hitherto had been legally and practically the first authority in the state, was almost totally deprived of its constitutional prerogatives. It was still to retain its previous powers in acts purely formal or in those which affected clan-relations—such as the vow of allegiance to be taken to the consul or to the dictator when they entered on office just as previously to the king (p. 63), and the legal dispensations requisite for an *arrogatio* or a testament—but it was not henceforward to perform any act of a properly political character. By the change of constitution the curial organisation was virtually rooted out, inasmuch as it was really based on the clan-organisation and the latter was to be found in its full purity exclusively among the old burgesses. When the plebeians were admitted into the curies, they were certainly also allowed to constitute themselves *de jure* as—what in the earlier period they could only have been *de facto* (p. 87)—families and clans; but it is distinctly recorded by tradition and in itself also very conceivable, that only a portion of the plebeians proceeded so far as to constitute *gentes*, and thus the new curiate assembly in opposition to its original character included numerous members who did not belong to any clan.

All the political prerogatives of the public assembly—as well the decision on appeals in criminal causes, which indeed were essentially political processes, as the nomination of magistrates and the adoption or rejection of laws—were transferred to, or were now acquired by, the assembled levy of those bound to military service; so that the centuries now received the rights, as they had previously borne the burdens, of citizens. In this way the small initial movements made by the Servian constitution—such as, in particular, the handing over to the army the right of assenting to the declaration of an aggressive war (p. 96)—attained such a development that the curies were completely and for ever cast into the shade by the assembly of the centuries, and people became accustomed to regard the latter as the sovereign people. There was no debate in this assembly any more than in that of the curies, except when the presiding magistrate chose himself to speak or bade others do so; of course in cases of appeal both parties had to be heard. A simple majority of the centuries was decisive.

This plan was evidently chosen, because in the curiate assembly those who were entitled to vote at all were on a footing of entire equality, and therefore after the admission of all the plebeians into the curies the result would have been a complete democracy if the decision of political questions had remained with that assembly; whereas the centuriate assembly placed the preponderating influence, not in the hands of the nobles certainly, but in those of the possessors of property, and the important privilege of priority in voting, which often practically decided the election, in the hands of the *equites* or, in other words, of the rich.

The senate was not affected by the reform of the constitution in the same way as the community. The previously existing college of elders not only continued exclusively patrician, but retained also its essential prerogatives—the right of appointing the interrex, and of confirming or rejecting the resolutions adopted by the community as constitutional or unconstitutional. In fact these prerogatives were enhanced by the reform of the constitution, because the appointment of the magistrates also, which fell to be made by election of the community, was thenceforth subject to the confirmation or rejection of the patrician senate. In cases of appeal alone its confirmation, so far as we know, was never deemed requisite, because in these the matter at stake was the pardon of the guilty and, when this was granted by the sovereign assembly of the people, any cancelling of such an act was wholly out of the question.

But, although by the abolition of the monarchy the constitutional rights of the patrician senate were increased rather than diminished, there yet took place—and that, according to tradition, immediately on the abolition of the monarchy—so far as regards other affairs which fell to be discussed in the senate and admitted of a freer treatment, an enlargement of that body, which brought into it plebeians also, and which in its consequences led to a complete remodelling of the whole. From the earliest times the senate had acted also, although not solely or especially, as a state-council; and, while probably even in the time of the kings it was not regarded as unconstitutional for non-senators in this case to take part in the assembly (p. 80), it was now arranged that for such discussions there should be associated with the patrician senate (*patres*) a number of non-patricians " added to the roll " (*conscripti*). This did not at all put them on a footing of equality; the plebeians in the senate did not become senators, but remained members of the equestrian order, were designated not *patres* but *conscripti*, and had no right to the insignia of senatorial dignity, the purple border and the red shoe (p. 78). Moreover, they not only remained absolutely excluded from the exercise of the magisterial prerogatives belonging to the senate (*auctoritas*), but were obliged, even where the question had reference merely to an advice (*consilium*), to rest content with the privilege of being present in silence while the question was put to the patricians in turn, and of only indicating their opinion by adding to the numbers when the division was taken—voting with the feet (*pedibus in sententiam ire, pedarii*) as the proud nobility expressed it. Nevertheless, the plebeians found their way through the new constitution not merely to the Forum, but also to the senate-house, and the first and most difficult step to equality of rights was taken in this quarter also.

Otherwise there was no material change in the arrangements affecting the senate. Among the patrician members a distinction of rank soon came to be recognised, especially in putting the vote: those who were proximately designated for the supreme magistracy, or who had already administered it, were entered on the list and were called upon to vote before the rest; and the position of the first of them, the foreman of the senate (*princeps senatus*), soon became a highly coveted place of honour. The consul in office, on the other hand, no more ranked as a member of senate than did the king, and therefore in taking the votes did not include his own. The selection of the members—both of the narrower patrician senate and of those added to the roll —fell to be made by the consuls just as formerly by the kings; but the nature of the case implied that, while the king had still perhaps some measure of regard to the representation of the several clans in the senate, this consideration was of no account so far as concerned the plebeians, among whom the clan-organisation was but imperfectly developed, and consequently the relation of the senate to that organisation in general fell more and more into abeyance. We have no information that the electing consuls were restricted from admitting more than a definite number of plebeians to the senate; nor was there need for such a regulation, because the consuls themselves belonged to the nobility. But probably from the outset the consul was in virtue of his very position practically far less free, and far more bound by the opinions of his order and by custom, in the appointment of senators than the king. The rule in particular, that the holding of the consulship should necessarily be followed by admission to the senate for life, if, as was probably the case at this time, the consul was not yet a member of it at the time of his election, must have in all probability very early acquired consuetudinary force. In like manner it seems to have become early the custom not to fill up the senators' places immediately on their falling vacant, but to revise and complete the roll of the senate on occasion of the census, consequently, as a rule, every fourth year; which also involved a not unimportant restriction of the authorities entrusted with the selection. The whole number of the senators remained as before, and in this the *conscripti* were also included; from which fact we are entitled to infer the numerical falling off of the patriciate.[1]

[1] That the first consuls admitted to the senate 164 plebeians, is hardly

Evidently in the Roman commonwealth, even on the conversion of the monarchy into a republic, the old was as far as possible retained. So far as a revolution in a state can be conservative at all, this one was so; not one of the constituent elements of the commonwealth was really overthrown by it. This circumstance indicates the character of the whole movement. The expulsion of the Tarquins was not, as the pitiful and deeply falsified accounts of it represent, the work of a people carried away by sympathy and enthusiasm for liberty, but the work of two great political parties already engaged in conflict, and clearly aware that their conflict would steadily continue— the old burgesses and the *metoeci*—who, like the English Whigs and Tories in 1688, were for a moment united by the common danger which threatened to convert the commonwealth into the arbitrary government of a despot, and differed again as soon as the danger was over. The old burgesses could not get rid of the monarchy without the co-operation of the new burgesses; but the new burgesses were far from being sufficiently strong to wrest the power out of the hands of the former at one blow. Compromises of this sort are necessarily limited to the smallest measure of mutual concessions obtained by tedious bargaining; and they leave the future to decide which of the constituent elements shall eventually preponderate, and whether they will work harmoniously together or maintain their antagonism. To look therefore merely to the direct innovations, or possibly the mere change in the duration of the supreme magistracy, is altogether to mistake the broad import of the first Roman revolution: its indirect effects were by far the most important, and vaster doubtless than even its authors anticipated.

This, in short, was the time when the Roman burgess-body in the later sense of the term originated. The plebeians had hitherto been *metoeci*, who were subjected to their share of taxes and burdens, but who were nevertheless in the eye of the law really nothing but tolerated aliens, between whose position and that of foreigners proper it may have seemed hardly necessary to draw a definite line of distinction. They were now enrolled as burgesses in the registers of the curies, and, although they were still far from being on a footing of legal equality—although the old burgesses still remained exclusively entitled to perform the acts of authority constitutionally pertaining to the council

to be regarded as an historical fact, but rather as a proof that the later Roman archaeologists were unable to point out more than 136 *gentes* of the Roman nobility. (*Röm. Forsch.* i. 121.)

of elders and solely eligible to the civil magistracies and priest-hoods, nay even exclusively entitled to participate in the usufructs of burgesses, such as the joint use of the public pasture —yet the first and most difficult step towards complete equalisa-tion was gained from the time when the plebeians no longer served merely in the common levy, but also voted in the common assembly and in the common council when its opinion was asked, and the head and back of the poorest *metoikos* were as well protected by the right of appeal as those of the noblest of the old burgesses.

One consequence of this amalgamation of the patricians and plebeians in a new corporation of Roman burgesses was the conversion of the old burgesses into a clan-nobility, which was incapable of receiving additions or even of filling up its own ranks, because the nobles no longer possessed the right of passing decrees in common assembly and the adoption of new families into the nobility by the decree of the community appeared still less admissible. Under the kings the ranks of the Roman nobility had not been thus closed, and the admission of new clans was no very rare occurrence: now this genuine characteristic of patricianism made its appearance as the sure herald of the speedy loss of its political privileges and of its importance in the community. The exclusion of the plebeians from all public magistracies and public priesthoods—while they were admissible to the position of officers and senators—and the maintenance, with perverse obstinacy, of the legal impossibility of marriage between old burgesses and plebeians, further impressed on the patriciate from the outset the stamp of an exclusive and wrongly privileged aristocracy.

A second consequence of the new union of the burgesses must have been a more definite regulation of the right of settle-ment, with reference both to the Latin confederates and to other states. It became necessary—not so much on account of the right of suffrage in the centuries (which indeed belonged only to the freeholder) as on account of the right of appeal, which was intended to be conceded to the plebeian, but not to the sojourner or the foreigner—to express more precisely the conditions of the acquisition of plebeian rights, and to mark off the enlarged burgess-body in its turn from those who were now the non-burgesses. To this epoch therefore we may trace back—in the views and feelings of the people—both the invidiousness of the distinction between patricians and plebeians, and the strict and haughty line of demarcation between *cives Romani* and aliens. But the former civic distinction was in its nature transient, while the latter political one was permanent; and the sense of political unity and rising greatness, which was thus implanted in the heart of the nation, was expansive enough first to undermine and then to carry away with its mighty current those paltry distinctions.

It was at this period, moreover, that law and edict were separated. The distinction indeed had its foundation in the essential character of the Roman state; for even the regal power in Rome was subordinate, not superior, to the law of the land. But the profound and practical veneration, which the Romans, like every other people of political capacity, cherished for the principle of authority, gave birth to the remarkable rule of Roman constitutional and private law, that every command of the magistrate not based upon a law was at least valid during his tenure of office, although it expired with that tenure. It is evident that in this view, so long as the presidents were nominated for life, the distinction between law and edict must have practically been almost lost sight of, and the legislative activity of the public assembly could acquire no development. On the other hand it obtained a wide field of action after the presidents were changed annually; and the fact was now by no means void of practical importance, that, if the consul in deciding a process committed a legal informality, his successor could institute a fresh trial of the cause.

It was at this period, finally, that the provinces of civil and military authority were separated. In the former the law ruled, in the latter the axe: the former was governed by the constitutional checks of the right of appeal and of regulated delegation; in the latter the general held an absolute sway like the king.[1] It was an established principle, that the general and the army as such should not under ordinary circumstances enter the city proper. That organic and permanently operative enactments could only be made under the superintendence of the civil power, was implied in the spirit, if not in the letter, of the constitution. Instances indeed occasionally occurred where a magistrate, disregarding this principle, convoked his forces in the camp as a burgess-assembly, nor was a decree passed under such circumstances legally void; but custom disapproved

---

[1] It may not be superfluous to remark, that the *iudicium legitimum*, as well as that *quod imperio continetur*, rested on the *imperium* of the directing magistrate, and the distinction only consisted in the circumstance that the *imperium* was in the former case limited by the *lex*, while in the latter it was free.

of such a proceeding, and it soon fell into disuse as though it had been forbidden. The distinction between Quirites and soldiers became more and more deeply rooted in the minds of the burgesses.

Time however was required for the development of these consequences of the new republicanism; vividly as posterity felt its effects, the revolution probably appeared to the contemporary world at first in a different light. The non-burgesses indeed gained by it burgess-rights, and the new burgess-body acquired in the *comitia centuriata* comprehensive prerogatives, but the right of rejection on the part of the patrician senate, which in firm and serried ranks confronted the *comitia* as if it were an Upper House, legally hampered their freedom of action precisely in the most important matters, and although not in a position to thwart the serious will of the collective body, yet practically interposed annoyance and delay. If the nobility in giving up their claim to be the sole representatives of the community did not seem to have lost much, they had in other respects decidedly gained. The king, it is true, was a patrician as well as the consul, and the nomination of the members of the senate belonged to the latter as to the former; but while his exceptional position raised the former no less above the patricians than above the plebeians, and while cases might easily occur in which he would be obliged to lean upon the support of the multitude even against the nobility, the consul—ruling for a brief term, but before and after that term simply one of the nobility, and obeying to-morrow the noble fellow-burgess whom he had commanded to-day—by no means occupied a position aloof from his order, and the spirit of the noble in him must have been far more powerful than that of the magistrate. Indeed, if at any time by way of exception a patrician disinclined to the rule of the nobility was called to the government, his official authority was paralysed partly by the priestly colleges which were pervaded by an intense aristocratic spirit, partly by his colleagues, and was easily suspended by the dictatorship; and, what was of still more moment, he wanted the first element of political power, time. The president of a commonwealth, whatever plenary authority may be conceded to him, will never gain possession of political power if he does not continue for some considerable time at the head of affairs; for a necessary condition of every dominion is duration. Consequently the senate appointed for life inevitably acquired—and that by virtue chiefly of its title to advise the magistrate in all points, so that we speak not of the narrower patrician, but of the enlarged patricio-plebeian, senate—so great an influence as contrasted with the annual rulers, that their legal relations became precisely inverted; the senate substantially assumed to itself the powers of government, and the former ruler sank into a president acting as its chairman and executing its decrees. In the case of every proposal to be submitted to the community for acceptance or rejection the practice of previously consulting the whole senate and obtaining its approval, while not constitutionally necessary, was consecrated by use and wont; and it was not lightly or willingly departed from. The same course was followed in the case of important state-treaties, of the management and distribution of the public lands, and generally of every act the effects of which extended beyond the official year; and nothing was left to the consul but the transaction of current business, the initial steps in civil processes, and the command in war. Especially important in its consequences was the change in virtue of which neither the consul, nor even the otherwise absolute dictator, was permitted to touch the public treasure except with the consent and by the will of the senate. The senate made it obligatory on the consuls to commit the administration of the public chest, which the king had managed or might at any rate have managed himself, to two standing subordinate magistrates, who were nominated by the consuls and had to obey them, but were, as may easily be conceived, much more dependent than the consuls themselves on the senate (p. 250). It thus drew into its own hands the management of finance; and this right of sanctioning the expenditure of the finances on the part of the Roman senate may be placed on a parallel in its effects with the right of sanctioning taxation in the constitutional monarchies of the present day.

The consequences followed as a matter of course. The first and most essential condition of all aristocratic government is, that the plenary power of the state be vested not in an individual but in a corporation. Now a preponderantly aristocratic corporation, the senate, had appropriated to itself the government, and at the same time the executive power not only remained in the hands of the nobility, but was also entirely subject to the governing corporation. It is true that a considerable number of men not belonging to the nobility sat in the senate; but as they were incapable of holding magistracies or even of taking part in the debates, and thus were excluded from all practical share in the government, they necessarily played a subordinate part in the senate, and were moreover kept in pecuniary dependence on the corporation through the economically important privilege of using the public pasture. The gradually recognised right of the patrician consuls to revise and modify the senatorial list at least every fourth year, however little may have been its effect in reference to the nobility, might very well be employed in their interest, and an obnoxious plebeian might by means of it be kept out of the senate or even be removed from its ranks.

It is therefore quite true that the immediate effect of the revolution was to establish the aristocratic government. It is not, however, the whole truth. While the majority of contemporaries probably thought that the revolution had brought upon the plebeians only a more inflexible despotism, we who come afterwards discern in that very revolution the germs of young liberty. What the patricians gained was gained at the expense not of the community, but of the magistrate's power. It is true that the community gained only a few narrowly restricted rights, which were far less practical and palpable than the acquisitions of the nobility, and which not one in a thousand probably had the wisdom to value; but they formed a pledge and earnest of the future. Hitherto the *metoeci* had been politically nothing, the old burgesses had been everything; now that the former were embraced in the community, the old burgesses were overcome; for, however much might be wanting to full civil equality, it is the first breach, not the occupation of the last post, that decides the fall of the fortress. With justice therefore the Roman community dated its political existence from the beginning of the consulship.

While however the republican revolution may, notwithstanding the aristocratic rule which in the first instance it established, be justly called a victory of the former *metoeci* or the *plebs*, the revolution even in this respect bore by no means the character which we are accustomed in the present day to designate as democratic. Pure personal merit without the support of birth and wealth could perhaps gain influence and consideration more easily under the regal government than under that of the patriciate. Then admission to the patriciate was not in law foreclosed; now the highest object of plebeian ambition was to be admitted as a dumb appendage to the senate. The nature of the case implied that the governing aristocratic order, so far as it admitted plebeians at all, would grant the

right of occupying seats in the senate not absolutely to the best
men, but chiefly to the heads of the wealthy and notable plebeian
families; and the families thus admitted jealously guarded
the possession of the senatorial stalls.   While a complete legal
equality therefore had subsisted within the old burgess-body,
the new burgess-body or former *metoeci* came to be in this way
divided from the first into a number of privileged families
and a multitude kept in a position of inferiority.   But the power
of the community now according to the centuriate organisation
came into the hands of that class which since the Servian
reform of the army and of taxation had borne mainly the
burdens of the state, namely the freeholders, and indeed not
so much into the hands of the great proprietors or into those
of the small cottagers, as into those of the intermediate class
of farmers—an arrangement in which the seniors were still so
far privileged that, although less numerous, they had as many
voting-divisions as the juniors.   While in this way the axe
was laid to the root of the old burgess-body and their clan-
nobility, and the basis of a new burgess-body was laid, the preponderance in the latter rested on the possession of land and
on age, and the first beginnings were already visible of a new
aristocracy based primarily on the actual consideration in which
the families were held — the future nobility.   There could
be no clearer indication of the fundamentally conservative
character of the Roman commonwealth than the fact, that the
revolution which gave birth to the republic laid down at the
same time the primary outlines of a new organisation of the
state, which was in like manner conservative and in like manner
aristocratic.

CHAPTER II

THE TRIBUNATE OF THE PLEBS AND THE DECEMVIRATE

UNDER the new organisation of the commonwealth the old
burgesses had attained by legal means full possession of political
power. Governing through the magistracy which had been
reduced to be their servant, preponderating in the senate, in
sole possession of all public offices and priesthoods, armed with
exclusive cognisance of things human and divine and familiar
with the whole routine of political procedure, influential in the
public assembly through the large number of pliant adherents
attached to the various families, and, lastly, entitled to examine
and to reject every decree of the community,—the patricians
might have long preserved their practical power, just because
they had at the right time abandoned their claim to sole legal
authority. It is true that the plebeians could not but be painfully
sensible of their political disabilities; but undoubtedly in the
first instance the nobility had not much to fear from a purely
political opposition, if it understood the art of keeping the
multitude, which desired nothing but equitable administration
and protection of its material interests, aloof from political
strife. In fact during the first period after the expulsion of the
kings we meet with various measures which were intended, or
at any rate seem to have been intended, to gain the favour
of the commons for the government of the nobility especially
on economic grounds. The port-dues were reduced; when
the price of grain was high, large quantities of corn were purchased on account of the state, and the trade in salt was made
a state-monopoly, in order to supply the citizens with corn and
salt at reasonable prices; lastly, the national festival was prolonged for an additional day. Of the same character was the
ordinance which we have already mentioned respecting property
fines (p. 248), which was not merely intended in general to set
limits to the dangerous fining-prerogative of the magistrates,
but was also, in a significant manner, calculated for the especial
protection of the man of small means. The magistrate was
prohibited from fining the same man on the same day to an

extent beyond two sheep or beyond thirty oxen, without granting leave to appeal; and the reason of these singular rates can only perhaps be found in the fact, that in the case of the man of small means possessing only a few sheep a different maximum appeared necessary from that fixed for the wealthy proprietor of herds of oxen—a considerate regard to the wealth or poverty of the person fined, from which modern legislators might take a lesson.

But these regulations were merely superficial; the main current flowed in the opposite direction. With the change in the constitution there was introduced a comprehensive revolution in the financial and economic relations of Rome. The government of the kings had probably abstained on principle from enhancing the power of capital, and had promoted as far as it could an increase in the number of farms. The new aristocratic government, again, appears to have aimed from the first at the destruction of the middle classes, particularly of the intermediate and smaller holdings of land, and at the development of a domination of landed and moneyed lords on the one hand, and of an agricultural proletariate on the other.

The reduction of the port-dues, although upon the whole a popular measure, chiefly benefited the great merchant. But a much greater accession to the power of capital was supplied by the indirect system of finance-administration. It is difficult to say what were the remote causes that gave rise to it: but, while its origin may probably be referred to the regal period, after the introduction of the consulate the importance of the intervention of private agency must have been greatly increased, partly by the rapid succession of magistrates in Rome, partly by the extension of the financial action of the treasury to such matters as the purchase and sale of grain and salt; and thus the foundation must have been laid for the system of farming the finances, the development of which became so momentous and so pernicious for the Roman commonwealth. The state gradually put all its indirect revenues and all its more complicated payments and transactions into the hands of middlemen, who gave or received a round sum and then managed the matter for their own benefit. Of course only considerable capitalists and, as the state looked strictly to tangible security, in the main only large landholders, could enter into such engagements: and thus there grew up a class of tax-farmers and contractors, who, in the rapid growth of their wealth, in their power over the state to which they appeared to be servants, and in the absurd and sterile basis of their moneyed dominion, are completely on a parallel with the speculators on the stock-exchange of the present day.

The new aspect assumed by the administration of finance showed itself first and most palpably in the treatment of the public lands, which tended almost directly to accomplish the material and moral annihilation of the middle classes. The use of the public pasture and of the state-domains generally was from its very nature a privilege of burgesses; formal law excluded the plebeian from the joint use of the common pasture. As however, apart from the conversion of the public land into private property or its assignation, Roman law knew no fixed rights of usufruct on the part of individual burgesses to be respected like those of property, it depended solely on the pleasure of the king, so long as the public land remained such, to grant and to define its joint enjoyment; and it is not to be doubted that he frequently made use of his right, or at least his power, as to this matter in favour of plebeians. But on the introduction of the republic the principle was again strictly insisted on, that the use of the common pasture belonged in law merely to the burgess of best right, or in other words to the patrician; and, though the senate still as before allowed exceptions in favour of the wealthy plebeian houses represented in it, the small plebeian landholders and the day-labourers, who stood most in need of the common pasture, had its joint enjoyment injuriously withheld from them. Moreover there had hitherto been paid for the cattle driven out on the common pasture a grazing-tax, which was moderate enough to make the right of using that pasture still be regarded as a privilege, and yet yielded no inconsiderable revenue to the public purse. The patrician quaestors were now remiss and indulgent in levying it, and gradually allowed it to fall into desuetude. Hitherto, particularly when new domains were acquired by conquest, allocations of land had been regularly arranged, in which all the poorer burgesses and *metoeci* were provided for; it was only the land which was not suitable for agriculture that was annexed to the common pasture. The ruling class did not venture wholly to give up such assignations, and still less to propose them merely in favour of the rich; but they became fewer and scantier, and were replaced by the pernicious system of occupation—that is to say, the cession of domain-lands, not in property or under formal lease for a definite term, but in special usufruct until further notice, to the first occupant and his heirs-at-law,

so that the state was at any time entitled to resume them, and
the occupier had to pay the tenth sheaf, or in oil and wine the
fifth part of the produce, to the exchequer. This was simply
the *precarium* already described (p. 192) applied to the state-
domains, and may have been already in use as to the public
land at an earlier period as a temporary arrangement until its
assignation should be carried out. Now, however, not only did
this occupation-tenure become permanent, but, as was natural,
none but privileged persons or their favourites participated, and
the tenth and fifth were collected with the same negligence as
the grazing-money. A threefold blow was thus struck at the
intermediate and smaller landholders: they were deprived of
the common usufructs of burgesses; the burden of taxation
was increased in consequence of the domain revenues no longer
flowing regularly into the public chest; and those land allocations were stopped, which had provided a constant outlet for
the agricultural proletariate somewhat as a great and well-
regulated system of emigration would do at the present day.
To these evils was added the farming on a large scale, which
was probably already beginning to come into vogue, dispossess-
ing the small agrarian clients, and in their stead cultivating the
estates by rural slaves; a blow which was more difficult to avert
and perhaps more pernicious than all those political usurpations
put together. The burdensome and partly unfortunate wars,
and the exorbitant taxes and taskworks to which these gave
rise, filled up the measure of calamity, so as either to deprive
the possessor directly of his farm and to make him the bondsman if not the slave of his creditor-lord, or to reduce him through
encumbrances practically to the condition of a temporary lessee
of his creditor. The capitalists, to whom a new field was here
opened of lucrative speculation unattended by trouble or risk,
sometimes augmented in this way their landed property; sometimes they left to the farmer, whose person and estate the law
of debt placed in their hands, nominal proprietorship and
actual possession. The latter course was probably the most
common as well as the most pernicious; for while utter ruin
might thereby be averted from the individual, this precarious
position of the farmer, dependent at all times on the mercy of his
creditor—a position in which he knew nothing of property but
its burdens—threatened to demoralise and politically to annihilate the whole farmer-class. The intention of the legislator,
when instead of mortgaging he prescribed the immediate
transfer of the property to the creditor with a view to prevent

insolvency and to devolve the burdens of the state on the real holders of the soil (p. 160), was evaded by the rigorous system of personal credit, which might be very suitable for merchants, but ruined the farmers. The free divisibility of the soil always involved the risk of an insolvent agricultural proletariate; and under such circumstances, when all burdens were increasing and all means of deliverance were foreclosed, distress and despair could not but spread with fearful rapidity among the agricultural middle class.

The distinction between rich and poor, which arose out of these relations, by no means coincided with that between the clans and the plebeians. If far the greater part of the patricians were wealthy landholders, opulent and considerable families were, of course, not wanting among the plebeians; and as the senate, which even then perhaps consisted in greater part of plebeians, had assumed the superintendence of the finances to the exclusion even of the patrician magistrates, it was natural that all those economic advantages, for which the political privileges of the nobility were abused, should go to the benefit of the wealthy collectively; and the pressure fell the more heavily upon the commons, since those who were the ablest and the most capable of resistance were by their admission to the senate transferred from the class of the oppressed to the ranks of the oppressors.

But this state of things prevented the political position of the aristocracy from being permanently tenable. Had it possessed the self-control to govern justly and to protect the middle class—as individual consuls from its ranks endeavoured, but from the reduced position of the magistracy were unable effectually to do—it might have long maintained itself in sole possession of the offices of state. Had it been willing to admit the wealthy and respectable plebeians to full equality of rights —possibly by connecting the acquisition of the patriciate with admission into the senate—both might long have governed and speculated with impunity. But neither of these courses was adopted; the narrowness of mind and short-sightedness, which are the proper and inalienable privileges of all genuine patricianism, were true to their character also in Rome, and rent the powerful commonwealth asunder in useless, aimless, and inglorious strife.

The immediate crisis however proceeded not from those who felt the disabilities of their order, but from the distress of the farmers. The rectified annals place the political revolution in the year $\frac{244}{510}$, the social in the years $\frac{259}{495}$ and $\frac{260}{494}$; they certainly appear to have been close upon each other, but the interval was probably longer. The strict enforcement of the law of debt— so runs the story—excited the indignation of the farmers at large. When in the year $\frac{259}{495}$ the levy was called forth for a dangerous war, the men bound to serve refused to obey the command; so that the consul Publius Servilius suspended for a time the application of the debtor-laws, and gave orders to liberate the persons already imprisoned for debt as well as prohibited further arrests. The farmers took their places in the ranks and helped to secure the victory. On their return from the field of battle the peace, which had been achieved by their exertions, brought back their prison and their chains: with merciless rigour the second consul, Appius Claudius, enforced the debtor-laws, and his colleague, to whom his former soldiers appealed for aid, dared not offer opposition. It seemed as if collegiate rule had been introduced not for the protection of the people, but to facilitate breach of faith and despotism; they endured, however, what could not be changed. But when in the following year the war was renewed, the word of the consul availed no longer. It was only when Manius Valerius was nominated dictator that the farmers submitted, partly from their awe of the higher magisterial authority, partly from their confidence in his friendly feeling to the popular cause— for the Valerii were one of those old patrician clans by whom government was esteemed a privilege and an honour, not a source of gain. The victory was again with the Roman standards; but when the victors came home and the dictator submitted his proposals of reform to the senate, they were thwarted by its obstinate opposition. The army still stood in its array, as usual, before the gates of the city. When the news arrived, the long threatening storm burst forth; the *esprit de corps* and the compact military organisation carried even the timid and the indifferent along with the movement. The army abandoned its general and its encampment, and under the leadership of the commanders of the legions—the military tribunes, who were at least in great part plebeians—marched in martial order into the district of Crustumeria between the Tiber and the Anio, where it occupied a hill and threatened to establish in this most fertile part of the Roman territory a new plebeian city. This secession showed in a palpable manner even to the most obstinate of the oppressors that such a civil war must end with economic ruin to themselves; and the senate gave way.

The dictator negotiated an agreement; the citizens returned within the city walls; unity was outwardly restored. The people gave Manius Valerius thenceforth the name of " the great " (*maximus*)—and called the mount beyond the Anio " the sacred mount." There was something mighty and elevating in such a revolution, undertaken by the multitude itself without definite guidance under generals whom accident supplied, and accomplished without bloodshed; and with pleasure and pride the citizens recalled its memory. Its consequences were felt for many centuries: it was the origin of the tribunate of the plebs.

In addition to temporary enactments, particularly for remedying the most urgent distress occasioned by debt, and for providing for a number of the rural population by the founding of various colonies, the dictator carried in constitutional form a law, which he moreover—doubtless in order to secure amnesty to the burgesses for the breach of their military oath—caused every individual member of the community to swear to, and then had it deposited in a temple under the charge and custody of two magistrates specially appointed from the plebs for the purpose, the two " house-masters " (*aediles*). This law placed by the side of the two patrician consuls two plebeian tribunes, who were to be elected by the plebeians assembled in curies. The power of the tribunes was of no avail in opposition to the military *imperium*, that is, in opposition to the authority of the dictator everywhere or to that of the consuls beyond the city; but it confronted, on a footing of independence and equality, the ordinary civil powers which the consuls exercised. There was, however, no partition of powers. The tribunes obtained on the one hand the right to cancel any command issued by a magistrate, by which the burgess whom it affected considered himself aggrieved, through a protest duly and personally tendered; and on the other hand they obtained or assumed the prerogative of pronouncing criminal sentences without limit and of defending them, if an appeal took place, before the assembled people. To these there was very soon attached the further prerogative of addressing the people in general and of procuring the adoption of resolutions.

The power of the tribunes therefore primarily involved the right of putting a stop at their pleasure to acts of administration and to the execution of the law, of enabling a person bound to military service to withhold himself from the levy with impunity, of preventing or cancelling the arrest of the con-

lemned debtor or his imprisonment during investigation, and
ther powers of the same sort. That this legal help might not
be frustrated by the absence of the helpers, it was further
ordained that the tribune should not spend a night out of the
ity, and that his door must stand open day and night. The
ribunes however could not prohibit the judge from pronouncing
his sentence, the senate from adopting its decree, or the centuries
rom giving their votes.

In virtue of their judicial office they could by their messengers
ummon before them any burgess, even the consul in office,
arrest him if he should refuse, imprison him during investiga-
ion or allow him to find bail, and then sentence him to death
or to a fine. For this purpose the two plebeian aediles, who
were appointed at the same time, were attached to the tribunes
as attendants and assistants; as were also the " ten men for
awsuits " (*iudices decemviri*, afterwards *decemviri litibus iudi-*
candis). The jurisdiction of the latter is not known; the
aediles had judicial powers like the tribunes, but principally in
the minor cases that might be settled by fines. If an appeal
took place from their sentence, it was directed not to the whole
body of the burgesses, with which the tribunes were not entitled
to transact business, but to the whole body of the plebeians,
who must in this case also have met and have voted by curies.
This sort of proceeding certainly savoured of violence rather
than of justice, especially when it was adopted against a non-
plebeian, as must in fact have been ordinarily the case. It was
not to be reconciled either with the letter or with the spirit of
the constitution, that a patrician should be called to account
by authorities who presided not over the body of burgesses, but
over an association formed within it, and that he should be
compelled to appeal not to the burgesses, but to this very
association. This was lynch justice; but it was carried into
effect, and there was at least an endeavour to clothe it in the
forms of law.

This new jurisdiction of the tribunes and aediles, and the
appellate decisions of the plebeian assembly thence arising,
were meant beyond doubt to be as much governed by the laws
as the jurisdiction of the consuls and quaestors and the judgments of the centuries on appeal. But the legal conceptions of
crime committed against the community (p. 150), and of offences
against order (p. 151), were themselves so little fixed, and their
statutory definition so difficult and indeed impossible, that the
administration of justice under these categories from its very

nature bore almost inevitably the stamp of arbitrariness. And at this epoch, when the very idea of right had become obscured amidst the struggles of the orders, and when the legal party-leaders on both sides were furnished with co-ordinate jurisdiction, that jurisdiction must have more and more approximated to a mere arbitrary police. It affected more especially the magistrate. By right the magistrate, according to Roman state-law, so long as he was in office, was amenable to no jurisdiction at all, and even after demitting his office he was not responsible for acts done within his proper province as a magistrate; even on the introduction of the *provocatio* there had been no attempt to depart from these principles (p. 248). But now the tribunician jurisdiction became practically a control exercised over every magistrate, sometimes immediately, sometimes in the sequel, and a control the more oppressive that neither the crime nor its punishment was formally defined by law. In reality, by means of the co-ordinate jurisdiction of the tribunes and consuls, the estates, limbs, and lives of the burgesses were abandoned to the pleasure or caprice of party-assemblies.

With this co-ordinate jurisdiction there was further associated a co-ordinate right of initiating legislation. As the tribunes had to address the people in defending their sentences in cases of penal procedure, it was natural that they should come to hold assemblies of the people for other purposes also, and that they should address the people or allow others to address them; a right that was specially guaranteed by the Icilian law ($\frac{262}{492}$), which threatened with severe punishment any one who should interrupt the tribune while speaking, or should bid the assembly disperse. It is evident that under such circumstances the tribune could not well be prevented from taking a vote on other proposals as well as on the confirmation of his sentences. Such "resolves of the multitude" (*plebi scita*) were not indeed strictly valid decrees of the people; on the contrary, they were at first little more than are the resolutions of our modern public meetings; but as the distinction between the comitia of the people and the councils of the multitude was of a formal nature rather than aught else, the validity of these resolves as autonomic determinations of the community was at once asserted at least on the part of the plebeians, and the Icilian law for instance was immediately carried in this way.

Thus were the tribunes of the people appointed as a shield and protection for individuals, and as leaders and managers for the collective body, provided with unlimited judicial power in criminal proceedings that in this way they might add emphasis to their command, and lastly even pronounced to be in their persons inviolable (*sacrosancti*). The people man by man swore for themselves and their children to defend the tribunes; and whoever laid hands upon them was regarded not merely as forfeited to the vengeance of the gods, but also as outlawed and proscribed among men.

The tribunes of the multitude (*tribuni plebis*) arose out of the military tribunes and derived from them their name; but constitutionally they had no further relation to them. On the contrary, in respect of powers the tribunes of the plebs stood on a level with the consuls. The appeal from the consul to the tribune, and the tribune's right of intercession in opposition to the consul, were precisely of the same nature with the appeal from consul to consul and the intercession of the one consul in opposition to the other; and both cases were simply applications of the general principle of law that, where two equal authorities differ, the veto prevails over the command. Moreover the original number (which indeed was soon augmented), the annual duration of the magistracy, which in the case of the tribunes changed its occupants on the 10th of December, and their irremovable tenure of office, were common to the tribunes and the consuls. They shared also the peculiar collegiate arrangement, which placed the full powers of the office in the hands of each individual consul and of each individual tribune, and, when collisions occurred within the college, did not count the votes, but gave the Nay precedence over the Yea; for which reason, when a tribune forbade, the vote of the individual was sufficient notwithstanding the opposition of his colleagues, while on the other hand when he brought an accusation he could be thwarted by any one of those colleagues. Both consuls and tribunes had full and co-ordinate criminal jurisdiction; and in its exercise, as the two quaestors were attached to the former, the two aediles were associated with the latter.[1] The consuls

---

[1] That the plebeian aediles were formed after the model of the patrician quaestors in the same way as the plebeian tribunes after the model of the patrician consuls, is evident both as regards their criminal functions (in which the distinction between the two magistracies seems to have lain in their tendencies only, not in their powers) and as regards their charge of the archives. The temple of Ceres was to the aediles what the temple of Saturn was to the quaestors, and from the former they derived their name. Significant in this respect is the enactment of the law of $\frac{305}{449}$ (Liv. iii. 55), that the decrees of the senate should be delivered over to the aediles there (p. 284), whereas, as is well known, according to the ancient—and, after

were necessarily patricians, the tribunes necessarily plebeians. The former had the ampler power, the latter the more unlimited; for the consul submitted to the prohibition and the judgment of the tribunes, but the tribune did not submit himself to the consul. Thus the tribunician power was a copy of the consular; but it was none the less a contrast to it. The power of the consuls was essentially positive, that of the tribunes essentially negative. Therefore the consuls alone were magistrates of the Roman people, not the tribunes; for the former were elected by the whole burgesses, the latter only by the plebeian association. In token of this the consul appeared in public with the apparel and retinue pertaining to state-officials; the tribune sat on a stool instead of the " chariot seat," and wanted the official attendants, the purple border, and generally all the insignia of magistracy: even in the senate the tribune had neither presidency nor seat. Thus in this remarkable institution absolute prohibition was in the most stern and abrupt fashion opposed to absolute command; the quarrel was settled by legally recognising and regulating the discord between rich and poor.

But what was gained by a measure which broke up the unity of the state; which subjected the magistrates to a controlling authority unsteady in its action and dependent on all the passions of the moment; which in the hour of peril might have brought the administration to a dead-lock at the bidding of any one of the opposition chiefs elevated to the rival throne; and which, by investing all the magistrates with co-ordinate jurisdiction in the administration of criminal law, as it were formally transferred that administration from the domain of law to that of politics and corrupted it for all time coming? It is true indeed that the tribunate, if it did not directly contribute to the political equalisation of the orders, served as a powerful weapon in the hands of the plebeians when these soon afterwards desired admission to the offices of state. But this was not the real design of the tribunate. It was a concession wrung not from the politically privileged order, but from the rich landlords and capitalists; it was designed to ensure to the commons equitable administration of law, and to promote a more judicious ad-

---

the settlement of the struggles between the orders, exclusively retained—practice those decrees were committed to the quaestors for preservation in the temple of Saturn. That the plebs also for a time had a chest of its own, and that the aediles managed it, is possible and, from the way in which the latter dealt with the *multae* paid to them, even probable; but it cannot be certainly proved.

ministration of finance. This design it did not, and could not, fulfil. The tribune might put a stop to particular iniquities, to individual instances of crying hardship; but the fault lay not in the unfair working of a righteous law, but in a law which was itself unrighteous, and how could the tribune regularly obstruct the ordinary course of justice? Could he have done so, it would have served little to remedy the evil, unless the sources of impoverishment were stopped—the perverse taxation, the wretched system of credit, and the pernicious occupation of the domain-lands. But such measures were not attempted, evidently because the wealthy plebeians themselves had no less interest in these abuses than the patricians. So this singular magistracy was instituted, which presented to the commons an obvious and available aid, and yet could not possibly carry out the necessary economic reform. It was no proof of political wisdom, but a wretched compromise between the wealthy aristocracy and the leaderless multitude. It has been affirmed that the tribunate of the people preserved Rome from tyranny. Were it true, it would be of little moment: a change in the form of the state is not in itself an evil for a people; on the contrary, it was a misfortune for the Romans that monarchy was introduced too late, after the physical and mental energies of the nation were exhausted. But the assertion is not even correct; as is shown by the circumstance that the Italian states remained as regularly free from tyrants as the Hellenic states regularly witnessed their rise. The reason lies simply in the fact that tyranny is everywhere the result of universal suffrage, and that the Italians excluded the burgesses who had no land from their public assemblies longer than the Greeks did: when Rome departed from this course, monarchy did not fail to emerge, and was in fact associated with this very tribunician office. That the tribunate had its use, in pointing out legitimate paths of opposition and averting many a wrong, no one will fail to acknowledge; but it is equally evident that, where it did prove useful, it was employed for very different objects from those for which it had been established. The bold experiment of allowing the leaders of the opposition a constitutional veto, and of investing them with power to assert it regardless of the consequences, proved to be an expedient by which the state was politically unhinged; and social evils were prolonged by the application of useless palliatives.

Now that civil war was organised, it pursued its course. The parties stood face to face as if drawn up for battle, each under

its leaders. Restriction of the consular and extension of the
tribunician power were the objects contended for on the one
side; the annihilation of the tribunate was sought on the other.
Legal impunity secured for insubordination, refusal to enter
the ranks for the defence of the land, impeachments involving
fines and penalties directed specially against magistrates who
had violated the rights of the commons or who had simply
provoked their displeasure, were the weapons of the plebeians;
and to these the patricians opposed violence, concert with the
public foes, and occasionally also the dagger of the assassin.
Hand-to-hand conflicts took place in the streets, and on both
sides the sacredness of the magistrate's person was violated.
Many families of burgesses are said to have migrated, and to
have sought more peaceful abodes in neighbouring communities;
and we may well believe it. The strong patriotism of the
people is obvious from the fact, not that they adopted this
constitution, but that they endured it, and that the community,
notwithstanding the most vehement convulsions, still held
together.

The best-known incident in these conflicts of the orders is the
history of Gaius Marcius, a brave aristocrat, who derived his
surname from the storming of Corioli. Indignant at the refusal
of the centuries to entrust to him the consulate in the year $\frac{263}{491}$,
he is reported to have proposed, according to one version, the
suspension of the sales of corn from the state-stores, till the
hungry people should give up the tribunate; according to
another version, the direct abolition of the tribunate itself.
Impeached by the tribunes so that his life was in peril, it is said
that he left the city, but only to return at the head of a Volscian
army; that when he was on the point of conquering the city of
his fathers for the public foe, the earnest appeal of his mother
touched his conscience; and that thus he expiated his first
treason by a second, and both by death. How much of this is
true cannot be determined; but the story, over which the naïve
misrepresentations of the Roman annalists have shed a patriotic
glory, affords a glimpse of the deep moral and political disgrace
of these conflicts between the orders. Of a similar stamp was
the surprise of the Capitol by a band of political refugees, led
by a Sabine chief, Appius Herdonius, in the year $\frac{294}{460}$; they
summoned the slaves to arms, and it was only after a violent
conflict, and by the aid of the Tusculans who hastened to render
help, that the Roman burgess-force overcame the Catilinarian
band. The same character of fanatical exasperation marks

rry it even amidst that stormy sea of passion and of weakness.
ıt he was mistaken. The nobles rose as one man; the rich
ebeians took part with them; the commons were dissatisfied
cause Spurius Cassius desired, in accordance with federal
ghts and equity, to give to the Latin confederates their share in
e assignation. Cassius had to die. There is some truth in
.e charge that he had usurped regal power, for he had indeed
.deavoured like the kings to protect the free commons against
.s own order. His law was buried along with him; but its
.ectre thenceforward incessantly haunted the eyes of the rich,
nd again and again it rose from the tomb against them, until
midst the conflicts to which it led the commonwealth perished.

A further attempt was made to get rid of the tribunician
.owvr by securing to the plebeians equality of rights in a more
.gular and more effectual way. The tribune of the people,
.aius Terentilius Arsa, proposed in $\frac{292}{462}$ the nomination of a
.mmission of five men to prepare a general code of law by
.hich the consuls should in future be bound in exercising their
.dicial powers. But the senate refused to sanction this pro-
.osal, and ten years elapsed ere it was carried into effect—years
.f vehement strife between the orders, and variously agitated
.oreover by wars and internal troubles. With equal obstinacy
.e party of the nobles hindered the concession of the law in the
.enate, and the plebs nominated again and again the same men
.s tribunes. Attempts were made to obviate the attack by other
.oncessions. In the year $\frac{297}{457}$ an increase of the tribunes from
.ve to ten was sanctioned—a very dubious gain; and in the
.ollowing year, by an Icilian *plebiscitum* which was admitted
.mong the sworn privileges of the plebs, the Aventine, which had
.itherto been a temple-grove and uninhabited, was distributed
.mong the poorer burgesses as sites for buildings in heritable
.ccupancy. The plebs took what was offered to them, but
.ever ceased to insist in their demand for a legal code. At
.ngth, in the year $\frac{300}{454}$, a compromise was effected; the senate
.ı substance gave way. The preparation of a legal code was
.esolved upon; for that purpose, as an extraordinary measure,
.he centuries were to choose ten men who were at the same time
.ɔ act as supreme magistrates in room of the consuls (*decemviri
.ɔnsulari imperio legibus scribundis*), and to this office not merely
.atricians, but plebeians also might be elected. These were
.ere for the first time designated as eligible, though only for an
.xtraordinary office. This was a great step in the progress
.owards full political equality; and it was not too dearly pur-

chased, when the tribunate of the people as well as the right of
appeal were suspended while the decemvirate lasted, and the
decemvirs were simply bound not to infringe the sworn liberties
of the plebs. Previously, however, an embassy was sent to
Greece to bring home the laws of Solon and other Greek laws,
and it was only on its return that the decemvirs were chosen
for the year $\frac{303}{451}$. Although they were at liberty to elect
plebeians, the choice fell on patricians alone—so powerful was
the nobility still—and it was only when the first commission did
not finish its business and a second election became necessary
for $\frac{304}{450}$, that some plebeians were chosen—the first non-patrician
magistrates that the Roman community had.

Taking a connected view of these measures, we can scarcely
attribute to them any other design than that of substituting for
tribunician intercession a limitation of the consular powers by
written law. On both sides there must have been a conviction
that things could not remain as they were, and the perpetuation
of anarchy, while it ruined the commonwealth, was in reality of
no benefit to any one. Sensible people could not but discern
that the interference of the tribunes in administration and their
action as prosecutors had an absolutely pernicious effect; and
the only real gain which the tribunate brought to the plebeians
was the protection which it afforded against a partial administration of justice, by operating as a sort of court of cassation to
check the caprice of the magistrate. Beyond doubt, when the
plebeians desired a written code, the patricians replied that in
that event the legal protection of tribunes would be superfluous;
and upon this there appears to have been concession by both
sides. It is not clear—and perhaps no definite arrangement was
entered into on the point—what was to be done after the preparation of the code was completed; the promise given to the
plebs, that their liberties were not to be touched, may certainly
bear merely the meaning that the tribunate of the people and the
other leading plebeian institutions were not to be abolished by
the impending codification, as in fact was not the case; but this
is very compatible with the intention that the decemvirs should,
on their retiring propose to the people to abandon the tribunician power and to leave themselves in the hands of the consuls,
whose sentences would no longer rest upon their arbitrary
pleasure, but on the written law.

The plan, if it should stand, was a wise one; all depended
on whether men's minds exasperated on either side with passion
would accept that peaceful adjustment. The decemvirs of the

ear $\frac{303}{451}$ submitted their law to the people, and it was confirmed
y them, engraven on ten tables of copper, and affixed in the
orum to the rostra in front of the senate-house. But as a
ipplement appeared necessary, decemvirs were again nominated
ı the year $\frac{304}{450}$, who added two more tables. Thus originated
ıe first and only Roman code, the law of the Twelve Tables. It
roceeded from a compromise between parties, and for that very
eason could not well include any changes of the existing law
ıore comprehensive than mere regulations of police or enact-
ıents adapted to existing circumstances. Even in the system
f credit no further alleviation was introduced than the estab-
shment of a—probably low—maximum of interest (10 per
ent.) and the threatening of heavy penalties against the usurer
—penalties, characteristically enough, far heavier than those of
he thief; the harsh procedure in actions of debt remained at
east in its leading features unaltered. Still less, as may easily
e conceived, were changes contemplated in the rights of the
rders. On the contrary the legal distinction between free-
olders and non-freeholders, and the invalidity of marriage
etween patricians and plebeians, were confirmed anew in the
ıw of the city. In like manner, with a view to restrict the
aprice of the magistrate and to protect the burgess, it was ex-
ressly enacted that the later law should uniformly have pre-
edence over the earlier, and that no decree of the people should
e issued against a single burgess. The most remarkable
eature was the exclusion of an appeal to the *comitia tributa* in
apital causes, while the privilege of appeal to the centuries was
uaranteed; which is perhaps to be explained by the circum-
tance that the penal jurisdiction was in fact usurped by the
lebs and its presidents (p. 270), and the decemvirs thought that,
vithout injuring its sworn liberties, they might do away at least
vith the worst case of this sort, the tribunician capital process.
'he real political significance of the measure resided far less in
he contents of the legislation than in the formal obligation
ıow laid upon the consuls to administer justice according to its
orms of process and its rules of law, and in the public exhibition
f the code, by which the administration of justice was subjected
o the control of publicity and the consul was compelled to dis-
ense equal and truly common justice to all.

The end of the decemvirate is involved in much obscurity.
t only remained—so runs the story—for the decemvirs to
ublish the last two tables, and then to give place to the ordinary
ıagistracy. But they delayed to do so: under the pretext that

the laws were not yet ready, they themselves prolonged the
magistracy after the expiry of their official year—a step qui
possible under Roman constitutional law, since even a magistra
appointed for a term only ceased to be magistrate by formal
demitting his office. The moderate section of the aristocrac
with the Valerii and Horatii at their head, are said to hav
attempted in the senate to compel the abdication of the dece
virate; but the head of the decemvirs Appius Claudius, origi
ally a rigid aristocrat, but now changing into a demagogue ar
a tyrant, gained the ascendancy in the senate, and the peop
submitted. The levy of two armies was accomplished witho
opposition, and war was begun against the Volscians as well
against the Sabines. Thereupon the former tribune of the peop
Lucius Siccius Dentatus, the bravest man in Rome, who ha
fought in a hundred and twenty battles and had forty-fi
honourable scars to show, was found dead in front of the cam
foully murdered, as it was said, at the instigation of the dece
virs. A revolution was fermenting in men's minds; and i
outbreak was hastened by the unjust sentence pronounced
Appius in the process as to the freedom of the daughter of t
centurion Lucius Verginius, the bride of the former tribu
Lucius Icilius—a sentence which wrested the maiden from h
relatives with a view to make her non-free and beyond the pa
of the law, and induced her father himself to plunge his kni
into the heart of his daughter in the open Forum, to rescue h
from certain shame. While the people in amazement at t
unprecedented deed surrounded the dead body of the fa
maiden, the decemvir commanded his lictors to bring the fath
and also the bridegroom before his tribunal, in order to rend
to him, from whose decision there lay no appeal, immedia
account for their rebellion against his authority. The cup w
now full. Protected by the furious multitude, the father an
the bridegroom of the maiden made their escape from the licto
of the despot, and while the senate trembled and wavered
Rome, the pair presented themselves, with numerous witness
of the fearful deed, in the two camps. The unparalleled tale w
told; the eyes of all were opened to the gap which the absen
of tribunician protection had made in the security of law; ar
what the fathers had done their sons repeated. Once more t
armies abandoned their leaders: they marched in warlike ord
through the city, and proceeded once more to the Sacred Moun
where they again nominated their own tribunes. Still t
decemvirs refused to resign their power; and the army appear

with its tribunes in the city, and encamped on the Aventine. Then at length, when civil war was imminent and the conflict in the streets might hourly begin, the decemvirs renounced their usurped and dishonoured power; and Lucius Valerius and Marcus Horatius negotiated a second compromise, by which the tribunate of the plebs was again established. The impeachment of the decemvirs terminated in the two most guilty, Appius Claudius and Spurius Oppius, committing suicide in prison, while the other eight went into exile and the state confiscated their property. The prudent and moderate tribune of the plebs, Marcus Duilius, prevented further judicial prosecutions by a seasonable use of his veto.

So runs the story as recorded by the pen of the Roman aristocrats; but, even leaving out of view the accessory circumstances, the great crisis out of which the Twelve Tables arose cannot possibly have had its termination in such romantic adventures, and in political issues so incomprehensible. The decemvirate was, after the abolition of the monarchy and the institution of the tribunate of the people, the third great victory of the plebs; and the exasperation of the opposite party against the institution and against its head Appius Claudius is sufficiently intelligible. The plebeians had through its means secured the right of eligibility to the highest magistracy of the community and a general code of law; and it was not they that had reason to rebel against the new magistracy, and to restore the purely patrician consular government by force of arms. This result can only have been sought by the party of the nobility, and if the patricio-plebeian decemvirs made the attempt to maintain themselves in office beyond their time, the nobility were certainly the first to enter the lists against them; on which occasion doubtless the nobles would not omit to urge that the stipulated rights of the plebs, and the tribunate in particular, should be also withheld. If the nobility thereupon succeeded in setting aside the decemvirs, it is certainly conceivable that after their fall the plebs should once more assemble in arms with a view to secure the results both of the earlier revolution of $\frac{260}{494}$ and of the latest movement; and the Valerio-Horatian laws of $\frac{305}{449}$ can only be understood as forming a compromise in this conflict.

The compromise as was natural proved very favourable to the plebeians, and again imposed severely felt restrictions on the power of the nobility. As a matter of course the tribunate of the people was restored, the code of law wrung from the aristocracy was adhered to and enforced, and the consuls were obliged to judge accordingly. Under that arrangement indeed the tribes lost their usurped jurisdiction in capital causes; but as an ample compensation for that loss, it was on the proposition of the consuls decreed by the centuries that in future every magistrate—and therefore the dictator among the rest—should be bound at his nomination to allow the right of appeal: any one who should nominate a magistrate on other terms was to expiate the offence with his life. In other respects the dictator retained his former powers; and, in particular, his official acts could not, like those of the consuls, be cancelled by a tribune. The tribunes retained, in the right to inflict fines without limitation and to submit their sentences to the *comitia tributa*, a sufficient means of driving an opponent out of the pale of the commonwealth.

The plenitude of the consular power was further restricted, in so far as the administration of the military chest was committed to two paymasters (*quaestores*) chosen by the community, who were nominated for the first time in $\frac{307}{447}$, but from the ranks of the aristocracy; while the nomination of the two paymasters administering the city-chest remained for the present with the consuls. The assembly, in which the military paymasters were elected under the superintendence of one of the consuls, was that of the whole patricio-plebeian freeholders, and voted by districts; an arrangement which likewise involved a concession to the plebeian farmers, who had far more command of these assemblies than of the centuriate *comitia*.

A concession of still greater consequence was that which allowed the tribunes to share in the discussions of the senate. To admit the tribunes to the hall where the senate sat, appeared to that body beneath its dignity; so a bench was placed for them at the door that they might from that spot follow its proceedings. But the tribunes could not be prevented from now interposing against any decree of the senate that displeased them; and the new principle became established, although only gradually, that any resolution of the senate or of the public assembly might be arrested by the intercession of a tribune. Lastly, to secure the decrees of the senate—with the validity of which indeed that of the most important *plebiscita* was bound up (p. 278)—from being tampered with or forged, it was enacted that in future they should be deposited not merely under charge of the patrician *quaestores urbani* in the temple of Saturn, but also under that of the plebeian aediles in the temple of Ceres.

Thus the struggle, which was begun in order to get rid of the tribunician power, terminated in the definite completion of its title to annul not only particular acts of administration on the appeal of the person aggrieved, but also any resolution of the constituent powers of the state at pleasure. The persons of the tribunes, and the uninterrupted maintenance of the college at its full number, were secured by the most sacred oaths and by every element of reverence that religion could present. No attempt to abolish this magistracy was ever from this time forward made in Rome.

CHAPTER III

THE EQUALISATION OF THE ORDERS, AND THE NEW ARISTOCRACY

THE tribunician movement appears to have mainly originated in social rather than political discontent, and there is good reason to suppose that some of the wealthy plebeians admitted to the senate were no less opposed to that movement than the patricians. For they benefited by the privileges against which the movement was mainly directed; and although in other respects they found themselves treated as inferior, it probably seemed to them by no means an appropriate time for asserting their claim to participate in the magistracies, when the exclusive financial power of the whole senate was assailed. This explains why during the first fifty years of the republic no step was taken aiming directly at the political equalisation of the orders.

But this league between the patricians and wealthy plebeians by no means bore within itself any guarantee of permanence. Beyond doubt from the very first a portion of the leading plebeian families had attached themselves to the movement-party, partly from a sense of what was due to the fellow-members of their order, partly in consequence of the natural bond which unites all who are treated as inferior, and partly because they perceived that concessions to the multitude were inevitable in the issue, and that, if turned to due account, they would result in the abrogation of the exclusive rights of the patriciate and would thereby give to the plebeian aristocracy a decisive preponderance in the state. Should this conviction become—as was inevitable—more and more prevalent, and should the plebeian aristocracy at the head of its order take up the struggle with the patrician nobility, it would wield in the tribunate a legalised instrument of civil warfare, and it might, with the weapon of social distress, so fight its battles as to dictate to the nobility the terms of peace and, in the position of mediator between the two parties, compel its own admission to the offices of state.

Such a crisis in the position of parties occurred after the fall of the decemvirate. It had now become perfectly clear hat the tribunate of the plebs could never be set aside; the plebeian aristocracy could not do better than seize this powerful lever and employ it for the removal of the political disabilities of their order.

Nothing shows so clearly the defencelessness of the patrician nobility when opposed to the united plebs, as the fact that the fundamental principle of the exclusive party—the invalidity of marriage between patricians and plebeians—fell at the first blow scarcely four years after the decemviral revolution. In the year $\frac{309}{445}$ it was enacted by the Canuleian law, that a marriage between a patrician and a plebeian should be valid as a true Roman marriage, and that the children begotten of such a marriage should follow the rank of the father. At the same time it was further carried that, in place of consuls, military tribunes—as a rule apparently six, as many as there were tribunes to the legion—with consular powers [1] and consular

---

[1] The hypothesis that legally the full *imperium* belonged to the patrician, and only the military *imperium* to the plebeian, consular tribunes, not only raises many questions which its advocates cannot answer—as to the course followed, for example, in the event of the election falling, as was by law quite possible, wholly on plebeians—but conflicts with the fundamental principle of Roman constitutional law, that the *imperium*, that is to say, the right of commanding the burgess in name of the community, was functionally indivisible and capable of no other limitation at all than a territorial one. There was a province of common law and a province of military law, in the latter of which the *provocatio* and other regulations of the common law were not applicable; there were magistrates, such as the proconsuls, who were empowered to discharge functions simply in the latter; but there were, in the strict sense of law, no magistrates with merely jurisdictional, as there were none with merely military, *imperium*. The proconsul was in his province, just like the consul, at once commander-in-chief and supreme judge, and was entitled to send to trial actions not only between non-burgesses and soldiers, but also between one burgess and another. Even when, on the institution of the praetorship, the idea arose of apportioning special functions to the *magistratus maiores*, this division of powers had more of a practical than of a strictly legal force; the *praetor urbanus* was primarily indeed the supreme judge, but he could also convoke the centuries, at least for certain cases, and could command the army; the consul in the city held primarily the supreme administration and the supreme command, but he too acted as a judge in cases of emancipation and adoption—the functional indivisibility of the supreme magistracy was therefore, even in these instances, very strictly adhered to on both sides. It thus appears that the military as well as jurisdictional authority, or, laying aside these abstractions foreign to the Roman law of this period, the absolute magisterial power, virtually pertained to the plebeian consular tribunes as well as to the patrician. But the supposition of Becker (*Handb.* ii. 2, 137) is highly probable, that—for the same reasons for which, at a subsequent period, the exclusively patrician praetorship was associated with the consulship common to both orders—during the consular tribunate the plebeian members of the college were practically excluded from jurisdiction, and so far certainly the consular tribunate prepared the way for the subsequent actual division of jurisdiction between consuls and praetors.

duration of office should be elected by the centuries. According to the ancient law every burgess or *metoikos* liable to service might attain the post of an officer (p. 96), and in virtue of that principle the supreme magistracy, after having been temporarily opened up to the plebeians in the decemvirate, was now after a more comprehensive fashion rendered equally accessible to all free-born burgesses. The question naturally occurs, what interest the aristocracy could have—now that it was under the necessity of abandoning its exclusive possession of the supreme magistracy and of yielding in the matter—in refusing to the plebeians the title, and conceding to them the consulate under this singular form? [1] But, in the first place, there were associated with the holding of the supreme magistracy various honorary rights, partly personal, partly hereditary; thus the honour of a triumph was regarded as legally dependent on the occupancy of the supreme magistracy, and was never given to an officer who had not administered the latter office in person; and the descendants of a curule magistrate were at liberty to set up the image of such an ancestor in the family hall and to exhibit it in public on fitting occasions, while this was not allowed in the case of other ancestors.[2] It is as easy to be explained as it is difficult to be vindicated, that the governing aristocratic order should have allowed the government itself to be wrested from their hands far sooner than the honorary rights associated with it, especially such as were hereditary; and therefore, when it was obliged to share the former with the plebeians, it gave to the actual supreme magistrate the legal standing not of the holder of a curule chair, but of a simple staff-officer, whose distinction was one purely personal. Of

[1] The defence, that the aristocracy clung to the exclusion of the plebeians from religious prejudice, mistakes the fundamental character of the Roman religion, and imports into antiquity the modern distinction between church and state. The admittance of a non-burgess to a religious ceremony of the citizens could not indeed but appear sinful to the orthodox Roman; but even the most rigid orthodoxy never doubted that admittance to civic communion, which absolutely and solely depended on the state, involved also full religious equality. All such scruples of conscience, the honesty of which in themselves we do not mean to doubt, were precluded, when once they granted to the plebeians *en masse* at the right time the patriciate. This only may perhaps be alleged by way of excuse for the nobility, that after it had neglected the right moment for this purpose at the abolition of the monarchy, it was no longer in a position subsequently of itself to retrieve the neglect (p. 258).

[2] Whether this distinction between these "curule houses" and the other families embraced within the patriciate was ever of serious political importance, cannot with certainty be either affirmed or denied; and as little do we know whether at this epoch there really was any considerable number of patrician families that were not yet curule.

greater political importance, however, than the refusal of the *ius imaginum* and of the honour of a triumph was the circumstance, that the exclusion of the plebeians sitting in the senate from debate necessarily ceased in respect to those of their number who, as designated or former consuls, ranked among the senators whose opinion had to be asked before the rest; so far it was certainly of great importance for the nobility to admit the plebeian only to a consular office, and not to the consulate himself.

But notwithstanding these vexatious disabilities the privileges of the clans, so far as they had a political value, were legally superseded by the new institution; and, had the Roman nobility been worthy of its name, it would now have given up the struggle. But it did not. Though a rational and legal resistance was thenceforth impossible, spiteful opposition still found a wide field of petty expedients, of chicanery and intrigue: and, far from honourable or politically prudent as such resistance was, it was still in a certain sense fruitful of results. It certainly procured at length for the commons concessions, which could not easily have been wrung from the united Roman aristocracy; but it also prolonged civil war for another century and enabled the nobility, in defiance of those laws, practically to retain the government in their exclusive possession for several generations longer.

The expedients of which the nobility availed themselves were as various as a paltry policy could suggest. Instead of deciding at once the question as to the admission or exclusion of the plebeians at the elections, they conceded what they were compelled to concede only with reference to the elections immediately impending. The vain struggle was thus annually renewed whether patrician consuls or military tribunes from both orders with consular powers should be nominated; and among the weapons of the aristocracy this mode of conquering an opponent by wearying and annoying him proved by no means the least effectual.

Moreover they broke up the supreme power which had hitherto been undivided, in order to delay their inevitable defeat by multiplying the points to be assailed. Thus the adjustment of the budget and of the burgess- and taxation-rolls, which ordinarily took place every fourth year and had hitherto been managed by the consuls, was entrusted in the year $\frac{319}{435}$ to two valuators (*censores*), nominated from among the nobles by the centuries for a period, at the most, of eighteen

months. The new office gradually became the palladium
of the aristocratic party, less even on account of its financial
influence than for the sake of the right annexed to it of filling
up the vacancies in the senate and in the equites, and of removing
individuals from the lists of the senate, equites, and burgesses
on occasion of their adjustment. At this epoch, however,
the censorship by no means possessed the great importance and
moral supremacy which afterwards were associated with it.

But the important change made in the year $\frac{333}{421}$ in respect
to the quaestorship amply compensated for this success of the
patrician party. There were at that time four quaestors, of
whom the two entrusted with the management of the city
chest were nominated by the consuls, and the two military
paymasters by the tribes, all however from the nobility. The
nomination of the city quaestors now passed to the patricio-
plebeian assembly of the tribes, and the consul retained merely
the superintendence of the election. And, what was of
still more moment, the commons—perhaps arguing that at
least the two military paymasters were in fact officers rather
than civil functionaries, and that accordingly the plebeians
appeared as well entitled to the quaestorship as to the military
tribuneship—acquired in this instance for the first time the
privilege of eligibility as well as the right of election for one of
the ordinary magistracies. With justice it was felt on the one
side as a great victory, on the other as a severe defeat, that
thenceforth patrician and plebeian were equally capable of
electing and being elected to the military as well as to the urban
quaestorship.

The nobility, in spite of their most obstinate resistance, only
sustained loss after loss; and their exasperation increased as
their power decreased. Attempts were doubtless still made
directly to assail the rights secured by agreement to the commons; but such attempts were not so much the well-calculated
manœuvres of party as the acts of an impotent thirst for
vengeance. Such in particular was the process against Maelius.
Spurius Maelius, a wealthy plebeian, during a severe dearth
($\frac{315}{439}$) sold corn at such prices as to put to shame and annoy
the patrician store-president (*praefectus annonae*) Gaius Minucius. The latter accused him of aspiring to kingly power; with
what amount of reason we cannot decide, but it is scarcely
credible that a man who had not even filled the tribunate
should have seriously thought of sovereignty. Nevertheless
the authorities took up the matter in earnest, and the cry of

" King " always produced on the multitude in Rome an effect similar to that of the cry of " Pope " on the masses in England. Titus Quinctius Capitolinus, who was for the sixth time consul, nominated Lucius Quinctius Cincinnatus, who was eighty years of age, as dictator without appeal, in open violation of the solemnly sworn laws (p. 284). Maelius, summoned before him, seemed disposed to disregard the summons; and the dictator's master of the horse, Gaius Servilius Ahala, slew him with his own hand. The house of the murdered man was pulled down, the corn from his granaries was distributed gratuitously to the people, and those who threatened to avenge his death were secretly made away with. This disgraceful judicial murder—a disgrace even more to the credulous and blind people than to the malignant party of young patricians —passed unpunished; but if that party hoped by such means to undermine the right of appeal, it violated the laws and shed innocent blood in vain.

Electioneering intrigues and priestly trickery proved in the hands of the nobility more efficient than any other weapons. The extent to which the former must have prevailed is best seen in the fact that in $\frac{322}{432}$ it appeared necessary to issue a special law against electioneering practices, which of course was of little avail. When the voters could not be influenced by corruption or threatening, the presiding magistrates stretched their powers—admitting, for example, so many plebeian candidates that the votes of the opposition were thrown away amongst them, or omitting from the list of candidates those whom the majority were disposed to choose. If in spite of all this an obnoxious election was carried, the priests were consulted whether no vitiating circumstance had occurred in the auspices or other religious ceremonies on the occasion; and some such law they seldom failed to discover. Taking no thought as to the consequences and unmindful of the wise example of their ancestors, the people allowed the principle to be established that the opinion of the skilled colleges of priests as to omens of birds, portents, and the like was legally binding on the magistrate, and thus put it into their power to cancel any state-act—whether the consecration of a temple or any other act of administration, whether law or election—on the ground of religious informality. Thus it happened that, although the eligibility of plebeians had been already established by law in $\frac{333}{421}$ and thenceforward continued to be legally recognised, it was only in $\frac{345}{409}$ that the first plebeian attained the quaestorship; in like manner patricians almost exclusively held the military tribunate with consular powers down to $\frac{354}{400}$. It was apparent that the legal abolition of the privileges of the nobles had by no means really and practically placed the plebeian aristocracy on a footing of equality with the gentile nobility. Many causes contributed to this result: the tenacious opposition of the nobility far more easily allowed itself to be theoretically superseded in a moment of excitement, than to be permanently kept down in the annually recurring elections; but the main cause was the inward disunion between the chiefs of the plebeian aristocracy and the mass of the farmers. The middle class, whose votes were decisive in the comitia, did not feel itself specially called on to advance the interests of the leading non-patricians, so long as its own demands were disregarded by the plebeian no less than by the patrician aristocracy.

During these political struggles social questions had lain altogether dormant, or were discussed at any rate with less energy. After the plebeian aristocracy had gained possession of the tribunate for its own ends, no serious notice was taken either of the question of the domains or of a reform in the system of credit; although there was no lack either of newly acquired lands or of impoverished or decaying farmers. Instances indeed of assignations took place, particularly in the recently conquered border-territories, such as those of the domain of Ardea in $\frac{312}{442}$, of Labici in $\frac{336}{418}$, and of Veii in $\frac{361}{393}$ —more however on military grounds than for the relief of the farmer, and by no means to an adequate extent. Individual tribunes doubtless attempted to revive the law of Cassius—for instance Spurius Maecilius and Spurius Metilius instituted in the year $\frac{337}{417}$ a proposal for the distribution of the whole state-lands—but they were thwarted, in a manner peculiarly characteristic of the existing state of parties, by the opposition of their own colleagues or in other words of the plebeian aristocracy. Some of the patricians also attempted to remedy the common distress; but with no better success than had formerly attended Spurius Cassius. A patrician like Cassius and like him distinguished by military renown and personal valour, Marcus Manlius, the saviour of the Capitol during the Gallic siege, came forward as the champion of the oppressed people, with whom he was connected by the ties of comradeship in war and of bitter hatred towards his rival, the celebrated general and leader of the optimate party, Marcus Furius Camillus. When a brave officer was about to be led away to a debtor's prison, Manlius interceded for him and released him with his own money; at the same time he offered his lands to sale, declaring loudly, that as long as he possessed a foot's breadth of land such iniquities should not occur. This was more than enough to unite the whole government party, patricians as well as plebeians, against the dangerous innovator. The trial for high treason, the charge of having meditated a renewal of the monarchy, wrought on the blind multitude with the insidious charm which belongs to stereotyped party-phrases. They themselves condemned him to death, and his renown availed him nothing save that it was deemed expedient to assemble the people for the bloody assize at a spot whence the voters could not see the rock of the citadel—the dumb monitor which might remind them how their fatherland had been saved from the extremity of danger by the hands of the very man whom they were now consigning to the executioner ($\frac{370}{384}$).

While the attempts at reformation were thus arrested in the bud, the social disorders became still more crying; for on the one hand the domain-possessions were ever extending in consequence of successful wars, and on the other hand debt and impoverishment were ever spreading more widely among the farmers, particularly from the effects of the severe war with Veii ($\frac{348-358}{406-396}$) and of the burning of the capital in the Gallic invasion ($\frac{364}{390}$). It is true that, when in the Veientine war it became necessary to prolong the term of service of the soldiers and to keep them under arms not—as hitherto at the utmost—only during the summer, but also throughout the winter, and when the farmers, foreseeing their utter economic ruin, were on the point of refusing their consent to the declaration of war, the senate resolved on making an important concession. It charged the pay, which hitherto the tribes had defrayed by contribution, on the state-chest, or in other words, on the produce of the indirect revenues and the domains ($\frac{348}{406}$). It was only in the event of the state-chest being at the moment empty that a general contribution (*tributum*) was imposed on account of the pay; and in that case it was considered as a forced loan and was afterwards repaid by the community. The arrangement was equitable and wise; but, as it was not based upon the essential condition of turning the domains to proper account for the benefit of the exchequer, there were added to the increased burden of service frequent contributions, which were none the less ruinous to the man of small means that they were officially regarded not as taxes but as advances.

Under such circumstances, when the plebeian aristocracy saw itself practically excluded by the opposition of the nobility and the indifference of the commons from equality of political rights, and the suffering farmers were powerless as opposed to the close aristocracy, it was natural that they should help each other by a compromise. With this view the tribunes of the people, Gaius Licinius and Lucius Sextius, submitted to the commons proposals to the following effect: first, to abolish the consular tribunate and to lay it down as a rule that at least one of the consuls should be a plebeian; secondly, to open up to the plebeians admission to one of the three great colleges of priests —that of the custodiers of oracles, whose number was to be increased to ten (*duoviri*, afterwards *decemviri sacris faciundis*, p. 180); thirdly, as respected the domains, to allow no burgess to maintain upon the common pasture more than a hundred oxen and five hundred sheep, or to hold more than five hundred *jugera* (about 300 acres) of the domain lands left free for occupation; fourthly, to oblige the landlords to employ in the labours of the field a number of free labourers proportioned to that of their rural slaves; and lastly, to procure alleviation for debtors by deduction of the interest which had been paid from the capital, and by the arrangement of set terms for the payment of arrears.

The tendency of these enactments is obvious. They were designed to deprive the nobles of their exclusive possession of the curule magistracies and of the hereditary distinctions of nobility therewith associated; which, it was characteristically conceived, could only be accomplished by the legal exclusion of the nobles from the place of second consul. They were designed, as a consequence, to emancipate the plebeian members of the senate from the subordinate position which they occupied as silent by-sitters (p. 255), in so far as those of them at least who had filled the consulate thereby acquired a title to deliver their opinion with the patrician consulars before the other patrician senators (pp. 255, 289). They were intended, moreover, to withdraw from the nobles the exclusive possession of spiritual dignities; and in carrying out this purpose for reasons sufficiently obvious the old Latin priesthoods of the augurs and pontifices were left to the old burgesses, but these were obliged to open up to the new burgesses the third great college of more recent origin and belonging to a worship that was originally foreign. They were intended, in fine, to procure a share in the common usufructs of burgesses for the poorer commons, alleviation for the suffering debtors, and employment for the day-labourers that were destitute of work. Abolition of privileges, social reform, civil equality—these were the three great ideas, of which it was the design of this movement to secure the recognition. Vainly the patricians exerted all the means at their command in opposition to these legislative proposals; even the dictatorship and the old military hero Camillus were able only to delay, not to prevent, their accomplishment. Willingly would the people have separated the proposals; of what moment to it were the consulate and custodiership of oracles, if only the burden of debt were lightened and the public lands were free! But it was not for nothing that the plebeian nobility had adopted the popular cause; it included the proposals in one single project of law, and after a long struggle—it is said of eleven years—the senate at length gave its consent and they passed in the year $\frac{387}{367}$.

With the election of the first non-patrician consul—the choice fell on one of the authors of this reform, the late tribune of the people, Lucius Sextius Lateranus—the gentile aristocracy ceased both in fact and in law to be numbered among the political institutions of Rome. When after the final passing of these laws the former champion of the clans, Marcus Furius Camillus, founded a sanctuary of Concord at the foot of the Capitol—upon an elevated platform, where the senate was wont frequently to meet, above the old meeting-place of the burgesses, the Comitium—we gladly cherish the belief that he recognised in the legislation thus completed the close of a dissension only too long continued. The religious consecration of the new concord of the community was the last public act of the old warrior and statesman, and a worthy termination of his long and glorious career. He was not wholly mistaken; the more judicious portion of the clans evidently from this time forward looked upon their exclusive political privileges as lost, and were content to share the government with the plebeian aristocracy. In the majority, however, the patrician spirit proved true to its incorrigible character. On the strength of the privilege which the champions of legitimacy have at all times claimed of obeying the laws only when these coincide with their party interests, the Roman nobles on various occasions ventured, in open violation of the stipulated arrangement, to nominate two patrician consuls. But, when by way of answer to an election of that sort for the year $\frac{411}{343}$ the community in the year following formally resolved to allow both consular positions to be filled by non-patricians, they understood the implied threat, and still doubtless desired, but never again ventured, to touch the second consular place.

In like manner the aristocracy simply injured itself by the attempt which it made, on the passing of the Licinio-Sextian laws, to save at least some remnant of its ancient privileges by means of a system of political clipping and paring. Under the pretext that the nobility were exclusively cognisant of law, the administration of justice was detached from the consulate when the latter had to be thrown open to the plebeians; and for this purpose there was nominated a special third consul, or, as he was commonly called, a praetor. In like manner the supervision of the market and the judicial police-duties connected with it, as well as the celebration of the city-festival, were assigned to two newly nominated aediles, who—by way of distinction from the plebeian aediles—were named from their standing jurisdiction " aediles of the judgment seat " (*aediles curules*). But the curule aedileship became immediately so far accessible to the plebeians, that it was held by patricians and plebeians alternately. Moreover the dictatorship was thrown open to plebeians in $\frac{398}{356}$, as the mastership of the horse had already been in the year before the Licinio-Sextian laws ($\frac{386}{368}$); both the censorships were thrown open in $\frac{403}{351}$, and the praetorship in $\frac{417}{337}$; and about the same time ($\frac{415}{339}$) the nobility were by law excluded from one of the censorships, as they had previously been from one of the consulships. It was to no purpose that once more a patrician augur detected secret flaws, hidden from the eyes of the uninitiated, in the election of a plebeian dictator ($\frac{427}{327}$), and that the patrician censor did not up to the close of our present period ($\frac{474}{280}$) permit his colleague to present the solemn sacrifice with which the census closed; such chicanery served merely to show the ill humour of patricianism. Of as little avail were the complaints which the patrician presidents of the senate would not fail to raise regarding the participation of the plebeians in its debates; it became a settled rule that not the patrician members, but those who had attained to one of the three supreme ordinary magistracies—the consulship, praetorship, and curule aedileship—should be summoned to give their opinion in this order and without distinction of class, while the senators who had held none of these offices still even now took part merely in the division. The right, in fine, of the patrician senate to reject a decree of the community as unconstitutional—a right, however, which in all probability it rarely ventured to exercise—was withdrawn from it by the Publilian law of $\frac{415}{339}$ and by the Maenian law which was not passed before the middle of the fifth century, in so far that it had to bring forward its constitutional objections, if it had any such, when the list of candidates was exhibited or the project of law was brought in; which practically amounted to a regular announcement of its consent beforehand. In this character, as a purely formal right, the confirmation of the decrees of the people still continued in the hands of the nobility down to the last age of the republic.

The clans retained, as may naturally be conceived, their religious privileges longer. Indeed, several of these, which were destitute of political importance, were never interfered with, such as their exclusive eligibility to the offices of the three supreme *flamines* and that of *rex sacrorum* as well as to the membership of the colleges of Salii. On the other hand the two colleges of pontifices and of augurs, with which a considerable influence over the courts and the comitia were associated, were too important to remain in the exclusive possession of the patricians. The Ogulnian law of $\frac{454}{300}$ accordingly threw these also open to plebeians, by increasing the number of pontifices from five to eight, and that of augurs from six to nine, and equally distributing the stalls in the two colleges between patricians and plebeians.

The two hundred years' strife was brought at length to a close by the law of the dictator Q. Hortensius ($\frac{465}{289}$, $\frac{468}{286}$) which was occasioned by a dangerous popular insurrection, and which declared that the decrees of the plebs should stand on an absolute footing of equality—instead of their earlier conditional equivalence—with those of the whole community. So greatly had the state of things been changed that that portion of the burgesses, which had once possessed exclusively the right of voting, thenceforth no longer took even a part in the most important and most frequent form of the votes which bound all the burgesses.

The struggle between the Roman clans and commons was thus substantially at an end. While the nobility still preserved out of its comprehensive privileges the *de facto* possession of one of the consulships and one of the censorships, it was excluded by law from the tribunate, the plebeian aedileship, the second consulship and censorship, and from participation in the votes of the plebs which were legally equivalent to votes of the whole body of burgesses. As a righteous retribution for its perverse and stubborn resistance, the patriciate had seen its former privileges converted into so many disabilities. The Roman gentile nobility, however, by no means disappeared because it had become an empty name. The less the significance and power of the nobility, the more purely and exclusively the patrician spirit developed itself. The haughtiness of the "Ramnians" survived the last of their class-privileges for centuries; after they had steadfastly striven "to rescue the consulate from the plebeian filth," and had at length become reluctantly convinced of the impossibility of such an achievement, they continued rudely and spitefully to display their aristocratic spirit. To understand rightly the history of Rome in the fifth and sixth centuries, we must never overlook this sulking patricianism; it could indeed do little more than irritate itself and others, but this it did to the best of its ability. Some years after the passing of the Ogulnian law ($\frac{458}{296}$) a characteristic instance of this sort occurred. A patrician matron, who was married to a leading plebeian that had attained to the highest dignities of the state, was on account of this misalliance expelled from the circle of noble dames and was refused admission to the common festival of Chastity; and in consequence of that exclusion separate patrician and plebeian goddesses of Chastity were thenceforward worshipped in Rome. Doubtless caprices of this sort were of very little moment, and the better disposed of the clans kept themselves entirely aloof from this miserable policy of peevishness; but it left behind on both sides a feeling of discontent, and, while the struggle of the commons against the clans was in itself a political and even moral necessity, these convulsive efforts to prolong the strife—the aimless combats of the rear-guard after the battle had been decided, as well as the empty squabbles as to rank and standing—needlessly irritated and disturbed the public and private life of the Roman community.

Nevertheless one object of the compromise concluded by the two portions of the plebs in $\frac{387}{367}$, the abolition of the patriciate, had in all material points been completely attained. The question next arises, how far the same can be affirmed of the two positive objects aimed at in the compromise?—whether the new order of things in reality checked social distress and established political equality? The two were intimately connected; for, if economic embarrassments ruined the middle class and broke up the burgesses into a minority of rich men and a suffering proletariate, such a state of things would at once annihilate civil equality and in reality destroy the republican commonwealth. The preservation and increase of the middle class, and in particular of the farmers, formed therefore for every patriotic statesman of Rome a problem not merely important, but the most important of all. The plebeians, moreover, recently called to take part in the government, greatly indebted as they were for their new political rights to the proletariate which was suffering and expecting help at their hands, were politically and morally under special obligation to attempt its relief by means of government measures, so far as relief was by such means at all attainable.

Let us first consider how far any real relief was contained in that part of the legislation of $\frac{387}{367}$ which bore upon the question. That the enactment in favour of the free day-labourers could not possibly accomplish its object—namely, to check the system of farming on a large scale and by means of slaves, and to secure to the free proletarians at least a share of work—is self-evident. In this matter legislation could afford no relief, without shaking the foundations of the civil organisation of the period in a way that would reach far beyond its immediate horizon. In the question of the domains, again, it was quite possible for legislation to effect a change; but what was done was manifestly inadequate. The new domain-arrangement, by granting the right of driving very considerable flocks and herds upon the public pastures, and that of occupying domain-land not laid out in pasture up to a maximum fixed on a high scale, conceded to the wealthy a very important and perhaps even disproportionate prior share in the produce of the domains; and by the latter regulation conferred upon the domain-tenure, although it remained in law liable to pay a tenth and revocable at pleasure, as well as upon the system of occupation itself, somewhat of a legal sanction. It was a circumstance still more suspicious, that the new legislation neither supplemented the existing and manifestly unsatisfactory provisions for the collection of the pasture-money and the tenth by compulsory measures of a more effective kind, nor prescribed any thorough revision of the domanial possessions, nor appointed a magistracy charged with the carrying of the new laws into effect. The distribution of the existing occupied domain-land partly among the holders up to a fair maximum, partly among the plebeians who had no property, in both cases in full ownership; the abolition in future of the system of occupation; and the institution of an authority empowered to make immediate distribution of any future acquisitions of territory, were so clearly demanded by the circumstances of the case, that it certainly was not through want of discernment that these comprehensive measures were neglected. We cannot fail to recollect that it was the plebeian aristocracy, in other words, a portion of the very class that was practically privileged in respect to the usufructs of the domains, which proposed the new arrangement, and that one of its very authors, Gaius Licinius Stolo, was among the first to be condemned for having exceeded the agrarian maximum; and we cannot but ask whether the legislators dealt altogether honourably, and whether they did not on the contrary designedly evade a solution, really tending to the common benefit, of the unhappy question of the domains. We do not mean, however, to express any doubt that the regulations of the Licinio-Sextian laws, such as they were, might and did substantially benefit the small farmer and the day-labourer. It must, moreover, be acknowledged that in the period immediately succeeding the passing of the law the authorities watched with at least comparative strictness over the observance of its rules as to the maximum, and frequently condemned the possessors of large herds and the occupiers of the domains to heavy fines.

In the system of taxation and of credit also efforts were made with greater energy at this period than at any before or subsequent to it to remedy the evils of the national economy, so far as legal measures could do so. The duty levied in $\frac{397}{357}$ of five per cent. on the value of slaves that were to be manumitted was—irrespective of the fact that it imposed a check on the undesirable multiplication of freedmen—the first tax in Rome that was really laid upon the rich. In like manner efforts were made to remedy the system of credit. The usury laws, which the Twelve Tables had established (p. 281), were renewed and gradually rendered more stringent, so that the maximum of interest was successively lowered from 10 per cent. (enforced in $\frac{397}{357}$) to 5 per cent. (in $\frac{407}{347}$) for the year of twelve months, and at length ($\frac{412}{342}$) the taking of interest was altogether forbidden. The latter foolish law remained formally in force, but, of course, it was practically inoperative; the standard rate of interest afterwards usual, viz. 1 per cent. per month, or 12 per cent. for the civil common year—which, according to the value of capital in antiquity, was probably at that time nearly the same as, according to its modern value, a rate of 5 or 6 per cent.—must have been already about this period established as the maximum of allowable interest. Any action at law for higher rates must have been refused, perhaps even judicial claims for repayment may have been allowed; moreover notorious usurers were not unfrequently summoned before the bar of the people and readily condemned by the tribes to heavy fines. Still more important was the alteration of the procedure in cases of debt by the Poetelian law ($\frac{428}{326}$ or $\frac{441}{313}$). On the one hand it allowed every debtor who declared on oath his solvency to save his personal freedom by the cession of his property; on the other hand it abolished the former summary proceedings in execution on a loan-debt, and laid down the rule that no Roman burgess could be led away to bondage except upon the sentence of jurymen.

It is plain that all these expedients might perhaps in some respects mitigate, but could not remove, the existing economic disorders. The continuance of the distress is shown by the appointment of a bank-commission to regulate the relations of credit and to provide advances from the state-chest in $\frac{402}{352}$, by the appointment of legal term-payments in $\frac{407}{347}$, and above all by the dangerous popular insurrection about $\frac{467}{287}$, when the people, unable to obtain new facilities for the payment of debts, marched out to the Janiculum, and nothing but a seasonable attack by external enemies, and the concessions contained in the Hortensian law, restored peace to the community. It is, however, very unjust to reproach these earnest attempts to check the impoverishment of the middle class with their inadequacy. The belief that it is useless to employ partial and palliative means against radical evils, because they only remedy them in part, is an article of faith, never preached unsuccessfully by baseness to simplicity, but it is none the less absurd. On the contrary, we may ask whether the vile spirit of demagogism had not even thus early laid hold of this matter, and whether expedients were really needed so violent and dangerous as, for example, the deduction of the interest paid from the capital. Our documents do not enable us to decide the question of right or wrong in the case. But we recognise clearly enough that the middle class of freeholders still continued economically in a perilous and critical position; that various endeavours were made by those in power to remedy it by prohibitory laws and by respites, but of course in vain; and that the aristocratic ruling class continued to be too weak in point of control over its members, and too much entangled in the selfish interests of its order, to relieve the middle class by the only effectual means at the disposal of the government—the entire and unreserved abolition of the system of occupying the state lands—and by that course to free the government from the reproach of turning to its own advantage the affliction of the governed.

A more effectual relief than any which the government was willing or able to give was derived by the middle classes from the political successes of the Roman community and the gradual consolidation of the Roman sovereignty over Italy. The numerous and large colonies which it was necessary to found for the securing of that sovereignty, the greater part of which were sent forth in the fifth century, furnished a portion of the agricultural proletariate with farms of their own, while the efflux gave relief to such as remained at home. The increase of the indirect and extraordinary sources of revenue, and the flourishing condition of the Roman finances in general, rendered it but seldom necessary to levy any contribution from the farmers in the form of a forced loan. While the earlier small holdings were probably lost beyond recovery, the rising average of Roman prosperity must have converted the former larger landholders into farmers, and in so far added new members to the middle class. People of rank sought principally to secure the large newly-acquired districts for occupation; the mass of wealth which flowed to Rome through war and commerce must have reduced the rate of interest; the increase in the population of the capital benefited the farmer throughout Latium; a wise system of incorporation united a number of neighbouring and formerly subject communities with the Roman state, and thereby strengthened especially the middle class; finally, the glorious victories and their mighty results silenced faction. If the distress of the farmers was by no means removed and still less were its sources stopped, it yet admits of no doubt that at the close of this period the Roman middle class was on the whole in a far less oppressed condition than in the first century after the expulsion of the kings.

Lastly civic equality was in a certain sense undoubtedly attained or rather restored by the reform of $\frac{387}{367}$, and the development of its legitimate consequences. As formerly, when the patricians still in fact formed the burgesses, these had stood upon a footing of absolute equality in rights and duties, so now in the enlarged burgess-body there existed in the eye of the law no arbitrary distinctions. The gradations to which differences of age, sagacity, cultivation, and wealth necessarily give rise in civil society, naturally also pervaded the sphere of public life; but the spirit animating the burgesses and the policy of the government uniformly operated so as to render these differences as little conspicuous as possible. The whole system of Rome tended to train up her burgesses to an average character of ability, but not to bring into prominence the gifts of genius. The growth of culture among the Romans did not at all keep pace with the development of the resources of the community, and it was instinctively repressed rather than promoted by those in power. That there should be rich and poor, could not be prevented; but (as in a genuine community of farmers) the farmer as well as the day-labourer personally guided the plough, and to the rich as well as the poor the good economic rule applied that they should live with uniform frugality and above all should hoard no unproductive capital at home—excepting the salt-cellar and the sacrificial ladle, no silver articles were at this period seen in any Roman house. Nor was this of little moment. In the mighty successes which the Roman community externally achieved during the century from the last Veientine down to the Pyrrhic war we perceive that the patriciate has now given place to the farmers; that the fall of the highborn Fabian would have been not more and not less lamented by the whole community than the fall of the plebeian Decian was lamented alike by plebeians and patricians; that the consulate did not of itself fall even to the wealthiest aristocrat; and that a poor husbandman from Sabina, Manius Curius, could conquer king Pyrrhus in the field of battle and chase him out of Italy, without ceasing to be a simple Sabine farmer and to cultivate in person his own bread-corn.

In regard however to this imposing republican equality, we must not overlook the fact that it was to a considerable extent only formal, and that an aristocracy of a very decided stamp grew out of it or rather was contained in it from the very first. The non-patrician families of wealth and consideration had long ago separated from the plebs, and leagued themselves with the patriciate in the participation of senatorial rights and in the prosecution of a policy distinct from that of the plebs and very often counteracting it. The Licinio-Sextian laws abrogated legal distinctions within the ranks of the aristocracy, and changed the character of the barrier which excluded the plebeian from the government, so that it was no longer an obstacle insurmountable in law, but a hindrance difficult to be surmounted in practice. In both ways fresh blood was mingled with the ruling order in Rome; but in itself the government still remained aristocratic. In this respect the Roman community was a genuine farmer-commonwealth, in which the rich holder of a whole hide was little distinguished externally from the poor cottager and held intercourse with him on equal terms, but aristocracy nevertheless exercised so all-powerful a sway that a man without means sooner rose to be master of the burgesses in the city than mayor in his own village. It was a very great and valuable gain, that under the new legislation even the poorest burgess might fill the highest office of the state; nevertheless it was a rare exception when a man from the lower ranks of the population reached such a position,[1] and not only so, but probably it was, at least towards the close of this period, possible only by means of an election carried by the opposition.

Every aristocratic government of itself calls forth a corresponding opposition party; and as the formal equalisation of the orders only modified the aristocracy, and the new ruling order not only succeeded the old patriciate but engrafted itself on it and intimately coalesced with it, the opposition also continued to exist and in all respects pursued a similar course. As it was now no longer the plebeians as such, but the common people, that were treated as inferior, the new opposition professed from the first to be the representative of the lower classes and particularly of the small farmers; and as the new aristocracy attached itself to the patriciate, so the first movements of this new opposition were interwoven with the final struggles against the privileges of the patricians. The first names in the series of these new popular leaders were Manius Curius (consul $\frac{464}{290}$, $\frac{479}{275}$, $\frac{480}{274}$; censor $\frac{482}{272}$) and Gaius Fabricius (consul $\frac{472}{282}$, $\frac{476}{278}$, $\frac{481}{273}$; censor $\frac{479}{275}$); both of them men without ancestral lineage and without wealth, both summoned—in opposition to the aristocratic principle of restricting re-election to the highest office of the state—thrice by the votes of the burgesses to the chief magistracy, both, as tribunes, consuls, and censors, opponents of patrician privileges and defenders of the small farmer class against the incipient arrogance of the leading houses. The future parties were already marked out; but the interests of party were still suspended on both sides in

---

[1] The statements as to the poverty of the consulars of this period, which play so great a part in the moral anecdote-books of a later age, mainly rest on a misunderstanding on the one hand of the old frugal economy—which might very well consist with considerable prosperity—and on the other hand of the beautiful old custom of burying men who had deserved well of the state from the proceeds of penny collections—which was far from being a pauper burial. The method also of explaining surnames by etymological guess-work, which has imported so many absurdities into Roman history, has furnished its quota to this belief (*Serranus*).

presence of the interests of the common-weal. The patrician Appius Claudius and the farmer Manius Curius—vehement in their personal antagonism—jointly by wise counsel and vigorous action conquered king Pyrrhus; and while Gaius Fabricius as censor inflicted penalties on Publius Cornelius Rufinus for his aristocratic sentiments and aristocratic habits, this did not prevent him from supporting the claim of Rufinus to a second consulate on account of his recognised ability as a general. The breach was already formed; but the adversaries still shook hands across it.

The termination of the struggles between the old and new burgesses, the various and comparatively successful endeavours to relieve the middle class, and the germs—already making their appearance amidst the newly acquired civic equality—of the formation of a new aristocratic and a new democratic party, have thus been passed in review. It remains that we describe the shape which the new government assumed amidst these changes, and the positions in which after the political abolition of the nobility the three elements of the republican commonwealth—the burgesses, the magistrates, and the senate—stood towards each other.

The burgesses in their ordinary assemblies continued as hitherto to be the highest authority in the commonwealth and the legal sovereign. But it was settled by law that—apart from the matters committed once for all to the decision of the centuries, such as the election of consuls and censors—voting by districts should be as valid as voting by centuries: a regulation introduced as regards the patricio-plebeian assembly by the Valerio-Horatian law of $\frac{305}{449}$ (p. 283) and extended by the Publilian law of $\frac{415}{339}$, but enacted as regards the plebeian separate assembly by the Hortensian law about $\frac{467}{287}$ (p. 297). We have already noticed that the same individuals, on the whole, were entitled to vote in both assemblies, but that—apart from the exclusion of the patricians from the plebeian separate assembly—in the general assembly of the districts all entitled to vote were on a footing of equality, while in the centuriate comitia the working of the suffrage was graduated with reference to the means of the voters, and in so far, therefore, the change was certainly a levelling and democratic innovation. It was a circumstance of far greater importance that, towards the end of this period, the primitive freehold basis of the right of suffrage began for the first time to be called in question. Appius Claudius, the boldest innovator known in Roman

history, in his censorship in $\frac{442}{312}$ without consulting the senate
or people so adjusted the burgess-roll, that a man who had
no land was received into whatever tribe he chose and then
according to his means into the corresponding century. But
this alteration was too far in advance of the spirit of the age to
obtain full acceptance. One of the immediate successors of
Appius, Quintus Fabius Rullianus, the famous conqueror of
the Samnites, undertook in his censorship of $\frac{450}{304}$ not to set it
aside entirely, but to confine it within such limits that the real
power in the burgess assemblies should continue to be vested
in the holders of land and of wealth. He incorporated all who
had no land, and also those freedmen possessed of land whose
property was valued at less than 30,000 sesterces (£300), in
the four city tribes, which were now made to rank not as the
first but as the last. The rural tribes, on the other hand, the
number of which gradually increased between $\frac{367}{387}$ and $\frac{513}{241}$
from seventeen to thirty-one—thus forming a majority, greatly
preponderating from the first and ever increasing in preponderance, of the voting-divisions—were reserved by law for the
whole of the freeborn burgesses who were freeholders, as well
as for the freedmen who held land exceeding the above-
mentioned limit. In the centuries the equalisation of the freeholders and non-freeholders who were of free birth remained
as Appius had introduced it; on the other hand, the freedmen
who were not admitted into the rural tribes were deprived of
the suffrage. In this manner provision was made for the
preponderance of the freeholders in the comitia of the tribes,
while in the centuriate comitia—in which, from the decided
preference given to the wealthy, fewer measures of precaution
sufficed—the freemen could at least do no harm. By this
wise and moderate arrangement on the part of a man who for
his warlike feats and still more for this peaceful achievement
justly received the surname of the Great (*Maximus*), the obligation of bearing arms was extended, as was fitting, to the non-
freehold burgesses, while a check was imposed on the increasing
power of the class who had once been slaves—a check which is
unfortunately in a state sanctioning slavery an indispensable
necessity. A peculiar moral jurisdiction, moreover, which
gradually came to be associated with the census and the making-
up of the burgess-roll, excluded from the burgess-body all
individuals notoriously unworthy, and guarded the full moral
and political purity of citizenship.

The powers of the comitia exhibited during this period a

tendency to enlarge their range, but in a manner very gradual. The increase in the number of magistrates to be elected by the people falls, to some extent, under this head; it is an especially significant fact that from $\frac{392}{362}$ the military tribunes of one legion, and from $\frac{443}{311}$ four tribunes in each of the first four legions respectively, were nominated no longer by the general, but by the burgesses. During this period the burgesses did not on the whole interfere in administration; only their right of declaring war was, as was reasonable, emphatically asserted, and held to extend also to cases in which a prolonged armistice concluded instead of a peace expired and what was not in law but in fact a new war began ($\frac{327}{427}$). In other instances a question of administration was only submitted to the people when the governing authorities came into collision and one of them referred the matter to the people, or when in difficult or invidious questions the government voluntarily placed the decision in their hands. Examples of such collisions occurred when the leaders of the moderate party among the nobility, Lucius Valerius and Marcus Horatius, in $\frac{305}{449}$, and the first plebeian dictator, Gaius Marcius Rutilus, in $\frac{398}{356}$, were not allowed by the senate to receive the triumphs they had earned; when the consuls of $\frac{452}{295}$ could not agree as to their respective provinces of jurisdiction; and when the senate, in $\frac{364}{390}$, resolved to give up to the Gauls an ambassador who had forgotten his duty, and a consular tribune carried the matter to the community. This was the first occasion on which a decree of the senate was annulled by the people; and heavily the community atoned for it. Instances of the decision being voluntarily left to the people occurred first, when Caere sued for peace, after the people had declared war against it but before war had actually begun ($\frac{401}{353}$), whereupon the senate hesitated to leave the resolution of the people unexecuted without their formal consent; and at a subsequent period, when the senate wished to reject the humble entreaty of the Samnites for peace, but shunning the odium of the declaration devolved it on the people ($\frac{436}{318}$). It is not till towards the close of this epoch that we find a considerable extension of the powers of the *comitia tributa* in affairs of administration, particularly through the practice of consulting it as to the conclusion of peace and of alliances: this extension probably dates from the Hortensian law of $\frac{467}{287}$.

Notwithstanding, however, these enlargements of the powers of the burgess-assemblies, their practical influence on state affairs began, particularly towards the close of this period, to wane.

First of all, the extension of the bounds of Rome deprived her collective assemblies of their original significance. An assembly of persons resident within the original territory of the city might very well meet in sufficiently full numbers, and might very well know its own wishes, even without discussion; but the Roman burgess-body had become less a civic community than a state. No doubt, in so far as the incorporated townships were associated together in the rural tribes—in the Papirian tribe, for instance, the votes of the Tusculans proved substantially decisive—the municipal sentiment, at all times so lively in Italy, pervaded also the Roman comitia and introduced into them, at least when voting by tribes, a sort of inward connection and a special *esprit de corps,* which thereupon gave rise to animosities and rivalries of all sorts. In this way, on extraordinary occasions, energy and independence were certainly infused into the voting; but under ordinary circumstances the composition of the comitia and their decision were left dependent on the person who presided or on accident, or were committed to the hands of the burgesses domiciled in the capital. It is, therefore, quite easy to understand how the assemblies of the burgesses, which had great practical importance during the first two centuries of the republic, gradually became a mere instrument in the hands of the presiding magistrates, and in truth a very dangerous instrument, because the magistrates called to preside were so numerous, and every resolution of the community was regarded as the ultimate legal expression of the will of the people. But the enlargement of the constitutional rights of the burgesses was not of much moment, inasmuch as practically they were less than ever capable of a will and action of their own, and there was as yet no demagogism, in the proper sense of that term, in Rome. Had any such demagogic spirit existed, it would have attempted not to extend the powers of the burgesses, but to remove the restrictions on political discussion in their presence; whereas throughout this whole period there was undeviating acquiescence in the old maxims, that the magistrate alone could convoke the burgesses, and that he was entitled to exclude all discussion and all proposal of amendments. At the time this incipient breaking up of the constitution made itself felt chiefly in the circumstance that the collective assemblies assumed an essentially passive attitude, and did not on the whole interfere in government either to help or to hinder it.

As regards the power of the magistrates, its diminution, although not the direct design of the struggles between the old and new burgesses, was doubtless one of their most important results. At the beginning of the struggle between the orders or, in other words, of the strife for the possession of the consular power, the consulate was still the one and indivisible, essentially regal, magistracy; and the consul, like the king in former times, still had the appointment of all subordinate functionaries left to his own free choice. At the termination of that contest its most important functions—jurisdiction, street-police, election of senators and equites, the census and financial administration —were separated from the consulship and transferred to magistrates, who like the consul were nominated by the community and occupied a position co-ordinate with him rather than subordinate. The consulate, formerly the single ordinary magistracy of the state, was no longer even absolutely the first. In the new arrangement as to the ranking and usual order of succession of the different offices the consulate stood indeed above the praetorship, aedileship, and quaestorship, but beneath the censorship, which—in addition to the most important financial duties—was charged with the adjustment of the rolls of burgesses, equites, and senators, and thereby wielded a wholly arbitrary moral control over the entire community and every individual burgess, the humblest as well as the most distinguished. The conception of limited magisterial power or special functions, which seemed to the older Roman constitutional law irreconcilable with the conception of magistracy, gradually gained a footing and mutilated and destroyed the earlier idea of the one and indivisible *imperium*. A first step was already taken in this direction by the institution of the collateral standing offices, particularly the quaestorship (p. 250); it was completely carried out by the Licinio-Sextian laws ($\frac{387}{367}$), which prescribed the functions of the three supreme magistrates, and assigned administration and the conduct of war to the two first, and the management of justice to the third. But the change did not stop here. The consuls, although they were in law wholly and everywhere co-ordinate, naturally from the earliest times divided between them in practice the different departments of duty (*provinciae*). Originally this was done simply by mutual concert, or in default of it by casting lots; but by degrees the other constituent authorities in the commonwealth interfered with this practical definition of functions. It became usual for the senate to define annually the spheres of duty; and, while it did not directly assign them to the co-ordinate magistrates, it exercised decided influence on the personal distribution by advice and request. In an extreme case the senate doubtless obtained a decree of the community, definitively to settle the question of distribution (p. 307); the government, however, very seldom employed this dangerous expedient. Further, the most important affairs, such as the concluding of peace, were withdrawn from the consuls, and they were in such matters obliged to have recourse to the senate and to act according to its instructions. Lastly, in cases of extremity the senate could at any time suspend the consuls from office; for, according to an usage never established by law but never violated in practice, the creation of a dictatorship depended simply upon the resolution of the senate, and the fixing of the person to be nominated, although constitutionally vested in the nominating consul, really under ordinary circumstances lay with the senate.

The old unity and plenary power of the *imperium* were retained longer in the case of the dictatorship than in that of the consulship. Although of course as an extraordinary magistracy it had in reality from the first its special functions, it had in law far less of a special character than the consulate. But it also was gradually affected by the new idea of definite powers and functions introduced into the legal life of Rome. In $\frac{391}{363}$ we first meet with a dictator expressly nominated from theological scruples for the mere accomplishment of a religious ceremony; and though that dictator himself, doubtless in formal accordance with the constitution, treated the restriction of his powers as null and took the command of the army in spite of it, such an opposition on the part of the magistrate was not repeated on occasion of the subsequent similarly restricted nominations, which occurred in $\frac{403}{351}$ and thenceforward very frequently. On the contrary, the dictators thenceforth accounted themselves bound by their powers as specially defined.

Lastly, further seriously felt restrictions of the magistracy were involved in the prohibition issued in $\frac{412}{342}$ against the accumulation of the ordinary curule offices, and in the enactment of the same date, that the same person should not again administer the same office under ordinary circumstances before an interval of ten years had elapsed, as well as in the subsequent regulation that the office which practically was the highest, the censorship, should not be held a second time at all ($\frac{489}{265}$). But the government was still strong enough not to be afraid of its instruments or to desist purposely on that account from employing those who were the most serviceable. Brave officers were very frequently released from these rules,[1] and cases still occurred like those of Quintus Fabius Rullianus, who was five times consul in eight-and-twenty years, and of Marcus Valerius Corvus ($\frac{384-483}{370-271}$) who, after he had filled six consul-ships, the first in his twenty-third, the last in his seventy-second year, and had been throughout three generations the protector of his countrymen and the terror of the foe, des-cended to the grave at the age of a hundred.

While the Roman magistrate was thus more and more com-pletely and definitely transformed from the absolute lord into the limited commissioner and administrator of the community, the old counter-magistracy, the tribunate of the people, was undergoing at the same time a similar transformation internal rather than external. It served a double purpose in the commonwealth. It had been from the beginning intended to protect the humble and the weak by its somewhat revolutionary assistance (*auxilium*) against the overbearing violence of the magistrates; it had subsequently been employed to get rid of the legal disabilities of the commons and the privileges of the gentile nobility. The latter end was attained. The original object was not only in itself a democratic ideal rather than a political possibility, but it was also quite as obnoxious to the plebeian aristocracy into whose hands the tribunate necessarily fell, and quite as incompatible with the new organisation which originated in the equalisation of the orders and had if possible a still more decided aristocratic hue than that which preceded it, as it was obnoxious to the gentile nobility and incompatible with the patrician consular constitution. But instead of abolishing the tribunate, they preferred to convert it from a weapon of opposition into an instrument of government, and now introduced the tribunes of the people, who were originally excluded from all share in administration and were neither

---

[1] Any one who compares the consular Fasti before and after $\frac{412}{342}$ will have no doubt as to the existence of the above-mentioned law respecting re-election to the consulate; for, while before that year a return to office, especially after three or four years, was a common occurrence, afterwards intervals of ten years and more were as frequent. Exceptions, however, occur in very great numbers, particularly during the severe years of war $\frac{434-443}{320-311}$. On the other hand, the principle of not allowing a plurality of offices was strictly adhered to. There is no certain instance of the com-bination of two of the three ordinary curule (Liv. xxxix. 39, 4) offices (the consulate, praetorship, and curule aedileship), but instances occur of other combinations, such as of the curule aedileship and the office of master of the horse (Liv. xxiii. 24, 30); of the praetorship and censorship (*Fast. Cap. a.* 501); of the praetorship and the dictatorship (Liv. viii. 12); of the consulate and the dictatorship (Liv. viii. 12).

magistrates nor members of the senate, into the class of governing authorities. While in jurisdiction they were from the beginning on a footing of equality with the consuls and in the early stages of the conflicts between the orders acquired like the consuls the right of initiating legislation, they now received—we know not exactly when, but probably at or soon after the final equalisation of the orders—a position of equality with the consuls as regarded the practically governing authority, the senate. Hitherto they had been present at the proceedings of the senate, sitting on a bench at the door; now they obtained, like the other magistrates and by their side, a place in the senate itself and the right to interpose their word in its discussions. If they were precluded from the right of voting, it was simply in virtue of the general principle of Roman state-law, that those only should give counsel who were not called to act; in accordance with which the whole of the acting magistrates possessed during their year of office only a seat, not a vote, in the council of the state (p. 256). But concession did not rest here. The tribunes received the distinctive prerogative of supreme magistracy, which among the ordinary magistrates belonged only to the consuls and praetors besides—the right of convoking the senate, of consulting it, and of procuring decrees from it.[1] This was only as it should be; the heads of the plebeian aristocracy had to be placed on an equality with those of the patrician aristocracy in the senate, when once the government had passed from the gentile nobility to the united aristocracy. Now that this opposition college, originally excluded from all share in the public administration, became—particularly with reference to strictly urban affairs—a second supreme executive and one of the most usual and most serviceable instruments of the government, or in other words of the senate, for managing the burgesses and especially for checking the excesses of the magistrates, it was certainly, as respected its original character, absorbed and politically annihilated; but this course was really enjoined by necessity. Clearly as the defects of the Roman aristocracy were apparent, and decidedly as the steady growth of aristocratic ascendancy was connected with the practical setting aside of the tribunate, none can fail to see that government could not be long carried on with an authority which was not only aimless and virtually calculated to put off the suffering proletariate with a deceitful prospect of relief,

---

[1] Hence despatches intended for the senate were addressed to Consuls, Praetors, Tribunes of the Plebs, and Senate (Cicero, *ad. Fam.* xv. 2, *et al.*).

but was at the same time decidedly revolutionary and possessed of an absolutely anarchical power of obstruction to the authority of the magistrates and even of the state itself. But that faith in an ideal, which is the foundation of all the power and of all the impotence of democracy, had come to be closely associated in the minds of the Romans with the tribunate of the plebs; and we do not need to recall the case of Cola Rienzi in order to perceive that, however unsubstantial might be the advantage thence arising to the multitude, it could not be abolished without a formidable convulsion of the state. Accordingly with genuine political prudence they contented themselves with reducing it to a nullity under forms that should attract as little attention as possible. The mere name of this essentially revolutionary magistracy was still preserved in the aristocratically governed commonwealth—an incongruity for the present, and for the future a sharp and dangerous weapon in the hands of a coming revolutionary party. For the moment, however, and for a long time to come the aristocracy was so absolutely powerful and so completely possessed control over the tribunate, that no trace is to be met with of a collegiate opposition on the part of the tribunes to the senate; and the government overcame the forlorn movements of opposition that now and then proceeded from independent tribunes, always without difficulty, and ordinarily by means of the tribune itself.

In reality it was the senate that governed the commonwealth, and that almost without opposition after the equalisation of the orders. Its very composition had undergone a change. The free prerogative of the chief magistrates in this matter, as it had been exercised after the setting aside of the old clan-representation (p. 78), had been subjected to very material restrictions on the abolition of the presidency for life (p. 255).

A further step towards the emancipation of the senate from the power of the magistrates took place, when the adjustment of the senatorial lists was transferred from the supreme magistrates to subordinate functionaries—from the consuls to the censors (p. 289). Certainly, whether immediately at that time or soon afterwards, the right of the magistrate entrusted with the preparation of the list to omit from it individual senators on account of a stain attaching to them and thereby to exclude them from the senate was, if not introduced, at least more precisely defined,[1] and in this way the foundations were laid

[1] This prerogative and the similar ones with reference to the equestrian and burgess-lists were perhaps not formally assigned by law to the censors,

of that peculiar jurisdiction over morals on which the high repute of the censors was chiefly based (p. 306). But censures of that sort, from the nature of the case—especially as the two censors had to be at one on the matter—while serving to remove particular persons who did not contribute to the credit of the assembly or were hostile to the spirit prevailing there, could not bring the body itself into dependence on the magistracy.

But the right of the magistrate to constitute the senate according to his judgment was decidedly restricted by the Ovinian law, which appears to have been carried, probably about the middle of this period, soon after the Licinio-Sextian laws. That law at once conferred a seat and vote in the senate provisionally on every one who had been curule aedile, praetor, or consul, and bound the next censors either formally to inscribe these expectants in the senatorial roll, or at any rate only to exclude them from the roll for such reasons as sufficed for the rejection of an actual senator. The number of those, however, who had been magistrates was far from sufficing to keep the senate up to the normal number of three hundred; and below that point it could not be allowed to fall, especially as the list of senators was at the same time that of jurymen. Considerable room was thus always left for the exercise of the censorial right of election; but those senators who were chosen not in consequence of having held office, but by selection on the part of the censor—frequently burgesses who had filled a non-curule public office, or distinguished themselves by personal valour, who had killed an enemy in battle or saved the life of a burgess—took part in voting, but not in debate (p. 297). The main body of the senate, and that portion of it in whose hands government and

but were always practically implied in their powers. It was the community, not the censor, that conferred burgess-rights; but the person whom the latter in making up his roll transferred from the list of burgesses to that of clients—although not losing his burgess-rights—could not exercise the privileges of a burgess till the preparation of a new list. The same was the case with the senate; the person omitted by the censor from his list ceased to attend the senate, so long as the list in question remained valid—unless the presiding magistrate should reject it and revive the earlier list. Evidently therefore the important question in this respect was not so much what was the legal liberty of the censors, as how far their authority availed with those magistrates who had to summon according to their lists. Hence it is easy to understand how this prerogative gradually rose in importance, and how with the increasing consolidation of the nobility such erasures assumed virtually the form of judicial decisions and were virtually respected as such. As to the adjustment of the senatorial list, undoubtedly the enactment of the Ovinian *plebiscitum* exercised a material share of influence—that the censors should admit to the senate " the best men out of all classes."

administration were concentrated, was thus according to the Ovinian law substantially constituted no longer by the arbitrary will of a magistrate, but by indirect popular election. The Roman state in this way made some approach to, although it did not reach, the great institution of modern times, representative popular government, while the aggregate of the non-debating senators furnished—what it is so necessary and yet so difficult to get in governing corporations—a compact mass of members capable of forming and entitled to pronounce an opinion, but voting in silence.

The powers of the senate underwent scarcely any change in form. The senate carefully avoided giving a handle to opposition or to ambition by unpopular changes, or manifest violations, of the constitution; it permitted, though it did not promote, the enlargement in a democratic direction of the power of the burgesses. But while the burgesses acquired the semblance, the senate acquired the substance of power—a decisive influence over legislation and the official elections, and the whole control of the state.

Every new project of law was subjected to a preliminary deliberation in the senate, and scarcely ever did a magistrate venture to lay a proposal before the community without or in opposition to the senate's opinion. If he did so, the senate had —in the intercessory powers of the magistrates and the annulling powers of the priests—an ample set of means at hand to nip in the bud, or subsequently to get rid of, obnoxious proposals; and in case of extremity it had in its hands as the supreme administrative authority not only the executing, but the power of refusing to execute, the decrees of the community. The senate further with tacit consent of the community claimed the right in urgent cases of absolving from the laws, under the reservation that the community should ratify the proceeding—a reservation which from the first was of little moment, and became by degrees so entirely a form that in later times they did not even take the trouble to propose the ratifying decree.

As to the elections, they passed, so far as they depended on the magistrates and were of political importance, practically into the hands of the senate. In this way it acquired, as has been mentioned already (p. 310), the right to appoint the dictator. Greater regard had certainly to be shown to the community; the right of bestowing the public magistracies could not be withdrawn from it; but, as has likewise been already observed, care was taken that this election of magistrates should not be construed into the conferring of definite functions, especially of the posts of supreme command when war was imminent. Moreover the newly introduced idea of special functions on the one hand, and on the other the right practically conceded to the senate of dispensation from the laws, gave to it an important share in official appointments. Of the influence which the senate exercised in settling the official spheres of the consuls in particular, we have already spoken (p. 309). One of the most important applications of the dispensing right was the dispensation of the magistrate from the legal term of his tenure of office—a dispensation which, as contrary to the fundamental laws of the community, might not according to Roman state-law be granted in the precincts of the city proper, but beyond these was at least so far valid that the consul or praetor, whose term was prolonged, continued after its expiry to discharge his functions " in a consul's or praetor's stead " (*pro consule, pro praetore*). Of course this important right of extending the term of office—essentially on a par with the right of nomination—belonged by law to the community alone, and at the beginning was in fact exercised by it; but in $\frac{447}{307}$, and regularly thenceforward, the command of the commander in chief was prolonged by mere decree of the senate. To this was added, in fine, the preponderating and skilfully concerted influence of the aristocracy over the elections, which guided them ordinarily, although not always, to the choice of candidates agreeable to the government.

Finally as regards administration, war, peace and alliances, the founding of colonies, the assignation of lands, building, in fact every matter of permanent and general importance, and in particular the whole system of finance, depended absolutely on the senate. It was the senate which annually issued general instructions to the magistrates, settling their spheres of duty and limiting the troops and moneys to be placed at the disposal of each; and recourse was had to its counsel in every case of importance. The keepers of the state-chest could make no payment to any magistrate with the exception of the consul, or to any private person, unless authorised by a previous decree of the senate. In the management, however, of current affairs and in the details of judicial and military administration the supreme governing corporation did not interfere; the Roman aristocracy had too much political judgment and tact to desire to convert the control of the commonwealth into a guardianship over the individual official, or to turn the instrument into a machine.

That this new government of the senate amidst all its retention of existing forms involved a complete revolutionising of the old commonwealth, is clear. That the free action of the burgesses should be arrested and benumbed; that the magistrates should be reduced to be the presidents of its sittings and its executive commissioners; that a corporation for the mere tendering of advice should seize the inheritance of both the authorities sanctioned by the constitution and should become, although under very modest forms, the central government of the state—these were steps of revolution and usurpation. Nevertheless, if any revolution or any usurpation appears justified before the bar of history by exclusive ability to govern, even its rigorous judgment must acknowledge that this corporation duly comprehended and worthily fulfilled its great task. Called to power not by the empty accident of birth, but substantially by the free choice of the nation; confirmed every fifth year by the stern moral judgment of the worthiest men; holding office for life, and so not dependent on the expiration of its commission or on the varying opinion of the people; having its ranks close and united ever after the equalisation of the orders; embracing in it all the political intelligence and practical statesmanship that the people possessed; absolute in dealing with all financial questions and in the control of foreign policy; having complete power over the executive by virtue of its brief duration and of the tribunician intercession which was at the service of the senate after the termination of the quarrels between the orders—the Roman senate was the noblest organ of the nation, and in consistency and political sagacity, in unanimity and patriotism, in grasp of power and unwavering courage, the foremost political corporation of all times—still even now an "assembly of kings," which knew well how to combine despotic energy with republican self-devotion. Never was a state represented in its external relations more firmly and worthily than Rome in its best times by its senate. In matters of internal administration it certainly cannot be concealed that the moneyed and landed aristocracy, which was especially represented in the senate, acted with partiality in affairs that bore upon its peculiar interests, and that the sagacity and energy of the body were often in such cases employed far from beneficially to the state. Nevertheless the great principle established amidst severe conflicts, that all Roman burgesses were equal in the eye of the law as respected rights and duties, and the opening up of a political career (or in other words, of admission to the senate) to every one, which was the result of that principle, concurred with the brilliance of military and political successes in preserving the harmony of the state and of the nation, and relieved the distinction of classes from that bitterness and malignity which marked the struggle of the patricians and plebeians. And, as the fortunate turn taken by external politics had the effect of giving the rich for more than a century ample space for themselves and rendered it unnecessary that they should oppress the middle class, the Roman people was enabled by means of its senate to carry out for a longer term than is usually granted to a people the grandest of all human undertakings—a wise and happy self-government.

CHAPTER IV

FALL OF THE ETRUSCAN POWER—THE CELTS

In the previous chapters we have presented an outline of the development of the Roman constitution during the first two centuries of the republic; we now recur to the commencement of that epoch for the purpose of tracing the external history of Rome and of Italy. About the time of the expulsion of the Tarquins from Rome the Etruscan power had reached its height. The Tuscans, and the Carthaginians who were in close alliance with them, possessed undisputed supremacy in the Tyrrhene Sea. Although Massilia amidst continual and severe struggles maintained her independence, the sea-ports of Campania and of the Volscian land, and after the battle of Alalia Corsica also (p. 142), were in the possession of the Etruscans. In Sardinia the sons of the Carthaginian general Mago laid the foundation of the greatness both of their house and of their city by the complete conquest of the island (about $\frac{260}{500}$); and in Sicily, while the Hellenic colonies were occupied with their internal feuds, the Phoenicians retained possession of the western half without material opposition. The vessels of the Etruscans were no less dominant in the Adriatic; and their pirates were dreaded even in the more eastern waters.

By land also their power seemed to be on the increase. To acquire possession of Latium was of the most decisive importance to Etruria, which was separated by the Latins alone from the Volscian towns which were dependent on it and from its possessions in Campania. Hitherto the firm bulwark of the Roman power had sufficiently protected Latium, and had successfully maintained against Etruria the frontier line of the Tiber. But now, when the whole Tuscan league, taking advantage of the confusion and the weakness of the Roman state after the expulsion of the Tarquins, renewed its attack more energetically than before under Larth Porsena king of Clusium, it no longer encountered the wonted resistance. Rome surrendered, and in the peace (assigned to $\frac{247}{507}$) not only ceded all her possessions on the right bank of the Tiber to the adjacent Tuscan communities and thus abandoned her exclusive command of the river, but

319

also delivered to the conqueror all her weapons of war and
promised to make use of iron thenceforth only for the plough-
share. It seemed as if the union of Italy under Tuscan supremacy was not far distant.

But the subjugation, with which the coalition of the Etruscan
and Carthaginian nations had threatened both Greeks and
Italians, was fortunately averted by the combination of peoples
drawn towards each other by family affinity as well as by
common peril. The Etruscan army, which after the fall of Rome
had penetrated into Latium, had its victorious career checked
in the first instance before the walls of Aricia by the well-timed
intervention of the Cumaeans who had hastened to the succour
of the beleaguered town ($\frac{248}{506}$). We know not how the war
ended, nor, in particular, whether Rome even at that time
broke the ruinous and disgraceful peace. This much only is
certain, that on this occasion also the Tuscans were unable to
maintain their ground permanently on the left bank of the Tiber.

But the Hellenic nation was soon forced to engage in a more
comprehensive and more decisive conflict with the barbarians
both of the west and of the east. It was about the time of the
Persian wars. The relation in which the Tyrians stood to the
great king led Carthage also to follow in the wake of Persian
policy—there exists a credible tradition even as to an alliance
between the Carthaginians and Xerxes—and, along with the
Carthaginians, the Etruscans. One of the grandest of political
combinations simultaneously directed the Asiatic hosts against
Greece, and the Phoenician hosts against Sicily, to extirpate at
a blow liberty and civilisation from the face of the earth. The
victory remained with the Hellenes. The battle of Salamis
($\frac{274}{480}$) saved and avenged Hellas proper; and on the same
day—so runs the story—the rulers of Syracuse and Agrigentum,
Gelon and Theron, vanquished the immense army of the Carthaginian general Hamilcar, son of Mago, at Himera so completely,
that the war was thereby terminated, and the Phoenicians, who
by no means cherished at that time the project of subduing the
whole of Sicily on their own account, returned to their previous
defensive policy. Some of the large silver pieces are still preserved which were coined for this campaign from the ornaments
of Damareta, the wife of Gelon, and other noble Syracusan
dames: and the latest times gratefully remembered the gentle
and brave king of Syracuse and the glorious victory whose
praises Simonides sang.

The immediate effect of the humiliation of Carthage was

the fall of the maritime supremacy of her Etruscan allies. Anaxilas, ruler of Rhegium and Zancle, had already closed the Sicilian straits against their privateers by means of a standing fleet (about $\frac{272}{482}$); soon afterwards ($\frac{280}{474}$) the Cumaeans and Hiero of Syracuse achieved a decisive victory near Cumae over the Tyrrhene fleet, to which the Carthaginians vainly attempted to render aid.   This is the victory which Pindar celebrates in his first Pythian ode; and there is still extant an Etruscan helmet, which Hiero sent to Olympia, with the inscription, " Hiaron son of Deinomenes and the Syrakosians to Zeus, Tyrrhane spoil from Kyma." [1]

While these extraordinary successes against the Carthaginians and Etruscans placed Syracuse at the head of the Greek cities in Sicily, the Doric Tarentum rose to undisputed pre-eminence among the Italian Greeks, after the Aachean Sybaris had fallen about the time of the expulsion of the Tarquins ($\frac{243}{511}$). The terrible defeat of the Tarentines by the Iapygians ($\frac{280}{474}$), the most severe disaster which a Greek army had hitherto sustained, served only, like the Persian invasion of Hellas, to unshackle the whole might of the national spirit in the development of an energetic democracy. Thenceforth the Carthaginians and the Etruscans were no longer paramount in the Italian waters; the Tarentines predominated in the Adriatic and Ionic, the Massiliots and Syracusans in the Tyrrhene, seas. The latter in particular restricted more and more the range of Etruscan piracy. After the victory at Cumae, Hiero had occupied the island of Aenaria (Ischia), and by that means interrupted the communication between the Campanian and the northern Etruscans. About the year $\frac{302}{452}$, with a view thoroughly to check Tuscan piracy, Syracuse sent forth a special expedition, which ravaged the island of Corsica and the Etrurian coast and occupied the island of Aethalia (Elba). Although Etrusco-Carthaginian piracy was not wholly repressed—Antium, for example, having apparently continued a haunt of privateering down to the beginning of the fifth century of Rome—the powerful Syracuse formed a strong bulwark against the allied Tuscans and Phoenicians. For a moment, indeed, it seemed as if the Syracusan power must be broken by the attack of the Athenians, whose naval expedition against Syracuse in the course of the Peloponnesian war ($\frac{339-341}{415-413}$) was supported by the Etruscans, old commercial friends of Athens, with three fifty-oared galleys.   But the victory remained, as is well known,

[1] Φιάρον ὁ Δεινομένεος καὶ τοὶ Συρακόσιοι τοὶ Δὶ Τύραν' ἀπὸ Κύμας.

both in the west and in the east with the Dorians. After the ignominious failure of the Attic expedition, Syracuse became so indisputably the first Greek maritime power that the men who were at the head of its affairs aspired to the sovereignty of Sicily and Lower Italy, and of both the Italian seas; while on the other hand the Carthaginians, who saw their dominion in Sicily now seriously in danger, were on their part also obliged to make, and made, the subjugation of the Syracusans and the reduction of the whole island the aim of their policy. We cannot here narrate the decline of the intermediate Sicilian states, and the increase of the Carthaginian power in the island, which were the immediate results of these struggles; we notice their effect only so far as Etruria is concerned. The new ruler of Syracuse, Dionysius (who reigned $\frac{348-387}{406-367}$), inflicted on Etruria blows which were severely felt. The far-scheming king laid the foundation of his new colonial power especially in the sea to the east of Italy, the more northern waters of which now became, for the first time, subject to a Greek maritime power. About the year $\frac{367}{387}$, Dionysius occupied and colonised the port of Lissus and island of Issa on the Illyrian coast, and the ports of Ancona, Numana, and Hatria, on the coast of Italy. The memory of the Syracusan dominion in this remote region is preserved not only by the " canal of Philistus " which was constructed at the mouth of the Po, beyond doubt by the well-known historian and friend of Dionysius who spent the years of his exile ($\frac{368}{386}$ et seq.) at Hatria, but also by the alteration in the name of the Italian eastern sea itself, which from this time forth, instead of its earlier designation of the " Ionic Gulf " (p. 130), received the appellation still current at the present day, and probably referable to this Syracusan occupation, of the sea " of Hatria." [1] But not content with these attacks on the possessions and commercial communications of the Etruscans in the eastern sea, Dionysius assailed the very heart of the Etruscan power by storming and plundering Pyrgi, the rich seaport of Caere ($\frac{369}{385}$). From this blow it never recovered. When the internal disturbances that followed the death of Dionysius in Syracuse gave the Carthaginians freer scope, and their fleet resumed in the Tyrrhene sea that ascendency which with but slight interruptions

---

[1] Hecataeus (+ after $\frac{257}{497}$) and Herodotus also ($\frac{270}{484}$—after $\frac{345}{409}$) only know Hatrias as the delta of the Po and the sea that washes its shores (O. Müller, *Etrusker*, i. p. 140; *Geogr. Graeci Min. ed. C. Müller*, i. p. 23). The appellation of Adriatic sea, in its more extended sense, first occurs in the so-called Scylax about $\frac{418}{336}$.

they thenceforth maintained, it proved a burden no less grievous to Etruscans than to Greeks; so that, when Agathocles of Syracuse in $\frac{444}{310}$ was making preparations for war with Carthage, he was even joined by eighteen Tuscan vessels of war. The Etruscans perhaps had their fears in regard to Corsica, which they probably still at that time retained. The old Etrusco-Phoenician symmachy, which still existed in the time of Aristotle ($\frac{370-432}{384-322}$), was thus broken up; but the Etruscans never recovered their maritime strength.

This rapid collapse of the Etruscan maritime power would be inexplicable but for the circumstance that, at the very time when the Sicilian Greeks were attacking them by sea, the Etruscans found themselves assailed with the severest blows on every side by land. About the time of the battles of Salamis, Himera, and Cumae a furious war raged for many years, according to the accounts of the Roman annals, between Rome and Veii ($\frac{271-280}{483-474}$). The Romans suffered in its course severe defeats. Tradition especially preserved the memory of the catastrophe of the Fabii ($\frac{277}{477}$), who had in consequence of internal commotions voluntarily banished themselves from the capital (p. 277) and had undertaken the defence of the frontier against Etruria, and who were slain to the last man capable of bearing arms at the rivulet of the Cremera. But the armistice for 400 months, which in room of a peace terminated the war, was so far favourable to the Romans that it at least restored the *status quo* of the regal period; the Etruscans gave up Fidenae and the district won by them on the right bank of the Tiber. We cannot ascertain how far this Romano-Etruscan war was connected directly with the war between the Hellenes and the Persians, and with that between the Sicilians and Carthaginians; but whether the Romans were or were not allies of the victors of Salamis and of Himera, there was at any rate a coincidence of interests as well as of results.

The Samnites as well as the Latins threw themselves upon the Etruscans; and hardly had their Campanian settlement been cut off from the mother-land in consequence of the battle of Cumae, when it found itself no longer able to resist the assaults of the Sabellian mountain tribes. Capua, the capital, fell in $\frac{330}{424}$; and the Tuscan population there was soon after the conquest extirpated or expelled by the Samnites. It is true that the Campanian Greeks, also isolated and weakened, suffered severely from the same invasion: Cumae itself was conquered by the Sabellians in $\frac{334}{420}$. But the Hellenes maintained their ground at Neapolis especially, perhaps with the aid of the Syracusans, while the Etruscan name in Campania disappeared from history—excepting some detached Etruscan communities, which prolonged a pitiful and forlorn existence there.

Events still more momentous, however, occurred about the same time in Northern Italy. A new nation was knocking at the gates of the Alps: it was the Celts; and their first pressure fell on the Etruscans.

The Celtic, Galatian, or Gallic nation received from the common mother endowments different from those of its Italian, Germanic, and Hellenic sisters. With various solid qualities and still more that were brilliant, it was deficient in those deeper moral and political qualifications which lie at the root of all that is good and great in human development. It was reckoned disgraceful, Cicero tell us, for the free Celts to till their fields with their own hands. They preferred a pastoral life to agriculture; and even in the fertile plains of the Po they chiefly practised the rearing of swine, feeding on the flesh of their herds, and staying with them in the oak forests day and night. Attachment to their native soil, such as characterised the Italians and the Germans, was wanting in the Celts; while on the other hand they delighted to congregate in towns and villages, which accordingly acquired magnitude and importance among the Celts earlier apparently than in Italy. Their political constitution was imperfect. Not only was the national unity recognised but feebly as a bond of connection—as is, in fact, the case with all nations at first—but the individual communities were deficient in unanimity and steady control, in earnest public spirit and consistency of aim. The only organisation for which they were fitted was a military one, where the bonds of discipline relieved the individual from the troublesome task of self-control. "The prominent qualities of the Celtic race," says their historian Thierry, "were personal bravery, in which they excelled all nations; an open impetuous temperament, accessible to every impression; much intelligence, but at the same time an extreme volatility, want of perseverance, aversion to discipline and order, ostentation and perpetual discord—the result of boundless vanity." Cato the Elder more briefly describes them, nearly to the same effect; "the Celts devote themselves mainly to two things—fighting and *esprit*." [1] Such qualities—those of good soldiers but of bad citizens—explain the historical fact, that the

---

[1] *Pleraque Gallia duas res industriosissime persequitur: rem militarem et argute loqui* (Cato, *Orig. l.* ii. *fr.* 2. Jordan.)

Celts have shaken all states and have founded none. Everywhere we find them ready to rove or, in other words, to march; preferring movable property to landed estate, and gold to everything else; following the profession of arms as a system of organised pillage or even as a trade for hire, and with such success that even the Roman historian Sallust acknowledges that the Celts bore off the prize from the Romans in feats of arms. They were the true soldiers-of-fortune of antiquity, as figures and descriptions represent them: with big but not sinewy bodies, with shaggy hair and long mustachios—quite a contrast to the Greeks and Romans, who shaved the head and upper lip; in variegated embroidered dresses, which in combat were not unfrequently thrown off; with a broad gold ring round the neck; wearing no helmets and without missile weapons of any sort, but furnished instead with an immense shield, a long ill-tempered sword, a dagger and a lance—all ornamented with gold, for they were not unskilful in working in metals. Everything was made subservient to ostentation, even wounds, which were often subsequently enlarged for the purpose of boasting a broader scar. Usually they fought on foot, but certain tribes on horseback, in which case every freeman was followed by two attendants likewise mounted; war-chariots were early in use, as they were among the Libyans and the Hellenes in the earliest times. Various traits remind us of the chivalry of the middle ages; particularly the custom of single combat, which was foreign to the Greeks and Romans. Not only were they accustomed during war to challenge a single enemy to fight, after having previously insulted him by words and gestures; during peace also they fought with each other in splendid suits of armour, as for life or death. After such feats carousals followed as a matter of course. In this way they led, whether under their own or a foreign banner, a restless soldier-life; they were dispersed from Ireland and Spain to Asia Minor, constantly occupied in fighting and so-called feats of heroism. But all their enterprises melted away like snow in spring; and nowhere did they create a great state or develop a distinctive culture of their own.

Such is the description which the ancients give us of this nation. Its origin can only be conjectured. Sprung from the same cradle from which the Hellenic, Italian, and Germanic peoples issued,[1] the Celts doubtless like these migrated from

---

[1] It has recently been maintained by expert philologists that there is a closer affinity between the Celts and Italians than there is even between

their eastern motherland into Europe, where at a very early period they reached the western ocean and established their headquarters in what is now France, crossing to settle in the British isles on the north, and on the south passing the Pyrenees and contending with the Iberian tribes for the possession of the peninsula. This, their first great migration, flowed past the Alps, and it was from the lands to the westward that they first began those movements of smaller masses in the opposite direction—movements which carried them over the Alps and the Haemus and even over the Bosporus, and by means of which they became and for many centuries continued to be the terror of the whole civilised nations of antiquity, till the victories of Caesar and the frontier defences organised by Augustus for ever broke their power.

The native legend of their migrations, which has been preserved to us mainly by Livy, relates the story of these later retrograde movements as follows.[1] The Gallic confederacy, which was headed then as in the time of Caesar by the canton

the latter and the Hellenes. In other words they hold that the branch of the great tree, from which the peoples of Indo-Germanic extraction in the west and south of Europe have sprung, divided itself in the first instance into Greeks and Italo-Celts, and that the latter at a considerably later period became subdivided into Italians and Celts. This hypothesis commends itself much to acceptance in a geographical point of view, and the existing historical facts may perhaps be also reconciled with it, because what has hitherto been regarded as Graeco-Italian civilisation may very well have been Graeco-Celto-Italian—in fact we know nothing of the earliest stage of Celtic culture. Linguistic investigation, however, seems not to have made as yet such progress as to warrant the insertion of its results in the primitive history of the peoples.

[1] The legend is related by Livy, v. 34, and Justin, xxiv. 4, and Caesar also has had it in view (*B.G.* vi. 24). But the association of the migration of Bellovesus with the founding of Massilia, by which the former is chronologically fixed down to the middle of the second century of Rome, undoubtedly belongs not to the native legend, which of course did not specify dates, but to later chronological research; and it deserves no credit. Isolated incursions and immigrations may have taken place at a very early period; but the great overflowing of northern Italy by the Celts cannot be placed before the age of the decay of the Etruscan power, that is, not before the second half of the third century of the city.

In like manner, after the judicious investigations of Wickham and Cramer, we cannot doubt that the line of march of Bellovesus, like that of Hannibal, lay not over the Cottian Alps (Mont Genèvre) and through the territory of the Taurini, but over the Graian Alps (the Little St. Bernard) and through the territory of the Salassi. The name of the mountain is given by Livy doubtless not on the authority of the legend, but on his own conjecture.

Whether the representation that the Italian Boii came through the more easterly pass of the Poenine Alps rested on the ground of a genuine legendary reminiscence, or only on the ground of an assumed connection with the Boii dwelling to the north of the Danube, is a question that must remain undecided.

M

of the Bituriges (around Bourges), sent forth in the days of king Ambiatus two great hosts led by the two nephews of the king. One of these nephews, Sigovesus, crossed the Rhine and advanced in the direction of the Black Forest, while the second, Bellovesus, crossed the Graian Alps (the Little St. Bernard) and descended into the valley of the Po. From the former proceeded the Gallic settlement on the middle Danube; from the latter the oldest Celtic settlement in the modern Lombardy, the canton of the Insubres with Mediolanum (Milan) as its capital. Another host soon followed, which founded the canton of the Cenomani with the towns of Brixia (Brescia) and Verona. Ceaseless streams thenceforth poured over the Alps into the beautiful plain; the Celtic tribes with the Ligurians whom they dislodged and swept along with them wrested place after place from the Etruscans, till the whole left bank of the Po was in their hands. After the fall of the rich Etruscan town Melpum (probably in the district of Milan), for the subjugation of which the Celts already settled in the basin of the Po had united with newly arrived tribes ($\frac{358}{396}$?), these latter crossed to the right bank of the river and began to press upon the Umbrians and Etruscans in their original abodes. Those who did so were chiefly the Boii, who are alleged to have penetrated into Italy by another route, over the Poenine Alps (the Great St. Bernard); they settled in the modern Romagna, where the old Etruscan town Felsina, with its name changed by its new masters to Bononia, became their capital. Finally came the Senones, the last of the larger Celtic tribes which made their way over the Alps; they took up their abode along the coast of the Adriatic from Rimini to Ancona. But isolated bands of Celtic settlers must have advanced even far in the direction of Umbria, and up to the border of Etruria proper; for stone-inscriptions in the Celtic language have been found even at Todi on the upper Tiber. The limits of Etruria on the north and east became more and more contracted, and about the middle of the fourth century the Tuscan nation found themselves substantially restricted to the territory which thenceforth bore and still bears their name.

Subjected to these simultaneous and, as it were, concerted assaults on the part of very different peoples—the Syracusans, Latins, Samnites, and above all the Celts—the Etrurian nation, that had just acquired so vast and sudden an ascendancy in Latium and Campania and on both the Italian seas, underwent a still more rapid and violent collapse. The loss of their maritime supremacy and the subjugation of the Campanian Etruscans belong to the same epoch as the settlement of the Insubres and Cenomani on the Po; and about this same period the Roman burgesses, who had not very many years before been humbled to the utmost and almost reduced to bondage by Porsena, first assumed an attitude of aggression towards Etruria. By the armistice with Veii in $\frac{280}{474}$ Rome had recovered its ground, and the two nations were restored in the main to the state in which they had stood in the time of the kings. When it expired in the year $\frac{309}{445}$, the warfare began afresh; but it took the form of border frays and pillaging excursions which led to no material result on either side. Etruria was still too powerful for Rome to be able seriously to attack it. At length the revolt of the Fidenates, who expelled the Roman garrison, murdered the Roman envoys, and submitted to Larth Tolumnius, king of the Veientes, gave rise to a more considerable war, which ended favourably for the Romans; the king Tolumnius fell in combat by the hand of the Roman consul Aulus Cornelius Cossus ($\frac{326}{428}$?), Fidenae was taken, and a new armistice for 200 months was concluded in $\frac{329}{425}$. During this truce the troubles of Etruria became more and more aggravated, and the Celtic arms were already approaching the settlements that hitherto had been spared on the right bank of the Po. When the armistice expired in the end of $\frac{346}{408}$, the Romans also on their part resolved to undertake a war of conquest against Etruria; and on this occasion the war was carried on not merely to vanquish Veii, but to crush it.

The history of the war against the Veientes, Capenates, and Falisci, and of the siege of Veii, which is said, like that of Troy, to have lasted ten years, rests on evidence little reliable. Legend and poetry have taken possession of these events as their own, and with reason; for the struggle in this case was waged, with unprecedented exertions, for an unprecedented prize. It was the first occasion on which a Roman army remained in the field summer and winter, year after year, till its object was attained. It was the first occasion on which the community paid the levy from the resources of the state. But it was also the first occasion on which the Romans attempted to subdue a nation of alien stock, and carried their arms beyond the ancient boundary of the Latin land. The struggle was vehement, but the issue was scarcely doubtful. The Romans were supported by the Latins and Hernici, to whom the overthrow of their dreaded neighbour was productive of scarcely less satisfaction and advantage than to the Romans themselves; whereas Veii was abandoned by its own nation, and only the adjacent towns of Capena and Falerii, along with Tarquinii, furnished contingents to its help. The contemporary attacks of the Celts would alone suffice to explain the non-intervention of the northern communities; it is affirmed however, and there is no reason to doubt, that the inaction of the other Etruscans was immediately occasioned by internal factions in the league of the Etruscan cities, and particularly by the opposition which the regal form of government retained or restored by the Veientes encountered from the aristocratic governments of the other cities. Had the Etruscan nation been able or willing to take part in the conflict, the Roman community would hardly have been able—undeveloped as was the art of besieging at that time—to accomplish the gigantic task of subduing a large and strong city. But isolated and forsaken as Veii was, it succumbed ($\frac{358}{396}$) after a valiant resistance to the persevering and heroic spirit of Marcus Furius Camillus, who first opened up to his countrymen the brilliant and perilous career of foreign conquest. The joy which this great success excited in Rome had its echo in the Roman custom, continued down to a late age, of concluding the festal games with a " sale of Veientes," at which, among the mock spoils submitted to auction, the most wretched old cripple who could be procured wound up the sport in a purple mantle and ornaments of gold as " king of the Veientes." The city was destroyed, and the soil was doomed to perpetual desolation. Falerii and Capena hastened to make peace; the powerful Volsinii, which with federal indecision had remained quiet during the agony of Veii and took up arms after its capture, likewise after a few years ($\frac{363}{391}$) consented to peace. The statement that the two bulwarks of the Etruscan nation, Melpum and Veii, yielded on the same day, the former to the Celts, the latter to the Romans, may be merely a melancholy legend; but it at any rate involves a deep historical truth. The double assault from the north and from the south, and the fall of the two frontier strongholds, were the beginning of the end of the great Etruscan nation.

For a moment, however, it seemed as if the two peoples, through whose co-operation Etruria saw her very existence put in jeopardy, were about to destroy each other, and the reviving power of Rome was to be trodden under foot by foreign barbarians. This turn of things, so contrary to what might naturally have been expected, the Romans brought upon themselves by their own arrogance and shortsightedness.

The Celtic swarms, which had crossed the river after the fall of Melpum, rapidly overflowed northern Italy—not merely the open country on the right bank of the Po and along the shore of the Adriatic, but also Etruria proper to the south of the Apennines. A few years afterwards ($\frac{363}{391}$) Clusium situated in the heart of Etruria (Chiusi, on the borders of Tuscany and the States of the Church) was besieged by the Celtic Senones; and so humbled were the Etruscans that the Tuscan city in its straits invoked aid from the destroyers of Veii. Perhaps it would have been wise to grant it and to reduce at once the Gauls by arms, and the Etruscans by according to them protection, to a state of dependence on Rome; but an intervention with aims so extensive, which would have compelled the Romans to undertake a serious struggle on the northern Tuscan frontier, was not embraced as yet within the horizon of the Roman policy. No course was therefore left but to refrain from all interference. Foolishly, however, while declining to send auxiliary troops, they despatched envoys. With still greater folly these sought to impose upon the Celts by haughty language, and, when this failed, they conceived that they might with impunity violate the law of nations in dealing with barbarians; in the ranks of the Clusines they took part in a skirmish, and in the course of it one of them stabbed and dismounted a Gallic officer. The barbarians acted in the case with moderation and prudence. They sent in the first instance to the Roman community to demand the surrender of those who had outraged the law of nations, and the senate was ready to comply with the reasonable request. But with the multitude compassion for their countrymen outweighed justice towards the foreigners; satisfaction was refused by the burgesses; and according to some accounts they even nominated the brave champions of their fatherland as consular tribunes for the year $\frac{364}{390}$,[1] which was to be so fatal in the Roman annals. Then the Brennus or, in other words, the "king of the army" of the Gauls broke up the siege of Clusium, and the whole Celtic host—the numbers of which are stated at 70,000 men—turned against Rome. Such expeditions into unknown and distant regions were not unusual for the Gauls, who marched as bands of armed emigrants, troubling themselves little as to the means of cover or of retreat; but it was evident that none in Rome anticipated the

---

[1] This is according to the current computation 390 B.C.; but, in fact, the capture of Rome occurred in Ol. 98, 1=388 B.C., and has been thrown out of its proper place merely by the confusion of the Roman calendar.

dangers involved in so sudden and so mighty an invasion. It was not till the Gauls had crossed the Tiber and were at the rivulet of the Allia, less than twelve miles from the gates, that a Roman military force sought to hinder their passage on the 18th July, $\frac{364}{390}$. And even now they went into battle with arrogance and foolhardiness,—not as against an army, but as against freebooters—under inexperienced leaders, Camillus having in consequence of the dissensions of the orders withdrawn from taking part in affairs. Those against whom they were to fight were but barbarians; what need was there of a camp, or of securing a retreat? These barbarians, however, were men whose courage despised death, and their mode of fighting was to the Italians as novel as it was terrible; sword in hand the Celts precipitated themselves with furious onset on the Roman phalanx, and shattered it at the first shock. Not only was the overthrow complete, but the disorderly flight of the Romans, who hastened to place the river between them and the pursuing barbarians, carried the greater portion of the defeated army to the right bank of the Tiber and towards Veii. The capital was thus needlessly left to the mercy of the invaders; the small force that was left behind, or that had fled thither, was not sufficient to garrison the walls, and three days after the battle the victors marched through the open gates into Rome. Had they done so at first, as they might have done, not only the city, but the state also must have been lost; the brief interval gave opportunity to carry away or to bury the sacred objects, and, what was more important, to occupy the citadel and to furnish it with provisions for the exigency. No one was admitted to the citadel who was incapable of bearing arms—there was not food for all. The mass of the defenceless dispersed among the neighbouring towns; but many, and in particular a number of old men of high standing, would not survive the downfall of the city and awaited death in their houses by the sword of the barbarians. They came, murdered all they met with, plundered whatever property they found, and at length set the city on fire on all sides before the eyes of the Roman garrison in the Capitol. But they had no knowledge of the art of besieging, and the blockade of the steep citadel rock was tedious and difficult, because subsistence for the great host could only be procured by armed foraging parties, and the citizens of the neighbouring Latin cities, the Ardeates in particular, frequently attacked the foragers with courage and success. Nevertheless the Celts persevered, with an energy which in their circumstances was unparalleled, for seven months beneath the rock, and the garrison, which had escaped a surprise on a dark night only in consequence of the cackling of the sacred geese in the Capitoline temple and the accidental awaking of the brave Marcus Manlius, already found its provisions beginning to fail, when the Celts received information as to the Veneti having invaded the Senonian territory recently acquired on the Po, and were thus induced to accept the ransom money that was offered to procure their withdrawal. The scornful throwing down of the Gallic sword, that it might be outweighted by Roman gold, indicated very truly how matters stood. The iron of the barbarians had conquered, but they sold their victory and by selling lost it.

The fearful catastrophe of the defeat and the conflagration, the 18th of July and the rivulet of the Allia, the spot where the sacred objects were buried, and the spot where the surprise of the citadel had been repulsed—all the details of this unparalleled event—were transferred from the recollection of contemporaries to the imagination of posterity; and we can scarcely realise the fact that two thousand years have actually elapsed since those world-renowned geese showed greater vigilance than the sentinels at their posts. And yet—although there was an enactment in Rome that in future, on occasion of a Celtic invasion no legal privilege should give exemption from military service; although dates were reckoned by the years from the conquest of the city; although the event resounded throughout the whole of the then civilised world and found its way even into the Grecian annals—the battle of the Allia and its results can scarcely be numbered among those historical events that are fruitful of consequences. It made no alteration at all in political relations. When the Gauls had marched off again with their gold—which only a legend of late and wretched invention represents the hero Camillus as having recovered for Rome—and when the fugitives had again made their way home, the foolish idea suggested by some faint-hearted prudential politicians, that the citizens should migrate to Veii, was set aside by a spirited speech of Camillus; houses arose out of the ruins hastily and irregularly—the narrow and crooked streets of Rome owed their origin to this epoch; and Rome again stood in her old commanding position. Indeed it is not improbable that this occurrence contributed materially, though not just at that moment, to diminish the antagonism between Rome and Etruria, and above all to knit more closely the ties of union between Latium and Rome. The conflict between the Gauls and the Romans was not, like that between Rome and Etruria or between Rome and Samnium, a collision of two political powers which affect and modify each other; it may be compared to those catastrophes of nature, after which the organism, if it is not destroyed, immediately resumes its equilibrium. The Gauls often returned to Latium: as in the year $\frac{387}{367}$, when Camillus defeated them at Alba—the last victory of the aged hero, who had been six times military tribune with consular powers, and five times dictator, and had four times marched in triumph to the Capitol; in the year $\frac{393}{361}$, when the dictator Titus Quinctius Pennus encamped opposite to them not five miles from the city at the bridge of the Anio, but before any encounter took place the Gallic host marched onward to Campania; in the year $\frac{394}{360}$, when the dictator Quintus Servilius Ahala fought with the hordes returning from Campania in front of the Colline gate; in the year $\frac{396}{358}$, when the dictator Gaius Sulpicius Peticus inflicted on them a signal defeat; in the year $\frac{404}{350}$, when they even spent the winter encamped upon the Alban mount and joined with the Greek pirates along the coast for plunder, till Lucius Furius Camillus, the son of the celebrated general, in the following year dislodged them—an incident, which came to the ears of Aristotle who was contemporary ($\frac{370-432}{384-322}$) in Athens. But these predatory expeditions, formidable and troublesome as they may have been, were rather incidental misfortunes than events of historical importance; and the chief result of them was, that the Romans were more and more regarded by themselves and by foreigners as the bulwark of the civilised nations of Italy against the assaults of the dreaded barbarians—a view which tended more than is usually supposed to further their subsequent claim to universal empire.

The Tuscans, who had taken advantage of the Celtic attack on Rome to assail Veii, had accomplished nothing, because they had appeared in insufficient force; the barbarians had scarcely departed, when the heavy arm of Latium descended on the Tuscans with undiminished weight. After the Etruscans had been repeatedly defeated, the whole of southern Etruria as far as the Ciminian hills remained in the hands of the Romans, who formed four new tribes in the territories of Veii, Capena, and Falerii ($\frac{367}{387}$), and secured the northern boundary by establishing the fortresses of Sutrium ($\frac{371}{383}$) and Nepete ($\frac{381}{373}$). With rapid steps this fertile region, covered with Roman colonists, became completely Romanised. About $\frac{396}{358}$ the neighbouring

Etruscan towns, Tarquinii, Caere, and Falerii, attempted to
revolt against Roman aggression, and the deep exasperation
which it had aroused in Etruria was shown by the slaughter
of the whole of the Roman prisoners taken in the first campaign,
three hundred and seven in number, in the market-place of
Tarquinii; but it was the exasperation of impotence. In the
peace $(\frac{403}{351})$ Caere, which as situated nearest to the Romans
suffered the heaviest retribution, was compelled to cede half
its territory to Rome, and with the diminished domain which
was left to it to withdraw from the Etruscan league, and to
enter into a relation of dependence on Rome. It seemed not
advisable however to force upon this more remote and alien
community full Roman citizenship, as had, under similar
circumstances, been done with the nearer and more cognate
Latin and Volscian communities. In its stead the Caerite
community received Roman citizenship without the privilege
of electing or of being elected (*civitas sine suffragio*)—a form
of political subjection, first occurring in this case, by which a
state that had hitherto been independent became converted into
a community not free, but administering its own affairs. Not
long afterwards $(\frac{411}{343})$ Falerii, which had preserved its original
Latin nationality even under Tuscan rule, abandoned the
Etruscan league and entered into perpetual alliance with Rome;
and thereby the whole of southern Etruria became in one form
or other subject to Roman supremacy. In the case of Tarquinii
and perhaps of northern Etruria generally, the Romans were
content with restraining them for a lengthened period by a
treaty of peace for 400 months $(\frac{403}{351})$.

In northern Italy likewise the peoples that had come into
collision and conflict gradually settled on a permanent footing
and within more defined limits. The migrations over the Alps
ceased, partly perhaps in consequence of the desperate defence
which the Etruscans made in their more restricted home, and
of the serious resistance of the powerful Romans, partly
perhaps in consequence of changes unknown to us on the north
of the Alps. Between the Alps and the Apennines, as far south
as the Abruzzi, the Celts were now generally the ruling nation,
and they were masters more especially of the plains and rich
pastures; but from the lax and superficial nature of their settlement their dominion took no deep root in the newly acquired
land and by no means assumed the shape of exclusive possession.
How matters stood in the Alps, and to what extent Celtic settlers
became mingled there with earlier Etruscan or other stocks,

our unsatisfactory information as to the nationality of the later Alpine peoples does not permit us to ascertain. It is on the other hand certain that the Etruscans or, as they were then called, the Raeti retained their settlements in the modern Grisons and Tyrol, and the Umbrians in like manner in the valleys of the Apennines. The Veneti, speaking a different language, kept possession of the north-eastern portion of the valley of the Po. Ligurian tribes maintained their footing in the western mountains, dwelling as far south as Pisa and Arezzo, and separating the Celt-land proper from Etruria. The Celts dwelt only in the intermediate flat country, the Insubres and Cenomani to the north of the Po, the Boii to the south, and—not to mention smaller tribes—the Senones on the coast of the Adriatic, from Ariminum to Ancona, in the so-called " territory of the Gauls " (ager Gallicus). But even there Etruscan settlements must have continued partially at least to exist, somewhat as Ephesus and Miletus remained Greek under the supremacy of the Persians. Mantua at any rate, which was protected by its insular position, was a Tuscan city even in the time of the empire, and Hatria on the Po also, where numerous discoveries of vases have been made, appears to have retained its Etruscan character; the description of the coasts that goes under the name of Scylax, composed about $\frac{418}{336}$, calls the district of Hatria and Spina a Tuscan land. This alone, moreover, explains how Etruscan corsairs could render the Adriatic unsafe till far into the fifth century, and why not only Dionysius of Syracuse covered its coasts with colonies, but even Athens, as a remarkable document recently discovered informs us, resolved about $\frac{429}{325}$ to establish a colony in the Adriatic for the protection of seafarers against the Tyrrhene pirates.

But while more or less of the Etruscan character continued to mark these regions, it was confined to isolated remnants and fragments of their earlier power; the Etruscan nation no longer reaped the benefit of such gains as were still acquired there by individuals in peaceful commerce or in maritime war. On the other hand it was probably from these half-free Etruscans that the germs proceeded of such civilisation as we subsequently find among the Celts and Alpine peoples in general (p. 216). The very fact that the Celtic hordes in the plains of Lombardy, to use the language of the so-called Scylax, abandoned their warrior-life and took to permanent settlement, must in part be ascribed to this influence; the rudiments moreover of handi-crafts and arts and the alphabet came to the Celts in Lombardy, and in fact to the Alpine nations as far as the modern Styria, through the medium of the Etruscans.

Thus the Etruscans, after the loss of their possessions in Campania and of the whole district to the north of the Apennines and to the south of the Ciminian forest, remained restricted to very narrow bounds; their season of power and of aspiration had for ever passed away. The closest reciprocal relations subsisted between this external decline and the internal decay of the nation, the seeds of which indeed were probably already deposited at a far earlier period. The Greek authors of this age are full of descriptions of the unbounded luxury of Etruscan life: poets of lower Italy in the fifth century of the city celebrate the Tyrrhenian wine, and the contemporary historians Timaeus and Theopompus delineate pictures of Etruscan unchastity and of Etruscan banquets, such as fall nothing short of the worst Byzantine or French demoralisation. Unattested as may be the details in these accounts, the statement at least appears to be well founded, that the detestable amusement of gladiatorial combats—the gangrene of the later Rome and of the last epoch of antiquity generally—first came into vogue among the Etruscans. At any rate on the whole they leave no doubt as to the deep degeneracy of the nation. It pervaded even its political condition. As far as our scanty information reaches, we find aristocratic tendencies prevailing, in the same way as they did at the same period in Rome, but more harshly and more perniciously. The abolition of royalty, which appears to have been carried out in all the cities of Etruria about the time of the siege of Veii, called into existence in the several cities a patrician government, which experienced but slight restraint from the laxity of the federal bond. That bond but seldom succeeded in combining all the Etruscan cities even for the defence of the land, and the nominal hegemony of Volsinii does not admit of the most remote comparison with the energetic vigour which the leadership of Rome communicated to the Latin nation. The struggle against the exclusive claim put forward by the old burgesses to all public offices and to all public usufructs, which must have destroyed even the Roman state, had not its external successes enabled it in some measure to satisfy the demands of the oppressed proletariate at the expense of foreign nations and to open up other paths to ambition—that struggle against the exclusive rule and (what was specially prominent in Etruria) the priestly monopoly of the clan-nobility—must have ruined Etruria politically, economically, and morally. Enormous wealth, particularly in landed property, became concentrated in the hands of a few nobles, while the masses were impoverished; the social revolutions which thence arose increased the distress which they sought to remedy; and, in consequence of the impotence of the central power, no course at last remained to the distressed aristocrats—*e.g.* in Arretium in $\frac{453}{301}$, and in Volsinii in $\frac{488}{266}$—but to call in the aid of the Romans, who accordingly put an end to the disorder but at the same time extinguished the remnant of independence.   The energies of the nation were broken from the day of Veii and Melpum.   Earnest attempts were still once or twice made to escape from the Roman supremacy, but in these instances the stimulus was communicated to the Etruscans from without—from another Italian stock, the Samnites.

CHAPTER V

SUBJUGATION OF THE LATINS AND CAMPANIANS BY ROME

THE great achievement of the regal period was the establishment of the sovereignty of Rome over Latium under the form of hegemony. It is in the nature of the case evident that the change in the constitution of Rome could not but powerfully affect both the relations of the Roman state towards Latium and the internal organisation of the Latium communities themselves; and that it did so is obvious from tradition. The fluctuations which the revolution in Rome occasioned in the Romano-Latin confederacy are attested by the legend, unusually vivid and various in its hues, of the victory at the lake Regillus, which the dictator or consul Aulus Postumius ($\frac{255}{499}$? $\frac{258}{496}$?) is said to have gained over the Latins with the help of the Dioscuri, and still more definitely by the renewal of the perpetual league between Rome and Latium by Spurius Cassius in his second consulate ($\frac{261}{493}$). These narratives, however, give us no information as to the main matter, the legal relation between the new Roman republic and the Latin confederacy; and what from other sources we learn regarding that relation comes to us without date, and can only be inserted here with an approximation to probability.

The nature of an hegemony implies that it becomes gradually converted into sovereignty by the mere inward force of circumstances; and the Roman hegemony over Latium formed no exception to the rule. It was based upon a complete equality of rights between the Roman state on the one side and the Latin confederacy on the other (p. 104); but this very equality of rights could not be carried out at all, more especially in reference to war and the treatment of its acquisitions, without practically annihilating the hegemony. According to the original constitution of the league not only was the right of making wars and treaties with foreign states—in other words, the full right of political self-determination—reserved in all probability both to Rome and to Latium, but, when a federal war took place, both

Rome and Latium contributed the like contingent. Each furnished, as a rule, an " army " of two legions, or 8400 men; [1] and they alternately appointed the commander-in-chief, who then nominated—by his own selection—the officers of his staff, six leaders-of-division (*tribuni militum*) for each of the four divisions of the army.   In case of victory the movable part of the spoil, as well as the conquered territory, was divided in equal portions between Rome and the confederacy; when the establishment of fortresses in the conquered territory was resolved on, their garrisons and population were composed partly of Roman, partly of confederate colonists; and not only so, but the newly-founded community was received as an independent federal state into the Latin confederacy and furnished with a seat and vote in the Latin diet.

These stipulations, the full execution of which would have annulled the reality of an hegemony, can have had but a limited practical significance, even during the regal period; in the republican epoch they must necessarily have undergone alterations also in form.   Among the first that fell into abeyance was, beyond doubt, the right of the confederacy to make wars and treaties with foreigners, [2] and their right to name the common commander every alternate year.   The decision on wars and treaties, as well as the supreme command, passed once for all to Rome.   It followed from this change that the staff-officers for the Latin troops also were now wholly nominated by the Roman commander-in-chief; and there was soon added the further innovation, that Roman burgesses alone were taken as staff-officers for the Roman half of the army, and if not alone, at any rate mainly, for the Latin half also. [3]   On the other hand, just as formerly, no stronger contingent could be demanded from the Latin confederacy as a whole than was furnished by

[1] The original equality of the two armies is evident from Liv. i. 52; viii. 8, 14, and Dionys. viii. 15; but most clearly from Polyb. vi. 26.

[2] Dionysius expressly states, that in the later federal treaties between Rome and Latium the Latin communities were expressly interdicted from calling out their contingents of their own motion and sending them into the field alone.

[3] The Latin staff-officers were the twelve *praefecti sociorum*, who had the charge of the two *alae* of the federal contingent, six to each *ala*, just as the twelve war-tribunes of the Roman army had charge of the two legions, six to each legion.   Polybius (vi. 26, 5) states that the consul nominated the former, as he originally nominated the latter.   Now according to the ancient maxim of law, that every person under obligation of service might become an officer (p. 96), it was legally allowable for the general to appoint a Latin as leader of a Roman, as well as conversely a Roman as leader of a Latin, legion; and this led to the practical result that the *tribuni militum* were wholly, and the *praefecti sociorum* at least ordinarily, Romans.

the Roman community; and the Roman commander-in-chief was likewise bound not to break up the Latin contingents, but to keep the contingent sent by each community as a separate division of the army under the leader whom that community had appointed.[1]   The right of the Latin confederacy to an equal share in the movable spoil and in the conquered land continued to subsist in form; in reality, however, the substantial fruits of war beyond doubt went, even at an early period, to the leading state.   Even in the founding of the federal fortresses or the so-called Latin colonies as a rule probably most, and not unfrequently all, of the colonists were Romans; and although by the transference they were converted from Roman burgesses into members of an allied community, the newly planted townships in all probability frequently retained a permanent—and for the confederacy dangerous—attachment to their actual mother-city.

The rights, on the contrary, which were secured by the federal treaties to the individual burgess of any of the allied communities in every city belonging to the league, underwent no restriction.   These included, in particular, full equality of rights as to the acquisition of landed property and movable estate, as to traffic and exchange, marriage and testament, and an unlimited liberty of migration; so that not only was a man who had burgess-rights in any of the federal towns legally entitled to settle in any other, but wherever he settled, he as a passive burgess (*municeps*) participated in all private and political rights and duties with the exception of eligibility to office, and was even—although in a limited sense—entitled to vote at least in the *comitia tributa*.[2]

Of some such nature, in all probability, was the relation between the Roman community and the Latin confederacy in the first period of the republic.   We cannot, however, ascertain

---

[1] These were the *decuriones turmarum* and *praefecti cohortium* (Polyb. vi. 21, 5; Liv. xxv. 14; Sallust. *Jug.* 69, *et al.*).   Of course, as the Roman consuls were ordinarily also the commanders-in-chief, the presidents of the community were very frequently in the dependent towns also placed at the head of the state-contingents (Liv. xxiii. 19; Orelli, *Inscr.* 7022). Indeed, the usual name given to the Latin magistrates (*praetores*) indicates that they were officers.

[2] Such a *metoikos* was not like an actual burgess assigned to a specific tribe once for all, but before each particular vote the tribe in which the *metoeci* were upon that occasion to vote was fixed by lot.   In reality this probably amounted to the concession to the Latins of one vote in the Roman *comitia tributa*.   The *metoeci* cannot have voted in the centuries, because a fixed place in some tribe was a preliminary condition of the centuriate suffrage.   On the other hand they must, like the plebeians, have taken part in the curies.

what elements are to be referred to earlier stipulations, and what
to the revision of the alliance in $\frac{261}{493}$.

With somewhat greater certainty the remodelling of the
organisation of the several communities belonging to the Latin
confederacy, after the pattern of the consular constitution in
Rome, may be characterised as an innovation and introduced
in this connection. For, although the different communities
may very well have arrived at the abolition of royalty in itself
independently of each other (p. 244), the identity in the
appellation of the new annual kings in the Roman and other
commonwealths of Latium, and the comprehensive application
of the peculiar principle of collegiateness,[1] evidently point to
some external connection. At some time or other after the
expulsion of the Tarquins from Rome the arrangements of the
Latin communities must have been throughout revised in
accordance with the scheme of the consular constitution. This
adjustment of the Latin constitutions in conformity with that
of the leading city may indeed belong to a later period; but

[1] Ordinarily, as is well known, the Latin communities were presided
over by two praetors. Besides these there occur in several communities
single magistrates, who in that case bear the title of dictator; as in Alba
(Orelli—Henzen, *Inscr.* 2293); Lanuvium (Cicero, *pro Mil.* 10, 27; 17, 45;
Asconius, *in Mil.* p. 32, *Orell.*; Orelli, n. 2786, 5157, 6086); Compitum
(Orelli, 3324); Nomentum (Orelli, 208, 6138, 7032; comp. Henzen, *Bullett.*
1858, p. 169); and Aricia (Orelli, n. 1455); the latter office was probably
connected with the consecration of the temple at Aricia by a dictator of the
Latin confederacy (Cato, *Origin. l.* ii. *fr.* 21, Jordan). There was a similar
dictator in the Latin colony of Sutrium (recently found inscription), and
in the Etruscan one of Caere (Orelli, n. 3787, 5772). All these magistracies
or priesthoods that originated in magistracies (for the praetors and dictators of commonwealths completely broken up, such as the Alban dictator, are to be explained in accordance with Liv. ix. 43: *Anagninis—
magistratibus praeter quam sacrorum curatione interdictum*), were annual
(Orelli, 208). The statement of Macer likewise and of the annalists who
borrowed from him, that Alba was at the time of its fall no longer under
kings, but under annual directors (Dionys. v. 74; Plutarch, *Romul.* 27;
Liv. i. 23), is probably a mere inference from the institution, with which he
was acquainted, of the sacerdotal Alban dictatorship which was beyond
doubt annual like that of Nomentum; a view in which, moreover, the
democratic partisanship of its author may have come into play. It may
be a question whether the inference is valid, and whether, even if Alba at
the time of its dissolution was under rulers holding office for life, the abolition of monarchy in Rome might not subsequently lead to the conversion
of the Alban dictatorship into an annual office.
An exception is presented by the two *dictatores* of Fidenae (Orelli, 112)
—a later and incongruous misuse of the title of dictator, which in all other
cases, even where it is transferred to non-Roman magistrates, implies an
exclusion of, and a contrast to, collegiateness.
All these Latin magistracies substantially coincide in reality, as well as
specially in name, with the arrangement established in Rome by the revolution in a way which is not adequately explained by the mere similarity
of the political circumstances in which they originated.

internal probability rather favours the supposition that the Roman nobility, after having effected the abolition of royalty for life at home, suggested a similar change of constitution to the communities of the Latin confederacy, and at length introduced aristocratic government everywhere in Latium—notwithstanding the serious resistance, imperilling the stability of the Romano-Latin league itself, which was probably offered on the one hand by the expelled Tarquins, and on the other by the royal clans and by partisans well affected to monarchy in the other communities of Latium. The mighty development of the power of Etruria that occurred at this very time, the constant assaults of the Veientes, and the expedition of Porsena, may have materially contributed to secure the adherence of the Latin nation to the once-established form of union, or, in other words, to the continued recognition of the supremacy of Rome, and disposed them for its sake to acquiesce in a change of constitution for which, beyond doubt, the way had been in many respects prepared even in the bosom of the Latin communities, nay perhaps to submit even to an enlargement of the rights of hegemony.

The permanently united nation was able not only to maintain, but also to extend on all sides its power. We have already (p. 320) mentioned that the Etruscans remained only for a short time in possession of supremacy over Latium, and that matters on the northern frontier soon returned to the position in which they stood during the regal period; but it was not till more than a century after the expulsion of the kings from Rome that any real extension of the Roman boundaries took place in this direction. The conquests of the earlier republican as of the regal period were entirely at the expense of Rome's eastern and southern neighbours,—the Sabines, between the Tiber and Anio; the Aequi, settled next to them, on the upper Anio; and the Volscians on the Tyrrhene sea.

The early period at which the Sabine land became dependent on Rome is shown by the position which it afterwards held. Even in the Samnite wars the Roman armies regularly marched through Sabina as through a peaceful land; and at an early epoch—much earlier than was the case, for instance, with the Volscian land—the Sabine district exchanged its original dialect for that of Rome. The Roman occupation here seems to have encountered but few obstacles. That the Sabines had a comparatively feeble sympathy with the desperate resistance offered by the Aequi and Volsci, is evident even from the accounts of

the annals; and—what is of more importance—we find no
fortresses to keep the land in subjection, such as were so
numerously established in the Volscian plain. Perhaps this
lack of opposition was connected with the fact that the Sabine
hordes probably about this very time poured themselves over
Lower Italy. Allured by the pleasantness of the settlements
on the Tifernus and Volturnus, they may have hardly disputed
the possession of their native land with the Romans; and these
may have mastered the half-deserted Sabine territory with little
opposition.

Far more vehement and lasting was the resistance of the
Aequi and Volsci. We do not intend to narrate the feuds
annually renewed with these two peoples—feuds which are
related in the Roman chronicles in such a way that the most
insignificant foray is scarcely distinguishable from a momentous
war, and historical connection is totally disregarded; it is sufficient to indicate the permanent results. We plainly perceive
that it was the especial aim of the Romans and Latins to separate
the Aequi from the Volsci, and to become masters of the communications between them. For this purpose the oldest federal
fortresses or so-called Latin colonies were founded, Cora, Norba
(assigned to $\frac{262}{492}$), and Signia (stated to have been reinforced in
$\frac{259}{495}$), all of which are situated at the points of connection between
the Aequian and Volscian districts. The object was attained
still more fully by the accession of the Hernici to the league of the
Romans and Latins ($\frac{268}{486}$), an accession which isolated the
Volscians completely, and provided the league with a bulwark
against the Sabellian tribes dwelling on the south and east; it
is easy therefore to perceive why this little people obtained the
concession of full equality with the two others in counsel and in
distribution of the spoil. The feebler Aequi were thenceforth
but little formidable; it was sufficient to undertake from time
to time a plundering expedition against them. The Volscians
opposed a more serious resistance, and it was only by gradually
advancing its fortresses that the league slowly gained ground
upon them. Velitrae had already been founded in $\frac{260}{494}$ as a
bulwark for Latium; it was followed by Suessa Pometia, Ardea
($\frac{312}{442}$), and, singularly enough, Circeii (founded or at least
strengthened in $\frac{361}{393}$), which, as long as Antium and Tarracina
continued free, can only have held communication with Latium
by sea. Attempts were often made to occupy Antium, and one
was temporarily successful in $\frac{287}{467}$; but in $\frac{295}{459}$ the town recovered
its freedom, and it was not till after the Gallic conflagration that,

in consequence of a violent war of thirteen years ($\frac{365-377}{389-377}$), the Romans gained a decided superiority in the Pomptine territory, which was secured by the founding of the fortresses Satricum ($\frac{369}{385}$) and Setia ($\frac{372}{382}$, strengthened in $\frac{375}{379}$), and was distributed into farm-allotments and tribes in the year $\frac{371}{383}$ and following years. After this date the Volscians still perhaps rose in revolt, but they carried on no further wars against Rome.

But the more decided the successes that the league of Romans, Latins, and Hernici achieved against the Etruscans, Sabines, Aequi, and Volsci, the more that league became liable to disunion. The reason lay partly in the increase of the hegemonic power of Rome, of which we have already spoken as necessarily springing out of the existing circumstances, but which nevertheless was felt as a heavy burden in Latium; partly in particular acts of odious injustice perpetrated by the leading community. Of this nature was especially the infamous sentence of arbitration between the Aricini and the Ardeates in $\frac{308}{446}$, in which the Romans, called in to be arbiters regarding a border territory in dispute between the two communities, took it to themselves; and when this decision occasioned in Ardea internal dissensions in which the people wished to join the Volsci, while the nobility adhered to Rome, these dissensions were still more disgracefully employed as a pretext for the despatch of Roman colonists to the wealthy city, amongst whom the lands of the adherents of the party opposed to Rome were distributed ($\frac{312}{442}$). The main cause however of the internal breaking up of the league was the very subjugation of the common foe; forbearance ceased on one side, devotedness ceased on the other, from the time when they thought that they had no longer need of each other. The open breach between the Latins and Hernici on the one hand and the Romans on the other was immediately occasioned partly by the capture of Rome by the Celts and the momentary weakness which it produced, partly by the definitive occupation and distribution of the Pomptine territory. The former allies soon stood opposed in the field. Already Latin volunteers in great numbers had taken part in the last despairing struggle of the Volsci: now the most famous of the Latin cities, Lanuvium ($\frac{371}{383}$), Praeneste ($\frac{372-374}{382-380}$, $\frac{400}{354}$), Tusculum ($\frac{373}{381}$), Tibur ($\frac{394}{360}$, $\frac{400}{354}$), and even several of the fortresses established in the Volscian land by the Romano-Latin league, such as Velitrae and Circeii, had to be subdued by force of arms, and the Tiburtines were not afraid even to make common cause against Rome with the once more advancing hordes of the Gauls. No concerted revolt however took place, and Rome mastered the individual towns without much trouble. Tusculum was even compelled (in $\frac{373}{381}$) to give up its commonwealth and to enter into the burgess-union of Rome—the first instance of a whole people being incorporated with the Roman commonwealth—while it still retained its walls and a sort of *de facto* communal independence. Soon afterwards Satricum met the same fate.

The struggle with the Hernici was more severe ($\frac{392-396}{362-358}$); the first consular commander-in-chief belonging to the plebs, Lucius Genucius, fell in it; but here too the Romans were victorious. The crisis terminated with the renewal of the treaties between Rome and the Latin and Hernican confederacies in $\frac{396}{358}$. The precise contents of these treaties are not known, but it is evident that both confederacies submitted once more, and probably on harder terms, to the Roman hegemony. The institution which took place in the same year of two new tribes in the Pomptine territory shows clearly the mighty advances made by the Roman power.

In manifest connection with this crisis in the relations between Rome and Latium stands the closing of the Latin confederation,[1]

---

[1] In the list given by Dionysius (v. 61) of the thirty Latin federal cities—the only list which we possess—there are named the Ardeates, Aricini, Bovillani, Bubentani (site unknown), Corni (Corani?), Corventani (site unknown), Circeienses, Coriolani, Corbintes, Cabani (perhaps the Cabenses on the Alban Mount, *Bull. dell' Inst.* 1861, p. 205), Fortinei (unknown), Gabini, Laurentes, Lanuvini, Lavinates, Labicani, Nomentani, Norbani, Praenestini, Pedani, Querquetulani (site unknown), Satricani, Scaptini, Setini, Tellenii (site unknown), Tiburtini, Tusculani, Tolerini (site unknown), Tricrini (unknown), and Veliterni. The occasional notices of communities entitled to participate, such as of Ardea (Liv. xxxii. 1), Laurentum (Liv. xxxvii. 3), Lanuvium (Liv. xli. 16), Bovillae, Gabii, Labici (Cicero, *pro Planc.* 9, 23) agree with this list. Dionysius gives it on occasion of the declaration of war by Latium against Rome in $\frac{256}{498}$, and it was natural therefore to regard—according to the view of Niebuhr—this list as derived from the well-known renewal of the league in $\frac{261}{493}$. But, as in this list drawn up according to the Latin alphabet the letter g appears in a position which it certainly had not at the time of the Twelve Tables and scarcely came to occupy before the fifth century (see my *Unteritalische Dial.* p. 33), it must be taken from a much more recent source; and it is by far the simplest hypothesis to recognise it as a list of those places which were afterwards regarded as the ordinary members of the Latin confederacy, and which Dionysius in accordance with his systematising custom specifies as its original component elements. It is to be noticed that the list presents not a single non-Latin community, not even Caere, but simply enumerates places originally Latin or occupied by Latin colonies—no one will lay stress on Corbio and Corioli as exceptions. Now if we compare with this list that of the Latin colonies, we find that of the nine which had been founded down to $\frac{369}{385}$—Suessa Pometia, *Cora*, Signia, *Velitrae*, *Norba*, Antium (if this was really a Latin colony, see p. 343), *Ardea*, *Circeii*, and *Satricum*—the six marked in italics, and on the other

which took place about the year $\frac{370}{384}$, although we cannot precisely determine whether it was the effect or, as is more probable, the cause of the revolt of Latium which we have just described. As the law had hitherto stood, every sovereign city founded by Rome and Latium took its place among the communes entitled to participate in the federal festival and federal diet, whereas every community incorporated with another city, and thereby politically annihilated, was erased from the ranks of the members of the league. At the same time, however, according to Latin use and wont the number once fixed of thirty confederate communities was so adhered to, that of the participating cities never more and never less than thirty were entitled to vote, and a number of the communities that were later in entering, or were disqualified for their trifling importance or for the crimes they had committed, were without the right of voting. In this way the confederacy was constituted about $\frac{370}{384}$ as follows. Of old Latin townships there were—besides some which have fallen into oblivion, or whose sites are unknown—still autonomous and entitled to vote, Nomentum, between the Tiber and the

hand of those founded later none but Setia established in $\frac{372}{382}$, occur in the Dionysian list. The Latin colonies therefore that were instituted before $\frac{370}{384}$ were, while those founded subsequently were not, members participating in the Alban festival. The circumstance that Suessa Pometia and Antium are wanting in Dionysius is not inconsistent with this view, for both were lost again soon after their colonisation, and Antium remained for a long time afterwards a chief fortress of the Volsci, while Suessa speedily perished. The only real inconsistency with the rule which we have laid down is the absence of Signia and the occurrence of Setia; so that it is natural either to suggest that ΣΗΤΙΝΩΝ should be changed into ΣΙΓΝΙΝΩΝ, or to assume that the foundation of Setia had been already determined on before $\frac{370}{384}$, and that Signia was among the non-voting communities. At any rate this isolated exception cannot affect a rule that otherwise so thoroughly applies. In entire harmony with what we might expect, all places are absent from this list which were incorporated with the Roman community before $\frac{370}{384}$—such as Ostia, Antemnae, and Alba; whereas those incorporated later are retained in it, such as Tusculum, Satricum, Cora, Velitrae, all of which must have forfeited their sovereignty between $\frac{370}{384}$ and $\frac{536}{218}$.

As regards the list given by Pliny of thirty-two townships extinct in his time which had formerly participated in the Alban festival, after deduction of eight that also occur in Dionysius (for the Cusuetani of Pliny appear to be the Corventani of Dionysius, and the Tutienses of the former to be the Tricrini of the latter) there remain twenty-four townships, most of them quite unknown, doubtless made up partly of those seventeen non-voting communities—many of which were perhaps the very oldest, subsequently disqualified members of the Alban festal league—partly of a number of other decayed or excluded members of the league, to which latter class in particular the ancient presiding township of Alba, also named by Pliny, belonged.

Anio; Tibur, Gabii, Scaptia, Labici,[1] Pedum, and Praeneste, between the Anio and the Alban range; Corbio, Tusculum, Bovillae, Aricia, Corioli, and Lanuvium on the Alban range; lastly, Laurentum and Lavinium in the plain along the coast. To these fell to be added the colonies instituted by Rome and the Latin league; Ardea in the former territory of the Rutuli, and Velitrae, Satricum, Cora, Norba, Setia and Circeii in that of the Volsci. Besides, seventeen other townships, whose names are not known with certainty, had the privilege of participating in the Latin festival without the right of voting. On this footing—of forty-seven townships entitled to participate and thirty entitled to vote—the Latin confederacy continued henceforward unalterably fixed. The Latin communities founded subsequently, such as Sutrium, Nepete (p. 333), Cales, and Tarracina, were not admitted into the confederacy, nor were the Latin communities subsequently divested of their autonomy, such as Tusculum and Satricum, erased from the list.

With this closing of the confederacy was connected the geographical settlement of the limits of Latium. So long as the Latin confederacy continued open, the bounds of Latium had advanced with the establishment of new federal cities: but as the later Latin colonies had no share in the Alban festival, they were not regarded geographically as part of Latium. For this reason doubtless Ardea and Circeii were reckoned as belonging to Latium, but not Sutrium or Tarracina.

But not only were the places on which Latin privileges were bestowed after $\frac{370}{384}$ kept aloof from the federal association; they were isolated also from one another as respected private rights. While each of them was allowed to have reciprocity of commercial dealings and probably also of marriage (*commercium et connubium*) with Rome, no such reciprocity was permitted with the other Latin communities. The burgess of Sutrium, for example, might possess in full property a piece of ground in

---

[1] Livy certainly states (iv. 47) that Labici became a colony in $\frac{336}{418}$. But—apart from the fact that Diodorus (xiii. 6) says nothing of it—Labici cannot have been a burgess-colony, for the town did not lie on the coast, and besides it appears subsequently as still in possession of autonomy; nor can it have been a Latin one, for there is not, nor can there be from the nature of these foundations, a single other example of a Latin colony established in the original Latium. Here as elsewhere it is most probable—especially as two *jugera* are named as the portion of land allotted—that a public assignation to the burgesses has been confounded with a colonial assignation (p. 188).

Rome, but not in Praeneste; and might have legitimate children with a Roman, but not with a Tiburtine, wife.[1]

Hitherto considerable freedom of movement had been allowed within the confederacy. A separate league for instance of the five old Latin communities, Aricia, Tusculum, Tibur, Lanuvium, and Laurentum, and of the three new Latin, Ardea, Suessa Pometia, and Cora, had been permitted to group itself round the shrine of the Aricine Diana. It is doubtless not the mere result of accident that we find no further instance in later times of such special confederations fraught with danger to the hegemony of Rome.

We may likewise assign to this epoch the further remodelling which the Latin municipal constitutions underwent, and their complete assimilation to the constitution of Rome. In after times two aediles, intrusted with the police-supervision of markets and highways and the administration of justice in connection therewith, make their appearance side by side with the two praetors as necessary elements of the Latin magistracy. The institution of these urban police functionaries, which evidently took place at the same time and at the instigation of the leading power in all the towns of the federation, certainly cannot have preceded the establishment of the curule aedileship in Rome, which occurred in $\frac{387}{367}$; probably it took place about that very time. Beyond doubt the arrangement was only one of a series of measures curtailing the liberties and modifying the organisation of the federal communities in the interest of aristocratic policy.

After the fall of Veii and the conquest of the Pomptine territory, Rome evidently felt herself powerful enough to tighten the reins of her hegemony and to reduce the whole of the Latin cities to a position so dependent that they became virtually her subjects. At this period ($\frac{406}{348}$) the Carthaginians, in a commercial treaty concluded with Rome, bound themselves to inflict no injury on the Latins who were subject to Rome, viz. the maritime towns of Ardea, Antium, Circeii, and Tarracina; if however, any one of the Latin towns should revolt from the Roman alliance, the Phoenicians were to be allowed to attack it but in the event of conquering it they were bound not to raze it

---

[1] This restriction of the ancient full reciprocity of Latin rights first occurs in the renewal of the treaty in $\frac{416}{338}$ (Liv. viii. 14); but as the system of isolation, of which it was an essential part, first began in reference to the Latin colonies settled after $\frac{370}{384}$, and was only generalised in $\frac{416}{338}$, it is proper to mention the alteration here.

but to hand it over to the Romans. This plainly shows by what chains the Roman community bound to itself its dependencies, and how much a town, which dared to withdraw from the native protectorate, sacrificed or risked by such a course.

It is true that even now the Latin confederacy at least—if not also the Hernican—retained its formal title to a third of the gains of war, and doubtless some other remnants of the former equality of rights; but what was palpably lost was important enough to explain the exasperation which at this period prevailed among the Latins against Rome. Not only did numerous Latin volunteers fight under foreign standards against the community at their head, wherever they found armies in the field against Rome; but in $\frac{405}{349}$ the Latin league itself resolved to refuse to the Romans its contingent. To all appearance a renewed rising of the whole Latin confederacy might be anticipated at no distant date; and at that very moment a collision was imminent with another Italian nation, which was able to encounter on equal terms the united strength of the Latin stock. After the overthrow of the Volscians no considerable people in the first instance opposed the Romans in the south; their legions unchecked approached the Liris. As early as $\frac{397}{357}$ they had contended successfully with the Privernates; and in $\frac{409}{345}$ with the Aurunci, from whom they wrested Sora on the Liris. Thus the Roman armies had reached the Samnite frontier; and the friendly alliance, which the two bravest and most powerful of the Italian nations concluded with each other in $\frac{400}{354}$, was the sure token of an approaching struggle for the supremacy of Italy— a struggle which threatened to become interwoven with the dangerous crisis in the Latin nation.

The Samnite nation, which, at the time of the expulsion of the Tarquins from Rome, had doubtless already been for a considerable period in possession of the hill-country which rises between the Apulian and Campanian plains and commands them both, had hitherto found its further advance impeded on the one side by the Daunians—the power and prosperity of Arpi fall within this period—on the other by the Greeks and Etruscans. But the fall of the Etruscan power towards the end of the third, and the decline of the Greek colonies in the course of the fourth century, made room for them towards the west and south; and now one Samnite host after another marched down to, and even moved across, the south Italian seas. They first made their appearance in the plain adjoining the bay, with which the name of the Campanians has been associated from the beginning of the fourth century; the Etruscans there were suppressed, and the Greeks were confined within narrower bounds; Capua was wrested from the former ($\frac{330}{424}$), Cumae from the latter ($\frac{334}{420}$). About the same time, perhaps even earlier, the Lucanians appeared in Magna Graecia: at the beginning of the fourth century they were involved in conflict with the people of Terina and Thurii; and a considerable time before $\frac{364}{390}$ they had established themselves in the Greek Laus. About this period their levy amounted to 30,000 infantry and 4000 cavalry. Towards the end of the fourth century mention first occurs of the separate confederacy of the Bruttii,[1] who had detached themselves from the Lucanians—not, like the other Sabellian stocks, as a colony, but through a quarrel—and had become mixed up with many foreign elements. The Greeks of Lower Italy tried to resist the pressure of the barbarians; the league of the Achaean cities was reconstructed in $\frac{361}{393}$; and it was determined that, if any of the allied towns should be assailed by the Lucanians, all should furnish contingents, and that the leaders of contingents which failed to appear should suffer the punishment of death. But even the union of Magna Graecia no longer availed; for the ruler of Syracuse, Dionysius the Elder, made common cause with the Italians against his countrymen. While Dionysius wrested from the fleets of Magna Graecia the mastery of the Italian seas, one Greek city after another was occupied or annihilated by the Italians. In an incredibly short time the circle of flourishing cities was destroyed or laid desolate. Only a few Greek settlements, such as Neapolis, succeeded with difficulty, and more by means of treaties than by force of arms, in preserving their existence and their nationality. Tarentum alone remained thoroughly independent and powerful, maintaining its ground in consequence of its more remote position and of its preparation for war—the result of its constant conflicts with the Messapians. Even that city, however, had constantly to fight for its existence with the Lucanians, and was compelled to seek for alliances and mercenaries in the mother-country of Greece.

About the period when Veii and the Pomptine plain came into the hands of Rome, the Samnite hordes were already in possession of all Lower Italy, with the exception of a few unconnected Greek colonies, and of the Apulo-Messapian coast. The Greek Periplus, composed about $\frac{418}{336}$, sets down the Samnites

---

[1] The name itself is very ancient; in fact it is the most ancient indigenous name for the inhabitants of the present Calabria (Antiochus, *Fr.* 5. Müll.). The well-known derivation is doubtless an invention.

proper with their " five tongues " as reaching from the one sea to the other; and specifies the Campanians as adjoining them on the Tyrrhene sea to the north, and the Lucanians to the south, amongst whom in this instance, as often, the Bruttii are included, and who already had the whole coast apportioned among them from Paestum on the Tyrrhene, to Thurii on the Ionic, sea. In fact to one who compares the achievements of the two great nations of Italy, the Latins and the Samnites, before they came into contact, the career of conquest on the part of the latter appears far wider and more splendid than that of the former. But the character of their conquests was essentially different. From the fixed urban centre which Latium possessed in Rome the dominion of the Latin stock spread slowly on all sides, and lay within limits comparatively narrow; but it planted its foot firmly at every step, partly by founding fortified towns of the Roman type with the rights of dependent allies, partly by Romanising the territory which it conquered. It was otherwise with Samnium. There was in its case no single leading community and therefore no policy of conquest. While the conquest of the Veientine and Pomptine territories was for Rome a real enlargement of power, Samnium was weakened rather than strengthened by the rise of the Campanian cities and of the Lucanian and Bruttian confederacies; for every swarm, which had sought and found new settlements, thenceforward pursued a path of its own.

The Samnite tribes filled a disproportionately large space, while yet they showed no disposition to make it thoroughly their own. The larger Greek cities, Tarentum, Thurii, Croton, Metapontum, Heraclea, Rhegium, and Neapolis, although weakened and often dependent, continued to exist; and the Hellenes were tolerated even in the open country and in the smaller towns, so that Cumae for instance, Posidonia, Laus, and Hipponium, still remained—as the Periplus already mentioned and coins show—Greek cities even under Samnite rule. Mixed populations thus arose; the bi-lingual Bruttii, in particular, included Hellenic as well as Samnite elements and even perhaps remains of the ancient autochthones; in Lucania and Campania also similar mixtures must to a lesser extent have taken place.

The Samnite nation, moreover, could not resist the dangerous charm of Hellenic culture; least of all in Campania, where Neapolis early entered into friendly intercourse with the immigrants, and where the sky itself humanised the barbarians. ||

Capua, Nola, Nuceria, and Teanum, although having a purely Samnite population, adopted Greek manners and a Greek civic constitution; in fact the indigenous cantonal form of constitution could not possibly subsist under these altered circumstances. The Samnite cities of Campania began to coin money, in part with Greek inscriptions; Capua became by its commerce and agriculture the second city in Italy in point of size—the first in point of wealth and luxury. The deep demoralisation, in which according to the accounts of the ancients that city surpassed all others in Italy, is especially reflected in the mercenary recruiting and in the gladiatorial sports, both of which pre-eminently flourished in Capua. Nowhere did recruiting officers find so numerous a concourse as in this metropolis of demoralised civilisation; while Capua knew not how to save itself from the attacks of the Samnites, the warlike Campanian youth flocked forth in crowds under self-elected *condottieri*, especially to Sicily. How deeply these soldiers of fortune influenced by their enterprises the destinies of Italy, we shall have afterwards to show; they form as characteristic a feature of Campanian life as the gladiatorial sports which likewise, if they did not originate, were at any rate carried to perfection in Capua. There sets of gladiators made their appearance even during banquets; and their number was proportioned to the rank of the guests invited. This degeneracy of the most important Samnite city—a degeneracy which beyond doubt was closely connected with the Etruscan habits that lingered there —must have been fatal for the nation at large; although the Campanian nobility knew how to combine chivalrous valour and high mental culture with the deepest moral corruption, it could never become to its nation what the Roman nobility was to the Latin. Hellenic influence had a similar, though less powerful, effect on the Lucanians and Bruttians as on the Campanians. The objects discovered in the tombs throughout all these regions show how Greek art was cherished there in barbaric luxuriance; the rich ornaments of gold and amber and the magnificent painted pottery, which are now disinterred from the abodes of the dead, enable us to conjecture how extensive had been their departure from the ancient manners of their fathers. Other indications are preserved in their writing. The old national writing which they had brought with them from the north was abandoned by the Lucanians and Bruttians, and exchanged for Greek; while in Campania the national alphabet, and perhaps also the language, developed itself under the influence of the Greek model into greater clearness and delicacy. We meet even with isolated traces of the influence of Greek philosophy.

The Samnite land, properly so called, alone remained un-affected by these innovations, which, beautiful and natural as they may to some extent have been, powerfully contributed to relax still more the bond of national unity which even from the first was loose. Through the influence of Hellenic habits a deep schism took place in the Samnite stock. The civilised "Philhellenes" of Campania were accustomed to tremble like the Hellenes themselves before the ruder tribes of the mountains, who were continually penetrating into Campania and disturbing the degenerate earlier settlers. Rome was a compact state, having the strength of all Latium at its disposal; its subjects might murmur, but they obeyed. The Samnite stock was dispersed and divided; and, while the confederacy in Samnium proper had preserved unimpaired the manners and valour of their ancestors, they were on that very account completely at variance with the other Samnite tribes and towns.

In fact, it was this variance between the Samnites of the plain and the Samnites of the mountains that led the Romans over the Liris. The Sidicini in Teanum, and the Campanians in Capua, sought aid from the Romans ($\frac{411}{343}$) against their own countrymen, who in swarms ever renewed ravaged their territory and threatened to establish themselves there. When the desired alliance was refused, the Campanian envoys made offer of the submission of their country to the supremacy of Rome: and the Romans were unable to resist the bait. Roman envoys were sent to the Samnites to inform them of the new acquisition, and to summon them to respect the territory of the friendly power. The further course of events can no longer be ascertained in detail;[1] we discover only that—whether after a

---

[1] Perhaps no section of the Roman annals has been more disfigured than the narrative of the first Samnite-Latin war, as it stands or stood in Livy, Dionysius, and Appian. It runs somewhat to the following effect. After both consuls had marched into Campania in $\frac{411}{343}$, first the consul Marcus Valerius Corvus gained a severe and bloody victory over the Samnites at mount Gaurus; then his colleague Aulus Cornelius Cossus gained another, after he had been rescued from annihilation in a narrow pass by the self-devotion of a division led by the military tribune Publius Decius. The third and decisive battle was fought by both consuls at the entrance of the Caudine Pass near Suessula; the Samnites were completely vanquished— forty thousand of their shields were picked up on the field of battle—and they were compelled to make a peace, in which the Romans retained Capua, which had given itself over to their possession, while they left Teanum to the Samnites ($\frac{413}{341}$). Congratulations came from all sides,

campaign, or without the intervention of a war—Rome and
Samnium came to an agreement, by which Capua was left at
the disposal of the Romans, Teanum in the hands of the Samnites, and the upper Liris in those of the Volscians. The
consent of the Samnites to treat is explained by the energetic
exertions made about this very period by the Tarentines to get
quit of their Sabellian neighbours. But the Romans also had
good reason for coming to terms as quickly as possible with the
Samnites; for the impending transition of the region bordering on the south of Latium into the possession of the Romans
converted the ferment that had long existed among the Latins
into open insurrection. All the original Latin towns, even the
Tusculans who had been received into the burgess-union of
Rome, declared against Rome, with the single exception of the
Laurentes, whereas all the Roman colonies in Latium, with the
exception of Velitrae, adhered to the Roman alliance. We can
readily understand how the Capuans, notwithstanding their
very recent and voluntarily offered submission to the Romans,
should eagerly embrace the first opportunity of again ridding
themselves of the Roman rule and, in spite of the opposition of

even from Carthage. The Latins, who had refused their contingent and
seemed to be arming against Rome, turned their arms not against Rome
but against the Paeligni, while the Romans were occupied first with a
military conspiracy of the garrison left behind in Campania $\left(\frac{4\,1\,2}{3\,4\,2}\right)$, then
with the capture of Privernum $\left(\frac{4\,1\,3}{3\,4\,1}\right)$ and the war against the Antiates.
But now a sudden and singular change occurred in the position of parties.
The Latins, who had demanded in vain Roman citizenship and a share in
the consulate, rose against Rome in conjunction with the Sidicines, who
had vainly offered to submit to the Romans and knew not how to save
themselves from the Samnites, and with the Campanians, who were already
tired of the Roman rule. Only the Laurentes in Latium and the *equites* of
Campania adhered to the Romans, who on their part found support among
the Paeligni and Samnites. The Latin army fell upon Samnium; the
Romano-Samnite army, after it had marched to the Fucine lake and from
thence, avoiding Latium, into Campania, fought the decisive battle against
the combined Latins and Campanians at Vesuvius; the consul Titus
Manlius Imperiosus, after he had himself restored the wavering discipline
of the army by the execution of his own son who had slain a foe in opposition to orders from head-quarters, and after his colleague Publius Decius
Mus had appeased the gods by sacrificing his life, at length gained the
victory by calling up the last reserves. But the war was only terminated
by a second battle, in which the consul Manlius engaged the Latins and
Campanians near Trifanum; Latium and Capua submitted, and were
mulcted in a portion of their territory.
   The judicious and candid reader will not fail to observe that this report
swarms with all sorts of impossibilities. Such are the statement of the
Antiates waging war after the surrender of $\frac{3\,7\,7}{3\,7\,7}$ (Liv. vi. 33); the independent campaign of the Latins against the Paeligni, in distinct contradiction to the stipulations of the treaties between Rome and Latium; the
unprecedented march of the Roman army through the Marsian and Samnite

the optimate party that adhered to the treaty with Rome, should make common cause with the Latin confederacy, and how the Volscians should no less recognise in this Latin revolt the last chance of recovering their freedom and should likewise take to arms; but we do not know through what motives the Hernici abstained like the Campanian aristocracy from taking part in the revolt. The position of the Romans was critical; the legions which had crossed the Liris and occupied Campania were cut off by the revolt of the Latins and Volsci from their home, and a victory alone could save them. The decisive battle was fought near Trifanum (between Minturnae, Suessa, and Sinuessa) in $\frac{414}{340}$; the consul Titus Manlius Imperiosus Torquatus achieved a complete victory over the united Latins and Campanians. In the two following years the several towns of the Latins and Volsci, so far as they still offered resistance, were reduced by capitulation or assault, and the whole country was brought into subjection.

The effect of the victory was the dissolution of the Latin league. It was transformed from an independent political federation into a mere association for the purpose of a religious

territory to Capua, while all Latium was in arms against Rome; to say nothing of the equally confused and sentimental account of the military insurrection of $\frac{412}{342}$, and the story of its compulsory leader, the lame Titus Quinctius, the Roman Götz von Berlichingen. Still more suspicious, perhaps, are the repetitions. Such is the story of the military tribune Publius Decius modelled on the courageous deed of Marcus Calpurnius Flamma, or whatever he was called, in the first Punic war; such is the recurrence of the conquest of Privernum by Gaius Plautius in the year $\frac{425}{329}$, which second conquest alone is registered in the triumphal Fasti; such is the self-immolation of Publius Decius, repeated, as is well known, in the case of his son in $\frac{459}{295}$. Throughout this section the whole representation betrays a different period and a different hand from the other more credible accounts of the annals. The narrative is full of detailed pictures of battles; of inwoven anecdotes, such as that of the praetor of Setia, who breaks his neck on the steps of the senate-house because he had been audacious enough to solicit the consulship, and the various anecdotes concocted out of the surname of Titus Manlius; and of prolix and somewhat suspicious archaeological digressions. In this class we include the history of the legion—of which the notice, most probably apocryphal, in Liv. i. 52, regarding the maniple of Romans and Latins intermingled formed by the second Tarquin, is evidently another fragment; the erroneous view given of the treaty between Capua and Rome (see my *Röm. Münzwesen*, p. 334, n. 122); the formularies of self-devotion, the Campanian *denarius*, the Laurentine alliance, and the *bina jugera* in the assignation (p. 347, n.). Under such circumstances it appears a fact of great importance that Diodorus, who follows other and often older accounts, knows absolutely nothing of any of these events except the last battle of Trifanum; a battle in fact that ill accords with the rest of the narrative, which, in accordance with the rules of poetical justice, ought to have concluded with the death of Decius.

festival; the ancient stipulated rights of the confederacy as to a maximum for the levy of troops and a share of the gains of war perished as such along with it, and assumed, where they were recognised in future, the character of acts of grace. Instead of the one treaty between Rome on the one hand and the Latin confederacy on the other, perpetual alliances were entered into between Rome and the several confederate towns. The principle of isolating the communities from each other, which had already been established in regard to the places founded after $\frac{370}{384}$ (p. 347), was thus extended to the whole Latin nation. In other respects the several places retained their former privileges and their autonomy. Tibur and Praeneste however had to cede portions of their territory to Rome, and with still greater harshness the rights of war were asserted against other Latin or Volscian communities. Roman colonists were sent to Antium, the most important and, by land as well as by sea, the strongest city of the Volsci, and the old burgesses were compelled not only to give up the necessary lands to the new comers, but also themselves to enter into the burgess-union of Rome ($\frac{416}{338}$). Roman settlers in like manner proceeded a few years afterwards ($\frac{425}{329}$) to Tarracina, the second of the Volscian coast towns in importance, and there too the old burgesses were either ejected or incorporated with the new colony. Lanuvium, Aricia, Nomentum, and Pedum also lost their independence and became Roman *municipia*. The walls of Velitrae were demolished, the senate was ejected *en masse* and deported to the interior of Roman Etruria, and the town was probably constituted a dependent community with Caerite rights. Of the land acquired a portion—the estates, for instance, of the senators of Velitrae—was distributed to the Roman burgesses: these special assignations and the numerous communities recently admitted into citizenship gave rise to the institution of two new tribes in $\frac{422}{332}$. The deep sense which prevailed in Rome of the enormous importance of the result achieved is attested by the honorary column, which was erected in the Roman Forum to the victorious dictator of $\frac{416}{338}$, Gaius Maenius, and by the decoration of the orators' platform in the same place with the beaks taken from the galleys of Antium that were found unserviceable.

In like manner, although with some difference of form, the dominion of Rome was established and confirmed in the south Volscian and Campanian territories. Fundi, Formiae, Capua, Cumae, and a number of smaller towns became communities

dependent on Rome with Caerite rights. To secure the pre-
minently important city of Capua, the breach between the
nobility and commons was artfully widened and the general
administration was revised and controlled in the interest of
Rome. The same treatment was measured out to Privernum,
whose citizens, supported by Vitruvius Vaccus a bold partisan
belonging to Fundi, had the honour of fighting the last battle
for Latin freedom; the struggle ended with the storming of the
town ($\frac{425}{329}$) and the execution of Vaccus in a Roman prison.
In order to rear a population devoted to Rome in these regions,
they distributed, out of the lands won in war particularly in the
Privernate and Falernian territories, so numerous allotments to
Roman burgesses, that a few years later ($\frac{436}{318}$) they were able
to institute there two new tribes. The establishment of two
fortresses as colonies with Latin rights finally secured the newly
won land. These were Cales ($\frac{420}{334}$) in the middle of the Campanian plain, whence the movements of Teanum and Capua
could be observed, and Fregellae ($\frac{426}{328}$), which commanded the
passage of the Liris. Both colonies were unusually strong, and
rapidly became flourishing, notwithstanding the obstacles which
the Sidicines interposed to the founding of Cales and the Samnites
to that of Fregellae. A Roman garrison was also despatched to
Sora, a step of which the Samnites, to whom this district had
been left by the treaty, complained with reason, but in vain.
Rome pursued her purpose with undeviating steadfastness, and
displayed her energetic and far-reaching policy—more even than
on the battle-field—in the securing of the territory which she
gained by enveloping it, politically and militarily, in a net whose
meshes could not be broken.

As a matter of course, the Samnites could not behold the
threatening progress of the Romans with satisfaction, and they
probably put obstacles in its way; nevertheless they neglected to
intercept the new career of conquest, while there was still perhaps
time to do so, with that energy which the circumstances required.
They appear indeed in accordance with their treaty with Rome
to have occupied and strongly garrisoned Teanum; for while
in earlier times that city sought help against Samnium from
Capua and Rome, in the later struggles it appears as the bulwark
of the Samnite power on the west. They spread, conquering
and destroying, on the upper Liris, but they neglected to establish themselves permanently in that quarter. They destroyed
the Volscian town Fregellae—by which they simply facilitated
the institution of the Roman colony there which we have just

M.—I   *N 542

mentioned—and they so terrified two other Volscian towns, Fabrateria (Falvaterra) and Luca (site unknown), that these, following the example of Capua, surrendered themselves to the Romans ($\frac{424}{330}$). The Samnite confederacy allowed the Roman conquest of Campania to be completed before they in earnest opposed it; and the reason for their doing so is to be sought partly in the contemporary hostilities between the Samnite nation and the Italian Hellenes, but principally in the remiss and distracted policy which the confederacy pursued.

CHAPTER VI

STRUGGLE OF THE ITALIANS AGAINST ROME

WHILE the Romans were fighting on the Liris and Volturnus, other conflicts agitated the south-east of the peninsula. The wealthy merchant-republic of Tarentum, daily exposed to more serious peril from the Lucanian and Messapian bands and justly distrusting its own sword, gained by good words and better coin the help of *condottieri* from the mother-country. The Spartan king, Archidamus, who with a strong band had come to the assistance of his fellow-Dorians, succumbed to the Lucanians on the same day on which Philip conquered at Chaeronea ($\frac{416}{338}$); a retribution, in the belief of the pious Greeks, for the share which nineteen years previously he and his people had taken in pillaging the sanctuary of Delphi. His place was taken by an abler commander, Alexander the Molossian, brother of Olympias the mother of Alexander the Great. In addition to the troops which he had brought along with him he united under his banner the contingents of the Greek cities, especially those of the Tarentines and Metapontines; the Poediculi (around Rubi, now Ruvo), who like the Greeks found themselves in danger from the Sabellian nation; and lastly, even the Lucanian exiles themselves, whose considerable numbers point to the existence of violent internal troubles in that confederacy. Thus he soon found himself superior to the enemy. Consentia (Cosenza), which seems to have been the federal head-quarters of the Sabellians settled in Magna Graecia, fell into his hands. In vain the Samnites came to the help of the Lucanians; Alexander defeated their combined forces near Paestum. He subdued the Daunians around Sipontum, and the Messapians in the south-eastern peninsula; he already commanded from sea to sea, and was on the point of arranging with the Romans a joint attack on the Samnites in their native abodes. But successes so unexpected went beyond the desires of the Tarentine merchants, and filled them with alarm. War broke out between them and their captain, who had come amongst them a hired mercenary and now appeared desirous to found an Hellenic empire in the west like his nephew in the east. Alexander had at first the advantage; he wrested Heraclea from the Tarentines, restored Thurii, and seems to have called upon the other Italian Greeks to unite under his protection against the Tarentines, while he at the same time tried to bring about a peace between them and the Sabellian tribes. But his grand projects found only feeble support among the degenerate and desponding Greeks, and the forced change of sides alienated from him his former Lucanian adherents: he fell at Posidonia by the hand of a Lucanian emigrant ($\frac{422}{332}$).[1] On his death matters substantially reverted to their old position. The Greek cities found themselves once more isolated and once more left to protect themselves as best they might by treaty or payment of tribute, or even by extraneous aid; Croton for instance repulsed the Bruttii about $\frac{430}{324}$ with the help of the Syracusans. The Samnite tribes acquired renewed ascendancy, and were able without troubling themselves about the Greeks, once more to direct their thoughts towards Campania and Latium.

But there during the brief interval a prodigious change had occurred. The Latin confederacy was broken and shattered the last resistance of the Volsci was overcome, the province of Campania, the richest and finest in the peninsula, was in the undisputed and well-secured possession of the Romans, and the second city of Italy was a dependency of Rome. While the Greeks and Samnites were contending with each other, Rome had almost without a contest raised herself to a position of power which no single people in the peninsula possessed the means of shaking, and which threatened to render all of them subject to her yoke. A joint exertion on the part of the peoples who were not severally a match for Rome might perhaps still burst the chains, ere they became fastened completely. But the clearness of perception, the courage, the self-sacrifice required for such a coalition of numerous peoples and cities that had hitherto been for the most part foes or at any rate strangers to each other, were not to be found at all, or were found only when it was already too late.

After the fall of the Etruscan power and the weakening of the Greek republics, the Samnite confederacy was beyond doubt, next to Rome, the most considerable power in Italy, and at the

---

[1] It may not be superfluous to mention that our knowledge of Archidamus and Alexander is derived from Greek annals, and that the synchronism between these and the Roman is in reference to the present epoch only approximately established. We must beware, therefore, of pursuing too far into detail the unmistakable general connection between the events in the west and those in the east of Italy.

ame time that which was most closely and immediately en-
langered by Roman encroachments. To its lot therefore fell
he foremost place and the heaviest burden in the struggle for
reedom and nationality which the Italians had to wage against
Rome. It might reckon upon the assistance of the small Sabel-
ian tribes, the Vestini, Frentani, Marrucini, and other smaller
cantons, who dwelt in rustic seclusion amidst their mountains,
but were not deaf to the appeal of a kindred stock calling them
to take up arms in defence of their common possessions. The
assistance of the Campanian Greeks and those of Magna Graecia
especially the Tarentines), and of the powerful Lucanians and
Bruttians would have been of greater importance; but the
negligence and supineness of the demagogues ruling in Tarentum
and the entanglement of that city in the affairs of Sicily, the
internal distractions of the Lucanian confederacy, and above
all the deep hostility that had subsisted for centuries between
the Greeks of Lower Italy and their Lucanian oppressors, scarcely
permitted the hope that Tarentum and Lucania would make
common cause with the Samnites. From the Marsi, who were
the nearest neighbours of the Romans and had long lived in
peaceful relations with Rome, little more could be expected than
lukewarm sympathy or neutrality. The Apulians, the ancient
and bitter antagonists of the Sabellians, were the natural allies
of the Romans. On the other hand it might be expected that
the more remote Etruscans would join the league if a first
success were gained; and even a revolt in Latium and the land
of the Volsci and Hernici was not impossible. But the Samnites
—the Aetolians of Italy, in whom national vigour still lived unimpaired—had mainly to rely on their own energies for such
perseverance in the unequal struggle as would give the other
peoples time for a generous sense of shame, for calm deliberation,
and for the mustering of their forces; a single success might then
kindle the flames of war and insurrection all around Rome.
History cannot but do the noble people the justice of acknow-
ledging that they understood and performed their duty.

Differences had already for several years existed between
Rome and Samnium in consequence of the continual aggressions
in which the Romans indulged on the Liris, and of which the
founding of Fregellae in $\frac{426}{328}$ was the most recent and most
important. But it was the Greeks of Campania that gave
occasion to the outbreak of the contest. The twin cities of
Palaeopolis and Neapolis, which seem to have been politically
united and to have ruled over the Greek islands in the bay,

were the only communities not yet reduced to subjection within
the Roman territory. The Tarentines and Samnites, informed
of the scheme of the Romans to obtain possession of these towns,
resolved to anticipate them; and while the Tarentines were too
remiss perhaps than too distant for the execution of this plan,
the Samnites actually threw a strong garrison into Palaeopolis.
The Romans immediately declared war nominally against the
Palaeopolitans, really against the Samnites ($\frac{427}{327}$), and began the
siege of Palaeopolis. After it had lasted a while, the Campanian
Greeks became weary of the disturbance of their commerce and
of the foreign garrison; and the Romans, whose whole efforts
were directed to keep states of the second and third rank by
means of separate treaties aloof from the coalition which was
about to be formed, hastened, as soon as the Greeks consented
to negotiate, to offer them the most favourable terms—full
equality of rights and exemption from land service, equal
alliance and perpetual peace. Upon these conditions, after the
Palaeopolitans had rid themselves of the garrison by stratagem,
a treaty was concluded ($\frac{428}{326}$).

The Sabellian towns to the south of the Volturnus, Nola,
Nuceria, Herculaneum, and Pompeii, took part with Samnium
in the beginning of the war; but their greatly exposed situation
and the machinations of the Romans—who endeavoured to
bring over to their side the optimate party in these towns by
all the levers of artifice and self-interest, and found a powerful
support to their endeavours in the precedent of Capua—
induced these towns to declare themselves either in favour of
Rome or neutral not long after the fall of Palaeopolis.

A still more important success befell the Romans in Lucania.
There also the people with true instinct was in favour of joining
the Samnites; but, as an alliance with the Samnites involved
peace with Tarentum and a large portion of the governing
lords of Lucania were not disposed to suspend their profitable
pillaging expeditions, the Romans succeeded in concluding an
alliance with Lucania — an alliance which was invaluable,
because it provided employment for the Tarentines and thus
left the whole power of Rome available against Samnium.

Thus Samnium stood on all sides unsupported; excepting
that some of the eastern mountain districts sent their contingents. In the year $\frac{428}{326}$ the war began within the Samnite land
itself: some towns on the Campanian frontier, Rufrae (between
Venafrum and Teanum) and Allifae, were occupied by the
Romans. In the following years the Roman armies penetrated

Samnium, fighting and pillaging, as far as the territory of the
Vestini, and even as far as Apulia, where they were received
with open arms; everywhere they had very decidedly the
advantage. The courage of the Samnites was broken; they
sent back the Roman prisoners, and along with them the dead
body of the leader of the war party, Brutulus Papius, who
had anticipated the Roman executioners, when the Samnite
national assembly determined to ask the enemy for peace and
to procure for themselves more tolerable terms by the surrender
of their bravest general. But when the humble, almost suppliant, request was not listened to by the Roman people ($\frac{432}{322}$),
the Samnites, under their new general Gavius Pontius, prepared
for the utmost and most desperate resistance. The Roman
army, which under the two consuls of the following year ($\frac{433}{321}$)
Spurius Postumius and Titus Veturius was encamped near
Calatia (between Caserta and Maddaloni), received accounts,
confirmed by the affirmation of numerous captives, that the
Samnites had closely invested Luceria, and that that important
town, on which depended the possession of Apulia, was in great
danger. They broke up in haste. If they wished to arrive in
good time, no other route could be taken than through the midst
of the enemy's territory—where afterwards, in continuation
of the Appian Way, a Roman road was constructed from Capua
by way of Beneventum to Apulia. This route led, between the
present villages of Arpaja and Montesarchio,[1] through a watery
meadow, which was wholly enclosed by high and steep wooded
hills and was only accessible through deep defiles at the entrance
and outlet. Here the Samnites had posted themselves in am-
bush. The Romans, who had entered the valley unopposed,
found its outlet obstructed by abattis and strongly occupied;
on marching back they saw that the entrance was similarly
closed, while at the same time the crests of the surrounding
mountains were crowned by Samnite cohorts. They perceived,
when it was too late, that they had suffered themselves to be
misled by a stratagem, and that the Samnites awaited them,
not at Luceria, but in the fatal pass of Caudium. They fought,
but without hope of success and without definite aim; the
Roman army was totally unable to manœuvre and was com-

---

[1] The general position of the place is certain enough, for Caudium certainly lay near Arpaja; but it is more doubtful whether the valley between
Arpaja and Montesarchio is meant, or that between Arienzo and Arpaja,
for the latter appears to have been since that time raised by natural
agencies at least one hundred palms. I follow the current hypothesis
without undertaking to defend it.

pletely vanquished without a struggle. The Roman generals
offered to capitulate. It is only a foolish rhetoric that represents
the Samnite general as shut up to the simple alternatives of
dismissing or of slaughtering the Roman army; he could not
have done better than accept the offered capitulation and
make prisoners of the hostile army—the whole force which for
the moment the Roman community could bring into action—
with both its commanders-in-chief. In that case the way to
Campania and Latium would have stood open; and in the then
existing state of feeling, when the Volsci and Hernici and the
larger portion of the Latins would have received him with open
arms, the political existence of Rome would have been in serious
danger. But instead of taking this course and concluding a
military convention, Gavius Pontius thought that he could at
once terminate the whole quarrel by an equitable peace; whether
it was that he shared that foolish longing of the confederates
for peace, to which Brutulus Papius had fallen a victim in the
previous year, or whether it was that he was unable to prevent
the party which was tired of the war from spoiling his unexampled
victory. The terms laid down were moderate enough; Rome
was to raze the fortresses which she had constructed in defiance
of the treaty—Cales and Fregellae—and to renew her equal
alliance with Samnium. After the Roman generals had agreed
to these terms, and had given six hundred hostages chosen from
the cavalry for their faithful execution—besides pledging their
own word and that of all their staff-officers on oath to the
same effect—the Roman army was dismissed uninjured, but
disgraced; for the Samnite army, drunk with victory, could
not resist the desire to subject their hated enemies to the
disgraceful formality of laying down their arms and passing
under the yoke.

But the Roman senate, regardless of the oath of their officers
and of the fate of the hostages, cancelled the agreement, and
contented themselves with surrendering to the enemy those
who had concluded it as personally responsible for its fulfilment.
Impartial history can attach little importance to the question
whether in so doing the casuistry of Roman advocates and priests
kept the letter of the law, or whether the decree of the Roman
senate violated it; under a human and political point of view
no blame in this matter rests upon the Romans. It was a
question of comparative indifference whether, according to
the formal state law of the Romans, the general in command
was or was not entitled to conclude peace without reserving

its ratification by the burgesses. According to the spirit and practice of the constitution it was quite an established principle that every state-agreement, not purely military, in Rome pertained to the province of the civil authorities, and a general who concluded peace without the instructions of the senate and the burgesses exceeded his powers. It was a greater error on the part of the Samnite general to give the Roman generals the choice between saving their army and exceeding their powers, than it was on the part of the latter that they had not the magnanimity absolutely to reject the suggestion; and it was right and necessary that the Roman senate should reject such an agreement. A great nation does not surrender what it possesses except under the pressure of extreme necessity: all treaties making concessions are acknowledgments of such a necessity, not moral obligations. If every people justly reckons it a point of honour to tear to pieces by force of arms treaties that are disgraceful, how could honour enjoin a patient adherence to a convention like the Caudine to which an unfortunate general was morally compelled, while the sting of the recent disgrace was keenly felt and the vigour of the nation subsisted unimpaired?

Thus the convention of Caudium did not produce the rest which the enthusiasts for peace in Samnium had foolishly expected from it, but only led to war after war with exasperation aggravated on either side by the opportunity forfeited, by the breach of a solemn engagement, by military honour disgraced, and by comrades that had been abandoned. The Roman officers given up were not received by the Samnites, partly because they were too magnanimous to wreak their vengeance on those unfortunates, partly because they would thereby have admitted the Roman plea that the agreement bound only those who swore to it, not the Roman state. Magnanimously they spared even the hostages whose lives had been forfeited by the rules of war, and preferred to resort at once to arms. Luceria was occupied by them and Fregellae surprised and taken by assault ($\frac{434}{320}$) before the Romans had reorganised their broken army; the junction of the Satricans with the Samnites shows what they might have accomplished, had they not allowed their advantage to slip through their hands. But Rome was only momentarily paralysed, not weakened; full of shame and indignation the Romans raised all the men and means they could, and placed the highly experienced Lucius Papirius Cursor equally distinguished as a soldier and as a general, at the head of the newly formed army. The army divided; the one half marched by Sabina and the Adriatic coast to appear before Luceria, the other proceeded to the same destination through Samnium itself, successfully engaging and driving before it the Samnite army. They formed a junction again under the walls of Luceria, the siege of which was prosecuted with the greater zeal, because the Roman *equites* lay in captivity there; the Apulians, particularly the Arpani, lent the Romans important assistance in the siege, especially by procuring supplies. After the Samnites had given battle for the relief of the town and been defeated, Luceria surrendered to the Romans ($\frac{435}{319}$). Papirius enjoyed the double satisfaction of liberating his comrades who had been given up for lost, and of retaliating the yoke of Caudium on the Samnite garrison of Luceria. In the next years ($\frac{435-437}{319-317}$) the war was carried on [1] not so much in Samnium itself as in the adjoining districts. In the first place the Romans chastised the allies of the Samnites in the Apulian and Frentanian territories, and concluded new conventions with the Teanenses of Apulia and the Canusini. At the same time Satricum was again reduced to subjection and severely punished for its revolt. Then the war turned to Campania, where the Romans conquered the frontier town towards Samnium, Saticula (perhaps S. Agata de' Goti) ($\frac{438}{316}$). But now the fortune of war seemed disposed once more to turn against them. The Samnites gained over the Nucerians ($\frac{438}{316}$), and soon afterwards the Nolans, to their side; on the upper Liris the Sorani of themselves expelled the Roman garrison ($\frac{439}{315}$); the Ausonians were preparing to rise, and threatened the important Cales; even in Capua the party opposed to Rome was vigorously stirring. A Samnite army advanced into Campania and encamped before the city, in the hope that its presence might place the national party in the ascendant ($\frac{440}{314}$). But Sora was immediately attacked by the Romans and recaptured after the defeat of a Samnite relieving force ($\frac{440}{314}$). The movements among the Ausonians were suppressed with cruel rigour ere the insurrection fairly broke out, and at the same time a special dictator was nominated to institute and decide political processes against the leaders of the Samnite party in Capua, so that the most illustrious of them died a voluntary death to escape from the Roman executioner ($\frac{440}{314}$). The Samnite army before Capua was defeated and compelled to retreat from Cam-

[1] That a formal armistice for two years subsisted between Rome and Samnium in $\frac{436-437}{318-317}$ is more than improbable.

pania; the Romans, following close at the heels of the enemy, crossed the Matese and encamped in the winter of $\frac{440}{314}$ before Bovianum, the capital of Samnium. Nola was thus abandoned by its allies; and the Romans had the sagacity to detach the town for ever from the Samnite party by a very favourable convention, similar to that concluded with Neapolis ($\frac{441}{313}$). Fregellae, which after the catastrophe of Caudium had fallen into the hands of the party adverse to Rome and had been their chief stronghold in the district on the Liris, finally fell in the eighth year after its occupation by the Samnites ($\frac{441}{313}$); two hundred of the citizens, the chiefs of the national party, were conveyed to Rome, and there openly beheaded in the Forum as an example and a warning to the patriots who were every-where bestirring themselves.

Apulia and Campania were thus in the hands of the Romans. In order finally to secure and permanently to command the conquered territory, several new fortresses were founded in it during the years $\frac{440-442}{314-312}$: Luceria in Apulia, to which on account of its isolated and exposed situation half a legion was sent as a permanent garrison; Pontiae (the Ponza islands) for the securing of the Campanian waters; Saticula on the Campano-Samnite frontier, as a bulwark against Samnium; and lastly Interamna (near Monte Cassino) and Suessa Aurunca (Sessa) on the road from Rome to Capua. Garrisons moreover were sent to Calatia, Sora, and other stations of military importance. The great military road from Rome to Capua, which with the necessary embankment for it across the Pomptine marshes the censor Appius Claudius caused to be constructed in $\frac{442}{312}$, completed the securing of Campania. The designs of the Romans were more and more fully developed; their object was the subjugation of Italy, which was enveloped more closely from year to year in a network of Roman fortresses and roads. The Samnites were already on both sides surrounded by the Roman meshes; already the line from Rome to Luceria severed north and south Italy from each other, as the fortresses of Cora and Norba had formerly severed the Volsci and Aequi; and Rome now rested on the Arpani, as it formerly rested on the Hernici. The Italians could not but see that the freedom of all of them was gone if Samnium succumbed, and that it was high time at length to hasten with all their might to the support of the brave mountain people which had now for fifteen years singly sustained the unequal struggle with the Romans.

The most natural allies of the Samnites would have been the

Tarentines; but it was part of that fatality that hung over Samnium and over Italy in general, that at this moment so fraught with the destinies of the future the decision lay in the hands of these Athenians of Italy. Since the constitution of Tarentum, which was originally after the old Doric fashion strictly aristocratic, had become changed to a complete democracy, a life of singular activity had sprung up in that city, which was inhabited chiefly by mariners, fishermen, and artisans. The sentiments and conduct of the population, more wealthy than noble, discarded all earnestness amidst the giddy bustle and brilliance of their daily life, and oscillated between the grandest boldness of enterprise and elevation of spirit on the one hand, and a shameful frivolity and childish whim on the other. It may not be out of place, in connection with a crisis wherein the existence or destruction of nations of noble gifts and ancient renown was at stake, to mention that Plato, who came to Tarentum some sixty years before this time, according to his own statement saw the whole city drunk at the Dionysia, and that the burlesque farce, or " merry tragedy " as it was called, was created in Tarentum about the very time of the great Samnite war. This licentious life and buffoon poetry of the Tarentine fashionables and literati had a fitting counterpart in the inconstant, arrogant, and short-sighted policy of the Tarentine demagogues, who regularly meddled in matters with which they had nothing to do, and kept aloof where their immediate interests called for action. After the Caudine catastrophe, when the Romans and Samnites stood opposed in Apulia, they had sent envoys thither to enjoin both parties to lay down their arms ($\frac{434}{320}$). This diplomatic intervention in the decisive struggle of the Italians could not rationally have any other meaning than that of an announcement that Tarentum had at length resolved to abandon the neutrality which it had hitherto maintained. It had in fact sufficient reason to do so. It was no doubt a difficult and dangerous thing for Tarentum to be entangled in such a war; for the democratic development of the state had directed its energies entirely to the fleet, and while that fleet, resting upon the strong commercial marine of Tarentum, held the first rank among the maritime powers of Magna Graecia, the land force, on which they were in the present case dependent, consisted mainly of hired soldiers and was sadly disorganised. Under these circumstances it was no light undertaking for the Tarentine republic to take part in the conflict between Rome and Samnium, even apart from the—

at least troublesome—feud in which Roman policy had contrived to involve them with the Lucanians. But these obstacles might be surmounted by an energetic will; and both the contending parties construed the summons of the Tarentine envoys that they should desist from the strife as meant in earnest. The Samnites, as the weaker, showed themselves ready to comply with it; the Romans replied by hoisting the signal for battle. Reason and honour dictated to the Tarentines the propriety of now following up the haughty injunction of their envoys by a declaration of war against Rome; but in Tarentum neither reason nor honour characterised the government, and they had simply been trifling in a very childish fashion with very serious matters. No declaration of war against Rome took place; in its stead they preferred to support the oligarchical party in the Sicilian towns against Agathocles of Syracuse who had at a former period been in the Tarentine service and had been dismissed in disgrace, and following the example of Sparta, they sent a fleet to the island—a fleet which would have rendered better service in the Campanian seas ($\frac{440}{314}$).

The peoples of northern and central Italy, who seem to have been roused especially by the establishment of the fortress of Luceria, acted with more energy. The Etruscans first drew the sword ($\frac{443}{311}$), the armistice of $\frac{403}{351}$ having already expired some years before. The Roman frontier-fortress of Sutrium had to sustain a two years' siege, and in the hot conflicts which took place under its walls the Romans as a rule were worsted, till the consul of the year $\frac{444}{310}$ Quintus Fabius Rullianus, a leader who had gained experience in the Samnite wars, not only restored the ascendancy of the Roman arms in Roman Etruria, but boldly penetrated into the land of the Etruscans proper, which had hitherto, from diversity of language and scanty means of communication, remained almost unknown to the Romans. His march through the Ciminian forest which no Roman army had yet traversed, and his pillaging of a rich region that had long been spared the horrors of war, raised all Etruria in arms. The Roman government, which had seriously disapproved the rash expedition and had when too late forbidden the daring leader from crossing the frontier, collected in the greatest haste new legions, in order to meet the expected onslaught of the whole Etruscan power. But a seasonable and decisive victory of Rullianus, the battle at the Vadimonian lake which long lived in the memory of the people, converted an imprudent enterprise into a celebrated feat of heroism and broke the resist-

ance of the Etruscans. Unlike the Samnites who had now for
eighteen years maintained the unequal struggle, three of the
most powerful Etruscan towns—Perusia, Cortona, and Arretium
—consented after the first defeat to a separate peace for three
hundred months ($\frac{444}{310}$), and after the Romans had once more
beaten the other Etruscans near Perusia in the following year,
the Tarquinienses also agreed to a peace of four hundred months
($\frac{446}{308}$); whereupon the other cities desisted from the contest,
and a temporary cessation of arms took place throughout
Etruria.

While these events were passing, the war had not been suspended in Samnium. The campaign of $\frac{443}{311}$ was confined like
the preceding to the besieging and storming of several strongholds of the Samnites; but in the next year the war took a more
vigorous turn. The dangerous position of Rullianus in Etruria,
and the reports which spread as to the annihilation of the
Roman army in the north, encouraged the Samnites to new
exertions; the Roman consul Gaius Marcius Rutilus was vanquished by them and severely wounded in person. But the
sudden change in the aspect of matters in Etruria destroyed their
newly kindled hopes. Lucius Papirius Cursor again appeared at
the head of the Roman troops sent against the Samnites, and
again remained the victor in a great and decisive battle ($\frac{445}{309}$),
in which the confederates had put forth their last energies.
The flower of their army—the wearers of the striped tunics and
golden shields, and the wearers of the white tunics and silver
shields—were there extirpated, and their splendid equipments
thenceforth on festal occasions decorated the rows of shops
along the Roman Forum. Their distress was ever increasing;
the struggle was becoming ever more hopeless. In the following
year ($\frac{446}{308}$) the Etruscans laid down their arms; and in the same
year the last town of Campania which still adhered to the
Samnites, Nuceria, simultaneously assailed on the part of the
Romans by water and by land, surrendered under favourable
conditions. The Samnites found new allies in the Umbrians of
northern, and in the Marsi and Paeligni of central, Italy, and
numerous volunteers from the Hernici joined their ranks; but
movements which might have decidedly turned the scale
against Rome, had the Etruscans still remained under arms,
now simply augmented the results of the Roman victory without seriously adding to its difficulties. The Umbrians, who
threatened to march on Rome, were intercepted by Rullianus
with the army of Samnium on the upper Tiber—a step which

the enfeebled Samnites were unable to prevent; and this sufficed to disperse the Umbrian levies. The war once more returned to central Italy. The Paeligni were conquered, as were also the Marsi; and, though the other Sabellian tribes remained nominally foes of Rome, in this quarter Samnium gradually came to stand practically alone. But unexpected assistance came to them from the district of the Tiber. The confederacy of the Hernici, called by the Romans to account for their countrymen discovered among the Samnite captives, now declared war against Rome (in $\frac{448}{306}$)—more doubtless from despair than from calculation. Some of the more considerable of the Hernican communities from the first kept aloof from hostilities; but Anagnia, by far the most eminent of the Hernican cities, carried out this declaration of war. In a military point of view the position of the Romans was undoubtedly rendered for the moment highly critical by this unexpected rising in the rear of the army occupied with the siege of the strongholds of Samnium. Once more the fortune of war favoured the Samnites; Sora and Calatia fell into their hands. But the Anagnines succumbed with unexpected rapidity before troops despatched from Rome, and these troops also gave seasonable relief to the army stationed in Samnium: all was once more lost. The Samnites sued for peace, but in vain; they could not yet come to terms. The final decision was reserved for the campaign of $\frac{449}{305}$. Two Roman consular armies penetrated—the one, under Tiberius Minucius and after his fall under Marcus Fulvius, from Campania through the mountain passes, the other, under Lucius Postumius, from the Adriatic upwards by Biferno—into Samnium, there to unite in front of Bovianum the capital; a decisive victory was achieved, the Samnite general Statius Gellius was taken prisoner, and Bovianum was carried by storm. The fall of the chief stronghold of the land terminated the twenty-two years' war. The Samnites withdrew their garrisons from Sora and Arpinum, and sent envoys to Rome to sue for peace; the Sabellian tribes, the Marsi, Marrucini, Paeligni, Frentani, Vestini, and Picentes followed their example. The terms granted by Rome were tolerable; cessions of territory were required from some of them, from the Paeligni for instance, but they do not seem to have been of much importance. The equal alliance was renewed between the Sabellian tribes and the Romans ($\frac{450}{304}$).

Probably about the same time, and in consequence doubtless of the Samnite peace, peace was also made between Rome

and Tarentum.   The two cities had not indeed directly opposed
each other in the field.   The Tarentines had been inactive
spectators of the long contest between Rome and Samnium
from its beginning to its close, and had only kept up hostilities
in league with the Sallentines against the Lucanians who were
allies of Rome.   In the last years of the Samnite war no doubt
they had shown some signs of more energetic action.   The
position of embarrassment to which the ceaseless attacks of the
Lucanians reduced them on the one hand, and on the other
hand the feeling ever obtruding itself on them more urgently
that the complete subjugation of Samnium would endanger
their own independence, induced them, notwithstanding their
unsatisfactory experience under Alexander, once more to
entrust themselves to a *condottiere*.   There came at their call
the Spartan prince Cleonymus, accompanied by five thousand
mercenaries; with whom he united a band equally numerous
raised in Italy, as well as the contingents of the Messapians and
of the smaller Greek towns, and above all the Tarentine civic
army of twenty-two thousand men.   At the head of this considerable force he compelled the Lucanians to make peace with
Tarentum and to install a government of Samnite tendencies;
in return for which Metapontum was abandoned to them.   The
Samnites were still in arms when this occurred; there was
nothing to prevent the Spartan from coming to their aid and
casting the weight of his numerous army and his military skill
into the scale in favour of freedom for the cities and peoples of
Italy.   But Tarentum did not act as Rome would in similar
circumstances have acted; and prince Cleonymus himself was
far from being an Alexander or a Pyrrhus.   He was in no hurry
to undertake a war in which he might expect more blows than
booty, but preferred to make common cause with the Lucanians
against Metapontum, and made himself comfortable in that
city, while he talked of an expedition against Agathocles of
Syracuse and of liberating the Sicilian Greeks.   Thereupon the
Samnites made peace; and when after its conclusion Rome
began to concern herself more seriously about the south-east
of the peninsula—in token of which in the year $\frac{447}{307}$ a Roman
force levied contributions, or rather reconnoitred by order of
the government, in the territory of the Sallentines—the
Spartan *condottiere* embarked with his mercenaries and surprised
the island of Corcyra, which was admirably situated as a basis
for piratical expeditions against Greece and Italy.   Thus
abandoned by their general, and at the same time deprived of

their allies in central Italy, the Tarentines and their Italian allies, the Lucanians and Sallentines, had now no course left but to solicit an accommodation with Rome, which appears to have been granted on moderate terms. Soon afterwards ($\frac{451}{303}$) even an incursion of Cleonymus, who had landed in the Sallentine territory and laid siege to Uria, was repulsed by the inhabitants with Roman aid.

The victory of Rome was complete; and she turned it to full account. It was not from magnanimity in the conquerors— for the Romans knew nothing of the sort—but from wise and far-seeing calculation that terms so moderate were granted to the Samnites, the Tarentines, and the more distant peoples generally. The first and main object was not so much to compel southern Italy at once formally to recognise the Roman supremacy as to supplement and complete the subjugation of central Italy, for which the way had been prepared by the military roads and fortresses already established in Campania and Apulia during the last war, and by that means to separate the northern and southern Italians into two masses cut off in a military point of view from direct contact with each other. To this object accordingly the next undertakings of the Romans were with consistent energy directed. Above all they embraced the welcome opportunity of dissolving the Hernican league, and thereby annihilating the last remnant of the old confederacies that competed with the isolated Roman power in the district of the Tiber. The fate of Anagnia and the other small Hernican communities which had taken part in the last stage of the Samnite war was, as might be expected, far harder than that which had under similar circumstances been meted out to the Latin communities in the previous generation. They all lost their autonomy and had to rest content with the citizenship without suffrage of Rome; out of a portion of their territory on the upper Trerus (Sacco), moreover, a new tribe was instituted, and another was formed at the same time on the lower Anio ($\frac{455}{299}$). The only regret was that the three Hernican communities next in importance to Anagnia, Aletrium, Verulae, and Ferentinum, had not also revolted; for, as they courteously declined the suggestion that they should voluntarily enter into the bond of Roman citizenship, and there existed no pretext for compelling them to do so, the Romans were obliged not only to respect their autonomy, but also to allow to them even the right of assembly and of intermarriage, and in this way still to leave a shadow of the old Hernican confederacy. No such considerations fettered their action in that portion of the Volscian country which had hitherto been held by the Samnites There Arpinum became subject, Frusino was deprived of a third of its domain, and on the upper Liris in addition to Fregellae the Volscian town of Sora, which had previously been garrisoned, was now permanently converted into a Roman fortress and occupied by a legion of 4000 men. In this way the old Volscian territory was completely subdued, and became rapidly Romanised. The region which separated Samnium from Etruria was penetrated by two military roads, both of which were secured by new fortresses. The northern road, which afterwards became the Flaminian, covered the line of the Tiber; it led through Ocriculum, which was in alliance with Rome, to Narnia, the name which the Romans gave to the old Umbrian fortress Nequinum when they settled a military colony there $(\frac{455}{299})$. The southern, afterwards the Valerian, ran along the Fucine lake by way of Carsioli and Alba, both of which places likewise received colonies $(\frac{451-453}{303-301})$; Alba in particular, important as the key of the Marsian land, received a garrison of 6000 men. The small tribes within whose bounds these colonies were instituted, the Umbrians who obstinately defended Nequinum, the Aequians who assailed Alba, and the Marsians who attacked Carsioli, could not arrest the course of Rome: the two strong curb-fortresses were inserted almost without hindrance between Samnium and Etruria. We have already mentioned the great roads and fortresses instituted for permanently securing Apulia and above all Campania: by their means Samnium was further surrounded on the east and west with the net of Roman strongholds. It is a significant token of the comparative weakness of Etruria that it was not deemed necessary to secure the defiles of the Ciminian forest in a similar mode—by a highway and corresponding fortresses. The former frontier fortress of Sutrium continued to be in this quarter the terminus of the Roman military line, and the Romans contented themselves with having the road leading thence to Arretium kept in a serviceable state for military purposes by the communities through whose territories it passed.[1]

---

[1] The operations in the campaign of $\frac{537}{217}$, and still more plainly the formation of the highway from Arretium to Bononia in $\frac{567}{187}$, show that the road from Rome to Arretium had already been rendered serviceable before that time. But it cannot at that period have been a Roman military road, because, judging from its later appellation of the "Cassian way," it cannot have been constructed as a *via consularis* earlier than $\frac{583}{171}$; no

The high-spirited Samnite nation perceived that such a peace was more ruinous than the most destructive war; and, what was more, it acted accordingly. The Celts in northern Italy were just beginning to bestir themselves again after a long suspension of warfare; moreover several Etruscan communities there were still in arms against the Romans, and brief armistices alternated in that quarter with furious but indecisive conflicts. All central Italy was still in ferment and partly in open insurrection; the fortresses were still only in course of construction; the way between Etruria and Samnium was not yet completely closed. Perhaps it was not yet too late to save freedom; but, if so, there must be no delay; the difficulty of attack increased, the power of the assailants diminished with every year by which the peace was prolonged. Five years had scarce elapsed since the contest ended, and all the wounds must still have been bleeding which the twenty-two years' war had inflicted on the rural communes of Samnium, when in the year $\frac{456}{298}$ the Samnite confederacy renewed the struggle. The last war had been decided in favour of Rome mainly through the alliance of Lucania with the Romans and the consequent standing aloof of Tarentum. The Samnites, profiting by that lesson, now threw themselves in the first instance with all their might on the Lucanians, and succeeded in bringing their party in that quarter to the helm of affairs, and in concluding an alliance between Samnium and Lucania. Of course the Romans immediately declared war; the Samnites had expected no other issue. It is a significant indication of the state of feeling, that the Samnite government informed the Roman envoys that it was not able to guarantee their inviolability, if they should set foot on Samnite ground.

The war thus began anew ($\frac{456}{298}$), and while a second army was fighting in Etruria, the main Roman army traversed Samnium and compelled the Lucanians to make peace and send hostages to Rome. The following year both consuls were able to proceed to Samnium; Rullianus conquered at Tifernum, his faithful comrade in arms, Publius Decius Mus, at Maleventum, and for five months two Roman armies encamped in the land of the enemy. They were enabled to do so, because the Tuscan states had on their own behalf entered into negotiations for peace with Rome. The Samnites, who from the beginning could not but see that their only chance of victory lay in the combination of

Cassian appears in the Roman consular Fasti between Spurius Cassius, consul in $\frac{252}{502}$, $\frac{261}{494}$, and $\frac{268}{486}$—who of course is out of the question—and Gaius Cassius Longinus, consul in $\frac{583}{171}$.

all Italy against Rome, exerted themselves to the utmost to prevent the threatened separate peace between Etruria and Rome; and when at last their general, Gellius Egnatius, offered to render aid to the Etruscans in their own country, the Etruscan federal council in reality agreed to hold out and once more to appeal to the decision of arms. Samnium made the most energetic efforts to place three armies simultaneously in the field, the first destined for the defence of its own territory, the second for an invasion of Campania, the third and most numerous for Etruria; and in the year $\frac{458}{296}$ the last, led by Egnatius himself, actually reached Etruria in safety through the Marsian and Umbrian territories, with whose inhabitants there was an understanding. Meanwhile the Romans were capturing some strong places in Samnium and breaking the influence of the Samnite party in Lucania; they were not aware in time to prevent the departure of the army led by Egnatius. When information reached Rome that the Samnites had succeeded in frustrating all the enormous efforts made to sever the northern from the southern Italians, that the arrival of the Samnite bands in Etruria had become the signal of an almost universal rising against Rome, and that the Etruscan communities were labouring with the utmost zeal to get their own forces ready for war and to take into their pay Gallic bands, every nerve was strained also in Rome; the freedmen and the married were formed into cohorts—it was felt on all hands that the decisive crisis was near. The year $\frac{458}{296}$ however passed away, apparently, in armings and marchings. For the following year ($\frac{459}{295}$) the Romans placed their two best generals, Publius Decius Mus and the aged Quintus Fabius Rullianus, at the head of their army in Etruria, which was reinforced with all the troops that could be spared from Campania, and amounted to at least 60,000 men, of whom more than a third were full burgesses of Rome. Besides this, two reserves were formed, the first at Falerii, the second under the walls of the capital. The rendezvous of the Italians was Umbria, towards which the roads from the Gallic, Etruscan, and Sabellian territories converged; towards Umbria the consuls also moved off their main force, partly along the left, partly along the right bank of the Tiber, while at the same time the first reserve made a movement towards Etruria, in order if possible to recall the Etruscan troops from the main scene of action for the defence of their homes. The first engagement did not prove fortunate for the Romans; their advanced guard was defeated by the combined Gauls and Samnites in the district of Chiusi.

But the diversion accomplished its object.   Less magnanimous than the Samnites, who had marched through the ruins of their towns that they might not be absent from the chosen field of battle, a great part of the Etruscan contingents withdrew from the federal army on the news of the advance of the Roman reserve into Etruria, and its ranks were greatly thinned when the decisive battle came to be fought on the eastern declivity of the Apennines near Sentinum.

Nevertheless it was a hotly contested day.   On the right wing of the Romans, where Rullianus with his two legions fought against the Samnite army, the conflict remained long undecided. On the left, which Publius Decius commanded, the Roman cavalry was thrown into confusion by the Gallic war chariots, and the legions also already began to give way.   Then the consul called to him Marcus Livius the priest, and bade him devote to the infernal gods both the head of the Roman general and the army of the enemy; and plunging into the thickest throng of the Gauls he sought death and found it.   This heroic deed of despair in so distinguished a man and so beloved a general was not in vain.   The fugitive soldiers rallied; the bravest threw themselves after their leader into the hostile ranks, to avenge him or to die with him; and just at the right moment the consular Lucius Scipio, despatched by Rullianus, appeared with the Roman reserve on the imperilled left wing.   The admirable Campanian cavalry, which fell on the flank and rear of the Gauls, turned the scale; the Gauls fled, and at length the Samnites also gave way, their general Egnatius falling at the gate of the camp. Nine thousand Romans strewed the field of battle; but dearly as the victory was purchased, it was worthy of such a sacrifice. The army of the coalition was dissolved, and with it the coalition itself; Umbria remained in the power of the Romans, the Gauls dispersed, the remnant of the Samnites still in compact order retreated homeward through the Abruzzi.   Campania, which the Samnites had overrun during the Etruscan war, was after its close re-occupied with little difficulty by the Romans.   Etruria sued for peace in the following year ($\frac{460}{294}$); Volsinii, Perusia, Arretium, and in general all the towns that had joined the league against Rome, promised a cessation of hostilities for four hundred months.

But the Samnites were of a different mind; they prepared for their hopeless resistance with the courage of free men, which shames fate if it may not overrule it.   When the two consular armies advanced into Samnium, in the year $\frac{460}{294}$, they encountered

everywhere the most desperate resistance; in fact Marcus
Atilius was discomfited near Luceria, and the Samnites were able
to penetrate into Campania and to lay waste the territory of the
Roman colony Interamna on the Liris. In the ensuing year
Lucius Papirius Cursor, the son of the hero of the first Samnite
war, and Spurius Carvilius, gave battle on a great scale near
Aquilonia to the Samnite army, the flower of which—the 16,000
in white tunics—had sworn a sacred oath to prefer death to
flight. Inexorable destiny, however, heeds neither the oaths
nor the supplications of despair; the Romans conquered and
stormed the strongholds where the Samnites had sought
refuge for themselves and their property. Even after this
great defeat the confederates still for years resisted the ever-
increasing superiority of the enemy with unparalleled perseverance in their fastnesses and mountains, and still achieved
various isolated advantages. The experienced arm of the old
Rullianus was once more called into the field against them ($\frac{462}{292}$),
and Gavius Pontius, a son perhaps of the victor of Caudium,
even gained for his nation a last victory, which the Romans
meanly enough avenged by causing him when subsequently
taken to be executed in prison ($\frac{463}{291}$). But there was no further
symptom of movement in Italy; for the war, which Falerii
began in $\frac{461}{293}$, scarcely deserves such a name. The Samnites
doubtless turned with longing eyes towards Tarentum, which
alone was still in a position to grant them aid; but it held aloof.
The same causes as before occasioned its inaction—internal
misgovernment, and the passing over of the Lucanians once
more to the Roman party in the year $\frac{456}{298}$; to which fell to
be added a not unfounded apprehension of Agathocles of Syracuse, who just at that time had reached the height of his
power and began to turn his views towards Italy. About $\frac{455}{299}$
the latter established himself in Corcyra whence Cleonymus
had been expelled by Demetrius Poliorcetes, and now threatened
the Tarentines from the Adriatic as well as from the Ionian sea.
The cession of the island to king Pyrrhus of Epirus in $\frac{459}{295}$
certainly removed to a great extent the apprehensions which
they had cherished; but the affairs of Corcyra continued to
occupy the Tarentines—in the year $\frac{464}{290}$, for instance, they helped
to protect Pyrrhus in possession of the island against Demetrius
—and in like manner Agathocles did not cease to give the Tarentines uneasiness by his Italian policy. When he died ($\frac{465}{289}$),
and with him the power of the Syracusans in Italy went to
wreck, it was too late; Samnium, weary of the thirty-seven

years' war, had concluded peace in the previous year ($\frac{464}{290}$) with the Roman consul Manius Curius Dentatus, and had in form renewed its league with Rome. On this occasion, as in the peace of $\frac{450}{304}$, no disgraceful or destructive conditions were imposed on the brave people by the Romans; no cessions even of territory seem to have taken place. The political sagacity of Rome preferred to follow the path which it had hitherto pursued, and to attach in the first place the Campanian and Adriatic coast more and more securely to Rome before proceeding to the direct conquest of the interior. Campania, indeed, had been long in subjection; but the far-seeing policy of Rome found it needful, in order to secure the Campanian coast, to establish two coast-fortresses there, Minturnae and Sinuessa ($\frac{459}{295}$), the new burgesses of which were admitted according to the settled rule in the case of maritime colonies to the full citizenship of Rome. With still greater energy the extension of the Roman rule was prosecuted in central Italy. There the whole of the Sabines after a brief and feeble resistance were forced to become subjects of Rome ($\frac{464}{290}$), and the strong fortress of Hatria was established in the Abruzzi, not far from the coast ($\frac{465}{289}$). But the most important colony of all was that of Venusia ($\frac{463}{291}$), whither the unprecedented number of 20,000 colonists was conducted. That city, founded at the boundary of Samnium, Apulia, and Lucania, on the great road between Tarentum and Samnium, in an uncommonly strong position, was destined as a curb to keep in check the surrounding tribes, and above all to interrupt the communications between the two most powerful enemies of Rome in southern Italy. Beyond doubt at the same time the southern highway, which Appius Claudius had carried to Capua, was prolonged thence to Venusia. Thus the compact Roman domain at the close of the Samnite wars extended on the north to the Ciminian forest, on the east to the Abruzzi, on the south to Capua, while the two advanced posts, Luceria and Venusia, established towards the east and south on the lines of communication of their opponents, isolated them on every side. Rome was no longer merely the first, but was already the ruling power in the peninsula, when towards the end of the fifth century of the city those nations, which had been raised to supremacy in their respective lands by the favour of the gods and by their own capacity, began to come into contact in council and on the battle-field; and, as at Olympia the preliminary victors girt themselves for a second and more serious struggle, so on the larger arena of the nations, Carthage, Macedonia, and Rome now prepared for the final and decisive contest.

CHAPTER VII

STRUGGLE BETWEEN PYRRHUS AND ROME, AND UNION
OF ITALY

AFTER Rome had acquired the undisputed mastery of the world, the Greeks were wont to annoy their Roman masters by the assertion that Rome was indebted for her greatness to the fever of which Alexander of Macedon died at Babylon on the 11th of June, $\frac{431}{323}$. As it was not very agreeable for them to reflect on the actual past, they were fond of allowing their thoughts to dwell on what might have happened, had the great king turned his arms—as was said to have been his intention at the time of his death—towards the west and contested the Carthaginian supremacy by sea with his fleet, and the Roman supremacy by land with his phalanxes. It is not impossible that Alexander may have cherished such thoughts; nor is it necessary to resort for an explanation of their origin to the mere difficulty which an autocrat, who is fond of war and is well provided with soldiers and ships, experiences in setting limits to his warlike career. It was an enterprise worthy of a great Greek king to protect the Siceliots against Carthage and the Tarentines against Rome, and to put an end to piracy on either sea; and the Italian embassies from the Bruttians, Lucanians, and Etruscans,[1] that along with numerous others made their appearance at Babylon, afforded him sufficient opportunities of becoming acquainted with the circumstances of the peninsula and of entering into relations with it. Carthage with its many connections in the east could not but attract the attention of the mighty monarch, and it was probably one or

[1] The story that the Romans also sent envoys to Alexander at Babylon rests on the testimony of Clitarchus (Plin. *Hist. Nat.* iii. 5, 57), from whom the other authorities who mention the fact (Aristus and Asclepiades, *ap* Arrian, vii. 15, 5; Memnon, *c.* 25), doubtless derived it. Clitarchus certainly was contemporary with these events; nevertheless, his Life of Alexander was decidedly an historical romance rather than a history: and, looking to the silence of the trustworthy biographers (Arrian, *l. c.* ; Liv. ix. 18) and the utterly romantic details of the account—which represents the Romans, for instance, as delivering to Alexander a chaplet of gold, and the latter as prophesying the future greatness of Rome—we cannot but set down the story as one of the many embellishments which Clitarchus introduced into the history.

his designs to convert the nominal sovereignty of the Persian
king over the Tyrian colony into a real one: the apprehensions of
the Carthaginians are shown by the Phoenician spy in the retinue
of Alexander. Whether, however, these ideas were dreams or
actual projects, the king died without having interfered in the
affairs of the west, and his ideas were buried with him. For a
few brief years a Greek ruler had held in his hand the whole intellectual vigour of the Hellenic race combined with the whole
material resources of the east. On his death the work to which
his life had been devoted—the establishment of Hellenism in
the east—was by no means undone; but his empire had barely
been united when it was again dismembered, and, amidst the
constant quarrels of the different states that were formed out
of its ruins, the object of world-wide interest which they were
destined to promote—the diffusion of Greek culture in the east—
though not abandoned, was prosecuted on a feeble and stunted
scale. Under such circumstances, neither the Greek nor the
Asiatico-Egyptian states could think of acquiring a footing in the
west or of turning their efforts against the Romans or the
Carthaginians. The eastern and western state-systems subsisted
side by side for a time without crossing, politically, each other's
path; and Rome in particular remained substantially aloof from
the quarrels of Alexander's successors. The only relations established with them were of a mercantile kind; as in the instance of
the free state of Rhodes, the leading representative of the policy
of commercial neutrality in Greece and in consequence the universal medium of intercourse in an age of perpetual wars, which
about $\frac{448}{306}$ concluded a treaty with Rome—a commercial convention of course, such as was natural between a mercantile
people and the masters of the Caerite and Campanian coasts.
Even in the supply of mercenaries from Hellas, the universal
recruiting field of those times, to Italy, and to Tarentum in
particular, political relations—such as subsisted, for instance,
between Tarentum and Sparta its mother-city—exercised but
a very subordinate influence. In general the raising of mercenaries was simply a matter of traffic, and Sparta, although
it regularly supplied the Tarentines with captains for their
Italian wars, was by that course as little involved in hostilities
with the Italians, as in the North American war of independence
the German states were involved in hostilities with the Union, to
whose opponents they sold the services of their subjects.

Pyrrhus, king of Epirus, was himself simply a military
adventurer. He was none the less a soldier of fortune that he

traced back his pedigree to Aeacus and Achilles, and that, had he been more peacefully disposed, he might have lived and died as the " king " of a small mountain tribe under the supremacy of Macedon or perhaps in isolated independence. He has been compared to Alexander of Macedon; and certainly the idea of founding an Hellenic empire of the west—which would have been based on Epirus, Magna Graecia, and Sicily, would have commanded both the Italian seas, and would have reduced Rome and Carthage to the rank of barbarian peoples bordering on the Hellenistic state-system, like the Celts and the Indians—was analogous in greatness and boldness to the idea which led the Macedonian king over the Hellespont. But it was not the mere difference of issue that formed the distinction between the expedition to the east and that to the west. Alexander with his Macedonian army, in which the staff especially was excellent, could fully make head against the great king; but the king of Epirus, which bore somewhat the same proportion to Macedon as Hesse lately bore to Prussia, could only raise an army worthy of the name by means of mercenaries and of alliances based on accidental political combinations. Alexander made his appearance in the Persian empire as a conqueror; Pyrrhus appeared in Italy as the general of a coalition of secondary states. Alexander left his hereditary dominions completely secured by the unconditional subjection of Greece, and by the strong army that remained behind under Antipater; Pyrrhus had no security for the integrity of his native dominions but the word of a doubtful neighbour. In the case of both conquerors, if their plans should be crowned with success, their native country would necessarily cease to be the centre of their new empire; but it was far more practicable to transfer the seat of the Macedonian military monarchy to Babylon than to found a soldier-dynasty in Tarentum or Syracuse. The democracy of the Greek republics— perpetual agony though it was—could not be at all coerced into the stiff forms of a military state; Philip had good reason for not incorporating the Greek republics with his empire. In the east no national resistance was to be expected; ruling and subject races had long lived there side by side, and a change of despot was a matter of indifference or even of satisfaction to the mass of the population. In the west the Romans, the Samnites, the Carthaginians, might be vanquished; but no conqueror could have transformed the Italians into Egyptian fellahs, or rendered the Roman farmers tributaries of Hellenic barons. Whatever we take into view—whether their own power, their allies, or the resources of their antagonists—in all points the plan of the Macedonian appears as a feasible, that of the Epirot as an impracticable, enterprise; the former as the completion of a great historical task, the latter as a remarkable blunder; the former as the foundation of a new system of states and of a new phase of civilisation, the latter as a mere episode in history. The work of Alexander outlived him, although its creator met an untimely death; Pyrrhus witnessed with his own eyes the wreck of all his plans, ere death called him away. Both had natures great and enterprising, but Pyrrhus was only the foremost general, Alexander was eminently the most gifted statesman, of his time; and, if it is insight into what is and what is not possible that distinguishes the hero from the adventurer, Pyrrhus must be numbered among the latter class, and may as little be placed on a parallel with his greater relative as the Constable of Bourbon may be put in comparison with Louis the Eleventh.

And yet a wondrous charm attaches to the name of the Epirot—a peculiar sympathy, evoked certainly in some degree by his chivalrous and amiable character, but still more by the circumstance that he was the first Greek that met the Romans in battle. With him began those direct relations between Rome and Hellas, on which the whole subsequent development of ancient, and an essential part of modern, civilisation are based. The struggle between phalanxes and cohorts, between a mercenary army and a militia, between military monarchy and senatorial government, between individual talent and national vigour—this struggle between Rome and Hellenism was first fought out in the battles between Pyrrhus and the Roman generals; and though the defeated party often afterwards appealed anew to the arbitration of arms, every succeeding day of battle simply confirmed the decision. But while the Greeks were beaten in the battle-field as well as in the senate-hall, their superiority was none the less decided on every other field of rivalry than that of politics; and these very struggles already betokened that the victory of Rome over the Hellenes would be different from her victories over Gauls and Phoenicians, and that the charm of Aphrodite only begins to work when the lance is broken and the helmet and shield are laid aside.

King Pyrrhus was the son of Aeacides, ruler of the Molossians (about Janina), who, spared as a kinsman and faithful vassal by Alexander, had been after his death drawn into the whirlpool of Macedonian family-politics, and lost in it first his kingdom and then his life ($\frac{441}{313}$). His son, then six years of age, was saved by Glaucias the ruler of the Illyrian Taulantii, and in the course of the conflicts for the possession of Macedonia he was, when still a boy, restored by Demetrius Poliorcetes to his hereditary principality ($\frac{447}{307}$)—but only to lose it again after a few years through the influence of the opposite party (about $\frac{452}{302}$), and to begin his military career as an exiled prince in the train of the Macedonian generals. Soon his peculiar genius asserted itself conspicuously. He shared in the last campaigns of Antigonus; and the old marshal of Alexander took delight in the born soldier, who in the judgment of the grey-headed general only wanted years to be already the first warrior of the age. The unfortunate battle at Ipsus brought him as a hostage to Alexandria, to the court of the founder of the Lagid dynasty, where by his daring and downright character, and his soldierly spirit thoroughly despising everything that was not military, he attracted the attention of the politic king Ptolemy no less than he attracted the notice of the royal ladies by his manly beauty, the effect of which was not impaired by the wildness of his countenance and the stateliness of his stride. Just at this time the enterprising Demetrius was once more establishing himself in a new kingdom, which on this occasion was Macedonia; of course with the intention of using it as a lever to revive the monarchy of Alexander. To keep down his ambitious designs, it was important to give him employment at home; and Ptolemy, who knew how to make admirable use of such fiery spirits as the Epirot youth in the prosecution of his subtle policy, not only met the wishes of his consort queen Berenice, but also promoted his own ends, by giving his step-daughter the princess Antigone in marriage to the young prince, and lending his aid and powerful influence to support the return of his beloved " son " to his native land ($\frac{458}{296}$). Restored to his paternal kingdom he soon carried all before him. The brave Epirots, the Albanians of antiquity, clung with hereditary loyalty and fresh enthusiasm to the high-spirited youth—the " eagle," as they called him. In the confusion that arose regarding the succession to the Macedonian throne after the death of Cassander ($\frac{457}{297}$), the Epirot extended his dominions: step by step he gained the regions on the Ambracian gulf with the important town of Ambracia, the island of Corcyra, and even a part of the Macedonian territory, and with forces far inferior he made head against king Demetrius to the admiration of the Macedonians themselves. Indeed, when Demetrius was by his own folly hurled from the Macedonian throne, it was voluntarily proffered by them to his chivalrous opponent, a kinsman of the Alexandrine house ($\frac{476}{287}$). No one was in reality worthier than Pyrrhus to wear the royal diadem of Philip and of Alexander. In an age of deep depravity, in which princely rank and baseness began to be synonymous, the personally unspotted and morally pure character of Pyrrhus shone conspicuous. For the free farmers of the hereditary Macedonian soil, who, although diminished and impoverished, were far from sharing in that decay of morals and of valour which the government of the Diadochi produced in Greece and Asia, Pyrrhus appeared exactly formed to be the fitting king,—Pyrrhus, who, like Alexander, in his household and in the circle of his friends preserved a heart open to all human sympathies, and constantly avoided the bearing of an oriental sultan which was so odious to the Macedonians; and who, like Alexander, was acknowledged to be the first tactician of his time. But the singularly overstrained national feeling of the Macedonians, which preferred the most paltry Macedonian sovereign to the ablest foreigner, and the irrational insubordination of the Macedonian troops towards every non-Macedonian leader, to which Eumenes the Cardian, the greatest general of the school of Alexander, had fallen a victim, put a speedy termination to the rule of the prince of Epirus. Pyrrhus, who could not exercise sovereignty over Macedonia with the consent of the Macedonians, and who was too powerless and perhaps too high spirited to force himself on the nation against its will, after reigning seven months left the country to its native misgovernment, and went home to his faithful Epirots ($\frac{467}{287}$). But the man who had worn the crown of Alexander, the brother-in-law of Demetrius, the son-in-law of Ptolemy Lagides and of Agathocles of Syracuse, the highly-trained tactician who wrote memoirs and scientific treatises on the military art, could not possibly spend his life in the ordinary routine of an Epirot prince—in inspecting at a set time yearly the accounts of the royal cattle-steward, in receiving from his brave Epirots their customary presents of oxen and sheep, in requiring thereafter the renewal of their oath of allegiance and repeating his own engagement to respect the laws at the altar of Zeus, and for the better confirmation of the whole carousing with them all night long. If there was no place for him on the throne of Macedonia, he could not remain in the land of his nativity at all; he was fitted for the first place, and he could not be content with the second. His views therefore turned abroad. The kings, who were quarrelling for the possession of Macedonia, although agreeing in nothing else, were ready and glad to concur in promoting the voluntary departure of their dangerous rival; and that his faithful war-comrades would follow him wherever he led, he knew full well. Just at that time the circumstances of Italy were such, that the project which had been meditated forty years before by Pyrrhus' kinsman, his father's cousin, Alexander of Epirus, and quite recently by his father-in-law Agathocles, once more seemed feasible; and so Pyrrhus resolved to abandon his Macedonian schemes and to found for himself and for the Hellenic nation a new empire in the west.

The interval of repose, which the peace with Samnium in $\frac{464}{290}$ had procured for Italy, was of brief duration; the impulse which led to the formation of a new league against Roman ascendancy came on this occasion from the Lucanians. This people, by taking part with Rome during the Samnite wars, paralysed the the action of the Tarentines and essentially contributed to the decisive issue; and in consideration of their services, the Romans gave up to them the Greek cities in their territory. Accordingly after the conclusion of peace they had, in concert with the Bruttians, applied themselves to subdue these cities in succession. The Thurines, repeatedly assailed by Stenius Statilius the general of the Lucanians and reduced to extremities, requested assistance against the Lucanians from the Roman senate, just as formerly the Campanians had asked the aid of Rome against the Samnites, and beyond doubt with a like sacrifice of their liberty and independence. In consequence of the founding of the fortress Venusia, Rome could dispense with the alliance of the Lucanians; so the Romans granted the prayer of the Thurines, and enjoined their friends and allies to desist from their designs on a city which had surrendered itself to Rome. The Lucanians and Bruttians, thus cheated by their more powerful allies of their share in the common spoil, entered into negotiations with the opposition-party among the Samnites and Tarentines to produce a new Italian coalition; and when the Romans sent an embassy to warn them, they detained the envoys in captivity and began the war against Rome with a new attack on Thurii (about $\frac{469}{285}$), while at the same time they invited not only the Samnites and Tarentines, but the northern Italians also—the Etruscans, Umbrians, and Gauls—to join them in the struggle for freedom. The Etruscan league actually revolted, and hired numerous bands of Gauls; the Roman army, which the praetor Lucius Caecilius was leading to the help of the Arretines who had remained faithful, was annihilated under the walls of Arretium by the Senonian mercenaries of the Etruscans: the general

himself fell with 13,000 of his men ($\frac{470}{284}$). The Senones were
reckoned allies of Rome; the Romans accordingly sent envoys
to them to complain of their furnishing soldiers to serve against
Rome, and to require the surrender of their captives without
ransom. But by the command of their chieftain Britomaris,
who had to take vengeance on the Romans for the death of his
father, the Senones slew the Roman envoys and openly took
the Etruscan side. All the north of Italy, Etruscans, Umbrians,
Gauls, were thus in arms against Rome; great results might be
achieved, if its southern provinces also would embrace the opportunity and declare, so far as they had not already done so,
against Rome. In fact the Samnites, ever ready to make a
stand on behalf of liberty, appear to have declared war against
the Romans; but weakened and hemmed in on all sides as they
were, they could be of little service to the league; and Tarentum
manifested its wonted delay. While her antagonists were
negotiating alliances, settling treaties as to subsidies, and col-
lecting mercenaries, Rome was acting. The Senones were first
made to feel how dangerous it was to gain a victory over the
Romans. The consul Publius Cornelius Dolabella advanced
with a strong army into their territory; all that were not put to
the sword were driven forth from the land, and this tribe was
erased from the list of the Italian nations ($\frac{471}{283}$). In the case of
a people subsisting chiefly on its flocks and herds such an expulsion *en masse* was quite practicable; and the Senones thus
expelled from Italy probably helped to compose the Gallic hosts
which soon after inundated the countries of the Danube, Macedonia, Greece, and Asia Minor. The next neighbours and kinsmen of the Senones, the Boii, terrified and exasperated by a
catastrophe which had been accomplished with so fearful a
rapidity, united instantaneously with the Etruscans, who still
continued the war, and whose Senonian mercenaries now fought
against the Romans no longer as hirelings, but as desperate
avengers of their native land. A powerful Etrusco-Gallic army
marched against Rome to retaliate the annihilation of the
Senonian tribe on the enemy's capital, and to extirpate Rome
from the face of the earth more completely than had been
formerly done by the chieftain of these same Senones. But the
combined army was decidedly defeated by the Romans at its
passage of the Tiber in the neighbourhood of the lake of Vadimo
($\frac{471}{283}$). After they had once more in the following year risked a
general engagement near Populonia with no better success, the
Boii deserted their confederates and concluded a peace on their

own account with the Romans ($\frac{472}{282}$). Thus the Gauls, the most formidable members of the league, were conquered in detail before the league was fully formed, and by that means the hands of Rome were left free to act against Lower Italy, where during the years $\frac{469-471}{285-283}$ the contest had not been carried on with any vigour. Hitherto the weak Roman army had with difficulty maintained itself in Thurii against the Lucanians and Bruttians; but now ($\frac{472}{282}$) the consul Gaius Fabricius Luscinus appeared with a strong army in front of the town, relieved it, defeated the Lucanians in a great engagement, and took their general Statilius prisoner. The smaller non-Doric Greek towns, recognising the Romans as their deliverers, everywhere voluntarily joined them. Roman garrisons were left behind in the most important places, in Locri, Croton, Thurii, and especially in Rhegium, on which latter town the Carthaginians seem also to have had designs. Everywhere Rome had most decidedly the advantage. The annihilation of the Senones had given to the Romans a considerable tract of the Adriatic coast. With a view, doubtless, to the smouldering feud with Tarentum and the already threatened invasion of the Epirots, they hastened to make themselves sure of this coast as well as of the Adriatic sea. A burgess colony was sent out (about $\frac{471}{283}$) to the seaport of Sena (Sinigaglia), the former capital of the Senonian territory; and at the same time a Roman fleet sailed from the Tyrrhene sea into the eastern waters, manifestly for the purpose of being stationed in the Adriatic and of protecting the Roman possessions there.

The Tarentines since the treaty of $\frac{450}{304}$ had lived at peace with Rome. They had been spectators of the long struggles of the Samnites, and of the rapid extirpation of the Senones; they had acquiesced without remonstrance in the establishment of Venusia, Hatria, and Sena, and in the occupation of Thurii and of Rhegium. But when the Roman fleet, on its voyage from the Tyrrhene to the Adriatic sea, now arrived in the Tarentine waters and cast anchor in the harbour of the friendly city, the long-cherished resentment at length overflowed. Old treaties, which prohibited the war-vessels of Rome from sailing to the east of the Lacinian promontory, were appealed to by popular orators in the assembly of the citizens. A furious mob fell upon the Roman ships of war, which, assailed suddenly in a piratical fashion, succumbed after a sharp struggle; five ships were taken and their crews executed or sold into slavery; the Roman admiral himself had fallen in the engagement. Only the supreme folly and supreme unscrupulousness of mob-rule can

account for those disgraceful proceedings. The treaties referred to belonged to a period long past and forgotten; it is
clear that they no longer had any meaning, at least subsequently
to the founding of Hatria and Sena, and that the Romans entered
the bay on the faith of the existing alliance; indeed, it was very
much their interest—as the further course of things showed—
—to afford the Tarentines no sort of pretext for declaring war.
In declaring war against Rome—if such was their wish—the
statesmen of Tarentum were only doing what they should have
done long before; and if they preferred to rest their declaration
of war upon the formal pretext of a breach of treaty rather than
upon the actual ground, no objection could be taken to that
course, seeing that diplomacy has always reckoned it beneath
its dignity to speak the plain truth in plain language. But to
make an armed attack upon the fleet without warning, instead of
summoning the admiral to retrace his course, was a foolish no
less than a barbarous act—one of those horrible barbarities of
civilisation, when moral principle suddenly forsakes the helm
and the merest coarseness emerges in its room, as if to warn us
against the childish belief that civilisation is able to extirpate
brutality from human nature.

And, as if what they had done had not been enough, the
Tarentines after this heroic feat attacked Thurii, the Roman
garrison of which capitulated in consequence of a surprise (in
the winter of $\frac{472-473}{282-281}$); and inflicted severe chastisement on
the Thurines—the same, who had so often been abandoned by
Tarentum itself in terms of agreement to the Lucanians, and
for that very reason had been compelled to yield to Rome—
for their desertion from the Hellenic party to the side of the
barbarians.

The barbarians, however, acted with a moderation which,
considering their power and the provocation they had received,
excites astonishment. It was the interest of Rome to maintain
as long as possible the Tarentine neutrality, and the leading
men in the senate accordingly rejected the proposal, which a
minority had with natural resentment submitted, to declare
war at once against the Tarentines. In fact, the continuance of
peace on the part of Rome was proffered on the most moderate
terms consistent with her honour—the release of the captives,
the restoration of Thurii, the surrender of the originators of the
attack on the fleet. A Roman embassy proceeded with these
proposals to Tarentum ($\frac{473}{281}$), while at the same time, to add
weight to their words, a Roman army under the consul Lucius

Aemilius advanced into Samnium. The Tarentines could, without forfeiting aught of their independence, accept these terms; and considering the little inclination for war in so wealthy a commercial city, the Romans had reason to presume that an accommodation was still possible. But the attempt to preserve peace failed, whether through the opposition of those Tarentines who recognised the necessity of meeting the aggressions of Rome, the sooner the better, by a resort to arms, or merely through the unruliness of the city rabble, which with characteristic Greek sauciness subjected the person of the envoy to an unworthy insult. The consul now advanced into the Tarentine territory; but instead of immediately commencing hostilities, he offered once more the same terms of peace; and, when this proved in vain, he began to lay waste the fields and country houses, and he defeated the civic militia. The principal persons captured, however, were released without ransom; and the hope was not abandoned that the pressure of war would give to the aristocratic party ascendancy in the city and so bring about peace. The reason of this reserve was, that the Romans were unwilling to drive the city into the arms of the Epirot king. His designs on Italy were no longer a secret. A Tarentine embassy had already gone to Pyrrhus and returned without having accomplished its object. The king had demanded more than it had powers to grant. It was necessary that they should come to a decision. That the civic militia knew only how to run away from the Romans, had been made sufficiently clear. There remained only the choice between a peace with Rome, which the Romans still were ready to agree to on equitable terms, and a treaty with Pyrrhus on any conditions that the king might think proper; or, in other words, the choice between submission to the supremacy of Rome, and subjection to the despotism of a Greek soldier. The parties in the city were almost equally balanced. At length the ascendancy remained with the national party—a result that was due partly to the justifiable predilection which led them, if they must yield to a master at all, to prefer a Greek to a barbarian, but partly also to the dread of the demagogues that Rome, notwithstanding the moderation now forced upon it by circumstances, would not neglect on a fitting opportunity to exact vengeance for the outrages perpetrated by the Tarentine rabble. The city, accordingly, came to terms with Pyrrhus. He obtained the supreme command of the troops of the Tarentines and of the other Italians in arms against Rome, along with the right of keeping a garrison in Tarentum. The expenses of the war were, of course, to be borne by the city. Pyrrhus, on the other hand, promised to remain no longer in Italy than was necessary; probably with the tacit reservation that his own judgment should fix the term during which he might be needed there. Nevertheless, the prey had almost slipped out of his hands. While the Tarentine envoys—the chiefs, no doubt, of the war party—were absent in Epirus, the state of feeling in the city, now hard pressed by the Romans, underwent a change. The chief command was already entrusted to Agis, a man favourable to Rome, when the return of the envoys with the concluded treaty, accompanied by Cineas the confidential minister of Pyrrhus, again brought the war party to the helm. A firmer hand now grasped the reins, and put an end to the pitiful vacillation. In the autumn of $\frac{473}{281}$ Milo, the general of Pyrrhus, landed with 3000 Epirots and occupied the citadel of the town. He was followed in the beginning of the year $\frac{474}{280}$ by the king himself, who landed after a stormy passage in which many lives were lost. He transported to Tarentum a respectable but miscellaneous army, consisting partly of household troops, Molossians, Thesprotians, Chaonians, and Ambraciots; partly of the Macedonian infantry and the Thessalian cavalry, which Ptolemy king of Macedonia had conformably to stipulation handed over to him; partly of Aetolian, Acarnanian, and Athamanian mercenaries. Altogether, it numbered 20,000 phalangitae, 2000 archers, 500 slingers, 3000 cavalry, and 20 elephants, and thus was not much smaller than the army with which fifty years before Alexander had crossed the Hellespont.

The affairs of the coalition were in no very favourable state when the king arrived. The Roman consul indeed, as soon as he saw the soldiers of Milo taking the field against him instead of the Tarentine militia, had abandoned the attack on Tarentum and retreated to Apulia; but, with the exception of the territory of Tarentum, the Romans virtually ruled all Italy. The coalition had no army in the field anywhere in Lower Italy; and in Upper Italy the Etruscans, who alone were still in arms, had in the last campaign ($\frac{473}{281}$) met with nothing but defeat. The allies had, before the king embarked, committed to him the chief command of all their troops, and declared that they were able to place in the field an army of 350,000 infantry and 20,000 cavalry. The reality formed a sad contrast to these great promises. The army, whose chief command had been committed to Pyrrhus, had still to be created; and for the time

being the main resources available for forming it were those of
Tarentum alone. The king gave orders for the raising of an
army of Italian mercenaries at the expense of Tarentum, and
called out the able-bodied citizens to serve in the war. But
the Tarentines had not so understood the agreement. They
had thought to purchase victory, like any other commodity, with
money; it was a sort of breach of contract, that the king should
compel them to fight for it themselves. The more glad the
citizens had been at first after Milo's arrival to be quit of the
burdensome service of mounting guard, the more unwillingly
they now rallied to the standards of the king: it was necessary
to threaten the negligent with the penalty of death. This
result now justified the peace party in the eyes of all, and communications were entered into, or at any rate appeared to have
been entered into, even with Rome. Pyrrhus, prepared for such
opposition, immediately treated Tarentum as a conquered city;
soldiers were quartered in the houses, the assemblies of the people
and the numerous clubs (συσσίτια) were suspended, the theatre
was shut, the promenades were closed, and the gates were
occupied with Epirot guards. A number of the leading men
were sent over the sea as hostages; others escaped the like fate
by flight to Rome. These strict measures were necessary, for
it was absolutely impossible in any sense to rely upon the Tarentines. It was only now that the king, in possession of that
important city as a basis, could begin operations in the field.

The Romans too were all aware of the conflict which awaited
them. In order first of all to secure the fidelity of their allies or,
in other words, of their subjects, the towns that could not be
depended on were garrisoned, and the leaders of the party of independence, where it seemed needful, were arrested or executed:
such was the case with a number of the members of the senate of
Praeneste. For the war itself great exertions were made; a war
contribution was levied; the full contingent was called forth from
all their subjects and allies; even the proletarians who were
properly exempt from obligation of service were called to arms.
A Roman army remained as a reserve in the capital. A second
advanced under the consul Tiberius Coruncanius into Etruria,
and dispersed the forces of Volci and Volsinii. The main force
was of course destined for Lower Italy; its departure was
hastened as much as possible, in order to reach Pyrrhus while
still in the territory of Tarentum, and to prevent him and his
forces from forming a junction with the Samnites and other
south Italian levies that were in arms against Rome. The

Roman garrisons, that were placed in the Greek towns of Lower Italy, were intended temporarily to check the king's progress. But the mutiny of the troops stationed in Rhegium—800 Campanians, and 400 Sidicines, under a Campanian captain Decius—deprived the Romans of that important town. It was not, however, transferred to the hands of Pyrrhus. While on the one hand the national hatred of the Campanians against the Romans undoubtedly contributed to produce this military insurrection, it was impossible on the other hand that Pyrrhus, who had crossed the sea to shield and protect the Hellenes, could receive as his allies troops who had put to death their Rhegine hosts in their own houses. Thus they remained isolated, in close league with their kinsmen and comrades in crime, the Mamertines, that is the Campanian mercenaries of Agathocles, who had by similar means gained possession of Messana on the opposite side of the straits; and they pillaged and laid waste for their own behoof the adjacent Greek towns, such as Croton, where they put to death the Roman garrison, and Caulonia, which they destroyed. On the other hand the Romans succeeded, by means of a weak corps which advanced along the Lucanian frontier and of the garrison of Venusia, in preventing the Lucanians and Samnites from uniting with Pyrrhus; while the main force—four legions as it would appear, and so, with a corresponding number of allied troops, at least 50,000 strong—marched against Pyrrhus, under the consul Publius Laevinus.

With a view to cover the Tarentine colony of Heraclea, the king had taken up a position with his own and the Tarentine troops between that city and Pandosia[1] ($\frac{474}{280}$). The Romans, covered by their cavalry, forced the passage of the Siris, and opened the battle with a fiery and successful cavalry charge; the king, who led his cavalry in person, was thrown from his horse, and the Greek horsemen, panic-struck by the disappearance of their leader, abandoned the field to the squadrons of the enemy. Pyrrhus, however, put himself at the head of his infantry, and began a fresh and more decisive engagement. Seven times the legions and the phalanx met in shock of battle, and still the conflict was undecided. Then Megacles, one of the best officers of the king, fell, and, because on this hotly contested day he had worn the king's armour, the army for the second time believed that the king had fallen; the ranks wavered; Laevinus already felt sure of the victory and threw the whole of

---

[1] Near the modern Anglona; not to be confounded with the better known town of the same name in the district of Cosenza.

his cavalry on the flank of the Greeks. But Pyrrhus, marching with uncovered head through the ranks of the infantry, revived the sinking courage of his troops. The elephants which had hitherto been kept in reserve were brought up to meet the cavalry; the horses took fright at them; the soldiers, not knowing how to encounter the huge beasts, turned and fled; the masses of disordered horsemen and the pursuing elephants at length broke the compact ranks of the Roman infantry, and the elephants in concert with the excellent Thessalian cavalry wrought great slaughter among the fugitives. Had not a brave Roman soldier, Gaius Minucius, the first hastate of the fourth legion, wounded one of the elephants and thereby thrown the pursuing troops into confusion, the Roman army would have been extirpated; as it was, the remainder of the Roman troops succeeded in retreating across the Siris. Their loss was great; 7000 Romans were found by the victors dead or wounded on the field of battle, 2000 were brought in prisoners; the Romans themselves stated their loss, including probably the wounded carried off the field, at 15,000 men. But Pyrrhus's army had suffered not much less: nearly 4000 of his best soldiers strewed the field of battle, and several of his ablest captains had fallen. Considering that his loss fell chiefly on the veteran soldiers who were far more difficult to be replaced than the Roman militia, and that he owed his victory only to the surprise produced by the attack of the elephants which could not be often repeated, the king, skilful judge of tactics as he was, may well at an after period have described this victory as resembling a defeat; although he was not so foolish as to communicate that piece of self-criticism to the public—as the Roman poets afterwards invented the story—in the inscription of the votive offering presented by him at Tarentum. Politically it mattered little in the first instance at what sacrifices the victory was bought; the gain of the first battle against the Romans was of inestimable value for Pyrrhus. His talents as a general had been brilliantly displayed on this new field of battle, and if anything could breathe unity and energy into the languishing league of the Italians, the victory of Heraclea could not fail to do so. But even the immediate results of the victory were considerable and lasting. Lucania was lost to the Romans: Laevinus collected the troops stationed there and marched to Apulia. The Bruttians, Lucanians, and Samnites joined Pyrrhus unmolested. With the exception of Rhegium, which pined under the oppression of the Campanian mutineers, the whole of the Greek cities joined the king, and Locri was even voluntarily surrendered to him by the Roman garrison; in his case they were persuaded, and with reason, that they would not be abandoned to the Italians. The Sabellians and Greeks thus passed over to Pyrrhus; but the victory produced no further effect. The Latins showed no inclination to get quit of the Roman rule, burdensome as it might be, by the help of a foreign dynast. Venusia, although now wholly surrounded by enemies, adhered with unshaken steadfastness to Rome. Pyrrhus proposed to the prisoners taken on the Siris, whose brave demeanour the chivalrous king requited by the most honourable treatment, that they should enter his army in accordance with the Greek fashion; but he learned that he was fighting not with mercenaries, but with a nation. Not one, either Roman or Latin, took service with him.

Pyrrhus proposed peace to the Romans. He was too sagacious a soldier not to recognise the precariousness of his footing, and too skilled a statesman not to profit opportunely by the moment which placed him in the most favourable position for the conclusion of peace. He now hoped that under the first impression made by the great battle on the Romans he should be able to secure the freedom of the Greek towns in Italy, and to call into existence between them and Rome a series of states of the second and third order as dependent allies of the new Greek power; for such was the tenor of his demands: the release of all Greek towns—and therefore of the Campanian and Lucanian towns in particular—from allegiance to Rome, and restitution of the territory taken from the Samnites, Daunians, Lucanians, and Bruttians, or in other words especially the surrender of Luceria and Venusia. A further struggle with Rome might be inevitable, but it was not desirable at any rate to begin it till the western Hellenes should be united under one ruler, till Sicily should be acquired and perhaps Africa be conquered.

Provided with such instructions, the Thessalian Cineas, the confidential minister of Pyrrhus, went to Rome. That dexterous negotiator, whom his contemporaries compared to Demosthenes so far as a rhetorician might be compared to a statesman and the minister of a sovereign to a popular leader, had orders to display by every means the respect which the victor of Heraclea really felt for his vanquished opponents, to make known the wish of the king to come to Rome in person, to influence men's minds in the king's favour by panegyrics which sound so well in the mouth of an enemy, by earnest flatteries, and, as opportunity offered, also by well-timed gifts—in short to try upon the

Romans all the arts of cabinet policy, as they had been tested at the courts of Alexandria and Antioch. The senate hesitated; to many it seemed a prudent course to draw back a step and to wait till their dangerous antagonist should have further entangled himself or should be no more. But the grey-haired and blind consular Appius Claudius (censor $\frac{442}{312}$, consul $\frac{447}{307}$, $\frac{458}{296}$), who had long withdrawn from state affairs but had himself conducted at this decisive moment to the senate, breathed the unbroken energy of this own vehement nature with words of fire into the souls of the younger generation. They gave to the message of the king the proud reply, which was first heard on this occasion and became thenceforth a maxim of the state, that Rome never negotiated so long as there were foreign troops on Italian ground; and to make good their words they dismissed the ambassador at once from the city. The object of the mission had failed, and the dexterous diplomatist, instead of producing an effect by his oratorical art, had on the contrary been himself impressed by such manly earnestness after so severe a defeat— he declared at home that every burgess in that city had seemed to him a king; in truth, the courtier had gained a sight of a free people.

Pyrrhus, who during these negotiations had advanced into Campania, immediately on the news of their being broken off marched against Rome, to co-operate with the Etruscans, to shake the allies of Rome, and to threaten the city itself. But the Romans as little allowed themselves to be terrified as cajoled. At the summons of the herald " to enroll in the room of the fallen," the young men immediately after the battle of Heraclea had pressed forward in crowds to enlist; with the two newly formed legions and the corps withdrawn from Lucania, Laevinus, stronger than before, followed the march of the king. He protected Capua against him, and frustrated his endeavours to enter into communications with Neapolis. So firm was the attitude of the Romans that, excepting the Greeks of Lower Italy, no allied state of any note dared to break off from the Roman alliance. Then Pyrrhus turned against Rome itself. Through a rich country, whose flourishing condition he beheld with astonishment, he marched against Fregellae which he surprised, forced the passage of the Liris, and reached Anagnia, which is not more than forty miles from Rome. No army crossed his path; but everywhere the towns of Latium closed their gates against him, and with measured step Laevinus followed him from Campania, while the consul Tiberius Coruncanius, who had just concluded a seasonable peace with the Etruscans, brought up a second Roman army from the north, and in Rome itself the reserve was preparing for battle under the dictator Gnaeus Domitius Calvinus. In these circumstances Pyrrhus could accomplish nothing; no course was left to him but to retire. For a time he still remained inactive in Campania in presence of the united armies of the two consuls; but no opportunity occurred of striking an effective blow. When winter came on, the king evacuated the enemy's territory, and distributed his troops among the friendly towns, taking up his own winter quarters in Tarentum. Thereupon the Romans also desisted from their operations. The army occupied standing quarters near Firmum in Picenum, where by command of the senate the legions defeated on the Siris spent the winter by way of punishment under tents.

Thus ended the campaign of $\frac{474}{280}$. The separate peace which at the decisive moment Etruria had concluded with Rome, and the king's unexpected retreat which entirely disappointed the sanguine hopes of the Italian confederates, counterbalanced in great measure the impression of the victory of Heraclea. The Italians complained of the burdens of the war, particularly of the bad discipline of the mercenaries quartered among them, and the king, weary of the petty quarrelling and of the impolitic as well as unmilitary conduct of his allies, began to feel that the problem which had fallen to him to solve might be, despite all tactical successes, politically insoluble. The arrival of a Roman embassy of three consulars, including Gaius Fabricius the conqueror of Thurii, again revived in him for a moment the hopes of peace; but it soon appeared that they had only power to treat for the ransom or exchange of prisoners. Pyrrhus rejected their demand, but at the festival of the Saturnalia he released all the prisoners on their word of honour. Their keeping of that word, and the repulse by the Roman ambassador of an attempt at bribery, were celebrated by posterity in a manner most unbecoming and betokening rather the dishonourable character of the later, than the honourable feeling of that earlier, epoch.

In the spring of $\frac{475}{279}$ Pyrrhus resumed the offensive, and advanced into Apulia, whither the Roman army marched to meet him. In the hope of shaking the Roman symmachy in these regions by a decisive victory, the king offered battle a second time, and the Romans did not decline it. The two armies encountered each other near Ausculum (Ascoli di Puglia).

Under the banner of Pyrrhus there fought, besides his Epirot
and Macedonian troops, the Italian mercenaries, the burgess-
force—the white shields, as they were called—of Tarentum,
and the allied Lucanians, Bruttians, and Samnites—altogether
70,000 infantry, of whom 16,000 were Greeks and Epirots, more
than 8000 cavalry, and nineteen elephants. The Romans were
supported on that day by the Latins, Campanians, Volscians,
Sabines, Umbrians, Marrucinians, Paelignians, Frentanians,
and Arpanians. They too numbered above 70,000 infantry, of
whom 20,000 were Roman citizens, and 8000 cavalry. Both
parties had made alterations in their military system. Pyrrhus,
perceiving with the sharp eye of a soldier the advantages of the
Roman manipular organisation, had on the wings substituted
for the long front of his phalanxes an arrangement by companies
with intervals between them in imitation of the cohorts, and—
perhaps for political no less than for military reasons—had
placed the Tarentine and Samnite cohorts between the subdivisions of his own men. In the centre alone the Epirot
phalanx stood in close order. For the purpose of keeping off
the elephants the Romans produced a species of war-chariot,
from which projected iron poles furnished with chafing-dishes,
and on which were fastened movable masts adjusted so as to
admit of lowering, and ending in an iron spike—in some degree
the model of the boarding-bridges which were to play so great
a part in the first Punic war.

According to the Greek account of the battle, which seems
less one-sided than the Roman account also extant, the Greeks
had the disadvantage on the first day, as they did not succeed in
deploying their line along the steep and marshy banks of the
river where they were compelled to accept battle, or in bringing
their cavalry and elephants into action. On the second day,
however, Pyrrhus anticipated the Romans in occupying the
intersected ground, and thus gained without loss the plain where
he could without disturbance draw up his phalanx. Vainly
did the Romans with desperate courage fall sword in hand on
the *sarissae*; the phalanx preserved an unshaken front under
every assault, but in its turn was unable to make any impression
on the Roman legions. It was not till the numerous escort
of the elephants had, with arrows and stones hurled from slings,
dislodged the combatants stationed in the Roman war-chariots
and had cut the traces of the horses, and the elephants pressed
upon the Roman line, that it began to waver. The giving way
of the guard attached to the Roman chariots formed the signal

for universal flight, which, however, did not involve the sacrifice
of many lives, as the adjoining camp received the fugitives.
The Roman account of the battle alone mentions the circumstance, that during the principal engagement an Arpanian corps
detached from the Roman main force had attacked and set
on fire the weakly-guarded Epirot camp; but, even if this were
correct, the Romans are not at all justified in their assertion
that the battle remained undecided. Both accounts, on the
contrary, agree in stating that the Roman army retreated
across the river, and that Pyrrhus remained in possession of
the field of battle. The number of the fallen was, according
to the Greek account, 6000 on the side of the Romans, 3505 on
that of the Greeks.[1] Amongst the wounded was the king himself, whose arm had been pierced with a javelin, while he was
fighting, as was his wont, in the thickest of the fray. Pyrrhus
had achieved a victory, but his were unfruitful laurels; the
victory was creditable to the king as a general and as a soldier,
but it did not promote his political designs. What Pyrrhus
needed was a brilliant success which should break up the Roman
army and give an opportunity and impulse to the wavering
allies to change sides; but the Roman army and the Roman
confederacy still remained unbroken, and the Greek army,
which was nothing without its leader, was fettered for a considerable time in consequence of his wound. He was obliged
to renounce the campaign and to go into winter quarters; which
the king took up in Tarentum, the Romans on this occasion in
Apulia. It was becoming daily more evident that in a military
point of view the resources of the king were inferior to those
of the Romans, just as, politically, the loose and refractory
coalition could not stand a comparison with the firmly established
Roman symmachy. The sudden and vehement style of the
Greek warfare and the genius of the general might perhaps
achieve another such victory as those of Heraclea and Ausculum,
but every new victory was wearing out his resources for further
enterprise, and it was clear that the Romans already felt themselves the stronger, and awaited with a courageous patience
final victory. Such a war as this was not the delicate game

[1] These numbers appear credible. The Roman account assigns, probably in dead and wounded, 15,000 to each side; a later one even specifies
5000 as dead on the Roman, and 20,000 on the Greek side. These accounts
may be mentioned here for the purpose of exhibiting, in one of the few
instances where it is possible to check the statement, the untrustworthiness—almost without exception—of the reports of numbers, which are
swelled by the unscrupulous invention of the annalists with avalanche-like
rapidity.

of art that was practised and understood by the Greek princes.
All strategical combinations were shattered against the full
and mighty energy of the national levy. Pyrrhus felt how
matters stood: weary of his victories and despising his allies,
he only persevered because military honour required him not
to leave Italy till he should have secured his clients from barbarian assault. With his impatient temperament it might
be presumed that he would embrace the first pretext to get rid
of the burdensome duty; and an opportunity of withdrawing
from Italy was soon presented to him by the affairs of Sicily.

After the death of Agathocles ($\frac{465}{289}$) the Greeks of Sicily
were without any leading power. While in the several Hellenic
cities incapable demagogues and incapable tyrants were re-
placing each other, the Carthaginians, the old rulers of the
western point, were extending their dominion unmolested.
After Agrigentum had surrendered to them, they believed that
the time had come for taking final steps towards the end
which they had kept in view for centuries, and for reducing
the whole island under their authority; they set themselves to
attack Syracuse. That city, which formerly by its armies and
fleets had disputed the possession of the island with Carthage,
had through internal dissension and the weakness of its government fallen so low that it was obliged to seek for safety in the
protection of its walls and in foreign aid; and none could afford
that aid but king Pyrrhus. Pyrrhus was the husband of
Agathocles's daughter, and his son Alexander, then sixteen
years of age, was Agathocles's grandson. Both were in every
respect natural heirs of the ambitious schemes of the ruler of
Syracuse; and if her freedom was at an end, Syracuse might
find compensation in becoming the capital of an Hellenic empire
of the West. So the Syracusans, like the Tarentines, and under
similar conditions, voluntarily offered their sovereignty to king
Pyrrhus (about $\frac{475}{279}$); and by a singular conjuncture of affairs
everything seemed to concur towards the success of the magnificent plans of the Epirot king, based as they primarily were on
the possession of Tarentum and Syracuse.

The immediate effect, indeed, of this union of the Italian and
Sicilian Greeks under one control was a closer concert also on
the part of their antagonists. Carthage and Rome now converted
their old commercial treaties into an offensive and defensive
league against Pyrrhus ($\frac{475}{279}$), the tenor of which was that, if
Pyrrhus invaded Roman or Carthaginian territory, the party
which was not attached should furnish that which was assailed

with a contingent on its own territory and should itself defray
the expense of the auxiliary troops; that in such an event
Carthage should be bound to furnish transports and to assist
the Romans also with a war fleet, but the crews of that fleet
should not be obliged to fight for the Romans by land; that
lastly, both states should pledge themselves not to conclude a
separate peace with Pyrrhus. The object of the Romans in
entering into the treaty was to facilitate their attack on Tarentum
and to cut off Pyrrhus from his own country, neither of which
ends could be attained without the co-operation of the Punic
fleet; the object of the Carthaginians was to detain the king
in Italy, so that they might be able without molestation to carry
into effect their designs on Syracuse.[1] It was accordingly the
interest of both powers in the first instance to secure the sea
between Italy and Sicily. A powerful Carthaginian fleet of
120 sail under the admiral Mago proceeded from Ostia, whither
Mago seems to have gone to conclude the treaty, to the Sicilian
straits. The Mamertines, who anticipated righteous punishment for their outrage upon the Greek population of Messana,
in the event of Pyrrhus becoming ruler of Sicily and Italy,
attached themselves closely to the Romans and Carthaginians,
and secured for them the Sicilian side of the straits. The allies
would willingly have brought Rhegium also on the opposite coast
under their power; but Rome could not possibly pardon the
Campanian garrison, and an attempt of the combined Romans
and Carthaginians to gain the city by force of arms miscarried.
The Carthaginian fleet sailed thence for Syracuse and blockaded
the city by sea, while at the same time a strong Phoenician army
began the siege by land ($\frac{476}{278}$). It was high time that Pyrrhus
should appear at Syracuse: but, in fact, matters in Italy were
by no means in such a condition that he and his troops could
be dispensed with there. The two consuls of $\frac{476}{278}$, Gaius Fabricius Luscinus and Quintus Aemilius Papus, both experienced
generals, had begun the new campaign with vigour, and although
the Romans had hitherto sustained nothing but defeat in this
war, it was not they but the victors that were weary of it and
longed for peace. Pyrrhus made another attempt to obtain

[1] The later Romans, and the moderns following them, give a version of
the league, as if the Romans had designedly avoided accepting the Carthaginian help in Italy. This would have been irrational, and the facts pronounce against it. The circumstance that Mago did not land at Ostia is
to be explained not by any such foresight, but simply by the fact that
Latium was not at all threatened by Pyrrhus and so did not need Carthaginian aid; and the Carthaginians certainly fought for Rome in front of
Rhegium.

an accommodation on tolerable terms. The consul Fabricius
had handed over to the king a wretch, who had proposed to
poison him on condition of being well paid for it. Not only did
the king in token of gratitude release all his Roman prisoners
without ransom, but he felt himself so moved by the generosity
of his brave opponents that he offered, by way of personal recompense, a singularly fair and favourable peace. Cineas appears
to have gone once more to Rome, and Carthage seems to have
been seriously apprehensive that Rome might come to terms.
But the senate remained firm, and repeated its former answer.
Unless the king was willing to allow Syracuse to fall into the
hands of the Carthaginians and to have his grand scheme thereby
disconcerted, no other course remained than to abandon his
Italian allies and to confine himself for the time being to the
occupation of the most important seaports, particularly Tarentum and Locri. In vain the Lucanians and Samnites conjured
him not to desert them; in vain the Tarentines summoned him
either to comply with his duty as their general or to give them
back their city. The king met their complaints and reproaches
with the consolatory assurance that better times were coming,
or with abrupt dismissal. Milo remained behind in Tarentum;
Alexander, the king's son, in Locri; and Pyrrhus, with his main
force, embarked in the spring of $\frac{476}{278}$ at Tarentum for Syracuse.

By the departure of Pyrrhus the hands of the Romans were
set free in Italy; none ventured to oppose them in the open
field, and their antagonists everywhere confined themselves to
their fastnesses or their forests. The struggle however was not
terminated so rapidly as might have been expected; partly in
consequence of its nature as a warfare of mountain skirmishes
and sieges, partly also, doubtless, from the exhaustion of the
Romans, whose fearful losses are indicated by a decrease of
17,000 in the burgess-roll from $\frac{473}{281}$ to $\frac{479}{275}$. In $\frac{476}{278}$ the consul
Gaius Fabricius succeeded in inducing the considerable Tarentine
settlement of Heraclea to enter into a separate peace, which was
granted to it on the most favourable terms. In $\frac{477}{277}$ a desultory
warfare was carried on in Samnium, where an attack thoughtlessly made on some entrenched heights cost the Romans many
lives, and thereafter in southern Italy, where the Lucanians and
Bruttians were defeated. On the other hand Milo, issuing from
Tarentum, anticipated the Romans in their attempt to surprise
Croton: whereupon the Epirot garrison made even a successful
sortie against the besieging army. At length, however, the
consuls ucceeded by a stratagem in inducing it to march forth,

nd in possessing himself to the undefended town ($\frac{477}{277}$). An
acident of more moment was the slaughter of the Epirot garrison
y the Locrians, who had formerly surrendered the Roman
arrison to the king, and now atoned for one act of treachery by
nother. By that step the whole south coast came into the
ands of the Romans, with the exception of Rhegium and Taren-
um. These successes, however, advanced the main object
ut little. Lower Italy itself had long been defenceless; but
*yrrhus was not subdued so long as Tarentum remained in his
ands and enabled him to renew the war at his pleasure, and the
.omans could not think of undertaking the siege of that city.
ven apart from the fact that in siege-warfare, which had been
evolutionised by Philip of Macedon and Demetrius Poliorcetes,
he Romans were at a very decided disadvantage when matched
gainst an experienced and resolute Greek commandant, a
trong fleet was needed for such an enterprise, and, although
he Carthaginian treaty promised to the Romans support by
ea, the affairs of Carthage herself in Sicily were by no means
a such a condition as to enable her to grant that support.

The landing of Pyrrhus on the island, which, in spite of the
arthaginian fleet, had taken place without interruption, had
hanged at once the aspect of matters there. He had immediately
elieved Syracuse, had in a short time united under his sway all
he free Greek cities, and at the head of the Sicilian confederation
ad wrested from the Carthaginians nearly their whole posses-
ions. It was with difficulty that the Carthaginians could, by
he help of their fleet which at that time ruled the Mediterranean
ithout a rival, maintain themselves in Lilybaeum; it was with
ifficulty, and amidst constant assaults, that the Mamertines
eld their ground in Messana. Under such circumstances,
greeably to the treaty of $\frac{475}{279}$, it would have been the duty of
.ome to lend her aid to the Carthaginians in Sicily, far rather
aan that of Carthage to help the Romans with her fleet to
onquer Tarentum; but on neither side was there much inclina-
on to secure or to extend the power of the other. Carthage
ad only offered help to the Romans when the real danger was
ast; they in their turn had done nothing to prevent the de-
arture of the king from Italy and the fall of the Carthaginian
ower in Sicily. Indeed, in open violation of the treaties Car-
aage had even proposed to the king a separate peace, offering,
a return for the undisturbed possession of Lilybaeum, to give
p all claim to her other Sicilian possessions and even to place at
ae disposal of the king money and ships of war, of course with

a view to his crossing to Italy and renewing the war against
Rome. It was evident, however, that with the possession of
Lilybaeum and the departure of the king the position of the
Carthaginians in the island would be nearly the same as it had
been before the landing of Pyrrhus; the Greek cities if left to
themselves were powerless, and the lost territory would be easily
regained. So Pyrrhus rejected the doubly perfidious proposal
and proceeded to build for himself a war fleet. Mere ignorance
and shortsightedness in after times censured this step; but it
was quite as necessary as it was, with the resources of the island,
easy of accomplishment. Apart from the consideration that
the sovereign of Ambracia, Tarentum, and Syracuse could not
dispense with a naval force, he needed a fleet to conquer Lilybaeum, to protect Tarentum, and to attack Carthage at home
as Agathocles, Regulus, and Scipio did before or afterwards so
successfully. Pyrrhus never was so near to the attainment of
his aim as in the summer of $\frac{478}{276}$, when he saw Carthage humbled
before him, commanded Sicily, and retained a firm footing in
Italy by the possession of Tarentum, and when the newly
created fleet, which was to connect, to secure, and to augment
these successes, lay ready for sea in the harbour of Syracuse.

The real weakness of the position of Pyrrhus lay in his faulty
internal policy. He governed Sicily as he had seen Ptolemy
rule in Egypt: he showed no respect to the local constitutions
he placed his confidants as magistrates over the cities whenever
and for as long as, he pleased; he made his courtiers judges
instead of the native jurymen; he pronounced arbitrary sentence
of confiscation, banishment, or death, even against those who
had been most active in promoting his coming thither; he placed
garrisons in the towns, and ruled over Sicily not as the leader
of a national league, but as a king. In so doing he probably
reckoned himself according to oriental-Hellenistic ideas a good
and wise ruler, and perhaps he really was so; but the Greek
bore this transplantation of the system of the Diadochi to Syracuse with all the impatience of a nation that in its long struggle
for freedom had lost all habits of discipline; the Carthaginian
yoke very soon appeared to the foolish people more tolerable
than their new military government. The principal cities
entered into communications with the Carthaginians, and even
with the Mamertines; a strong Carthaginian army ventured
again to appear on the island; and everywhere supported by the
Greeks, it made rapid progress. In the battle which Pyrrhus
fought with it fortune was, as usual, with the "Eagle;" but the

circumstances served to show what the state of feeling was in
the island, and what might and must ensue when the king should
depart.

To this first and most essential error Pyrrhus added a second;
he proceeded with his fleet, not to Lilybaeum, but to Tarentum.
It was evident, looking to the very ferment in the minds of the
Sicilians, that he ought first of all to have driven the Carthaginians wholly from the island, and thereby to have cut off the
discontented from their last support, before he turned his attention to Italy; in that quarter there was nothing to be lost, for
Tarentum was safe enough, and the other allies were of little
moment now that they had been abandoned. It is not unlikely that his soldierly spirit impelled him to wipe off the stain
of his not very honourable departure in $\frac{476}{278}$ by a brilliant return, and that his heart bled when he heard the complaints of
the Lucanians and Samnites. But problems, such as Pyrrhus
had proposed to himself, can only be solved by men of iron
nature who are able to control their feelings of compassion and
even their sense of honour; and Pyrrhus was not one of these.
The fatal embarkation took place towards the end of $\frac{478}{276}$.
On the voyage the new Syracusan fleet had to sustain a sharp
engagement with the Carthaginians, and lost a considerable
number of vessels. The departure of the king and the accounts
of this first misfortune sufficed for the fall of the Sicilian kingdom. On the arrival of the news all the cities refused to the
absent king money and troops; and the brilliant state collapsed
even more rapidly than it had arisen, partly because the king
had himself undermined in the hearts of his subjects the loyalty
and affection on which every state depends, partly because the
people lacked the devotedness to renounce freedom for perhaps
but a short term in order to save their nationality. Thus the
enterprise of Pyrrhus was wrecked, and the plan of his life was
ruined irretrievably; he was thenceforth an adventurer, who
felt that he had been great and was so no longer, and who now
waged war not as a means to an end, but in order to drown
thought amidst the reckless excitement of the game and to find,
if possible, in the tumult of battle a soldier's death. Arrived
on the Italian coast, the king began by an attempt to get possession of Rhegium; but the Campanians repulsed the attack
with the aid of the Mamertines, and in the heat of the conflict
before the town the king himself was wounded in the act of
striking down an officer of the enemy. On the other hand he
surprised Locri, whose inhabitants suffered severely for their

slaughter of the Epirot garrison, and he plundered the rich treasury of the temple of Persephone there, to replenish his empty exchequer. Thus he arrived at Tarentum, it is said, with 20,000 infantry and 3000 cavalry. But these were no longer the experienced veterans of former days, and the Italians no longer hailed them as deliverers; the confidence and hope with which they had received Pyrrhus five years before were gone; the allies were destitute of money and of men.

The king took the field in the spring of $\frac{479}{275}$ with the view of aiding the hard-pressed Samnites, in whose territory the Romans had passed the previous winter; and he forced the consul Manius Curius to give battle near Beneventum on the *campus Arusinus*, before he could form a junction with his colleague advancing from Lucania. But the division of the army, which was intended to take the Romans in flank, lost its way during a night march in the woods, and failed to appear at the decisive moment; and after a hot conflict the elephants again decided the battle, but decided it in favour of the Romans, for, thrown into confusion by the archers who were stationed to protect the camp, they attacked their own people. The victors occupied the camp; there fell into their hands 1300 prisoners and four elephants—the first that were seen in Rome—besides an immense spoil, from the proceeds of which the aqueduct, which conveyed the water of the Anio from Tibur to Rome, was subsequently built. Without troops to keep the field and without money, Pyrrhus applied to his allies who had contributed to his equipment for Italy, the kings of Macedonia and Asia; but even in his native land he was no longer feared, and his request was refused. Despairing of success against Rome and exasperated by these refusals, Pyrrhus left a garrison in Tarentum, and went home himself in the same year ($\frac{479}{275}$) to Greece, where some prospect of gain might open up to the desperate player sooner than amidst the steady and measured course of Italian affairs. In fact, he not only rapidly recovered the portion of his kingdom that had been taken away, but once more grasped, and not without success, at the Macedonian throne. But his last plans also were thwarted by the calm and cautious policy of Antigonus Gonatas, and still more by his own vehemence and inability to tame his proud spirit; he still gained battles, but he no longer gained any lasting success, and met his death in a miserable street combat in Peloponnesian Argos ($\frac{482}{272}$).

In Italy the war came to an end with the battle of Beneventum; the last convulsive struggles of the national party died slowly away. So long indeed as the warrior prince, whose mighty arm had ventured to seize the reins of destiny in Italy, was still among the living, he held, even when absent, the stronghold of Tarentum against Rome. Although after the departure of the king the peace party recovered ascendancy in the city, Milo, who commanded there on behalf of Pyrrhus, rejected their suggestions and allowed the citizens favourable to Rome, who had erected a separate fort for themselves in the territory of Tarentum, to conclude peace with Rome as they pleased, without on that account opening his gates. But when after the death of Pyrrhus a Carthaginian fleet entered the harbour, and Milo saw that the citizens were on the point of delivering up the city to the Carthaginians, he preferred to hand over the citadel to the Roman consul Lucius Papirius ($\frac{482}{272}$), and by that means to secure a free departure for himself and his troops. For the Romans this was an immense piece of good fortune. After the experiences of Philip before Perinthus and Byzantium, of Demetrius before Rhodes, and of Pyrrhus before Lilybaeum, it may be doubted whether the strategy of that period was at all able to compel the surrender of a town well fortified, well defended, and freely accessible by sea; and how different a turn matters might have taken, had Tarentum become to the Phoenicians in Italy what Lilybaeum was to them in Sicily! What was done, however, could not be undone. The Carthaginian admiral, when he saw the citadel in the hands of the Romans, declared that he had only appeared before Tarentum conformably to the treaty to lend assistance to his allies in the siege of the town, and set sail for Africa; and the Roman embassy, which was sent to Carthage to demand explanations and make complaints regarding the attempted occupation of Tarentum, brought back nothing but a solemn confirmation on oath of that assertion as to its friendly design, with which accordingly the Romans had for the time to rest content. The Tarentines obtained from Rome, probably on the intercession of emigrants, the restoration of their autonomy; but their arms and ships had to be given up and their walls had to be pulled down.

In the same year, in which Tarentum became Roman, the Samnites, Lucanians, and Bruttians finally submitted. The latter were obliged to cede the half of the lucrative, and for ship-building important, forest of Sila.

At length also the band that for ten years had sheltered themselves in Rhegium were duly chastised for the breach of their military oath, as well as for the murder of the citizens of Rhegium and of the garrison of Croton. In this instance Rome, while vindicating her own rights, vindicated the general cause of the Hellenes against the barbarians. Hiero, the new ruler of Syracuse, accordingly supported the Romans before Rhegium by sending supplies and a contingent, and in combination with the Roman expedition against the garrison of Rhegium he made an attack upon their fellow-countrymen and fellow-criminals, the Mamertines of Messana. The siege of the latter town was long protracted. On the other hand Rhegium, although the mutineers resisted long and obstinately, was stormed by the Romans in $\frac{484}{270}$; the survivors of the garrison were scourged and beheaded in the public market at Rome, while the old inhabitants were recalled and, as far as possible, reinstated in their possessions. Thus all Italy was, in $\frac{484}{270}$, reduced to subjection. The Samnites alone, the most obstinate antagonists of Rome, still in spite of the official conclusion of peace continued the struggle as " robbers," so that in $\frac{485}{269}$ both consuls had to be once more despatched against them. But even the most high-spirited national courage—the bravery of despair—comes to an end; the sword and the gibbet at length carried quiet even into the mountains of Samnium.

For the securing of these immense acquisitions a new series of colonies was instituted: Paestum and Cosa in Lucania ($\frac{481}{273}$); Beneventum ($\frac{486}{268}$), and Aesernia (about $\frac{491}{263}$) to hold Samnium in check; and, as outposts against the Gauls, Ariminum ($\frac{486}{268}$), Firmum in Picenum (about $\frac{490}{264}$), and the burgess colony of Castrum Novum. Preparations were made for the continuation of the great southern highway—which acquired in the fortress of Beneventum a new station intermediate between Capua and Venusia—as far as the seaports of Tarentum and Brundisium, and for the colonisation of the latter seaport, which Roman policy had selected as the rival and successor of the Tarentine emporium. The construction of the new fortresses and roads gave rise to some further wars with the small tribes, whose territory was thereby curtailed: with the Picentes ($\frac{485}{269}$, $\frac{486}{268}$), a number of whom were transplanted to the district of Salernum; with the Sallentines ($\frac{487}{267}$, $\frac{488}{266}$); and with the Umbrian Sassinates ($\frac{487}{267}$, $\frac{488}{266}$), who seem to have occupied the territory of Ariminum after the expulsion of the Senones. By these establishments the dominion of Rome was extended over the interior of Lower Italy, and generally from the Apennines to the Ionian sea.

Before we describe the political organisation of the Italy which was thus united under the government of Rome, it remains that we should glance at the maritime relations that subsisted in the fourth and fifth centuries. At this period Syracuse and Carthage were the main competitors for the dominion of the western waters. On the whole, notwithstanding the great temporary successes which Dionysius ($\frac{348-}{406-}$ $\frac{389}{365}$), Agathocles ($\frac{437-465}{317-289}$), and Pyrrhus ($\frac{476-478}{278-276}$) obtained at sea, Carthage had the preponderance, and Syracuse sank more and more into a second-rate naval power. The maritime importance of Etruria was wholly gone (p. 321); the hitherto Etruscan island of Corsica, if it did not quite pass into the possession, fell under the maritime supremacy, of the Carthaginians. Tarentum, which for a time had played a considerable part, had its power broken by the Roman occupation. The brave Massiliots maintained their ground in their own waters; but they exercised no material influence over the course of events in those of Italy. The other maritime cities hardly require to be taken into serious account.

Rome itself was not exempt from a similar fate; its own waters were likewise commanded by foreign fleets. It was indeed from the first a maritime city, and in the period of its vigour never was so untrue to its ancient traditions as wholly to neglect its war marine or so foolish as to desire to be a mere continental power. Latium furnished the finest timber for ship-building, far surpassing the famed growths of Lower Italy; and the very docks constantly maintained in Rome showed that the Romans never abandoned the idea of possessing a fleet of their own. During the perilous crises, however, which the expulsion of the kings, the internal disturbances in the Romano-Latin confederacy, and the unhappy wars with the Etruscans and Celts brought upon Rome, the Romans could take but little interest in the state of matters in the Mediterranean; and, in consequence of the policy of Rome directing itself more and more decidedly to the subjugation of the Italian continent, the growth of its naval power was arrested. There is hardly any mention of Latin vessels of war up to the end of the fourth century, except that the votive offering from the Veientine spoil was sent to Delphi in a Roman vessel ($\frac{360}{394}$). The Antiates indeed continued to prosecute their commerce with armed vessels and thus, as occasion offered, to practise the trade of piracy also, and the "Tyrrhene corsair" Postumius, whom Timoleon captured about $\frac{415}{339}$, may certainly have been an

Antiate; but the Antiates were scarcely to be reckoned among the naval powers of that period, and, had they been so, the fact must from the attitude of Antium towards Rome have been anything but an advantage to the latter. The extent to which the Roman naval power had declined about the year $\frac{400}{350}$ is shown by the plundering of the Latin coasts by a Greek, probably a Sicilian, war fleet in $\frac{405}{349}$, while at the same time Celtic hordes were traversing and devastating the Latin land. In the following year ($\frac{406}{348}$), and beyond doubt under the immediate impression produced by these disastrous events, the Roman community and the Phoenicians of Carthage, acting respectively for themselves and for their dependent allies, concluded a treaty of commerce and navigation—the oldest Roman document whose text has reached us, although only in a Greek translation.[1] In that treaty the Romans had to come under obligation not to navigate, except under pressure of necessity, the waters beyond the Fair Promontory (Cape Bon) on the Libyan coast. On the other hand they obtained the privilege of freely trading, like the natives, in Sicily, so far as it was Carthaginian; and in Africa and Sardinia they obtained at least the right to dispose of their merchandise at a price fixed with the concurrence of the Carthaginian officials and guaranteed by the Carthaginian community. The privilege of free trading seems to have been granted to the Carthaginians in Rome at least, perhaps in all Latium; only they bound themselves neither to do violence to the subject Latin communities (p. 345), nor, even if they should set foot as enemies on Latin soil, to take up their quarters for a night on shore—in other words, not to extend their piratical inroads into the interior—nor to construct any fortresses in the Latin land.

We may probably assign to the same period the already mentioned (p. 389) treaty between Rome and Tarentum, respecting the date of which we are only told that it was concluded a considerable time before $\frac{472}{282}$. By it the Romans bound themselves—for what concessions on the part of Tarentum is not stated—not to navigate the waters to the east of the Lacinian promontory; a stipulation by which they were wholly excluded from the eastern basin of the Mediterranean.

These were disasters no less than the defeat on the Allia, and the Roman senators seem to have felt them as such and to have

---

[1] The grounds for assigning the document given in Polybius (iii. 22) not to $\frac{245}{509}$, but to $\frac{406}{348}$, are set forth in my *Röm. Chronologie*, p. 320 *et seq.* [translated in the Appendix to this volume].

1ade use of the favourable turn, which their Italian relations
ssumed soon after the conclusion of the humiliating treaties
ith Carthage and Tarentum, with all their energy to improve
heir depressed maritime position. The most important of the
past towns were furnished with Roman colonies: Pyrgi, the
eaport of Caere, the colonisation of which probably falls within
his period; along the Latin coast, Antium in $\frac{416}{338}$ (p. 356),
'arracina in $\frac{425}{329}$ (p. 356), the modern isle of Ponza in $\frac{441}{313}$
. 367), so that, as Ostia, Ardea, and Circeii had previously
eceived colonists, all the Latin seaports of consequence were
ow Latin or burgess colonies; on the Campanian and Lucanian
pasts, Minturnae and Sinuessa in $\frac{459}{295}$ (p. 379), Paestum and
osa in $\frac{481}{273}$ (p. 408); and on the coast of the Adriatic, Sena
allica and Castrum Novum about $\frac{471}{283}$ (p. 388), and Ariminum
1 $\frac{486}{268}$ (p. 408), to which falls to be added the occupation of
irundisium, which took place immediately after the close of the
'yrrhic war. In the greater part of these places—the burgess
r maritime colonies [1]—the young men were exempted from
erving in the legions and destined solely for the watching of the
pasts. The well-judged preference given at the same time to
ae Greeks of Lower Italy over their Sabellian neighbours,
articularly to the considerable communities of Neapolis,
.hegium, Locri, Thurii, and Heraclea, and their similar exemp-
ion under the like conditions from furnishing contingents to
ae land army, completed the network drawn by Rome around
ae coasts of Italy.

But with a statesmanlike sagacity, from which the succeeding
enerations might have drawn a lesson, the leading men of the
.oman commonwealth perceived that all these coast fortifica-
ions and coast garrisons would prove inadequate, unless the
ar marine of the state were again placed on a footing that should
ommand respect. Some sort of nucleus for this purpose was
lready furnished on the subjugation of Antium ($\frac{416}{338}$) by the
erviceable war-galleys which were carried off to the Roman
ocks; but the enactment at the same time, that the Antiates
1ould abstain from all maritime traffic,[2] is a very clear and

---

[1] These were Pyrgi, Ostia, Antium, Tarracina, Minturnae, Sinuessa, Sena
allica, and Castrum Novum.

[2] This statement is as distinct (Liv. viii. 14; *interdictum mari Antiati
ipulo est*) as it is intrinsically credible; for Antium was inhabited not
.erely by colonists, but also by its former citizens who had been nursed
. enmity to Rome (p. 356). This view is, no doubt, inconsistent with the
reek accounts, which assert that Alexander the Great ($+\frac{431}{323}$) and Deme-
ius Poliorcetes ($+\frac{471}{283}$) lodged complaints at Rome regarding Antiate

distinct indication how weak the Romans then felt themselve
at sea, and how completely their maritime policy was sti
summed up in the occupation of places on the coast. There
after, when the Greek cities of southern Italy, Neapolis leadin
the way in, $\frac{428}{326}$ were admitted to the clientship of Rome, th
war-vessels, which each of these cities bound itself to furnish a
a war contribution under the alliance to the Romans, formed a
least a renewed nucleus for a Roman fleet. In $\frac{443}{311}$, moreover
two fleet-masters (*duoviri navales*) were nominated in conse
quence of a resolution of the burgesses specially passed to tha
effect, and this Roman naval force co-operated in the Samnit
war at the siege of Nuceria (p. 370). Perhaps even the remark
able mission of a Roman fleet of twenty-five sail to found
colony in Corsica, which Theophrastus mentions in his *Histor
of Plants* written about $\frac{447}{307}$, belongs to this period. But hov
little was immediately accomplished with all this preparation
is shown by the renewed treaty with Carthage in $\frac{448}{306}$. Whil
the stipulation of the treaty of $\frac{406}{348}$ relating to Italy and Sicil
(p. 410) remained unchanged, the Romans were now prohibite
not only from the navigation of the eastern waters, but als
from that of the Atlantic Ocean which was previously per
mitted, as well as debarred from holding commercial intercours
with the subjects of Carthage in Sardinia and Africa, and also
in all probability, from effecting a settlement in Corsica; [1] s
that only Carthaginian Sicily and Carthage itself remained ope
to their traffic. We recognise here the jealousy of the dominan
maritime power, gradually increasing with the extension of th
Roman dominion along the coasts. Carthage compelled th
Romans to acquiesce in her prohibitive system, to submit to b
excluded from the seats of production in the west and east (con
nected with which exclusion is the story of a public rewar

pirates. The former statement is of the same stamp, and perhaps fron
the same source, with that regarding the Roman embassy to Babylo
(p. 380). It seems more likely that Demetrius Poliorcetes may have trie
by edict to put down piracy in the Tyrrhene sea which he had never se
eyes upon, and it is not at all inconceivable that the Antiates may hav
even as Roman citizens, in defiance of the prohibition, continued for
time their old trade in an underhand fashion: much dependence mus
not, however, be placed even on the second story.

[1] According to Servius (*in Aen.* iv. 628) it was stipulated in the Romano
Carthaginian treaties, that no Roman should set foot on (or rather occupy
Carthaginian, and no Carthaginian on Roman, soil, but Corsica was t
remain in a neutral position between them (*ut neque Romani ad litor
Carthaginiensium accederent neque Carthaginienses ad litora Romanorun
. . . Corsica esset media inter Romanos et Carthaginienses*). This appear
to refer to our present period, and the colonisation of Corsica seems t
have been prevented by this very treaty.

bestowed on the Phoenician mariner who at the sacrifice of his own ship decoyed a Roman vessel, steering after him into the Atlantic Ocean, to perish on a sand-bank), and to restrict their navigation under the treaty to the narrow space of the western Mediterranean—and all this for the mere purpose of averting pillage from their coasts and of securing their ancient and important trading connection with Sicily. The Romans were obliged to yield to these terms; but they did not desist from their efforts to rescue their marine from its condition of impotence.

A comprehensive measure with that view was the institution of four quaestors of the fleet (*quaestores classici*) in $\frac{487}{267}$: of whom the first was stationed at Ostia the port of Rome; the second, stationed at Cales then the capital of Roman Campania, had to superintend the ports of Campania and Magna Graecia; the third, stationed at Ariminum, superintended the ports on the other side of the Apennines; the district assigned to the fourth is not known. These new standing officials were intended to exercise not the sole, but a conjoint, guardianship of the coasts, and to form a war marine for their protection. The objects of the Roman senate—to recover their independence by sea, to cut off the maritime communications of Tarentum, to close the Adriatic against fleets coming from Epirus, and to emancipate themselves from Carthaginian supremacy—were very obvious. Their already explained relations with Carthage during the last Italian war discover traces of such views. King Pyrrhus indeed drove the two great cities once more—it was for the last time—to conclude an offensive alliance; but the lukewarmness and faithlessness of that alliance, the attempts of the Carthaginians to establish themselves in Rhegium and Tarentum, and the immediate occupation of Brundisium by the Romans after the termination of the war, show clearly how much their respective interests already came into collision.

Rome very naturally sought to find support against Carthage from the Hellenic maritime states. Her old and close relations of amity with Massilia continued uninterrupted. The votive offering sent by Rome to Delphi, after the conquest of Veii, was preserved there in the treasury of the Massiliots. After the capture of Rome by the Celts there was a collection in Massilia for the sufferers by the fire, in which the city chest took the lead; in return the Roman senate granted commercial advantages to the Massiliot merchants, and, at the celebration of the games, assigned a position of honour to the Massiliots by the side of the platform for the senators (*Graecostasis*). To the same category belong the treaties of commerce and amity concluded by the Romans about $\frac{448}{306}$ with Rhodes and not long after with Apollonia, a considerable mercantile town on the Epirot coast, and especially the closer relations, so fraught with danger for Carthage, which immediately after the end of the Pyrrhic war sprang up between Rome and Syracuse (p. 408).

While the Roman power by sea was thus very far from keeping pace with the immense development of their power by land, and the war marine belonging to the Romans in particular was by no means such as from the geographical and commercial position of the city it ought to have been, yet it began gradually to emerge out of the complete nullity to which it had been reduced about the year $\frac{400}{350}$; and, considering the great resources of Italy, the Phoenicians might well follow its efforts with anxious eyes.

The crisis in reference to the supremacy of the Italian waters was approaching; by land the contest was decided. For the first time Italy was united into one state under the sovereignty of the Roman community. What political privileges the Roman community on this occasion withdrew from the various other Italian communities and took into its own sole keeping, or in other words, what conception of political power is to be associated with this sovereignty of Rome, we are nowhere expressly informed, and—a significant circumstance, indicating prudent calculation—there does not even exist any generally recognised expression for that conception.[1] The only privileges that demonstrably belonged to it were the right of making war, of concluding treaties, and of coining money. No Italian community could declare war against any foreign state, or even negotiate with it, or coin money for circulation. On the other hand every war and every state-treaty resolved upon by the Roman people were binding in law on all the other Italian communities, and the silver money of Rome was legally current throughout all Italy. It is probable that formerly the general rights of the leading community extended no further. But to

---

[1] The clause, by which a dependent people binds itself " to uphold in a friendly manner the sovereignty of that of Rome " (*maiestatem populi Romani comiter conservare*), is certainly the technical appellation of that mildest form of subjection, but it probably did not come into use till a considerable later period (Cic. *pro Balbo*, 16, 35). The appellation of clientship derived from private law, aptly as in its very indefiniteness it denotes the relation (Dig. xlix. 15, 7, 1), was scarcely applied to it officially in earlier times.

these rights there was necessarily attached a prerogative of
sovereignty that practically went far beyond them.

The relations, which the Italians sustained to the leading
community, exhibited in detail great inequalities. In this
point of view, in addition to the full burgesses of Rome, there
were three different classes of subjects to be distinguished.
The full franchise itself, in the first place, was extended as far
as was possible, without wholly abandoning the idea of an urban
commonwealth in the case of the Roman commune. Not only
was the old burgess-domain extended by individual assignation
far into Etruria on the one hand and into Campania on the
other, but, after the example was first set in the case of Tusculum, a great number of communities more or less remote were
gradually incorporated with the Roman state and merged in it
completely. It has been already mentioned (pp. 345, 356), that
in consequence of the repeated insurrections of the Latins against
Rome a considerable portion of the original members of the
Latin league were compelled to enter the ranks of the full
Roman burgesses. The same course was followed in $\frac{486}{268}$ with
all the communities of the Sabines, who were closely related
to the Romans, and had sufficiently approved their fidelity
in the last severe war. In a similar way and for the like
reasons, a number of communities of the former Volscian territory appear to have been about the same time transferred
from the class of subjects to that of burgesses. These originally
Sabine and Volscian, but probably by that time essentially
Romanised, communes were the first members of properly alien
lineage incorporated in the Roman burgess-union. To these
there fell to be added the just-mentioned maritime or burgess
colonies, as they were called, in which the whole inhabitants
likewise possessed the full Roman franchise. Accordingly the
Roman burgess-body probably extended northward as far as
the neighbourhood of Caere, eastward to the Apennines, and
southward as far as, or beyond, Formiae. In its case, however,
we cannot use the term "boundaries" in a strict sense. Isolated
communities within this region, such as Tibur, Praeneste, Signia,
and Norba, had not the Roman franchise; others beyond its
bounds, such as Sena, possessed it; and it is probable that
families of Roman farmers were already dispersed throughout
all Italy, either altogether isolated or associated in villages.

Among the subject communities the most privileged and
most important class was that of the Latin towns, which now
embraced but few of the original participants in the Alban

festival (and these, with the exception of Tibur and Praeneste, altogether insignificant communities), but on the other hand obtained accessions equally numerous and important in the autonomous communities founded by Rome in and even beyond Italy—the Latin colonies, as they were called—and was always increasing in consequence of new settlements of the same nature. These new urban communities of Roman origin, but with Latin rights, became more and more the real buttresses of the Roman rule. These Latins, however, were by no means those with whom the battles of the lake Regillus and Trifanum had been fought. They were not those old members of the Alban league, who reckoned themselves originally equal to, if not better than, the community of Rome, and who felt the dominion of Rome to be an oppressive yoke, as the fearfully rigorous measures of security taken against Praeneste at the beginning of the war with Pyrrhus, and the collisions that long continued to occur with the Praenestines in particular, show. The Latins of the later times of the republic, on the contrary, consisted almost exclusively of communities, which from the beginning had honoured Rome as their capital and parent city; which, settled amidst peoples of alien language and of alien habits, were attached to Rome by community of language, of law, and of manners; which, as the petty tyrants of the surrounding districts, were obliged doubtless to lean on Rome for their very existence, like advanced posts leaning upon the main army; and which, in fine, in consequence of the increasing material advantages of Roman citizenship, were ever deriving very considerable benefit from their equality of rights with the Romans, limited though it was. A portion of the Roman domains, for instance, was usually assigned to them for their separate use, and participation in the state leases was open to them as to the Roman burgess. A certain danger no doubt threatened the Romans from this quarter. Venusian inscriptions of the time of the Roman republic, and Beneventine inscriptions recently brought to light,[1] show that Venusia as well as Rome had its plebs and its tribunes of the people, and that the chief magistrates of Beneventum bore the title of consul at least about the time of the Hannibalic war. Both communities are among the most recent of the Latin colonies with older rights: we perceive what pretensions were stirring in them about the middle of the fifth century. These so-called

---

[1] *V. Cervio A. f. cosol dedicavit* and *Iunonei Quiritei sacra. C. Falcilius L. f. consol dedicavit.*

Latins, issuing from the Roman burgess-body and feeling themselves in every respect on a level with it, could not but on their part begin to view with displeasure their subordinate federal rights and to strive after full equalisation. Accordingly the senate exerted itself to curtail these Latin colonies,—however important they were for Rome—as far as possible in their rights and privileges, and to convert their position from that of allies to that of subjects, so far as this could be done without removing the line of demarcation between them and the non-Latin communities of Italy. We have already described the abolition of the league itself, and the loss of the most important political privileges belonging to the communities as well as of their former complete equality of rights. On the complete subjugation of Italy a further step was taken, and a movement was made towards the restriction of the personal rights—that had not hitherto been touched—of the individual Latin, especially the important right of freedom of settlement. It is true that the privileges secured by stipulation to the older communities were not touched; but in the case of Ariminum founded in $\frac{486}{268}$ and of all the autonomous communities constituted afterwards, the privilege of acquiring by settlement in Rome the passive franchise and even a sort of suffrage there (p. 340) was no longer conceded. The main advantage enjoyed by them, as compared with other subjects, consisted in their equalisation with burgesses of the Roman community so far as regarded private rights—those of traffic and barter as well as those of inheritance. The Roman franchise was in future conferred only on such citizens of these townships as had filled a public magistracy in them: in that case, however, it was, apparently from the first, conferred without any limitation of rights.[1] This clearly shows

[1] According to the testimony of Cicero (*pro Caec.* §35) Sulla gave to the Volaterrans the former *jus* of Ariminum, that is—adds the orator—the *jus* of the "twelve colonies" which had not the Roman *civitas* but had full *commercium* with the Romans. Few things have been so much discussed as the question to what places this *jus* of the twelve towns refers; and yet the answer is not far to seek. There were in Italy and Cisalpine Gaul— laying aside some places that soon disappeared again—thirty-four Latin colonies established in all. The twelve most recent of these—Ariminum, Beneventum, Firmum, Aesernia, Brundisium, Spoletium, Cremona, Placentia, Copia, Valentia, Bononia, and Aquileia—are those here referred to; and because Ariminum was the oldest of these and the town in reference to which this new organisation was primarily established, partly perhaps also because it was the first Roman colony founded beyond Italy, the *jus* of these colonies rightly took its name from Ariminum. This at the same time demonstrates the truth of the view—which already had on other grounds very high probability—that all the colonies established in

the complete revolution in the position of Rome. So long as Rome was still but one among the many urban communities of Italy, although that one might be the first, admission even to the unrestricted Roman franchise was universally regarded as a gain for the admitting community and as a loss of privilege for those admitted; and the acquisition of that franchise by non-burgesses was facilitated in every way, and was in fact often imposed on them as a punishment. But after the Roman community became sole sovereign and all the others were its servants, the state of matters changed. The Roman community began jealously to guard its franchise, and accordingly put an end in the first instance to the old full liberty of migration; although the statesmen of that period were wise enough still to keep admission to the Roman franchise legally open at least to the men of eminence and of capacity in the highest class of subject communities. The Latins were thus made to feel that Rome, after having subjugated Italy mainly by their aid, had now no longer need of them as before.

The two other classes of Roman subjects, the subject Roman burgesses and the non-Latin allied communities, were in a far inferior position. The communities having the Roman franchise without the privilege of electing or being elected (*civitas sine suffragio*), approached nearer in form to the full Roman burgesses than the Latin communities that were legally autonomous. Their members were, as Roman burgesses, liable to all the burdens of citizenship, especially to the levy and taxation, and were subject to the Roman census; whereas, as their very designation indicates, they had no claim to its honorary rights. They lived under Roman laws, and had justice administered by Roman judges; but the hardship was lessened by the fact that their common law was, after undergoing revision by Rome, restored to them as Roman local law, and a " deputy " (*praefectus*) annually nominated by the Roman praetor [1] was sent to

Italy (in the wider sense of the term) after the founding of Aquileia belonged to the class of burgess colonies.

We cannot fully determine the extent to which the curtailment of the rights of the later Latin towns was carried, as compared with the earlier. Of course the right of settlement in itself was not withdrawn from the burgesses of these towns, for in law every one who was not an enemy, or interdicted from fire and water, was at liberty to take up his abode in Rome. If intermarriage, as is not improbable but is in fact anything but definitely established (p. 105 *supra*; Diodor. p. 590, 62, *fr.* Vat. p. 130, *Dind.*), formed a constituent element of the original federal equality of rights, it was, at any rate, no longer conceded to the Latin colonies of more recent origin.

[1] In my *Corpus Inscr. Lat.* i. p. 47, I have shown that these praefects

them to conduct its administration. In other respects these communities retained their own administration, and chose for that purpose their own chief magistrates. This relation, which was first instituted in $\frac{403}{351}$ for Caere (p. 334), and subsequently was applied to Capua (p. 356) and a number of other communities more remote from Rome, was probably in reality the most oppressive among the different forms of subjection. Lastly, the relations of the non-Latin allied communities were subject, as a matter of course, to very various rules, just as each particular treaty of alliance had defined them. Many of these perpetual treaties of alliance, such as that with the Hernican communities (p. 373) and those with Neapolis (p. 361), Nola (p. 367), and Heraclea (p. 402), granted rights comparatively comprehensive, while others, such as the Tarentine and Samnite treaties, probably approximated to despotism.

As a general rule, it may be taken for granted that not only the Latin and Hernican national confederations—as to which the fact is expressly stated—but all such confederations subsisting in Italy, and the Samnite and Lucanian leagues in particular, were legally dissolved or at any rate reduced to insignificance, and that in general no Italian community was allowed the right of acquiring property or of intermarriage, or even the right of joint consultation and resolution, with any other. Further, provision must have been made, under different forms, for placing the military and financial resources of all the Italian communities at the disposal of the leading community. Although the burgess militia on the one hand, and the contingents of the " Latin name " on the other, were still alone regarded as the main and integral constituents of the Roman army, and in that way its national character was on the whole preserved, the Roman *cives sine suffragio* were called forth to join its ranks, and not only so, but beyond doubt the non-Latin allied communities also were either bound to furnish ships of war, as was the case with the Greek cities, or were placed on the roll of contingent-furnishing Italians (*formula togatorum*), as must have been decreed at once or gradually in the case of the Apulians, Sabellians, and Etruscans. In general this contingent, like that of the Latin communities, appears to have had its numbers definitely fixed, although, in case of necessity, the leading com-

---

were down to the seventh century nominated by the praetors, and not by the burgesses, and that, if Livy (ix. 20) in using the word *creari* has meant it to refer to popular election, he has erroneously transferred the arrangement adopted in the last period of the republic to an earlier epoch.

munity was not precluded from making a larger requisition. This at the same time involved an indirect taxation, as every community was bound itself to equip and to pay its own contingent. Accordingly it was not without design that the supply of the most costly requisites for war devolved chiefly on the Latin, or non-Latin allied, communities; that the war marine was for the most part kept up by the Greek cities; and that in the cavalry service the allies, at least subsequently, were called upon to furnish a proportion thrice as numerous as the Roman burgesses, while in the infantry the old principle, that the contingent of the allies should not be more numerous than the burgess army, still remained in force for a long time at least as the rule.

The system, on which this fabric was constructed and kept together, can no longer be ascertained in detail from the few notices that have reached us. Even the numerical proportions of the three classes, relatively to each other and to the full burgesses, can no longer be determined even approximately; [1]

---

[1] It is to be regretted that we are unable to give satisfactory information as to the proportional numbers. We may estimate the number of Roman burgesses capable of bearing arms in the later regal period as about 20,000 (p. 98). Now from the fall of Alba to the conquest of Veii the immediate territory of Rome received no material extension; in perfect accordance with which we find that from the first institution of the twenty-one tribes about $\frac{259}{495}$ (p. 277), which involved little or no extension of the Roman bounds, no new tribes were instituted till $\frac{367}{387}$. However abundant allowance we make for increase by the excess of births over deaths, by immigration, and by manumissions, it is absolutely impossible to reconcile with the narrow limits of a territory of hardly 650 square miles the traditional accounts of the census, according to which the number of Roman burgesses capable of bearing arms in the second half of the third century varied between 104,000 and 150,000, and in $\frac{362}{392}$, regarding which a special statement is extant, amounted to 152,573. These numbers are on a parallel with the 84,700 burgesses of the Servian census; and in general the whole lists of the census, carried back to the four earlier lustres of Servius Tullius and furnished with copious numbers, belong to the class of those apparently documentary traditions which delight in, and betray themselves by the very fact of, such numerical details.

It was only with the second half of the fourth century that the large extensions of territory on the one hand, and the incorporation of whole communities with Rome on the other (p. 345) which must have suddenly and considerably augmented the burgess roll, began. It is reported on reliable authority and is intrinsically credible, that about $\frac{416}{338}$ the Roman burgesses numbered 165,000; which very well agrees with the statement that ten years previously, when the whole militia was called out against Latium and the Gauls, the first levy amounted to ten legions, that is, to 50,000 men. Subsequently to the great extensions of territory in Etruria, Latium, and Campania, in the fifth century the effective burgesses humbered, on an average, 250,000; immediately before the first Punic war, 280,000 to 290,000. These numbers are certain enough, but they are of

and in like manner the geographical distribution of the several categories over Italy is but imperfectly known. The leading ideas on which the structure was based, on the other hand, are so obvious that it is scarcely necessary specially to set them forth. First of all, as we have already said, the immediate circle of the ruling community was extended as far as was possible without completely decentralising the Roman community, which was urban and was intended to remain so. When the system of incorporation was extended up to and perhaps even beyond its natural limits, the communities that were subsequently added had to submit to a position of subjection; for a pure hegemony as a permanent relation was intrinsically impossible. Thus not through any arbitrary monopolising of sovereignty, but through the inevitable force of circumstances, a class of subjects took its place by the side of the class of ruling burgesses. It was one of the primary expedients of Roman rule to subdivide the governed by breaking up the Italian confederacies and instituting as large a number as possible of comparatively small communities, and to graduate the pressure of that rule according to the different categories of subjects. As Cato in the government of his household took care that the slaves should not be on too good terms with one another, and designedly fomented variances and factions among them, so the Roman community acted on a great scale. The expedient was not generous, but it was effectual.

It was but a wider application of the same expedient, when in each dependent community the constitution was remodelled after the Roman pattern and a government of the wealthy and respectable families was installed, which was naturally more or less keenly opposed to the multitude and was induced by its material interests and by its wish for local power to lean on Roman support. The most remarkable instance of this sort is furnished by the treatment of Capua, which appears to have

little service historically for another reason, namely, that in them, beyond doubt, the Roman full burgesses and the " burgesses without vote," such as the Caerites and Campanians, are mixed up together, while practically the latter must be reckoned decidedly as subjects, and Rome could count with much more certainty on the contingents of the Latins not included in these numbers than on the Campanian legions. If the statement in Livy (xxiii. 5) that 30,000 infantry and 4000 horse could be raised from Capua, was drawn, as hardly admits of doubt, from the Roman census rolls, we may—seeing that the Campanians probably formed the main body of the passive burgesses and are directly put as equivalent to them in Polyb. ii. 24, 14—estimate these passive burgesses at nearly 50,000 men capable of bearing arms; but this number is not sufficiently certain to form the basis of further calculations.

been from the first treated with suspicious precaution as the
only Italian city that could come into possible rivalry with
Rome. The Campanian nobility received the rights of a privileged order, separate places of assembly, and a peculiar position
in all respects; indeed they even obtained not inconsiderable
pensions—sixteen hundred of them at 450 *stateres* (about £29)
annually—charged on the Campanian exchequer. It was these
Campanian equites, whose refusal to take part in the great
Latino-Campanian insurrection of $\frac{414}{340}$ mainly contributed to its
failure, and whose brave swords decided the day in favour of
the Romans at Sentinum in $\frac{459}{295}$ (p. 377); whereas the Campanian infantry at Rhegium was the first body of troops that in
the war with Pyrrhus revolted from Rome (p. 393). Another
remarkable instance of the Roman practice of turning to account
for their own interest the variances between the orders in the
dependent communities by favouring the aristocracy, is furnished
by the treatment which Volsinii met with in $\frac{489}{265}$. There, just
as in Rome, the old and new burgesses must have stood opposed
to one another, and the latter must have attained by legal means
equality of political rights. In consequence of this the old burgesses of Volsinii resorted to the Roman senate with a request
for the restoration of their old constitution—a step which the
ruling party in the city naturally viewed as high treason, and
inflicted legal punishment accordingly on the petitioners. The
Roman senate, however, took part with the old burgesses, and,
when the city showed no disposition to submit, not only destroyed by military violence the communal constitution of
Volsinii which was in recognised operation, but also, by razing
the old capital of Etruria, exhibited to the Italians a fearfully
palpable proof of the despotism of Rome.

But the Roman senate had the wisdom not to overlook the
fact, that the only means of giving permanence to despotism
is moderation on the part of the despots. On that account the
dependent communities either had the full Roman franchise
granted in lieu of independence, or were left in possession of a
species of autonomy, which included a shadow of independence,
a special share in the military and political successes of Rome,
and above all a free communal constitution—so far as the
Italian confederacy extended, there existed no community of
Helots. On that account also Rome from the very first, with
a clearsightedness and magnanimity perhaps unparalleled in
history, waived the most dangerous of all the rights of government, the right of taxing her subjects. At the most tribute

was perhaps imposed on the dependent Celtic cantons: so far as
the Italian confederacy extended, there was no tributary community. On that account, lastly, while the duty of bearing
arms was partially devolved on the subjects, the ruling burgesses
were by no means exempt from it; it is probable that the latter
were proportionally far more numerous than the body of the
allies; and in that body, again, probably the Latins as a whole
were liable to far greater demands upon them than the passive
burgesses or at least the non-Latin allied communities. There
was thus a certain reasonableness in the appropriation by which
Rome ranked first, and the Latins next to her, in the distribution of the spoil acquired in war.

The central administration at Rome solved the difficult
problem of preserving its supervision and control over the mass
of the Italian communities liable to furnish contingents, partly
by means of the four Italian quaestors, partly by the extension
of the Roman censorship over the whole of the dependent communities. The quaestors of the fleet (p. 413), along with their
more immediate duty, had to raise the revenues from the newly
acquired domains and to control the contingents of the new
allies; they were the first Roman functionaries to whom a
residence and district out of Rome were assigned by law, and
they formed the necessary intermediate authority between the
Roman senate and the Italian communities. Moreover, as is
shown by the later municipal constitution, the chief functionaries in every Italian community,[1] whatever might be their
title, had to undertake a valuation every fourth or fifth year;
an institution, the suggestion of which must necessarily have
emanated from Rome, and which can only have been intended
to furnish the senate with a view of the resources in men and
money of the whole of Italy, corresponding to the census in
Rome.

Lastly, with this military administrative union of the whole
peoples dwelling to the south of the Apennines, as far as the
Iapygian promontory and the straits of Rhegium, was connected the rise of a new name common to them all—that of
" the men of the toga " (togati), which was their oldest designation in Roman state law, or that of the " Italians," which was
the appellation originally in use among the Greeks and thence
became universally current. The various nations inhabiting

---

[1] Not merely in every Latin one; for the censorship or so-called *quin-
quennalitas* occurs, as is well known, also among communities whose constitution was not formed according to the Latin scheme.

those lands were probably first led to feel and own their unity, partly through their common contrast to the Greeks, partly and mainly through their common resistance to the Celts; for, although an Italian community may now and then have made common cause with the Celts against Rome and employed the opportunity to recover independence, yet in the long run sound national feeling necessarily prevailed. As the Gallic territory down to a late period stood contrasted in law with the Italian, so the "men of the toga" were thus named in contrast to the Celtic "men of the hose" (*braccati*); and it is probable that the repelling of the Celtic invasions played an important diplomatic part as a reason or pretext for centralising the military resources of Italy in the hands of the Romans. Inasmuch as the Romans on the one hand took the lead in the great national struggle and on the other hand compelled the Etruscans, Latins, Sabellians, Apulians, and Hellenes (within the bounds to be immediately described) alike to fight under their standards, that unity, which hitherto had been undefined and latent rather than expressed, obtained firm consolidation and recognition in state law; and the name *Italia*, which originally and even in the Greek authors of the fifth century—in Aristotle for instance—pertained only to the modern Calabria, was transferred to the whole land of these wearers of the toga.

The earliest boundaries of this great armed confederacy led by Rome, or of the new Italy, reached on the western coast as far as the district of Leghorn south of the Arnus,[1] on the east as far as the Aesis north of Ancona. The places colonised by Italians, lying beyond these limits, such as Sena Gallica and Ariminum beyond the Apennines, and Messana in Sicily, were reckoned geographically as situated out of Italy—even when, like Ariminum, they were members of the confederacy or, like Sena, were Roman burgess communities. Still less could the Celtic cantons beyond the Apennines be reckoned among the *togati*, although perhaps some of them were already among the clients of Rome.

The new Italy had thus become a political unity; it was also in the course of becoming a national unity. Already the ruling Latin nationality had assimilated to itself the Sabines and Volscians and had scattered isolated Latin communities over all

---

[1] This earliest boundary is probably indicated by the two small places *Ad Fines*, of which one lay north of Arezzo on the road to Florence, the second on the coast not far from Leghorn. Somewhat further to the south of the latter, the brook and valley of Vada are still called *Fiume della Fine, Valle della Fine* (Targioni Tozzetti, *Viaggj*, iv. 430).

Italy; these germs were merely developed, when subsequently the Latin language became the mother-tongue of every one entitled to wear the Latin toga. That the Romans already clearly recognised this as their aim, is shown by the familiar extension of the Latin name to the whole body of contingent-furnishing Italian allies.[1] Whatever can still be recognised of this grand political structure testifies to the great political sagacity of its nameless architects; and the singular cohesion, which that confederation composed of so many and so diversified ingredients subsequently exhibited under the severest shocks, stamped their great work with the seal of success. From the time when the threads of this net drawn skilfully and firmly around Italy were concentrated in the hands of the Roman community, it became a great power, and took its place in the system of the Mediterranean states in the room of Tarentum, Lucania, and other intermediate and minor states erased by the last wars from the list of political powers. Rome received, as it were, an official recognition of its new position by means of the two solemn embassies, which in $\frac{481}{273}$ were sent from Alexandria to Rome and from Rome to Alexandria, and which, though primarily they regulated only commercial relations, beyond doubt prepared the way for a political alliance. As Carthage was contending with the Egyptian government regarding Cyrene and was soon to contend with that of Rome regarding Sicily, so Macedonia was contending with the former for the predominant influence in Greece, with the latter proximately for the sovereignty of the Adriatic coasts. The new struggles, which were preparing on all sides, could not but influence each other, and Rome, as mistress of Italy, could not fail to be drawn into the wide arena which the victories and projects of Alexander the Great had marked out as the field of conflict to his successors.

[1] In strict official language, indeed, this was not the case. The fullest designation of the Italians occurs in the agrarian law of $\frac{643}{111}$, line 21;— [ceivis] Romanus sociumve nominisve Latini, quibus ex formula togatorum [milites in terra Italia imperare solent]; in like manner at the 29th line of the same the peregrinus is distinguished from the Latinus, and in the decree of the senate as to the Bacchanalia in $\frac{568}{186}$ the expression is used: ne quis ceivis Romanus neve nominis Latini neve socium quisquam. But in common use very frequently the second or third of these three subdivisions is omitted, and along with the Romans sometimes only those Latini nominis are mentioned, sometimes only the socii (Weissenborn on Liv. xxii. 50, 6), while there is no difference in the meaning. The designation homines nominis Latini ac socii Italici (Sallust. Jug. 40), correct as it is in itself, is foreign to the official usus loquendi, which employs Italia, but not Italici.

CHAPTER VIII

LAW—RELIGION—MILITARY SYSTEM—ECONOMIC CONDITION—NATIONALITY

In the development of law during this period within the Roman commonwealth, probably the most important material innovation was that peculiar control which the community itself, and in a subordinate degree its office-bearers, began to exercise over the manners and habits of the individual burgesses. The germ of it is to be sought not so much in the religious anathemas which had served in the earliest times as a sort of substitute for police (p. 176), as in the right of the magistrates to inflict property fines (*multae*) for offences against order (p. 151). In the case of all fines of more than two sheep and thirty oxen or, after the cattle-fines had been by the decree of the people in $\frac{324}{430}$ commuted into money, of more than 3020 libral *asses* (£30), the decision soon after the expulsion of the kings passed by way of appeal into the hands of the community (p. 248); and thus procedure by fine acquired an importance which it was far from originally possessing. Under the vague category of offences against order men might include any accusations they pleased, and by the higher grades in the scale of fines they might accomplish whatever they desired. The dangerous character of such arbitrary procedure was brought to light rather than obviated by the mitigating proviso, that these property-fines, where they were not fixed by law at a definite sum, should not exceed half the estate of the person fined. To this class belonged the police laws, which from the earliest times were especially abundant in the Roman commonwealth. Such were those enactments of the Twelve Tables, which prohibited the anointing of a dead body by persons hired for the purpose, the dressing it out with more than one cushion or more than three purple-edged coverings, the decorating it with gold or gaudy chaplets, the use of dressed wood for the funeral pile, and the perfuming or sprinkling of the pyre with frankincense or myrrh wine; which limited the number of flute-players in the funeral procession to ten at most; and which forbade wailing women and funeral banquets—in a certain sense the earliest Roman legislation against luxury. Such also were the laws—originating in the conflicts of the orders—directed against an immoderate use of the common pasture and a disproportionate appropriation of the occupiable domain-land, as well as those directed against usury. But far more fraught with danger than these and similar police laws, which at least explicitly set forth the offence and often prescribed also its precise punishment, was the general prerogative of every magistrate who exercised jurisdiction to inflict a fine for an offence against order, and if the fine reached the amount necessary to found an appeal and the person fined did not submit to the penalty, to bring the case before the community. Already in the course of the fifth century quasi-criminal proceedings had been in this way instituted against immorality of life both in men and women, against the fore-stalling of grain, witchcraft, and similar practices. Closely akin to this was the quasi-jurisdiction of the censors, which likewise sprang up at this period. They were invested with authority to adjust the Roman budget and the burgess-roll, and they availed themselves of it partly to impose of their own accord taxes on luxury which differed only in form from penalties, partly to abridge or withdraw the political privileges of the burgess who was reported to have been guilty of any infamous action. The extent to which this surveillance was already carried is shown by the fact that penalties of this nature were inflicted for the negligent cultivation of a man's own land, and that such an one as Publius Cornelius Rufinus (consul in $\frac{464}{290}$, $\frac{477}{277}$) was struck off the list of senators by the censors of $\frac{479}{275}$, because he possessed silver plate to the value of 3360 sesterces (£34). No doubt, according to the rule generally applicable to the edicts of magistrates (p. 259), the sentences of the censors had legal force only during their censorship, that is on an average for the next five years, and might be renewed or not by the next censors at pleasure. Nevertheless this censorial pre-rogative was of so immense importance, that in virtue of it the censorship, originally one of the least of the Roman public magistracies, became in rank and consideration the first of all (pp. 290, 309). The government of the senate rested essentially on this twofold police control supreme and subordinate, vested in the community and its officials, and furnished with powers as extensive as they were arbitrary. Like every such arbitrary government, it was productive of much good and much evil, and we do not mean to combat the view of those who hold that the evil preponderated. But we must not forget that—amidst the morality external no doubt but stern and energetic, and the vigorous development of public spirit, that were the genuine characteristics of this period—these institutions remained exempt as yet from any really vulgar abuse; and if they were the chief instruments in repressing individual freedom, they were also the means by which the public spirit and the good old manners and order of the Roman community were with might and main upheld.

Along with these changes a humanising and modernising tendency showed itself slowly but yet clearly enough in the development of Roman law. Most of the enactments of the Twelve Tables, which coincide with the laws of Solon and therefore may with reason be considered as in substance innovations, bear this character; such as the securing the right of free association and the autonomy of the societies that originated under it; the enactment that forbade the ploughing up of boundary-balks; and the mitigation of the punishment of theft, so that a thief not caught in the act might henceforth release himself from the plaintiff's suit by payment of double compensation. The law of debt was modified in a similar sense, but not till a century afterwards, by the Poetelian law (p. 301). The right freely to dispose of property, which according to the earliest Roman law was accorded to the owner in his lifetime but in the case of death had hitherto been conditional on the consent of the community, was liberated from this restriction, inasmuch as the law of the Twelve Tables or its interpretation assigned to private testaments the same force as pertained to those confirmed in the curies. This was an important step towards the breaking up of the clanships, and towards the full carrying out of individual liberty in the disposal of property. The fearfully absolute paternal power was restricted by the enactment, that a son thrice sold by his father should not relapse into his power, but should thenceforth be free; which— by a legal inference that, strictly viewed, was no doubt inconsistent with the spirit of the Roman law—was soon construed to imply that a father might voluntarily divest himself of dominion over his son by emancipation. In the law of marriage civil marriage was permitted (p. 89); and although the full marital power was associated as necessarily with a true civil as with a true religious marriage, yet the permission of a connection formed without that power in the place of marriage (p. 57, *note*) constituted a first step towards relaxation of the

full power of the husband. The first step towards a legal enforcement of married life was the tax on old bachelors (*uxorium*),
with the introduction of which Camillus began his public career
as censor in $\frac{351}{403}$.

Changes more comprehensive than those effected in the law
itself were introduced into—what was more important in a
political point of view, and more easily admitted of alteration—
the system of judicial administration. First of all came the
important limitation of the supreme judicial power by the embodiment of the common law in a written code, and the obligation of the magistrate thenceforth to decide no longer according
to varying usage, but according to the written letter in civil as
well as in criminal procedure ($\frac{303}{451}$, $\frac{304}{450}$). The appointment of a
supreme magistrate in Rome exclusively for the administration
of justice in $\frac{387}{367}$ (p. 296), and the establishment of separate police
functionaries which took place contemporaneously in Rome, and
was imitated under Roman influence in all the Latin communities
(p. 296), secured greater speed and precision of justice. These
police-magistrates or aediles had, of course, a certain jurisdiction
at the same time assigned to them. On the one hand, they were
the ordinary civil judges for sales concluded in open market, for
the cattle and slave markets in particular; and on the other
hand, they ordinarily acted in processes of fines and amerce-
ments as judges of first instance or—which was in Roman law
the same thing—as public prosecutors. In consequence of this
the administration of the laws imposing fines, and the equally
indefinite and politically important right of fining in general,
were vested mainly in them. Similar but subordinate functions,
having especial reference to the poorer classes, pertained to the
tres viri nocturni or *capitales*, first nominated in $\frac{465}{289}$; they were
entrusted with the duties of nocturnal police as regards fire and
the public safety and with the superintendence of executions,
with which a certain jurisdiction was very soon, perhaps even
from the outset, associated.[1] Lastly from the increasing extent

---

[1] The view formerly adopted, that these *tres viri* belonged to the earliest
period, is erroneous, for colleges of magistrates with odd numbers are
foreign to the oldest state-arrangements (*Chronol.* p. 15, note 12). Probably the well-accredited account, that they were first nominated in $\frac{465}{289}$
(Liv. *Ep.* 11), should simply be retained, and the otherwise suspicious inference of the falsifier Licinius Macer (in Liv. vii. 46), which makes mention
of them before $\frac{450}{304}$, should be simply rejected. At first undoubtedly the
tres viri were nominated by the superior magistrates, as must have been
the case with most of the later *magistratus minores ;* the Papirian *plebiscitum*, which transferred the nomination of them to the community, and
at the same time extended their powers to the collection of process-fines

of the Roman community it became necessary, out of regard to the convenience of litigants, to station in the more remote places special judges competent to deal at least with minor civil causes. This arrangement was applied regularly throughout the communities of burgesses *sine suffragio* (p. 418), and was perhaps even extended to the more remote communities of full burgesses,[1] —the first germs of a Romano-municipal jurisdiction developing itself by the side of that which was strictly Roman.

In civil procedure (which, however, according to the ideas of that period included most of the crimes committed against fellow-citizens) the division of a process into the settlement of the question of law before the magistrate (*ius*), and the decision of the question of fact by a private person nominated by the magistrate (*iudicium*)—a division doubtless customary even in earlier times—was on the abolition of the monarchy prescribed by law (p. 248); and to that separation the private law of Rome was mainly indebted for its logical clearness and practical precision.[2] In actions regarding property, the decision as to what constituted possession, which hitherto had been left to the arbitrary caprice of the magistrate, was subjected gradually to legal rules; and, besides the right of property, a right of posses-

(*sacramenta*, Festus, *v. sacramentum*, p. 344, Müll.), was at any rate not issued till after the institution of the office of *praetor peregrinus*, or at the earliest towards the middle of the sixth century, for it names the praetor *qui inter cives ius dicit.*

[1] This inference is suggested by what Livy says (ix. 20) as to the reorganisation of the colony of Antium twenty years after it was founded; and it is self-evident that, while the Romans might very well impose on the inhabitant of Ostia the duty of settling all his law-suits in Rome, the same course could not be followed with places like Antium and Sena.

[2] People are in the habit of praising the Romans as a nation specially privileged in respect to jurisprudence, and of gazing with wonder on their admirable law as a mystical gift of heaven; not improbably by way of excuse for the worthlessness of their own legal system. A glance at the singularly varying and undeveloped criminal law of the Romans might show the untenableness of ideas so confused even to those who may think the proposition too simple, that a sound people has a sound law, and a morbid people an unsound. Apart from the more general political conditions on which jurisprudence also, and indeed jurisprudence especially depends, the causes of the excellence of the Roman civil law lie mainly in two features: first, that the plaintiff and defendant were specially obliged to explain and embody in due and binding form the grounds of the demand and of the objection to comply with it; and secondly, that the Romans appointed a permanent machinery for the edictal development of their law, and associated it immediately with practice. By the former the Romans precluded the pettifogging practices of advocates, by the latter they obviated incapable law-making, so far as such things can be prevented at all; and by means of both in conjunction they satisfied, as far as is possible, the two conflicting requirements, that law shall constantly be fixed, and that it shall constantly be in accordance with the spirit of the age.

sion was established—another step, by which the magisterial
authority lost an important part of its powers. In criminal
processes, the tribunal of the people, which hitherto had exercised
the prerogative of mercy, became a court of legally secured
appeal. If the accused was condemned by a magistrate and
appealed to the people, the cause was discussed in three public
assemblies, the magistrate who had given judgment defending
his sentence and so in reality appearing as public prosecutor;
it was not till the fourth diet that the question was put
(*anquisitio*), when the people confirmed or reversed the sentence.
Modification was not allowed. A similar republican spirit
breathed in the principles, that the house protected the burgess,
and that an arrest could only take place out of doors; that
imprisonment during investigation was to be avoided; and that
it was allowable for every accused and not yet condemned
burgess by renouncing his citizenship to withdraw from the
consequences of condemnation, so far as they affected not his
property but his person—principles which certainly were not
embodied in formal laws and accordingly did not legally bind
the prosecuting magistrate, but yet were by their moral weight
of the greatest influence, particularly in limiting capital punishment. But, if the Roman criminal law furnishes a remarkable
testimony to the strong public spirit and to the increasing
humanity of this epoch, it on the other hand suffered injury in
its practical working from the struggles between the orders,
which in this respect were specially baneful. The co-ordinate
primary jurisdiction of all the public magistrates in criminal
cases, that arose out of these conflicts (p. 272), led to the result,
that there was no longer any fixed authority for preparing
indictments, or any serious preliminary investigation, in Roman
criminal procedure. And, as the ultimate criminal jurisdiction
was exercised in the forms and by the organs of legislation, and
never forgot its origin from the prerogative of mercy; as, moreover, the adjudication of police fines had an injurious reaction
on the criminal procedure which was externally very similar;
the decision in criminal causes was pronounced—and that not
so much by way of abuse, as in some degree by virtue of the
constitution—not according to fixed law, but according to the
arbitrary pleasure of the judges. In this way the Roman
criminal procedure was completely void of principle, and was
degraded into the sport and instrument of political parties; a
result which can the less be excused, seeing that this procedure,
while especially introduced for political crimes proper, was

applicable also to others, such as murder and arson. The evil was aggravated by the clumsiness of that procedure, which in concert with the haughty republican contempt for non-burgesses gave rise to a growing custom of tolerating, side by side with the more formal process, a summary criminal, or rather police, procedure against slaves and persons of inferior consideration. Here too the passionate strife regarding political processes overstepped natural limits, and introduced institutions which materially contributed to estrange the Romans step by step from the idea of a fixed moral order in the administration of justice.

We are less able to trace the progress of the religious ideas of the Romans during this epoch. In general they adhered with simplicity to the simple piety of their ancestors, and kept equally aloof from superstition and from unbelief. How vividly the idea of spiritualising all earthly objects, on which the Roman religion was based, still prevailed at the close of this epoch, is shown by the new god " of silver " (*Argentinus*), who probably came into existence in consequence of the introduction of the silver currency in $\frac{485}{269}$, and who naturally was the son of the older god " of copper " (*Aesculanus*).

The relations to foreign lands were the same as heretofore; but here, and here especially, Hellenic influences were on the increase. It was only now that temples began to rise in Rome itself in honour of the Hellenic gods. The oldest was the temple of Castor and Pollux, which had been vowed in the battle at lake Regillus (p. 338) and was consecrated on 15th July $\frac{269}{485}$. The legend associated with it, that two youths of superhuman size and beauty had been seen fighting on the battle-field in the ranks of the Romans, and immediately after the battle watering their foaming steeds in the Roman Forum at the fountain of Iuturna, and announcing the great victory, bears a stamp thoroughly un-Roman, and was beyond doubt at a very early period modelled on the appearance of the Dioscuri—similar down to its very details—in the famous battle fought about a century before between the Crotoniates and Locrians at the river Sagras. The Delphic Apollo too was not only consulted—as was usual with all peoples that felt the influence of Grecian culture—and presented moreover after special successes, such as the capture of Veii, with a tenth of the spoil ($\frac{360}{394}$, but also had a temple built for him in the city ($\frac{323}{431}$, renewed $\frac{401}{353}$). The same honour was towards the close of this period accorded to Aphrodite ($\frac{459}{295}$), who was in some enigmatical way identified with the old Roman garden goddess, Venus;[1] and to Asklapios or Aesculapius, who was obtained by special request from Epidaurus in the Peloponnesus and solemnly conducted to Rome ($\frac{463}{291}$). Isolated complaints were heard in serious emergencies as to the intrusion of foreign superstition, probably the art of the Etruscan *haruspices* (as in $\frac{326}{428}$); but in such cases the police did not fail to take proper cognisance of the matter.

In Etruria on the other hand, while the nation stagnated and decayed in political helplessness and indolent opulence, the theological monopoly of the nobility, stupid fatalism, wild and meaningless mysticism, the system of soothsaying, and of mendicant prophecy gradually developed themselves, till they reached the height at which we afterwards find them.

In the sacerdotal system no comprehensive changes, so far as we know, took place. The more stringent enactments, that were made about $\frac{465}{289}$ regarding the tax on actions at law destined to defray the cost of public worship, point to an increase in the religious expenses of the state—a necessary result of the increase in the number of its gods and its temples. It has already been mentioned as one of the evil effects of the dissensions between the orders that a greater influence began to be conceded to the colleges of men of lore, and that they were employed for the annulling of political acts (p. 291)—a course by which on the one hand the faith of the people was shaken, and on the other hand the priests were permitted to exercise a very injurious influence on public affairs.

A complete revolution occurred during this epoch in the military system. The primitive Graeco-Italian military organisation, which was probably based, like the Homeric, on the selection of the most distinguished and effective warriors—who ordinarily fought on horseback—to form a special vanguard, had in the later regal period been superseded by the old Dorian phalanx of hoplites, probably eight file deep (p. 95). This phalanx thenceforth undertook the chief burden of the battle, while the cavalry were stationed on the flanks, and, mounted or dismounted according to circumstances, were chiefly employed as a reserve. From this arrangement there were developed nearly at the same time the phalanx of *sarissae* in Macedonia and the manipular legion in Italy, the former formed by closing and deepening, the latter by breaking up and multiply-

---

[1] Venus probably first appears in the later sense as Aphrodite on occasion of the dedication of the temple consecrated in this year (Liv. x. 31; Becker, *Topographie*, p. 472).

ing, the ranks. The old Doric phalanx had been wholly adapted to close combat with the sword and especially with the spear, and only an accessory and subordinate position in the order of battle was assigned to missile weapons. In the manipular legion the thrusting-lance was confined to the third division, and instead of it the two first were furnished with a new and peculiar Italian missile weapon, the *pilum*—a square or round piece of wood, four and a half feet long, with a triangular or quadrangular iron point—which had been originally perhaps invented for the defence of the ramparts of the camp, but was soon transferred from the rear to the front ranks, and was hurled by the advancing line into the ranks of the enemy at a distance of from ten to twenty paces. At the same time the sword acquired far greater importance than the short knife of the phalangite could ever have had; for the volley of javelins was intended in the first instance merely to prepare the way for an attack sword in hand. While, moreover, the phalanx had, as if it were a single mighty lance, to be hurled at once upon the enemy, in the new Italian legions the smaller units, which existed in the phalanx system but were in battle array held together by an indissolubly firm bond, were again separated from each other. The close square was separated in the direction of its depth into the three divisions of the *hastati*, *principes*, and *triarii*, each of a moderate depth probably amounting in ordinary cases to only four files; and was broken up along the front into ten bands (*manipuli*), in such a way that between every two divisions and every two maniples there was left a perceptible interval. It was a mere continuation of the same process of individualising, by which the collective mode of fighting was discouraged even in the diminished tactical unit and the single combat became prominent, as is evident from the (already mentioned) decisive part played by hand-to-hand encounters and combats with the sword. The system of entrenching the camp assumed also a peculiar development. The place where the army encamped, even were it only for a single night, was invariably provided with a regular circumvallation and as it were converted into a fortress. Little change took place on the other hand in the cavalry, which in the manipular legion retained the secondary place which it had occupied by the side of the phalanx. The system of officering the army also continued in the main unchanged; yet it was at this period probably that the clear line of demarcation became established between the subaltern officers, who as common soldiers had to gain their place at the head of the maniples by the sword and passed by regular promotion from the lower to the higher maniples, and the military tribunes placed at the head of whole legions—six to each—in whose case there was no regular promotion, and who were usually taken from the better classes. In this respect it must have become a matter of importance that, while previously the subaltern as well as the staff officers had been uniformly nominated by the general, after $\frac{392}{362}$ some of the latter posts were filled up through election by the burgesses (p. 307). Lastly, the old, fearfully strict, military discipline remained unaltered. Still, as formerly, the general was at liberty to behead any man serving in his camp, and to scourge with rods the staff officer as well as the common soldier; nor were such punishments inflicted merely on account of common crimes, but also when an officer had allowed himself to deviate from the orders which he had received, or when a division had allowed itself to be surprised or had fled from the field of battle. On the other hand, the new military organisation necessitated a far more serious and prolonged military training than the previous phalanx system, in which the solidity of the mass kept even the inexperienced in their ranks. As, however, no special soldier-class sprang up, but on the contrary the army still remained, as before, a burgess army, this object was chiefly attained by abandoning the former mode of ranking the soldiers according to property (p. 92) and arranging them according to length of service. The Roman recruit now entered among the light-armed " skirmishers " (*rorarii*), who fought out of the line and especially with stone slings, and he advanced from this step by step to the first and then to the second division, till at length the soldiers of long service and experience were associated together in the corps of the *triarii*, which was numerically the weakest but imparted its tone and spirit to the whole army.

The excellence of this military organisation, which became the primary cause of the superior political position of the Roman community, chiefly depended on the three great military principles of maintaining a reserve, of combining the close and distant modes of fighting, and of combining the offensive and the defensive. The system of a reserve was already foreshadowed in the earlier employment of the cavalry, but it was now completely developed by the partition of the army into three divisions and the reservation of the flower of the veterans for the last and decisive shock. While the Hellenic phalanx had developed the close, and the oriental squadrons of horse armed with bows and light missile spears the distant, modes of fighting respectively, the Roman combination of the heavy javelin with the sword produced results similar, as has justly been remarked, to those attained in modern warfare by the introduction of bayonet muskets; the volley of javelins prepared the way for the sword encounter, exactly in the same way as a volley of musketry now precedes a charge with the bayonet. Lastly, the thorough system of encampment allowed the Romans to combine the advantages of defensive and offensive war and to decline or give battle according to circumstances, and in the latter case to fight under the ramparts of their camp just as under the walls of a fortress—the Roman, says a Roman proverb, conquers by sitting still.

That this new military organisation was in the main a Roman, or at any rate Italian, remodelling and improvement of the old Hellenic tactics of the phalanx, is plain. If some germs of the system of reserve and of the individualising of the smaller sub-divisions of the army are found to occur among the later Greek strategists, especially Xenophon, this only shows that they felt the defectiveness of the old system, but were not well able to remedy it. The manipular legion appears fully developed in the war with Pyrrhus; when and under what circumstances it arose, whether at once or gradually, can no longer be ascertained. The first tactical system which the Romans encountered, fundamentally different from the earlier Italo-Hellenic system, was the Celtic sword-phalanx. It is not impossible that the subdivision of the army and the intervals between the maniples in front were arranged with a view to resist, as they did resist, its first and only dangerous charge; and it accords with this hypothesis that Marcus Furius Camillus, the most celebrated Roman general of the Gallic epoch, is presented in various detached notices as the reformer of the Roman military system. The further traditions associated with the Samnite and Pyrrhic wars are neither sufficiently accredited, nor can they be arranged in proper order;[1] although it is in itself probable that the pro-

---

[1] According to Roman tradition the Romans originally carried square shields, after which they borrowed from the Etruscans the round hoplite shield (*clupeus*, ἀσπίς), and from the Samnites the later square shield (*scutum*, θυρεός), and the javelin (*veru*) (Diodor. *Vat. Fr.* p. 54; Sallust. *Cat.* 51, 38; Virgil, *Aen.* vii. 665; Festus, *Ep. v. Samnites*, p. 327, *Müll.*; and the authorities cited in Marquardt, *Handb.* iii. 2, 241). But it may be regarded as certain that the hoplite shield or, in other words, the tactics of the Doric phalanx were imitated not from the Etruscans, but directly from the Hellenes. As to the *scutum*, that large, cylindrical, convex leather shield must certainly have taken the place of the flat copper *clupeus*, when the phalanx was broken up into maniples; but the indisput-

onged Samnite mountain warfare exercised a lasting influence on the individual development of the Roman soldier, and that the struggle with one of the first masters of the art of war, belonging to the school of the great Alexander, effected an improvement in the technical features of the Roman military system.

In the national economy agriculture was, and continued to be, the social and political basis both of the Roman community and of the new Italian state. The common assembly and the army consisted of Roman farmers; what as soldiers they had acquired by the sword, they secured as colonists by the plough. The insolvency of the middle class of landholders gave rise to the formidable internal crises of the third and fourth centuries, amidst which it seemed as if the young republic could not but be destroyed. The revival of the Latin farmer-class, which was produced during the fifth century partly by the large assignations of land and incorporations, partly by the fall in the rate of interest and the increase of the Roman population, was at once the effect and the cause of the mighty development of Roman power. The acute soldier's eye of Pyrrhus justly recognised the cause of the political and military ascendancy of the Romans in the flourishing condition of the Roman farms. But the rise also of husbandry on a large scale among the Romans appears to fall within this period. In earlier times indeed there existed landed estates of—at least comparatively—large size; but their management was not farming on a large scale, it was simply a husbandry of numerous small parcels (p. 192). On the other hand the enactment in the law of $\frac{387}{367}$, which is not inapplicable to the earlier mode of management but yet is far more appropriate to the later, viz. that the landholder should be bound to employ along with his slaves a proportional number of free persons (p. 294), may well be regarded as the oldest trace of the later centralised farming of estates; [1] and it deserves notice that even here at its first emergence it essentially rests on slaveholding. How it arose, must remain an undecided point; possibly the Carthaginian plantations in Sicily served as models to the oldest Roman landholders, and perhaps even the appearance of wheat in husbandry by the side of spelt (p. 188), which

---

able derivation of the word from the Greek casts suspicion on the derivation of the thing itself from the Samnites. From the Greeks the Romans derived also the sling (*funda* from σφενδόνη, like *fides* from σφίδη), (p. 227). The pilum was considered by the ancients a thoroughly Roman invention.

[1] Varro (*De R. R.*, i. 2, 9) evidently conceives the author of the Licinian agrarian law as farming in person his extensive lands; although the story may easily have been invented to explain the cognomen (*Stolo*).

Varro places about the period of the decemvirs, was connected
with that altered style of management. Still less can we ascertain how far this method of husbandry had already during this
period spread; but the history of the wars with Hannibal leaves
no doubt that it cannot yet have become the rule, nor can it have
yet absorbed the Italian farmer-class. Where it did come into
vogue, however, it annihilated the older clientship based on the
precarium; just as the modern system of large farms has been
formed by the suppression of petty holdings and the conversion
of hides into farm-fields. It admits of no doubt that the restriction of this agricultural clientship very materially contributed
towards the distress of the class of small cultivators.

Respecting the internal intercourse of the Italians with each
other our written authorities are silent; coins alone furnish
some information. We have already mentioned (p. 196) that
in Italy, with the exception of the Greek cities and of the
Etruscan Populonia, there was no coinage during the first three
centuries of Rome, and that cattle in the first instance, and
subsequently copper by weight, served as the medium of exchange. Within the present epoch occurred the transition on
the part of the Italians from the system of barter to that of
money; and in their money they were naturally led at first to
Greek models. The circumstances of central Italy led however
to the adoption of copper instead of silver as the metal for their
coinage, and the unit of coinage was primarily based on the
previous unit of value, the copper pound; hence they cast their
coins instead of stamping them, for no die would have sufficed
for pieces so large and heavy. There seems from the first to have
been a fixed ratio for the relative value of copper and silver
(250 : 1), and with reference to that ratio the copper coinage
seems to have been issued; so that, for example, in Rome the
large copper piece, the *as*, was equal in value to a scruple ($\frac{1}{288}$
of a pound) of silver. It is a circumstance historically more
remarkable, that coining in Italy most probably originated in
Rome, and in fact with the decemvirs, who found in the Solonian
legislation a pattern for the regulation of their coinage; and
that from Rome it spread over a number of Latin, Etruscan,
Umbrian, and East Italian communities,—a clear proof of the
superior position which Rome from the beginning of the fourth
century held in Italy. As all these communities subsisted side
by side in formal independence, the monetary standard for each
was in law entirely local, and the territory of every city had its
own monetary system. Nevertheless the standards of copper

coinage in central and northern Italy may be comprehended in three groups, within which the coins in common intercourse seem to have been treated as identical. These groups are, first, the coins of the cities of Etruria lying north of the Ciminian forest and those of Umbria; secondly, the coins of Rome and Latium; and lastly, those of the eastern seaboard. We have already observed that the Roman coins held a certain ratio to silver by weight; on the other hand we find those of the east coast of Italy placed in a definite proportional relation to the silver coins which were current from an early period in southern Italy, and the standard of which was adopted by the Italian immigrants, such as the Bruttians, Lucanians, and Nolans, by the Latin colonies in that quarter, such as Cales and Suessa, and even by the Romans themselves for their possessions in Lower Italy. Accordingly the inland traffic of Italy must have been divided into corresponding provinces, which dealt with one another like foreign nations.

In transmarine commerce the relations we have previously described (p. 201) between Sicily and Latium, Etruria and Attica, the Adriatic and Tarentum, continued to subsist during the epoch before us or rather, strictly speaking, belonged to it; for although facts of this class, which as a rule are mentioned without a date, have been placed together for the purpose of presenting a general view under the first period, the statements made apply equally to the present. The clearest evidence in this respect is, of course, that of the coins. As the striking of Etruscan silver money after an Attic standard (p. 201), and the penetrating of Italian and especially of Latin copper into Sicily (p. 203) testify to the two former routes of traffic, so the equivalence, which we have just mentioned, between the silver money of Magna Graecia and the copper coinage of Picenum and Apulia, forms, with numerous other indications, an evidence of the active traffic which the Greeks of Lower Italy, the Tarentines in particular, held with the east Italian seaboard. The commerce again, which was at an earlier period perhaps still more active, between the Latins and the Campanian Greeks seems to have been disturbed by the Sabellian immigration, and to have been of no great moment during the first hundred and fifty years of the republic. The refusal of the Samnites in Capua and Cumae to supply the Romans with grain in the famine of $\frac{343}{411}$ may be regarded as an indication of the altered relations which subsisted between Latium and Campania, till at the commencement of the fifth century the Roman arms restored and gave increased impetus to the old intercourse.

Touching on details, we may be allowed to mention, as one of the few dated facts in the history of Roman commerce, the notice drawn from the annals of Ardea, that in $\frac{454}{300}$ the first barber came from Sicily to Ardea; and to dwell for a moment on the painted pottery which was sent chiefly from Attica, but also from Corcyra and Sicily, to Lucania, Campania, and Etruria, to serve there for the decoration of tombs—a traffic, as to the circumstances of which we are accidentally better informed than as to any other article of transmarine commerce. The commencement of this import trade probably falls about the period of the expulsion of the Tarquins; for the vases of the oldest style, which are of very rare occurrence in Italy, were probably painted in the second half of the third century of the city, while those of the chaste style, occurring in greater numbers, belong to the first half, those of the most finished beauty to the second half, of the fourth century; and the immense quantities of the other vases, often marked by showiness and size but seldom by excellence in workmanship, must be assigned as a whole to the following century. It was from the Hellenes undoubtedly that the Italians derived this custom of embellishing tombs; but while the moderate means and fine discernment of the Greeks confined the practice in their case within narrow limits, it was stretched in Italy by barbaric opulence and barbaric extravagance far beyond its original and proper bounds. It is a significant circumstance, however, that in Italy this extravagance meets us only in the lands that had an Hellenic semi-culture. Any one who can read such records will perceive in the cemeteries of Etruria and Campania—the mines whence our museums have been replenished—a significant commentary on the accounts of the ancients as to the Etruscan and Campanian semi-culture stifled amidst wealth and arrogance (p. 336, 352). The homely Samnite character on the other hand remained at all times a stranger to this foolish luxury; the absence of Greek pottery from the tombs exhibits, quite as palpably as the absence of a Samnite coinage, the slight development of commercial intercourse and of urban life in this region. It is still more worthy of remark that Latium also, although not less near to the Greeks than Etruria and Campania, and in closest intercourse with them, almost wholly refrained from such sepulchral decorations. It is more than probable that in this result we have to recognise the influence of the stern Roman morality or—if the expression be preferred—of the rigid Roman police.   Closely connected with this subject are the already-mentioned interdicts, which the law of the Twelve Tables fulminated against purple bier-cloths and gold ornaments placed beside the dead; and the banishment of all silver plate, excepting the salt-cellar and sacrificial ladle, from the Roman household, so far at least as sumptuary laws and the terror of censorial censure could banish it: even in architecture we shall again encounter the same spirit of hostility to luxury whether noble or ignoble.   Although, however, in consequence of these influences Rome probably preserved a certain outward simplicity longer than Capua and Volsinii, her commerce and trade—on which, in fact, along with agriculture her prosperity from the beginning rested—must not be regarded as having been inconsiderable, or as having less sensibly experienced the influence of her new commanding position.

No urban middle class in the proper sense of that term, no body of independent tradesmen and merchants, was ever developed in Rome.   The cause of this was—in addition to the disproportionate centralisation of capital which occurred at an early period—mainly the employment of slave labour.   It was usual in antiquity, and was in fact a necessary consequence of slavery, that the minor trades in towns were very frequently carried on by slaves, whom their master established as artisans or merchants; or by freedmen, in whose case the master not only frequently furnished the capital, but also regularly stipulated for a share, often the half, of the profits.   Retail trading and dealing in Rome were undoubtedly constantly on the increase; and there are proofs that the trades which minister to the luxury of great cities began to be concentrated in Rome —the Ficoroni casket for instance was designed in the fifth century of the city by a Praenestine artist and was sold to Praeneste, but was nevertheless manufactured in Rome.[1]   But as the net proceeds even of retail business flowed for the most part into the coffers of the great houses, no industrial and commercial middle-class arose to an extent corresponding to that increase.   As little were the great merchants and great manufacturers marked off as a distinct class from the great landlords. On the one hand, the latter were from ancient times (p. 204, 265) simultaneously traders and capitalists, and combined in their

[1] The conjecture that Novius Plautius, the artist who wrought at this casket in Rome for Dindia Macolnia, may have been a Campanian, is refuted by the old Praenestine tombstones recently discovered, on which, among other Macolnii and Plautii, there occurs also a Lucius Magolnius, son of Plautius (L. Magolnio Pla. f.).

hands lending on security, trafficking on a great scale, the undertaking of contracts, and the executing of works for the state. On the other hand, from the emphatic moral importance which in the Roman commonwealth attached to the possession of land, and from its constituting the sole basis of political privileges— a basis which was infringed for the first time only towards the close of this epoch (p. 306)—it was undoubtedly at this period usual for the fortunate speculator to invest part of his capital in land.   It is clear enough also from the political privileges given to freedmen possessing freeholds (p. 306), that the Roman statesmen sought in this way to diminish the dangerous class of the rich who had no land.

But while neither an opulent civic middle class nor a strictly close body of capitalists grew up in Rome, it was constantly acquiring more and more the character of a great city. This is plainly indicated by the increasing number of slaves crowded together in the capital (as attested by the very serious slave conspiracy of $\frac{335}{419}$), and still more by the increasing multitude of freedmen, which was gradually becoming inconvenient and dangerous, as we may safely infer from the considerable tax imposed on manumissions in $\frac{397}{357}$ (p. 300) and from the limitation of the political rights of freedmen in $\frac{450}{304}$ (p. 306). For not only was it implied in the circumstances that the great majority of the persons manumitted had to devote themselves to trade or commerce, but manumission itself among the Romans was, as we have already said, less an act of liberality than an industrial speculation, the master often finding it more for his interest to share the profits of the trade or commerce of the freedman than to assert his title to the whole proceeds of the labour of his slave. The increase of emancipations must therefore have necessarily kept pace with the increase of the commercial and industrial activity of the Romans.

A similar indication of the rising importance of urban life in Rome is presented by the great development of the urban police. To this period probably belong in great measure the enactments under which the four aediles divided the city into four police districts, and made provision for the discharge of their equally important and difficult functions—for the efficient repair of the network of drains small and large by which Rome was pervaded, as well as of the public buildings and places; for the proper cleansing and paving of the streets; for preventing the nuisances of ruinous buildings, dangerous animals, or foul smells; for the removing of waggons from the highway except during the hours of evening and night, and generally for the keeping open of the communication; for the uninterrupted supply of the market of the capital with good and cheap grain; for the destruction of unwholesome articles, and the suppression of false weights and measures; and for the special oversight of baths, taverns, and houses of bad fame.

In respect to buildings the regal period, particularly the epoch of the great conquests, probably accomplished more than the first two centuries of the republic. Structures like the temples on the Capitol and on the Aventine and the great Circus were probably as offensive to the frugal fathers of the city as to the burgesses who gave their taskwork; and it is remarkable that perhaps the most considerable building of the republican period before the Samnite wars, the temple of Ceres in the Circus, was a work of Spurius Cassius ($\frac{261}{493}$), who in more than one respect sought to lead the commonwealth back to the traditions of the kings. The governing aristocracy moreover repressed private luxury with a rigour such as the rule of the kings, if prolonged, would certainly not have displayed. But at length even the senate was no longer able to resist the superior force of circumstances. It was Appius Claudius who in his epoch-making censorship ($\frac{442}{312}$) threw aside the antiquated rustic system of parsimonious hoarding, and taught his fellow-citizens to make a worthy use of the public resources. He began that noble system of public works of general utility, which justifies, if anything can justify, the military successes of Rome when viewed in the light of the well-being of the nations, and which even now in its ruins furnishes some idea of the greatness of Rome to thousands on thousands who have never read a page of her history. To him the Roman state was indebted for its first great military road, and the city of Rome for its first aqueduct. Following in the steps of Claudius, the Roman senate wove around Italy that network of roads and fortresses, the formation of which has already been described (p. 408), and without which, as the history of all military states from the Achaemenides down to the creator of the road over the Simplon shows, no military hegemony can subsist. Following in the steps of Claudius, Manius Curius built from the proceeds of the Pyrrhic spoil a second aqueduct for the capital ($\frac{482}{272}$); and some years previously ($\frac{464}{290}$) with the gains of the Sabine war he opened up for the Velino, at the point above Terni where it falls into the Nera, that broader channel in which the stream still flows, with a view to drain the beautiful valley of Rieti and thereby to gain space for a large burgess settlement along with a modest farm for himself. Such works, in the eyes of persons of intelligence, threw into the shade the aimless magnificence of the Hellenic temples. The style of living also among the citizens now was altered. About the time of Pyrrhus silver plate began to make its appearance on Roman tables, and the chroniclers date the disappearance of shingle roofs in Rome from $\frac{470}{284}$.[1] The new capital of Italy gradually laid aside its village-like aspect, and now began to embellish itself. It was not yet indeed customary to strip the temples in conquered towns of their ornaments for the decoration of Rome; but the beaks of the galleys of Antium were displayed at the orator's platform in the Forum (p. 356); and on public festival days the gold-mounted shields brought home from the battlefields of Samnium were exhibited along the stalls of the market (p. 370). The proceeds of fines were specially applied to the paving of the highways in and near the city, or to the erection and embellishment of public buildings. The wooden booths of the butchers, which stretched along the Forum on both sides, gave way, first on the Palatine side, then on that also which faced the Carinae, to the stone stalls of the money-changers; so that this place became the Exchange of Rome. Statues of the famous men of the past, of the kings, priests, and heroes of the legendary period, and of the Grecian *hospes*, who was said to have interpreted to the decemvirs the laws of Solon; honorary columns and monuments dedicated to the great burgomasters who had conquered the Veientes, the Latins, the Samnites, to state envoys who had perished while executing their instructions, to rich women who had bequeathed their property to public objects, nay even to celebrated Greek philosophers and heroes such as Pythagoras and Alcibiades, were erected on the Capitol or in the Forum. Thus, now that the Roman community had become a great power, Rome itself became a great city.

Lastly Rome, as head of the Romano-Italian confederacy, not only entered into the Hellenistic state-system, but also conformed to the Hellenic system of moneys and coins. Up to this time the different communities of northern and central Italy, with few exceptions, had struck only a copper currency; the

---

[1] We have already mentioned the censorial stigma attached to Publius Cornelius Rufinus (consul $\frac{464}{290}$, $\frac{477}{277}$) for his silver plate (p. 427). The strange statement of Fabius (in Strabo, v. p. 228) that the Romans first became given to luxury (αἰσθέσθαι τοῦ πλούτου) after the conquest of the Sabines, is evidently only another version of the same story; for the conquest of the Sabines took place in the first consulate of Rufinus.

south Italian towns again universally had a currency of silver; and there were as many legal standards and systems of coinage as there were sovereign communities in Italy. In $\frac{485}{269}$ all these local mints were restricted to the issuing of small coin; a general standard of currency applicable to all Italy was introduced, and the coining of the currency was centralised in Rome; Capua alone continued to retain its own silver coinage struck in the name of Rome, but after a different standard. The new monetary system was based on the legal ratio subsisting between the two metals, as it had long been fixed (p. 438). The common monetary unit was the piece of ten *asses*, or the *denarius*, which weighed in copper $3\frac{1}{2}$ and in silver $\frac{1}{72}$, of a Roman pound, a trifle more than the Attic *drachma*. At first copper money still predominated in the coinage; and it is probable that the earliest silver *denarius* was coined chiefly for Lower Italy and for intercourse with other lands. As the victory of the Romans over Pyrrhus and Tarentum and the Roman embassy to Alexandria could not but engage the thoughts of the contemporary Greek statesman, so the sagacious Greek merchant might well ponder as he looked on these new Roman *drachmae*. Their flat, unartistic, and monotonous stamping appeared poor and insignificant by the side of the marvellously beautiful contemporary coins of Pyrrhus and the Siceliots; nevertheless they were by no means, like the barbarian coins of antiquity, slavishly imitated and unequal in weight and alloy, but, on the contrary, worthy from the first by their independent and careful execution to be placed on a level with any Greek coin.

Thus, when the eye turns from the development of constitutions and from the national struggles for dominion and for freedom which agitated Italy, and Rome in particular, from the banishment of the Tarquinian house to the subjugation of the Samnites and the Italian Greeks, and rests on those calmer spheres of human existence which history nevertheless pervades and rules, it everywhere encounters the reflex influence of the great events, by which the Roman burgesses burst the bonds of patrician sway, and the rich variety of the national cultures of Italy gradually perished to enrich a single people. While the historian may not attempt to follow out the great course of events into the infinite multiplicity of individual detail, he does not overstep his province when, laying hold of detached fragments of scattered tradition, he indicates the most important changes which during this epoch took place in the national life of Italy. The fact that in such an inquiry the life of Rome becomes still more prominent than in the earlier epoch is not merely the result of the accidental blanks of our tradition; it was an essential consequence of the change in the political position of Rome, that the Latin nationality should more and more cast the other nationalities of Italy into the shade. We have already referred to the fact, that at this epoch the neighbouring lands—southern Etruria, Sabina, the land of the Volscians, and even Campania—began to become Romanised, as is attested by the almost total absence of monuments of the old native dialects, and by the occurrence of very ancient Roman inscriptions in those regions. The numerous individual assignations and colonial establishments scattered throughout Italy were, not only in a military but also in a linguistic and national point of view, the advanced posts of the Latin stock. It is true that the Latinising of the Italians was scarcely at this time the aim of Roman policy; on the contrary, the Roman senate seems to have intentionally upheld the distinction between the Latin and other nationalities, and to have by no means absolutely allowed the introduction of Latin into official use among the communities dependent on Rome. The force of circumstances, however, is stronger than even the strongest government: the language and customs of the Latin people immediately shared its ascendancy in Italy, and already began to undermine the other Italian nationalities.

These nationalities were at the same time assailed from another quarter and by an ascendancy resting on another basis —by Hellenism. This was the period when Hellenism began to become conscious of its intellectual superiority to the other nations, and to diffuse itself on every side. Italy did not remain unaffected by it. The most remarkable phenomenon of this sort is presented by Apulia, which after the fifth century of Rome gradually laid aside its barbarian dialect and silently became Hellenised. This change was brought about, as in Macedonia and Epirus, not by colonisation, but by civilisation, which seems to have gone hand in hand with the land commerce of Tarentum; at least that hypothesis is favoured by the facts, that the districts of the Poediculi and Daunii who were on friendly terms with the Tarentines carried out their Hellenisation more completely than the Sallentines who lived nearer to Tarentum but were constantly at feud with it, and that the towns that were soonest Graecised, such as Arpi, were not situated on the coast. The stronger influence exerted by Hellenism over Apulia than over any other Italian region is explained partly by its position, partly by the slight development of any national culture of its own, and partly perhaps by its nationality presenting a character less alien to the Greek stock than that of the rest of Italy (p. 10). We have already called attention (p. 352) to the fact that the southern Sabellian stocks, although at the outset in concert with the tyrants of Syracuse they crushed and destroyed the Hellenism of Magna Graecia, were at the same time affected by contact and mingling with the Greeks, so that some of them, such as the Bruttians and Nolans, adopted the Greek language by the side of their native tongue, and others, such as the Lucanians and part of the Campanians, adopted at least Greek writing and Greek manners. Etruria likewise showed tendencies towards a kindred development in the remarkable vases which have been discovered (p. 440) belonging to this period, rivalling those of Campania and Lucania; and though Latium and Samnium remained mere strangers to Hellenism, there were not wanting there also traces of an incipient and ever-growing influence of Greek culture. In all branches of the development of Rome during this epoch, in legislation and coinage, in religion, in the formation of national legend, we encounter traces of the Greeks; and from the commencement of the fifth century in particular, in other words, after the conquest of Campania, the Greek influence on Roman life appears rapidly and constantly on the increase. In the fourth century occurred the erection of the "Graecostasis"— remarkable in the very form of the word—a platform in the Roman Forum for eminent Greek strangers and primarily for the Massiliots (p. 413). In the following century the annals began to exhibit Romans of quality with Greek surnames, such as Philippus or in Roman form Pilipus, Philo, Sophus, Hypsaeus. Greek customs gained ground: such as the non-Italian practice of placing inscriptions in honour of the dead on the tomb—of which the epitaph of Lucius Scipio (consul in $\frac{456}{298}$) is the oldest example known to us; the fashion, also foreign to the Italians, of erecting without any decree of the state honorary monuments to ancestors in public places—a system begun by the great innovator Appius Claudius, when he caused bronze shields with images and eulogies of his ancestors to be suspended in the new temple of Bellona ($\frac{442}{312}$); the distribution of branches of palms to the competitors, introduced at the Roman national festival in $\frac{461}{293}$; above all, the Greek manners and habits at table. The custom not of sitting as formerly on benches, but of reclining on couches, at table; the postponement of the chief meal from noon to between two and three o'clock in the afternoon according to our mode of reckoning; the institution of masters of the revels at banquets, who were appointed from among the guests present, generally by throwing the dice, and who then prescribed to the company what, how, and when they should drink; the table-chants sung in succession by the guests, which, however, in Rome were not *scolia*, but lays in praise of ancestors—all these were not primitive customs in Rome, but were borrowed from the Greeks at a very early period, for in Cato's time these usages were already common and had in fact partly fallen into disuse again. We must therefore place their introduction in this period at the latest. A characteristic feature also was the erection of statues to "the wisest and the bravest Greek" in the Roman Forum, which took place by command of the Pythian Apollo during the Samnite wars. The selection fell on Pythagoras and Alcibiades, the saviour and the Hannibal of the western Hellenes. The extent to which an acquaintance with Greek was already diffused in the fifth century among the leading Romans is shown by the embassies of the Romans to Tarentum—when their mouthpiece spoke, if not in the purest Greek, at any rate without an interpreter—and of Cineas to Rome. It scarcely admits of a doubt that from the fifth century the young Romans who devoted themselves to state affairs universally acquired a knowledge of what was then the general language of the world and of diplomacy.

Thus in the intellectual sphere Hellenism made advances quite as incessant as the efforts of the Romans in their career of outward conquest; and the secondary nationalities, such as the Samnites, Celts, and Etruscans, hard pressed on both sides, were ever losing their inward vigour as well as narrowing their outward bounds.

When the two great nations, both arrived at the height of their development, began to mingle in hostile or in friendly contact, their antagonism of character was at the same time prominently and fully brought out—the total want of individuality in the Italian and especially in the Roman character, as contrasted with the boundless variety, lineal, local, and personal, of Hellenism. There was no epoch of mightier vigour in the history of Rome than the epoch from the institution of the republic to the subjugation of Italy. That epoch laid the foundations of the commonwealth both within and without; it created a united Italy; it gave birth to the traditional groundwork of the national law and of the national history; it originated the *pilum* and the maniple, the construction of roads and of aqueducts, the farming of estates and the monetary system; it moulded the she-wolf of the Capitol and designed the Ficoroni casket. But the individuals, who contributed the several stones to this gigantic structure and cemented them together, have disappeared without leaving a trace, and the nations of Italy did not merge into that of Rome more completely than the single Roman burgess merged in the Roman community. As the grave closes alike over all whether important or insignificant, so in the roll of the Roman burgomasters the empty scion of nobility stands undistinguishable by the side of the great states- man. Of the few records that have reached us from this period none is more venerable, and none at the same time more char- acteristic, than the epitaph of Lucius Cornelius Scipio, who was consul in $\frac{456}{298}$, and three years afterwards took part in the decisive battle of Sentinum (p. 377). On the beautiful sarcophagus, in noble Doric style, which eighty years ago still enclosed the dust of the conqueror of the Samnites, the following sentence is inscribed:—

> Cornélius Lucius—Scipió Barbátus,
> Gnaivód patré prognátus,—fórtis vír sapiénsque,
> Quoiús fórma virtu—téi parisuma fúit,
> Consól censór aidilis—quei fuit apúd vos,
> Taurásiá Cisaúna—Sámnió cépit,
> Subigit omné Loucánam—ópsidésque abdoúcit.

$$\smile -' \smile -' \smile - ' \smile \underset{\smile}{-} \; \| \; -' \smile -' \smile -' \smile$$

Innumerable others who had been at the head of the Roman commonwealth, as well as this Roman statesman and warrior, might be commemorated as having been of noble birth and of manly beauty, valiant and wise; but there was no more to record regarding them. It is no mere fault of tradition that among all these Cornelii, Fabii, Papirii and the like, we nowhere encounter a distinct individual figure. The senator was sup- posed to be no worse and no better than other senators, nor at all to differ from them. It was not necessary and not desirable that any burgess should surpass the rest, whether by showy silver plate and Hellenic culture, or by uncommon wisdom and excel- lence. Excesses of the former kind were reproved by the censor, and for the latter the constitution gave no scope. The Rome to this period belonged to no individual; it was necessary for all the burgesses to be alike, that each of them might be like a king.

No doubt, even now Hellenic individual development began to assert its claims by the side of that levelling system; and the genius and force which it exhibited bear, no less than the tendency to which it opposed itself, the full stamp of that great age. We can but name a single man in connection with it; but he was, as it were, the incarnation of the idea of progress. Appius Claudius (censor $\frac{442}{312}$; consul, $\frac{447}{307}$, $\frac{458}{296}$), the great-great-grandson of the decemvir, was a man of the old nobility and proud of the long line of his ancestors; but yet it was he who set aside the restriction which confined the full franchise of the state to the freeholders (p. 306), and who broke up the old system of finance (p. 443). From Appius Claudius date not only the Roman aqueducts and highways, but also Roman jurisprudence, eloquence, poetry, and grammar. The publication of a table of the *legis actiones*, speeches committed to writing and Pythagorean sentences, and even innovations in orthography, are attributed to him. We may not on this account call him absolutely a democrat or include him in that opposition-party which found its champion in Manius Curius (p. 305); in him on the contrary the spirit of the ancient and modern patrician kings predominated — the spirit of the Tarquins and the Caesars, between whom he forms a connecting link in that five hundred years' interregnum of extraordinary deeds and ordinary men. So long as Appius Claudius took an active part in public life, in his official conduct as well as his general carriage he disregarded laws and customs on all hands with the hardihood and sauciness of an Athenian; till, after having long retired from the political stage, the blind old man, returning as it were from the tomb at the decisive moment, overcame king Pyrrhus in the senate and first formally and solemnly proclaimed the complete sovereignty of Rome (p. 396). But the gifted man came too early or too late; the gods made him blind on account of his untimely wisdom. It was not individual genius that ruled in Rome and through Rome in Italy; it was the one immovable idea of a policy—propagated from generation to generation in the senate—with the leading maxims of which the sons of the senators were imbued, when in the company of their fathers they made their appearance in the senate hall and there listened to the wisdom of the men whose seats they were destined at some future time to fill. Immense successes were thus obtained at an immense price; for Nike too is followed by her Nemesis. In the Roman commonwealth there was no special dependence on any one man, either on soldier or on general, and under the rigid discipline of its moral police all the idiosyncrasies of human character were extinguished. Rome reached a greatness such as no other state of antiquity attained; but she dearly purchased her greatness at the sacrifice of the graceful variety, of the easy *abandon*, and of the inward freedom of Hellenic life.

CHAPTER IX

ART AND SCIENCE

THE growth of art, and of poetic art especially, in antiquity was intimately associated with the development of national festivals. The extraordinary thanksgiving - festival of the Roman community which had been organised in the previous period mainly under Greek influence, the *ludi maximi* or *Romani* (p. 228), acquired during the present epoch a longer duration and greater variety in the amusements. Originally limited to one day, the festival was prolonged by an additional day after the happy termination of each of the three great revolutions of $\frac{245}{509}$, $\frac{260}{494}$, and $\frac{387}{367}$, and thus at the close of this period it had already a duration of four days.[1]

A still more important circumstance was, that, probably on the institution of the curule aedileship ($\frac{387}{367}$) which was from the first entrusted with the preparation and oversight of the festival (p. 296), it lost its extraordinary character and its reference to a special vow made by the general, and took its place in the series of the ordinary annual festivals as the first of all. Nevertheless the government adhered to the practice of allowing the spectacle proper—namely the chariot-race which was the principal performance—to take place not more than once at the close of the festival. On the other days the multitude were probably left mainly to furnish amusements for themselves, although

[1] The account given by Dionysius (vi. 95; comp. Niebuhr, ii. 40) and by Plutarch deriving his statement from another passage in Dionysius (*Camill.* 42), regarding the Latin festival, must be understood to apply to the Roman rather than the Latin games, as, apart from other grounds, is strikingly evident from comparing the latter passage with Liv. vi. 42 (Ritschl, *Parerg.* i. p. 313). Dionysius has perseveringly, according to his wont when in error, misunderstood the expression *ludi maximi*.

There was, moreover, a tradition which referred the origin of the national festival not, as in the common version, to the conquest of the Latins by the first Tarquinius, but to the victory over the Latins at the lake Regillus (Cicero, *de Div.* i. 26, 55; Dionys. vii. 71). That the important statements preserved in the latter passage from Fabius really relate to the ordinary thanksgiving-festival, and not to any special votive solemnity, is evident from the express allusion to the annual recurrence of the festival, and from the exact agreement of the sum of the expenses with the statement in the Pseudo-Asconius (p. 142 *Or.*).

musicians, dancers, rope-walkers, jugglers, jesters, and such-like would not fail to make their appearance on the occasion, whether hired or not. But about the year $\frac{390}{364}$ an important change occurred, which must have been connected with the fixing and prolongation of the festival shortly before. A scaffolding of boards was erected at the expense of the state in the Circus for the first three days, and suitable representations were provided on it for the entertainment of the multitude. That matters might not be carried too far however in this way, a fixed sum of 200,000 *asses* (£2055) was once for all appropriated from the exchequer for the expenses of the festival; and the sum was not increased up to the period of the Punic wars. The aediles, who had to expend this sum, were obliged to defray any additional expense out of their own pockets; and it is not probable that they contributed often or much from their own resources. That the new stage was generally under Greek influence, is proved by its very name (*scaena*, σκηνή). It was no doubt at first designed merely for musicians and buffoons of all sorts, amongst whom the dancers to the flute, particularly those then so celebrated from Etruria, were probably the most distinguished; but a public stage had now arisen in Rome and thus became accessible to the Roman poets.

There was no want of such poets in Latium. Latin "strolling minstrels" or "ballad-singers" (*grassatores*, *spatiatores*) went from town to town and from house to house, and recited their chants (*saturae*, p. 28), gesticulating and dancing to the accompaniment of the flute. The measure was of course the only one that then existed, the so-called Saturnian (p. 225). No distinct plot lay at the basis of the chants, and as little do they appear to have been in the form of dialogue. We must conceive of them as resembling those monotonous—sometimes improvised, sometimes recited—ballads and *tarantelle*, such as one may still hear in the Roman hostelries. Songs of this sort accordingly early came upon the public stage, and certainly formed the first nucleus of the Roman theatre. But not only were these beginnings of the drama in Rome, as everywhere, modest and humble; they were, in a remarkable manner, accounted from the very outset disreputable. The Twelve Tables denounced evil and worthless song-singing, imposing severe penalties not only upon incantations but even on lampoons composed against a fellow-citizen or recited before his door, and forbidding the employment of wailing-women at funerals. But far more severely than by such legal restrictions, the incipient exercise of art was affected by the moral anathema, which was denounced against these frivolous and mercenary trades by the sober earnestness of the Roman character. "The trade of a poet," says Cato, "in former times was not respected; if any one occupied himself with it or addicted himself to banquets, he was called an idler." But now any one who practised dancing, music, or ballad-singing for money was visited with a double stigma, in consequence of the more and more confirmed disapproval of the acquisition of a livelihood by services rendered for hire. While accordingly the taking part in the masked farces with stereotyped characters, that formed the usual native amusement (p. 226), was looked upon as a pardonable youthful frolic, the appearing on a public stage for money and without a mask was considered as directly infamous, and the singer and poet were in this respect placed quite on a level with the rope-dancer and the harlequin. Persons of this stamp were regularly pronounced by the censors (p. 426) incapable of serving in the burgess-army or of voting in the burgess-assembly. Moreover, not only was the direction of the stage regarded as pertaining to the province of the city police—a fact significant enough even in itself—but the police was probably, even at this period, invested with arbitrary powers of an extraordinary character against professional artists. Not only did the police magistrates sit in judgment on the performance after its conclusion—on which occasion wine flowed as copiously for those who had acquitted themselves well, as stripes fell to the lot of the bungler—but all the urban magistrates were legally entitled to inflict bodily chastisement and imprisonment on any actor at any time and at any place. The necessary effect of this was that dancing, music, and poetry, at least so far as they appeared on the public stage, fell into the hands of the lowest classes of the population, and especially into those of foreigners; and while at this period poetry still played altogether too insignificant a part to attract foreign artists to its cultivation, the statement on the other hand, that in Rome all the music, sacred and profane, was really Etruscan, may be regarded as already applicable to this period; so that the ancient Latin art of the flute, which was evidently at one time held in high esteem (p. 226), had been supplanted by foreign music.

There is no mention of any poetical literature. Neither the masked plays nor the recitations of the stage can have had any definitely settled text; on the contrary, they were ordinarily improvised by the performers themselves as circumstances required. Of works composed at this period posterity could point to nothing but a sort of Roman " Works and Days "— counsels of a farmer to his son,[1] and the already-mentioned Pythagorean poems of Appius Claudius (p. 450), the first commencement of Roman poetry after the Hellenic type. Nothing of the poems of this epoch has survived but one or two epitaphs in Saturnian measure (p. 449).

Along with the rudiments of the Roman drama, the rudiments of Roman historical composition belong to this period; both as regards the contemporary recording of remarkable events, and as regards the conventional settlement of the early history of the Roman community.

The writing of contemporary history was associated with the register of the magistrates. The register reaching farthest back, which was accessible to the later Roman inquirers and is still indirectly accessible to us, seems to have been derived from the archives of the temple of the Capitoline Jupiter; for it records the names of the annual presidents of the community onward from the consul Marcus Horatius, who consecrated that temple on the 13th September in his year of office, and it also notices the vow which was made on occasion of a severe pestilence under the consuls Publius Servilius and Lucius Aebutius (according to the reckoning now current, $\frac{291}{463}$), that thenceforward a nail should be driven every hundredth year into the wall of the Capitoline temple. Subsequently it was the state officials who were learned in measuring and in writing, or in other words, the pontifices, that kept an official record of the names of the annual chief magistrates, and thus combined an annual, with the earlier monthly, calendar. Both these calendars were afterwards comprehended under the name of Fasti—which strictly belonged only to the list of court-days. This arrangement was probably adopted not long after the abolition of the monarchy; for in fact an official record of the annual magistrates was of urgent practical necessity for the purpose of determining the order of succession of official documents. But, if there was an official register of the consuls so old, it probably perished in the Gallic conflagration ($\frac{364}{390}$); and the list of the pontifical college

---

[1] A fragment has been preserved:—

  Hiberno pulvere, verno luto, grandia farra
  Camille metes—

We do not know by what right this was afterwards regarded as the oldest Roman poem (Macrob. *Sat.* v. 20; Festus, *Ep. v. flaminius*, p. 93, M.; Serv. on Virg. *Georg.* i. 101; Plin. xvii. 2. 14).

was subsequently completed from the Capitoline register which was not affected by that catastrophe, so far as this latter reached. That the list of presidents which we now have—although in collateral matters, and especially in genealogical statements, it has been supplemented from the family pedigrees of the nobility —is in substance based from the beginning on contemporary and credible records, admits of no doubt. But it reproduces the calendar years only imperfectly and approximately: for the consuls did not enter on office with the new year, or even on a definite day fixed once for all; on the contrary from various causes the day of entering on office was fluctuating, and the *interregna* that frequently occurred between two consulates were entirely omitted in the reckoning by official years. Accordingly, if the calendar years were to be reckoned by this list of consuls, it was necessary to note the days of entering on and of demitting office in the case of each pair, along with such *interregna* as occurred; and this too was probably early done. But besides this, the list of the consuls was adjusted to the list of calendar years in such a way that a pair of magistrates were by accommodation assigned to each calendar year, and, where the list did not suffice, intercalary years were inserted, which are denoted in the later (Varronian) tables by the figures 379-383, 421, 430, 445, 453. From $\frac{291}{463}$ the Roman list demonstrably, not indeed in detail but yet on the whole, coincides with the Roman calendar, and is thus chronologically certain, so far as the defectiveness of the calendar itself allows. The 47 years preceding that date cannot be checked, but must likewise be at least in the main correct.[1] Whatever lies beyond $\frac{245}{509}$ remains, chronologically, in oblivion.

No era was formed for ordinary use; but in ritual matters they reckoned from the year of the consecration of the temple of the Capitoline Jupiter, with which the list of magistrates also started.

The idea naturally suggested itself that, along with the names of the magistrates, the most important events occurring under their magistracy might be noted; and from such notices appended to the catalogue of magistrates the Roman annals arose, just as the chronicles of the middle ages arose out of the memoranda attached to the table of Easter. But it was not until a late period that the pontifices formed the scheme of a formal chronicle

---

[1] The first places in the list alone excite suspicion, and may have been subsequently added with a view to round off the number of years between the flight of the king and the burning of the city to 120.

(*liber annalis*), which should steadily year by year record the names of all the magistrates and the remarkable events. Before the eclipse of the sun noticed under the 5th of June $\frac{351}{403}$, by which is probably meant that of the 20th June $\frac{354}{400}$, no solar eclipse was found recorded from observation in the later chronicle of the city: its statements as to the numbers of the census only begin to sound credible after the beginning of the fifth century (pp. 98, 420); the cases of fines brought before the people, and the prodigies expiated on behalf of the community, appear to have been regularly introduced into the annals only after the second half of the fifth century began.[1] To all appearance the institution of an organised book of annals, and—what was certainly associated with it—the revision (which we have just explained) of the earlier list of magistrates so as to make it a year-calendar by the insertion, where chronologically necessary, of intercalary years, must have taken place in the first half of the fifth century. But even after it became a practically recognised duty of the *pontifex maximus* to record year after year campaigns and colonisations, pestilences and famines, eclipses and portents, the deaths of priests and other men of note, the new decrees of the people, and the results of the census, and to deposit these records in his official residence for permanent preservation and for any one's inspection, these records were still far removed from the character of real historical writings. How scanty the contemporary record still was at the close of this period and how ample room it left for the caprice of subsequent annalists, is shown with especial clearness by a comparison of the accounts as to the campaign of $\frac{456}{298}$ in the annals and in the epitaph of the consul Scipio.[2] The later historians were evidently unable to construct a readable and in some measure connected narrative out of these notices from the book of annals; and we should have difficulty, even if the book of annals still lay before us with its original contents, in writing thence a methodical history of the times. Such chronicles, however, did not exist merely in Rome; every Latin city possessed its

---

[1] Such isolated notices with definite dates as are found with reference to the earlier period can hardly perhaps bear strict examination. The statement as to the removal of the old fig-tree from the Roman Forum in $\frac{260}{494}$ is now shown to lack manuscript attestation (p. 190, note), and grave doubts have also arisen as to the apparently very credible account that twenty-one tribes were instituted in $\frac{259}{495}$ (p. 277).

[2] P. 449. According to the annals Scipio commands in Etruria and his colleague in Samnium, and Lucania is during this year in league with Rome; according to the epitaph Scipio conquers two towns in Samnium and all Lucania.

annals as well as its pontiffs, as is clear from isolated notices relative to Ardea for instance, Ameria, and Interamna on the Nar; and from the collective mass of these city-chronicles some result might perhaps have been attained similar to what has been accomplished for the earlier middle ages by a comparison of the different monastic chronicles. Unfortunately the Romans in later times preferred to supply the defect by Hellenic or Hellenising falsehoods.

Besides these official arrangements, meagre in plan and uncertain in treatment, for the commemoration of past times and past events, there can scarcely have existed at this epoch any other records immediately serviceable for Roman history. Of private chronicles we find no trace. The leading houses, however, were careful to draw up genealogical tables, so important in a legal point of view, and to have the family pedigree painted for a perpetual memorial on the walls of the entrance-hall. These lists, which at least named the magistracies held by the family, not only furnished a basis for family tradition, but doubtless at an early period had biographical notices attached to them. The memorial orations, which in Rome could not be omitted at the funeral of any distinguished person, and were ordinarily pronounced by the nearest relative of the deceased, consisted not merely in an enumeration of the virtues and excellences of the dead, but also in a recital of the deeds and virtues of his ancestors; and so they were doubtless, even in the earliest times, transmitted traditionally from one generation to another. Many valuable notices may by this means have been preserved; but many daring perversions and falsifications also were in this way introduced into tradition.

But as the first steps towards writing actual history belonged to this period, to it belonged also the first attempts to record, and to give conventional shape to, the primitive history of Rome. The sources whence it was formed were of course the same as they are everywhere. Isolated names and facts, the kings Numa Pompilius, Ancus Marcius, Tullus Hostilius, the conquest of the Latins by king Tarquinius and the expulsion of the Tarquinian royal house, probably continued to live in a genuine tradition widely diffused and orally transmitted. Further materials were furnished by the traditions of the patrician clans, such as the various stories that relate to the Fabii. Other tales gave a symbolic and historical version of primitive national institutions, especially setting forth with great vividness the origin of rules of law. The sacredness of the walls was thus

illustrated in the tale of the death of Remus, the abolition of
blood-revenge in the tale of the end of king Tatius (p. 149, note),
the necessity of the arrangement as to the *pons sublicius* in the
legend of Horatius Cocles,[1] the origin of the *provacatio* in the
beautiful tale of the Horatii and Curiatii, the origin of manumission and of the burgess-rights of freedmen in the tale of the
Tarquinian conspiracy and the slave Vindicius. To the same
class belongs the history of the foundation of the city itself,
which was designed to connect the origin of Rome with Latium
and with Alba, the general metropolis of the Latins. Historical
glosses were annexed to the surnames of distinguished Romans;
that of Publius Valerius the "servant of the people" (*Poplicola*), for instance, gathered around it a whole group of such
anecdotes. Above all, the sacred fig-tree and other spots and
notable objects in the city were associated with a great multitude
of sexton-tales of the same nature as those out of which, upwards
of a thousand years afterwards, there grew up on the same
ground the Mirabilia Urbis. Some attempts to link together
these different tales—the adjustment of the series of the seven
kings, the reckoning of the duration of the monarchy at 240
years in all, which was undoubtedly based on a calculation of the
length of generations,[2] and even the commencement of an official
record of these assumed facts—probably took place in this epoch.
The outlines of the narrative, and in particular its quasi-chrono-
logy, make their appearance in the later tradition so unalterably
fixed, that for that very reason the fixing of them must be placed
not in, but previous to, the literary epoch of Rome. If a bronze
casting of the twins Romulus and Remus sucking the teats of
the she-wolf was already placed beside the sacred fig-tree in
$\frac{458}{296}$, the Romans who subdued Latium and Samnium must have
heard the history of the origin of their ancestral city in a form
not greatly differing from what we read in Livy. Even the
Aborigines—*i.e.* "those from the beginning"—that simple
starting-point in the historical speculation of the Latin race,
present themselves about $\frac{465}{289}$ in the Sicilian author Callias.
It is of the very nature of a chronicle that it should attach pre-
historic speculation to history and endeavour to go back, if not

---

[1] This object of the legend is clear from Pliny the Elder (*H. N.* xxxvi.
15, 100).

[2] They appear to have reckoned three generations to the hundred years
and to have rounded off the figures 233⅓ to 240, just as the epoch between
the king's flight and the burning of the city was rounded off to 120 years
(p. 455, note). The reason why these precise numbers suggested themselves
is apparent from the similar adjustment (above explained, p. 207) of the
measures of surface.

to the origin of heaven and earth, at least to the origin of the community; and there is express testimony that the table of the pontifices specified the year of the foundation of Rome. Accordingly it may be assumed that, when the pontifical college in the first half of the fifth century proceeded to substitute for the former scanty records—ordinarily confined to the names of the magistrates—the scheme of a formal yearly chronicle, it also supplied the lack of a beginning by the history of the monarchy and of its abolition, and, by placing the institution of the republic on the day of the consecration of the Capitoline temple, the 13th of September $\frac{245}{509}$, furnished a semblance of connection between the dateless and the annalistic narrative. That in this earliest record of the origin of Rome the hand of Hellenism was at work, can scarcely be doubted. The speculations as to the primitive and subsequent population and as to the priority of pastoral life over agriculture, and the transformation of the man Romulus into the god Quirinus (p. 168), have quite a Greek aspect, and even the obscuring of the genuinely national forms of the pious Numa and the wise Egeria by an admixture of alien elements of Pythagorean primitive wisdom appears by no means to be one of the most recent additions to the Roman pre-historic annals.

The pedigrees of the noble clans were completed in a manner analogous to these *origines* of the community, and were, in the favourite style of heraldry, universally traced back to illustrious ancestors. The Aemilii, for instance, Calpurnii, Pinarii, and Pomponii professed to be descended from the four sons of Numa, Mamercus, Calpus, Pinus, and Pompo; and the Aemilii, yet further, from Mamercus, the son of Pythagoras, who was named the " winning speaker " ($a i \mu \acute{u} \lambda o s$).

But, notwithstanding the Hellenic reminiscences that are everywhere apparent, these pre-historic annals of the community and of the leading houses may be designated at least relatively as national, partly because they originated in Rome, partly because they were primarily intended to form links of connection not between Rome and Greece, but between Rome and Latium.

It was Hellenic story and fiction that undertook the task of connecting Rome and Greece. Hellenic legend exhibits throughout an endeavour to keep pace with the gradual extension of geographical knowledge, and to form a dramatised geography by the aid of its numerous stories of voyagers and emigrants. In this, however, it seldom follows a simple course. An account like that of the earliest Greek historical work which mentions

Rome, the " Sicilian History " of Antiochus of Syracuse (which ended in $\frac{330}{424}$)—that a man named Sikelos had migrated from Rome to Italia, that is, to the Bruttian peninsula—such an account, simply giving an historical form to the family affinity between the Romans, Siculi, and Bruttians, and free from all Hellenising colouring, is a rare phenomenon. Greek legend as a whole is pervaded—and the more so, the later its rise—by a tendency to represent the whole barbarian world as having either issued from the Greeks or having been subdued by them; and it early in this sense spun its threads also around the west. For Italy the legends of Herakles and of the Argonauts were of less importance—although Hecataeus ($+$ after $\frac{257}{497}$) is already acquainted with the Pillars of Herakles, and carries the Argo from the Black Sea into the Atlantic Ocean, from the latter into the Nile, and thus back to the Mediterranean—than were the homeward voyages connected with the fall of Ilion. With the first dawn of information as to Italy Diomedes begins to wander in the Adriatic, and Odysseus in the Tyrrhene Sea (p. 139); indeed the latter localisation at any rate was naturally suggested by the Homeric conception of the legend. Down to the times of Alexander the countries on the Tyrrhene Sea belonged in Hellenic fable to the domain of the legend of Odysseus; Ephorus, who ended his history with the year $\frac{414}{340}$, and the so-called Scylax (about $\frac{418}{336}$) still substantially follow it. Of Trojan voyages the whole earlier poetry has no knowledge; in Homer Aeneas after the fall of Ilion rules over the Trojans that remained at home.

It was the great remodeller of myths, Stesichorus ($\frac{122-201}{632-553}$) who first in his " Destruction of Ilion " brought Aeneas to the land of the west, that he might poetically enrich the world of fable in the country of his birth and of his adoption, Sicily and Lower Italy, by the contrast of the Trojan heroes with the Hellenic. With him originated the poetical outlines of the fable as thenceforward fixed, especially the group of the hero and his wife, his little son and his aged father bearing the household gods, departing from burning Troy, and the important identification of the Trojans with the Sicilian and Italian autochthones, which is especially apparent in the case of the Trojan trumpeter Misenus who gave his name to the promontory of Misenum.[1]

---

[1] The " Trojan colonies " in Sicily, mentioned by Thucydides, the pseudo-Scylax, and others, as well as the designation of Capua as a Trojan foundation in Hecataeus, must also be traced to Stesichorus and his identification of the natives of Italy and Sicily with the Trojans.

The old poet was guided in this view by the feeling that the barbarians of Italy were less widely removed from the Hellenes than other barbarians were, and that the relation between the Hellenes and Italians might, when measured poetically, be conceived as similar to that between the Homeric Achaeans and the Trojans. This new Trojan fable soon came to be mixed up with the earlier legend of Odysseus, while it spread at the same time more widely over Italy. According to Hellanicus (who wrote about $\frac{350}{400}$) Odysseus and Aeneas came through the country of the Thracians and Molottians (Epirus) to Italy, where the Trojan women whom they had brought with them burnt the ships, and Aeneas founded the city of Rome and named it after one of these Trojan women. To a similar effect, only with less absurdity, Aristotle ($\frac{370-432}{384-322}$) related that an Achaean squadron cast upon the Latin coast had been set on fire by Trojan female slaves, and that the Latins had originated from the descendants of the Achaeans who were thus compelled to remain there and of their Trojan wives. With these tales were next mingled elements from the indigenous legend, the knowledge of which had been diffused as far as Sicily by the active intercourse between Sicily and Italy, at least towards the end of this epoch. In the version of the origin of Rome, which the Sicilian Callias gave about $\frac{465}{289}$, the fables of Odysseus, Aeneas, and Romulus were intermingled.[1]

But the person who really completed the conception subsequently current of this Trojan migration was Timaeus of Tauromenium in Sicily, who concluded his historical work with $\frac{492}{262}$. It is he who represents Aeneas as first founding Lavinium with its shrine of the Trojan Penates, and as thereafter founding Rome; he must also have interwoven the Tyrian princess Elisa or Dido with the legend of Aeneas, for with him Dido is the foundress of Carthage, and Rome and Carthage are said by him to have been built in the same year. These alterations were manifestly suggested by certain accounts that had reached Sicily respecting Latin manners and customs, in conjunction with the critical struggle which at the very time and place where Timaeus wrote was preparing between the Romans and the Carthaginians. In the main, however, the story cannot have been derived from Latium, but can only have been the good-for-

---

[1] According to his account Romé, a woman who had fled from Ilion to Rome, married Latinus, king of the Aborigines, and bore to him three sons, Romus, Romylus, and Telegonus. The last, who undoubtedly emerges here as founder of Tusculum and Praeneste, belongs, as is well known, to the legend of Odysseus.

nothing invention of the old "gossip-monger" himself. Timaeus
had heard of the primitive temple of the household gods in
Lavinium; but the statement, that these were regarded by the
Lavinates as the Penates brought by the followers of Aeneas
from Ilion, is as certainly an addition of his own, as the ingenious
parallel between the Roman October horse and the Trojan horse,
and the exact inventory of the sacred objects of Lavinium—there
were, our worthy author affirms, heralds' staves of iron and
copper, and an earthen vase of Trojan manufacture. It is
true that these same Penates were not shown to any one for
centuries afterwards; but Timaeus was one of the historians
who upon no matter are so fully informed as upon things un-
knowable. It is not without reason that Polybius, who knew
the man, advises that he should in no case be trusted, and least
of all where, as in this instance, he appeals to documentary
proofs. In fact the Sicilian rhetorician, who professed to point
out the grave of Thucydides in Italy, and who could find no
higher praise for Alexander than that he had finished the conquest
of Asia sooner than Isocrates finished his " Panegyric," was
exactly the man to knead the naïve fictions of the earlier time
into that confused medley on which the play of accident has
conferred so singular a celebrity.

How far the Hellenic fables regarding Italian matters, such
as they at first arose in Sicily, gained credit during this period
in Italy itself, cannot be ascertained with precision. Those
links of connection with the Odyssean cycle, which we subsequently meet with in the legends of the foundation of Tusculum,
Praeneste, Antium, Ardea, and Cortona, must probably have
been invented at this period; and even the belief in the descent
of the Romans from Trojan men or women must have been
established at the close of this epoch in Rome, for the first
demonstrable contact between Rome and the Greek east is the
intercession of the senate on behalf of the " kindred " Ilians
in $\frac{472}{282}$. That the fable of Aeneas was nevertheless of comparatively recent origin in Italy, is shown by the extremely
scanty measure of its localisation as compared with the legend
of Odysseus; and at any rate the final adjustment of these tales,
as well as their reconciliation with the legend of the origin of
Rome, belongs only to the following age.

While in this way historical composition, or what was so called
among the Hellenes, busied itself in its own fashion with the
pre-historic times of Italy, it left the contemporary history of
Italy almost untouched—a circumstance as significant of the

sunken condition of Hellenic history, as it is to be for our sakes regretted. Theopompus of Chios (who ended his work with $\frac{418}{336}$) barely noticed in passing the capture of Rome by the Celts; and Aristotle (p. 333), Clitarchus (p. 380), Theophrastus (p. 412), Heraclides of Pontus (+ about $\frac{450}{300}$), incidentally mention particular events relating to Rome. It is only with Hieronymus of Cardia, who as the historian of Pyrrhus described also his Italian wars, that Greek historiography becomes an authority for the history of Rome.

Among the sciences, that of jurisprudence acquired an invaluable basis in the committing to writing of the laws of the city in the years $\frac{303}{451}$, $\frac{304}{450}$. This code, known under the name of the Twelve Tables, is perhaps the oldest Roman document that deserves the name of a book. The nucleus of the so-called *leges regiae* was probably not much more recent. These were certain precepts chiefly of a ritual nature, which rested upon traditional usage, and were probably promulgated to the general public under the form of royal enactments by the college of pontifices, which was entitled to point out but not to prescribe the law. Moreover it is probable that from the commencement of this period the more important decrees of the senate— although not those of the people—were regularly recorded in writing; for already in the earliest conflicts between the orders disputes took place as to the mode of their preservation (pp. 273, 284).

While the mass of written laws and documents thus increased, the foundations of jurisprudence in the proper sense were also firmly laid. It was necessary that both the magistrates who were annually changed and the jurymen taken from the people should be enabled to resort to advisers (*auctores*), who were acquainted with the course of law and knew how to suggest a decision accordant with precedents or, in the absence of these, resting on reasonable grounds. The pontifices who were wont to be consulted by the people regarding court-days and on all questions of difficulty and points of ceremony relating to the worship of the gods, delivered also, when asked, counsels and opinions on other points of law, and thus developed in the bosom of their college that tradition which formed the basis of Roman private law, more especially the formulae of action proper for each particular case. A set of formulae which embraced all these actions, along with a calendar which specified the court-days, was published to the people about $\frac{450}{300}$ by Appius Claudius or by his clerk, Gnaeus Flavius. This attempt, how-

ever, to formulise a science, that as yet hardly recognised itself,
stood for a long time completely isolated.

That the knowledge of law and the exposition of it were even
now a means of recommendation to the people and of attaining
offices of state, may be readily conceived, although the story,
that the first plebeian *pontifex* Publius Sempronius Sophus
(consul $\frac{450}{304}$), and the first plebeian *pontifex maximus* Tiberius
Coruncanius (consul $\frac{474}{280}$), were indebted for their honorary
offices to their knowledge of law, is probably rather a conjecture
of posterity than a statement of tradition.

That the real genesis of the Latin and doubtless also of the
other Italian languages was anterior to this period, and that
even at its commencement the Latin language was substantially
complete, is evident from the fragments of the Twelve Tables,
which, however, have been largely modernised by their semi-
oral tradition. They contain a number of antiquated words
and harsh combinations, particularly in consequence of omitting
the indefinite subject; but their meaning by no means presents,
like that of the Arval chant, any real difficulty, and they exhibit
far more agreement with the language of Cato than with that of
the ancient litanies. If the Romans at the beginning of the
seventh century had difficulty in understanding documents of
the fifth, the difficulty doubtless proceeded merely from the fact
that there existed at that time in Rome no real research, least
of all any study of documents. On the other hand it must have
been at this period, when the exposition and the compilation of
law began, that the Roman technical style first established itself
—a style which at least in its developed shape is nowise inferior
to the modern legal phraseology of England in stereotyped
formulae and turns of expression, endless enumeration of
particulars, and long-winded periods; and which commends
itself to the initiated by its clearness and precision, while the
uninitiated who do not understand it listen according to their
character and humour with reverence, impatience, or chagrin.
Moreover at this epoch began the methodical treatment of the
native languages. About its commencement the Sabellian as
well as the Latin idiom threatened, as we saw (p. 228), to become
barbarous, and the mutilation of endings and the corruption of
the vowels and more delicate consonants spread on all hands,
just as was the case with the Romanic languages in the fifth and
sixth centuries of the Christian era. But a reaction set in: the
sounds which had coalesced in Oscan, *d* and *r*, and the sounds
which had coalesced in Latin, *g* and *k*, were again separated,

and each was provided with its proper sign; *o* and *u*, for which from the first the Oscan alphabet had lacked separate signs, and which had been in Latin originally separate but threatened to coalesce, again became distinct, and in Oscan even the *i* was resolved into two signs different in sound and in writing; lastly, the writing again came to follow more closely the pronunciation —the *s* for instance among the Romans being in many cases replaced by *r*. Chronological indications point to the fifth century as the period of this reaction; the Latin *g* for instance was not yet in existence about $\frac{300}{450}$, but was so probably about $\frac{500}{250}$; the first of the Papirian clan, who called himself Papirius instead of Papisius, was the consul of $\frac{418}{336}$; the introduction of *r* instead of *s* is attributed to Appius Claudius (censor in $\frac{442}{312}$). Beyond doubt the re-introduction of a more delicate and precise pronunciation was connected with the increasing influence of Greek civilisation, which is observable at this very period in all departments of Italian life; and, as the silver coins of Capua and Nola are far more perfect than the contemporary *asses* of Ardea and Rome, writing and language appear also to have been more speedily and fully reduced to rule in the Campanian land than in Latium. How little, notwithstanding the labour bestowed on it, the Roman language and mode of writing had become settled at the close of this epoch, is shown by the inscriptions preserved from the end of the fifth century, in which the greatest arbitrariness prevails, particularly as to the insertion or omission of *m, d* and *s* in final sounds and of *n* in the body of a word, and as to the distinguishing of the vowels *o u* and *e i*.[1] It is probable that the contemporary Sabellians were in these points further advanced, while the Umbrians were but slightly affected by the regenerating influence of the Hellenes.

In consequence of this progress of jurisprudence and grammar, elementary instruction also, though it did not now spring up for the first time, must have undergone a certain improvement. As Homer was the oldest Greek, and the Twelve Tables was the

[1] In the two epitaphs, of Lucius Scipio consul in $\frac{456}{298}$, and of the consul of the same name in $\frac{495}{259}$, *m* and *d* are ordinarily wanting in the termination of cases, yet *Luciom* and *Gnaivod* respectively occur once; there occur alongside of one another the nominatives *Cornelio, filios ; cosol, cesor,* alongside of *consol, censor ; aidiles, dedet, ploirume* (=*plurimi*) *hec* (nom. sing.) alongside of *aidilis, cepit, quei, hic.* Rhotacism is already carried out completely; we find *duonoro* (=*bonorum*), *ploirume,* not as in the chant of the Salii *foedesum, plusima.* Our surviving inscriptions do not in general precede the age of rhotacism; of the earlier usage only isolated traces occur, such as afterwards *honos, labos* alongside of *honor, labor ;* and the similar feminine *praenomina, Maio* (=*maios, maior*) and *Mino* in recently found epitaphs at Praeneste.

oldest Roman, book, each became in its own land the essential basis of instruction; and the learning by heart the juristico-political catechism was a chief part of Roman juvenile training. Alongside of the Latin " writing-masters " (*litteratores*) there were of course, from the time when an acquaintance with Greek was indispensable for every statesman and merchant, also Greek " language-masters " (*grammatici*),[1] partly tutor-slaves, partly private teachers, who at their own dwelling or that of their pupil gave instructions in the reading and speaking of Greek. As a matter of course, the rod played its part in instruction as well as in military discipline and in police.[2] The instruction of this epoch cannot however have passed beyond the elementary stage: there was no material shade of difference, in a social respect, between the educated and the non-educated Roman.

That the Romans at no time distinguished themselves in the mathematical and mechanical sciences is well known, and is attested, in reference to the present epoch, by almost the only fact which can be adduced under this head with certainty—the regulation of the calendar attempted by the decemvirs. They wished to substitute for the previous calendar based on the old and very imperfect *trieteris* (p. 211) the contemporary Attic calendar of the *octaeteris*, which retained the lunar month of $29\frac{1}{2}$ days but assumed the solar year at $365\frac{1}{4}$ days instead of $368\frac{3}{4}$, and therefore, without making any alteration in the length of the common year of 354 days, intercalated, not as formerly 59 days every 4 years, but 90 days every 8 years. With the same view the improvers of the Roman calendar intended—while otherwise retaining the current calendar—in the two intercalary years of the four years' cycle to shorten not the intercalary months, but the two Februaries by 7 days each, and consequently to fix that month in the intercalary years at 22 and 21 days respectively instead of 29 and 28. But want of mathematical precision and theological scruples, especially in reference to the annual festival of Terminus which fell within

---

[1] *Litterator* and *grammaticus* are related nearly as elementary teacher and teacher of languages with us; the latter designation belonged by earlier usage only to the teacher of Greek, not to a teacher of the mother-tongue. *Litteratus* is more recent, and denotes not a schoolmaster but a man of culture.

[2] It is at any rate a true Roman picture, which Plautus (*Bacch.* 431) produces as a specimen of the good old mode of training:—

> . . . *ubi revenisses domum,*
> *Cincticulo praecinctus in sella apud magistrum adsideres ;*
> *Si, librum cum legeres, unam peccavisses syllabam,*
> *Fieret corium tam maculosum, quam est nutricis pallium.*

those very days in February, disarranged the intended reform, so that the Februaries of the intercalary years came to be of 24 and 23 days, and thus the new Roman solar year in reality ran to 366¼ days. Some remedy for the practical evils resulting from this was found in the practice by which, setting aside the reckoning by calendar months or ten months (p. 211) as now no longer applicable from the inequality in the length of the months, wherever more accurate specifications were required, they reckoned by terms of ten months of a solar year of 365 days, or by the so-called ten-month year of 304 days. Over and above this, there came early into use in Italy, especially for agricultural purposes, the farmers' calendar based on the Egyptian solar year of 365¼ days by Eudoxus (who flourished $\frac{366}{388}$).

A higher idea of what the Italians were able to do in these departments is furnished by their works of structural and plastic art, which are closely associated with the mechanical sciences. Here too we do not find phenomena of real originality; but if the impress of borrowing, which the plastic art of Italy bears throughout, diminishes its artistic interest, there gathers around it an historical interest all the more lively, because on the one hand it affords the most remarkable evidences of an international intercourse of which other traces have disappeared, and on the other hand, amidst the well-nigh total loss of the history of the non-Roman Italians, art is almost the sole surviving index of the life and activity which the different peoples displayed. No novelty is to be reported in this period; but what we have already shown (p. 240) may be illustrated in this period with greater precision and on a broader basis, namely, that the stimulus derived from Greece powerfully affected the Etruscans and Italians on different sides, and called forth among the former a rich and luxurious, among the latter, where it had any influence at all, a more intelligent and genuine, art.

We have already shown how wholly the architecture of all the Italian lands was, even in its earliest period, pervaded by Hellenic elements. Its city walls, its aqueducts, its tombs with pyramidal roofs, and its Tuscanic temple, are not at all, or not materially, different from the oldest Hellenic structures. No trace has been preserved of any advance in architecture among the Etruscans during this period; we find among them neither any really new reception, nor any original creation, unless we ought to reckon as such the magnificent tombs, *e.g.* the so-called tomb of Porsena at Chiusi described by Varro, which vividly recalls the strange and meaningless grandeur of the Egyptian pyramids.

In Latium too, during the first century and a half of the republic, it is probable that they moved solely in the previous track, and it has already been stated that the exercise of art rather sank than rose with the introduction of the republic (p. 443). There can scarcely be named any Latin building of architectural importance belonging to this period, except the temple of Ceres built in the Circus at Rome in $\frac{261}{493}$, which was regarded in the period of the empire as a model of the Tuscanic style. But towards the close of this epoch a new spirit appeared in Italian and particularly in Roman architecture (p. 443); the building of the magnificent arches began. It is true that we are not entitled to pronounce the arch and the vault Italian inventions. It is well ascertained that at the epoch of the genesis of Hellenic architecture the Hellenes were not yet acquainted with the arch, and therefore had to content themselves with a flat ceiling and a sloping roof for their temples; but the arch may very well have been a later invention of the Hellenes originating in more scientific mechanics; as indeed the Greek tradition refers it to the natural philosopher Democritus ($\frac{294}{460}$-$\frac{397}{357}$). With this priority of Hellenic over Roman arch-building the hypothesis, which has been often and perhaps justly propounded, is quite compatible, that the vaulted roof of the Roman great *cloaca*, and that which was afterwards thrown over the old Capitoline well-house (which originally had a pyramidal roof—p. 235), are the oldest extant structures in which the principle of the arch is applied; for it is more than probable that these arched buildings belong not to the regal but to the republican period (p. 111), and that in the regal period the Italians were acquainted only with flat or overlapped roofs (p. 235). But whatever may be thought as to the invention of the arch itself, the application of a principle on a great scale is everywhere, and particularly in architecture, at least as important as its first exposition; and this application belongs indisputably to the Romans. With the fifth century began the building of gates, bridges, and aqueducts based mainly on the arch, which is thenceforth inseparably associated with the Roman name. Akin to this was the development of the form of the round temple with the dome-shaped roof, which was foreign to the Greeks, but was a peculiar favourite with the Romans and was especially applied by them in the case of their peculiar non-Grecian worships, particularly that of Vesta.[1]

[1] The round temple certainly was not, as has been supposed, an imita‧tion of the oldest form of the house; on the contrary, house architecture

Something the same may be affirmed as true of various subordinate, but not on that account unimportant, performances in this field. They do not lay claim to originality or artistic accomplishment; but the firmly-jointed slabs of the Roman streets, the indestructible highways, the broad hard ringing tiles, the everlasting mortar of their buildings, proclaim the indestructible solidity and the energetic vigour of the Roman character.

Like architectural art, and, if possible, still more completely, the plastic and delineative arts were not so much matured by Grecian stimulus as developed from Greek seeds on Italian soil. We have already observed (p. 237) that these, although only younger sisters of architecture, began to develop themselves at least in Etruria, even during the regal period; but their principal development in Etruria, and still more in Latium, belongs to the present epoch, as is very evident from the fact that in those districts which the Celts and Samnites wrested from the Etruscans in the course of the fourth century there is scarcely a trace of the practice of Etruscan art. The plastic art of the Tuscans applied itself first and chiefly to works in terra-cotta, in copper, and in gold—materials which were furnished to the artists by the rich strata of clay, the copper mines, and the commercial intercourse of Etruria. The activity with which moulding in clay was prosecuted is attested by the immense number of bas-reliefs and statuary works in terra-cotta, with which the walls, gables, and roofs of the Etruscan temples were formerly decorated as their still extant ruins show, and by the trade which can be shown to have existed in such articles between Etruria and Latium. Casting in copper occupied no inferior place. Etruscan artists ventured to make colossal statues of bronze fifty feet in height, and Volsinii, the Etruscan Delphi, was said to have

uniformly starts from the square form. The later Roman theology associated this round form with the idea of the terrestrial sphere or of the universe surrounding like a sphere the central sun (Fest. *v. retundam*, p. 282; Plutarch, *Num.* 11; Ovid, *Fast.* vi. 267, *seq.*). In reality it rests simply on the fact, that the circular shape was recognised as the most convenient and the safest form of a space destined for enclosure and custody. That was the rationale of the round *thesauroi* of the Greeks as well as of the round structure of the Roman store-chamber, or temple of the Penates. It was natural, also, that the fireplace—that is, the altar of Vesta—and the fire-chamber—that is, the temple of Vesta—should be constructed of a round form, just as was done with the cistern and the well-enclosure (*puteal*). The round style of building in itself was Graeco-Italian as was the square form, and the former was appropriated to the store-place, the latter to the dwelling-house; but the architectural and religious development of the simple *tholos* into the round temple with pillars and columns was Latin.

possessed about the year $\frac{489}{265}$ two thousand bronze statues. Sculpture in stone, again, began in Etruria, as probably everywhere, at a far later date, and was prevented from development not only by internal causes, but also by the want of suitable material; the marble quarries of Luna (Carrara) were not yet opened. Any one who has seen the rich and elegant gold decorations of the south-Etruscan tombs, will have no difficulty in believing the statement that Tyrrhene gold cups were valued even in Attica. Gem-engraving also, although more recent, was in various forms practised in Etruria. Equally dependent on the Greeks, but otherwise quite on a level with the workers in the plastic arts, were the Etruscan designers and painters, who manifested extraordinary activity both in contour-drawing on metal and in monochromatic fresco-painting.

On comparing with this the domain of the Italians proper, it appears at first, contrasted with the Etruscan riches, almost poor in art. But on a closer view we cannot fail to perceive that both the Sabellian and the Latin nations must have had far more capacity and aptitude for art than the Etruscans. It is true that in the proper Sabellian territory, in Sabina, in the Abruzzi, in Samnium, there are hardly found any works of art at all, and even coins are wanting. But those Sabellian stocks, which reached the coasts of the Tyrrhene or Ionic seas, not only appropriated Hellenic art externally, like the Etruscans, but more or less completely acclimatised it. Even in Velitrae, where in spite of the conversion of the city into a Latin colony and afterwards into a Roman *municipium* the Volscian language and peculiarities appear to have maintained themselves longest, painted terra-cottas have been found, displaying vigorous and characteristic treatment. In Lower Italy Lucania was to a less degree influenced by Hellenic art; but in Campania and in the land of the Bruttii, Sabellians and Hellenes became completely intermingled not only in language and nationality, but also and especially in art, and the Campanian and Bruttian coins in particular stand so entirely in point of artistic treatment on a level with the contemporary coins of Greece, that the inscription alone serves to distinguish the one from the other.

It is a fact less known, but not less certain, that Latium also, while inferior to Etruria in the copiousness and massiveness of its art, was not inferior in artistic taste and practical skill. It is true that there the art of gem-engraving so diligently prosecuted in luxurious Etruria is entirely wanting, and we find no indication that the Latin workshops were, like those of the

Etruscan goldsmiths and clay-workers, occupied in supplying a foreign demand. It is true that the Latin temples were not like the Etruscan overloaded with bronze and clay decorations, that the Latin tombs were not like the Etruscan filled with gold ornaments, and their walls shone not, like those of the Tuscan tombs, with paintings of various colours. Nevertheless, on the whole the balance does not incline in favour of the Etruscan nation. The invention of the effigy of Janus, which, like the god himself, may be attributed to the Latins (p. 167), is not unskilful, and is of a more original character than that of any Etruscan work of art. The activity of celebrated Greek masters in Rome is attested by the very ancient temple of Ceres; the sculptor Damophilus, who with Gorgasus prepared the painted terracotta figures for it, appears to have been no other than Demophilus of Himera, the teacher of Zeuxis (about $\frac{300}{450}$). The most instructive illustrations are furnished by those branches of art in which we are able to form a comparative judgment, partly from ancient testimonies, partly from our own observation. Of Latin works in stone scarcely anything else survives than the stone sarcophagus of the Roman consul Lucius Scipio, wrought at the close of this period in the Doric style; but its noble simplicity puts to shame all similar Etruscan works. Many beautiful bronzes of an antique chaste style of art, particularly helmets, candelabra, and the like articles, have been taken from Etruscan tombs; but which of these works is equal to the bronze she-wolf erected in $\frac{458}{296}$ from the proceeds of fines at the Ruminal fig-tree in the Roman Forum, and still forming the finest ornament of the Capitol? And that the Latin metal-founders as little shrank from great enterprises as the Etruscans, is shown by the colossal bronze figure of Jupiter on the Capitol erected by Spurius Carvilius (consul in $\frac{461}{293}$) from the melted equipments of the Samnites, the chisellings of which sufficed to cast the statue of the victor that stood at the foot of the Colossus; this statue of Jupiter was visible even from the Alban Mount. Amongst the cast copper coins by far the finest belong to southern Latium; the Roman and Umbrian are tolerable, the Etruscan almost destitute of any image and often really barbarous. The fresco-paintings, which Gaius Fabius executed in the temple of Health on the Capitol, dedicated in $\frac{452}{302}$, obtained in design and colouring the praise even of connoisseurs trained in Greek art in the Augustan age; and the art-enthusiasts of the empire commended the frescoes of Caere, but with still greater emphasis those of Rome, Lanuvium, and

Ardea, as masterpieces of painting. Engraving on metal, which in Latium decorated not the hand-mirror, as in Etruria, but the toilet-casket with its elegant outlines, was practised to a far less extent in Latium and almost exclusively in Praeneste. There are excellent works of art among the copper mirrors of Etruria as among the caskets of Praeneste; but it was a work of the latter kind, and in fact a work which most probably originated in the workshop of a Praenestine master at this epoch,[1] regarding which it could with truth be affirmed that scarcely another product of the graving of antiquity bears the stamp of an art so finished in its beauty and characterisation, and yet so perfectly pure and chaste, as the Ficoroni *cista*.

The general character of Etruscan works of art is, on the one hand, a sort of barbaric extravagance in material as well as in style; on the other hand, an utter absence of original development. Where the Greek master lightly sketches, the Etruscan disciple lavishes a scholar's diligence; instead of the light material and moderate proportions of the Greek works, there appears in the Etruscan an ostentatious stress laid upon the size and costliness, or even the mere singularity, of the work. Etruscan art cannot imitate without exaggerating; the chaste in its hands becomes harsh, the graceful effeminate, the terrible hideous, and the voluptuous obscene; and these features become more prominent, the more the original stimulus falls into the background and Etruscan art finds itself left to its own resources. Still more surprising is the adherence to traditional forms and a traditional style. Whether it was that a more friendly contact with Etruria at the outset allowed the Hellenes to scatter there the seeds of art, and that a later epoch of hostility impeded the introduction of the more recent developments of Greek art, or whether, as is more probable, the intellectual torpor that rapidly came over the nation was the main cause of the phenomenon, art in Etruria remained substantially stationary at the primitive stage which it had occupied on its first entrance. This, as is well known, forms the reason why Etruscan art, the stunted daughter, was so long regarded as the mother, of Hellenic art. Still more even than the rigid adherence to the style traditionally transmitted in the older branches of art, the sadly inferior handling of those branches that came into vogue afterwards, particularly of sculpture in

[1] Novius Plautius (p. 489) cast perhaps only the feet and the group on the lid; the casket itself may have proceeded from an earlier artist, but hardly from any other than a Praenestine, for the use of these caskets was substantially confined to Praeneste.

stone and of copper-casting as applied to coins, shows how
quickly the spirit of Etruscan art evaporated. Equally instructive are the painted vases, which are found in so enormous
numbers in the later Etruscan tombs. Had these come into
current use among the Etruscans as early as the metal plates
decorated with contouring or the painted terra-cottas, beyond
doubt they would have learned to manufacture them at home
in considerable quantity, and of a quality at least relatively
good; but at the period at which this luxury arose, the power
of independent reproduction wholly failed—as the isolated vases
provided with Etruscan inscriptions show—and they contented
themselves with buying instead of making them.

But even within Etruria there appears a further remarkable
distinction in artistic development between the northern and
southern districts. It is South Etruria, particularly in the
districts of Caere, Tarquinii, and Volci, that has preserved the
great treasures of art which the nation boasted, especially in
frescoes, temple decorations, gold ornaments, and painted vases.
Northern Etruria is far inferior; no painted tomb, for example,
has been found to the north of Chiusi. The most southern
Etruscan cities, Veii, Caere, and Tarquinii, were accounted in
Roman tradition the primitive and chief seats of Etruscan art;
the most northerly town, Volaterrae, with the largest territory
of all the Etruscan communities, stood most of all aloof from
art. While a Greek semi-culture prevailed in South Etruria,
Northern Etruria was marked by the absence of all culture.
The causes of this remarkable contrast may be sought partly in
differences of race—South Etruria being largely peopled in all
probability by non-Etruscan elements (p. 122)—partly in the
varying intensity of Hellenic influence, which must have made
itself very decidedly felt at Caere in particular. The fact itself
admits of no doubt. The more injurious on that account must
have been the early subjugation of the southern half of Etruria
by the Romans, and the Romanising—which there began very
early—of Etruscan art. What Northern Etruria, confined to
its own efforts, was able to produce in the way of art, is shown
by the copper coins which mainly belong to it.

Let us now turn from Etruria to glance at Latium. The
latter, it is true, created no new art; it was reserved for a far
later epoch of culture to develop on the basis of the arch a new
architecture different from the Hellenic, and then to unfold in
harmony with that architecture a new style of sculpture and
painting. Latin art is nowhere original and often insignificant;

but the fresh sensibility and the discriminating tact, which appropriate what is good in others, constitute a high artistic merit. Latin art seldom became barbarous, and in its best products it comes quite up to the level of Greek technical execution. We do not mean to deny that the art of Latium, at least in its earlier stages, had a sort of dependence on the certainly earlier Etruscan (p. 238); Varro may be quite right in supposing that, previous to the execution by Greek artists of the clay figures in the temple of Ceres (p. 471), only "Tuscanic" figures adorned the Roman temples; but that, at all events, it was mainly the direct influence of the Greeks that led Latin art into its proper channel, is self-evident, and is very obviously shown by these very statues as well as by the Latin and Roman coins. Even the application of graving on metal in Etruria solely to the toilet mirror, and in Latium solely to the toilet casket, indicates the diversity of the art-impulses that affected the two lands. It does not appear, however, to have been exactly at Rome that Latin art put forth its freshest vigour; the Roman *asses* and Roman *denarii* are far surpassed in fineness and taste of workmanship by the Latin copper, and the rare Latin silver, coins, and the masterpieces of painting and design belong chiefly to Praeneste, Ardea, and Lanuvium. This accords completely with the realistic and sober spirit of the Roman republic which we have already described—a spirit which can hardly have prevailed with equal intensity in other parts of Latium. But in the course of the fifth century, and especially in the second half of it, there was a mighty activity in Roman art. This was the epoch in which the construction of the Roman arches and Roman roads began; in which works of art like the she-wolf of the Capitol originated; and in which a distinguished man of an old Roman patrician clan took up his pencil to embellish a newly constructed temple and thence received the honorary surname of the "Painter." This was not accident. Every great age lays its grasp on all the powers of man; and, rigid as were Roman manners, strict as was Roman police, the impulse received by the Roman burgesses as masters of the peninsula or, to speak more correctly, by Italy united for the first time as one state, became as evident in the stimulus given to Latin and especially to Roman art, as the moral and political decay of the Etruscan nation was evident in the decline of art in Etruria. As the mighty national vigour of Latium subdued the weaker nations, it impressed its imperishable stamp also on bronze and on marble.

APPENDIX

I

THE PATRICIAN CLAUDII

[THIS paper, which was subjoined to the former English edition of the History as exhibiting the grounds which had induced Dr. Mommsen to modify the views given in that and the earlier German editions regarding Appius Claudius the decemvir and Appius Claudius the censor, may retain a place here as more fully explaining the views now embodied in the text. It was read at the sitting of the Prussian Academy on March 4, 1861, and has since been reprinted among the author's *Römische Forschungen*. I have given it almost entire.—TR.]

The patrician clan of the Claudii, probably one of the *gentes maiores*, played a leading part in the history of Rome for five hundred years. Our object in this inquiry is to arrive at a proper estimate of its political position.

We are accustomed to regard this Claudian *gens* as the very incarnation of the patriciate, and its leaders as the champions of the aristocratic party and of the conservatives in opposition to the plebeians and the democrats; and this view, in fact, already pervades the works which form our authorities. In the little, indeed, which we possess belonging to the period of the republic, and particularly in the numerous writings of Cicero, there occurs no hint of the kind; for the circumstance that Cicero in one special instance (*ad Fam.* iii. 7, 5), when treating of the persons of Appius and Lentulus, uses *Appietas* and *Lentulitas* as—what they were—superlative types of the Roman nobility, by no means falls under this category. It is in Livy that we first meet with the view which is now current. At the very beginning of his work the Claudii are introduced as the *familia superbissima ac crudelissima in plebem Romanam* (ii. 56), and throughout the first decad, whenever an ultra aristocrat is needed, a Claudius appears on the stage. For instance, the very first consul of this name, Appius Claudius consul in 259, is contrasted with the gentle Servilius as *vehementis ingenii vir* (ii. 23 seq.), and it was no fault of his that on the secession of the plebs to the Sacred Mount the quarrel was not decided by arms (ii. 29). The next consul of this *gens*, in 283, vehemently opposes the Publilian law as to the election of the tribunes of the plebs by the tribes, while his colleague—on this occasion a Quinctius—vainly counsels moderation (ii. 56). The third consul C. Claudius, in 294, unreasonably obstructs the law for preparing a national code, which

475

his colleague of the Valerian *gens* had shortly before his glorious death promised to the people (iii. 19); and although this C. Claudius, as compared with the still more hateful decemvir Appius, plays a mediating and conciliatory part, he afterwards in the dispute regarding the *conubium* contends for the most extreme aristocratic view (iv. 6). The son of the decemvir, who was military tribune in 330, although there is nothing to be told about him, is not allowed to pass without mention of his hereditary hatred towards the tribunes and the plebs (iv. 36). The same character is ascribed on different occasions to the grandson of the decemvir, who was military tribune in 351 and perhaps consul in 405 (iv. 48, v. 2-6, 20); and in the discussions on the Licinio-Sextian laws a detailed defence of the government of the nobility is placed in his mouth (vi. 40, 41, comp. vii. 6). Lastly, on occasion of the censorship of Caecus the annalist once more sums up the roll of the Claudian sins (ix. 34).

The Claudii are treated in a similar style by Dionysius on these same occasions and a number of others: it is needless to enumerate here the several passages, or to dwell on the speeches in the senate attributed to them, so intolerable from their insipid wordiness.

The authors of the time of Tiberius, Valerius Maximus and Velleius, naturally indulge in no invectives against the Claudian house; but Tacitus again speaks, just like Livy and Dionysius, of the *vetus atque insita Claudiae familiae superbia* (*Ann.* i. 4); and Suetonius in his Lives of the Caesars (*Tib.* 2) says still more expressly, that all the patrician Claudii, with the exception of the tribune of the people P. Clodius, had been conservative (*optimates*) and the most zealous champions of the standing and power of the patriciate as opposed to the plebs. These testimonies add no strength to the proof. The later Romans derived their views of men and things under the republic entirely from Livy—that remarkable writer, who, standing on the confines of the old and new periods, still possessed on the one hand the republican inspiration without which the history of the Roman republic could not be written, and, on the other hand, was sufficiently imbued with the refined culture of the Augustan age to work up the older annals, which were uninteresting in conception and rude in composition, into an elegant narrative written in good Latin. The combination of these qualities produced a book which is still as readable now as it was well-nigh two thousand years ago, and this must be reckoned no mean praise; but the annals of Livy are no more a history in the true sense of the term—in the sense in which Polybius wrote history—than the annals of Fabius. A certain systematic aim is observable in his work; but that aim is not historical, tracing the causes and effects of things; it is poetical, demanding a narrative unbroken by historic doubts, and requiring representative men and more particularly leading champions of the political parties. Thus he needed, by way of contrast to the liberal-conservative Valerii, a prototype of the proud patrician clans; and, if he and in like manner Dionysius—whether after the precedent of some earlier annalist, or of their own choice (a point to which we shall hereafter advert)—have used the Claudii for this purpose, their representations must not be held as absolutely binding on the historical inquirer.

Materials for a revision of their judgment in this respect are not wholly wanting: in fact, from the honesty with which Livy reproduces the positive accounts which lay before him, most of the materials of this nature have been preserved by him, while Dionysius with his affectation of critical sagacity has in this instance effaced every trace of the genuine truth.

Among the general characteristics of the Claudian *gens* nothing strikes us so much as the fact, that no notable patrician clan has given to the community so few famous warriors as the Claudian house, although it flourished for so many centuries. Suetonius [1] records among the honours of the clan six triumphs and two ovations; of the former four can be pointed out with certainty, viz. that of Appius Crassus over the Picentes in 486, that of Gaius Nero over Hasdrubal in 547, that of Gaius Pulcher over the Istrians and Ligurians in 577, and that of Appius Pulcher over the Salassi in 611; of the latter one, viz. that of Appius over the Celtiberians in 580; the missing triumph or missing ovation was perhaps that of the dictator in 392. But, as is well known, there was not among the Romans one general in ten triumphators; and of the triumphs just named one alone commemorated an important military success—the gain of the battle of Sena by the two consuls M. Livius and C. Nero; the latter, moreover, belonged to a collateral branch of the patrician house little spoken of in the republican period, the Claudii Nerones. Among the Claudii proper there is not a single soldier of note, and it can be proved that the most important of them did not owe their reputation to their services in the field. How far different was the case with the noble houses of equal standing with the Claudii, such as Fabii, Aemilii, Cornelii!

On the other hand, no *gens* of the Roman nobility displayed so much activity in science and literature from the earliest times as the Claudian house. From the decemvir Appius Claudius proceeded, as is well known, the Roman code of law, which, as the oldest Roman book, as modelled after the laws of Solon, and as including the earliest calendar that was publicly promulgated, exercised in a literary and scientific point of view the deepest and most permanent influence. To the achievements of the censor Appius Claudius in this respect we shall return. Even in subsequent times, when culture was general, there are various evidences that the patrician Claudii continued to have at heart the interests of science. I may refer to the different aedileships of men of this *gens*, which form epochs in the history of the theatre; to the adept in the Greek mysticism who was contemporary with Cicero, Appius Claudius consul in 700, and his Eleusinian Propylaeum, the votive inscription of which has been recently found; [2] and to the emperors Tiberius and Claudius, both of whom cherished a deeper interest in philology and archaeology than is common with princely *dilettanti*.

It will be allowed that neither of these observations tells exactly in favour of the current view of the Claudian family. The aristo-

---

[1] *Tib.* 1: *Patricia gens Claudia—duodetriginta consulatus, dictaturas quinque, censuras septem, triumphos sex* (or *septem*), *duas ovationes adepta est . . .*

[2] *Corp. Inscr. Lat.* I. n. 619.

cratic party at all times set a higher value on martial prowess than
on mental gifts; democracy on the contrary, and above all the
Roman democracy down to a late age, sought its sphere in the
Forum beyond the reach of the sword, and found powerful levers in
science and art. How is all this reconcilable with the *familia superbissima ac crudelissima in plebem Romanam ?* And various other
considerations might be adduced. The statement that the Claudii
only migrated to Rome in the sixth year after the expulsion of the
kings is not merely untrustworthy as to date, but decidedly at
variance with the requirements of republican state law; moreover
the Claudian *gens*, which gave its name to a Roman tribe, and which
appears at an early date in the Fasti, cannot possibly have migrated
to Rome at so recent a period. But, apart from the date, the fact
itself of the migration of the Claudii from Sabina is attested by a
highly credible family tradition; and it is a surprising circumstance
that this same patrician clan, which was almost the only one to
preserve and to value the recollection of its having come from
abroad, should have furnished the champion of the native patricians. The Claudii, too, were almost the only patrician *gens* which
had a counterpart of the same name and of kindred origin among
the old plebeian nobility; [1] for that more than a mere nominal kin-
ship was assumed to exist between the patrician Claudii and the
plebeian Marcelli, is attested by the competing claims of the two
houses in the case of heritages passing to *gentiles* (Cic. *de Orat.* i. 39,
176). One would think that this relation must have constituted a
connecting bond between the patrician Claudii and the plebs rather
than the reverse.

But general considerations of this sort do not determine the
matter. The question depends on the political position which the
prominent men of the Claudian *gens* took up, and by which they
determined that of the whole clan, so far as in the case of the latter
we can speak of such a position at all. Now of such prominent men
the Claudian clan in the earlier centuries of the republic produced
two,—Appius the Decemvir and Appius the Censor: of the other
Claudii of this epoch we know, laying aside idle inventions, just
about as much as we know of the Egyptian kings—their names and
their years of office. We shall have to treat accordingly in the first
instance of the two former, and then to subjoin what is to be said
regarding the far less important Claudii of later regular history.

The accounts given in the annals which have reached us regarding the Ap. Claudius who was consul in 283 and decemvir in 303
can certainly make no claim to historical credibility, and are still
more corrupted and disfigured than other accounts of the same
epoch. Authors, who record under the year 284 the death of the
man who was decemvir twenty years afterwards, will receive credit
from nobody when they report his speeches in the Forum and the
senate and the history of his impeachment. Yet the most important facts relating to the origin of the Twelve Tables are as
little doubtful as the Twelve Tables themselves; and in this case it
is not difficult to separate an historical kernel from the loose tissue of
fable. First of all, it is clear and undisputed that the committal of

---

[1] The Veturii alone were in the same position.

the public law to writing was a measure directed against the patrician magistrates and consequently against the patrician government itself. Moreover, it is no less certain that the decemvirs were not all patricians. For, if there is anything good and reliable in what has been handed down to us, the list of magistrates is so; and we know also the patrician clans sufficiently to be certain that, while the decemvirs first nominated were all patricians, of those elected in 304 at least the three described by Dionysius (x. 58) as plebeian, and probably two others — or, in other words, one-half — were plebeians. The circumstance that Livy in his narrative itself says nothing of the quality of the members of this college, and afterwards in a speech (iv. 3) calls all the decemvirs patricians, is of no moment. Niebuhr, who did not fail to see the conclusive force of the evidence in favour of the plebeian character of a portion of the second decemvirs, supposed (and Schwegler assents to his view) that the first and second decemvirate were different in kind,—the former being an extraordinary legislative commission, the latter a college of archons organised as a permanent institution and composed of both orders. But this hypothesis is opposed to all tradition, as well as to all probability; the two sets of magistrates occurring in so close succession, both occupied with the preparation of the legal code, and both comprehended under the same title *decemviri consulari imperio legibus scribundis* in the roll of magistrates, must have been in constitutional law homogeneous. Consequently nothing remains but the hypothesis that the decemvirate stood open from the first to both orders; and this view is necessarily demanded by the analogy of the military tribunate *consulari potestate*. For the essential features—the substitution of a larger number of magistrates for the pair, and the assigning to these magistrates not the title and rank of consul with the relative honours (right to celebrate a triumph and to carry images of ancestors), but only delegated consular power—are common to the military tribunate and the decemvirate; and, as the military tribunate was notoriously organised in this way just in order to make the supreme magistracy, but not the highest honours of that magistracy, accessible to the plebeians, the decemvirate cannot well be conceived otherwise than common from the first to both orders. The fact that the first college consisted exclusively of patricians is not inconsistent with this hypothesis, but agreeable to all analogy; the military tribunate in like manner, although always common in law, remained practically for many years in the hands of the patricians. Lastly, Livy himself narrates the course of the matter as if the plebs had demanded at first a commission composed of plebeians, and then one in which the two orders were to be mixed (iii. 9, 5; iii. 31, 7 *plebeiae leges*), and yet the ten commissioners were at last chosen from the patricians: *placet creari decemviros—admiscerenturne plebei, controversia aliquamdiu fuit ; postremo concessum patribus, modo ne lex Icilia de Aventino aliaeque sacratae leges abrogarentur* (iii. 31). It is easy to see how the older view has here been not really altered, but merely obscured by the omission of the circumstance that the plebeians carried their demand for the appointment of a mixed magistracy. What was true of the election, viz., that patricians only were fixed upon, was erroneously referred to the institution itself—an error which might be the more readily excused, as the point related not to a magistracy that was often to recur, but to a college which was to finish within its year of office the compilation of the code for which preparations had long been making, and consequently was to be elected only once.

If we reflect on these surely-established facts, first, that the obtaining of a written body of law was in itself a severe defeat of the nobility, and secondly, that men of both orders might be and were placed on the legislative commission and the eligibility of the plebeians to the supreme magistracy was in its case first legally and practically recognised, it is plainly preposterous to make the head of the decemvirate the leader of the patrician party. This, however, is what Livy has done; but that the older annals, characterised by less literary taste and by a more vivid realisation of the matters which they narrate, did not give any such version, may be proved from his own pages. He introduces his narrative of the second decemvirate by the remark that a new spirit had possessed Appius and the furious patrician had all at once become a mob-courtier (*plebicola*, iii. 33)—that, surrounded by the leading men of the plebs, the Duellii and Icilii, he had appeared in the Forum, and had by vile demagogic arts carried his re-election for the next year and the nomination of men of little standing as his colleagues (iii. 36). By this view Livy thenceforth abides on the whole, although he now and again falls back on the earlier, representing the decemvirs for instance as afterwards appearing with a retinue of young patricians and perpetrating their deeds of violence under its protection (iii. 37). This new spirit, which is alleged to have strangely taken possession of Appius at the close of 303, is evidently none other than that which has been eliminated from his character by the misrepresentations of later historians, but is ascribed to him by the earlier annals generally, and alone befits the part that he played—the spirit of a patrician demagogue who ends as a tyrant to patricians as well as plebeians. How much in the story of his fall is historical, and what may have been the real incidents of the process of Verginia—the murder of Siccius seems to have been a late addition—cannot of course be ascertained, and is a matter of comparative indifference; but the import of that story of Verginia, given in Diodorus and consequently proceeding from Fabius, may be easily perceived, and is significant enough, even should it be an invention. The unjust judicial sentence pronounced in his own personal interest, not in that of his order, the coming forward of the complaisant accommodating retainer, the greedy lust from which the burgher-maiden only saves her honour in death—these are all well-known traits in the picture of the ancient *tyrannus;* and, in fact, the charge of usurping the *tyrannis* is brought up very distinctly in many passages by Livy against the second decemvirs generally (iii. 36; *decem regum species erat, c. 32; id vero regnum haud dubie videri, c.* 39; *decem Tarquinios*. The emperor Claudius also speaks of *decem-virale regnum* on the Lyons Tables, i. 33). There was certainly good reason also for placing the demagogic *gens* of the Icilii in the foreground both at the second election of Appius and at the catastrophe. The oldest annals, written in a patrician spirit, showed at this point—when they were compelled to relate the momentous victory of the plebs over the nobility—by an instructive example, what fruit the people themselves derived from such a success of the popular party; how every demagogue naturally turns into a tyrant; how the honest plebeian, who had helped to place Appius in the judgment seat, himself suffered most at the hands of the judge; and how the plebs, thoroughly cured of its blindness by such consequences of its own act, took up arms against the self-constituted tyrant, was brought back by its true aristocratic protectors, the Valerii and Horatii, to that old constitution which could alone give happiness, and at length received from them as a free gift the real prize for which the plebs had contended, but which the demagogues who had turned tyrants had neglected to confer—the completion of the legal code. This no doubt is not history; but it approaches nearer to the reality than the well-written but ill-concocted *epideixis* of Livy.

Respecting Appius Claudius Caecus, censor in 442, consul in 447 and 458, the accounts are both more trustworthy and more copious. Niebuhr has already formed a judgment substantially correct regarding him, and I have in my *History of Rome* given a short sketch of him, in the main outlines of which I have no occasion to make any change, although, in consequence of my not then possessing an insight into the very peculiar character of the traditional accounts of the Claudii, there are various misapprehensions in the details. He was not only no representative of conservative tendencies, but a decided revolutionist, although he employed the forms and handles furnished by the constitution for the purpose of overthrowing it. Let us briefly review the accounts handed down in regard to him. First of all, the story of his blindness has perhaps arisen solely from the misunderstanding of a surname. That the current story, which represents him as struck with blindness by Hercules on account of a sacrilegious offence committed in his censorship of 442, is absurd in reference to a man who was twice afterwards consul, has long been seen; and it is also evident that the version of Diodorus (xx. 10), according to which he feigned himself blind in order that he might have a suitable pretext for keeping aloof from the senate which was hostile to him, is simply a second absurdity which has arisen out of a perception of the first. The view now usually adopted, that Appius had grown blind in his old age, is inconsistent with the Capitoline Fasti, which already under 442 register him as *Ap. Claudius C. f. Ap. n. Caecus ;* for, as they distinctly specify surnames acquired after entering on office as such (recording, for instance, in the very case of his colleague, *C. Plautius C. f. C. n. qui in hoc honore Venox appellatus est*), their compilers appear to have regarded *Caecus* as a simple cognomen, and the fact of his being blind at all is thus rendered doubtful. It is possible, indeed, that they may either have fallen into an error or may have wished in this way to avoid those absurdities of the older annals, and that the current hypothesis may still be the truth; certainty is not on such a question to be attained.

Of the martial deeds of Appius there is little to tell. Although

he was once dictator, twice consul, and twice praetor, and took the
field against the Samnites and Etruscans, and although his activity
fell within the epoch of Rome's greatest military glory, yet he never
triumphed. He built a temple to Bellona; but it is well known
that man not unfrequently pays the most zealous homage to the
divinity that scorns him. The really significant activity of Appius
belongs to the field of civil life. In particular, that speech of the
venerable old man who had long retired from all state affairs, which
vanquished the first Greek diplomatist that appeared in the Roman
senate, and at a decisive moment gave fresh courage and power to
the Roman government—the speech against Pyrrhus—remained
indelibly engraven on the memory of posterity. This result was
partly due to the fact that it was the first speech which, so far as we
know, was committed to writing in Rome—at least Cicero, who
read it, had no doubt of its genuineness. Nor have we any reason
to regard his poetical " sayings " (*sententiae*), which Panaetius had
read, as spurious; they were maxims of a general nature, such as
that " he who gets a sight of a friend forgets his grief " (Prisc. viii.
18), and the well-known saying, " every one is the architect of his
own fortune " (Sallust, *de Ord. Rep.* i. 1); when Cicero called them
Pythagorean, he was undoubtedly thinking of the pseudo-Pytha-
gorean " Golden Words," and this oldest Latin poem must in fact
have been formed under the influence of such Greek collections.
He is said also to have introduced the practice of writing the *r*
between two vowels instead of the earlier *s* (Dig. i. 2, 2, 36), and to
have banished the use of *z*,[1] doubtless bringing the writing into
conformity with the pronunciation. The same bold and far-seeing
spirit of innovation, which is discernible in his literary activity,
marks also his political career; and it is remarkable how he in this
respect walks in the steps of his great-great-grandfather, the
decemvir. The publication of the *legis actiones*, which was carried
out by his clerk Cn. Flavius, beyond all doubt at his suggestion—
by some indeed it was attributed to himself (Dig. *l. c.*)—was virtually
the publication of a revised and enlarged code. The Twelve Tables,
indeed, were in substance a regulation of civil procedure; and the
object in both cases, as in all similar instances, was to emancipate
the humble burgess from dependence on the caprice of the aristocratic magistrate and on the advice of the no less aristocratic men
of lore, by means of a written code accessible to all. The same
remark applies to the Fasti, which at that time were still in the
main what the name indicates, a list of court days: as the calendar
had been an integral part of the Twelve Tables, it now became a
part of the legal directory of Flavius, and was diffused along with
the latter in the form of a book.

A mere notice may suffice for the innovations of Appius in ritual
matters; viz., the transference of the public worship of Hercules in
the Forum Boarium from the *gens* of the Potitii to the charge of

---

[1] Mart. Cap. i. 3, § 261, Kopp.: *z idcirco Appius Claudius detestatur,
quod dentes mortui dum exprimitur imitatur*, where we should perhaps read
dentis morsus. Appius, it is probable, only assigned (or was alleged to
have assigned) this as a reason for the banishment of the *z* from the
language and writing.

public slaves, and the ejection of the guild of *tibicines* from the temple of Jupiter, which in the following year led to the well-known quarrel so happily ended by the jocose diplomatic intervention of the Tiburtines and the yielding of the senate.

The conversion of the burgess-qualification hitherto in force from landed property into a money-rating was materially modified by the successor of Appius in the censorship, the great Quintus Fabius; but enough of his innovations remained both as regards the *comitia tributa* and the *comitia centuriata*, but more especially the latter, to associate the censorship of Appius with perhaps the most material constitutional change which ever took place in republican Rome. The nomination of sons of freedmen as senators, the omission to purge the senatorial and equestrian rolls of disreputable and infamous individuals, and the election, at the suggestion of Appius, of his clerk Cn. Flavius the son of a freedman to a curule office; the spending of the moneys accumulated in the treasury, without the previous sanction of the senate, on magnificent structures called—a thing hitherto unheard of—after the builder's name; the Appian aqueduct and the Appian highway; lastly, his prolongation of the censorship beyond the legal term of eighteen months; are each and all measures diametrically opposed to Roman conservatism and to Roman reverence for the constitution and for use and wont, and belonging to the most advanced demagogism—measures which savour more of Cleisthenes and Pericles than of a statesman of the Roman commonwealth. "Such a character," Niebuhr aptly remarks, "would not surprise us in the history of Greece; in that of Rome it appears very strange." It is not my intention at present to do more than merely to indicate these several undertakings of Appius, which in general are sufficiently well known, and which could not be adequately estimated without lengthened and minute explanation. I shall only advert to a general opinion regarding the character of his proceedings in the censorship, and to an isolated notice which has not hitherto been correctly apprehended. The opinion to which I refer is that of Fabius, preserved by Diodorus (xx. 36). He says under the year 444-5, "One of the censors of this year, Appius Claudius, on whom his colleague was entirely dependent, disturbed many matters of use and wont, for, gratifying the multitude, he troubled himself little about the senate." The notice to which I refer occurs in Suetonius (*Tib.* 2). In enumerating the injuries done by the Claudii to the commonwealth, he says, *Claudius Drusus, statua sibi diademata ad Appi Forum posita, Italiam per clientelas occupare temptavit.* According to the order in which this statement occurs, it falls between the decemvirate and the first Punic war. It has at all times, and very justly, excited extreme suspicion; few perhaps will be inclined with Niebuhr to hold it, simply as it stands, as historical, and to see in this Claudius Drusus an otherwise totally unknown tyrant of Italy. The name in fact is demonstrably corrupt, not only because *Claudii Drusi* do not occur elsewhere, but more especially because Suetonius after discussing the paternal ancestors of the emperor Tiberius passes on to the maternal and treats minutely of the *Livii Drusi* and of the origin of that cognomen. He could not but have noticed so singular

a coincidence of the two families in the possession of a cognomen
anything but frequent, had that name of Claudius Drusus been the
real one; while on the other hand the subsequent occurrence of the
cognomen Drusus might lead a copyist to anticipate it at the wrong
place.   How the passage should be amended, I know not; [1] in point
of fact beyond all doubt no other can be meant but Appius
Caecus; for he not only falls in point of time exactly within the
requisite epoch and is the only one of all the Claudii against whom
such a charge as that indicated by Suetonius is rationally conceivable, but the Forum Appii, the present Foro Appio between Tre-
ponti and Terracina not far from Sezza, was itself, like the Appian
way, a work of his—situated in the middle of that immense embankment of hewn stone carried across the Pomptine marshes, in the
construction of which, as Diodorus says, Appius exhausted the
treasure of the state and left an eternal monument to his name.   To
him alone could the idea occur of having a statue erected to himself
at this otherwise inconsiderable place; and it is further easy to
understand how the—at that time novel—institution of a market
village along the highway, and the naming of it after its originator,
might give rise to the allegation that its founder designed to bring
all Italy under his power by forming client-communities.   Valerius
Maximus also assigns to Caecus *plurimas clientelas* (viii. 13, 5).

The portrait of Caecus, as it has just been sketched, is delineated
in our tradition in strong, clear, mutually harmonious lines.   At the
same time it must be added that it strictly suits only Appius as
censor; in the two consulships which he held after his censorship
and in his other later activity we encounter nothing more of that
vehemently revolutionary spirit.   It must probably be assumed
that he himself in his later years abandoned the career on which he
had entered at first, and became reconciled in some measure to the
existing conservative government—if not, we do not see how he
could have ended otherwise than like the Gracchi or like Caesar.
But though this be granted, it is clear that Appius Caecus was not,
any more than the decemvir Appius, an appropriate representative
of the strict aristocratic party; and Livy, when he treats Caecus in
this light, has certainly assigned to him a part most incongruous to
his character.   It is necessary, not in order to complete our view of
Caecus, but in order to perceive the character of Livy and of that
mode of writing history which he represents, that we should dwell
for a moment on the false colours with which this Claudius like all
the rest has been overlaid.   I do not include in this category the
statement that the builder of the temple of Bellona placed in it the
escutcheons of his ancestors with a list of the curule offices filled by
each (Plin. *H. N.* xxxv. 3, 12, where this is erroneously referred to
the consul of 259); aristocratic pride is very compatible with the
character of a Pericles, and Caesar with all his demagogism boasted
of his descent from Venus.   But the view given of the censorship
of Appius, as we read it in Livy (ix. 29, 30, 33, 34), is very strange,
not so much on account of the occasional attacks on the " inborn
arrogance " of the Claudii, " that family destined by fate to quarrel

---

[1] Perhaps it ran thus: *Caecus rursus statua sibi diademata ad Appi Forum
posita Italiam per clientelas occupare temptavit.*

with the plebs " (ix. 29, 33), as because all his palpably demagogic measures are passed over in silence—a silence which is the more evidently intentional, seeing that the most important of these, the enrolment of persons who had no landed property in the tribes, is afterwards mentioned incidentally under the censorship of Fabius (x. 7). It is no less remarkable that Livy (x. 15) represents Appius Caecus as again heading the opposition to the Ogulnian law of 454, which abolished the last substantial privilege of the patricians as respected the great priestly colleges; and here, at the close of the whole strife between the orders, once more contrasts him as the incarnation of patricianism with the figure of the pure plebeian hero Decius Mus. Nor is this even enough. At the consular elections for 458 the same Appius is said to have attempted unconstitutionally to bring in a second patrician, Q. Fabius Rullianus, as consul along with himself, and the project is said to have been thwarted solely by the loyal magnanimity of the said Fabius (x. 15). A different, but analogous story is given by Cicero (*Brut.* 14, 55); according to which Caecus in the capacity of interrex presiding at the elections (he filled this office according to Livy, x. 11, in 455—on which occasion, however, as the first interrex he could not have conducted the election—and according to his *elogium* on two other occasions unknown to us) is said to have rejected the votes given for a plebeian consular candidate, and thus to have led the tribune of the people, M'. Curius, to propose a further restriction of patrician privileges. That these evidently kindred stories are highly incredible, is plain to every one conversant with the matter; how is it possible that, at a time when the patricians had been divested almost without resistance of the last privileges of their order, and when the plebeians had had their title to share in the consulship not only constitutionally secured ever since men could remember, but also long confirmed by usage, the idea of such a restoration should have entered the mind of a mature statesman? And these accounts, in themselves more than suspicious, are coupled with the names of men than whom none could have been selected more unsuitable. The crazy patrician, who brings forward those preposterous projects, is no other than the censorial demagogue Appius Caecus who was for good reasons at bitterest feud with the ruling conservative party; and the person, whom he unconstitutionally selects as his colleague for 458, is no other than Fabius Rullianus, who had checked the unbounded demagogism of Appius on succeeding him in the censorship. We might be disposed to recognise in this one of those singular political conversions which have occurred at various epochs in the history of the world. But, as abrupt transition from one party-extreme to another and renegade arrogance have at no time been regarded as specially honourable, and as so much is said about Caecus more especially in the way of censure, such a change of sides, which must have produced the greatest sensation, would certainly have been prominently noticed in the accounts. But we nowhere meet with any hint of the sort: on the contrary, we have seen even the censorship of Appius, clearly as it bears on the face of it the stamp of demagogism, divested as far as possible of any such character in the narrative of Livy. To this

falls to be added the spirit of perversion and invention hostile to the
Claudii, noticed at the outset as pervading the older annals generally.
The delineation of the character of Caecus—towards whom the ninth
and tenth books of Livy exhibit various traces of an altogether
peculiar hatred—cannot be separated from the history of the trial
and suicide of Appius Claudius, consul in 283, as told by Dionysius
and Livy, which has been demonstrated to be a pure lie foreign to
the earlier annals by the mention of the same man in the Capitoline
Fasti twenty years later; from those constantly recurring consular
and senatorial speeches of Claudii hostile to the people; from that
irrational misrepresentation of the decemvir; or, generally, from
the whole class of anti-Claudian stories. Nothing remains accordingly but the hypothesis that the anti-popular anecdotes attached
to the demagogue Caecus—turning, it may be remarked, throughout on easily invented trifles and nowhere affecting his leading and
well-known actions—have been designedly perverted or invented.

It thus appears that at a pretty early period a pencil not merely
hostile generally to the Claudii, but specially assailing them as the
hereditary foes of progress and of democracy, has been at work in
the Roman annals, and has caricatured its portraits with more good-
will than judgment. Who it was that wielded it, can only be
guessed inferentially. That the earliest annalists, and Fabius in
particular, knew nothing of these lies, is clear from what we have
said above. On the other hand they cannot well have originated
with Livy; this far from honourable species of libel concealing itself
under the falsifying of documents is by no means consistent with
the morally pure character of his work, and besides there was no
ostensible ground for it in his case. For, when Livy wrote the first
decad, there remained no man of note belonging to the main stock
of the patrician Claudii, and probably none of them remained at all
except the son of P. Clodius, who was utterly insignificant and was
ruining himself by reckless debauchery; the collateral branch of
the Nerones was then obscure, Tiberius the future emperor was still
a boy. Further, it is far from credible that Dionysius, whose books
are evidently pervaded by the same tendency, and who professes to
give us antidemocratic speeches of the Claudii even in numerous
cases when Livy is silent, should have in this matter rested solely on
Livy and invented in a similar spirit what he did not find there.
Besides, if the notice in Cicero's *Brutus* has been correctly estimated
above, this series of falsifications must have already existed in
Cicero's time; but the " Claudian arrogance " was certainly not
yet at that time generally recognised and familiar, otherwise as-
suredly Cicer would not have allowed so suitable a handle for
invective against his mortal enemy Clodius wholly to escape him.
Lastly, these falsifications bear on the face of them the stamp of a
democratic origin. Putting together all these indications, we may
at all events suggest a name to which the suspicion of having set
afloat these plebeian libels on the Claudian house may not without
warrant be attached. It is that of Licinius Macer. Macer was, as
is well known, a contemporary of Cicero, senior to him by a few
years (tribune of the people in 681, he died, after having served the
praetorship, in 688), a notorious democrat and the author of ill

written and not much read annals, which however, it can be shown, formed a main authority both with Livy and with Dionysius. I have shown in my *Chronologie* that this man, who had been legally condemned for extortion and probably on that account committed suicide, was not only a thief, but at the same time a thoroughly shameless falsifier. It is true that nothing is known of any special quarrel between him and the patrician Claudii; but all the latter were, in the period of Sulla and the subsequent times, in the oligarchic camp and most decidedly opposed to Macer and his party, and we may perhaps even point out the individual who specially attracted the hatred of the democrats. Few of the acts of Gaius Claudius consul in 662 are recorded; but his extraordinary influence in the state is more than once (Cic. *pro Planc.* 21, 51, *Brut.* 45, 166) prominently referred to in so striking a manner, that we may certainly recognise him as one of the leaders of the senate at this time, and one who may be presumed accordingly to have been specially obnoxious to the party of progress.

Until further investigation shall confirm or remove this suspicion resting on the credibility of Macer and the annalists who derived their accounts from him, we may be allowed to regard it as a reason for cautiously receiving whatever is connected with his authority, especially seeing that it affects a man whose reputation is not thereby rendered worse than it is already.

It remains that we cast a glance at the Claudii of the later purely historical times, and their political position. This, however, need not detain us long. For that there was no clan-policy at all in the sense which not a few modern historians associate with the term, the inquiry which we have just concluded shows by an instructive example; the far-famed Claudian policy would seem, from that review, to have been nothing else than a caricature invented by a partisan falsifier of history. In the sixth and seventh centuries the Claudii had no remarkable prominence; the good and bad qualities which pretty uniformly marked the Roman oligarchy characterised them also, and there are few of the numerous men of this family known to us in the later times of the republic, as to whom we can tell more than their names and titles. Of course the Claudii of this period were, like the rest of the clans of the high nobility, generally found in the conservative camp; yet no notable champion of the oligarchy appeared among them, while there were various men who professed oppositional sentiments or milder views leaning to the popular side. This is especially the case with all those of whose characters any sketches or even any isolated vivid traits have been preserved. The well-known stories regarding P. Pulcher consul in the first Punic war, who audaciously killed the sacred fowls at Drepana and, in defiance of the senate, nominated Glicia his former clerk as dictator, indicate great insolence doubtless, but not aristocratic arrogance; they rather betoken that pride which disregards traditional views and class-prejudices and is in fact truly democratic. In the nomination of Glicia, which excited the utmost horror in all genuine patricians for centuries, he was, beyond doubt, influenced by the recollection that his ancestor Caecus had introduced his clerk Flavius into the senate. C. Pulcher, when censor in 585,

prevented his colleague Ti. Gracchus from depriving the freedmen
by censorial authority of their right of suffrage, because, as he
affirmed, none could be deprived of that right without a decree of
the people (Liv. xlv. 15)—a course which was very proper and
highly commendable, but not specially oligarchic.   Appius Claudius,
consul in 611, is known as one of the most conspicuous promoters
of the agitation of the Gracchi; he himself along with the two
Gracchi, the elder of whom was his son-in-law, presided over the
execution of the scheme of reform as a commissioner for the distribution of lands.   As to the tribune of the people P. Clodius, the
adopted son of the plebeian Fonteius, it is hardly necessary to prove
that he at least was no pearl of conservatism.   If, therefore, the
very moderate measure of historical truth and importance, which
lies at the root of the hypothesis of a hereditary family policy, is to
be in future brought to bear on the case of the Claudii, it will be
well at least utterly to abandon the current tradition, and to regard
this patrician house not as the defenders of an obdurate aristocracy,
but as the predecessors of the Gracchi and of Caesar.   In this respect
the Claudii were justly called to ascend, in combination with the
Julian house, the imperial throne, and even on that throne they did
not wholly forget the traditional policy of their clan; for it is only
in the light of that traditional policy that we can rightly understand why Tiberius and Claudius declined the title of *Imperator*,
and various similar traits.

II

THE TREATIES BETWEEN ROME AND CARTHAGE

THE earliest treaty between Rome and Carthage, given by Polybius,
is stated by him to have been concluded κατὰ Λεύκιον Ἰούνιον Βροῦτον
καὶ Μάρκον Ὡράτιον.[1]   I have formerly endeavoured to defend this
date as documentary, but I have now to confess myself mistaken.   Painful as it is to witness the disappearance of the last
star which seemed to light the anxious pilot in navigating the
dark seas of early history, an unprejudiced consideration shows
that the Polybian date is not documentary and is probably erroneous.

Respecting the treaties between Rome and Carthage, we have, in
addition to the evidence of Polybius, the following statements.

406 U.C.—Diodorus,[2] undoubtedly on the authority of Fabius:
Ἐπὶ δὲ τούτων (under the consuls of this year) Ῥωμαίοις μὲν πρὸς
Καρχηδονίους πρῶτον συνθῆκαι ἐγένοντο.   Livy:[3]—*Cum Carthaginiensibus legatis foedus ictum, cum amicitiam ac societatem petentes
venissent.*

---

[1] Polyb. iii. 22.   [2] xvi. 69.
[3] vii. 27; and thence Orosius, iii. 7: *primum illud ictum cum Carthaginiensibus foedus.*

448 U.C.—Livy:[1]—*Cum Carthaginiensibus eodem anno foedus tertio renovatum legatisque eorum, qui ad id venerant, comiter munera missa.*

475 U.C.—Livy:[2]—*Cum Carthaginiensibus quarto foedus renovatum est.* This treaty is indisputably the third of Polybius.

The inconsistency between Polybius on the one hand and Fabius on the other is manifest. The former too says expressly that even in his time the oldest men, and those most cognisant of public matters in Rome and in Carthage, were unacquainted with these documents,[3] and, as on that account he excuses Philinus for having remained ignorant of them, he must have held a similar view regarding the expression of Fabius, that the treaty of 406 was the first treaty between Rome and Carthage. On the other hand Polybius by no means says—what he has often been made to say—that he had himself discovered the documents and that no one had made use of them before him. On the contrary, it is probable that they came to light on occasion of the endless diplomatic negotiations which preceded the third Punic war, and that it then became apparent that they were unknown to the leading statesmen in the Roman and Carthaginian senates. Perhaps they were brought to light by Cato, who had sufficient inducement to search for them in the Roman archives, and who, when he charged the Carthaginians with having six times before 536 broken their compacts with Rome,[4] must have taken some trouble to ascertain the contents of the earlier treaties. Polybius either gained his knowledge of them from the oral communications of Cato or of some third person, or—as there is nothing to prevent us from assuming—derived them from Cato's historical work. Livy follows, as he so often does, different authorities—as to 406 Fabius, as to 448 and 475 an authority agreeing with Polybius.[5]

The position of the testimony therefore is this: the one party reckons the treaties of 245, 448, 475, as first, third, and fourth; the other reckons that of 406 as the first, and therefore, beyond doubt, those of 448 and 475 as the second and third. In the first place,

---

[1] ix. 43. [2] Ep. 13.

[3] iii. 26, 2 ταῦτα—καθ᾿ ἡμᾶς ἔτι καὶ ʿΡωμαίων καὶ Καρχηδονίων οἱ πρεσβύτατοι καὶ μάλιστα δοκοῦντες περὶ τὰ κοινὰ σπουδάζειν ἠγνόουν.

[4] Cato, *Orig. l.* iv. *ap.* Nonium, *v. duodevicesimo*, p. 100 M.: *Deinde duodevicesimo* (rather *duoetvicesimo*) *anno post dimissum bellum, quod quattuor et viginti annos fuit, Carthaginiensis sextum de foedere decernere* (rather *decessere*). The fifth breach of the peace was probably constituted in his view by the occurrences which led to the cession of Sardinia in 517, the fourth by the declaration of war in 490, the third by the attempt on Tarentum in 482. The first two I know no means of determining. In reference to the number and order of the treaties—to throw light on which the passage has often been employed—nothing is deducible from it.

[5] The proposal to harmonise the statements of Livy by counting the diplomatic congratulations of the Carthaginians in 411 (Liv. vii. 43) as a second treaty, simply substitutes one piece of negligence for another, because Livy ought to have said this, had he meant it. It is, moreover, highly improper, when an inconsistency between Fabius and Polybius is established, to explain away the traces of the same inconsistency in Livy.

the latter view is supported by the fact that it has the older authorities in its favour. In the second place, it is evident that there were in the Roman archives in Cato's time only two treaties with Carthage, which preceded that of 475; which would suit very well, if that were the third, but not if it were the fourth, treaty, especially as the missing treaty must have been not the first, but either the second or the third, of the four. In the third place, it would be very delightful to meet with a document dating from the legendary period; but on that very account such an occurrence is far from probable.

While all these considerations tell in favour of the earlier and evidently more unbiassed tradition, in reality neither on internal nor external grounds can the Polybian date be vindicated. The document does not bear internal traces of so great an antiquity; if it lay before us without date, we should simply infer from it that it must be earlier than 416. That in the seventh century treaties of alliance had the date officially attached to them, at least if they were concluded by the senate, is no doubt evident from the treaty with the community of Astypalaea (*Corp. Inscr. Graec.* 2485), and that relating to Asclepiades the Clazomenian and others (*C. I. Gr.* 5879); but the age of this custom is not incontestably established, and the only inference which it warrants is, that the first treaty with Carthage might, not that it must, have been dated. Polybius himself by no means refers his statement of the year to this source which would dispel all doubt, and moreover he specifies the time of the second and third treaties in so general and reserved a manner, that in these cases at least he cannot possibly have found a specification of the year. The circumstance (to which I was formerly disposed to attach some weight) that the second treaty of Polybius seemed not to suit the year 448 well, because Tyre after the time of Alexander the Great can hardly have had the independent right of stipulating with a foreign power, was of some importance, so long as the choice between 406 and 448 seemed open: but the constitutional relations subsisting between the Greek and Phoenician mercantile cities and the crown of Asia, as well as those between Tyre and Carthage, are far from being ascertained to such an extent that on that ground we should refuse to believe other important testimonies. The only grounds that remain are, the impossibility of discovering the source of the mistake, and the weight of the authority of Polybius. But, desirable as it is, with a view to complete conviction, to point out not only the error, but also the truth from which every error proceeds, we cannot possibly be required, in the case of such a specification of time presenting itself wholly apart from its original connection, to hold it as true until we have shown in what way the author came by the erroneous number. Lastly, the authority of Polybius is undoubtedly, in his own field of investigation, one of the highest furnished to us by antiquity; but in this case his account refers to an epoch which he did not seek independently to investigate, and as to which he took his facts in good faith from some Roman work. He specifies the year of the foundation of the city, and the duration of the reigns of the kings; but we do not regard fables as converted into history because he has placed them on record. Historical criticism must therefore place the first treaty between Rome and Carthage in 406, and the two following, accordingly, in 448 and 475. It follows that no proof can be drawn from the statement of Polybius in favour of the historical character of the pair of consuls marking the year at the head of our list; while conversely, after their unhistorical character has been otherwise demonstrated, the Polybian date necessarily falls with them.

MADE AT THE TEMPLE PRESS LETCHWORTH IN GREAT BRITAIN